Business Environment in a Global Context

Business Environment in a Global Context

SECOND EDITION

Andrew Harrison

OXFORD

UNIVERSITY PRESS

Great Clarendon Street, Oxford, OX2 6DP,
United Kingdom

Oxford University Press is a department of the University of Oxford.
It furthers the University's objective of excellence in research, scholarship,
and education by publishing worldwide. Oxford is a registered trade mark of
Oxford University Press in the UK and in certain other countries

Published in the United States of America by Oxford University Press
198 Madison Avenue, New York, NY 10016, United States of America

British Library Cataloguing in Publication Data

Data available

Library of Congress Control Number: 2013946492

ISBN 978-0-19-967258-5

Printed in Great Britain by
Bell & Bain Ltd, Glasgow

For my wife, Heather, our children, David and Rachel,
and in memory of my parents, John and Betty Harrison.

About the Author

 Andrew Harrison was formerly Principal Lecturer in Economics at Teesside University, and is a Visiting Lecturer at the Technical University of Košice, Slovakia. He holds qualifications from London, Salford, and Leeds Universities and Trinity College of Music, London. Andrew began his career in accountancy and held teaching appointments in further education before moving to Teesside University. In the course of his career Andrew has also been a visiting lecturer in Germany, Ukraine, and Singapore. In 2008, Andrew Harrison was awarded an honorary doctorate by the Technical University of Košice. He is married to Heather, has two grown-up children, David and Rachel, and is a keen amateur pianist and organist.

Acknowledgements

I should like to thank Francesca Griffin, Melanie Smith, Amanda George, Emily Spicer, Sian Jenkins, and their colleagues at Oxford University Press for their continual support, advice, patience, and encouragement during the writing of this book and its preparation for publication; colleagues and students at Teesside University and the Technical University of Košice, especially Lynton Bussell, Ertuğrul Dalkiran, Ena Elsey, Julian Gough, Oto Hudec, Stephen James, and Bill Suthers, for the many insights I have gained from them during the course of my teaching career; my colleague, Neil Smith, for the author's photograph; the anonymous reviewers, both of the first edition and draft chapters of the second edition, for their helpful comments and constructive criticisms; and above all, my wife, Heather, for her love, encouragement, and wise counsel, my son, David, for his helpful suggestions on some of the scientific and statistical aspects of the book, and my daughter, Rachel, for reminding me of the important things in life when I became too absorbed in writing the book.

Finally, I should like to thank the following for permission to reproduce copyright material: Business Alliance of Slovakia; European Commission; IMD World Competitiveness Center; International Monetary Fund; www.internetworldstats.com; Office for National Statistics (PSI Licence C2009000761); Organization for Economic Cooperation and Development; Oxford University Press; Professor Geert Hofstede and Geert Hofstede B.V.; Professor Angus Maddison; Professor Jeffrey Sachs; Statistical Office of the Slovak Republic; United Nations; US Bureau of Economic Analysis; US Bureau of Labor Statistics; World Economic Forum; and World Trade Organization.

Notwithstanding the valued contributions of all the above, I accept full responsibility for any remaining errors or omissions and for opinions expressed in the book. Whilst every effort has been made to present ideas in a balanced and fair way and to obtain permission for the use of copyright material, I will undertake to rectify any errors or omissions notified to me at the earliest opportunity.

About the Book

Aims and themes of the book

This book is intended to provide in-depth understanding of the external business environment for undergraduate and postgraduate students of business and management or related disciplines. It should also be useful for practising managers who want to deepen their understanding of the business environment. Clearly, in-depth analysis is important for postgraduate and advanced undergraduate students, but it is hoped that first-year undergraduates will also appreciate the way the book offers a more rigorous approach than is commonly found at this level.

Organizations operate in an increasingly complex domestic and international environment and many degree courses now include modules on the business environment, international business environment, or global economy. The book guides the reader through the major themes and issues in the business environment at regional, national, and international levels, setting them in the context of globalization and the global economy. It then explores key dimensions of the business environment at each of these levels and geopolitical developments taking place in the main regions of the world. At all times, concepts and theories are juxtaposed with practical examples and insights. Without practical applications theory is sterile, but without theoretical underpinning there is no real understanding.

Whilst various approaches are often used to explore the business environment, it is the author's conviction that there is no substitute for in-depth understanding of the underlying issues. This requires theoretical knowledge and techniques as well as the ability to apply knowledge in practice. The book therefore provides extensive theoretical and conceptual analysis to underpin the reader's understanding of the business environment, together with a variety of practical applications – including opening scenarios, practical insights, assignment topics, and case studies in each of the main chapters and emerging scenarios in the geopolitical chapters towards the end of the book. The reader can also keep up to date with recent developments by consulting the Online Resource Centre at the following website:

www.oxfordtextbooks.co.uk/orc/harrison2e/.

The structure of the book

The structure of the book is encapsulated in the diagram that follows. After an introductory chapter, which outlines the scope of the book, globalization provides the overarching theme for the book as a whole. Global issues permeate each of the main spatial levels of the business environment (regional, national, and international) in Part One, the major dimensions of the business environment in Part Two, and the main regions of the world in Part Three. Organizations operate at a variety of overlapping levels both within and between countries, but always within a broader global context. Part One explores the factors that influence the environment at each of these levels. The dimensions covered in Part Two represent important components of the business environment and the concepts and theories that help to explain them. Particular attention is paid to cultural and ethical issues, the internationalization process, markets and competition, technology, and risk in the international environment. Part Three surveys the major geopolitical and related developments in Europe, the Americas, Asia, and Africa – helping to provide the backdrop to the action in the earlier parts of the book. The book therefore encompasses many of the themes and issues facing an organization in its external environment.

Theoretical material is derived from various academic disciplines, including business and management, history, ethics, and the social sciences, though particular emphasis is placed on economic concepts because of the crucial role they play in the business environment. In all cases, key concepts are explained when first introduced to make the analysis accessible to readers who have not previously studied the business environment or its underlying disciplines in a formal sense.

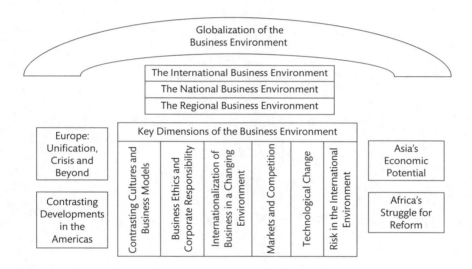

The importance of studying the business environment

Business and management courses often equip their students with sophisticated knowledge and skills in areas such as people management, financial management, marketing, and strategic management. This is entirely appropriate. However, the external environment is often treated as a more peripheral area of study, offering students a broadening experience but not core knowledge. Given the complexity of the external environment, this is hardly sufficient. It is the author's hope that this book will help to remedy this deficiency, both for students embarking on a business or management career and for practising managers keen to improve their understanding of the external environment. Indeed, it is hoped that in-depth understanding of the business environment will ultimately contribute towards better decision making, more successful organizations, improved economic performance – and, for the reader, the satisfaction that comes from gaining new insights and enjoying a more fulfilling career.

Contents

Detailed contents

List of Abbreviations

ACP	African, Caribbean, and Pacific group of countries
AD	Aggregate Demand
AFTA	ASEAN Free Trade Area
AFTZ	Africa Free Trade Zone
AGOA	African Growth and Opportunity Act
AMU	Arab Maghreb Union
APEC	Asia Pacific Economic Cooperation
AS	Aggregate Supply
ASEAN	Association of Southeast Asian Nations
BRIC	Brazil, Russia, India, and China
BRICS	Brazil, Russia, India, China, and South Africa
BSE	Bovine Spongiform Encephalopathy (mad cow disease)
CACM	Central American Common Market
CAD	Computer-Aided Design
CAFTA	Central American Free Trade Agreement or China ASEAN Free Trade Area
CAFTA-DR	Central American–Dominican Republic Free Trade Agreement
CAM	Computer-Aided Manufacturing
CAP	Common Agricultural Policy
Caricom	Caribbean Community
CEE	Central and Eastern Europe
CEN-SAD	Community of Sahel-Saharan States
CFA	Communauté Financière Africaine
CIS	Commonwealth of Independent States
CMEA	Council for Mutual Economic Assistance (also known as Comecon)
CO_2	Carbon Dioxide
COMESA	Common Market for Eastern and Southern Africa
CSR	Corporate Social Responsibility
DNA	Deoxyribonucleic Acid (carrying the genetic information of living organisms)
DOS	Disk Operating System
EAC	East African Community
EAFRD	European Agricultural Fund for Rural Development
EAGLES	Emerging and Growth Leading Economies
EBRD	European Bank for Reconstruction and Development
ECCAS	Economic Community of Central African States
ECOWAS	Economic Community of West African States

ECSC	European Coal and Steel Community
EEA	European Economic Area
EEC	European Economic Community
EFTA	European Free Trade Association
EMFF	European Maritime and Fisheries Fund
ERDF	European Regional Development Fund
ESF	European Social Fund
EU	European Union
FDI	Foreign Direct Investment
FIFA	International Federation of Association Football
FTAA	Free Trade Area of the Americas
G6/G7/G8	Group of 6/7/8 leading industrialized economies
G20	Group of 20 major industrialized and developing economies
GATS	General Agreement on Trade in Services
GATT	General Agreement on Tariffs and Trade
GDP	Gross Domestic Product
GM	Genetically Modified
GNI	Gross National Income
GSP	Generalized System of Preferences
HD	High Definition
HIPC	Heavily Indebted Poor Country
HIV/AIDS	Human Immunodeficiency Virus/Acquired Immune Deficiency Syndrome
IBRD	International Bank for Reconstruction and Development
ICSID	International Centre for the Settlement of Investment Disputes
ICT	Information and Communication Technology
IDA	International Development Association
IFC	International Finance Corporation
IGAD	Intergovernmental Authority on Development
IMD	International Institute for Management Development
IMF	International Monetary Fund
IP	Intellectual Property
IPA	Instrument for Pre-Accession Assistance
IT	Information Technology
LDC	Least Developed Country
LEP	Local Enterprise Partnership
LRAS	Long-Run Aggregate Supply
MEC	Marginal External Cost
MERCOSUR	Common Market of the South
MFN	Most Favoured Nation

MIGA	Multilateral Investment Guarantee Agency
MITI	Ministry of International Trade and Industry
MNC	Multinational Corporation
MNE	Multinational Enterprise
MPC	Marginal Private Cost or Marginal Propensity to Consume
MPM	Marginal Propensity to Import
MPS	Marginal Propensity to Save
MRSA	Methicillin-Resistant *Staphylococcus aureus*
MRT	Marginal Rate of Taxation
MSC	Marginal Social Cost
N-11	Next Eleven emerging countries
NAFTA	North American Free Trade Agreement
NAIRU	Non-Accelerating Inflation Rate of Unemployment
NATO	North Atlantic Treaty Organization
NGO	Non-Governmental Organization
NIC	Newly Industrializing Country
NUTS	Nomenclature of Territorial Units for Statistics
OAU	Organization of African Unity
OECD	Organisation for Economic Co-operation and Development
OEEC	Organization for European Economic Co-operation
OLI	Ownership, Location, Internalization
OPEC	Organization of Petroleum Exporting Countries
OSCE	Organization for Security and Co-operation in Europe
PEST	Political, Economic, Social, and Technological
PESTLE	Political, Economic, Social, Technological, Legal, and Environmental
PPP	Purchasing Power Parity
PTA	Preferential Trading Agreement
R&D	Research and Development
RER	Real Exchange Rate
SACU	Southern Africa Customs Union
SADC	Southern African Development Community
SAFTA	South Asian Free Trade Agreement
SCP	Structure, Conduct, Performance
SICA	Central American Integration System (Systema de la Integración entroamericana)
SO_2	Sulphur Dioxide
SRAS	Short-Run Aggregate Supply
STEEPLE	Social, Technological, Economic, Environmental, Political, Legal, and Ethical
STEP	Social, Technological, Economic, and Political

SWOT	Strengths, Weaknesses, Opportunities, and Threats
TNC	Transnational Corporation
TRIMS	Trade-Related Investment Measures
TRIPS	Trade-Related Aspects of Intellectual Property Rights
UN	United Nations
UNCTAD	United Nations Conference on Trade and Development
USSR	Union of Soviet Socialist Republics
VAT	Value Added Tax
WEF	World Economic Forum
WTO	World Trade Organization

List of Features

List of tables

List of figures

List of opening scenarios

List of practical insights

List of case studies

How to use the Book

Learning outcomes

 Chapter learning outcomes

On completion of this chapter the reader should be ab
- Identify the nature of globalization and the forces t
- Explore the implications of globalization for the ch
- Discuss the rationale for and the institutions of glol
- Analyse the impact and theoretical basis of globali

Learning outcomes

Each chapter starts with a set of bulleted learning outcomes, which indicate what you can expect to learn from the chapter.

Opening scenario: Singapore – a globalized

The tiny country of Singapore covers an area of around 700 sq
of a little under five and a half million, it is one of the most den
in the world, effectively making it a city state. It lies at the south
north of the equator, but unlike many of the world's equatorial
country with the world's fifth highest GDP per capita on a purc
population is predominantly of Chinese ethnicity, but there are
Indians, and the country has a large migrant population of fo

Opening scenario

The opening scenario sets the scene at the beginning of a chapter by describing an event, the activities of an organization, or developments in a particular region or country. By focusing on a topical issue at the outset, the opening scenario gives the topic immediate practical relevance, raising questions and issues that are explored throughout the chapter.

Practical insight **2.2:** Dyson's global repositio

In 2002, Dyson reluctantly moved its main vacuum cleaner pro
to Malaysia. The company already had a plant in Malaysia servi
but the new plant was to become the main international produ
machine production was also transferred to Malaysia in 2003. U
UK were controversial because of the loss of jobs and what ma
manufacturing capability. However, the move enabled Dyson to
competitive as a relatively small player in a challenging intern

Practical insights

The text is interspersed with a number of practical insights. These include discussion of detailed practical examples and pose questions for reflection. They are designed to enhance your understanding of a topic or issue as you progress through a chapter.

Summary

Globalization is a process that is 'flattening' the barri
of people, and the flow of information around the wc
between countries. Globalization is being driven by
forces. These forces are gradually changing the worl
to the growing influence of China and the other BRIG

Chapter summary

The chapter summary provides a brief overview of the issues covered in a particular chapter, helping you to review what you have learned.

Discussion questions

1. Which do you consider to be the most important dr
   or technological drivers?
2. To what extent do you think US political and econor
   next few years?

Discussion questions

The end-of-chapter discussion questions help you to test your understanding of a chapter and can be used either by an independent reader or as the basis for a seminar discussion or coursework.

Suggested assignment topics

1. Choose a company and investigate the impact of g
   including its products, labour force, the location of i
   evant factors.
2. Choose a country and investigate the impact of glo
   culture in recent years.

Suggested research topics

The research topics are designed as the basis for individual or group investigative projects. Such projects are a good way to relate theory and concepts to topical issues in the changing international business environment.

Case study: Globalization of the car i

The international car manufacturing industry provides a useful i
responding to globalization. Looking back to the 1950s and 196
developed economies had one or more major national car mar
Motors and Ford in the United States, Volkswagen and Daimler-
the former British Leyland (later Rover Group) in the UK. Many

Case study

The end-of-chapter case study provides an opportunity to apply theories and concepts to a detailed example. The term 'case study' is used to include organizations and industries as well as regions, countries, and other issues that are relevant to the business environment in its global context.

Suggestions for further reading

Detailed analyses of globalization from an economic perspecti
Bhagwati, J. (2007), *In Defense of Globalization*, Oxford U
Wolf, M. (2005), *Why Globalization Works*, Yale Universi

A passionate account of the way in which ICT is facilitating glo

Suggestions for further reading

An annotated list of recommended reading is provided to enable you to explore each of the main topic areas in more depth.

Key terms introduced in this chapter

Bipolar world order A world dominated by two
United States and USSR during the cold war period.

BRICs /BRICS The four largest emerging economies
coined by a Goldman Sachs report in 2001, later joined

De-industrialization A relative decline in the sha

Key terms

A list of key terms is included at the end of a chapter to provide you with a brief explanation of any technical terms introduced in the chapter.

Emerging scenario: Europe coming of age

One of the biggest challenges facing Europe in the twenty-firs
fringe, from Russia in the north-east to the Balkans and Turkey
that make up these regions were communist republics in the f
they have generally followed a more difficult path to market d
European neighbours who have been joining the EU and NAT
2000s after economic and political upheaval in the 1990s by r

Emerging scenario

The geopolitical chapters in Part Three end with an emerging scenario. Each of these scenarios focuses on a key issue raised in the chapter that has potential implications for future developments in the region.

Glossary

Absolute monarchy A political system where the
state is governed by a hereditary ruler with absolute
power.

   **Bipol
   power
   and U

Glossary

The glossary at the end of the book provides a complete alphabetical listing of the end-of-chapter key terms and their brief explanations.

How to use the Online Resource Centre

www.oxfordtextbooks.co.uk/orc/harrison2e/

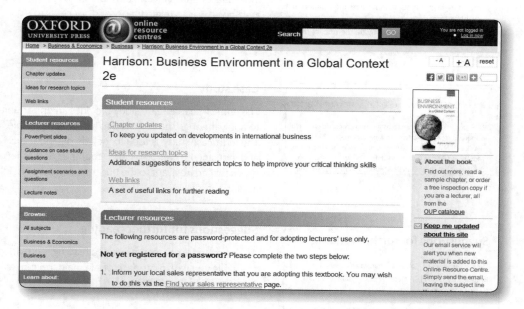

For students

Chapter update: Recovery of th

This chapter provides an overviev
in more detail throughout the rest
types of organization are affected

Chapter updates

To ensure that the book remains current and topical, the author will provide annual updates to the general chapter content, opening scenarios, practical insights, and case studies.

Chapter 01

Introduction to the Business Environment

- Choose a company which has successfully adapte
  environment during the 2008-9 world recession. Ide

Ideas for research topics

Additional suggestions for research topics will be provided to supplement and update those discussed at the end of each chapter.

For those who want to delve further into the idea of an eco
as a complex system:
Brian Arthur Papers, Santa Fe Institute: http://tuvalu.santa
/Papers.html

For an example of a fourth sector organization:
Fourth Sector Strategies: http://www.fourthsectorstrategie

Web links

A set of annotated links to useful websites is provided to help you search for relevant information and statistical data.

For lecturers

1.4 Developments in the Business Envir

Globalization:

* Huge growth in trade, capital flows, ability to tr communicate and work across an interconnect

PowerPoint® lecture slides and lecture notes

A set of PowerPoint® slides has been provided by the author, highlighting the main points from each chapter. These can easily be customized to match your own lecture style. Lecture notes are also provided to expand on the details included in the slides.

Guidance on answering the ca

Case Study Questions

1. How would you describe Tesco's competitive env

Answer: Competition in the UK retail grocery marke around 75 per cent of the market in the hands of the

Guidance on case study questions

Suggested answers are provided to the end-of-chapter case study questions. These questions test the application of theory and concepts to detailed practical examples. The answers include brief explanations as well as alternative perspectives on the issues.

Assignment scenarios and questions

1. Identify a significant change or event in the busin and discuss the extent to which it relates to politic technological, or ethical aspects of the business e

2. Use each of the following approaches to produce environment facing an organization of your choice

Assignment scenarios and questions

Suggestions for assignment topics and other learning activities are provided. These will be updated in the light of changing events.

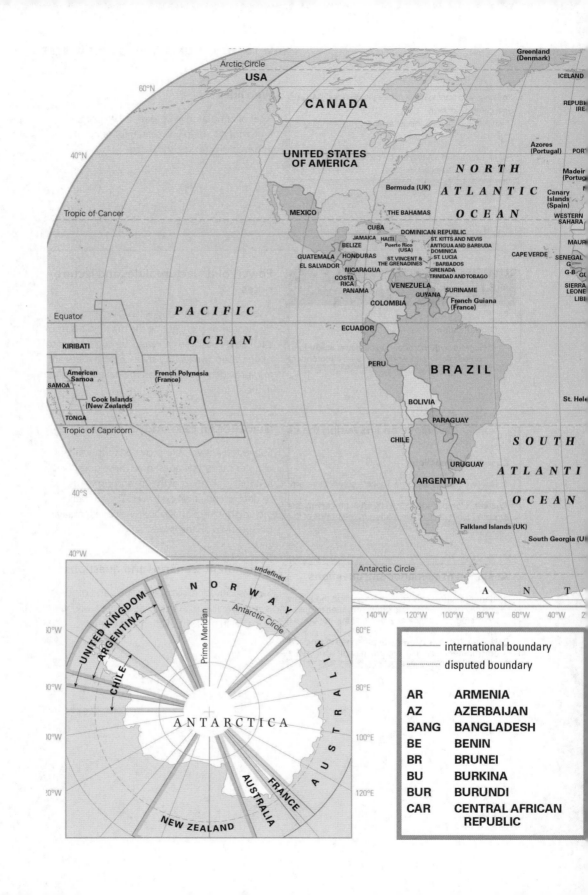

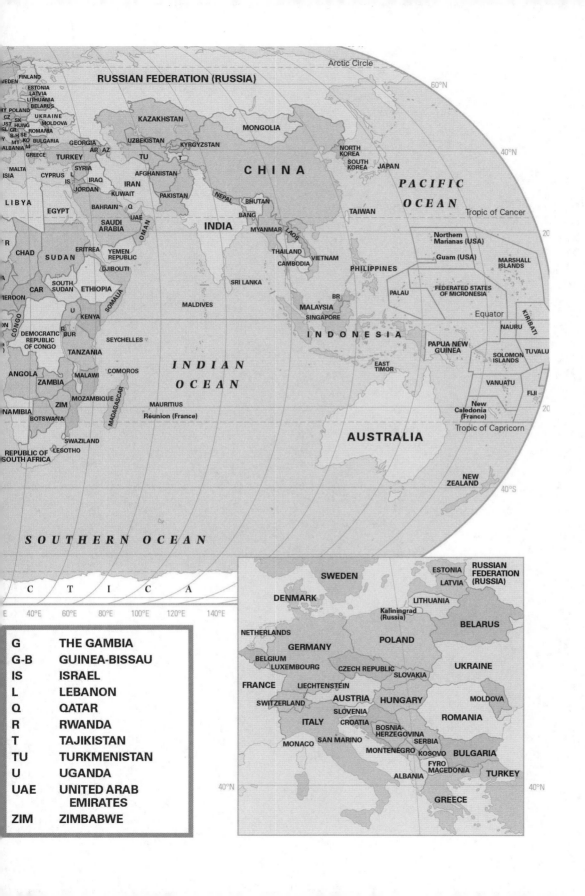

RUSSIAN FEDERATION (RUSSIA)

Arctic Circle

60°N

FINLAND
WEDEN
ESTONIA
LATVIA
LITHUANIA
BELARUS
RY POLAND
CZ SK   UKRAINE
JST HUNG   MOLDOVA
SL CR   ROMANIA
B-H SE
Y   KO BULGARIA
ALBANIA M GEORGIA
MT
GREECE
TURKEY
SYRIA
MALTA
ISIA   CYPRUS   L   IRAQ
IS
JORDAN   KUWAIT

KAZAKHSTAN

UZBEKISTAN   KYRGYZSTAN
AR AZ
TU   T
AFGHANISTAN

MONGOLIA

NORTH
KOREA
SOUTH
KOREA   JAPAN

40°N

CHINA

PACIFIC

OCEAN

IRAN
PAKISTAN

NEPAL

BHUTAN

BANG

TAIWAN

Tropic of Cancer

LIBYA

EGYPT

BAHRAIN   Q
UAE
SAUDI
ARABIA

OMAN

INDIA

MYANMAR

LAOS

20

Northern
Marianas (USA)

R

CHAD   SUDAN

ERITREA   YEMEN
REPUBLIC
DJIBOUTI

THAILAND
CAMBODIA

VIETNAM

Guam (USA)

MARSHALL
ISLANDS

MEROON

CAR   SOUTH
SUDAN   ETHIOPIA

SRI LANKA

PHILIPPINES

FEDERATED STATES
OF MICRONESIA

PALAU

MALDIVES

BR

ON

U

DEMOCRATIC R
REPUBLIC   BUR
OF CONGO

KENYA

SEYCHELLES

MALAYSIA

SINGAPORE

Equator

KIRIBATI

CONGO

TANZANIA

INDONESIA

NAURU

PAPUA NEW
GUINEA

SOLOMON
ISLANDS   TUVALU

ANGOLA
ZAMBIA

MALAWI   COMOROS

INDIAN

OCEAN

EAST
TIMOR

VANUATU

FIJI

ZIM
NAMIBIA
BOTSWANA

MOZAMBIQUE

MADAGASCAR

MAURITIUS

Réunion (France)

20

New
Caledonia
(France)

Tropic of Capricorn

SWAZILAND
REPUBLIC OF   LESOTHO
SOUTH AFRICA

AUSTRALIA

NEW
ZEALAND

40°S

SOUTHERN   OCEAN

C   T   I   C   A

E   40°E   60°E   80°E   100°E   120°E   140°E

G	THE GAMBIA
G-B	GUINEA-BISSAU
IS	ISRAEL
L	LEBANON
Q	QATAR
R	RWANDA
T	TAJIKISTAN
TU	TURKMENISTAN
U	UGANDA
UAE	UNITED ARAB EMIRATES
ZIM	ZIMBABWE

SWEDEN

DENMARK

ESTONIA
LATVIA

RUSSIAN
FEDERATION
(RUSSIA)

LITHUANIA

Kaliningrad
(Russia)

BELARUS

NETHERLANDS

POLAND

GERMANY

BELGIUM
LUXEMBOURG

CZECH REPUBLIC
SLOVAKIA

UKRAINE

FRANCE   LIECHTENSTEIN

SWITZERLAND

AUSTRIA   HUNGARY

MOLDOVA

SLOVENIA

ITALY   CROATIA

ROMANIA

MONACO   SAN MARINO

BOSNIA-
HERZEGOVINA

SERBIA

MONTENEGRO   KOSOVO   BULGARIA

FYRO
MACEDONIA

ALBANIA

TURKEY

40°N

GREECE

40°N

Part One

The Business Environment in a Changing World

The Business Environment: An Overview

◉ Chapter learning outcomes

On completion of this chapter the reader should be able to:

- Identify the meaning and relevance of the external business environment
- Relate the business environment to its organizational context
- Outline the major international developments in the business environment in recent years
- Evaluate alternative approaches to the analysis of the business environment

---

Opening scenario: The Olympic effect

Events such as the 2012 London Olympic and Paralympic Games can have numerous effects on a business or other organization, expected and unexpected, positive and negative. Many of the effects were felt in the immediate vicinity of the sporting venues because of the need for transport, accommodation, and a variety of retail services. Some of the effects were more widely distributed as we rushed out to buy Olympic merchandise or brought forward the decision to buy the high-definition television we had been promising ourselves so that we could experience the full impact of the television coverage. The huge television audiences also gave the advertising industry a much-needed boost. Other effects were negative, including the impact on non-Olympic tourists who stayed away in order to avoid London's increased congestion and inflated hotel prices or the displacement effect on tourism in other parts of the UK as the Olympics became the main attraction.

Of course, an event like the Olympic Games also has a more lasting effect both during the years of preparation and in terms of the 'Olympic legacy'. Much of the expenditure by the Olympic organizers was incurred before the events themselves in the building of sporting venues and related transport infrastructure. The Olympic legacy is often measured in non-economic terms, including the positive image of London and the UK as a whole, the potential for increased participation in sport and related health benefits, and increased public awareness of disability issues following the huge interest in the London Paralympic Games. Some of these effects can also be translated into economic benefits such as the boost given to UK brands and tourism, and the investment in facilities for sport and the disabled.

The 2016 Olympic Games in Rio de Janeiro will experience many of these effects, but it is also the first time the event has been staged in South America. Together with the FIFA World Cup in Brazil in 2014, the economic and reputational impact of these events on one of the world's largest emerging economies may be even more significant than the London Olympics.

As in London, the organizers of the Rio Olympics will also face a number of potential risks. In London, for example, a breakdown in security arrangements was only averted at the last minute when additional troops were deployed to make up for under-recruitment by the main private security contractor and a diplomatic incident had to be rapidly diffused when the South Korean flag was inadvertently used

(continued...)

to represent the North Korean football team. The range of potential risks is, of course, huge and the management of internal and external risk is now an important requirement for the organizers of any major event.

Most of the above effects describe the impact of the external environment. Of course, the Olympic Games and World Cup are only microcosms of that environment but, if a single event (or short series of events) lasting just a few weeks can have such a widespread impact, the environment as a whole is clearly of major significance. In this chapter we explore the nature of the external environment and consider ways in which we can analyse its impact.[1]

1.1 The environment as an eclectic concept

No organization exists within a vacuum. Its strategies and operations are influenced by and must take account of its external environment. The term 'environment' in this sense is all-encompassing. The same term is also used to refer to the ecological or natural environment, so to distinguish between them we often describe the broader concept as the external environment or **business environment**. The natural environment is an important subset of the business environment, but the latter term also includes the activities of consumers and competitors, the policies of governments and international organizations, developments in technology, the social and cultural context, and many other factors. Sometimes these factors are described as environmental 'forces', implying that they exert pressure on business organizations. Whilst this is often true, the process may not be entirely one way. As we shall see later in this chapter, there is a growing tendency to view organizations as interacting with their environment and perhaps even able to influence their environment to some extent.

It is important to note here that the terms 'business organization' and 'business environment' are not restricted to private sector profit-making organizations. Government departments and charitable organizations, for example, also interact with their external environment in the course of their normal activities or 'business', though the relative importance of different factors may vary.

A common way to describe the business environment is to identify its key aspects or perspectives. These are illustrated in Figure 1.1. Sometimes these perspectives are described as separate 'environments', though in reality they are integral parts of the environment as a whole. Figure 1.1 includes the major perspectives on the business environment, but other perspectives such as the natural environment could easily be added to the diagram. It is often difficult to separate political, economic, legal, and other issues, so we have adopted an eclectic approach in this book. Whatever element of the environment is under consideration, we explore each of the relevant perspectives as well as the interrelationships between them.

The business environment can be described as a '**complex adaptive system**'. A complex system is a structure made up of many elements that operate independently and also interact with each other, absorbing information from their surrounding elements. Complex systems and their individual elements adapt or evolve over a period of time. This concept is derived from the natural sciences, but is increasingly being applied to economic systems or economies.[2] It may also be a useful way of thinking about the wider business environment. A fuller

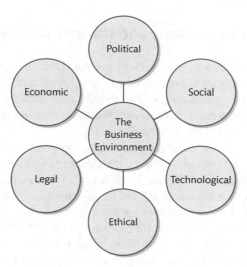

Figure 1.1 Key perspectives on the business environment

discussion of evolutionary approaches to the business environment, including 'complexity theory' as this topic is known, can be found in the context of how competition works in Section 9.3.5. The important thing to note at this stage is that, in order to understand the business environment, we need to explore the interrelationships between its various elements or perspectives. Whilst this book will sometimes focus on a particular environmental context, such as the operation of markets and competition, we will discover that what appears to be a purely economic issue is often embedded in a wider political, legal, social, ethical, and technological context. This is certainly true of the Olympic effect outlined in the opening scenario. It is also illustrated in Practical Insight 1.1.

Practical insight 1.1:   The EU services directive

The European Union (EU) services directive went through a tortuous process as it passed between the EU's major institutions, the European Commission, the Council of Ministers, and the European Parliament. Although finally agreed in December 2006, it did not become legally enforceable in each member state until the end of 2009. Its intention is to remove barriers to the provision of services across internal EU borders or the establishment of a service operation in another EU country, to create more open competition, and to allow consumers to choose the price and type of service they want. However, the way the directive operates may be affected by business customs and practices at a local level and, where cross-border financial transfers are involved, its effect will depend on the availability of integrated electronic transmission networks for financial services.

Question

- In this case, are we describing the political environment, the legal environment, the economic environment, the social environment, or the technological environment? Or is the freedom to operate throughout the EU internal market also an ethical issue?

1.2 Organizations, strategy, and the environment

An understanding of the business environment and the ability to analyse the business environment are essential tools for any organization. In fact, there should be a sequential development from the organization's mission and objectives, its analysis of the external environment, and the analysis of its own organizational capabilities to the formulation of strategy, planning, and operations. This process is illustrated in Figure 1.2.

An organization's mission describes its overall aims, purpose, and values – what it is ultimately trying to achieve. Its mission is then translated into more specific objectives against which the organization's performance can be measured. The organization needs to develop strategies to indicate how it intends to achieve its objectives, but these strategies should be informed by analyses of the organization's own capabilities as well as the external environment. The strategies, in turn, will inform the planning process and the organization's operations. The analysis of organizational capabilities and the environment is often undertaken using a **SWOT analysis**, identifying the *strengths* and *weaknesses* of the organization (sometimes known as the internal environment) and the *opportunities* and *threats* posed by the external environment. SWOT analysis was designed to enable an organization to take into account internal and external factors that may affect its strategic planning decisions and thus to improve its prospects of success.

In this book we are primarily concerned with the external environment, and it is important to appreciate how an understanding of the external environment can contribute to the success of an organization. However, the identification and awareness of environmental factors in a simple form of SWOT analysis is only the starting point. A more sophisticated approach might be to consider assigning probability values to the likelihood of an event occurring or the likely consequences of an event, or to find ways of tracking the interrelationships between different environmental factors. Some of these approaches are considered in Section 1.5, but whichever form of environmental analysis is used, an in-depth understanding of the underlying principles and issues will be of great benefit. In order to do this, we need to use a number of concepts, theories, and models that explain the processes and linkages at work in the external environment. This is the main purpose of this book.

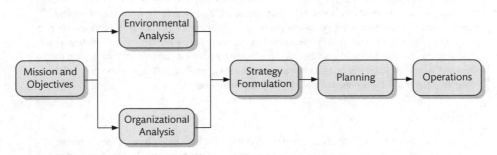

Figure 1.2 The strategic planning process

1.3 Types of organization

The term 'organization' encompasses large, medium, and small **private sector** businesses, central and local government, public corporations, and other **public sector organizations**, a variety of '**third-sector' organizations** such as charities, community groups, social enter- prises, cooperatives, and other non-profit organizations, as well as '**fourth-sector' organiza- tions** which exist to meet social needs but are operated as profit-making businesses. These organizations are extremely varied so they are not all affected in the same way by the business environment. Environmental analysis therefore has to be tailored to the needs of each organ- ization. All organizations are, however, affected by external forces and, in many cases, have an impact on their external environment as well as on other organizations. An understanding of the environment is therefore a prerequisite for undertaking an effective environmental analysis. Some of the key features of organizations are identified below.

1.3.1 **Private sector organizations**

The largest national and multinational companies are typically public limited liability com- panies. Examples include oil companies such as Exxon or Shell, manufacturers like Ford or General Electric, and financial institutions such as HSBC or Banco Santander. The shares of public companies are normally traded on stock exchanges, allowing them to raise capi- tal from the general public and institutional investors (banks, insurance companies, invest- ment companies, pension funds etc.), though the balance between equity (share) capital and loan capital varies between countries. US and UK companies rely mainly on equity capital, whereas German and Japanese companies have tended to rely more on loan capital from the banks. This, together with the UK's more liberal takeover rules, makes British companies more susceptible to hostile takeovers than German companies. Smaller companies are likely to be private limited liability companies or perhaps unincorporated businesses such as a partnership or sole trader. Even quite large companies like the German car maker, BMW, may sometimes be private, family-owned companies. Incorporation and limited liability provide legal protection in the event of business failure, whereas sole or joint ownership al- lows greater freedom of operation and sometimes considerable rewards for successful small business owners.

1.3.2 **Public sector organizations**

National government departments and local government are normally funded directly from tax revenue and are accountable to parliament or local councils. In the main, they provide public services such as education, health care, or defence, though they may also be more di- rectly involved in business activities such as road building or business advisory services. Like private sector organizations, however, they have customers or service users, employ people, and have to respond to changes in government policy and other external factors. Other pub- lic sector organizations include public corporations or state-owned enterprises (also known as nationalized industries if they control the major part of an industry) and publicly funded bodies such as the competition authorities, most universities and colleges, and agencies responsible for a variety of public issues such as equal opportunities or child support. Agencies or companies that are funded wholly or partly by government and perform functions of public importance are sometimes described as '**parastatals**': hybrid organizations which have their own governance structures but are also accountable to the state. Until recently, many of Europe's utility industries were state owned, though the majority of these public corporations have now been privatized.

1.3.3 **Third-sector organizations**

The term 'third sector' has come into use in recent years to describe a large number of non-profit organizations. These organizations occupy the middle ground between the private and public sectors. Their funding is predominantly from private and often voluntary sources, though they may also attract public funds. They range from international non-governmental organizations (NGOs) such as the Red Cross or Red Crescent through to cooperatives (shared-ownership business ventures), charities, voluntary and community groups, foundations and trusts, and a growing number of 'social enterprises'. Social enterprises are non-profit businesses that exist to promote socially desirable activities.[3] Third-sector organizations are also affected by their external environment as they respond to the needs of the communities they serve and their resources depend on the availability of private and public funds.

1.3.4 **Fourth-sector organizations**

The term 'fourth sector' is now also starting to come into use. Although not yet clearly defined, the fourth sector describes organizations which combine business (including profit-making) objectives with social or environmental objectives. Some of these organizations are similar to 'social enterprises', though a distinction can be made between a private entrepreneur whose business promotes social projects and a social enterprise which is run primarily as a non-profit activity. Other examples include organizations providing finance for micro businesses (microfinance) or venture capital for socially desirable purposes (venture philanthropy), and businesses whose intention is to minimize their environmental impact (sustainable businesses). This hybrid type of organization, in its various forms, is now becoming more common.[4] Practical Insight 1.2 focuses on how different types of organization are affected by their external environment.

1.4 Developments in the business environment

The business environment has been undergoing considerable change in recent years. This situation is not unique to modern times, but the pace of change seems to have been increasing. Of course, not all aspects of the environment are constantly changing; for example, an Act of Parliament may remain in force for many years. However, the Act may be reinterpreted or changes in society may alter its impact or make it obsolete. So changes in some aspects of the business environment may bring about changes in others – or, to express it in terms of a

Practical insight 1.2: The impact of a world recession

The international financial crisis and subsequent world recession of 2008–9 left a trail of struggling banks, government debt, depressed share prices, falling sales and profit, business insolvency, rising unemployment, declining income and consumption, and growing social hardship in many of the advanced and some of the developing economies. The subsequent recovery initially seemed promising and the emerging and developing economies grew rapidly in 2010. However, the onset and escalation of the eurozone crisis following the emergence of the Greek debt crisis in December 2009 and even a relative slowdown in the world's new manufacturing heartland, China, in 2012 have caused the IMF to revise its projections for world economic growth downwards for a number of advanced and emerging economies.[5]

Question

In what ways might a slow recovery from the world recession affect each of the following?

- A major charity such as Oxfam
- A bank that lends mortgages to house buyers
- A car manufacturer dependent on domestic and export markets
- A government finance department

complex system, the elements of the complex system are responding and adapting to each other and thus causing changes in the system as a whole.

In order to evaluate change, it is important to view an issue in its historical context, sometimes over a relatively recent period, sometimes over a longer period. Where appropriate, we incorporate this historical perspective into the analysis, helping to provide continuity in the understanding of an issue. History is in effect one of several dimensions of the business environment that enable us to explore an issue fully; other dimensions include politics, economics, law, ethics, and culture.

Another major theme within the changing environment is 'internationalization'. Like change itself, the internationalization of the business environment is not new, but it has become a more dominant feature in recent years. The international nature of the business environment has strongly influenced the design of this book, especially the study of globalization at an early stage in Chapter 2 and the focus on the major regions of the world in Part Three. Even at the sub-national level, it is difficult to explore the environment without being aware of international issues. We now proceed to outline some of the major changes that have been occurring in recent years.

1.4.1 **Political change**

The last quarter of the twentieth century witnessed the gradual re-emergence of China as an economic power (from 1978 onwards) and the collapse of communism in the former Soviet bloc (from 1989 to 1991 onwards). These two events continue to have significant implications for international relations and the world economy in the twenty-first century. Numerous other developments have also been important in recent years. Among these are the USA's confirmation as the world's only 'superpower' (for the time being at least), the economic success of Asia's 'tiger economies' (mainly from the 1980s onwards), India's rapid economic growth (since the early 1990s), the growing importance of Latin America's larger states, Brazil and Mexico (especially since the late 1990s), and the Arab uprising or 'Arab Spring' in a succession of North African and Middle Eastern countries, which began in Tunisia in December 2010 but gathered momentum during the spring of 2011.

The opening up of China and the former Soviet bloc is still transforming the international business environment, though the course of events has been very different in each case. The transition to market democracy in Russia and Eastern Europe since 1989 has brought about a complete political and economic transformation in most of these countries. China's rise to prominence, on the other hand, has been less dramatic but the pace of China's economic development is now taking the world by storm. The importance of these developments should not be underestimated, though we need to keep a balanced view of the issues. The fact that China is becoming dominant in manufacturing and exporting, and that its economic and political influence will inevitably increase, should not draw us to the conclusion that all is lost for the rest of the world. As our study of globalization will demonstrate in Chapter 2, it is probably a mistake to think of the changing international scene as a zero-sum game, where one country's gain is another country's loss.

1.4.2 Globalization

The huge growth in international trade, international capital flows, and the ability of people to travel, communicate, and work across an increasingly interconnected world has become generally known as **globalization**. Clearly, globalization has major implications for business organizations; even a small business operating locally may find itself competing with a foreign multinational company or have to respond to a change in world oil prices, for example. Globalization has allowed many businesses and some countries to prosper (not only in the developed world), but in some respects has increased global inequalities. It has also brought to prominence a number of multinational institutions such as the United Nations, World Bank, and World Trade Organization (WTO), in the belief that international coordination is beneficial for the world as a whole.

As the world's nations and their economies have become more open to trade and investment, they have become more interdependent. Interdependence seems to emphasize the power of some nations and the dependence of others. This has led some observers to focus their attention on the apparent 'unfairness' of free trade and on the issue of poverty in the countries that have been left behind, many of which are in sub-Saharan Africa. All these issues raise political, economic, ethical, and many other questions, some of which will be addressed in subsequent chapters. Many of the issues undoubtedly have far-reaching implications for business organizations in an increasingly global environment.

1.4.3 Technological change

Technology is one of the main driving forces behind globalization. As with other aspects of globalization, technological change is not new. 'Modern' methods of transport such as the motor vehicle and the aeroplane were first developed in something like their modern form during the years just before and after 1900 respectively. Even the computer has antecedents that date back to the mid-twentieth century in a form recognizable to us today (and much earlier in more limited forms). Although technological discoveries often draw on the work of many individuals over a long period of time, the pace of technological change seems to have been accelerating since the late 1970s. This is particularly evident in the case of computer technology, including computerized control systems, computer-aided design and manufacturing (CAD and CAM), and information and communication technology (ICT). The use of computers has affected almost every type of business organization, from the recording and processing of information to the worldwide provision of goods, services, and information via the internet. The use of computers also has a number of other business implications. For example, a computerized network, such as the internet, allows relatively small businesses, in terms of the number of employees, to operate internationally. On the other hand, a computer platform, such as Microsoft's Windows operating system, gives the company that controls the platform a potential competitive advantage over its rivals.

1.4.4 The international financial crisis, world recession, and their aftermath

In 2008, the difficulties that were being experienced by one or two smaller financial institutions began to spread rapidly to the financial sector as a whole. The crisis emerged in the US sub-prime mortgage market, where falling house prices and mortgage defaults among high-risk borrowers left lending institutions with bad debts. These debts had been 'parcelled' into securities which were bought by other financial institutions, a process known as 'securitization'. As a result, banks sometimes quite remote from the original high-risk mortgages became involved in a lending chain. As long as the mortgages were believed to be sound, financial institutions were holding valuable assets. Once the mortgages started to lose value, the institutions found themselves holding 'toxic' assets whose value had suddenly fallen. This type of practice was not unique to US mortgage lending institutions and before long banks in the UK, Iceland, Ireland, other parts of Europe and America, and across the world began to be affected. Institutions with a large amount of bad debts or toxic securities were most seriously affected and a number of US and UK institutions, in particular, either went into liquidation or had to be bailed out by their respective governments. Famous names included Lehman Brothers, Merrill Lynch, and AIG in the United States and the Royal Bank of Scotland in the UK.

The financial crisis put pressure on government finances in the countries worst affected and led to falling exchange rates and share prices, and a shortage of credit finance for businesses and consumers. Consumer spending was soon affected, businesses were struggling with falling sales, and rising unemployment became inevitable. By late 2008 the financial crisis had not only spread across much of the world but had also caused a general economic downturn. Whereas in China the downturn involved a slower rate of economic growth, for many countries it meant recession or negative economic growth. After 2009, the world economy began to recover, though at a much quicker pace in the emerging and developing countries than in the advanced economies. Recovery has remained slow in North America and Western Europe, exacerbated by government debt crises in Greece, Ireland, Portugal, Spain, and Italy and the resulting eurozone crisis (see Section 3.2.5), and even the Chinese economy, the world's fastest-growing large economy, began to slow down more than expected in 2012.

The effect of the economic downturn and patchy recovery in different parts of the world can be seen in the International Monetary Fund (IMF) GDP growth rates for 2009–10 and

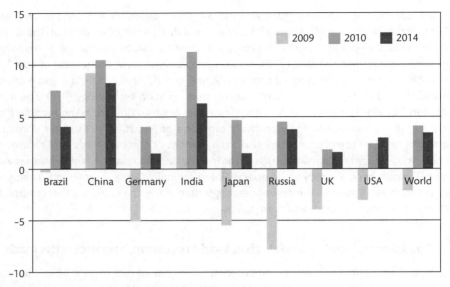

Figure 1.3 Real GDP percentage growth rates, 2009–10 and projections for 2014

Source: IMF, *World Economic Outlook Database,* April 2013.

growth rate projections for 2014, illustrated in Figure 1.3. As output fell, business and government revenue also fell. This slowed down the growth of consumer income and even those
with secure employment and access to finance generally became more cautious in their
spending decisions. The income of third-sector organizations was also affected by declining individual, corporate, and public finances. Whilst not everyone was affected in the same
way, the world recession had a significant impact in countries as diverse as the United States,
Japan, and Brazil. The relatively weak recovery in the advanced economies is also having a
dampening effect on the emerging and developing economies. This is another example of the
interdependent world that globalization has brought.

1.4.5 Consensus and contrast in national government policy

The interconnectedness that comes with globalization has brought a degree of consensus
in national policy making among the world's leading economies, particularly on macroeconomic policy. This has come about because of three key developments: the apparent 'triumph'
of the market economies over the centrally planned economies, symbolized by the end of
state economic planning in the former Soviet bloc and China; a gradual synthesis of ideas in
modern macroeconomics; and the growing influence of international economic institutions
such as the IMF, World Bank, and World Trade Organization, which have promoted common
economic policies among their member countries. In outline, the macroeconomic policy
consensus requires national governments to set a budget that balances tax revenue and current expenditure over the economic cycle (fiscal policy), whilst pursuing a policy of monetary
stability by raising or lowering interest rates to maintain low inflation (monetary policy). This
type of prudent fiscal and monetary policy has been adopted by several developed countries

in recent years and also by a number of developing and emerging countries, often at the in-sistence of the IMF or World Bank. Countries that have been less successful in pursuing these policies, including European countries such as Greece and Italy, have been criticized for their 'excessive' public debts or high rates of inflation.

The macroeconomic consensus was tested during the 2008–9 economic downturn and in countries left with large government debts during the recovery. The steady economic growth with low inflation common to many of the developed countries during the late 1990s and early 2000s came to an abrupt end in 2008. Even during this difficult period, however, a reasonable degree of consensus in favour of economic stimulus measures was achieved among the world's leading developed and developing countries at the G20 London summit in April 2009. In effect, this represented a return to **Keynesian policy**, where an increase in government spending or reduction in taxes provides a stimulus to aggregate demand during a recession (see Section 4.4.3). However, this type of **fiscal stimulus** has not met with universal approval, either during the world recession (with no-table dissent from Germany), or among governments trying to reduce their debt during the recovery (for example in the UK) and many of those who advocated this approach still seem to share the view that a fiscal stimulus is at best a temporary measure before a return to more prudent economic management. In this sense, the consensus has broadly survived. However, agreement on how to achieve economic growth while managing a budget deficit after a recession is proving more elusive.

There is generally greater policy divergence on microeconomic policy. The key debate here relates to the role of government. During the 1970s and 1980s, when Japan and South Korea were apparently building their economic success on government intervention to promote key industries, active industrial policy received considerable acclaim. Japan's economic slow-down in the 1990s, followed by the Asian financial crisis that affected countries like South Korea and Thailand in 1997–8, then cast doubt on the wisdom of active government inter-vention. Similar debates have been heard in Europe, contrasting the social market policies of continental Western Europe with the free-market policies of the UK and USA. Examples of the social market approach include the extensive labour market regulation and generous social insurance found in countries like Germany and France. Examples of the free-market approach include the privatization and market liberalization of industries like telecommunications and energy in the UK during the 1980s and 1990s. Of course, these contrasting approaches con-tain many nuances and anomalies that require more in-depth analysis.

1.4.6 **Free markets and social responsibility**

Just as free-market policies had apparently triumphed as the world was approaching the new millennium, pressure on governments and companies to moderate the harsher aspects of free markets was increasing. For some of the 'anti-globalization' protesters, globalization represents everything that is wrong with market economics (or the more pejorative term 'capitalism'). However, even neutral observers are now increasingly emphasizing the need for those engaged in any form of economic activity to be socially responsible. Examples of this trend include the following: the 'fairtrade' and 'trade justice' movements; Jubilee 2000 (calling for the cancellation of poor countries' debts); the United Nations Millennium Development Goals (targets to improve conditions in developing countries); concerns about the impact of production and trade on the natural environment; and pressure on companies to take full account of their **corporate social responsibilities**.

Although there are different ethical views on whether a company's responsibilities are to its shareholders or to its wider stakeholders, there is a growing expectation that a company should at least be aware of its impact on society and the environment. This raises issues not only for companies but also for the role of government in regulating the activities of companies and for industry regulators who exercise these powers on behalf of government. A recent example is the introduction of tradable pollution permits for the control of industrial pollution (also known as 'emissions trading'). These permits have been issued in industries such as power generation and chemical manufacturing, imposing pollution limits but also creating an incentive for companies to reduce their pollution and make money by selling their permits. This issue is discussed more fully in Section 7.6. Corporate social responsibility, whether left to individual companies or encouraged by government, is now very much a feature of the business environment.

1.4.7 Socio-cultural change

Globalization has far-reaching consequences for the way people live their lives. Not only does it bring opportunities for international travel and allow the local supermarket to stock goods from around the world, it also exposes people to unfamiliar cultures and practices. Cultural change can be regarded both positively and negatively. There is a view that the world's cultures are converging and that 'western' or American culture is becoming dominant. Examples cited to illustrate this 'dominance' include the prevalence of western dress, fast food, and the English language. However, nothing is ever quite as straightforward as it seems. Whilst some degree of cultural convergence has taken place, there is also evidence of cultural diversity. For example, European citizens enjoy a much more varied choice of cuisine today than they would have fifty years ago. It is also curious that neighbouring countries such as the UK and France, or even neighbouring communities in a single country such as the Walloons (French speakers) and Flemings (Flemish speakers) in Belgium, still retain their distinctive cultural identities after many centuries of coexistence. Even the ubiquitous English language may not be quite as widely spoken as is commonly imagined,[6] and the use of standard British English is increasingly giving way to a wide range of variants in different parts of the world and different contexts.

Culture is often influenced by religious beliefs. Only a few years ago it might have been argued that religion was becoming less important in the western world. This can hardly be claimed today. Huntington's thought-provoking analysis of what he calls the 'clash of civilizations' has religious fault lines at its heart.[7] Most of the world's major civilizations are characterized by their religious traditions. Of particular interest is the revival in the influence of Islam, not only in predominantly Muslim countries in Asia, the Middle East, and North Africa, but also in the USA and Europe. Sometimes these religious traditions represent important differences of outlook and beliefs, including their perspectives on political issues and business practices. In reality, therefore, it is by no means certain that cultural convergence predominates over cultural diversity. What is certain, however, is that the study of culture and social change leads to fascinating insights into the complexities of the business environment, as illustrated in Practical Insight 1.3.

Practical insight **1.3:** Continuity and change in one of Europe's newest states

Slovakia is one of the former communist countries of Central and Eastern Europe that has been transforming its economic and political system since 1989 and joined the European Union in 2004. Slovakia is, in many ways, becoming more like its Western European neighbours, opening its borders, adopting modern technology and market-based policies, and adapting to international business practices. Yet a foreign traveller venturing beyond the cosmopolitan hotels of the country's capital, Bratislava, will encounter a country trying to forge its own identity after centuries of foreign occupation, the major part of 75 years as the junior partner in the Czechoslovak state (1918–92 with the exception of the World War II years), and 40 years of Soviet communism (1948–89). The traveller will also find the unfamiliar Slovak language (recognizable only to Slovakia's Slavic neighbours) and wide variations in landscape, culture, and outlook across the country's western, central, and eastern regions. Slovakia is, in effect, a microcosm of the changing business environment in recent years, illustrating both the general and the individual impact of change as well as the continuity of human development.

Question

● Why are some cultural characteristics more enduring than others?

1.5 Alternative approaches to analysis of the business environment

1.5.1 **PESTLE-type analysis**

One of the most common methods of analysing the business environment is to identify and explain the key external factors that are likely to affect the performance of an organization. It is normally specific to a particular organization, though some of the external factors may be common to other organizations. Its simplest form is known as PEST analysis (or, by reordering the initials, STEP analysis). PEST analysis focuses on four key aspects of the external environment: political, economic, social, and technological. Individual factors are identified under each of these headings and their impact on the organization is explored. Some writers have argued that other aspects of the environment should be specifically included in the analysis, so acronyms such as PESTLE and STEEPLE have also come into use. PESTLE (political, economic, social, technological, legal, and environmental or ecological) is now probably the most common form, though STEEPLE adds an additional dimension (ethical). It is not difficult to imagine that other dimensions could be added.

PESTLE-type analysis provides a starting point for environmental analysis though, despite its popularity, on its own it is of relatively limited value. The identification of environmental factors might be regarded as the first stage in environmental analysis, but it is more important to be able to understand and analyse these factors, not only individually, but also the interactions between them. This does not preclude the use of **PESTLE analysis**; in fact, it may well help to make it a more useful tool. However, it is hoped that the book may encourage more sophisticated approaches to the analysis of the business environment. The types of factor that might be included in a PESTLE analysis are illustrated in Table 1.1. The list of factors in each column could clearly be extended and the factors could be made more specific to a particular organization. A number of factors could also appear in more than one column; for

Table 1.1 Illustrative factors used in a PESTLE analysis

Political	Economic	Social	Technological	Legal	Environmental
• Political stability • Political complexion of government • Government or local government policies • Government attitudes towards inward investment • EU policies	• Economic growth rate • Inflation • Unemployment • Interest rates • Government expenditure & taxation • Consumer expenditure • Foreign direct investment • Exchange rates • Nature of competition	• Social structure • Demographic factors • Income distribution • Education • Indicators of happiness or wellbeing • Health factors • Fashion • Trends in work and leisure	• Computer availability, speed & capacity • Software developments • Cost, availability & speed of internet access/use • Developments in production technology or biotechnology	• Consumer protection • Employment law • Competition law/policy • Health & safety legislation • Equality legislation • Disability discrimination legislation	• Environmental regulations • Emissions trading scheme • Pollution taxes • Congestion charging • Vehicle emissions standards • Recycling regulations • Global warming

example, taxation is set by a political decision but has an economic impact and competition law or policy is set by government, but has the force of law as well as economic implications. This illustrates something of the complexity of the business environment, which we started to explore in the opening scenario on the Olympic Games, and the importance of being able to analyse the interactions between its various elements. The external environment also poses considerable risk to an organization (see Practical Insight 1.4).

Practical insight 1.4: Microsoft and business environmental risk

In recent years Microsoft has been investigated by the US and EU competition authorities for allegedly abusing its market power in relation to access to its software codes (allowing interoperability for rival software) and the 'bundling' of Media Player and other software with its Windows operating system to the detriment of its competitors (see case study at the end of Chapter 9). The European Commission ruled against Microsoft in 2004 and this decision was upheld by the European Court of First Instance in 2007. Following the court decision, the Commission imposed a heavy fine on Microsoft for non-compliance and for overcharging for access to interoperability information. This decision was subsequently upheld by the European General Court (formerly Court of First Instance) in 2012. Open access to Microsoft's interoperability information has now allowed a number of new products to enter the market, potentially reducing Microsoft's influence over related software markets.

The question as to whether Microsoft is likely to retain its dominant position is also complicated by the challenge posed by rival operating systems, especially with the arrival of 'cloud computing' (where web platforms replace the need for desktop software and files are stored online) and the development of smartphones and hand-held computer devices which use touch screens rather than Windows operating systems. The competition investigations and technological developments clearly carry external risks for Microsoft.

Question

● To what extent are these risks economic, legal, technological, or even political risks?

1.5.2 Measures of competition at the industry level

A more detailed picture of an organization's competitive environment can be gained by analysing the industry or market in which it operates. The competitive environment is really a subset of the wider business environment, taking account of the number, relative size, and behaviour of competitors in the market, the nature of entry barriers, and the degree of product differentiation, among other things. However, unlike the business environment in its broader sense, the competitive environment focuses on the factors that influence the way organizations compete with each other. This in turn affects the price and quality of their products or services and their ability to survive. Competitive analysis has long been the focus of industrial economics, which takes an objective view of the nature of competition. This type of analysis is explored in depth in Section 9.3.

A widely used method of competitive analysis from an organizational perspective is Michael Porter's five forces model.[8] This type of analysis is also known as industry analysis. Porter provides a framework for the analysis of competition where rivalry between firms is influenced by five forces: supplier power, buyer power, the threat of entry by new firms, the threat from substitute products, and the nature of the rivalry between the firms themselves. This model can in principle be applied to any industry or market but, as with PESTLE analysis, the basic model provides only a starting point for environmental analysis and needs to be underpinned by an in-depth understanding of the competitive process. Indeed, Porter's five forces model draws its inspiration from the structure-conduct-performance paradigm, which is explained in Section 9.3.3, and the model itself is developed in more detail in Section 9.3.6.

1.5.3 Measures of competitiveness at the national level

Studies of the business environment at a national level are becoming increasingly common. Although these studies are essentially engaged in analysis of the business environment, they are generally expressed in terms of a country's international **competitiveness**. They compare key elements of the business environment in a variety of countries, attaching a score to each of the elements and then ranking the countries' international competitiveness according to their aggregate scores. The term 'international competitiveness' is not without its critics as 'competitiveness' implies the ability to compete. It is therefore more appropriate when applied to business organizations than to countries, since businesses buy and sell goods and services and compete with other businesses and, in the main, countries do not.[9] However, in this context a country that ranks highly in terms of its international competitiveness is one that provides an environment that enables business organizations to be internationally competitive, for example by providing a stable economic and political environment, a high-quality infrastructure, or a highly skilled workforce. These advantages are, of course, available to foreign investors as well as domestic firms, so China's international competitiveness is beneficial for American, European, and Japanese investors, not only for China and its own indigenous firms.

Systematic comparisons of international competitiveness have been undertaken by Michael Porter and by organizations such as the International Institute for Management Development (IMD) and the World Economic Forum (WEF). Porter and his team carried out extensive empirical research in ten countries and his work now provides an important analytical basis for studies of international competitiveness.[10] Both IMD and the WEF are based in Switzerland. The WEF is also known for its gatherings of world political and business leaders in Davos in January each year.

Porter found that 'advanced factors', including communication systems, skilled labour, and specialized services, were more important than 'basic factors' like natural resources in determining national competitive advantage. This helps to explain why countries rich in natural resources, such as Nigeria or Ukraine, are not necessarily rich countries. Countries like Japan, which has invested in education, technology, and other sophisticated developments, have tended to do much better. It also casts doubt on the widely accepted view that countries with low labour costs represent the greatest competitive threat. Arguably, China's increasingly educated workforce, adoption of new technology, and huge increases in productivity are much more significant for the country's economic prosperity than its present relatively low labour costs. According to Porter, the key determinants of national competitive advantage are as follows: firm strategy, structure, and rivalry (effective strategies and competition); factor conditions (especially advanced factors); demand conditions (demanding and discerning consumers); and related and supporting industries (to provide competitively priced, high-quality inputs and business services). These four factors are sometimes represented diagrammatically as the four corners of a diamond and are known as 'Porter's Diamond'. Porter also argues that governments have an important role to play in helping to create favourable conditions for each of the four factors.

The IMD World Competitiveness Scoreboard has been published annually since 1989 and is still widely respected. The IMD Scoreboard 2012 includes 59 countries and 337 individual competitiveness criteria relating to four main areas of competitiveness: economic performance, government efficiency, business efficiency, and infrastructure. The work of IMD in this field and Porter's work on national competitive advantage have been influential in the development of the WEF's Global Competitiveness Reports. The 2012–13 WEF Global Competitiveness Report ranks 144 countries in relation to 12 main pillars (categories): institutions, infrastructure, macroeconomic environment, health and primary education, higher education and training, goods market efficiency, labour market efficiency, financial market development, technological readiness, market size, business sophistication, and innovation.

Like Porter, these international competitiveness rankings place particular emphasis on the quality of a country's 'advanced factors', including its intellectual capital, rather than basic low-cost factors. This helps to explain why the high-cost developed countries fill most of the top positions in the rankings, as can be seen in Table 1.2. Although six of the top ten countries

Table 1.2: Top 10 countries in major international competitiveness rankings

Rank	IMD World Competitiveness Scoreboard 2012	World Economic Forum Global Competitiveness Index 2012–13
1	Hong Kong	Switzerland
2	United States	Singapore
3	Switzerland	Finland
4	Singapore	Sweden
5	Sweden	Netherlands
6	Canada	Germany
7	Taiwan	United States
8	Norway	United Kingdom
9	Germany	Hong Kong
10	Qatar	Japan

Source: World Competitiveness Yearbook 2012, IMD Switzerland, and the Global Competitiveness Report 2012–13, ©World Economic Forum.

Practical insight 1.5:   International competitiveness rankings

Switzerland, Sweden, and Singapore were ranked among the top five countries in both the IMD and WEF international competitiveness rankings in 2012 and 2012–13 respectively. In fact, all the top ten countries in both rankings might be regarded as developed countries if we include the two newly developed countries, Taiwan and Qatar. On the other hand, two of the world's leading emerging economies, China and India, ranked twenty-third and thirty-second in the IMD scoreboard and twenty-ninth and fifty-ninth in the WEF index respectively.

Questions

- Why do you think Switzerland, Sweden, and Singapore appear near the top of these international competitiveness rankings?
- Why do you think China and India come further down the rankings, despite their low-cost production?
- What does this tell us about the importance IMD and the WEF attach to production costs relative to other factors as determinants of a country's international competitiveness?

appear in both the IMD and WEF rankings in Table 1.2, the choice of criteria and the weightings attached to each of the criteria clearly affect the rank order. Competitiveness rankings also reflect prevailing views about the desirability of open, competitive market economies with transparent and efficient public services – characteristics more commonly found in the developed countries (see Practical Insight 1.5).

1.5.4 Forecasting and risk assessment

One of the problems with many types of business environmental analysis is that they lack precision in the evaluation of the impact of environmental factors. Of course, the nature of many environmental factors makes them difficult to measure, especially in a quantifiable way. For example, whilst the impact of an event like the Olympic Games may be estimated in advance, an accurate assessment can only be made after the event. With hindsight, it is even possible to evaluate the impact of an extreme event such as the Japanese earthquake and tsunami on 11 March 2011. Predicting the effect and the possibility of such an event in advance is much more difficult, though developments in geological techniques may help to provide more accurate predictions of natural disasters in the future. More generally, however, various methods are available to help predict the likelihood of future events.

Forecasting is a method commonly used to estimate the future course of events that have some degree of predictability. For example, many business organizations use sales forecasts to project their past sales figures into the future. If sales figures follow a regular pattern, perhaps with seasonal variations, and have a steady growth trend year on year, forecasts over a relatively short period of time may be reasonably accurate. Even here, however, there is likely to be a range of possible sales forecasts, allowing for small errors and variations in the data. Known or expected events can also be incorporated into the forecast without undue loss of accuracy. This process is known as time series analysis, with seasonal adjustment if appropriate, and there are relatively straightforward techniques for undertaking this type of analysis. Businesses also take advantage of published forecasts relating to national economic statistics such as the growth of gross domestic product (GDP), or international statistics in a publication such as the IMF's *World Economic Outlook* (including international comparisons of GDP, trade, prices, and other economic indicators). These published forecasts may then influence an individual firm's sales forecasts, allowing the firm to take account of swings in the economic cycle and other national or international trends.

In effect, forecasting involves a set of techniques designed to make future trends more predictable and to reduce business risk. In relation to particular events where the risks are quantifiable, the likelihood of a future event occurring and the consequences of such an event can also be estimated using probability calculations. When they are less predictable or more difficult to quantify, probability calculations and statistical forecasting may be unreliable or even impossible. Indeed, the complex nature of the business environment means that numerical estimates are often subject to significant errors. Other methods of risk assessment are increasingly being used, often in relation to the more immediate financial risks facing a business but also in relation to external environmental risk. Whilst environmental risk assessment is at a relatively early stage of development, various techniques are available for analysing the less quantifiable risks. Possible techniques include index construction, where scores or weights are attached to risk factors, and scenario planning, where potential risk scenarios are worked out in detail (an approach used by the emergency services as a method of crisis management, for example).

1.5.5 Analysis of alternative futures

Although not yet mainstream, the study of possible **future scenarios** is becoming more widely accepted as an alternative way of planning for future events. Whilst the future is to a large extent unknown, it is argued that it is better to attempt to influence events in a positive direction than simply to allow negative events to happen. An example of this approach is the exhortation of most climate scientists that we should modify our behaviour to reduce the future impact of global warming. Whilst climate change requires collective action on a large scale, even a small business can make the decision to conserve energy or reduce harmful emissions from its production processes. Neither the climate scientist nor the environmentally conscious business would describe themselves as 'futurists' (the name given to those who study 'futures' or future scenarios), but they are engaging in the same kind of activity.

In this way, futurists argue that an organization can to some extent influence its own future by taking actions that will maximize the likelihood of positive outcomes and minimize the likelihood of negative outcomes. This type of approach to the planning of future scenarios is known as **strategic foresight**.[11] Governments and international organizations have also been urged to use strategic foresight when planning for the future. This approach is not unlike the strategic approach taken by many of the more successful companies. It does not of course preclude the possibility of unforeseen events or evaluation errors. As with other methods of analysing the external environment, strategic foresight also benefits considerably from in-depth knowledge of the factors involved. The use of alternative approaches to the analysis of the business environment is illustrated in Practical Insight 1.6.

Practical insight 1.6: Eurotunnel

Eurotunnel, the Anglo-French company which operates the channel tunnel between Britain and France, reported an increase in revenue and profit in 2011 and the volume of traffic using the tunnel continued to increase during the first nine months of 2012, with the exception of rail freight traffic. From 1 January to 30 September 2012 freight truck and passenger car numbers using the shuttle service grew by 19 and 7 per cent respectively and the number of passengers using the Eurostar train service grew by 2 per cent. However, freight train numbers and tonnage fell by 6 and 13 per cent respectively over the same period. Eurotunnel has historically suffered from a lack of price competitiveness compared with the channel ferry operators, but its recent improved performance may partly reflect the stimulus effect of the 2012 London Olympics. The company attributes its relatively poor performance in rail freight services to constraints imposed by the company responsible for the French rail infrastructure, though Eurotunnel has never really achieved its potential in terms of freight traffic.

An understanding of the competitive environment is crucial for an organization like Eurotunnel, as is the ability to monitor and evaluate changes in the wider external environment. Cross-channel traffic between Britain and continental Europe may be affected by the general economic climate, the euro/pound exchange rate, EU internal market legislation, relations between France and the UK, strike action by trade unions in the haulage industry, and a number of other factors.[12]

Question

- What could you learn about Eurotunnel's external environment from each of the following: (a) a competitive analysis using Porter's five forces model; (b) a PESTLE analysis of the company's current external environment; and (c) the use of alternative future scenarios describing potential changes affecting the company's external environment?

Summary

The business environment describes the external context in which all organizations operate. Its various elements, including political, economic, social, technological, legal, environmental, and ethical factors, may be separately analysed, but it is important to understand how they interact with each other in a complex economic system. Private, public, third-sector, and fourth-sector organizations are all affected by their external environment in the normal course of their 'business'. The business environment has undergone significant changes in recent years, including the opening up of China and the former Soviet bloc, the impact of globalization and technological change, and the world recession. Whilst profound, these changes have not necessarily had the same effect on all regions or countries because of the distinctive contribution of politics, history, culture, and other factors. It is clear, however, that the international dimension of the business environment is becoming increasingly important. There are a number of different ways of analysing the business environment, but the main purpose of this book is to provide the underpinning knowledge and understanding necessary for in-depth environmental analysis.

Discussion questions

1. What role should an understanding of the business environment play in determining an organization's strategic planning?

2. In what sense can the business environment be described as a complex adaptive system?

3. In what ways have the opening up of China's economy and the end of communist central planning in the former Soviet bloc changed the international business environment in recent years?

4. PESTLE analysis is perhaps the most widely used method of assessing an organization's business environment. What are the limitations of this approach?

5. Why does the World Economic Forum focus predominantly on qualitative factors as the main determinants of a country's international competitiveness?

6. What are the main advantages and disadvantages of the development of scenarios as a way of planning for the future?

Suggested assignment topics

1. Choose a company or other organization and investigate the main domestic and international changes that have affected the organization's business environment in the last five years.

2. Choose a specific event (e.g. a new law, policy, technological development, international incident, etc.) that has affected the business environment within the last year. Investigate the impact of this event on the businesses and industries concerned.

3. Choose a specific country other than your own and identify the main features of the country's business environment from a foreign investor's perspective.

 Case study: Tesco and the changing retail environment

Tesco's founder, Jack Cohen, started the business as a market trader in the East End of London in 1919 and opened his first Tesco shop in 1929. From these humble beginnings Tesco has become the UK market leader, with a market share in the UK grocery market of 31 per cent in June 2012. Tesco was also the third largest retailer in the world, behind Wal-Mart Stores and Carrefour, measured by annual sales in 2012, though at $104 billion it was still considerably smaller than the world's largest retailer, Wal-Mart, with sales of $447 billion.[13] Wal-Mart is also the owner of Tesco's nearest UK rival, Asda, which had a market share of 17 per cent, closely followed by Sainsbury at 16.6 per cent and Morrison at 11 per cent.

  Although well ahead of its competitors in terms of UK market share, Tesco's three main rivals became more equally balanced after Morrison's takeover of Safeway in 2003. The UK market also contains a number of smaller supermarket chains, including the Cooperative (6.5 per cent), Waitrose (4.6 per cent), and two German discounters, Aldi and Lidl (each with 2.8 per cent). A third continental European discounter, the Danish company Netto, sold its UK stores to Asda in 2011, some of which have now been resold to comply with competition policy rules. Opportunities for further expansion in the UK market are now limited to some extent by competition rules and planning restrictions, but significant growth was achieved by Aldi, Lidl, Waitrose, and Asda during the twelve months to June 2012.[14]

  Tesco has pursued a strategy of rapid growth in the UK for a number of years, with considerable success, though its market share has now stabilized and the company is in the process of reorganizing and upgrading many of its UK stores. Its growth strategy has included organic growth through the opening of new stores, a move into smaller convenience stores, increasing emphasis on non-food sales such as clothing and electronic goods, the development of telecommunication services, and the launch of its internet business and Tesco Bank.

Like many UK retailers, Tesco was relatively slow to go international. Despite the company's long history, it was only in the 1990s that Tesco started to venture abroad, initially to Ireland and continental Europe, then to Asia, and more recently to the United States. One of the company's early international ventures was its acquisition of the northern French chain, Catteau, but Tesco soon pulled out of France after facing stiff competition in the mature French market. Its main European operations outside the UK are now in Ireland and four of the Central European countries, the Czech Republic, Poland, Hungary, and Slovakia. Tesco also has stores in China, Malaysia, South Korea, Thailand, Turkey, the United States, and Japan, though the company is now withdrawing from the USA and Japan.

Tesco's international expansion has often involved the acquisition of an existing retail chain, followed by the opening of new stores, but its expansion to the United States was more cautious. The experience of other UK retailers, such as Marks and Spencer and Dixons, may have discouraged Tesco from early US market entry. Despite the familiar language, the US market is highly competitive and US shopping habits are not as uniform as might be expected. Tesco extended its internet business to the United States in 2001 and opened its first 'Fresh and Easy' convenience stores there in 2007, though after persistent losses, the company decided to close its US stores in 2013. Although it is now clearly a multinational business, around two-thirds of the company's retail sales revenue still came from its UK operations in 2012.

Tesco's business has grown during a period of unprecedented change in the retail sector. From a one-man market stall to a small chain of conventional stores during the first half of the twentieth century, Tesco adopted the self-service and supermarket formats during the 1960s and 1970s, followed by a succession of takeovers and new stores as the food market became dominated by the large supermarket chains in the 1980s and 1990s. By 1995, Tesco had become the UK retail grocery market leader. The company's international expansion was clearly a response to international developments such as the end of communism in Central and Eastern Europe, the rapid expansion of Asia's tiger economies, and the opening up of China. On the other hand, the world's more mature markets in Western Europe and North America have proved difficult to penetrate.

The world's retail markets have clearly become more international in recent years, but more especially in Asia and Central Europe than in the more mature markets of Western Europe and North America. International competition is beginning to penetrate some of the latter markets, but the change has been gradual rather than dramatic.[15]

Case study questions

1. How would you describe Tesco's competitive environment in the UK market?

2. How is this environment likely to differ in the markets for food, clothing, electronic goods, and financial services respectively?

3. Why do you think UK retailers were generally slow to venture abroad until the 1990s?

4. How would you describe Tesco's competitive environment in its international markets?

5. To what extent do you think it is significant that three of the fastest-growing grocery retailers in the UK market are foreign-owned firms?

6. Why do you think Tesco's international expansion has, up to now, been more successful in Ireland, Central Europe, and Asia than in Western Europe and the United States?

7. On what factors is Tesco's future success in international markets likely to depend?

8. What changes in the business environment are likely to be on the horizon for Tesco in the near future?

Notes

1. Grobel, W. (2010), 'What are the London 2012 Olympics worth?' *Marketing Week* (15 April) and Jennings, W. (2012), 'The Olympics as a story of risk management', *Harvard Business Review* Blog Network (13 August).

2. For a discussion of complex systems in relation to an economy see, for example, Foster, J. (2005), 'From simplistic to complex systems in economics', *Cambridge Journal of Economics*, vol. 29, pp. 873–92.

3. See, for example, UK National Audit Office (2005), 'Working with the Third Sector', Report by the Comptroller and Auditor General (29 June).

4. For a discussion of the emerging fourth sector, see www.fourthsector.net.

5. IMF, *World Economic Outlook Database*, April 2012.

6. The total number of speakers of English as a first language is estimated to be 341 million, which is similar to Spanish (358 million) and Hindi (366 million), but much lower than Mandarin Chinese (874 million). The number of speakers of English as a second or foreign language is unknown, with estimates ranging from 200 million to a billion or more. These figures are taken from Janson, T. (2002), *Speak: A Short History of Languages*, Oxford University Press, p. 260.

7. Huntington, S. P. (2002), *The Clash of Civilizations and the Remaking of World Order*, The Free Press.

8. See Porter, M. E. (2004), *Competitive Strategy: Techniques for Analyzing Industries and Competitors*, Free Press, a division of Simon and Schuster.

9. For a fuller discussion of the difficulties with the concept of international competitiveness, see Krugman, P. R. (1996), 'Making sense of the competitiveness debate', *Oxford Review of Economic Policy*, vol. 12, no. 3, pp. 17–25.

10. See Porter, M. E. (1998), *The Competitive Advantage of Nations*, Palgrave Macmillan.

11. See, for example, Fuller, T., and Warren, L. (2006), 'Entrepreneurship as foresight: A complex social network perspective on organisational foresight', *Futures*, vol. 38, pp. 956–71.

12. Main sources: Groupe Eurotunnel Registration Document 2011 and Eurotunnel press release, 23 October 2012 (http://www.eurotunnelgroup.com).

13. Fortune Global 500, 2012.

14. Market share data are taken from *Retail Week* (19 June 2012).

15. Main sources: *Retail Week* (19 June 2012); http://www.tescoplc.com (accessed on 3 November 2012); and BBC News (17 April 2013), 'Tesco profits fall as supermarket pulls out of US'.

Suggestions for further reading

Books with a broad coverage of the business environment in an international context

Brooks, I., Weatherston, J., and Wilkinson, G. (2010), *The International Business Environment*, FT Prentice Hall

Hamilton, L., and Webster, P. (2012), *The International Business Environment*, Oxford University Press

Morrison, J. (2011), *The Global Business Environment: Meeting the Challenges*, Palgrave Macmillan

More advanced treatment of the business environment in an international context

Baron, D. (2009), *Business and its Environment*, Pearson

Guy, F. (2009), *The Global Environment of Business*, Oxford University Press

For those who want to explore the idea of the business environment as a complex adaptive system
Dopfer, K. (2006), *The Evolutionary Foundations of Economics*, Cambridge University Press

 Take your learning further: Online Resource Centre
http://www.oxfordtextbooks.co.uk/orc/harrison2e/
Visit the Online Resource Centre that accompanies this book to enrich your understanding of Chapter 1: The Business Environment: An Overview. Among other resources explore web links and keep up to date with the latest developments in the area.

Key terms introduced in this chapter

Business environment The external political, economic, social, legal, technological, ethical, and other factors which affect an organization.

Competitiveness When applied to an organization, the ability to compete effectively against rivals; when applied to a country, the ability to create an environment which is conducive to good economic and business performance.

Complex adaptive system A structure made up of many elements that operate independently and also interact with each other, absorbing information from their surrounding elements.

Corporate social responsibility The responsibility of an organization for the economic, social, ethical, and environmental impacts of its activities.

Fiscal stimulus An increase in government expenditure or reduction in taxation used to boost aggregate demand during a recession.

Fourth-sector organization An organization which combines business (including profit-making) objectives with social or environmental objectives.

Future scenario An evaluation of how alternative future events may materialize and their potential implications for an organization.

Globalization A set of interrelated political, economic, and social processes involving international flows of goods, services, people, and capital which lead to the increasing interdependence of countries.

Keynesian policy Interventionist government policy used to manage the level of aggregate demand in an economy in order to stimulate economic growth and employment or control inflation and reduce a balance of payments deficit.

Parastatal An agency, company, or other organization that is funded wholly or partly by government and performs functions of public importance, but has its own governance structure.

PESTLE analysis The identification of political, economic, social, technological, legal, and environmental factors as a basis for analysing an organization's external environment.

Private sector organization A public or private limited company or unincorporated business owned by a private individual, group of individuals, or organization.

Public sector organization A central or local government department, public corporation, or other organization owned by the state.

Strategic foresight The ability to develop future scenarios and/or influence the likely outcome of future events facing an organization.

SWOT analysis The identification of an organization's strengths and weaknesses and the opportunities and threats it faces in the external environment used as a basis for developing strategies or reviewing progress.

Third-sector organization A not-for-profit organization such as a charity, cooperative, voluntary or community group, foundation, trust, or social enterprise.

Globalization of the Business Environment

 Chapter learning outcomes

On completion of this chapter the reader should be able to:

- Identify the nature of globalization and the forces that drive globalization
- Explore the implications of globalization for the changing world order
- Discuss the rationale for and the institutions of global governance
- Analyse the impact and theoretical basis of globalization
- Evaluate alternative perspectives on globalization

Opening scenario: Singapore – a globalized city state

The tiny country of Singapore covers an area of around 700 square kilometres, but with a population of a little under five and a half million, it is one of the most densely populated and urbanized countries in the world, effectively making it a city state. It lies at the southern tip of the Malaysian peninsula just north of the equator, but unlike many of the world's equatorial regions, Singapore is a highly developed country with the world's fifth highest GDP per capita on a purchasing power parity basis.[1] Singapore's population is predominantly of Chinese ethnicity, but there are also sizeable groups of Malays and Indians, and the country has a large migrant population of foreign citizens, many of whom work in the large number of multinational companies operating in Singapore.

Although governed by a democratic system, Singapore has been ruled by the People's Action Party since it gained independence in 1965 and Lee Kwan Yew was prime minister throughout this period until 1990. His son, Lee Hsien Loong, has also been prime minister since 2004 and Lee Kwan Yew continued to occupy the position of 'minister mentor' in the cabinet until his resignation in May 2011. Political stability has helped Singapore to maintain continuity in its economic and foreign policies and these policies have promoted an open economy with strong links to the main trading nations, but effective single-party rule has also facilitated a system of tight government control over the country's affairs.

Despite having a relatively authoritarian government, Singapore is one of the most open liberalized economies, with international trade accounting for over two and a half times its GDP and inward FDI over 20 per cent of GDP in 2011, making it one of the most 'globalized' countries in the world.[2] It is also a member of the Association of South-East Asian Nations (ASEAN), the main trade grouping in the region and was the first ASEAN member country to sign a free trade agreement with the European Union in 2012. However, the country's economic openness can also be contrasted with its highly organized society, dominant Chinese ruling elite, and distinctive blend of cultural influences.

Singapore's size and location make the country reliant on imports for most of its natural resources – even its water supplies are piped in from neighbouring Malaysia. However, the country has made up for these shortages by investing in education and high-tech industries such as electronics, information technology, pharmaceuticals, and financial services. The government also places great emphasis on the

(continued...)

learning of English throughout the education system, making it easy for skilled workers and multinational companies to enter or leave the country, and its modern, highly developed economy and administrative system consistently place Singapore among the top few countries in international competitiveness rankings (see Table 1.2). For these and other reasons, Singapore provides a good example of many of the key features of globalization discussed in this chapter, as well as reminding us that, even in an open global economy, countries often retain many of their distinctive political and cultural characteristics.[3]

2.1 Globalization as a process

Globalization describes a process, not a completed state.[4] It implies that the world is 'globalizing', not necessarily that it is fully 'globalized', though descriptions such as the 'global village' suggest that, in some respects, the process has been completed.[5] So what does this process involve? It is probably more accurate to describe it as a set of interrelated processes rather than a single process. At its core, there is what the *New York Times* journalist and author, Thomas Friedman, calls a 'flattening' process.[6] According to Friedman, the world is being flattened in the sense that technology is creating a 'flat' or level playing field by allowing developing countries like China and India to become participants in international business on a par with the richer developed countries. This view implies that all countries could potentially participate in globalization, though in practice a number of obstacles may prevent this.

The idea that globalization involves the removal of barriers between countries is widely held. In a purely economic sense, a barrier-free world economy is effectively a world of free trade or laissez-faire as it was described in the nineteenth century. In this sense, the concept is not new, though the fact that free trade has gone further than before, both in volume terms and in its geographical spread, makes it different in degree at least. The idea of a borderless world can be extended to include the breaking down of political, social, and cultural borders, allowing the international movement of people, policies, ideas, customs, and beliefs and making nation states more interdependent in a political as well as an economic sense.

Globalization also seems to imply that the whole world is becoming involved in this process, for example that business activity is becoming 'global', with global resources being used by global companies that sell their products in global markets. This picture of globalization is of course exaggerated, as many companies and markets are not global, though resources seem to possess more of the characteristics of a global economy. This is especially true of capital, which flows apparently seamlessly from one country to another. Even bulk raw materials like coal or oil can easily be transported around the world at relatively low cost. People can also be transported quickly and easily and do so in large numbers for business and pleasure, though international labour migration is proportionately less today than it was in the latter half of the nineteenth century when many Europeans were emigrating to the 'new world'.

Another aspect of globalization is the growth of supranational activities, especially through organizations such as the United Nations (UN), International Monetary Fund (IMF), World Bank, and World Trade Organization (WTO). In this respect, globalization seems to be at least partially replacing 'territorialism' and the sovereignty of the nation state, with increasing political and social connections between states and their people.[7] Sometimes this argument is extended to suggest that nations, particularly smaller states, have limited power in a globalizing world and that multinational companies wield the real power. Comparisons between the worldwide turnover of some of the world's largest multinational companies and many countries' gross domestic product (GDP) seem to support this argument, but in the main the influence of companies is in a more limited sphere of activity than that of countries (commercial activities rather than defence, law and order, education, etc.).

Underlying many of these features of globalization is technological change. This is particularly true of information and communication technology. The widespread use of personal computers, smartphones, and hand-held computer devices, coupled with the development of the internet and the worldwide web, has enabled businesses and individuals to communicate and share information across the world. It has increased the connections between different parts of the world, making the world appear smaller (reinforcing the concept of the global village). This characteristic of globalization has been described as the 'death of distance', implying that distance or spatial separation no longer has any significance when conducting business or personal affairs.[8] Whilst this is largely true in relation to communication and information flows, it does not necessarily apply to all areas of business or personal activity. For example, where face-to-face contact is required, as in conventional retailing, or where physical goods have to be transported, distance and location still matter. There may also be a number of other reasons why proximity to the customer is important, including the need for cultural awareness. Nevertheless, technology has allowed us to overcome many of the barriers that distance used to present (see Practical Insight 2.1).

Practical insight 2.1: Technology and remote development

'... computers became cheaper and dispersed all over the world, and there was an explosion of software – e-mail, search engines like Google, and proprietary software that can chop up any piece of work and send one part to Boston, one part to Bangalore, and one part to Beijing, making it easy for anyone to do **remote development**'.[9] Thomas Friedman's analysis of the global operations made possible by information and communication technology sees few limits to the way technology is connecting the world and flattening the barriers between rich and poor countries.

Question

● Are there any limits to the remote development of business operations?

2.2 Drivers of globalization

The search to identify the forces driving globalization has exercised many minds since the early 1990s. To some extent, our view of globalization will influence the priority we attach to particular drivers. A broad view of globalization as a set of political, economic, and social processes might lead to the conclusion reached by the sociologist, Anthony Giddens, that globalization is an inevitable consequence of the historical processes of modernization in contemporary society.[10] In what follows we view globalization as essentially an economic process, though one which is driven by political and technological as well as economic forces. We also recognize that it is a complex set of processes involving many poorly understood interactions and feedback mechanisms, and that economic processes may have far-reaching political and social consequences. A popular view is that multinational companies are the main drivers of globalization, though most analysts consider that these companies are responding to global forces rather than driving them. Broadly speaking, the key drivers of globalization are political, technological, and economic, though the economic drivers are separated into their main components in the following subsections.

2.2.1 Political drivers

Numerous political forces are at work in the modern world. One of the most important is the relative peace and security that has existed in much of the world since 1945. Of course, there have been many localized wars during this period, which is no doubt a reason why some of the world's poorest countries remain relatively isolated from globalization. Among the major trading nations, however, peace and security have brought opportunities to do business with much of the world in a relatively safe environment. There is nothing like good international relations for promoting economic prosperity. The opening up of China and the countries of the former Soviet bloc has also been a significant driver of trade and investment between regions formerly closed to each other. It is reassuring to note that the fall of the Berlin Wall, which symbolized the end of communism in Eastern Europe, took place on 9 November 1989 – 11/9, signifying the dawn of a new era after the end of the 'cold war' – in contrast to 9/11 (11 September 2001), the date of the Al-Qaeda attacks in New York, Washington, and Pennsylvania.[11] A number of transnational and supranational organizations may also be regarded as helping to drive globalization. The former category includes a large number of regional groupings such as the European Union (EU) or North American Free Trade Agreement (NAFTA), which promote integration within regions, though arguably at the expense of inter-regional integration (see Section 3.3); the latter includes organizations such as the IMF or WTO (see Section 2.4 below).

2.2.2 Technological drivers

Some people regard technology as the main driver of globalization. Certainly its impact is all-pervasive, from the alarm clock that wakes us up in the morning to the car we drive to work, the computers we use at work, and the automatic timer that switches on the oven for our evening meal. Technology has numerous applications, but information and communication technology almost certainly has the most widespread implications, allowing worldwide communication, information sharing, and the operation and control of remote activities (including **outsourcing** and **offshoring**, which are explained in Section 8.4.5). Above all the microprocessor, facilitating the development of ever more powerful computers, and the internet, enabling global communication and the creation of the worldwide web, have been of enormous significance. Reductions in transport costs have also facilitated the creation of more efficient worldwide distribution networks, where goods can easily be transferred from one mode of transport to another with the advent of containerization. The establishment of communication and transport networks often involves high initial fixed costs, but additional users, both businesses and consumers, incur falling variable costs as the network size increases. These increasing returns to scale create huge benefits, known as network externalities, as the network expands (see Sections 10.2.3 and 10.3.3).

2.2.3 Economic liberalization

One of the features modern globalization has in common with earlier periods of internation-alization, especially in the late nineteenth century, is greater economic openness or free trade. **Economic liberalization**, in its modern form, usually describes internal economic reform such as **deregulation** and **privatization** and the removal of barriers to trade in services as well as the more conventional view of free trade as the removal of tariffs on physical imports. Economic liberalization has come about as a result of the following: the succession of trade rounds since 1948 under the General Agreement on Tariffs and Trade (GATT), incorporated into the policies of the WTO from 1995, which have brought a gradual reduction in trade barriers between the main trading nations; the revival of free-market policies under Margaret Thatcher in the UK (1979–90) and Ronald Reagan in the USA (1981–9), supported by renewed interest in free-market economics generally and the adoption of a free-market approach by the IMF and, to a lesser extent, the World Bank (the so-called **Washington consensus**)[12] during the 1980s and 1990s; and the apparent triumph of free-market capitalism after the collapse of communist central planning in the Soviet bloc in 1989–91, together with China's gradual but growing success in its experimentation with free-market economics after 1978. Each of these events was of course politically driven, but the forces unleashed were undoubt-edly economic. In effect, economic liberalization enables a business to take advantage of resources outside its traditional industrial or geographical boundaries, facilitating a global reallocation of resources.

2.2.4 Market drivers

As domestic sales growth in the more developed countries slows down or these markets become saturated, businesses increasingly rely on international markets to allow continued expansion. Rising income in international markets will inevitably encourage this expansion. Two of the world's most rapidly growing markets are China and India, though companies were initially attracted to these countries by the ready supply of low-cost skilled labour. China's own rapid economic growth has also been made possible by its access to export markets in North America, Europe, and other parts of the world. World population growth may also be a significant factor in the growth of world markets. World population more than doubled from 3 billion in 1960 to just over 7 billion in 2013, though the rate of growth has been slowing down since about 1970.[13] More specifically, proximity to markets seems to have become the most important driver of foreign direct investment (FDI), one of the key components of economic globalization. A joint venture or alliance with a foreign partner provides an alternative method of entry into a foreign market. This suggests that, despite the distance-reducing effects of globalization, location is still important (see Section 8.4).

2.2.5 Cost drivers

The increased openness of the world economy exposes the differences in resource costs in different countries. This allows companies to search for lower costs, either by purchasing raw materials or components abroad, relocating a production process or service operation abroad (offshoring), or outsourcing some of their activities to other businesses abroad. Internationali-zation also enables a firm to take advantage of **economies of scale**, with the larger interna-tional market allowing increased scale of operations, hence lower average production costs.

This is especially important in industries like motor manufacturing where product development costs are high. This helps to account for the large number of alliances in the car industry, where companies share common production platforms, research and development costs, and purchasing and distribution costs (see Section 8.4.4).

2.2.6 Competition drivers

International competition also drives cost reductions, but its impact is more far-reaching, prompting improvements in quality, efficiency, and productivity in all aspects of a firm's activities. The need to be internationally competitive, even in the home market, increases as international barriers come down and the world's economies become more interdependent. Competitive pressures may not have initiated the process of globalization, but they undoubtedly drive companies to become more international in order to be internationally competitive (see Practical Insight 2.2). The drive to create internationally competitive products and services through differentiation is a powerful force. Even smaller companies can engage in this kind of specialized competition, helping to dispel the idea that only large multinational companies can be successful in international markets.[14]

2.3 Globalization and the changing world order

Globalization is connecting the world's economies, but countries do not of course play an equal role in this process. Throughout much of the period since 1945, international business activity has been dominated by the 'Triad': North America, Western Europe, and Japan.

Practical insight 2.2:   Dyson's global repositioning

In 2002, Dyson reluctantly moved its main vacuum cleaner production plant from Malmesbury in the UK to Malaysia. The company already had a plant in Malaysia serving the East Asian and Australian market, but the new plant was to become the main international production operation. The company's washing machine production was also transferred to Malaysia in 2003. Understandably, the plant closures in the UK were controversial because of the loss of jobs and what many people perceived as a loss of the UK's manufacturing capability. However, the move enabled Dyson to cut its production costs and remain competitive as a relatively small player in a challenging international market. Many of its suppliers were already located in East Asia, so this created further cost savings. The company retained its design and research and development (R&D) teams in the UK and quadrupled its R&D expenditure between 2005 and 2010, leading to the introduction of new products such as the Air Multiplier fan and Airblade hand dryer, and almost 1,500 of the company's 3,600 employees worked in the UK in 2012. Competitive repositioning has also allowed the company to gain a leading position in the North American and other markets.[15] This story is not untypical of the way in which companies have improved their performance or ensured their survival by responding to the cost, market, and competition drivers of globalization.

Question

- What have been the overall consequences of Dyson's decision to offshore its production to Malaysia and retain its design and R&D capabilities in the UK?

The relative importance of these economies has changed over time, but even today the Triad account for just over half of world merchandise exports, about 60 per cent of world exports of commercial services, and about 70 per cent of world FDI outflows (see Section 3.2). The dominant position of the Triad in world economic activity is gradually declining, but it would be premature to suggest that these countries are no longer important. What is clear, however, is that countries like China and India are becoming gradually more important in the world economy. In 2001, Goldman Sachs coined the term '**BRIC**' to describe the world's four largest emerging economies, Brazil, Russia, India, and China.[16] These economies have all been growing rapidly and, in a subsequent paper, Goldman Sachs estimated that by 2039 the BRIC economies may have overtaken the G6 (France, Germany, Italy, Japan, UK, and USA) and that by 2050 they were likely to be the world's largest group of economies by a considerable margin.[17]

Of course, these projections depend on the BRICs' ability to sustain something like their recent economic growth performance for another thirty or forty years, but even if the projections are optimistic, there is nevertheless likely to be a change in the balance of economic power during the first half of the twenty-first century. Arguably, China is already beginning to assume a more prominent role, having become the world's second largest economy and largest exporter of merchandise goods, and having survived the 2008–9 world economic downturn in a stronger economic and financial position than any of the Triad countries. Other countries beyond the BRICs could also be considered to be potential economic leaders of the future, and South Africa officially joined the '**BRICS**' in 2010. Goldman Sachs proposed a further list of eleven large emerging economies with growth potential, described as the Next Eleven (N-11), including Bangladesh, Egypt, Indonesia, Iran, Mexico, Nigeria, Pakistan, Philippines, Turkey, South Korea, and Vietnam, though apart from South Korea and Mexico, these countries are generally less developed.[18] The term 'EAGLES' has also been suggested to describe the 'emerging and growth leading economies' of the next few years (Brazil, China, India, Indonesia, South Korea, Mexico, Russia, Taiwan, and Turkey).[19] This probably represents a more realistic set of countries with growth potential than the N-11, but it should also be recognized that most of these countries, including the BRICS, although large, will have considerably lower GDP per capita than the Triad even in 2050.

The world political order has been somewhat different. The post-war settlement left the world divided between the North Atlantic Treaty Organization (NATO), led by the United States, and the Warsaw Pact countries, led by the USSR. This **bipolar world order** continued until the collapse of the Soviet Union in 1991. Since then, the United States has been dominant politically and militarily. For the United States, political power has been reinforced by economic power, but this was not the case with the Soviet Union, whose economic power was largely confined to the group of countries in its own sphere of influence, mainly in Central and Eastern Europe. Since 1991, not only has the United States confirmed its political and economic position, but some of the countries formerly under Soviet influence have joined NATO and the EU. Whilst NATO's role is now less clear than it was during the cold war, the EU has become a powerful economic force alongside the United States. This is not, however, true to the same extent in the political sphere, except perhaps in relation to their influence over trade policy at the WTO.

How long the US **unipolar world order** will continue is uncertain. It is clear that China is now becoming a significant economic power and, despite its current reluctance to play a global role comparable to that of the United States, it is likely that Chinese political influence will gradually increase over the coming years. The extent to which China will be joined by the other BRICS countries or other emerging economies to create a **multipolar world order** is less

Key Dates	Global Governance: Key International Institutions	Political Power: Key Countries and Groupings	Economic Power: Key Countries and Groupings
1945 End of World War II	UN, IMF, World Bank G7 (1975/76)	Bipolar world: USA (Nato), USSR (Warsaw Pact)	Triad: N. America, W. Europe, Japan
1991 End of the 'Cold War'	UN, IMF, World Bank WTO (1995) G7/G8 (1997) G20 (1999)	Unipolar World: USA	USA, EU, Japan China (emerging)
2010 Recovery from world recession	UN, IMF, World Bank WTO G20 G7/G8?	USA – end of unipolar world? Growing influence of China	USA, EU, China BRIC?
2050 A new world order?	New institutional arrangements?	Bipolar World: USA, China Multipolar World?	China, USA, EU BRIC, Others?

Figure 2.1 The changing world order: an emerging scenario

clear. What is clearer, however, is that the world political and economic order is likely to change significantly during the next few decades. This has potentially huge implications for international economic activity, the policies of the major international institutions, and the relative importance of different regions of the world. This emerging scenario is illustrated in Figure 2.1 and can be discussed in more detail as three alternative scenarios in Practical Insight 2.3.

2.4 Global governance and the need for international regulation

The immediate post-World War II years heralded a move towards **multilateralism** in world political and economic affairs. The League of Nations, an earlier attempt to establish a framework for multinational cooperation and security, had failed to prevent World War II, but

Practical insight 2.3:   The changing world order: alternative scenarios in 2050

Consider the following alternative scenarios representing visions of the world in 2050. Try to describe each of the possible scenarios in more detail, drawing out their implications for the pattern of international business activities.

- Scenario 1: The Bipolar World – a world dominated by the United States and China, two superpowers jostling for position in political and economic affairs.

- Scenario 2: The Multipolar World – a world dominated by powerful individual countries or groups of countries such as the USA, China, and the other BRICS countries, characterized by a changing balance of economic and political power.

- Scenario 3: The Fragmented World – a world with no overall political leadership where there is little consensus on political or economic issues.

renewed efforts were made after the devastation of two world wars in less than half a century. The UN was formed in 1945 and the International Monetary Fund (IMF) and International Bank for Reconstruction and Development (IBRD, now part of the World Bank group) came into operation in 1946. Multilateral cooperation on trade began with the General Agreement on Tariffs and Trade (GATT), which came into effect in 1948. A variety of other international organizations were set up during the early post-war years, most notably the Council of Europe in 1949 and the European Coal and Steel Community (ECSC) in 1951, which led to the formation of the European Economic Community (EEC), now known as the EU, in 1957.

Multilateralism has become more established in recent years, reinforced by the belief that international problems require international rules enforced by international authorities. This system of **global governance**, as it is sometimes known, is not without its critics, both because of its inability to enforce compliance when individual countries flout its rules and because of the alleged unfairness of the rules themselves. This is a particular concern in the area of trade policy, which now comes under the remit of the World Trade Organization (WTO).

2.4.1 The World Trade Organization

The WTO has its origins in the General Agreement on Tariffs and Trade. The GATT was an attempt by some of the developed countries to encourage free trade by lowering the level of tariffs on industrial goods, and the general level of tariffs has been significantly reduced since the 1940s. The GATT operated through a series of trade rounds or negotiations, the last completed round being the **Uruguay Round** (1986–94). The Uruguay Round led to a reduction in tariffs on industrial goods in developed countries from an average of 6.3 to 3.8 per cent. It also included negotiations on agricultural products for the first time. Sometimes member countries slip back on their commitment to reduce trade barriers and there has also been a tendency to rely on non-tariff barriers such as product regulations in place of tariffs. The most important outcome of the Uruguay Round was the establishment of the WTO in January 1995. This has formalized the process of multilateral trade negotiations and strengthened the disputes procedure when things go wrong.

As well as the GATT, which continues to be one of the agreements managed by the WTO, there is also a General Agreement on Trade in Services (GATS), an agreement on Trade-Related Aspects of Intellectual Property Rights (TRIPS), and an agreement on Trade-Related Investment Measures (TRIMS). The GATS framework was agreed during the Uruguay Round, but subsequent agreement has been reached by a number of member countries, though not all, on the liberalization of telecommunications and financial services. Although merchandise goods still dominate international trade, access to international service sectors is becoming an important issue. Less progress has been made on intellectual property rights (TRIPS), including patents, copyright, trade marks, and geographical indications (names linking a product to a place such as Champagne or Scotch). The TRIMS agreement is designed to prevent investment rules, such as local content requirements, being used to circumvent trade rules.

In each of these areas, the WTO applies a number of important trade principles:

- The *most favoured nation principle* (MFN), whereby every WTO member is expected to treat all other members in the same way as it treats its most favoured partner;
- *Equal national treatment* of foreign and local goods, services, and intellectual property once they have entered a market (the national principle);

- Gradual movement towards *freer trade* through negotiation;
- Binding and transparent trade agreements that are *predictable*;
- *Fair competition* without distorting subsidies or dumping (selling exports below cost in order to gain market share); and
- A trading system which *encourages development and economic reform* among the three-quarters of WTO member countries that are developing countries or countries in transition to market economies.

There are inevitably some exceptions to these principles, most notably the recognition of regional economic groupings like the EU as well as many bilateral agreements between individual countries or groups of countries. However, preferential trading agreements that provide favourable market access to developing countries are covered by the final principle above; these include arrangements such as the generalized system of preferences (GSP) or the Cotonou Agreement between the EU and the African, Caribbean, and Pacific (ACP) group of countries (see Section 3.3).

Although dominated by the large developed countries, the WTO had 159 members in March 2013, including many developing countries. After almost 15 years of negotiations, China was finally admitted to the WTO in December 2001. This marked a major step towards the WTO becoming a global institution, though China's reluctance to remove obstacles to its domestic market made WTO entry negotiations a tortuous process. Russia also finally joined the WTO in August 2012 after 18 years of negotiations. The developing member countries are increasingly exerting their influence over trade negotiations and the most recent trade round, the **Doha Round**, has a strong focus on what is known as the Doha Development Agenda. The Doha Round began in Qatar in November 2001 and was originally supposed to be completed by 1 January 2005, but tensions between the developed and developing countries have effectively brought progress to a halt. The developing countries had experienced difficulties in implementing agreements on agricultural tariffs made under the Uruguay Round, but a major stumbling block under the Doha Round has been the reluctance of the EU and United States to reduce their agricultural support policies. These policies have restricted access to the world's largest internal markets and, more controversially, have sometimes distorted international trade through the use of export subsidies. Progress on future trade negotiations will depend on the willingness of both sides to reduce their long-established dependence on agricultural protection.

The fact that almost three-quarters of the world's nations belong to the WTO suggests there is broad support for free trade, or at least the necessity of gaining access to other countries' markets. The WTO also requires commitment to a rule-based multinational trading system. Sometimes the rules are broken or tested to the limit, as when the United States initially resisted attempts to remove its emergency steel tariffs between 2002 and 2003 or in the long-running dispute over the EU's preferential treatment of banana imports from the African, Caribbean, and Pacific countries (see Practical Insight 2.4). On the whole, the multinational trading system has helped to open the world's markets to freer competition, though often painfully slowly. However, the actions of many of the WTO members suggest an ambivalent attitude towards free trade, supporting the ideal, but often resisting the removal of their own trade barriers, with an apparently unshakeable belief that protection is normally in their national interests, despite frequent evidence to the contrary.

Practical insight 2.4: The banana dispute

Even before the European Union introduced its preferential banana regime for imports from the African, Caribbean and Pacific (ACP) countries in 1993, some of the Latin American banana-producing countries raised their objections under the General Agreement on Tariffs and Trade. The EU regime allowed ACP bananas to be imported at reduced tariffs and with preferential quotas compared with bananas from Latin America and other regions, effectively safeguarding the ACP countries' share of the EU market. This preferential treatment had in fact been provided by some individual EU countries prior to 1993 in order to protect the exports of their former colonies among the ACP countries after they gained independence. The Latin American producers, supported by the United States where their major distributors are based, have understandably been unhappy with these arrangements and have repeatedly been in dispute with the EU at the WTO. Indeed, an acceptable resolution to the dispute was only achieved in 2009 under the Geneva Agreement on Trade in Bananas, an agreement which was finally ratified by all the parties concerned in 2012.

Essentially, the preferential banana regime contravenes the WTO's most-favoured nation principle and national principle, but WTO rulings against the regime have been delayed by EU attempts to reduce their impact and by the failure to reach agreement on agricultural trade under the stalled Doha process. However, the Geneva Agreement now establishes a tariff-only banana regime (without special quotas), where tariffs on Latin American imports are being gradually reduced over the period up to 2017. Whether this will finally end the banana dispute is open to question. It may well depend on how satisfied the various parties are with any future agreement on agricultural trade in general – assuming the aims of the Doha development agenda are eventually achieved.[20]

Question

● What lessons can be learned from this case for the conduct of international trade policy?

The WTO has come under increasing criticism for its stance on free trade. Critics argue that the organization is controlled by the developed countries, whose interests and those of the major multinational companies tend to dominate its policy agenda. Whereas free trade may be good for the mature developed economies, some form of import protection may be necessary for the weaker economies of the developing countries, an issue that is discussed at greater length in Section 3.5.2. A more serious criticism is that the developed countries do not always practise what they preach. The EU Common Agricultural Policy (CAP) provides a good example of this, though the USA, Japan, and other developed countries also have extensive agricultural protection policies. The CAP offers price support for some agricultural products (though not as many as formerly), allowing farmers to gain high prices, but restricts foreign access to this lucrative market through import levies. If farmers are unable to sell all their produce at the high support prices, the EU provides export subsidies to allow them to sell off their surplus production on world markets. This policy limits access to the EU market for some of the developing countries (others have preferential access agreements such as the Cotonou Agreement), but more importantly some of the world's poorest producers find it difficult or even impossible to compete with the EU's subsidized export prices. The reluctance of some EU member states and the USA to reduce their reliance on agricultural protection has been a major stumbling block during the Doha Round negotiations.

The WTO is at the centre of two major debates. First, at its core is a belief that economic liberalism is good for the world economy and that developing countries will gain as much as developed countries from free trade and liberal domestic economic policies such as privatization and deregulation. This view is widely held in economic and political circles, especially by those on the right and centre-right of politics, but it is challenged by those on the left and centre-left, including a number of influential charities such as Oxfam and Christian Aid. This debate is explored more fully in Section 3.5. The second debate is about the need for supranational or global governance. Some free-market economists and politicians argue that trade relations are best left to market forces or that countries should be left to make bilateral agreements where it is in their mutual interest, a system that existed before 1945. Others believe that international cooperation is essential but do not always agree on the form it should take. Failure to make progress in the Doha Round has led some people to question whether the WTO will continue to exist in its present form.

2.4.2 **The International Monetary Fund and World Bank**

The IMF and World Bank Group play a major role in promoting international financial stability. The IMF was originally set up to establish a **fixed exchange rate system** between the major trading nations and to provide financial assistance to countries with short-term balance of payments difficulties. This helped to create the conditions for increased international trade during the 1950s and 1960s. However, a period of exchange rate volatility, rising inflation, and economic stagnation in the 1970s, exacerbated by soaring oil prices, helped to bring about a refocusing of the IMF's role. Since the 1980s the IMF has turned its attention more towards longer-term finance for countries facing financial turbulence or economic transition. Like the WTO, the IMF operates largely on free-market principles and has therefore been subject to similar criticisms. In particular, its insistence on liberal economic reforms as a precondition for financial assistance, even in the poorest countries, has brought considerable criticism.[21]

The World Bank Group includes the following organizations: the International Bank for Reconstruction and Development (IBRD), its original branch set up to help with European reconstruction after World War II but which now lends to middle-income and low-income creditworthy countries; the International Development Association (IDA), which provides subsidized loans to the poorest countries; the International Finance Corporation (IFC), which provides finance for private businesses in developing countries; the Multilateral Investment Guarantee Agency (MIGA), which promotes foreign direct investment into developing countries; and the International Centre for the Settlement of Investment Disputes (ICSID), which provides conciliation and arbitration facilities for countries involved in investment disputes. The World Bank has received some of the same criticisms as the IMF, though on the whole it has been less doctrinaire in its approach to free-market reforms. The World Bank Evaluation Group, set up to monitor the activities of the World Bank, has commended the Bank for helping to remove obstacles to trade in developing countries, but argues that the Bank's policies have been less effective in boosting export growth and alleviating poverty in these countries.[22]

2.5 **The impact of globalization**

Globalization is moving the world's economies closer to being a single, interconnected global economy. Of course, in reality there are still numerous barriers between the world's economies, including a plethora of import and investment restrictions, market regulations, and many other discriminatory government policies as well as natural barriers imposed by history, culture, or geography. However, there is plenty of evidence of increased global economic activity, international competition, and interdependence between national economies. Some of the main economic effects of globalization on the business environment are as follows:

- The internationalization of markets, including the development of increasingly global products and the use of global marketing strategies.
- The internationalization of production, including global production strategies such as outsourcing and the offshoring of manufacturing and service operations.
- Rapid international communication, data transmission, and technology transfer.
- Increasing opportunities for **economies of scope** (adopting common production platforms to produce differentiated variants of standardized products).
- Change in the relative importance of economies of scale at plant and organizational levels – shifting the focus away from conventional large-scale production towards scale economies in global sourcing, marketing, and strategic planning at the level of the organization as a whole.
- The changing structure of industry, as the relative share of manufacturing in national output and employment declines in developed 'industrialized' countries and increases in newly industrializing countries. '**De-industrialization**' in developed countries generally gives way to an increase in service industries, though some developing countries such as India are also building large service sectors, especially in services linked to information technology.
- Changes in the demand for labour: as the structure of industry changes, developed countries increase their demand for educated and skilled labour in high-tech and service industries but reduce their demand for low-skilled labour, while traditional manufacturing jobs are created in developing countries.

These effects of globalization help to increase efficiency in the global allocation of resources, but bring a number of transitional problems and lifestyle changes in their wake. The ability of people, organizations, and economies to adapt is clearly crucial (see Practical Insight 2.5). In Section 2.6 we explore the economic principles underlying globalization.

2.6 The economics of globalization

There is no specific economic theory of globalization. However, there are various theories we can use to shed light on the processes involved. Conventional economic theory provides a useful starting point for our analysis. The conventional theory of market economics is derived from **neoclassical microeconomics**, that is, principles explaining the detailed working of markets that have been developed from the ideas of 'classical' economists like Adam Smith (1723–90) and Alfred Marshall (1842–1924).[23] The basic idea is that markets allocate resources by equating supply with demand (where **demand curve** D_1 and **supply curve** S intersect at the initial equilibrium price p_1 in Figure 2.2a). If demand increases, producers will

Practical insight 2.5: De-industrialization

The proportion of the working population employed in industry in the developed countries fell from an estimated 27.6 to 23.4 per cent between 1999 and 2009. In the developing countries the corresponding proportion increased from 18.4 to 21.3 per cent over the same period.[24] These changes are part of a long-term trend, indicating both the higher level of historical industrialization in the developed countries and the recent global shift in manufacturing towards the developing countries. Of course, industrialized countries are now able to produce more goods with fewer workers because of technological progress, but a gradual change in the relative importance of manufacturing in different parts of the world is also under way. The loss of manufacturing jobs has caused considerable concern in some of the 'de-industrializing' countries and this issue has been a hot topic among rival politicians in the United States, United Kingdom, and elsewhere.

Question

- To what extent are politicians in the developed countries right to argue that their governments should do more to prevent the loss of manufacturing jobs?

be attracted into a market by the prospect of profit (illustrated by a shift in the demand curve to D_2, a movement up the supply curve S, and a higher price p_2 in Figure 2.2a). If demand falls, producers will leave the market and pursue opportunities for profit elsewhere (a shift in the demand curve to D_2, a movement down the supply curve S, and a lower price p_2 in Figure 2.2b).

If supply conditions change, perhaps because of the introduction of new technology leading to increased or lower-cost production, the supply curve will shift to the right from S_1 to S_2 and the price will fall from p_1 to p_2 in Figure 2.3. In pure economic theory price plays an important role, acting as a **market signal** to both consumers and producers, and **market equilibrium** is reached where demand and supply are equal at a particular price. As firms enter or leave the market they are allocating resources to the production of different goods and services. This process of resource allocation is known as the **market mechanism**.

We can now extend the concept of market equilibrium to an economy as a whole or indeed to the global economy. An economy is made up of many different markets, including markets for goods, services, labour, and capital. If all these markets are free from entry barriers,

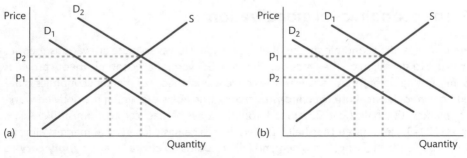

Figure 2.2: The market mechanism when demand changes

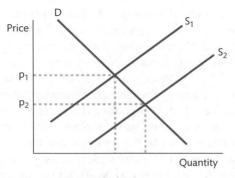

Figure 2.3: The market mechanism when supply increases

one of the characteristics of globalization, competition will drive prices and costs down and firms will move from one market to another in search of profit. When market equilibrium is reached in all markets throughout an economy, **general equilibrium** has been achieved. General equilibrium means that competition has promoted efficient resource allocation on a national or even global scale. Clearly, general equilibrium analysis relies on a number of restrictive assumptions. In the real world, competition is based on product differentiation and quality of service as well as on price and costs, and not all markets are free from barriers and other restrictions. However, the outcomes of conventional microeconomic theory are not very far removed from some of the effects of globalization. Global competition does in fact force prices and costs down. This is why Marks and Spencer replaced some of its high-cost British suppliers with low-cost foreign suppliers when faced with falling profit, why Dyson transferred its vacuum cleaner production to Malaysia, or why Norwich Union (now Aviva) transferred some of its call centres to India (though some of them have been retained in or returned to the UK in response to customer concerns).

Price and cost pressures do indeed seem to be significant features of globalization, but they are not the only pressures. Competitive firms are continually innovating by developing new products, using new technology, and improving customer service. These are dynamic features of competition and globalization is above all a dynamic process. Its effects are chang- ing constantly as the drivers pull in different directions and interact with each other. Dynamic theories of competition help to explain how this process works (see Section 9.3.5). Instead of seeing competition as a process leading to a state of market equilibrium, dynamic theories view competition as a process of continual turbulence and change. Entrepreneurs develop new products or differentiate their products from their competitors. Sometimes they suc- ceed, sometimes they fail. Through experience they learn how to do things better as good decisions are more often rewarded than bad ones. Markets are imperfect but competition gradually makes them work better. The result is not a steady state of equilibrium, but a pro- cess of continual change. However, although this view of the competitive process is very dif- ferent from the conventional view, the pressures on firms to be competitive are very much the same.[25]

It is also important to note that globalization is not a zero-sum game. A zero-sum game is one where one player can only gain at another's expense as the size of the pay-off is fixed (i.e. zero growth). In the game of globalization the players are consumers, producers, workers, and governments. Let us consider the example of offshoring, such as moving call centres to India. Offshoring helps to reduce a firm's production costs to enable it to remain competitive. It results in a loss of jobs in the home country and the creation of jobs in the host country. But this is not simply one country's loss and another country's gain. Lower production costs mean that the firm can reduce its price. Consumers will therefore have to pay less for its products. This may increase the company's sales, but consumers will also have more disposable income to spend on a variety of other goods and services, which will create jobs in these other industries, some of them at home and some abroad. Of course, the workers who lose their jobs through offshoring may not be the ones who gain the new jobs. The jobs could be anywhere in the country. However, if an economy is functioning well, jobs are being lost and created continually, so the net effect may well be at least neutral for the home country and positive for the host country. This is an increasing-sum game. In a similar way, international trade theory reinforces the view that international activity creates net benefits for the world as a whole (see Section 3.4).

There are of course a number of problems with this scenario. For a variety of reasons displaced workers do not always find jobs quickly and their new jobs are not always as well paid as their old ones. This is a transitional problem of globalization and may become a longer-term problem for the workers concerned and their families. There is also a fear that manufacturing and, increasingly, service jobs are moving from developed to developing countries. This is part of a process of changing industrial structure as countries like China and India develop the skills to perform these activities at lower cost. On the whole, however, the developed countries have been successful in adjusting to manufacturing and services that create higher added value. China is already finding that its labour costs are rising as the demand for labour increases (even with its huge population). Its future success will then depend on its ability to improve productivity and product quality, and other countries will take over as lower-cost producers. Again, it is a mistake to think of China's gain, as an exporter of cheap manufactured goods, as the old industrialized countries' loss. After all, China's cheap exports benefit Europe's and North America's consumers, giving them surplus income to spend on other goods and services, thus increasing their standard of living. As China's income per capita rises, world demand will also increase and competition from Chinese goods will encourage other countries to improve the quality of their goods – as competition from Japanese cars and electronic goods did in the 1970s and 1980s. This is clearly not a zero-sum game.

Despite the economic benefits of globalization, industrialized and newly industrializing countries alike are wrestling with the problems of change. The developed countries have to come to terms with their changing industrial structure and labour markets, the developing countries with the problems of industrialization: poor factory working conditions, urban congestion, air and river pollution, and associated social problems. Basically, there are two options for the developed countries in response to globalization: either they attempt to slow down or prevent the impact of globalization – using protective measures such as import controls, regulation, or financial subsidies, or they accept that globalization is inevitable and take measures to improve competitiveness by promoting education and training, research and development, productivity, and market reforms. For political and social reasons most governments use a combination of these approaches, though the logic of the economics of globalization clearly points in the latter direction. Practical Insight 2.6 considers how these issues are viewed by industrialists and consumers.

Practical insight 2.6:   Changing views on free trade and protection

During the 1970s and 1980s many North American and Western European industrialists argued for import protection when faced with intense Japanese competition, especially in the car and electronics industries. Governments were also persuaded by this argument and imposed quotas or voluntary export restraints (agreed rather than imposed quotas) on Japanese goods. By the 1990s many of these industrialists were arguing for free trade, often in the face of opposition from consumer organizations and trade unions.

Question

● What do you think had changed?

2.7 Alternative perspectives on globalization

Current mainstream economic analysis, sometimes described as free-market economics or economic liberalism, broadly takes a positive view of globalization. One of the most rigorous analyses of the free-market view of globalization has been provided by the *Financial Times* journalist, Martin Wolf.[26] There are of course many alternative perspectives. Some take a more negative position; others focus on different aspects of globalization. Analysis of these alternative perspectives helps us to explore the implications of globalization more fully, though in each case we need to test the validity of the arguments carefully. Whatever position one takes on globalization, however, most writers seem to agree that, whilst some aspects of globalization may be inevitable, human beings are not simply bystanders while globalization washes over them. We can actually do something to help mitigate its more harmful effects. Precisely what we should do is often more difficult to determine. In what follows, we discuss some of the alternative contentions.

2.7.1 Globalization is not new

A number of writers have pointed out that some aspects of what we now call globalization have occurred before. The internationalization of business activity is certainly not new. Perhaps the main contender for the globalization label is the latter half of the nineteenth century and the early twentieth century, particularly the period 1870–1914. This was the height of the policy of laissez-faire when international trade was arguably freer than it is today. International trade reached roughly the same proportion of world output in 1913 as it did in the mid-1990s (after years of decline during two world wars and the Great Depression of the 1930s). International labour migration was in fact greater as a proportion of world population in the latter part of the nineteenth century than it is today.[27] Some writers date the concept of globalization back to a much earlier period. For example, Friedman describes three 'globalizations': Globalization 1.0 began with Christopher Columbus's voyage to America in 1492; Globalization 2.0 began in 1800, when the industrial revolution was taking off and English and Dutch companies were starting to expand abroad; and Globalization 3.0 began in 2000 when the technological revolution was reaching its maturity.[28] Whilst some writers take the view that the similarities between these periods of 'globalization' are significant, others consider the recent period to be qualitatively different, especially because of the impact of technology.

2.7.2 Globalization is a threat

Just as globalization seemed to be reaching its peak as we approached the year 2000, the anti-globalization movement started to emerge as a powerful dissenting voice, first at the Seattle summit of the WTO in 1999, then at a series of other international gatherings in Prague (2000), Genoa (2001), Stockholm (2002), and Cancún (2003). The anti-globalization protestors represent a large number of different causes but are united by their hostility towards what they see as the destructive forces of global capitalism. Sometimes their concerns are incompatible with each other or are only tenuously linked with globalization, but antipathy towards globalization has become the rallying cry.

Globalization is variously seen as one or more of the following: a threat to poor developing countries that cannot compete with developed countries; a threat to jobs in developed countries that cannot compete with low-cost industries in developing countries; a threat to consumers who are at the mercy of multinational companies; a threat to the environment as resources are depleted and pollution proliferates; and a threat to national sovereignty and traditional ways of life (in all countries). Many of the protestors feel a sense of powerlessness in the face of all-powerful multinational companies and international institutions. One of the most powerful indictments of the activities of multinational companies, especially in relation to their use of 'sweat-shop' labour, can be found in the writings of Naomi Klein.[29] Some academics and politicians have seen globalization not so much as a threat to national sovereignty in a nationalistic sense, but as a constraint on the ability of governments to maintain independent economic and social policies.[30] A particular concern in Europe has been that the pressures of global competition may make it difficult for governments to keep taxes at a level that will enable them to maintain their expensive education, health, and social welfare systems (see Practical Insight 2.7). On a wider international scale, the global activities of multinational companies have been seen as having excessive influence over government policy, especially in some of the smaller host countries.

2.7.3 Globalization increases the gap between rich and poor

It is almost certainly the case that the unfettered operation of free markets increases income inequalities between rich and poor. This is true both within countries and regions and also across the world as a whole. This is not to say that the poor necessarily become poorer as the rich become richer, but rather that the income of the rich increases at a faster rate than the income of the poor – though some people in the poorest parts of the world have seen very little increase in their income for many years. Statistics can, of course, give a completely different impression if they are presented in different ways. For example, if we compare the richest 5 per cent of the world's population with the poorest 5 per cent, the income gap has almost certainly widened in recent years, whereas if we compare the top half with the bottom half, the gap has narrowed. This is because income in China and India, for example, which are still in the lower income group and together account for almost one-third of the world's population, has been

Practical insight 2.7: 'Baumol's disease' and the pressures of globalization

Developed countries often enjoy high levels of education, health, and welfare provision, along with a variety of leisure and other personal services. These services tend to be labour intensive and, even when technological innovations are introduced, it may be difficult to reduce the labour input. There is therefore limited scope for productivity improvements in comparison with other industries. If labour and other costs increase in response to inflationary pressures, the cost of these services will rise relative to other parts of an economy, as rising costs cannot be offset against productivity gains. This phenomenon has been described as 'Baumol's cost disease' (or simply Baumol's disease), after one of the US economists who first described it.[31] As these services are often financed by government, it means that increasing amounts of tax revenue are needed to pay for them. There is therefore understandable pressure on governments to impose efficiencies or cuts on publicly funded services (including the arts) during difficult economic times in an open global economy. However, in a recent book, Baumol argues that, provided significant productivity improvements continue to occur in an economy as a whole, the cost of these services may actually fall if measured in terms of the labour hours needed to pay for them.[32] Whether this argument is sufficient to persuade hard-pressed governments to abandon their austerity measures is debatable.

Question

● To what extent should Europe's expensive public services be reduced in order to relieve the tax burden on businesses struggling to compete in the global economy?

growing much faster than income in the world's richer countries (see Table 2.1). In fact, GDP per capita grew faster in the developing countries as a whole than in the developed countries during the 1990s and in every developing region except Oceania during the first decade of the twenty-first century. This means that the relative income gap between developing and developed countries has decreased during this period, though the absolute difference between the dollar value of GDP per capita in the richest and poorest regions has increased.

The problem arises not so much with our understanding of the statistics, but with the allocation of responsibility. The fact that globalization increases the gap between the richest and

Table 2.1 GDP per capita in different regions of the world, 1992–2010

Region	Real Growth in GDP per capita (%)		GDP per capita at current prices (US$)
	1992–2000	2000–2010	2010
World	1.7	1.6	9,178
Developing economies	3.0	4.6	3,703
Africa	0.7	2.7	1,676
America	1.4	2.3	8,558
Asia	4.3	5.9	3,508
Oceania	−0.4	0.7	3,313
Least developed countries	1.8	4.8	737
Transition economies	−1.7	5.8	6,989
Developed economies	2.3	1.0	39,445

Source: UNCTAD, *Development and Globalization: Facts and Figures*, 2012, section 2.1.

poorest countries, and the richest and poorest people, does not necessarily mean we should abandon globalization (if in fact this were possible). A system that allows some people's income to rise at a faster rate than that of others is not necessarily a bad system, as it is likely that overall income per capita will be rising. It may, however, be an unfair system. Whether poverty in some parts of the world is a consequence of globalization or whether the poorest countries are in some way excluded from globalization is a different question. Perhaps the apportionment of blame is less relevant than the fact that, if left alone, the problems of the world's poorest countries will remain. These problems relate not only to low income, though this is a major underlying issue, but also to other aspects of the poverty trap in which these countries find themselves, such as poor governance, disease, dependence on basic commodities, lack of educational provision, gender inequalities, poor access to technology (the digital divide), and the burden of excessive debt.[33] These issues have inevitably become caught up in the globalization debate, but mainstream opinion now seems to accept the need for policies to alleviate the problems of poverty in the poorest countries, whatever their cause.

2.7.4 Globalization leads to cultural convergence

The link between globalization and culture is often bound up in the debate on national sovereignty. National culture is regarded as something to be protected and globalization brings products and values that represent an assault on national culture. There is a feeling that, increasingly, we all wear the same clothes, eat the same food, use the same technology, and buy the same cars, watches, and household goods, and that these consumption patterns are 'westernizing', 'Americanizing' or even 'McDonaldizing' national cultures around the world.[34] There is of course some truth in this view, but modern culture is almost certainly not as homogeneous as we imagine. International cultural influences are clearly very prevalent during a period of globalization, but culture in all but the most remote regions has always been an amalgam of numerous international influences. What we associate with particular countries often originates from another part of the world. Potatoes have long been a staple diet of the Irish and chilli peppers are widely used in Asian cooking, but both of these vegetables came originally from the Americas. In-depth study of the culture of any nation illustrates the diversity of cultural influences within a single country. Tyler Cowen, for example, points out that 'to varying degrees, Western cultures draw their philosophical heritage from the Greeks, their religions from the Middle East, their scientific base from the Chinese and Islamic worlds, and their core populations and languages from Europe'.[35] It is probably best to think of national culture as a hybrid of many influences over a long period of time.

2.7.5 Globalization harms the environment

All economic activity has an impact on the environment, either because it uses resources or because it creates externalities such as waste products or pollution. Resource use in itself is not necessarily harmful, though it may be if resources are overused or non-renewable. The accumulation of waste products creates a number of problems and pollution is almost always harmful. The rapid increase in global economic activity potentially multiplies the harmful effects. This happens not only because of the growth of world output, the increased demand for the world's resources, and the global impact of pollution on the world's natural environment,

Practical insight **2.8**: The deregulation of air transport

Deregulation of the EU air transport market during the 1980s and 1990s encouraged the growth of low-cost airlines such as easyJet and Ryanair. Similar activity accompanied US airline deregulation in 1978. The proliferation of new routes and low fares has significantly increased the demand for air travel. However, no sooner had the low-cost airlines started to celebrate their success than governments were being lobbied to increase the tax on air travel to discourage passenger demand and reduce the carbon dioxide (CO_2) emissions from aircraft.

Question

● Are the benefits of cheap flights sufficient to justify the increased air pollution?

but also because of the huge increase in trade flows as more and more goods are transported between countries. Airlines, in particular, have received criticism from environmentalists for their contribution to air pollution (see Practical Insight 2.8). The problem of international trade is sometimes illustrated by calculations of the 'food miles' travelled by the food we eat before it reaches our table, contrasting this with the more traditional reliance on local produce.

However, there is another dimension to this picture. Globalization, with its competitive pressures, encourages more efficient production and methods of transport. Production and transport efficiencies bring more efficient use of resources, therefore less resource depletion, waste, and pollution per unit of output. If a developing African or South American country can produce food more efficiently, and with less resource use, than a developed European or North American country, it makes sense for the latter to buy its food from the former. Globalization therefore facilitates global specialization and more efficient resource use, allowing each country to specialize in what it does best. In practice, of course, there are many distortions in the global economy, such as subsidies paid to farmers in the EU or USA, so the benefits of international specialization are sometimes lost – but this is the result of distorting policies, not globalization. It is clear that economic activity causes environmental problems and that world population growth brings about an increase in economic activity. Whether globalization, the breaking down of barriers between nations, is specifically responsible for these problems is another matter.

2.7.6 Globalization is really regionalization

A few years ago Alan Rugman, a respected international business scholar, wrote a book with the provocative title *The End of Globalization* in which he argued that most 'global' activity is in fact regional.[36] A significant proportion of world trade in merchandise goods and services is between the Triad nations of North America, Western Europe, and Japan (see Section 3.2), though the relative importance of other regions of the world is now increasing. The **regionalization** of international business activity is even stronger in relation to FDI. Although the balance of international activity is beginning to change as countries like China and India develop, it is still to a large extent dominated by the Triad. Two of the world's major regional economic groupings or trade blocs also operate within these regions, the EU and NAFTA. Regional integration is therefore an important element of the international business environment. The implication of the above argument is that some countries and regions play a much more prominent part in what we call globalization than others. The process of globalization may be gradually encompassing an increasing number of countries, but its effects are uneven in a variety of ways.

2.8 Implications of globalization at local, national, and international levels

Whilst the impact of globalization can be seen on an international scale, its effects permeate all levels of economic, political, and social activity. At a national level governments are faced with decisions such as whether to intervene to prevent industrial closure or whether to discourage foreign takeovers of their 'national champions'. Sub-national regions are also affected by global activity, sometimes more acutely than the country as a whole, and competition between regions to attract high-profile investors is often intense. In this and many other ways globalization is having a significant impact at all levels of economic activity and is therefore an important element of the business environment.

Summary

Globalization is a process that is 'flattening' the barriers to trade, investment, the movement of people, and the flow of information around the world. It is also increasing the connections between countries. Globalization is being driven by political, economic, and technological forces. These forces are gradually changing the world political and economic order, leading to the growing influence of China and the other BRIC(S) countries. Alongside these developments, a number of international institutions have been created to help regulate relations between countries. The most important, and sometimes controversial, institutions affecting the business environment are the International Monetary Fund, the World Bank, and the World Trade Organization. Markets and production are becoming more international, as multinational companies take advantage of opportunities to sell their products and source their supplies in different parts of the world. These activities are aided by developments in information and communication technology. Globalization is also changing the structure of industries and labour markets, as manufacturing is replaced by service industries in developed countries and developing countries are becoming the new manufacturing centres. This process is leading to a global reallocation of resources and has a significant impact on the way we live our lives. Inevitably, there are a number of alternative perspectives on globalization, reflecting different assessments of its costs and benefits. Whatever its costs and benefits, globalization has a major impact at all levels of political, economic, and social activity.

Discussion questions

1. Which do you consider to be the most important drivers of globalization: political, economic, or technological drivers?

2. To what extent do you think US political and economic influence is likely to diminish over the next few years?

3. Why do you think it has been difficult for the member countries of the World Trade Organization to reach agreement on the Doha trade round?

4. Do you agree that the demand for low-skilled labour is likely to fall in developed countries? If so, what are the implications for workers in these countries?

5. To what extent does globalization increase the inequality of income both within and between countries? Why do you think this happens?

6. Is globalization leading to cultural homogeneity or cultural diversity?

Suggested assignment topics

1. Choose a company and investigate the impact of globalization on the company's activities, including its products, labour force, the location of its production and markets, and other relevant factors.

2. Choose a country and investigate the impact of globalization on the country's economy and culture in recent years.

3. Investigate a trade dispute that has been brought before the World Trade Organization during the last five years and evaluate the arguments on both sides of the dispute.

 Case study: Globalization of the car industry

The international car manufacturing industry provides a useful illustration of the way an industry is responding to globalization. Looking back to the 1950s and 1960s, we see that most of the larger developed economies had one or more major national car manufacturers; among them were General Motors and Ford in the United States, Volkswagen and Daimler-Benz in Germany, Renault in France, and the former British Leyland (later Rover Group) in the UK. Many of these companies had grown by acquiring smaller independent businesses either at home or abroad. Car manufacturing was also developing in countries like Japan and South Korea, though these firms were not yet major multinational companies.

By the late 1960s Japanese manufacturers were engaged in a coordinated export drive, an example of the Japanese 'convoy system' where companies in a particular industry ventured abroad together, with the backing of the Japanese government and banks. Companies like Toyota, Honda, and Nissan (formerly Datsun) soon became household names in North America and Western Europe. At first, Japanese cars were lacking in style but were well engineered and included many 'extras' as standard features. By the 1970s Japanese competition was regarded as a major threat to the established western car producers and by the early 1980s a raft of trade restrictions were being introduced to limit imports of Japanese cars. In fact, the voluntary export restraints 'agreed' between European countries and Japan were not finally lifted until 1999. During the 1970s and 1980s many of Europe's larger car manufacturers were lagging behind their Japanese counterparts in their production methods and reliability. Restrictions on Japanese imports seemed to be the only solution.

European and US import restrictions did not of course hold back the flow of Japanese cars for very long. The Japanese simply built their car plants in Europe and America instead. Although the Japanese presence was viewed by western manufacturers as a threat to their survival, in many ways it forced them to revitalize themselves. Inevitably, some firms found this more difficult than others. British Leyland was taken into state ownership during the 1970s and, after a long struggle to revive itself, the privatization and break-up of the business into separate companies in the 1980s, and six years under

(continued...)

BMW ownership (1994–2000), the residual MG Rover company finally succumbed to insolvency in 2005 and was sold to Nanjing Automobile Group of China. France's state-owned Renault company revived its fortunes after major restructuring in the 1980s and 1990s and privatization in 1996. Other companies like Volkswagen, Daimler, and BMW were stronger challengers and became market leaders in their sectors of the car market. Japanese production methods, such as just-in-time production and *kaizen* (continuous improvement), were also adopted by US and European companies, helping to improve their efficiency and the quality of their products.

Some of these developments took place during the early stages of modern globalization, though the term itself did not come into use until later. However, the relative isolation of the US and Western European car markets was becoming a thing of the past. European consumers had bought cars from other European countries, but Asian or even US cars (other than those made in Europe) were still rare until the Japanese arrived. Since that time national car markets have been gradually opening up to international competition and most of the major manufacturers are now multinational companies. As markets have opened, mergers and acquisitions have become more common. Ford, for example, bought Volvo's car division (later sold to Zhejiang Geely of China), Jaguar and Land Rover (sold to Tata Motors of India), Aston Martin (sold to an investor consortium), and a partial shareholding in Mazda (now mainly sold). General Motors acquired control of Saab's and Daewoo's car divisions and significant shareholdings in Isuzu, Suzuki, and Fiat, though most of these shareholdings have now been sold. Other prominent mergers since the 1980s have included DaimlerChrysler (dissolved in 2007), Volkswagen's acquisition of Seat, Skoda, Bentley, and Porsche (together with its earlier acquisition of Audi), BMW's acquisition of Rover (now only the Mini) and the Rolls-Royce (which BMW manufacture at a new UK plant after acquiring the Rolls-Royce trade mark), and Fiat's alliance with and gradual acquisition of Chrysler.

Another significant development has been the large number of strategic alliances between the world's car manufacturers. The most notable alliance has been Renault's joint venture with Nissan since 1999, in which Renault now owns 44.4 per cent of Nissan's shares and Nissan owns 15 per cent of Renault's shares, but more importantly Renault has management control of Nissan. This type of arrangement between a French and a Japanese company would have been unthinkable only a few years earlier. After all, in the 1980s Nissan was a rising star and Renault was trying to revive its struggling business. Japanese companies were also fiercely protected from foreign predators. However, the 1990s brought growing success for Renault and growing problems for Nissan. Nissan remained a highly productive car manufacturer, with strong products and state-of-the art production facilities, but the close-knit Japanese *keiretsu* system had allowed Nissan to take out large loans to finance its international expansion, leaving the company heavily indebted by the 1990s. The Renault-Nissan alliance has helped Nissan to restructure its business and finances and has provided a new synergy to both companies. Although one of the most successful of the recent alliances, Renault-Nissan is by no means an isolated example. General Motors, for instance, had an unsuccessful alliance with Fiat in the early 2000s and formed a new alliance with PSA Peugeot-Citroën in 2012. Many looser forms of alliance also exist between the world's major car manufacturers.

These various mergers and alliances have helped to restructure the international car manufacturing industry. A few small independent car manufacturers still survive, but the world market is dominated by the larger mass-market and specialized multinational companies. The ten largest car firms ranked by sales revenue in 2012 are listed in Table 2.2. General Motors and Ford have dominated the rankings for many years, but recent problems at these companies have allowed Toyota, Volkswagen, and Daimler to rival them for the top positions. The Renault-Nissan alliance would also rank among the top three on the basis of their combined sales revenue in 2012. Both General Motors and Chrysler were subject to 'Chapter 11' bankruptcy proceedings in the United States in 2009, but their fortunes have been gradually improving since then. Chapter 11 of the US Bankruptcy Code allows a company time to reorganize its activities, whilst technically insolvent, with a view to re-emerging as a going concern.

Table 2.2: Top 10 motor manufacturers ranked by sales revenue, 2012

Rank	Company
1	Toyota Motor
2	Volkswagen
3	General Motors
4	Daimler
5	Ford
6	Nissan Motor
7	Honda Motor
8	BMW
9	Peugeot
10	Hyundai

Source: Fortune Global 500, 2012.

The car industry is also responding to a number of other international developments. The BRIC and CEE (Central and Eastern European) countries have attracted significant inward investment in recent years. Most of the major car manufacturers now have production plants in these countries and indigenous car manufacturers are becoming significant players in countries like China and India. Even small countries like Hungary, the Czech Republic, and Slovakia have become car manufacturing centres. These investments have been driven by cost pressures and market opportunities, and car production in the high-cost, mature markets of the United States and Western Europe has been declining. Environmental pressures have also focused the attention of the car manufacturers and some of the alliances discussed above have been helping them to share their physical and intellectual resources in an effort to improve fuel efficiency or search for alternative fuel sources. The international expansion of car production has also outstripped demand. This has led to a problem of overcapacity and increasing competitive pressures, a problem which was exacerbated by the 2008–9 world recession. Inevitably, some firms are adjusting to these pressures better than others. These and many other influences have been reshaping the international car industry in an increasingly global economy.[37]

Case study questions

1. To what extent was the international expansion of Japanese car manufacturers beneficial to the development of the US and Western European car industries in the 1970s and 1980s?

2. Did US and European import restrictions on Japanese cars in the 1980s and 1990s have any beneficial effects?

3. How have consumers been affected by the gradual globalization of the car industry?

4. Why have there been a large number of international mergers in the car industry? To what extent have these mergers been beneficial for the companies concerned?

5. What benefits has the Renault-Nissan joint venture brought for each company? Why was this alliance a significant step for a Japanese company to take?

6. Why do competing companies frequently form alliances?

7. Toyota, Volkswagen, General Motors, Daimler, and Ford have been battling for the top sales positions in the international car market. On what factors is their future success likely to depend?

8. What are the implications of the gradual shift in car manufacturing from North America and Western Europe to Asia, Latin America, and Central and Eastern Europe?

Notes

1. CIA, *World Factbook*, 2012.

2. IMF, *World Economic Outlook Database*, 2012 and UNCTAD, *World Investment Report*, 2012.

3. Main sources: Tselichtchev, I., and Debroux, P. (2009), *Asia's Turning Point: An Introduction to Asia's Dynamic Economies at the Dawn of the New Century*, John Wiley & Sons; CIA, World Factbook, 2012; IMF, *World Economic Outlook Database*, 2012; and UNCTAD, *World Investment Report*, 2012.

4. The term 'globalization' came into common use in the 1980s, though its origin is uncertain.

5. The term 'global village' was first used by P. Wyndham Lewis (1948), *America and Cosmic Man*, and used in the sense of a world connected by electronic communication by H. Marshall McLuhan (1962), *The Gutenberg Galaxy: The Making of Typographic Man*, Toronto University Press.

6. Friedman, T. L. (2007), *The World is Flat: The Globalized World in the Twenty-First Century*, Penguin.

7. For the development of this view see, for example, Scholte, J. A. (2005), *Globalization: A Critical Introduction*, Palgrave Macmillan.

8. Frances Cairncross is thought to have coined the phrase 'the death of distance' in her article: Cairncross, F. (1995), 'The death of distance', *The Economist* (30 September); she later developed her argument in her book: Cairncross, F. (1997), *The Death of Distance: How the Communications Revolution Will Change Our Lives*, Harvard Business School Press.

9. From a discussion with Nandan Nilekani, the CEO of Infosys Technologies Ltd, in Friedman, T. L. (2007), *The World is Flat: The Globalized World in the Twenty-First Century*, Penguin.

10. Giddens, A. (1990), *The Consequences of Modernity*, Polity Press.

11. The author is grateful to Thomas Friedman (2007), *The World is Flat: The Globalized World in the Twenty-First Century*, Penguin, p. 51, for pointing out the significance of these dates.

12. The term 'Washington consensus' was coined by John Williamson in relation to the neo-liberal policy prescriptions of the IMF and World Bank when lending to Latin America: Williamson, J. (1989), 'What Washington means by policy reform', in Williamson, J. (ed.) *Latin American Readjustment: How Much Has Happened?* Institute for International Economics.

13. UN Department of Economic and Social Affairs, Population Division, Population Estimates and Projections Section (http://esa.un.org/unpd/wpp/Excel-Data/population.htm).

14. For a discussion of the increasing importance of small specialized firms in international markets, see Anderson, C. (2009), *The Long Tail: How Endless Choice is Creating Unlimited Demand*, Random House Business Books.

15. Main sources: the *Telegraph* (6 February 2002), '800 jobs to go as Dyson goes to the Far East'; the *Telegraph* (21 August 2003), 'Dyson production moves to Malaysia'; the *Telegraph* (28 February 2005), 'Dyson is making pots of money for Britain by going to Malaysia'; Company press release (25 April 2010): 'Dyson doubles the number of UK engineers' (http://content.dyson.co.uk); and the *Telegraph* (5 November 2012), 'Dyson to create UK jobs as turnover tops £1bn'.

16. Goldman Sachs Global Economics Paper (30 November 2001), 'Building Better Global Economic BRICs'.

17. Goldman Sachs Global Economics Paper (2003), 'Dreaming with BRICs: The path to 2050'.

18. Goldman Sachs Global Economics Paper (2007), 'The N-11: More than an acronym'.

19. BBVA Research, 2012 EAGLES Annual Report (http://www.bbvaresearch.com); the 2011 EAGLES Annual Report also included Egypt.

20. WTO press release (15 December 2009): 'Lamy hails accord ending long running banana dispute' and WTO news item (8 November 2012): 'Historic signing ends 20 years of EU-Latin American banana disputes', http://www.wto.org.

21. Notably from Joseph Stiglitz, a former chief economist at the World Bank, in Stiglitz, J. (2003), *Globalization and its Discontents*, Penguin.

22. Independent Evaluation Group (2006), 'Assessing World Bank support for trade: 1987–2004: An IEG evaluation', World Bank.

23. Smith, A. (2012), *An Inquiry into the Nature and Causes of the Wealth of Nations*, CreateSpace Independent Publishing Platform, first published in 1776, and Marshall, A. (2009), *Principles of Economics*, Cosimo, first published in 1890.

24. International Labour Organization, *Global Employment Trends 2011: The Challenge of a Jobs Recovery*, Table A10, p. 67.

25. A powerful exposition of the dynamic economic benefits of globalization can be found in Wolf, M. (2005), *Why Globalization Works*, Yale University Press.

26. Wolf, M. (2005), *Why Globalization Works*, Yale University Press.

27. See, for example, Hirst, P., Thompson, G., and Bromley, S. (2009), *Globalization in Question*, Polity Press, or Nayyar, D. (2006), 'Globalisation, history and development: a tale of two centuries', *Cambridge Journal of Economics*, vol. 30, pp. 137–59.

28. Friedman, T. L. (2007), *The World is Flat: The Globalized World in the Twenty-First Century*, Penguin.

29. In particular, Klein, N. (2010), *No Logo*, Fourth Estate.

30. For example, Gray, J. (2009), *False Dawn: The Delusions of Global Capitalism*, Granta Books.

31. Baumol, W. J., and Bowen, W. G. (1965), 'On the performing arts: The anatomy of their economic problems', *American Economic Review*, vol. 55, no. 1/2, pp. 495–502.

32. Baumol, W. J. (2012), *The Cost Disease: Why Computers Get Cheaper and Health Care Doesn't*, Yale University Press.

33. For a polemical but challenging discussion of these issues see, for example, Isaak, R. A. (2005), *The Globalization Gap*, FT Prentice Hall.

34. See, for example, Ritzer, G. (2010), *The McDonaldization of Society*, Sage Publications.

35. Cowen, T. (2004), *Creative Destruction: How Globalization is Changing the World's Cultures*, Princeton University Press, p. 6.

36. Rugman, A. (2001), *The End of Globalization: What it Means for Business*, Random House.

37. Main sources: Library of Congress Business Reference Services, Business and Economics Research Advisor (BERA), Issue 2, Fall 2004: 'The Automotive Industry' (http://www.loc.gov), BBC News (28 February 2007), 'Globalising the car industry' (http://www.news.bbc.co.uk), and the websites of major automotive manufacturers, including Nissan (http://www.nissan-global.com), Renault (http://www.renault.com), and General Motors (http://www.gm.com).

Suggestions for further reading

Detailed analyses of globalization from an economic perspective

Bhagwati, J. (2007), *In Defense of Globalization*, Oxford University Press

Wolf, M. (2005), *Why Globalization Works*, Yale University Press

A passionate account of the way in which ICT is facilitating globalization

Friedman, T. L. (2007), *The World is Flat: A Brief History of the Globalized World in the 21st Century*, Penguin

More sceptical perspectives on globalization

Gray, J. (2009), *False Dawn: The Delusions of Global Capitalism*, Granta Books

Hirst, P., Thompson, G., and Bromley, S. (2009), *Globalization in Question*, Polity Press

Stiglitz, J. E. (2007), *Making Globalization Work: The Next Steps to Global Justice*, Penguin

On globalization and cultural differences

Cowen, T. (2004), *Creative Destruction: How Globalization is Changing the World's Cultures*, Princeton University Press

Take your learning further: Online Resource Centre
http://www.oxfordtextbooks.co.uk/orc/harrison2e/
Visit the Online Resource Centre that accompanies this book to enrich your understanding of Chapter 2: Globalization of the Business Environment. Among other resources explore web links and keep up to date with the latest developments in the area.

Key terms introduced in this chapter

Bipolar world order A world dominated by two powerful countries, as for example the United States and USSR during the cold war period.

BRICs /BRICS The four largest emerging economies, Brazil, Russia, India, and China, a term coined by a Goldman Sachs report in 2001, later joined by South Africa at their summit meetings.

De-industrialization A relative decline in the share of manufacturing output or employment in a country's GDP or workforce.

Demand curve A line or curve on a graph representing the quantities of a good or service that consumers are willing and able to buy at a range of prices.

Deregulation The removal of regulatory barriers allowing open competition in a market.

Doha Round The latest round of trade negotiations at the WTO, which began in 2001.

Economic liberalization Policies designed to open up markets to competition, either through internal economic reform such as deregulation or privatization, or through the removal of external trade barriers.

Economies of scale Lower unit costs which result from large-scale operations (internal economies of scale) or location close to other organizations engaged in complementary activities (external economies of scale); internal economies may be achieved either in the production process or in the sourcing, marketing, and strategic planning of the organization as a whole.

Economies of scope Lower unit costs which result from the use of a common production platform or standardized product to produce a number of differentiated variants.

Fixed exchange rate system An exchange rate system where two or more currencies have an agreed exchange rate maintained by the authorities.

General equilibrium The situation where all markets in an economy are simultaneously operating under perfectly competitive conditions.

Global governance Policies and rules set by supranational institutions such as the UN, IMF, and WTO.

Market equilibrium The point at which supply and demand are equal (where the supply and demand curves intersect).

Market mechanism The process by which supply and demand interact with each other to allocate resources in a market.

Market signalling The process by which consumers and producers respond to price, quality, and other signals in a market.

Multilateralism Trade and other international agreements made collectively by a group of countries, as for example at the WTO.

Multipolar world order A world where power is shared by a number of countries, possibly including the USA, China, and one or two other countries.

Neoclassical (micro) economics The mainstream economic theory of firms and markets in the tradition of Adam Smith and Alfred Marshall.

Offshoring The relocation of production or other business operations to another country, either by outsourcing to an independent operator or by establishing a wholly or partially owned subsidiary.

Outsourcing The contracting out of production operations or services to external suppliers either at home or abroad.

Privatization The transfer of state-owned industries, assets, or public services to the private sector.

Regionalization Economic and other activities between groups of countries in specific regions of the world, as distinct from globalization if this term is used to imply activity between all the main regions of the world.

Remote development Undertaking all or part of a business operation at a distant location, often in another country.

Supply curve A line or curve on a graph representing the quantities of a good or service that firms are willing and able to produce at a range of prices.

Triad The name used to describe the major economies during the post-war period, including North America, Western Europe, and Japan.

Unipolar world order A world dominated by a single powerful country, as for example the post-cold war period dominated by the USA.

Uruguay Round The last completed round of trade negotiations, signed in 1994 and leading to the creation of the WTO in 1995.

Washington consensus The free-market approach favoured by the US government and major institutions such as the IMF and World Bank.

3 The International Business Environment

Chapter learning objectives

On completion of this chapter the reader should be able to:

- Outline the main trends in international business activity since World War II and the political context in which international business takes place

- Examine the role played by international trade, foreign direct investment, and international finance

- Explore the role of regional integration in the international business environment

- Analyse the main theoretical ideas that underpin international trade and investment

- Evaluate the issues surrounding the free trade, fair trade, and trade justice debates

Opening scenario: A Vietnamese renaissance?

Although Vietnam may not have caught the public imagination as much as its neighbour, China, the country has been following in China's footsteps in opening up its economy to market forces whilst retaining its communist political system. Vietnam emerged from a long period of conflict when the Vietnam war ended in 1975 as one of East Asia's poorest countries. Although peace brought unification between North and South Vietnam, the war left a legacy of tension between the two communities and with the North's former enemy, the United States. Given the difficulties in the neighbouring countries of Cambodia and Laos, the future for Vietnam looked bleak in the late 1970s.

However, since 1986 when the country introduced its *doi moi* (or 'renovation') reform programme, Vietnam has been opening up its economy to market forces. By the 1990s, Vietnam was starting to outperform many of its South-East Asian neighbours, achieving an average growth rate of 7.5 per cent per annum from 1990 to 2007, only falling to 6.1 per cent during the world economic slowdown and its aftermath from 2008–11. This growth was to a large extent fuelled by exports, which increased by 545 per cent between 2001 and 2011; this compares with increases of 613 per cent for China and 602 per cent for India over the same period.[1] Although agricultural products and fish still account for around 20 per cent of Vietnam's exports, textiles and other manufactured goods have become increasingly important, making up around 45 per cent of exports, with petroleum being the other major export at around 20 per cent of the total.[2]

Although further reforms are needed to modernize Vietnam's economy, the country started to attract foreign direct investors after the *doi moi* reforms and especially during the years following its landmark reconciliation and bilateral trade agreement with the United States in 2000. Vietnam also signalled its desire to become an open trading economy by joining the Association of Southeast Asian Nations

(ASEAN) in 1995, Asia Pacific Economic Cooperation (APEC) in 1998, and the World Trade Organization (WTO) in January 2007. Dependence on export markets and FDI made Vietnam vulnerable to the 2008–9 world economic slowdown, but with the help of a government stimulus package, the country recovered relatively quickly after a brief downturn in late 2008 and early 2009.

Vietnam illustrates the way in which a number of the world's poorer countries have been taking advantage of the more open international business environment in recent years. However, like China, Vietnam retains its communist political system and the government still exerts considerable influence over the economy, both through its regulatory powers and through the large number of state enterprises that account for about 40 per cent of the country's GDP. As in China, Vietnam's economic reforms have been gradual and there are still a number of restrictions on foreign ownership. The country's financial system is also heavily indebted and corruption is an endemic problem in the corridors of power. In many ways, Vietnam illustrates both the successes and challenges of an emerging economy trying to gain the benefits of internationalization without losing its political control and cultural identity.[3]

3.1 The international political context

Post-World War II international relations were dominated by the 'cold war' between the world's two superpowers, the United States and the USSR. This east–west political divide led to a build-up of military power and periodic tensions between the two sides. It also created two separate economic spheres, one where the United States traded mainly with its partners in Western Europe and Japan (sometimes known as the 'Triad'), the other where the USSR and its satellite states traded in the Council for Mutual Economic Assistance (CMEA) area that was largely cut off from the rest of the world.[4] Most of the world's economic activity was dominated by the Triad, while the economies of the Soviet bloc gradually fell behind. Even in 2012 the Triad accounted for a significant share of world trade and foreign direct investment.

However, a number of other events have had a major impact on the international business environment since the 1980s. The collapse of communism in the Soviet bloc, at the end of 1989 in much of Eastern Europe and in 1991 in the USSR, brought about the end of the cold war. These events were accompanied by a wave of optimism as old enmities were forgotten and the 'iron curtain' between east and west was torn down. On 9 November 1989 the fall of the Berlin Wall, which had divided East and West Berlin since 1961, came to symbolize the reuniting of Eastern and Western Europe. The end of almost seventy-five years of communism in the USSR, or over forty years in most of Eastern Europe, would have been unimaginable only a few years earlier.

The period of optimism that followed the end of the cold war brought democracy to much of the former Soviet bloc, enthusiastically in Western Europe's closest neighbours such as Poland or the former Czechoslovakia, more reluctantly in many of the former Soviet republics like Belarus or Kazakhstan. The 1990s also witnessed a transition from state planned economies to market economies in this region. Most of the Central European states, as we now call them, and the three Baltic republics that were formerly part of the USSR have made relatively good progress and joined the European Union (EU) in 2004. Most of the other former Soviet republics have made more faltering progress, though after a difficult initial transition in the 1990s the Russian economy grew much faster during the early 2000s.

Even before the collapse of Soviet communism, China had already embarked on its policy of economic reform in 1978 after Deng Xiaoping came to power. China's 'economic revolution' has been more gradual than that of the countries of Central and Eastern Europe (CEE), but its impact on international business has been more significant. Both these developments have led to the opening up of important regions of the world that had been largely closed to international business during most of the post-World War II years. The opening up of Central and Eastern Europe also brought political fragmentation and the creation of new states such as Slovakia and Slovenia. The new political map of the world is also changing the patterns of international business activity.

Along with these events, several East and South-East Asian developing countries (formerly known as the 'tiger economies') have been expanding rapidly since the 1980s and 1990s, or earlier in the case of South Korea. In Vietnam's case, a communist country has achieved rapid economic growth by following China's example in introducing gradual market reforms. Economic development in Latin America has been more fitful, though Mexico and Brazil have been attracting large amounts of foreign investment since the 1990s, along with Argentina until its financial crisis came to a head in December 2001. On the other hand, the world's least developed countries, many of them in Africa, have been lagging behind. These countries are not excluded from international business, but they are only just beginning to enjoy some of the benefits in terms of their economic development.

Another significant recent development has been the so-called 'Arab uprising' or Arab spring'. With a few exceptions, the countries of North Africa and the Middle East have generally underperformed in terms of international business activity. The main exceptions are Gulf states such as Saudi Arabia, the world's leading oil producer, and Qatar, the country with the world's highest GDP per capita. The Arab uprising spread rapidly across the region during the spring of 2011, starting with anti-government protests, but in some cases leading to civil conflict and the removal of long-established political leaders. Although the long-term effects of the Arab uprising are difficult to predict, the disruption and upheaval in these countries is likely to make them less attractive as a place to do business in the short term (see Practical Insight 3.1).

The emerging economies of CEE, Asia and Latin America, together with the renewed vitality of the US economy in the 1990s, all contributed to a massive growth in international trade and investment and an acceleration of the forces of globalization up to the year 2000. Optimism rarely lasts indefinitely, however. Even before globalization had apparently reached its peak, the chorus of 'anti-globalization' protestors was becoming more audible. Protest groups, from anti-capitalists to environmentalists and campaigners against third world poverty, were berating multinational companies and rich nations for the perceived inequalities and injustices of the world trading system. This pessimism was soon accompanied by a slowdown in world economic growth and the collapse of 'new economy' share prices and businesses at the end of 2000 and the beginning of 2001. World trade fell briefly in 2001, then quickly recovered. Foreign direct investment (FDI) took longer to recover after falling in 2001–3 but gradually began to grow as investor confidence returned in 2004. Similar effects were seen more strongly during and after the 2008–9 financial crisis and world recession, though a growing divide became evident between the developed

Practical insight 3.1: The Arab uprising

The Arab uprising started in Tunisia in December 2010, then spread like a tidal wave to Egypt, Yemen, Algeria, Bahrain, Libya, Oman, Morocco, Syria, and other neighbouring countries during the spring of 2011. In four cases, Tunisia, Egypt, Libya, and Yemen, leaders were removed from office and, at the time of writing, fierce civil war was raging between government and opposition forces in Syria, with considerable loss of human life and destruction of property. The Arab uprising was triggered by the death of a young Tunisian fruit seller, Mohammed Bouazizi, who set fire to himself as a protest against the authorities in his country, but his act unleashed a groundswell of unrest against repressive regimes throughout the Arab region. In the case of Tunisia, the government fell remarkably quickly; in other cases, notably Libya and Syria, full-scale civil wars have ensued.

In the west, there has been a tendency to think that the uprisings will lead to rapidly emerging democracies and more open societies, but the transition process is often slow and faltering; in some cases little real change has occurred (as for example in Egypt), and in others protest has been effectively repressed (as for example in Bahrain). Even if a democratic outcome is achieved, as in Egypt where the Muslim Brotherhood's Mohamed Morsi was elected, it is unlikely that a western-style democracy will emerge. Clearly, there is underlying tension in each of these countries and the story of the Arab uprising has some way to go. For these and other reasons, the short-term international business impact is likely to be either negative or limited. The longer-term impact could potentially be far-reaching.[5]

Question

- What are the main short- and long-term implications of the Arab uprising for the international business environment?

countries, where growth was sluggish, and the developing countries, whose economies were more resilient.

Pessimism took hold in earnest after the terrorist attacks of '9/11' (11 September 2001). Despite the relative resilience of the world economy, 9/11 brought growing tensions between the Islamic and western worlds to public attention. Although most Muslims condemn the atrocities of 9/11, there has been increasing awareness of a rift between western and Muslim perceptions of the world. There was a measure of tolerance for the US-led retaliatory invasion of Afghanistan in October 2001, but Muslims were almost universally opposed to the invasion of Iraq in March 2003. The tensions that underlie these differences are deep-rooted, especially Muslim perceptions of the west's role in the failure to find a solution to the Palestinian question in the Middle East.

The period since the end of the cold war has given rise to two main alternative interpretations of world events: Francis Fukuyama's view of the 'end of history' and Samuel Huntington's 'clash of civilizations'.[6] Fukuyama argues that democratic capitalism has triumphed and that successful states will gradually adopt this system, while Huntington is less sanguine about the difficulties that will accompany the resurgence of diverse civilizations. International business flourished under post-cold war optimism in the 1990s and has remained remarkably resilient during the tense years that followed 2001. With the exception of the 2008–9 economic downturn, most of the indicators of international business activity have been healthy. National governments and international institutions have also been more supportive towards international business in recent years, though the regulatory environment has become more complicated. International relations are rarely straightforward, but a number of new dimensions have been added to our study of the international business environment in recent years.

3.2 Nature and patterns of international business activity

3.2.1 The location of business activity

For much of the latter half of the twentieth century international business activity was predominantly based in the Triad countries of North America, Western Europe, and Japan. At the beginning of the twenty-first century this is still broadly true, though the Triad are now being joined by some of the other East Asian countries, notably China and South Korea, and gradually by India and the larger Latin American countries, especially Brazil and Mexico. Most of these countries are developing countries, as can be seen by their GDP per capita in Table 3.1, but their economies are large.

Using the purchasing power parity (PPP) method of measuring gross domestic product (see Section 4.4.1), China, India, Russia, and Brazil were among the ten largest economies in the world in 2011 (see Table 3.1). However, it would be wrong to suggest that they have almost caught up with the world's leading economies as their economic wealth is consumed by large populations, leaving them well behind in terms of their standard of living. Nevertheless, as locations of economic activity, these countries are becoming increasingly significant. Given their generally faster rates of economic growth, they are also gradually converging with the richer economies. This is especially true in the case of China and, to a lesser extent, India. Brazil has a large economy but has been growing more slowly and Russia has been recovering its position after a period of economic decline during most of the 1990s.

Until recently, much of the world's international business activity was located in North America, Western Europe, and Japan. These countries are still the richest nations, but their dominance is gradually being challenged by the emerging economies of Asia and Latin America (see Practical Insight 3.2).

Table 3.1: The world's leading economies, 2012

Rank	Country	GDP PPP basis ($ billion)	GDP current prices ($ billion)	GDP per capita PPP basis ($)	Annual Average GDP Growth Rates (%) 2000-8	2009-12
1	United States	15,685	15,685	49,922	2.3	0.8
2	China	12,406	8,227	9,162	10.4	9.2
3	India	4,684	1,825	3,830	7.0	7.0
4	Japan	4,628	5,964	36,266	1.2	0.1
5	Germany	3,197	3,401	39,028	1.6	0.7
6	Russia	2,513	2,022	17,709	7.0	1.1
7	Brazil	2,356	2,396	11,875	3.7	2.7
8	United Kingdom	2,336	2,441	36,941	2.6	−0.3
9	France	2,254	2,609	35,548	1.8	0.1
10	Italy	1,833	2,014	30,136	1.3	−1.4

Source: IMF, *World Economic Outlook Database*, April 2012 and April 2013.

Practical insight 3.2: G20 and global economic recovery

A communiqué issued by G20 finance ministers and central bank governors towards the end of Mexico's presidency in November 2012 included the following statement:[7]

> We will do everything necessary to strengthen the overall health and growth of the global economy. Our main focus in the period ahead will be to rebuild confidence and to reduce risks and volatility in international financial markets; contribute to a faster pace of economic recovery and job creation, and promote the foundations for strong, sustainable, and balanced growth. We are firmly committed to open trade and investment, expanding markets and resisting protectionism in all its forms.[8]

Leaders of nineteen of the world's most important economies, together with representatives of the EU (collectively known as G20), now meet regularly to agree a coordinated response to global issues. The Mexico City communiqué indicated an agreed commitment to restore confidence in the international financial system, promote recovery and growth in the global economy, and reaffirm G20's commitment to resist **protectionism**. The G20 finance ministers clearly indicated their willingness to take shared responsibility for the problems facing the global economy and, beyond that, to adopt a broadly liberal approach to international trade. Whether G20 is having a real impact on global economic problems is debatable, but their summits nevertheless demonstrate remarkable progress in achieving a common sense of purpose among a large group of developed and developing countries, including countries as diverse as China, Brazil, and the United States.

Question

- To what extent does the increasing role played by G20 suggest that the locus of international economic power is gradually shifting towards countries like China and Brazil?

3.2.2 International trade

For many centuries international trade has been the mainstay of cross-border business activity. In terms of the value of world exports and imports this is still true today, though international trade's share of international business activity has declined as FDI and other modes of international market entry have become more popular (see Section 8.4). Despite this, there has been a persistent increase in the proportion of world output traded internationally since the 1950s (see Figure 3.1). Between 1950 and 1990 the rate of increase in trade was on average half as much again as the rate of increase in world GDP. In the 1990s the increase in trade was about two and half times the increase in output, from 2001–7 it was twice as much, despite the world economic slowdown in 2001, and from 2005–10 **merchandise exports** exceeded world GDP by 75 per cent.

The increase in trade during the post-war years may be attributable to a period of relative peace and stability among the major trading nations, to a general reduction in trade barriers (encouraged by GATT and the WTO), and to the exchange rate stability and trade-financing facilities of the IMF, among other factors. However, there was a marked increase in the proportion of goods traded after 1990. This corresponds with the opening up of China and CEE, as well as the rapid development of ICT and improvements in transportation which have largely eliminated distance as a barrier to international business. Indeed, it was about this time that the term 'globalization' started to come into widespread use.

Figure 3.1: World production and merchandise exports, 1950–2010 (average annual change in volume, %)

Source: WTO International Trade Statistics 2008, table A1, p. 174 and WTO International Trade Statistics 2011, table I.1, p. 19.

The relative importance of international trade to different countries and regions can be seen in Table 3.2, as well as the massive increase in the value of world exports since World War II. Although US exports have been increasing, its share of world exports has declined as Europe's and especially Asia's shares have increased. In Europe's case, the growth reflects its

Table 3.2: World merchandise exports by region and selected economy, 1948–2011

	1948	1953	1963	1973	1983	1993	2003	2011
Exports ($ billion)								
World	59	84	157	579	1,838	3,675	7,377	17,816
Share of World Exports (%)								
N. America	28.1	24.8	19.9	17.3	16.8	18.0	15.8	12.8
United States	21.7	18.8	14.9	12.3	11.2	12.6	9.8	8.3
S. & C. America	11.3	9.7	6.4	4.3	4.4	3.0	3.0	4.2
Brazil	2.0	1.8	0.9	1.1	1.2	1.0	1.0	1.4
Europe	35.1	39.4	47.8	50.9	43.5	45.4	45.9	37.1
Germany[a]	1.4	5.3	9.3	11.7	9.2	10.3	10.2	8.3
CIS	–	–	–	–	–	1.5	2.6	4.4
Africa	7.3	6.5	5.7	4.8	4.5	2.5	2.4	3.3
Middle East	2.0	2.7	3.2	4.1	6.8	3.5	4.1	7.0
Asia	14.0	13.4	12.5	14.9	19.1	26.1	26.2	31.1
China	0.9	1.2	1.3	1.0	1.2	2.5	5.9	10.7
Japan	0.4	1.5	3.5	6.4	8.0	9.9	6.4	4.6
India	2.2	1.3	1.0	0.5	0.5	0.6	0.8	1.7

[a] Federal Republic of Germany from 1948–83.

Source: WTO, *International Trade Statistics*, 2012, table 1.5, p. 24.

Table 3.3: Leading exporters and importers in world merchandise trade, 2011

Rank	Exporters	Value ($ bn)	Share (%)	Rank	Importers	Value ($ bn)	Share (%)
1	China	1,898	10.4	1	United States	2,266	12.3
2	United States	1,480	8.1	2	China	1,743	9.5
3	Germany	1,472	8.1	3	Germany	1,254	6.8
4	Japan	823	4.5	4	Japan	855	4.6
5	Netherlands	661	3.6	5	France	714	3.9
6	France	596	3.3	6	Hong Kong, China[a]	641	3.5
7	South Korea	555	3.0	7	United Kingdom	638	3.5
8	Italy	523	2.9	8	Netherlands	599	3.2
9	Russia	522	2.9	9	Italy	557	3.0
10	Belgium	477	2.6	10	South Korea	524	2.8
	Extra-EU (27)	2,133	14.9		Extra-EU (27)	2,350	16.2

[a] including imports for re-export.

Source: WTO International Trade Statistics 2012, tables 1.7 and 1.8, pp. 26–7.

post-war recovery and the success of the EU in generating intra-EU trade. In Asia's case, the growth is a reflection of the rapid development of China and the South-East Asian tiger economies. It is also worth noting that international trade is still dominated by North America and Europe, including some of the smaller European countries, though China and South Korea have risen up the rankings in recent years (see Table 3.3).

Broadly the same picture applies to trade in **commercial services**, though the ranking of countries is slightly different and the Triad have a larger share of world trade (see Table 3.4).

Table 3.4: Leading exporters and importers in commercial services, 2011

Rank	Exporters	Value ($ bn)	Share (%)	Rank	Importers	Value ($ bn)	Share (%)
1	United States	581	13.9	1	United States	395	10.0
2	United Kingdom	274	6.6	2	Germany	289	7.3
3	Germany	253	6.1	3	China	237	6.0
4	China	182	4.4	4	United Kingdom	170	4.3
5	France	167	4.0	5	Japan	166	4.2
6	Japan	142	3.4	6	France	143	3.6
7	Spain	140	3.4	7	India	124	3.1
8	India	137	3.3	8	Netherlands	118	3.0
9	Netherlands	134	3.2	9	Ireland	114	2.9
10	Singapore	129	3.1	10	Italy	114	2.9
	Extra-EU (27)	784	24.7		Extra-EU (27)	644	21.1

Source: WTO International Trade Statistics 2012, tables 1.9 and 1.10, pp. 28–9.

Table 3.5: World exports of merchandise trade and commercial services, 2011

	Value ($ billion)	Share (%)
Merchandise trade	18,255	81.4
Commercial services	4,170	18.6

Source: WTO International Trade Statistics 2012, tables 1.7 and 1.9, pp. 26 and 28.

It is interesting to note that India and Spain appear among the top ten exporters of commercial services, and India and Ireland appear among the top ten importers. India's recent development has been predominantly in the service sector, especially in IT services, Spain is a major player in tourism and financial services, and Ireland has attracted inward investment in financial and telecommunication services. It is perhaps surprising that international trade is still predominantly in merchandise goods rather than commercial services (see Table 3.5), despite the developed countries' increasing reliance on services in their domestic economies. This is likely to change gradually in the next few years, though for the time being manufacturing and other merchandise trade remain an important component of most countries' balance of payments. The changing patterns of international trade are considered further in Practical Insight 3.3.

Practical insight 3.3:   Changing patterns of trade

Despite the fact that multinational companies are increasingly using alternative modes of entry when venturing abroad, both the volume and value of international trade have grown significantly since the late 1940s. Trade has also been important for the world's rapidly growing economies in various parts of the world, from Ireland to Vietnam, and remains important for the United States, Germany, and other leading economies.

Questions

- Why do you think international trade has generally increased at a faster rate than world output throughout the post-war period (Figure 3.1)?
- How would you explain the changes in Europe's share of world exports between 1948 and 2011 (Table 3.2)?
- China has been rapidly climbing up the table of the world's leading exporters and importers of merchandise trade in recent years. What other countries would you expect to be following on behind (Table 3.3)? Try checking the latest edition of the WTO International Trade Statistics to verify your answer.
- Why do you think the United States now has a larger share of exports of commercial services than of merchandise trade (Tables 3.3 and 3.4)?
- Why do you think the value of world merchandise trade still far outweighs trade in commercial services, despite services representing a larger share of the economies of most of the major trading nations (Table 3.5)?

Table 3.6: World FDI stock, 1990–2011 ($ billions)

	FDI Inward Stock			FDI Outward Stock		
	1990	2000	2011	1990	2000	2011
World	2,081	7,450	20,438	2,093	7,953	21,168
Developed economies	1,564	5,654	13,056	1,947	7,074	17,056
European Union	762	2,324	8,081	886	3,751	10,444
France	98	391	964	112	926	1,373
Germany	111	272	714[a]	152	542	1,442[a]
United Kingdom	204	439	1,199	229	898	1,731
Japan	10	50	226	201	278	963
United States	540	2,783	3,509	732	2,694	4,500
Developing economies	517	1,735	6,625	146	857	3,705
Asia	343	1,072	3,991	68	607	2,573
China[b]	21[a]	193[a]	712[a]	4[a]	28[a]	366[a]
India	2	16	202	–	2	111
Latin America & Caribbean	111	507	2,048	58	205	1,006
Brazil	37	122	670	41[a]	52	203
Mexico	22	102	302	3	8	112
Africa	61	154	570	21	45	126
South Africa	9	43	130	15	32	72
CIS	–	54	672	–	20	397
Russia	–	32	457	–	20	362

[a] Estimates
[b] Excludes Hong Kong.
Source: UNCTAD World Investment Report 2012, Annex Table I.2, pp. 173–6.

3.2.3 Foreign direct investment

Foreign direct investment is by no means a new international business activity, but it has become much more prominent in recent years. This has been especially true since 1990. As Table 3.6 illustrates, the cumulative world **stock of FDI** increased dramatically from 1990 to 2011. Whilst the rate of growth of international trade also accelerated during the 1990s, the growth of FDI might be described as an 'explosion'. The world economic slowdown in 2001 led to a significant decline in **FDI flows** from 2001 to 2003, but a steep recovery had occurred by 2007. The slowdown affected FDI more than trade, probably because decisions to invest abroad have longer-term implications and are influenced by investor confidence, which was badly damaged after the events of 9/11. This effect has been mirrored to some extent during the 2008–9 world economic downturn and its aftermath. However, the decline in FDI was more marked in the developed countries than in the developing countries, where it recovered more quickly.

Multinational companies have been locating their activities abroad at an unprecedented rate in recent years. FDI involves the establishment or acquisition of production or other facilities in a foreign country over which the investing firm has some degree of control. It may involve a **greenfield investment**, a **takeover**, or partial equity ownership in a **joint venture**. 'Control' is what distinguishes direct investment from **portfolio investment** (discussed in

Section 3.2.4), though control is sometimes defined as an equity stake as low as 10 per cent.[9] For a variety of reasons multinational companies have been seeking greater control over their foreign operations rather than simply exporting at a distance. At first sight, this seems surprising at a time when technology is reducing the impact of distance. However, it makes more sense when we consider the increasing importance attached to knowledge of local markets and culture and the global aspirations of many companies.

It is clear from Table 3.6 that most FDI was undertaken by the developed countries during the 1990s and early 2000s (81 per cent of FDI outward stock up to 2011) and that most FDI went into developed countries (64 per cent of FDI inward stock up to 2011). Among individual countries, the USA, UK, France, Germany, and Japan have been the leading outward investors. With the exception of Japan, they have also been the main recipients of inward investment, though China and other emerging economies have been closing the gap (see Table 3.7). FDI flows are gradually being attracted to the emerging economies of Asia, Latin America, and to a lesser extent Africa, and the annual flow of FDI into the developing countries was 45 per cent of total FDI inflows in 2011.

FDI is an indicator of the level of multinational production and service operations around the world. Until recently, these multinational operations were predominantly in the manufacturing sector, especially in the electronics, motor manufacturing, and oil industries. Companies like Shell, Toyota, and General Electric still rank among the world's largest multinational companies, but they are increasingly being joined by companies such as Wal-Mart Stores, ING, and E.ON in the retail, financial services, and energy sectors and by companies from the emerging economies such as China's Sinopec or Russia's Gazprom.[10] Even more than international trade, FDI seems to symbolize the interconnectedness of the global economy and the important role played by multinational companies.

Despite its importance, the measurement of FDI is notoriously difficult. Whilst the overall scale of FDI is clearly evident, even the most authoritative figures may sometimes be misleading. FDI figures are taken from national balance of payments accounts and are converted into US dollars at the prevailing exchange rate. It involves the ownership of equity capital in a

Table 3.7: World FDI Flows, 2009–11 ($ billions)

	FDI Inward Flows			FDI Outward Flows		
	2009	2010	2011	2009	2010	2011
World	1,198	1,309	1,524	1,175	1451	1694
Developed economies	606	619	748	858	990	1238
European Union	357	318	421	394	483	562
United States	144	198	227	267	304	397
Developing economies	519	617	684	268	400	384
Asia	315	384	423	211	273	280
China	95	115	124	57	69	65
Latin America & Caribbean	149	187	217	54	120	100
Africa	5	1	6	1	0	−1
CIS	63	69	85	47	61	73

Source: UNCTAD World Investment Report 2012, Annex Table I.1, pp. 169–72.

foreign operation, but it also includes the international transfer of funds within multinational companies as well as profit made and reinvested in foreign operations. The treatment of these components leads to a variety of interpretations of the scale of a particular firm or country's FDI. In addition, the 10 per cent minimum definition of control used in the *World Investment Report* is not applied uniformly by every country. The result is that the value of FDI flowing between two countries may be reported quite differently by the countries involved. For example, FDI flows into China in 2002 were reported as $21.8 billion by the major investing countries but $31.0 billion by China itself.[11] This problem also accounts for the discrepancies between inward and outward stocks and flows in Tables 3.6 and 3.7. Worldwide inward and outward investments should of course be equal as the same investment leaves one country and enters another, but this is rarely the case in the recorded statistics. Notwithstanding the measurement problems, however, there has clearly been a significant increase in the importance of FDI since 1990. Nowhere has this been more evident than in China (see Practical Insight 3.4).

3.2.4 International financial markets

International financial flows are necessary to facilitate trade, FDI, portfolio investment, and lending by banks, governments, and international financial institutions. The major international financial markets include the capital market, foreign exchange market, commodity markets, insurance market, and **derivatives** markets. Multinational companies finance their international operations through share issues on the world's major stock markets, by borrowing from a bank, or by selling **bonds** via a bank or securities trader (the '**over-the-counter' market**) or sometimes on a stock market; these financial operations are collectively known as the capital market. The foreign exchange market enables currencies to be exchanged; currency exchange occurs in most international transactions, either immediately or at an agreed future date, whether it involves trade in goods or services, investment, borrowing and

---

Practical insight 3.4:   China's FDI

Tables 3.6 and 3.7 indicate the growing importance of inward FDI in China. Whilst outward FDI is still much lower, as in most of the developing countries, the rate of increase of China's outward FDI has been significant during this period. Much of the inward investment has been in manufacturing industries and some of China's indigenous companies have also grown rapidly in recent years. One of the main reasons for the growth in outward investment has been cross-border **mergers** and **acquisitions**, including Nanjing Automobile Group's acquisition of the UK's MG Rover from BMW, Lenovo's acquisition of IBM's personal computer division, both in 2005, and Geely's acquisition of Volvo in 2010. However, the vast financial surpluses generated by China's rapid export growth have also facilitated large investments in the property market in other Asian countries, in natural resources and infrastructure projects throughout Africa, and increasingly in Latin America's natural resource industries.[12]

Question

- What are the implications of the increase in Chinese investment in Africa, Asia, and Latin America for China's role in the world economy?

lending, insurance, or any other financial transaction. The foreign exchange market therefore plays a particularly important role in international business.

Commodity markets involve the buying and selling of metals, oil, coffee, wheat, and other primary products; these products serve as raw materials, energy, or unprocessed food supplies that are needed for the production of goods and services and ultimately to meet the demand from consumers. International insurance markets enable companies to cover many of the risks of international business, either through individual insurance companies or through insurance syndicates such as Lloyd's of London, which insures a large proportion of the world's shipping, airlines, and other specialist activities or events. Finally, derivatives markets create opportunities for trading in a wide range of financial products that are 'derived' from an underlying asset such as a **share**, bond, commodity, or currency; derivatives typically involve an option to buy a share or currency, for example, at a fixed price on an agreed future date, allowing a firm to hedge against the risk of price fluctuations.

Many of the funds used to buy shares, bonds, commodities, and currencies are provided by portfolio investors, including individuals, companies, and financial institutions. Unlike direct investment, portfolio investment is concerned with the acquisition of financial assets or commodities for the purpose of earning a return on surplus funds. Investors in these markets are interested in the financial return on an investment that does not involve control of a business operation. Many of these financial markets are highly specialized and involve transactions in the legal title to assets rather than the direct handling of commodities, for example. They also facilitate the movement of vast funds around the world. Although these activities may appear to be peripheral to the movement of 'real' goods and services, or simply lining the pockets of successful portfolio investors, the financial markets do in fact oil the wheels of the world economy. By making finance available, in the required form at the required time, the financial markets allow trade and investment to take place.

Of course, financial markets do not always work as efficiently as described above. This was certainly the case during the 2008 international financial crisis, following problems in the US sub-prime mortgage market which emerged in 2007. In this case, the complex derivatives markets had allowed high-risk assets to be bundled into securities and sold on to investment companies and other financial institutions. Whilst this process appeared to spread the risk, it also meant that large amounts of assets held by a variety of financial institutions were at risk when sub-prime mortgage holders started to default on their mortgage commitments. A number of banks had in fact expanded their lending to business and personal customers by borrowing heavily on the inter-bank market and the collapse in asset values caused this source of funds to dry up, leaving the banks short of liquid assets to finance their day-to-day operations.

Financial markets are often highly flexible markets, where prices respond immediately to fluctuations in supply and demand, unlike many markets for goods and services, and they rapidly take account not only of current information but also of expectations about future events. This property of financial markets can be seen in the process of 'arbitrage', where funds are moved between markets whenever a higher return can be earned, causing asset prices to equalize provided there is free movement of funds between markets. However, the view that financial markets always operate efficiently, known as the *efficient market hypothesis*, has increasingly been challenged in recent years (see Section 9.2.5).[13] Financial markets certainly respond quickly to a change in market conditions, but this does not appear to prevent them from allowing a high-risk situation to develop in the first place, especially when unpredictable events precipitate a financial crisis. The response of the international community to the 2008 financial crisis was to call for stronger national and international regulatory frameworks to reduce the risk of financial collapse in the future.

3.2.5 Exchange rates and the eurozone sovereign-debt crisis

One of the most influential factors affecting the international flow of goods, services, and investment is the movement of exchange rates. Further discussion of exchange rates can be found in Section 11.4.3. Here we note the significance of exchange rates for patterns of trade and investment and for the stability of the international financial system. Most of the world's major currencies, including the US dollar, the euro, the Japanese yen, and the British pound, are fully convertible floating currencies, that is, they can be traded anywhere in the world and their value normally depends on market forces.

The euro/US dollar exchange rate since the launch of the euro in January 1999 provides a vivid illustration of the impact of exchange rate movements. On 4 January 1999, the first day of trading in the new currency, the euro was worth $1.18. By October 2000 the euro had slipped to $0.85, but by the end of December 2004 the euro had climbed back to $1.34. During the course of 2005 the rate settled down to around $1.20 as the dollar recovered in value. These movements represent a depreciation in the value of the euro of 28 per cent between January 1999 and October 2000, an appreciation of 58 per cent between October 2000 and December 2004, and a depreciation of 10 per cent in the euro's value during 2005.[14] Such large fluctuations had a massive impact on the terms of trade between Europe and the USA during this period, that is, on the relative prices of European and American goods and services.

The prevailing view from 1945 to 1970 was that exchange rates should be stabilized in order to provide certainty in trading relationships. This period was one of fixed exchange rates under the Bretton Woods system, with the dollar as the anchor currency, and the relative stability it brought probably helped to encourage the steady growth in trade during the post-war years. Exchange rate stability was one of the early roles of the IMF, along with the provision of lending facilities for countries with balance of payments deficits. The Bretton Woods system of fixed exchange rates was abandoned during the early 1970s and the automatic adjustment mechanism of floating exchange rates is now generally favoured. A floating rate finds its own level and a country with a trade deficit will find that its falling currency helps to boost exports and restrain imports, thus helping to correct the deficit.

The main exception to the above is where countries choose to link their currencies together in a fixed or semi-fixed exchange rate system or adopt a common currency, usually within a regional economic group (see Section 3.3). The most prominent example of the latter is the European single currency, currently used by seventeen of the twenty-eight EU member countries. The euro is designed to create a stable area for trade and investment and the movement of people and capital. It also eliminates the transaction costs incurred in currency exchange and removes the risk of internal currency fluctuations when doing business within the eurozone. However, a common currency requires a good deal of policy coordination and its members stand together when things go wrong. This is the case with the eurozone sovereign-debt crisis which began in Greece in late 2009, then gradually spread to Ireland, Portugal, Spain, Italy, and Cyprus.

The debt crisis was caused by excessive budget deficits and rising government debt (sovereign debt) in several EU countries, which in some cases led to a downgrading by the credit rating agencies, making it more difficult for these countries to continue borrowing to finance their deficits. This problem was exacerbated by the international financial crisis and world recession and the need to bail out struggling banks, leaving some countries in difficulties. Although the underlying problem was within each of the debtor countries, the eurozone shared some responsibility for not having kept tight control of its Stability and Growth Pact, which places limits on the size of budget deficits and gross public debt. The eurozone countries, especially Germany, have also had to help bail out the countries in difficulties in order to protect the stability of their shared currency, the euro.

3.2.6 Illicit international business activities

Not all international business activity is legitimate. The opportunities for illicit trade are enormous. Greater openness of borders and modern communication technology are making it easier to move all kinds of illegal goods and services around the world. Like legal trade, these activities are not new, but large income differentials between countries in a more open global economy increase the incentives to move people, capital, goods, and services across borders. Open borders also make it more difficult for national authorities to police these movements.

Large quantities of drugs, arms, counterfeit branded goods, stolen artefacts, human organs, illegal immigrants, and people sold into slavery or prostitution are 'traded' internationally. Income from these activities may then be 'laundered' through legitimate financial institutions. Demand is often the fuel for trade in drugs and arms and suppliers are willing to meet the demand without regard for the consequences for human welfare. In countries like Colombia or Afghanistan, with lax controls and powerful mafia-style organizations, the supply of drugs is difficult to restrict. Arms are often readily available in former Soviet republics where large armies can no longer be afforded, weapons are stockpiled, and there is no effective control by the authorities. Demand also fuels the trade in human beings and human organs. Sometimes desperation leads people to offer themselves in these trades, sometimes they are 'sold' against their will. Illegal immigrants are lured by the prospect of a better life in a rich country and may be willing to pay large amounts of money to secure their dream. Counterfeit watches, CDs, and designer clothing are commonplace in many of the developing countries. When these goods can be copied cheaply, sold profitably below the high prices of the well-known brands, and international enforcement of intellectual property rights is weak, it is not difficult to see why this trade flourishes. Even legitimate banks sometimes make it easy for the proceeds to be laundered when they respect the confidentiality of their customers.

A number of measures are now being taken, both nationally and internationally, to restrict this trade, but it is a difficult battle. The issue is discussed at length in a book by Moises Naim.[15] Naim argues that illicit trade has grown dramatically in recent years, both in value and in the range of products and activities. He also claims that brokers and other intermediaries have become more important than suppliers in encouraging this trade and in their ability to cream off the profits. Indeed, one of the successes of the illicit traders has been their ability to use legitimate channels to carry out their illegal activities, making it more difficult for the authorities to stop them. Naim estimates that the value of the counterfeit supply of drugs (including beneficial as well as harmful drugs) and copies of branded goods amounts to about $500 billion a year. This is relatively small compared to the value of legitimate trade,

> ## Practical insight 3.5:   Tax havens
>
> In its 2008 assessment on tax cooperation, the OECD Global Forum on Taxation published the names of countries which were not completely open in sharing information on their tax havens.[16] The document's intention was to encourage greater exchange of information in order to increase transparency and remove the distorting effects of unfair tax competition in an increasingly open global economy. Whilst tax havens may not be illegal, they make it more difficult for financial regulators to keep track of financial movements. They also allow multinational companies and rich individuals to avoid paying tax by transferring their income or wealth to offshore locations. The OECD document was revealed at the G20 London summit in April 2009, following discussions on the extent to which tax havens may have contributed to the 2008 international financial crisis. By 2012, the OECD reported considerable progress in information sharing among its 109 member countries, but most of them still had some deficiencies to address and only 12 countries were found to have all the necessary requirements in place.[17] Clearly, further progress is needed, even in some of the countries with long experience of financial transparency, but more especially among those with little or no experience.
>
> ### Question
>
> - In what ways may the lack of financial transparency in many of the world's tax havens have contributed towards instability in the global financial system?

but it is certainly a significant sum. Perhaps an even bigger issue for the global economy is the international avoidance of taxation and its implications for the stability of the international financial system (see Practical Insight 3.5).

3.3 Regional integration

An important feature of the international business environment in recent years has been the development of regional economic groupings in many parts of the world. By far the most integrated grouping is the EU, which not only has expanded to include 28 countries, but also has developed an extensive range of policies and a high level of policy coordination. Other well-established regional groupings include the North American Free Trade Agreement (NAFTA), the Association of Southeast Asian Nations (ASEAN), and the Common Market of the South (Mercosur) in South America. A large number of other groupings also exist in most regions of the world. Extensive discussion of regional integration in Europe, the Americas, Asia, and Africa can be found in the four geopolitical chapters in Part Three (see Sections 12.2, 13.3, 13.4, 14.5, and 15.3). Regional integration normally involves cooperation and trade within a group of neighbouring countries, but the type or level of integration varies considerably. The main levels of regional integration are now considered in turn (see also Figure 3.2).

Preferential trading agreement

A **preferential trading agreement** (PTA) is one allowing preferential access for the exports of a particular country or group of countries. Typically, this type of agreement enables developing

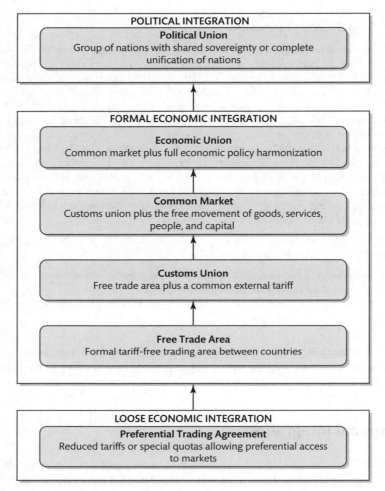

Figure 3.2 Levels of integration between countries

Source: Harrison, A., Dalkiran, E., and Elsey, E. (2000), *International Business*, Figure 7.1, p. 150. By permission of Oxford University Press.

countries to sell their goods in the markets of developed countries. The most widely used form of PTA is the Generalized System of Preferences (GSP), which is a scheme operated under the auspices of the WTO by the EU, United States, and several other countries, granting reduced **tariffs** and other preferential arrangements to the products of a large number of developing countries. Other PTAs include the Cotonou Agreement between the EU and the African, Caribbean, and Pacific (ACP) group,[18] and the US African Growth and Opportunity Act (AGOA).[19]

Free trade area

This is the first level of more formal regional integration, involving a tariff-free area between a group of countries. Other barriers such as quotas are also likely to be eliminated. This type of integration forms the basis of NAFTA, ASEAN, and the recently formed Africa Free Trade Zone (AFTZ), for example – though free trade is a more distant prospect in the case of the AFTZ. The EU is also a **free trade area**, though it is much more than this. The most ambitious attempt to create a free trade area is being made by Asia Pacific Economic Cooperation (APEC), which is made up of a diverse group of countries around the Pacific rim. APEC is a loose economic grouping, including the United States, China, Russia, and a number of smaller countries, which has made some progress towards its aim of achieving free trade (by 2010 and 2020 for its developed and developing member countries respectively), but this aim is unlikely to be fully achieved in the near future. A free trade area linking the United States and the EU has also been proposed.[20]

Customs union

The next level of integration combines a free trade area with a common external tariff. This means that the member countries forgo the right to set their own national tariffs, but it avoids the problem of importers trying to find the lowest-tariff entry point into the trading area. **Customs unions** normally have arrangements to share the tariff revenues. This requires them to establish more formal institutional processes. Examples of customs unions include the EU, Mercosur, and the Caribbean Community (Caricom), though in each case steps have been taken to progress to higher or deeper levels of integration.

Common market

This was the term used by the European Economic Community (EEC) before it became known as the EU to describe its original economic aim and was widely used to describe the EEC as a whole in its early years. However, it is also the textbook name for the next level of integration. It incorporates a customs union as well as the free movement of goods, services, people, and capital (the 'four freedoms'). It therefore goes beyond the removal of tariffs and quotas to tackle non-tariff barriers such as restrictions on the supply of services, the failure to recognize qualifications, or restrictions on foreign ownership. Mercosur, Caricom, and the African Union have all been attempting to create a **common market**, with varying degrees of success, but the most extensive common market has been achieved by the EU. The European single or internal market, as it is known, has created something approaching a common market, though complete free movement has proved difficult to achieve when there are significant economic and cultural differences between countries (see Section 12.2.1).

Economic union

This is the most comprehensive level of economic integration between a group of independent nations. It involves a common market and the harmonization of economic policies. The EU is the closest example of an **economic union**, having a number of common policies, but it has only achieved a partial monetary union (a subset of economic union) and has not yet achieved tax harmonization, among other things. A higher degree of political integration is also required as a regional grouping progresses to the higher levels of economic integration.

Political union

Complete **political union** would involve the unification of one or more formerly independent states, such as the unification of East and West Germany in October 1990. However, in the context of regional integration, it is more likely to involve close political coordination supported by a unified decision-making structure.

The primary purpose of regional integration is to achieve economic benefits for the countries concerned. The potential benefits include a combination of static and dynamic effects. Static effects are those which create once-for-all benefits. Dynamic effects are those which create recurring benefits. Static effects of regional integration include the cost savings and other benefits that result from the removal of border controls, the simplification of trade documentation, and the adoption of harmonized standards, as well as the economies of scale and changing patterns of trade that arise in a large barrier-free market.

Changing trade patterns include **trade creation**, involving new trade previously prevented by trade barriers, and **trade diversion**, where trade is diverted from countries outside the trading area to countries inside. If the level of external trade barriers is no higher than it was for each individual country before integration occurred, the trade effects will generally be positive, allowing goods and services to be sourced from the most efficient producers. Dynamic effects include the way in which competitive pressures cause price reductions and stimulate efficiency, innovation, and overall economic growth in a large internal market. Efficiency applies not only to production methods, work practices, and competitive sourcing at the level of the firm, but also to the way in which industrial reorganization occurs through mergers, alliances, and other market entry strategies.

It should be noted, however, that these benefits are likely to be greater where there is a high level of integration, where the countries concerned have similar economic and political structures, and where goods, capital, and labour markets operate flexibly enough to enable the necessary adjustment processes to work effectively. Some of the difficulties that can arise in regional groupings involving countries at different levels of economic development are illustrated in Practical Insight 3.6.

Practical Insight 3.6:   A Trans-Pacific Free Trade Area

APEC Member Countries[21]

Australia	Indonesia	Papua New Guinea	South Korea
Brunei	Japan	Peru	Taiwan
Canada	Malaysia	Philippines	Thailand
Chile	Mexico	Russia	United States
China	New Zealand	Singapore	Vietnam
Hong Kong			

Asia Pacific Economic Cooperation (APEC) is a loose grouping of Pacific-rim countries. Although not a formal regional economic grouping like the EU or NAFTA, it is nevertheless attempting to create free trade and investment by the years 2010 and 2020 for its developed and developing economy members respectively. However, this is no mean task given the diversity of its members' economies and political systems. A number of APEC countries have been trying to speed up the integration process and a Trans-Pacific Strategic Economic Partnership Agreement was signed by four APEC members, Brunei, Chile, New Zealand, and Singapore, in 2005. By the end of 2008, Australia, Japan, Peru, Vietnam, and notably the United States had expressed an interest in joining this group to create a Trans-Pacific free trade area. These were followed by Malaysia in 2010 and Mexico and Canada in 2012. If successful, this free trade area will be unique in including developed and developing countries in Asia, Oceania, and both North and South America. There is clearly a desire for more open trade among APEC members, but the practical difficulties will be considerable. In particular, there has been criticism that some aspects of the draft agreement appear to strengthen the access of multinational companies at the expense of national authorities.[22]

Questions

- To what extent is a Trans-Pacific free trade area likely to bring mutual benefits for APEC member countries?
- Do you think trade agreements of this type are a useful stepping stone or a hindrance to global free trade?

3.4 Explanations of trade and investment

3.4.1 Conventional theories

Many economists have tried to explain why international trade takes place. At the country level, the most successful explanation is almost certainly David Ricardo's **theory of comparative advantage**.[23] Although not the originator of the theory, Ricardo provided its most comprehensive explanation. The theory basically asserts that a country should specialize in producing goods where it has a comparative advantage. Ricardo illustrated this using two goods, wine and cloth, which could be produced in both Portugal (his parental country of origin) and England (where he was born and lived). He argued that Portugal was more productive (required less labour) in the production of both wine and cloth than England, but that Portugal had a greater productivity advantage in the production of wine and a smaller advantage in the production of cloth. Portugal therefore had a comparative advantage in wine production and England had a comparative advantage (or was less unproductive) in cloth production. If Portugal specialized in wine and England in cloth, then traded with each other, Portugal would be able to use its labour more productively and increase its wine production, while England would be able to use its labour less unproductively and increase its cloth production. After trade, the 'world' as a whole would be better off (see Practical Insight 3.7).

Although apparently crude, the theory of comparative advantage was a significant advance on Adam Smith's earlier theory of absolute advantage.[24] Clearly, if one country has an absolute advantage over another in producing a good (has greater productivity), it will be better off if it specializes in what it does best. The problem is that not every country can be the best. Ricardo overcame this problem because almost every country is comparatively better at producing some goods than others (unless they are equally good or bad at everything). Thus, even a poor Caribbean country will be comparatively more productive when producing bananas than when producing computers compared with the United States or Japan. This is not to denigrate Adam Smith's work, however, as Smith's belief that it was better to specialize in what you do best and trade with other countries was a vast improvement on the **mercantilist** ideas that were preva-lent at that time. Mercantilists believed a country could prosper by promoting its exports and restricting its imports – a policy that, if taken to the extreme, would require a country to be self-sufficient, no matter how unproductive its industry might be. Despite the poverty of mercantil-ist thought, this view is still surprisingly prevalent today, even sometimes among politicians.

An important feature of the theory of comparative advantage is that countries can only maxi-mize the benefits of specialization if there is free trade. If trade barriers exist, this will reduce the flow or increase the cost of trade and reduce the benefits from specialization. The original version of the theory also requires perfect competition. In neoclassical economic theory, per-fect competition exists where firms have complete freedom to enter and leave a market (in this case an international market) and are selling homogeneous products. Thus, Ricardo envisaged a world where free trade and perfect competition would allow countries to maximize the bene-fits from exploiting their comparative advantages and the world as a whole would be better off.

The theory of comparative advantage has also been developed by later economists, most notably by the Swedish economists Eli Heckscher and Bertil Ohlin.[25] The Heckscher–Ohlin model, also known as factor endowment theory, suggests that countries will specialize in pro-ducing goods whose inputs are in relatively abundant supply and can therefore be used at rel-atively low cost. Thus, a country with an abundant labour supply will specialize in producing labour-intensive goods. Or, more generally, specialization will depend on a country's factor endowments. The Heckscher–Ohlin refinements give the theory of comparative advantage more intuitive appeal. However, it is by no means certain that countries always specialize in producing goods that exploit their abundant resources, as shown in an empirical study by Wassily Leontief – the so-called Leontief Paradox that countries sometimes specialize in pro-ducing goods using relatively scarce resources, which suggests that other factors such as the quality of resources or level of technology may also be important.[26]

Clearly, the theory of comparative advantage needs to be updated in the modern world. The source of comparative advantage is not restricted to the productivity of labour or natural resources and it is probably unwise for a country to specialize too narrowly. However, a more serious criticism of the theory is that it applies to countries rather than firms. After all, it is firms that make decisions to produce and trade, not countries. The theory also relies on the unrealistic assumptions of free trade and perfect competition. These criticisms have led to a number of theoretical and empirical developments. Nevertheless, after a period of neglect, the theory of comparative advantage is now generally regarded by economists as providing a fundamental explanation of the benefits of international trade, and free trade in particular. The theory also provides a basic explanation for the location of FDI, at least at the national level, in that investment will be attracted to countries that offer a comparative advantage in the production of particular goods. Firm-based theories of FDI are explored in Section 8.5.

3.4.2 **Modern theories**

In 1961, Staffan Linder suggested that demand was more important as a determinant of coun-try specialization than factor endowments.[27] The Linder hypothesis, also known as income similarities theory, postulates that countries with similar income levels will have similar de-mands and develop similar industries. Thus, for example, high-income countries developed car-manufacturing industries during the twentieth century and traded in similar, though dif-ferentiated products. This theory has intuitive and empirical appeal in the modern world though it does not necessarily provide a complete explanation for trade patterns.

Raymond Vernon then applied his product cycle theory to international trade and investment in 1966.[28] Based on empirical evidence from the US economy, Vernon explained how a country like the United States would initially produce technologically advanced products for the home market. The market for the product would then grow and the product would be exported. Gradually, international rivals would catch up with it, production would be standardized and components sourced abroad in order to reduce costs. Finally, production would be transferred to low-cost countries which would serve as an export base, allowing the product cycle to be extended while gradually being replaced by more sophisticated products. Vernon's theory explains patterns of trade and FDI that are appropriate to industries such as textiles and textile-machinery manufacture, which have been largely relocated from the United States and Europe to Asia in recent years, but it is probably more relevant to old than to new industries. Thus, the theory may help to explain why some firms 'offshore' their manufacturing and service operations to low-cost countries such as China or Vietnam, but it is less useful as an explanation for the development of high-tech industries in emerging economies. Vernon's product cycle theory is explained more fully in Section 8.5.3.

Other explanations have focused on the way firms behave in imperfect markets. Most prominent among these is the so-called *new trade theory* developed by Paul Krugman and others during the 1970s and 1980s.[29] New trade theory was an attempt to explain why some countries seem to specialize in producing goods where they have no obvious comparative advantage. The theory relaxes one of the main assumptions of the theory of comparative advantage in that competition is viewed as imperfect. Industrial organization theory is used to explain how firms take advantage of economies of scale and differentiated products in international markets that operate under **monopolistic competition** or **oligopoly**. Monopolistic competition describes a market structure where firms are small in relation to the market as a whole but their differentiated product marks them out from their rivals. Oligopoly represents a market dominated by a few large firms with considerable influence over the market. Firms therefore derive cost advantages from economies of scale and market power from their differentiated products. A firm may expand its scale of production, using a large production base to supply the world market. Such economies are known as internal economies of scale (or increasing returns to scale).

External economies of scale are also possible when a number of firms cluster around the same geographical location. External economies are the advantages that arise when a cluster of firms do business with each other, develop specialized local resources, and attract supporting industries to the area. In this model, large specialized firms or clusters of smaller firms take advantage of their economies of scale and differentiated products in their search for customers with specialized preferences around the world.

New trade theory helps to explain why countries often trade in similar goods, buying each other's cars or mobile phones because consumers have tastes and preferences that are satisfied by the products of different firms in different countries. For this reason it is sometimes known as **intra-industry trade** theory. The theory provides a fuller explanation for the phenomenon identified by Linder. It also allows for the existence of bigger, more powerful firms that increasingly dominate international markets. More controversially, new trade theorists have also offered support for protective import policies in certain circumstances. This issue is discussed in Section 3.5.2 below. Many new trade theorists now view their contributions as an overlay on the foundation of comparative advantage theory – complementary to rather than replacing conventional theory (see Practical Insight 3.7).

Practical insight 3.7: The enduring appeal of comparative advantage

Assume two countries with the following production capacities (maximum production if all resources are used to produce one product only):

	Cars	Computers
Country A	1,000	2,000
Country B	1,000	800

If each country uses half its resources to produce cars and half to produce computers, but no trade takes place (self-sufficiency):

	Cars	Computers
Country A	500	1,000
Country B	500	400
World output	1,000	1,400

If each country specializes in the product in which it has a comparative advantage (where it can produce more output using the same resources):

	Cars	Computers
Country A	–	2,000
Country B	1,000	–
World output	1,000	2,000

If each country trades half its output with the other:

	Cars	Computers
Country A	500	1,000
Country B	500	1,000
World output	1,000	2,000

Specialization increases world output. Trade leaves at least one country better off and neither country worse off. There is therefore a net gain for the world as a whole.

Questions

- What factors may give a country a comparative advantage?
- Given that cars and computers are highly differentiated products, why might car and computer producers exist in both countries and still engage in trade?
- Does this mean that a country's comparative advantage is no longer relevant?

Porter's diamond of national competitive advantage is also sometimes cited as a modern theory of international trade because it adopts a more sophisticated view of a country's factor endowments than comparative advantage theory and emphasizes the importance of demand conditions, related and supporting industries, rivalry between firms, and the role of government as location advantages in a particular country (see Section 11.4.3).[30] However, it is probably more accurate to view Porter's diamond as an explanation of the competitive advantages individual firms can gain from location, whether they trade abroad or not, rather than as an explanation of international trade. By emphasizing the 'competitive advantages' of a country, Porter's model appears to offer an alternative explanation to comparative advantage theory, but competition between countries implies that one country gains at another's expense (a zero-sum game), which would suggest that international trade brings no advantage to the world as a whole. Comparative advantage theory, on the other hand, explains why international trade is beneficial for the world as a whole.[31] Further discussion of the concept of international competitiveness in relation to countries and firms can be found in Section 11.4.2.

3.5 Free trade and trade protection

3.5.1 The case for free trade

Economists and politicians have debated the merits of free trade since Adam Smith's time. As the conventional theory of international trade developed during the late eighteenth and nineteenth centuries, the case for free trade became more compelling. If the theory of comparative advantage is correct, the full benefits of specialization can only be attained in a world of completely free trade. This view is strengthened by the conventional economic analysis of tariffs. An import duty or tariff increases the price and reduces the demand for a good in the protected country. The higher price allows higher-cost domestic producers to enter the market and enjoy increased revenue from the sale of their products. Lower-cost imports have therefore been replaced by higher-cost domestic supplies. The government also gains from the tariff revenue. However, the combined gains to domestic producers and the government are outweighed by the loss suffered by domestic consumers. This is a loss of consumer surplus (the difference between the price paid and the price consumers are willing and able to pay as shown by their demand curve).

This can be seen more clearly in Figure 3.3, which is a supply and demand graph, let us say for wheat, within a particular country. The world price (p_w) applies both within the country and internationally if there is no tariff. The domestic price (p_d) is the price the consumer pays within the country if a tariff is imposed. At the world price (p_w), domestic consumers will demand output qt_1 but only output qd_1 will be supplied by domestic producers. After the tariff is imposed, domestic consumers will demand qt_2 and domestic producers will increase their output to qd_2. Imports will fall from qt_1 minus qd_1 to qt_2 minus qd_2 as a result of the tariff. The imposition of the tariff means that consumers pay a higher price (p_d) and lose consumer surplus equal to areas A + B + C + D. In other words, there is a smaller surplus between what they are willing and able to pay (shown by the demand curve) and the price they actually pay. This leaves consumers with less money to save or spend on other goods and services. Domestic producers gain area A after the tariff (which represents an increase in their income though not necessarily profit if higher-cost

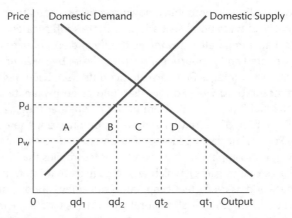

Figure 3.3 The welfare loss from a tariff

producers have entered the market). The country's government gains the tariff revenue represented by area C. However, areas B and D, which are known as the **deadweight loss** or welfare loss from the tariff, are a loss to the domestic economy as a whole. The loss of consumer surplus therefore outweighs the gain to domestic producers and the government.

Thus, as well as replacing efficient foreign producers with less efficient domestic producers, the tariff has the perverse effect of harming the very country it is supposed to protect. Of course, the foreign importer also loses out. Similar logic can be used to explain the effect of a quota, restricting the quantity of imports allowed into the country. When the supply of goods available in the country is reduced, the price rises just as it does with a tariff. The main difference is that the foreign importer enjoys a higher price, though fewer sales, so area C goes to the importer rather than the government. The net welfare loss to the country is therefore greater than with a tariff. Whilst there are some specific circumstances in which a tariff or quota may be beneficial to an individual country, tariffs generally lead to welfare losses for both the country concerned and the world as a whole. This is why the WTO is trying to reduce or eliminate tariffs and why the participant countries of the G20 have stated their intention to avoid protectionist trade policies.

The case for free trade was made forcefully in mid-nineteenth-century Britain by Richard Cobden and other members of the Anti-Corn Law League, and the corn laws that had protected British agriculture were eventually repealed by Prime Minister Sir Robert Peel in 1846. In fact, the free trade (or 'laissez-faire') debate was a dominant political issue in Britain throughout much of the nineteenth century. In more recent times, the US Administration was criticized for introducing tariffs on imported steel in March 2002. These tariffs were designed to protect US steel producers by allowing them time to adjust to increased imports of low-priced steel from China and other emerging economies. After a chorus of criticism from the EU and other steel-producing countries, the case was brought before the WTO and the United States finally removed the tariffs in December 2003. Perhaps unsurprisingly, US steel consumers were among the protestors against the tariffs. At times, however, the protectionists are more persuasive than the free traders and there is a widespread belief that protection is necessary in some situations.

3.5.2 **The case for trade protection**

The case for import protection has also been explored in the academic literature. The most widely accepted case for trade protection is the so-called *infant industry argument*. This argument is usually attributed to the German economist, Friedrich List (1841), but it was also developed by the British economist and philosopher, John Stuart Mill (1848).[32] The infant industry argument is that protection might be justified to enable a new industry to become established, especially in a developing country where factor markets for labour and capital are often underdeveloped. The core of the argument is that market failures or distortions prevent efficient resource allocation in these markets and leave infant industries at a disadvantage. A similar case was made by new trade theorists in the 1980s, though they argued that import protection might be justified because of imperfect competition in product markets rather than factor markets.[33] Their arguments were also directed more towards the developed countries facing increased competition from Japanese goods at that time.

Despite these attempts to qualify the case for free trade, the free traders became more dominant as the policies of Margaret Thatcher and Ronald Reagan took hold in the UK and USA respectively during the 1980s. Free-market economics also received a boost from the apparent triumph of capitalism after the collapse of Soviet communism, and became the basis for the lending policies of the IMF and World Bank and the trade policies of the WTO (the so-called Washington consensus). But as free-market economics was approaching its peak in the late 1990s, anti-globalization protestors were increasingly questioning the merits of unfettered competition. These protests have been accompanied by a more cogent theoretical case for protection from economists such as Ha-Joon Chang.[34] Chang has studied the use of trade protection by countries in the early stages of their development. He argues that Britain and other developed countries made extensive use of import protection when their industries were less developed during the eighteenth and nineteenth centuries. Now that these countries have reached economic maturity, they extol the virtues of free trade, not only for themselves but also (hypocritically, according to Chang) for today's developing countries.

There is also a case for strategic trade policy, that is, trade policy designed to protect a vulnerable group or a strategically important industry. Although the benefits of trade protection to domestic producers are normally outweighed by the cost in terms of higher prices to domestic consumers, there may still be a case for protecting domestic producers. The economic and social cost to production workers will probably cause more hardship than a relatively small price increase spread thinly across a country's consumers. There may also be a political imperative for the government to protect jobs or to protect an industry of national strategic importance. It is important to remember, however, that a policy that favours one group at the expense of another may still have a negative overall economic impact on society. It may well be better to tackle the problem of job losses through domestic policies targeted at this group rather than by creating a trade distortion. In principle, there would appear to be a stronger case for trade protection designed to correct (rather than create) a market distortion. This may be especially true in the case of developing countries with immature markets and a difficult institutional environment. The problem is that in practice the argument for trade protection is overused and the costs of protection frequently outweigh the benefits, even for the protected industries, in the long term. These arguments are considered further in the case of the EU textile quotas in Practical Insight 3.8.

Practical insight 3.8: EU quotas on Chinese textile imports

On 31 December 2004 the ten-year multi-fibre agreement was terminated. The agreement had allowed its signatories to impose quotas on textile and clothing imports to protect their domestic textile industries. It was a response to growing competition from cheap textile products from the developing countries, especially in Asia. Almost as soon as the multi-fibre agreement had ended, however, Chinese and other low-cost textile products started to flood into European and American markets. Pressure soon grew on the EU to reimpose controls and the EU agreed to reintroduce quotas on Chinese textiles and clothing in June 2005. Almost immediately, clothing importers and retailers were complaining that their orders were piling up at the ports. Many of these goods had been ordered before the new quotas were imposed, but the quota limits for 2005 were soon reached. The European Commission responded by allowing the goods to be imported as an advance on the following year's quotas.

Pressure for the new quotas had come from Europe's struggling textile producers who feared the loss of their livelihoods as cheap Chinese clothing flooded the market. Before long, however, the large retail chains were looking for alternative sources of cheap clothing from countries like India, Vietnam, and Cambodia. They argued that their customers demanded low-priced clothing and that local producers were unable to supply their needs. The European Commission claimed in its defence that it was trying not only to protect European textile producers, but also to safeguard production and jobs in the EU's Mediterranean neighbours, Tunisia and Morocco, which would have been squeezed out by the Chinese imports.

The quotas were finally withdrawn at the end of 2007, with an agreement between the EU and the Chinese government that they would continue to operate a joint monitoring system for a further year. Since the beginning of 2009, there has been a more open trading system and Chinese products now account for about 39 per cent of EU textile imports. However, the European Commission claims that the EU textile industry has responded by improving productivity and concentrating production on the high added-value end of the market.[35]

Question

- Taking all the above factors into account, do you think the EU textile quotas were justifiable?

3.6 'Fair trade' and 'trade justice'

Not everyone is convinced that free trade is as beneficial to the poor countries as it is to the rich. Farm workers and agricultural production are often poorly organized in the developing countries and international trade in agricultural products is dominated by large multinational companies that buy, process, and distribute these products or by large retailers that sell the products in the developed countries. World markets are also subject to big fluctuations in price as good or bad harvests increase or reduce the world supply of these products. Perversely, a good harvest leads to excess supply and a fall in the world price. The buying power of large traders and reductions in world prices combine to depress the incomes and destroy the livelihoods of farm workers in developing countries. This situation has led to the formation of a number of 'fair trade' organizations dedicated to the protection of these workers. Their aim is to ensure a reasonable price for the primary producers of a range of products such as cocoa, coffee, fruit, rice, tea, and cotton. In some cases they also help to ensure that money goes into local community development or environmentally sustainable production, among other things. Consumers in the developed countries are encouraged to support these schemes by buying products bearing the 'fair trade mark'. Sometimes, the multinational companies are bypassed when products are brought directly to the market, though increasingly the large food-processing companies, distributors, and retail chains are themselves taking part in fair trade schemes – guaranteeing to buy their supplies from 'fair trade' sources.

As a contribution to the survival of farming communities in the developing world, many of these schemes are achieving tangible benefits. They are also helping to moderate the excessive buying power of multinational companies in the absence of any effective international regulation of their activities. Even if consumers in rich countries pay a small premium for 'fair trade' products, this seems a reasonable price to pay for the protection of farm workers and their families in poor countries. Arguably, fair trade also helps these communities to stand on their own feet without having to depend on development aid – though they are of course dependent on the success of fair trade organizations in mobilizing international support for their cause.

Unfortunately, this picture represents only a 'micro' view of the situation. If the underlying problem is world overproduction, the higher prices guaranteed by 'fair trade' schemes will only exacerbate the problem on a 'macro' scale as it will encourage workers to remain in or move into agricultural production and increase agricultural output. If there were only a few 'fair trade' schemes, the impact on world output would be minimal, but as these schemes become more successful, overproduction will increase. This will depress world prices even more, making prices less 'fair' for workers who are not protected by a 'fair trade' scheme. It might also be argued that 'fair trade' encourages workers in developing countries to remain in agriculture, which may hold back their country's progress towards greater economic development.

A raft of controversial issues surrounds this debate and some in the 'fair trade' movement may be happy to protect agricultural communities rather than to promote industrialization and the social and environmental problems that accompany industrial development. On the other hand, very few countries in the modern world have significantly increased their standard of living, and brought the benefits of access to better education and health care, without relinquishing their dependence on basic agricultural commodities. Whatever view one takes on these issues, it must be borne in mind that 'fair trade' potentially has macro as well as micro implications. In the short term, it may be necessary to provide 'fair trade' support to meet the immediate needs of farming communities in the poorest countries. It may also be sensible to moderate the power of multinational companies, as happens under the competition policies of most developed countries. However, 'fair trade' may also encourage overproduction and inefficient labour-intensive production, and is unlikely to promote the long-term economic development of the world's poorest countries. Despite this, it is almost certainly better than doing nothing to help the poorest communities.

The 'trade justice' movement is concerned with broader issues. This movement caught the public imagination during the Make Poverty History campaign that reached a climax around the time of the G8 summit in Gleneagles, Scotland, in July 2005. The Make Poverty History campaign had a bigger agenda than 'trade justice', including debt relief and increased aid for poor countries, but it also encompassed the 'trade justice' agenda. Supporters of 'trade justice' argue that international trade rules are biased against poor countries and that free trade is not necessarily in the interests of these countries. In particular, they call for more effective regulation of the activities of large multinational companies, the removal of agricultural subsidies by the developed countries, and more protective policies for the developing countries.

The world's most powerful multinational companies almost certainly wield great influence over the policies of the WTO, though comparisons with the size and power of countries are sometimes exaggerated. Certainly, these companies are keen to promote trade liberalization in developed and developing countries alike and these policies have been adopted by the WTO, IMF, and World Bank. Governments in the developed countries have also promoted this agenda. Essentially, the 'trade justice' movement is challenging the wisdom of global free trade and claiming that the trade liberalization policies of the WTO, IMF, and World Bank have been harmful to the developing countries. There is no doubt that the agricultural support policies of the EU, the United States, and other developed countries have had damaging effects on the agricultural trade and industries of many of the poorest developing countries. Not only has the EU common agricultural policy (CAP) used tariffs to protect EU markets but, more perniciously, it has subsidized its exports of high-priced food in order to sell off its surpluses on world markets. This has been devastating to agricultural producers in many of the developing countries as it has made both their exports and their domestic produce uncompetitive. Of course, resistance to the removal of EU agricultural subsidies has come from farmers and politicians in Europe, not from supporters of free trade.

The more controversial aspect of the 'trade justice' agenda for free traders has been the insistence on trade protection for the developing countries. Intellectually, there is support for this view from the infant industry argument and from the historical lessons drawn by Chang, as discussed in Section 3.5.2. The former chief economist at the World Bank, Joseph Stiglitz, has also criticized the IMF and World Bank for their structural adjustment policies that insist on trade liberalization, privatization, and other free-market policies when making loans to developing countries.[36] A number of academic research studies have provided additional support for the view that trade liberalization increases developing countries' imports more than their exports and has a negative effect on their national income.[37] This seems to be particularly true for the least developed countries.

Even if one accepts that free trade is too harsh a remedy for these countries, tariffs alone may not provide a complete answer to their difficulties. In fact, the removal of EU and US export subsidies may well alleviate the need for tariffs to some extent, as developing countries can counter the superior productivity of the rich countries with their low-cost production. Developing countries also need to import manufactured goods and other supplies so any tariff protection would need to be selective. Economic development in these countries will probably depend on a number of factors, including improvements in their political, social, and economic institutions, so trade protection alone is unlikely to provide a complete answer.

Summary

There has been a general increase in the level of international business activity since World War II. This increase began to accelerate after the end of the cold war and the gradual liberalization of the Chinese economy during the 1980s and 1990s. The economic slowdown of 2001 and the events of 9/11 had a negative effect on business confidence but the overall impact on the world economy was relatively small. However, the world financial crisis and recession of 2008–9 had a more significant impact on the level of international business activity. Although most international trade and FDI are still undertaken by businesses in North America, Western Europe, and Japan, China and other developing countries are catching up. An important feature of the recent international business environment has been the development of regional integration in most parts of the world. Trade and investment theories provide a measure of support for the changing patterns of international business activity and, on the whole, favour free trade. However, these views are increasingly being challenged by critics of trade liberalization, especially in relation to the developing countries.

Discussion questions

1. What do you consider to be the relative importance of political change, trade liberalization, and technological developments as explanations for the growth in world trade since World War II?

2. To what extent is the 'clash of civilizations' likely to have a negative effect on international business activity?

3. Why do you think FDI increased by more than international trade during the last decade of the twentieth century?

4. Under what circumstances is regional integration likely to be most beneficial to the economies of the countries concerned?

5. Do experience and conventional theories of international trade provide sufficient justification for a general policy of free trade?

6. To what extent does the infant industry argument provide support for the 'trade justice' case in favour of import protection for the poorest countries?

Suggested assignment topics

1. Investigate the implications of Vietnam's dependence on exports for the stability of the country's future economic growth.

2. With respect to a specific regional economic grouping, investigate the impact integration has had on one of its member countries' economies.

3. Investigate a specific 'fair trade' project and evaluate the short-term and long-term implications of the project for the community or communities concerned.

 Case study: The Doha development agenda

The Doha Round is the first trade round to be initiated since the formation of the WTO in 1995, though it is the ninth trade round since the first GATT round began in 1948. The Doha Round started in November 2001 in Doha, the capital of Qatar, and is the first trade round to focus specifically on issues relating to the developing countries. For this reason, it has been dubbed the Doha Development Agenda. In the main, trade negotiations have been dominated by the developed countries, especially the USA, the EU, and Japan, and whilst this situation is unlikely to change significantly in the short term, major developing countries such as China, India, Brazil, and South Africa are beginning to demand a bigger role in trade negotiations.

The Doha declaration, produced at the outset in November 2001, aimed to reach agreement on a wide range of issues relating to agriculture, non-agricultural goods, services, intellectual property

(continued...)

rights, trade-related investment measures, and a number of other matters, though some of these issues were later dropped from the agenda. As the round progressed, the main attention focused on the reform of agricultural subsidies, improvements in market access, and reductions in the general level of tariff and other trade barriers, whilst respecting the need for sustainable economic development in the developing countries.

Throughout this process, progress has been slow and negotiations have been suspended and resumed and deadlines passed on numerous occasions, including an original target completion date of 2005 and an 'absolute deadline' set by the WTO for 31 December 2011. There are a number of possible explanations for this situation. First, the role of the developed countries in setting the trade agenda has been seriously challenged for the first time. Secondly, whilst the ultimate aim of freer trade is important for all WTO members, there is no universal agreement on how to achieve this goal. Thirdly, the developing countries believe they need to use trade protection measures in the short term to allow their economies time to adjust to global markets. Fourthly, even when trade negotiators from the EU or USA are willing to offer concessions to the developing countries, powerful domestic lobby groups sometimes make this difficult. Fifthly, it has proven impossible to achieve universal agreement on all the measures simultaneously.

In the case of agriculture, which is an important issue for many developing countries, the main stumbling block relates to the use of export subsidies by the EU and other developed countries. The EU CAP allows the use of export subsidies as a way of selling off high-priced European surplus production on world markets. This practice allows European producers to undercut the prices of producers in developing countries, making it difficult for them to compete either in their home markets or on the world market. However, although these subsidies are not as widely used as formerly, European farmers sometimes depend on them for their livelihood. This creates a clash of interests and is clearly a barrier to reaching agreement on agricultural issues. Tariffs, domestic subsidies, and other forms of trade barrier may also hinder market access in the developed countries.

Another ongoing issue relates to the general level of tariffs. This applies to manufactured goods as well as agricultural commodities, but although tariffs are generally lower as a result of the eight previous trade rounds, average agricultural tariffs are higher than tariffs on manufactured goods. This is a more difficult issue for the developing countries, as their tariffs are generally higher than those of the developed countries. In the short term, high levels of tariff protection for developing countries may be justifiable, but the developed countries are pressing for market access for their products, partly for commercial reasons and partly to strengthen the case for making concessions with their home constituencies in mind.

Failure to reach agreement on these issues has inevitably led to frustration with the Doha process and smaller groups of countries have resorted to forming their own multilateral or bilateral trade agreements. Such agreements may help the countries concerned, but often hinder trade with other countries and make it more difficult to reach universal agreement within the WTO. These political and economic concerns have caused the Doha development agenda to falter, but the stakes for the international trading environment could hardly be higher.[38]

Case study questions

1. What are the implications of the fact that previous GATT trade rounds have been driven mainly by the interests of the developed countries?

2. Why do you think the interests of developing countries have finally risen to the top of the trade agenda?

3. Is free trade generally in the interests of developed and developing countries alike?

4. Why has the Doha Round apparently reached an impasse?

5. To what extent, if any, is there a case for the use of agricultural export subsidies by the EU and other developed countries?

6. To what extent, if any, is there a case for the use of tariff protection by the developing countries?

7. To what extent do you think social and environmental issues should influence trade negotiators when considering trade protection for the developing countries?

8. What is at stake for the world economy if the Doha Round fails to create a more open international trading system?

Notes

1. WTO, *International Trade Statistics*, 2012, table A6, p. 214.

2. UNCTAD, *Investment Policy Review: Vietnam*, 2008, table 1.8, p. 25.

3. Main sources: UNCTAD, *Investment Policy Review: Vietnam*, 2008; *Asia Times* (15 August 2003), 'Vietnam: the deep end of doi moi'; BBC News (26 October 2006), 'Challenges for Vietnam's economy'; and *The Economist* (15 September 2012), 'Vietnam: A tiger at bay'.

4. The Council for Mutual Economic Assistance (CMEA) or Comecon as it was also known, included the communist states of Cuba, Mongolia, and Vietnam as well as the former Soviet-bloc countries.

5. Main source: Lynch, M. (2012), *The Arab Uprising: The Unfinished Revolutions of the New Middle East*, PublicAffairs.

6. Fukuyama, F. (2012), *The End of History and the Last Man*, Penguin; and Huntington, S. P. (2002), *The Clash of Civilizations and the Remaking of World Order*, The Free Press.

7. G20 includes Argentina, Australia, Brazil, Canada, China, France, Germany, India, Indonesia, Italy, Japan, Mexico, South Korea, Russia, Saudi Arabia, South Africa, Turkey, UK, USA, and EU.

8. A Communiqué of Ministers of Finance and Central Bank Governors of the G20, Mexico City, 4–5 November 2012 (http://www.g20.org/en).

9. UNCTAD, *World Investment Report*, 2005, Box 1.1, p. 4.

10. Fortune Global 500 (2012).

11. For a discussion of measurement problems relating to FDI, see UNCTAD, *World Investment Report*, 2005, Box 1.1, p. 4.

12. Main sources: UNCTAD, *World Investment Report*, 2006, ch. II, pp. 50–9; BBC News (26 November 2007), 'China in Africa: developing ties'; and *China Daily* (10 September 2012), '"Massive overseas mergers" on horizon'.

13. Black, F. and Scholes, M. (1973), 'The pricing of options and corporate liabilities', *Journal of Political Economy*, vol. 81, pp. 637–54.

14. Historical data on exchange rates can be found, for example, at http://www.x-rates.com.

15. Naim, M. (2007), *Illicit: How Smugglers, Traffickers and Copycats are Hijacking the Global Economy*, Arrow.

16. OECD Global Forum on Taxation, Tax Co-operation: Towards a Level Playing Field, 2008 Assessment.

17. OECD Global Forum on Transparency and Exchange of Information for Tax Purposes, Progress Report to the G20, Los Cabos, Mexico, June 2012.

18. The Cotonou Agreement, signed in 2000, and earlier agreements dating back to 1975, allow preferential trade access to EU markets for the 79 African, Caribbean, and Pacific (ACP) group of countries, most of which are former colonies of EU countries.

19. The AGOA grants preferential trade access to sub-Saharan African countries which meet specified criteria relating to their progress in establishing political pluralism, the rule of law, a market-based economy, and basic levels of welfare provision.

20. A US/EU Transatlantic Trade and Investment Partnership was proposed in early 2013.

21. APEC member economies as at November 2012, http://www.apec.org.

22. *Financial Times* (19 November 2008), 'Australia to join trans-Pacific free trade pact'; New Zealand Ministry of Foreign Affairs and Trade, http://www.mfat.govt.nz, accessed 10 May 2009; APEC Secretariat, APEC at a glance, 2012; and Palacios, J. J. (2012), 'Mexico and the Trans-Pacific Partnership', East Asia Forum, 26 September.

23. Ricardo, D. (2004), *The Principles of Political Economy*, Dover Publications, first published in 1817 under the title *On the Principles of Political Economy and Taxation*.

24. Smith, A. (2012), *An Inquiry into the Nature and Causes of the Wealth of Nations*, CreateSpace Independent Publishing Platform, first published in 1776.

25. Heckscher and Ohlin's original work was published in Heckscher, E. (1919), 'The effect of foreign trade on the distribution of income', *Ekonomisk Tidskriff*, pp. 497–512, and Ohlin, B. (1933), *Interregional and International Trade*, Harvard University Press.

26. Leontief, W. (1953), 'Domestic production and foreign trade: the American capital position re-examined', *Proceedings of the American Philosophical Society*, vol. 97, pp. 332–49.

27. Linder, S. B. (1961), *An Essay on Trade and Transformation*, Almqvist and Wicksell.

28. Vernon, R. (1966), 'International investment and international trade in the product cycle', *Quarterly Journal of Economics*, May, vol. 80, pp. 190–207.

29. See, for example, Krugman, P. R. (1979), 'Increasing returns, monopolistic competition, and international trade', *Journal of International Economics*, vol. 9, issue 4, pp. 469–79 and Krugman, P. R. (1991), 'Increasing returns and economic geography', *The Journal of Political Economy*, vol. 99, no. 3, pp. 483–99.

30. Porter, M. E. (1998), *The Competitive Advantage of Nations*, Palgrave Macmillan.

31. A useful discussion of Porter's diamond in relation to trade theory can be found in Smit, A. J. (2010), 'The competitive advantage of nations: is Porter's Diamond Framework a new theory that explains the international competitiveness of countries?' *Southern African Business Review*, vol. 14, no. 1, pp. 105–30.

32. List, F. (2005), *National System of Political Economy*, Cosimo, vols. 1–3, first published in 1841, and Mill, J. S. (2004), *Principles of Political Economy*, Prometheus Books, first published in 1848.

33. See, for example, Krugman, P. R. (1987), 'Is free trade passé?', *Journal of Economic Perspectives*, vol. 1, pp. 131–44.

34. Chang, H.-J. (2002), *Kicking Away the Ladder: Development Strategy in Historical Perspective*, Anthem Press.

35. The *Guardian* (23 August 2005), 'Retailers rip into Chinese textile quotas'; the *Independent* (24 August 2005), 'The EU-China dispute is not just about cheap clothes'; European Commission trade document (9 October, 2007), 'EU and China decide on textile import monitoring'; and European Commission (http://ec.europa.eu/enterprise/sectors/textiles/external-dimension/bilateral-dialogues/index_en.htm), accessed on 15 November 2012.

36. Stiglitz, J. E. (2003), *Globalization and its Discontents*, Penguin.

37. See, for example, Santos-Paulino, A. U. and Thirlwall, A. P. (2004), 'The effects of trade liberalisation on imports in selected developing countries', *Economic Journal*, vol. 114, F50–F72.

38. Main sources: World Trade Organization (http://www.wto.org); European Commission (ec.europa.eu); Office of the United States Trade Representative (http://www.ustr.gov); World Bank (July 2008), The Doha Development Agenda: What's on the Table?; and *The Economist* (8 September 2012), 'Goodbye Doha, hello Bali'.

Suggestions for further reading

For a broad understanding of the international business environment, international business operations, and international trade theory

Krugman, P. R., and Obstfeld, M. (2011), *International Economics: Theory and Policy*, Pearson Education

Rugman, A. M., and Collinson, S. (2012), *International Business*, Pearson

The political context of the international business environment

Fukuyama, F. (2012), *The End of History and the Last Man*, Penguin

Huntington, S. P. (2002), *The Clash of Civilizations and the Remaking of World Order*, The Free Press

The case for free trade in its historical context

Bhagwati, J. (2003), *Free Trade Today*, Princeton University Press

The case against free trade with respect to developing countries

Chang, H.-J. (2008), *Bad Samaritans: The Guilty Secrets of Rich Nations and the Threat to Global Prosperity*, Random House

Trade, globalization, and the developing countries

Sachs, J. D. (2009), *Common Wealth: Economics for a Crowded Planet*, Penguin

Stiglitz, J. E. (2007), *Making Globalization Work: The Next Steps to Global Justice*, Penguin

 Take your learning further: Online Resource Centre
http://www.oxfordtextbooks.co.uk/orc/harrison2e/
Visit the Online Resource Centre that accompanies this book to enrich your understanding of Chapter 3: The International Business Environment. Among other resources explore web links and keep up to date with the latest developments in the area.

Key terms introduced in this chapter

Acquisition The purchase of a majority ownership stake in another organization (also known as a takeover).

Bond An interest-bearing investment in a company or public sector debt.

Commercial services Traded services such as transport, financial services, or telecommunications.

Common market A tariff-free trading area with a common external tariff and the free movement of goods, services, people, and capital.

Comparative advantage theory The idea that countries should specialize in producing goods where they have a relative productivity advantage, then trade with each other.

Customs union A tariff-free trading area with a common external tariff.

Deadweight loss The loss of consumer surplus as a result of a price or tax increase.

Derivative A financial asset which is 'derived' from an underlying asset such as a share, bond, commodity, or currency, for example an option to buy or sell a share or currency at a fixed price on an agreed future date.

Economic union A tariff-free trading area with a common external tariff, the free movement of goods, services, people, and capital, and common economic policies.

FDI flow The amount of inward or outward FDI in a particular year.

FDI stock The cumulative amount of inward or outward FDI up to and including the current period.

Foreign direct investment (FDI) The establishment or acquisition of production or other facilities in a foreign country over which the investing firm has some degree of control.

Free trade area A tariff-free trading area.

Greenfield investment FDI involving the building of a new production plant or other facility.

Intra-industry trade International trade between firms in the same industry.

Joint venture An agreement between two or more companies involving joint equity ownership and control.

Mercantilism The idea that exports should be encouraged and imports discouraged as a means of achieving economic prosperity, contrary to the ideas of comparative advantage theory.

Merchandise trade Trade in physical goods and resources such as food, cars, or oil.

Merger Either an agreement between two or more companies to form a combined company or the general term for a combination of two or more previously separate companies, including a takeover.

Monopolistic competition A form of market structure where there is freedom of entry and exit and a large number of small firms selling differentiated products.

Oligopoly A form of market structure where there are entry barriers and a few dominant firms selling differentiated products.

Over-the-counter market The sale of bonds or other securities via a bank, securities trader, or other intermediary without the use of a stock market.

Political union A group of countries with a unified policy-making structure.

Portfolio investment The acquisition of financial assets or commodities for the purpose of earning a return on surplus funds rather than to gain corporate control.

Preferential trading agreement An agreement allowing preferential market access for the exports of a particular country or group of countries.

Protectionism A policy intended to restrict imports as a means of protecting output and employment in an economy.

Share An investment creating ownership (or equity) rights in a company.

Stock A non-equity investment in a company or public sector debt, including bonds and other securities.

Takeover The purchase of a majority stake in another organization (also known as an acquisition).

Tariff A percentage tax or duty on goods imported into a country.

Trade creation An increase in trade between the members of a regional economic grouping as a result of the removal of internal tariffs and other trade barriers.

Trade diversion Trade which is diverted from countries outside a regional economic grouping to countries inside as a result of the removal of internal tariffs and other trade barriers.

4 The National Business Environment

 Chapter learning outcomes

On completion of this chapter the reader should be able to:

- Identify the main factors affecting the national business environment
- Appreciate the role of government in maintaining political and economic stability
- Analyse the impact of fiscal, monetary, and supply-side policies on a country's economic performance
- Evaluate the factors affecting a country's industrial structure and labour market, and the impact of alternative government policy approaches
- Determine the implications of globalization for the national business environment

Opening scenario: The changing fortunes of the US economy

The 1990s was a period of strong growth in the US economy. This in itself was not so unusual except that it signalled a revival in US economic fortunes after a period of relative decline when compared with the post-war successes of the German and Japanese economies. The 1990s growth phase in the US **economic cycle** was, however, unusual in that economic growth accelerated in the latter half of the 1990s whereas growth usually slows down by this stage in the cycle (see Figure 4.1). This economic growth was accompanied by rising profitability, high rates of investment, rising **productivity**, low **inflation**, and falling **unemployment** in the US economy. By 2000, the federal government enjoyed a considerable budget surplus of tax revenue over government expenditure (see Figure 4.2).

The year 2000 was also the presidential election year when George W. Bush defeated Al Gore in the race to succeed Bill Clinton at the White House. The healthy economic situation meant that the candidates enjoyed the luxury of being able to offer tax cuts and/or increases in government spending without apparently having to worry about more conventional economic concerns like inflation or unemployment. However, no sooner had George Bush taken office in January 2001 than it became clear that the US economy was already slowing down, consumer and investor confidence was weakening, and share prices were falling. Many of the 'new economy' businesses whose inflated share prices had reflected expectations rather than reality were now facing bankruptcy. The tragic events of 11 September 2001 (often referred to as 9/11) added a further blow to the problems facing the US economy.

The economic downturn brought rising unemployment, lower consumer spending and falling profitability, but the US economy gradually recovered during the years that followed, reaching annual growth rates of over 3 per cent in 2004–5. The economic recovery was accompanied by strong growth in profitability and productivity but a decline in average incomes. By this time the federal budget surplus of 1998–2000 had become a significant deficit. The US economy also had a large external trade deficit and the value of the US dollar weakened against major foreign currencies, especially from 2006

(continued...)

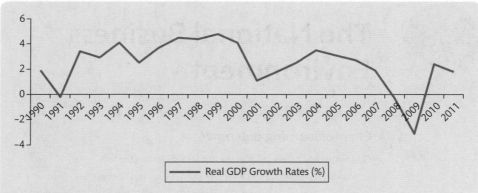

Figure 4.1: US real GDP growth rates, 1990–2011

Source: US Bureau of Economic Analysis.

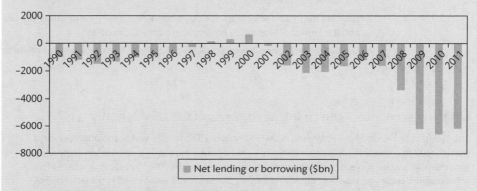

Figure 4.2: US government net lending or borrowing, 1990–2011

Source: US Bureau of Economic Analysis

to 2009. In 2008, the international financial crisis started to take hold, leaving the government with a growing budget deficit as it bailed out struggling financial institutions and the economy headed towards recession.

The US recession deepened in 2009, but with the help of a huge fiscal stimulus package introduced by President Obama and **quantitative easing** (sometimes called 'printing money') undertaken by the Federal Reserve, the economy returned to modest growth in 2010. However, the combined cost of bailing out the financial institutions and General Motors, which only narrowly survived 'Chapter 11' bankruptcy proceedings in 2009, left the US with a huge budget deficit and mounting public debt. Since then, along with other developed economies, the US has struggled to maintain economic growth and reduce unemployment, and President Obama faced the difficult task of trying to revitalize the US economy as he began his second term in January 2013.

Whilst the above picture provides a broad view of the impact of changes in the US economy and hints at some of the links between different national and international factors, it leaves a number of unanswered questions. This chapter explores the underlying forces at work within an economy and the way in which it is affected by the political system, national **institutions**, and government policy.[1]

4.1 Political and economic systems

4.1.1 Political systems

The most important determinant of the business and social environment in a country is its political system. The main types of political system are represented in Figure 4.3, though in practice there are many variants of these systems.

Democracy is increasingly becoming the dominant form of political system in the modern world, including the countries of North America and Europe, most of the countries of Latin America and the Caribbean, Australia, New Zealand, several Asian countries, and a growing number of African countries. This was not always so, as until the end of the 1980s the Soviet Union and Eastern Europe, China and some of its neighbouring states, Cuba, and several African countries had some kind of communist regime (sometimes described as **state socialism**). In fact modern **communism**, which began in Russia in 1917, was one of the major world political systems during the latter half of the twentieth century. Although some form of democracy has now taken root in the developed world and significant parts of the developing world, there are also a number of dictatorships or **absolute monarchies** (for example, in parts of Africa and the Middle East), a small number of communist states (notably China, Vietnam, North Korea, Laos, and Cuba), and one or two other types of **authoritarian** state such as the Islamic Republic of Iran (a **theocracy** or theocratic **oligarchy**) and Burma or Myanmar (effectively a military oligarchy or **dictatorship**).

Although it is common to consider communism and dictatorship, or in the extreme **fascism**, to be at opposite ends of the political spectrum, as illustrated in Figure 4.3, in some ways it may be more accurate to think of them as two points close together on the circumference of a circle. Whereas the spectrum from communism to democracy and then to dictatorship takes us round most of the circle, the two extremes lie next to each other, representing different forms of **totalitarian** state. Although at odds in terms of their political ideology, they share a belief in the one-party state and tend to use censorship, secret police, and other forms of repression as means of social control. The way they run the economy, however, is often quite different. Communist systems, or state socialist systems as they are sometimes known, favour extensive state ownership and a **central planning system** for the allocation of economic resources. Dictatorships are more likely to operate a capitalist system, though

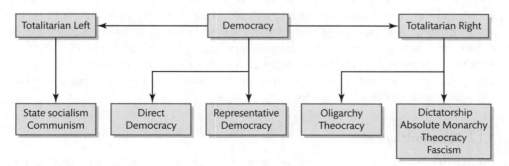

Figure 4.3:   The main political systems

there will be a large amount of state intervention in the economy and people's everyday lives. In reality, there is sometimes considerable overlap between these systems, so for example North Korea is effectively both a communist state with a central planning system and also a military dictatorship. A number of countries also have a democratic system but are effectively ruled by a single political party or individual, such as in Singapore or Zimbabwe.

Democracy has, if anything, even more variants than the totalitarian systems. The most common form is **representative democracy**, where the people elect a parliament and/or a president to govern on their behalf. In the UK, for example, the government is formed by the political party or parties with a majority in the House of Commons, the lower house of parliament, whereas in the United States the government is formed by the president who is elected separately from the Senate and House of Representatives (the upper and lower houses of parliament or Congress). **Direct democracy** involves the people making decisions on individual policies or issues; this system is not generally applied at the national level in its pure form, but in Switzerland, for example, referendums are held on all important issues, so the political system is somewhere between a representative and a direct democracy. Representative democracies also have many different political complexions, ranging from social democracy or democratic forms of socialism through to traditional or libertarian conservatism.

Social democracy has been particularly associated with Germany and the Scandinavian countries, whose social market economies combine a market system with a high level of social protection, though the Christian Democratic-led government of Angela Merkel (2005–) in Germany, for example, has been more conservative. Some countries combine a democratic system with more overtly socialist policies, such as Hugo Chávez's government in Venezuela (1999–2013). Conservatism gained popularity in North America and Europe from the 1980s onwards, following the election of Margaret Thatcher in the UK (1979–90) and Ronald Reagan in the United States (1981–9). This form of libertarian free-market conservatism influenced governments of various political complexions during the 1990s and 2000s, including those of George W. Bush (2001–9) in the USA and Tony Blair (1997–2007) in the UK. On the other hand, the Obama Presidency (from January 2009) has signalled a move towards a more progressive social policy and a willingness to intervene in the economy, though without necessarily abandoning a broadly liberal approach to economic policy.

The influence of religion can be seen most clearly in Islamic states such as Iran, Saudi Arabia, or Pakistan, though unlike the former two countries which have authoritarian rulers, Pakistan has oscillated between military dictatorship and democracy. In western democracies, religion is most visible in Christian democratic politics, which tends to be moderately conservative in Europe but more socially radical in Latin America, reflecting the different Catholic traditions in the two regions as well as the influence of the Orthodox, Lutheran, and Calvinist traditions in Europe. Each of the various political systems also has a significant influence on the economic system, the institutional environment, and the approach to economic policy.[2] These elements of the national business environment are now considered in more detail.

4.1.2 Economic systems

Politics and history have a major influence on the type of economic system adopted by a particular country. From the late 1940s until the end of the 1980s, it was convenient to divide the world into communist centrally planned economies and capitalist economies. The major centrally planned economies were the Soviet Union, together with its satellite states in Eastern Europe, and China. A number of smaller communist states also had planned or partially planned economies, notably Cuba, Vietnam (initially North Vietnam, then the whole of the country after the Vietnam war and the US withdrawal in the 1970s), and several African countries following the end of colonial rule. The rest of the world had some form of capitalist economic system. This led to a variety of studies of the differences between capitalist systems (the 'first world') and communist state planning systems (occasionally referred to as the 'second world'); some studies also contrasted these systems with 'third world' economies and the subject became generally known as comparative economic systems.[3]

However, the collapse of communism in Eastern Europe (from late 1989) and in the Soviet Union (in 1991), together with gradual market liberalization in China (from 1978), made this approach largely redundant. More recently, attention has turned towards the many 'varieties of capitalism' that exist throughout most of the world. In particular, a distinction is sometimes made between **coordinated market economies** such as Germany or Japan and **liberal market economies** such as the United States or United Kingdom.[4]

Communist central planning had a significant impact on the economies of the hard-line communist states. Rather than leaving decisions on what to produce, how much to produce, and what price to charge to individual firms or market forces, these decisions were made by the state planning authorities. The development of industries and products was therefore largely determined by the state rather than by market forces. For example, the Soviet Union allocated vast resources to the military and to scientific research, including space exploration, but fewer resources to the production of consumer goods. This enabled them to impress their 'cold war' opponents, but sometimes left ordinary citizens short of basic provisions. Capitalist or market systems, on the other hand, allocate resources mainly according to market forces, depending on the independent decisions of producers and consumers. As most of the world's economies are now predominantly market economies, this chapter focuses on the way in which market economies operate at the national level. This includes the role of government in managing or influencing the national economy as, in all the many varieties of capitalism, governments are reluctant to leave their economies entirely to market forces. The various forms of capitalism are explored in more detail in Section 6.6.

4.2 The national institutional environment

In Section 4.4 we explore the macroeconomic principles underlying the working of a market economy at the national level. These principles can be applied to all economies, but the way in which an economy operates also depends on the institutional environment within a particular country. Institutions, in this sense, are the rules by which a country and its economy operate. At the formal level, they include its political system, legal system, government policies, and the procedures adopted by organizations such as the central bank or stock market. At an informal level, they include the customs, practices, and ways of thinking that influence producers and consumers. The role of institutions is now increasingly regarded as central to our understanding of the working of an economy.[5]

Practical insight **4.1:** The Scottish housing market

The Scottish housing market behaves differently from the English and Welsh housing market because Scots law requires house buyers to make a sealed bid and, once accepted by the vendor, an agreement becomes legally binding. This is not the case in England and Wales, where offers are accepted informally and only become legally binding when contracts are exchanged towards the end of the house-buying process. The Scottish system relies more on formal institutions, while the English and Welsh system is more informal.

Question

- How is this likely to affect the behaviour of buyers and sellers in each case?

If the rules of a game are changed, different incentives are created and this inevitably affects the way the game is played. Thus, for example, the introduction of the tie-break in all but the final set of a five-set tennis match has changed the dynamics for players and spectators alike, as well as shortening some of the more closely fought matches. If there are no rules at all, a game soon becomes a free-for-all. In the same way, an efficient market economy needs rules or institutions. Without rules, it would soon descend into chaos and there would be no protection of the rights of consumers or producers. Even a black market or mafia-style market has informal institutions, though the rights of the strongest players may well be enforced at the expense of the weaker players (sometimes by violent means). An efficient market, on the other hand, is one where the rights of all the players are adequately protected and there is an effective process for resolving disputes. Property rights are therefore crucial in setting the rules of a market economy. They include contractual obligations, sale of goods legislation, employment law, and intellectual property rights such as patents, copyrights, and trademarks. Practical Insight 4.1 illustrates how different institutional arrangements can affect the way a market works.

4.3 Government policy priorities

Whatever the political or economic system, governments have a number of responsibilities which must be undertaken. These include defence and national security, foreign policy, law and order, and oversight of the economy. Most governments also regard some form of educational, health, and social provision as priority objectives, though the way they implement these objectives varies considerably. Political stability is of overriding importance in creating public confidence and providing a business environment which is attractive to domestic and foreign investors. Indeed, political stability seems to be a major factor in determining the development potential of an economy. Internal national security has become a particular concern since 9/11, given the negative impact of terrorist attacks on normal business activity and public confidence.

Stability is also a primary requirement in the economic sphere. As with political stability, it is difficult to conduct normal business activity without economic stability. Fundamentally, this means achieving stability at the macroeconomic level, though a stable institutional environment is also important when carrying out business transactions at the microeconomic level. The problems caused by economic instability were clearly evident during the 2008–9 international financial crisis and world recession. As illustrated in the opening scenario to this chapter, it is difficult to keep an economy on a stable course when the financial system is in crisis, economic growth is slowing down and the public finances come under pressure. The main government policy objectives usually considered necessary to ensure macroeconomic stability are as follows:

- **steady economic growth** – enabling an economy to stimulate business activity, raise living standards, and generate a surplus that can be used to finance public services or unforeseen emergencies;
- **stable prices** – to maintain stability in the value of money, allowing it to perform its normal role in market transactions and as a store of value, to enable prices to give reliable signals to producers and consumers, and to maintain confidence in the economic system;
- **full employment** – allowing an economy to utilize its labour resources to the full and operate at or close to its productive potential (in addition to the social benefits of full employment);
- **balance of payments equilibrium** – enabling an economy to earn sufficient foreign currency from its exports and other international activities to pay for its imports and other international financial commitments.

4.4 The national economy and macroeconomic policy

4.4.1 Measuring national economic performance

The main indicators of the size of a country's economy are **gross domestic product** (GDP) and **gross national income** (GNI). GDP measures the total value of a country's domestic output of goods and services in a given year, including exports but excluding imports. In fact, it is the sum of the value added at each stage of production, otherwise the output of one industry would be doubled-counted if it became an input of another industry and was then included in the second industry's output. GNI is the term now generally used in place of gross national product (GNP) to measure GDP plus net factor income from abroad, that is, factor income (interest, rent, profit, and labour income) from abroad minus factor income taken abroad by foreign nationals. Both these measures of an economy's size may be valued at 'market prices' (including indirect taxes and subsidies) or at 'factor cost' (excluding indirect taxes and subsidies). The most common indicator to use when considering the growth rate of an economy is the annual percentage change in real GDP at factor cost as this reflects changes in the value of domestic output in terms of the cost of employing labour, capital, and other factors of production after allowing for inflation.

Comparisons of the size of different economies are problematic as each country measures its GDP in its own currency, not to mention differences in statistical methods. US dollars are normally used to make international comparisons, but fluctuating exchange rates can make an economy appear to grow or shrink if the value of its currency rises or falls against the dollar, even though its **real output** remains constant. Similar problems arise with non-convertible currencies such as the Chinese renminbi.[6] In this case, the official exchange rate is fixed by the authorities rather than by market forces. Although China increased the renminbi's dollar exchange rate in 2005, allowing greater flexibility against a basket of currencies, many observers believe that the exchange rate has for a number of years been undervalued against the dollar, with the result that the size of the Chinese economy is almost certainly underestimated when measured on an exchange rate basis.[7]

A more reliable comparison can be made by estimating the size of an economy on a **purchasing power parity** (PPP) basis. This involves comparing the dollar value of a 'basket' of goods and services in the United States with the renminbi value of the same basket of goods and services in China, for example. If the goods and services cost $100 in the United States and 400 renminbi in China, the PPP exchange rate is $1 = 4 renminbi (sometimes expressed as an 'international dollar' – a dollar that has the same purchasing power as a US dollar in the United States). If the official exchange rate is $1 = 8 renminbi, the Chinese economy will be twice the size on a PPP basis as it will be on an exchange rate basis when measured in US dollars. The problem of fluctuating exchange rates can be mitigated by using the average rate of exchange over a period of time, and even adjusting for differences in inflation rates between countries,[8] but PPP exchange rates are more widely used as a reliable indicator of the size of a country's economy. The difference the method of estimating the size of an economy can make is illustrated in Practical Insight 4.2.

Of course, the overall size of an economy is not everything. GDP or GNI per capita is a better measure of the relative level of national income in a country, taking account of the size of its population. GDP per capita is often used to indicate a country's level of economic development or to make comparisons between the standards of living in different countries. A country's economic performance over a period of time is usually measured by its **economic growth rate** (annual percentage change in real GDP) or the growth rate of its real GDP per capita. However, a number of other indicators may also be used. The most widely used macroeconomic indicators, in addition to the growth rate, are measures of inflation, unemployment, and the **balance of payments**. Microeconomic indicators such as measures of productivity or labour costs may also be used. The remainder of this chapter is concerned

Practical insight **4.2**: Measuring the size of the Russian economy

During August and September 1998, at the height of the Russian financial crisis, the Russian rouble lost more than half its value against the US dollar – at one point over 70 per cent of its value.[9] Russia's already weak financial system had been affected by the Asian financial crisis of 1997–8. In exchange rate terms, the currency depreciation left the Russian economy's dollar value less than half the size it had been only a few weeks earlier. In reality, Russia's real GDP fell by 4.9 per cent during 1998 as a whole, which was a significant decline but hardly as drastic as its dollar value suggested.[10]

Question

● Would GDP based on a purchasing power parity exchange rate have provided a more reliable indicator of the size of the Russian economy?

with the relationships between these variables and the way in which government policies or unforeseen events may affect the performance of an economy and therefore the economic and political environment in which businesses operate.

Of course, economic indicators are not the only way to measure an economy's performance, as ultimately society's welfare also depends on social factors such as the distribution of income and wealth, the health and general well-being of the population, and other qualitative factors. A number of researchers have tried to explain why economic prosperity does not necessarily lead to increased 'happiness' and recent studies of the economics of happiness have attempted to identify the factors most likely to make people happy. Richard Layard, who has pioneered work in this field, argues that happiness is increased by factors such as social contact, trust, preservation of the status quo, work-life balance, and inner mental and spiritual well-being.[11] In this chapter we focus mainly on the operation of an economy at the national level in order to understand the processes that lead to economic stability or instability, but it is important to remember that other factors also need to be taken into consideration.

4.4.2 The importance of macroeconomic stability

It is now widely accepted that economies and businesses generally perform better if there is a stable economic environment. Economic growth enables a country to improve its standard of living, but a stable economic environment requires a steady rate of economic growth which is consistent with low inflation, relatively full employment and something approaching balance of payments equilibrium. Of course, general economic stability does not mean that an economy will never face problems. Such problems may include a structural change in an industry or region or an external event such as the effect of a crisis in the Middle East on the world price of oil or the world recession caused by the 2008 international financial crisis. It does mean, however, that in normal circumstances there should be a reasonable degree of stability in the economic cycle rather than dramatic changes as an economy moves from boom to recession.

The term 'economic cycle', or 'business cycle' as it is also known, describes the way in which GDP fluctuates above or below an economy's long-run trend rate of economic growth. The **trend growth rate** is determined by increases in an economy's productive capacity over a period of time. The productive capacity of an economy depends on the quantity and quality of labour, capital, technology, and other resources available to a country at a particular time. In modern advanced economies, the main way to increase the productive capacity and therefore the trend growth rate is by increasing productivity, that is, by increasing the output derived from a given set of inputs. Technological advances are important sources of productivity growth, but an economy can also become more productive by improving the quality of its labour force through education and training, by stimulating competition, or by increasing the flexibility with which resources are used, among other things.

At any particular time, real GDP may exceed or fall below its trend growth rate. There are a number of alternative explanations for these fluctuations, but they seem to reflect changes in consumer and investor confidence and the impact of these changes on the overall level of demand for goods and services (**aggregate demand**).[12] Even in periods of economic slowdown economic growth is often still positive, but the growth rate speeds up during an economic recovery. Occasionally a recession or boom occurs, where economic growth is negative or

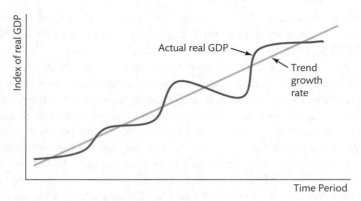

Figure 4.4   Trends and fluctuations in an economy

particularly strong. These fluctuations arise with some regularity though the length of a cycle (from peak to peak or trough to trough) may vary considerably, so it may be more accurate to speak of economic fluctuations rather than an economic cycle. These fluctuations can be seen in Figure 4.1 for the US economy, though it should be noted that the 1990s cycle was a little longer than usual, as explained in the opening scenario to this chapter. Figure 4.4 illustrates the long-run trend growth rate and short-run fluctuations for a typical economy.

The trend growth rate can only be increased if the productive capacity of an economy is increased. Without an immediate increase in a country's labour force, stock of machinery, and other resources, improvements in its productive capacity can normally only be achieved in the medium to long term. In the short term, it is possible to raise output above the trend growth rate by using existing resources more intensively, for example by increasing working hours or operating machinery 24 hours a day. Output may also fall temporarily below the trend growth rate if resources are under-utilized. However, short-run fluctuations around the trend growth rate may cause problems for an economy. Output may rise in the short run in response to an increase in the demand for goods and services. This leads to increased demand for existing resources and bids up the price of these resources, leading to increases in wages, the cost of machinery, and land prices, for example. Increased demand and intensive resource use combine to cause inflation. If demand falls and resources are under-utilized, as in the 2008–9 world economic downturn, workers will become unemployed. In more normal times, a government will try to avoid these two possibilities by keeping the level of demand as close as possible to its economy's trend growth rate. This helps to minimize the risk of inflation and unemployment, unless these problems are caused by long-term structural factors, in which case they may require more radical policy solutions. To reduce the risk of short-term fluctuations in the economic cycle and achieve macroeconomic stability, governments generally use a combination of fiscal and monetary policies.

4.4.3 Government policies for macroeconomic stability

In recent years, the primary focus of macroeconomic stabilization policy has been on the control of inflation. Inflation is regarded as a problem because it distorts market decision making. Consumers defer spending decisions or prefer to borrow rather than save; producers make cuts in their workforce or defer investment and training decisions to keep costs under control. The uncertainty caused by inflation has a generally negative effect on an economy and may lead to rising unemployment. This is why it is important to keep the level of demand in line with an economy's ability to supply goods and services: its productive capacity. Once inflation becomes established, it is difficult to regain control without imposing severe restraints on demand or wages, or a more drastic solution in the case of hyperinflation. This lesson was clear from the experience of the transition economies in Central and Eastern Europe during the early 1990s and notable recent examples include Venezuela and the extreme case of Zimbabwe.[13] The avoidance of inflation is therefore paramount. A consensus has now emerged around the use of **monetary policy** as the main instrument for influencing the short-term level of demand, though this was not always the case.

The experience of the Great Depression in the UK in the late 1920s and early 1930s led the British economist, John Maynard Keynes, to propose more active government intervention as a way of preventing the collapse of demand that occurred at that time.[14] By increasing public investment, the government could stimulate demand, not only because of the initial investment but also through the **multiplier** effect. Investment in public works would create income for construction workers, who would spend a proportion of their additional income, which would then become income for the sellers of goods and services, who would in turn spend a proportion of their extra income, and so on. The resulting 'multiplier effect' would depend on the marginal propensity to consume, the proportion of additional income spent by consumers (see Practical Insight 4.3).

The Keynesian approach was adopted by UK Labour and Conservative governments alike during the post-war years from 1945 to the 1970s and by a number of other governments during this period. In essence, Keynesian economics argues for the use of **fiscal policy** to manage the level of demand over the economic cycle (sometimes described as a policy of demand management). During an economic upturn taxes are raised or government spending is reduced in order to restrain aggregate demand in the economy (deflationary policy), helping

---

Practical insight 4.3: The national income multiplier

The multiplier can be calculated using the following formula:

$$\frac{1}{1 - MPC} \tag{4.1}$$

where MPC is the marginal propensity to consume: the proportion of additional gross income spent on goods produced in a particular country. If the marginal propensity to save (MPS) is 0.1 (or 10 per cent), the marginal rate of taxation (MRT) is 0.2 and the marginal propensity to import (MPM) is 0.1, MPC = 1 − (MPS + MRT + MPM) = 0.6. In this example the multiplier is 1/(1 − 0.6) = 2.5. Therefore an increase in investment of €1 billion will generate additional income of €2.5 billion after the multiplier effect has run its course.

Question

• What would the value of the multiplier be in the above example if the marginal rate of taxation (MRT) were increased to 0.3?

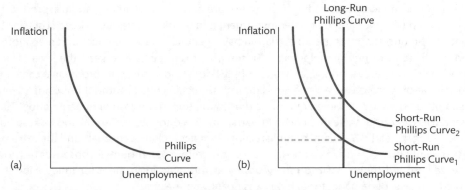

Figure 4.5   The Phillips Curve: (a) The Basic Phillips Curve. (b) The Expectations-Augmented Phillips Curve

to reduce inflation but leading to rising unemployment. During an economic downturn taxes are reduced or government spending is increased to stimulate aggregate demand (reflationary policy), helping to reduce unemployment but at the expense of higher inflation. This has often resulted in a 'stop-go' policy cycle of deflation and reflation, but, until the late 1960s, the policy was remarkably successful in keeping both inflation and unemployment at historically low levels in the UK. However, the policy led to the view that there was an inevitable trade-off between inflation and unemployment. This trade-off seemed to be supported by historical data showing a correlation between money wages (or inflation) and unemployment, as represented by the Phillips Curve (see Figure 4.5a).[15]

During the 1970s, rising inflation was accompanied by rising unemployment in the UK. This led many observers to question the trade-off between inflation and unemployment and indeed the whole basis of Keynesian policy, especially in the long run. The arrival of Margaret Thatcher in the UK (1979–90) and Ronald Reagan in the USA (1981–9) brought a new 'monetarist' approach to macroeconomic policy, based predominantly on the work of Milton Friedman.[16] Monetarists argued that a Keynesian fiscal stimulus caused inflation without any lasting increase in output or employment and that active demand management was likely to have a long-run 'crowding-out' effect, where public sector intervention stifled private sector activity and adversely affected the working of an efficient market economy. Friedman believed that governments should balance their budget over the economic cycle and use monetary policy instead of fiscal policy to control inflation. In particular, he urged governments to restrict the growth of the **money supply** in line with the demand for money. This policy approach formed the basis of UK government policy during the 1980s and early 1990s and variants of it were adopted in countries as diverse as Chile, the United States, and New Zealand. However, while the policy achieved some success in controlling inflation, the supply-side reforms that accompanied it were often achieved at the expense of rising unemployment (see Section 4.4.6).

The monetarist approach was accompanied by a free-market view of economics and a number of measures were introduced to increase private ownership and competition in a wide range of developed and emerging economies during the 1990s. These measures included the privatization of state industries and deregulation of monopoly markets in industries such as gas, electricity, and telecommunications. **Supply-side policies** were used to promote economic growth in the belief that only by improving the productive potential of an economy could there be a sustainable increase in output and employment. Underlying this conviction was the view that there was a 'natural rate of unemployment' at any particular time, which depended on the productive capacity of an economy. The natural rate of unemployment was the level of unemployment an economy could sustain without causing an acceleration in the rate of inflation (also known as the 'non-accelerating inflation rate of unemployment' or NAIRU).[17]

If this view is incorporated into the Phillips Curve (Figure 4.5b), the trade-off between inflation and unemployment may remain in the short run though sometimes at higher levels of inflation and unemployment (for example, short-run Phillips Curve$_2$), but in the long run any attempt to reduce unemployment by fiscal expansion will result in increased inflation without any lasting increase in employment, as shown by the vertical long-run Phillips Curve. The long-run Phillips Curve also reflects the view that people generally expect inflation to be the consequence of fiscal expansion and it is therefore sometimes known as the expectations-augmented Phillips Curve. The main legacy of this period in terms of economic policy has been the shift away from interventionist fiscal policy and demand management towards an emphasis on monetary policy to control inflation and the use of supply-side policies to promote economic growth. Although **monetarism** no longer carries the influence it did in the 1980s, the long-held view that stable prices and full employment are incompatible because of the trade-off between the two is no longer considered inevitable in mainstream macroeconomics.

From the late 1990s until the international financial crisis and world recession of 2008–9 there was a growing consensus around macroeconomic policy. The monetarist emphasis on monetary policy was retained, though the focus shifted from control of the money supply to the targeting of inflation itself, as the money supply appears to be only loosely related to the level of demand in an economy. Interest rates, on the other hand, are seen as having a more direct effect on the demand for credit, consumer spending, and aggregate demand. Supply-side measures also emerged as the most effective way to increase the productive capacity and trend growth rate of an economy, though free-market economists emphasize the role of competition while interventionists favour government investment in the infrastructure. Keynes's preference for discretionary policy at different points of the economic cycle went out of favour in mainstream macroeconomics during this period and the importance of targeting inflation became widely accepted by monetary authorities when setting interest rates.

However, there is now a growing recognition that fiscal policy may have more than simply a passive role to play in economic policy.[18] Even classic Keynesian policy was revived, if only temporarily, when the US, UK, Chinese, and a number of other governments used increases in government spending or tax cuts to create a fiscal stimulus during the 2008–9 economic downturn (see Practical Insight 4.4). The period since 2009 has also witnessed increasing tension in countries with large government deficits and debts between those who favour strict adherence to budgetary discipline by prioritizing government deficit and debt reduction and those who argue that economic growth should be the main priority. The tension between these two views arises because attempts to reduce government expenditure or increase taxes at a low point in the economic cycle are likely to reduce aggregate demand at a time when unemployment is already high; they may also reduce tax receipts and increase pressure on

Practical insight 4.4:   The return of Keynesian policy?

The US and UK governments effectively nationalized some of their leading financial institutions, including the US mortgage corporations, Fannie Mae and Freddie Mac, and the UK's Royal Bank of Scotland, during the 2008–9 financial crisis. In some countries government protection was extended beyond the financial sector to other high-profile companies, notably in the automotive sector. These measures led to a new wave of state intervention, but were motivated by a desire to prevent financial collapse rather than by interventionist political ideology. The speed with which the financial crisis led to an economic downturn also convinced several governments that a fiscal stimulus package was needed. For example, President Obama announced a package of government spending and tax cuts amounting to around $800 billion as soon as he came into office in January 2009 and the Chinese government had previously announced additional government spending of 4 trillion yuan (about $586 billion) in November 2008. Fiscal stimulus measures were also endorsed by the G20 countries at their London summit in April 2009.

Question

● Do you think the 2008–9 fiscal stimulus packages represent a return to conventional Keynesian policy or simply emergency measures before a return to more prudent fiscal policy?

welfare spending, making it even more difficult to reduce the budget deficit. On the other hand, if a Keynesian stimulus is used to boost aggregate demand using conventional fiscal policy, this will increase the budget deficit and may create inflationary pressures. Policy makers must also keep one eye on the bond market, as government borrowing may become more expensive if investors perceive the risk of lending to governments to have increased – a problem that became severe in Greece and some of the other weaker eurozone economies from late 2009 onwards.

Faced with the seemingly intractable conflict between austerity measures to reduce the deficits and stimulus measures to generate growth, monetary authorities have found a creative way of circumventing the problem. The US Federal Reserve, UK Bank of England, and European Central Bank have all used a policy of quantitative easing (or printing money as it also known) to inject money into the banking system in the hope of stimulating bank lending and generating economic activity; the Bank of Japan probably also adopted the policy in the early 2000s. The process of quantitative easing is explained more fully in Section 4.4.5. The US and UK authorities have injected vast sums into their economies since 2008,[19] but the policy has been criticized either as being ineffective if the banks do not respond by increasing their lending or as potentially leading to inflation if demand is overstimulated. The Chinese authorities have also claimed that US quantitative easing is flooding the foreign exchange market with dollars, causing the dollar to depreciate – a policy which China suspects may be designed to boost US exports at China's expense.

4.4.4 The role of fiscal policy

Until the 2008–9 financial crisis and world recession at least, there was broad agreement that the active use of fiscal policy to provide a short-run stimulus to an economy should normally

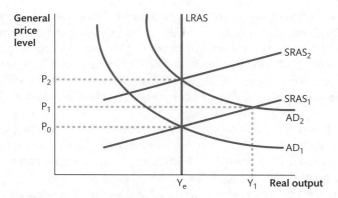

Figure 4.6 The aggregate demand and supply model

be avoided. Under normal circumstances, a fiscal stimulus is likely to result in an increase in inflation without any lasting increase in output or employment. In the short run, it will create additional demand but this will bid up the price of scarce resources. An economy will not be able to sustain this level of resource use, as in the long run output is determined by an economy's productive capacity. Inflation, once established, will be difficult to reduce.

This scenario can be illustrated using an aggregate demand and supply diagram (see Figure 4.6). Aggregate demand represents the total of all consumer expenditure, capital investment, government expenditure, and net export expenditure (exports minus imports), that is, total expenditure on goods and services produced in a particular country. **Aggregate supply** represents the planned real output of all goods and services. In the short run, an increase in net government expenditure (expenditure minus taxation) will cause aggregate demand to rise (from AD_1 to AD_2). This will create a short-run equilibrium between aggregate demand and aggregate supply at price P_1 and output Y_1, bringing about additional but higher-cost output as shown by the upward-sloping short-run aggregate supply curve ($SRAS_1$). In the long run, however, the economy will not be able to sustain this level of output and will return to the long-run aggregate supply curve (LRAS) at the long-run equilibrium output level Y_e. The price level will have risen to P_2. Any further attempt to stimulate aggregate demand will be met by a short-run increase in output (along $SRAS_2$) and yet another increase in inflation. This outcome is reinforced by the Phillips Curve analysis explained in Section 4.4.3.

Hence, the overall effect of the increase in net government expenditure is to cause inflation without any sustained increase in output. An increase in output can only be achieved in the long run by increasing an economy's productive capacity, which would be shown by a shift in the long-run aggregate supply curve to the right. Within this model governments should therefore maintain a broadly neutral fiscal policy stance. This does not necessarily mean that net government expenditure should remain constant. During a slowdown in the economic cycle net expenditure might be allowed to increase slightly to compensate for the lack of demand. Similarly, a small reduction might be necessary during an upturn in the cycle. In most modern economies there are in fact some fiscal safeguards (sometimes known as automatic stabilizers) that allow government expenditure and taxation to fluctuate at different points in the cycle. These include progressive income taxes and unemployment benefits.

In general, however, the government's budget should balance over the economic cycle as a whole. Although not always quite so strictly applied, this proposition forms the basis of fiscal policy advice offered to its members by the Organisation for Economic Co-operation and Development (OECD) and by the International Monetary Fund (IMF) when lending to countries in financial difficulties.[20] It is also a normal requirement of the Stability and Growth Pact of the European Union (EU) that member governments limit their budget deficits to 3 per cent of GDP.

Despite the broad consensus on the need for fiscal discipline as a long-term objective, a view is emerging that fiscal policy may have a more active role to play in certain circumstances. The UK Labour government (1997–2010), for example, adopted a policy of balancing revenue and current expenditure over the economic cycle, but of allowing a net increase in borrowing to finance capital expenditure, which has a longer-term impact on the economy; this was known as the 'golden rule'. In a different context, the Japanese government found that monetary policy alone was unable to stabilize the country's economy during its prolonged slowdown in the 1990s and early 2000s. Even with interest rates approaching zero per cent, the Japanese economy continued to stagnate and a moderate fiscal and monetary expansion was needed to promote economic growth.[21] It seems that fiscal policy may sometimes be needed to reinforce the effects of monetary policy, especially during periods of severe instability such as a financial crisis or world recession. Even in these circumstances, however, it is possible that inflationary pressure may re-emerge when the world economy starts to recover and a return to more passive macroeconomic stabilization policies is likely to be desirable in the long term.

4.4.5 **The role of monetary policy**

Monetary policy has taken over from fiscal policy as the main means of controlling inflation. Inflation indicates a general increase in prices and affects the purchasing power or 'value' of money. As it is a monetary phenomenon, it seems appropriate to use monetary policy. Initially, monetarists advocated that governments should control the money supply in line with the demand for money, which in turn relates to the demand for goods and services. However, experience has shown that it is often quite difficult to control the money supply, a small proportion of which is in the form of cash but most of which is made up of bank lending. In any case, the relationship between the money supply, the demand for money, and the demand for goods and services is often a complex and unpredictable one. As a result, the monetary authorities now generally prefer to use a much simpler policy instrument, the interest rate, and to target the ultimate goal, inflation, rather than an intermediate goal, the money supply.

Basically, a rise in interest rates increases the cost of borrowing and therefore has a dampening effect on credit-financed consumer expenditure and business investment, which helps to reduce aggregate demand and inflation. However, the process by which interest rates achieve this outcome, known as the **monetary policy transmission mechanism**, is a little more complex in reality. When the central bank raises its official interest rate (sometimes known as 'bank rate'), this puts pressure on other banks to follow suit, not least because the cost of borrowing short-term funds from the central bank has increased. The increase in interest rates also attracts international capital flows, which cause an increase in the demand for the country's currency and an increase in its exchange rate. The combined effect of higher domestic interest rates and the higher exchange rate is to reduce domestic and external demand for the country's goods and services. The reduction in demand helps to reduce inflationary pressures.[22]

In practice, interest rates have proved to be quite an effective means of controlling inflation, though there is normally a time lag between interest rate rises and a reduction in demand. It is therefore important for the authorities to keep a close eye on inflationary pressures so they can anticipate the need for an interest rate rise before inflation has actually increased. Moreover, it appears that the beneficial effect of interest rates may be reinforced by the expectations created. If people expect inflation to be low and the monetary authorities have a credible record of maintaining low inflation, this may have a moderating effect on price, wage, and spending decisions. There is also some evidence to suggest that monetary policy is more effective when government imposes a clear inflation target and where the monetary authorities have operational independence in setting interest rates and responsibility for achieving the target.[23] This allows them to focus single-mindedly on the control of inflation and avoids the political pressures that governments face. In Europe, this approach was pioneered by the German Bundesbank but it is now common throughout Europe and in other parts of the world, and has been adopted by the European Central Bank for the countries in the eurozone.

Monetary policy has also been used to stimulate demand. For example, expansionary monetary policy was used by the US, UK, and eurozone central banks when holding interest rates at very low levels from 2008 onwards. More controversially, they also resorted to a policy of quantitative easing as a means of stimulating their economies when low interest rates appeared to have lost their effectiveness. Quantitative easing involves the central bank creating new money to buy bonds (mainly government securities, but also high-quality company bonds) from banks and other financial institutions, which hold them as part of their investment portfolios. This money is credit money created electronically rather than cash, but it is equivalent to 'printing' money. Quantitative easing is therefore a means of expanding the money supply in the economy. The money helps to provide additional liquidity for the banks and it is hoped that they will respond by lending to their customers. The central bank's bond purchases also increase the demand for bonds, which raises their price but reduces the effective yield for bond holders (as the fixed rate of interest now represents a smaller percentage of the higher priced bonds). This has the effect of reducing long-term interest rates, which should also encourage individuals and businesses to borrow money. However, whether increasing demand by reducing the cost of borrowing or by increasing the money supply, the authorities run the risk of creating inflationary pressures and other problems when recovery begins to emerge (see Practical Insight 4.5).

4.4.6 Supply-side policies

How can a country increase its productive capacity? Essentially there are two ways to achieve this: it can either increase the quantity of resources available for production or increase the productivity of its existing resources. In the early stages of economic development, countries are often able to employ increasing amounts of land, labour, and machinery to develop manufacturing industries. This happened during Britain's industrial revolution in the eighteenth and nineteenth centuries and has been happening in recent times in China and other newly industrializing Asian economies. China's manufacturing sector, for example, has attracted a large number of migrant workers from its rural northern and western regions.

Practical insight 4.5: Quantitative easing: solution or problem?

Within the broad macroeconomic policy consensus, the main role of monetary policy is to control inflation. However, the 2008–9 financial crisis and world recession presented a dilemma for the monetary authorities in Europe and North America. The US Federal Reserve, UK Bank of England, and European Central Bank responded to the crisis with drastic cuts in interest rates and, despite emerging inflationary pressures, reinforced the monetary stimulus with a policy of quantitative easing. Notwithstanding continual criticism that the banks have strengthened their liquidity rather than increased their lending, the monetary authorities have persisted with low interest rates and quantitative easing, arguing that the economic situation would have been worse without these measures. It has also been suggested that low bond yields, caused by quantitative easing, have reduced the investment earnings of pension funds with the effect of increasing the deficit of company pension schemes and reducing the pensions received by pension-fund members. Whilst quantitative easing is a form of monetary policy, not the more pernicious policy of printing money to finance a government deficit, and the policy can be withdrawn or reversed (by re-selling bonds) when necessary, there are nevertheless a number of potential risks with any form of monetary policy expansion.

Question

● Is quantitative easing a solution to the problem of reduced bank lending following a financial crisis and recession, or does it simply create its own problems?

Even China, however, with its vast supply of low-cost labour, would be unable to sustain its industrialization indefinitely without improvements in productivity. As an economy becomes more developed, or even during a strong growth phase in its development, improvements in productivity are essential to achieve long-run economic growth. This was clearly the case during the long US growth phrase of the 1990s. For most countries, it is simply not possible to increase the labour supply continually. This has sometimes been true even for China, as the supply of workers willing to work long hours in difficult factory conditions dries up. The huge demand for labour also bids up wage rates, gradually eroding the advantage of low-cost labour. Long-term success therefore depends on productivity rather than the quantity of resources.

The most common measure of productivity is output per worker or per hour worked. This is a measure of labour productivity. The productivity of other resources is also important though more difficult to measure. The combined productivity of resources is known as total factor (or multi-factor) productivity. The productivity of labour can be increased in a number of ways: through education and training, improvements in work practices, and measures to improve motivation, build teams, or develop leadership skills, among other things. Another important source of productivity improvements is technology. In many manufacturing industries, and increasingly in service industries like banking or retailing, the use of technology is helping to reduce costs of production and increase output. Technology is in fact probably the biggest single cause of productivity improvements in most advanced and many developing economies.

At a more general level, improvements in the quality of a country's education, health care, transport, communication, and legal and financial systems are likely to aid its economic development. Its capacity for innovation and enterprise are also important, as well as the intensity of competition in goods and factor markets. There has been an increasing focus on policies such as privatization, deregulation, and trade liberalization as a means of stimulating productivity through competition and other market pressures. In some cases, governments have also used the tax system to create economic incentives.

Increasing emphasis is now being placed on the creation and diffusion of knowledge, the development of **human capital** (including the knowledge, skills, health, and values that people possess), and an economy's capacity for innovation, which combines the effects of human and other forms of capital. There are of course different views on the relative importance of each of the above factors; those of a free-market persuasion argue for competition, flexible labour markets, minimal regulation, privatization, and trade liberalization; others make the case for public investment in education, technology, and infrastructure. However, it is now widely accepted that long-run economic growth is largely determined by internal conditions within an economy – that the rate of economic growth is endogenously determined (see Section 10.3.2 on endogenous growth theory).

Whether the conditions for economic growth are restricted to supply-side factors is a different question. If they are, it suggests that supply creates its own demand (a proposition sometimes known as 'Say's Law' after the French economist, Jean-Baptiste Say, 1767–1832). In the aggregate demand and supply model, aggregate demand needs to be sufficient to convert aggregate supply from planned to actual real output, but additional demand beyond this level is inflationary. There may also be a role for demand in attracting additional productive capacity; this issue is discussed further in relation to the development of technology markets in Section 10.2.5.

4.5 Industrial structure and policy

4.5.1 Changing industrial structure

One of the main characteristics of a country's national environment is its industrial structure. The pattern of industries in a country may change significantly even over relatively short periods of time. This can clearly be seen in the declining share of agriculture and other primary industries in countries like Ireland, Mexico, South Korea, and Turkey between 1970 and 2010 or 2011 (see Table 4.1). On the other hand, in France, Germany, Italy, Japan, the UK, and USA, there is a marked shift from manufacturing to services over the same period. Whilst Mexico, South Korea, and Turkey have become more industrialized as well as more service-oriented, Ireland was more industrialized in 1970 but has also changed its economic structure from agriculture to industry and then to services within a relatively short period of time. This reflects Ireland's rapid economic development during the 1990s and early 2000s (see case study at the end of this chapter).

Underlying these changes in industrial structure there appears to be some kind of development process at work. One of the most influential explanations for this process since the 1960s has been Rostow's theory of the stages of economic growth.[24] Rostow, an economic historian, suggested that countries progress through five stages of economic growth:

- the traditional society;
- the preconditions for take-off into self-sustaining growth;
- the take-off;

Table 4.1: Main industrial sectors in selected OECD countries, 1970–2011 (% of total value added)

	Primary		Secondary		Tertiary	
	1970[a]	2011	1970[a]	2011	1970[a]	2011
France	7.6	1.8	35.2	18.7	56.1	79.5
Germany	3.6	0.9	48.4	30.8	48.8	68.2
Ireland	17.4	1.7[b]	36.0	30.9[b]	47.9	67.4[b]
Italy	8.6	2.0	40.0	24.6	51.3	73.4
Japan	5.8	1.2[b]	43.7	27.5[b]	50.2	71.3[b]
Mexico	11.9	3.5[b]	25.8	34.3[b]	66.1	62.2[b]
South Korea	31.0	2.7	24.2	39.7	44.7	57.6
Turkey	37.9	9.2	23.1	27.7	38.5	63.2
United Kingdom	2.9	0.7	42.5	23.1	54.5	76.2
United States	3.4	1.2	33.9	20.0	62.3	78.8

[a] Even allowing for rounding errors, most of the percentage shares for 1970 do not quite add up to 100%. This reflects minor errors in the data. However, the main trends are clearly indicated.
[b] 2010.
Source: OECD Statistics.

- the drive to maturity; and
- the age of high mass consumption.

However, with the exception of the role played by investment, the theory provides only a limited explanation of how a country can progress from one stage to the next.

Despite its limitations, Rostow's theory has intuitive appeal as a description of the stages of economic development experienced by the major developed countries. Although it is difficult to map a country's stage of development accurately to one of Rostow's five stages, in broad terms the UK developed from being an economy based on agriculture, 'cottage' industries, and other commercial activity (the preconditions for take-off) to being a factory-based industrial economy during its industrial revolution in the late eighteenth and nineteenth centuries (the take-off stage). From the late nineteenth century and throughout much of the twentieth century the UK economy was using more advanced production methods and becoming more technologically developed (the drive to maturity). By the end of the twentieth century it had reached the age of mass consumption and services had taken over from manufacturing. The relative decline in manufacturing output and especially employment in the latter stages of this process are sometimes described as 'de-industrialization'. On the other hand, Germany's manufacturing and construction (secondary) sector was still relatively large in 1970, probably because post-war reconstruction had given its manufacturing industry a new lease of life. However, by 2011 the trend towards services (the tertiary sector) is clearly evident in both the UK and Germany.

An alternative explanation of the stages of economic development is offered by the US economist, Jeffrey Sachs.[25] According to Sachs, there are four main stages of economic development: the pre-commercial, commercial, industrial, and knowledge stages. Although this is similar in conception to Rostow's theory, Sachs places more emphasis on the transformation process between each of the stages and on the role of knowledge rather than consumption at the final stage (see Figure 4.7). In pre-commercial societies there is a clear separation between

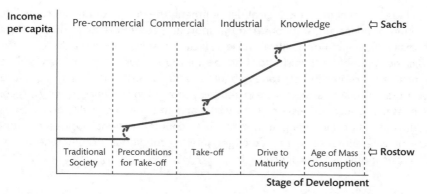

Figure 4.7 Stages of economic development

Source: adapted from Sachs, J.D. (19 June 2004), 'Stages of Economic Development', transcript of a speech delivered at the Chinese Academy of Arts and Sciences, http://earth.columbia.edu.

the rural and urban economies and most of society is made up of isolated rural communities. In the commercial stage these economies become more integrated, allowing a basic division of labour and trade between the rural and urban sectors, though urban manufacturing is still relatively small-scale. Industrialization, involving mechanization, large-scale production, and international trade, occurs during the industrial stage. The final stage involves the transition to a knowledge-based economy characterized by technological innovation and rising productivity. Sachs considers many of the sub-Saharan African nations to be predominantly at the pre-commercial stage while China and India are somewhere between the industrial and knowledge stages, though he accepts that the stages may overlap and different regions within a country may be at different stages of economic development.

It is now widely recognized that the process of development within a country depends on a number of different factors (see Practical Insight 4.6). Some of these factors are economic;

Practical insight 4.6: Industrial structure and the stage of economic development

All the countries in Table 4.1 experienced a decline in the share of primary industries like agriculture and all of them apart from Mexico experienced an increase in the share of services in total value added between 1970 and 2010 or 2011. The developed countries also experienced a relative decline in manufacturing industry. The less developed countries, if we include South Korea which became a developed country during this period, saw an increase in the share of manufacturing. This suggests they have been at different stages of economic development, but also that the development process has been continuing in each case.

Question

● What factors are likely to explain how a country's economy progresses from agriculture to manufacturing and from manufacturing to services over a period of time?

they include the level of technological development, the quality of human capital, the sophistication of financial institutions, the transport and communication infrastructure, and the intensity of competition. Political and legal factors are also important; the former include the efficiency of public administration and the appropriateness of government policies; the latter include the protection of property rights and the fairness and efficiency of the judicial system. Cultural and social factors are increasingly thought to influence the way an economy operates as they affect business practices, values and attitudes, the quality of education, and the health of a nation. Even geography may affect a country's national business environment, particularly where intense heat and drought, infertile conditions, or remote location make even basic economic activity difficult.

4.5.2 Industrial policy approaches

The industrial environment is also influenced by government policy. Industrial policy may take a number of different forms depending on the political convictions and economic philosophy of a particular government. Whilst free-market policies are generally associated with governments of the political right and more interventionist policies with the political left, these distinctions are not always as clear-cut in practice. Different policy approaches may also be associated with different national cultures. Thus, for example, Anglo-Saxon governments have in the main pursued market-based policies since Thatcher and Reagan in the 1980s and post-war East Asian governments have generally pursued highly interventionist policies. In each case, however, there are exceptions and countries may change course over a period of time. The various approaches to industrial policy may be summarized as follows:

Free-market approaches

A pure free-market policy would involve a complete absence of government intervention. However this is rarely the case in practice. Even in Margaret Thatcher's Britain (1979–90), a proactive free-market approach was adopted, removing regulatory barriers that restricted competition (the policy of deregulation) or introducing legislation to restrict the activities of trade unions in the belief that market forces were being hampered by trade union power. Rather than simply opting out of markets, Thatcher proactively created the legal framework she believed was necessary to allow markets to work better. There were also instances where the government refused to intervene in a sensitive foreign takeover or unilaterally removed foreign exchange controls to promote free international trade and investment, for example.

More generally, pro-market or neo-liberal policies have been adopted in a wide range of emerging economies, often at the instigation of the IMF, World Bank, or a regional development bank such as the European Bank for Reconstruction and Development (EBRD). These include the CEE transition economies, many of the Latin American economies, one or two African economies such as Botswana, India since the early 1990s, and South Korea, an economy that has been dismantling its interventionist policies in favour of a market-oriented approach since the Asian financial crisis of 1997–8.[26] Neo-liberalism encompasses policies like privatization, deregulation, trade liberalization, and in general a less regulated type of industrial organization.

Interventionist approaches

Government intervention may range from state ownership of an entire industry at one extreme to temporary support for an individual company at the other extreme. The most extensive form of state ownership is usually found in communist countries; thus, for example, even small shops and restaurants were normally state owned in the former Soviet Union and many of its satellite states. Nationalization of utilities, transport, and other key industries such as steel, aerospace, and shipbuilding has also been common in many non-communist countries, though there has been a marked trend away from state ownership in many parts of the world since the 1980s.

Directive intervention, where government influences resource planning decisions in the private sector, is another form of intervention particularly associated with Japan, South Korea, and other East Asian countries, but also with France during the early post-war years. For this reason it is often known by the French term '**dirigisme**', though in English the term 'indicative economic planning' is also used. The Japanese government worked closely with major companies such as Toyota, Nissan, and Sony during most of the post-war years until the 1980s, providing support for their international expansion. Whilst French governments are no longer as *dirigiste* as they were in the late 1940s and 1950s, even today they take a close interest in the fortunes of key French companies in what they regard as strategically important industries such as air transport, telecommunications, or even motor manufacturing.

In addition to these forms of intervention, there are many examples of governments intervening to bail out a struggling (or 'lame duck') company or providing capital for a new venture; these approaches are sometimes known as 'decelerative' and 'accelerative' intervention respectively. The practical implications of selective intervention, where particular companies are the target of government support, are explored further in Section 4.5.3.[27]

Supportive approaches

Governments often play a supportive role towards industry without intervening in an active sense. Perhaps the best example of this approach is the German social market economy, which is discussed more fully in Section 6.6.3. Germany's social market provides extensive welfare protection and strict market regulation to ensure industrial consensus or fair competition, and to protect companies from hostile takeovers (see Practical Insight 4.7). Another example of a supportive approach is the use of public-private partnerships to finance health services, education, and a variety of infrastructure projects. These projects have been common in a number of European countries since the 1990s, allowing public amenities to be built without the need for public finance but also attracting criticism from opponents of the 'creeping privatization' of public services.

4.5.3 **Selective intervention in practice**

Most governments find it difficult to resist intervening in industry when their national interest appears to be at stake. In many countries there is a public expectation that this should be so. Thus, for example, many French people would consider it quite proper for their government to protect the French language by restricting the number of foreign language programmes

Practical insight 4.7:   The 'VW Law'

Strict German takeover rules, especially in the case of hostile takeovers, have been used to protect the consensus approach that is integral to Germany's social market model. Since 1960, there has even been a law that prevented any shareholder from holding more than 20 per cent of Volkswagen's voting rights. This is known as the 'VW law'. This law has effectively given Volkswagen's home state of Lower Saxony, which owns just over 20 per cent of the shares, the power to veto a takeover of the company. In October 2007, a European Court decision declared the law an unlawful restriction on the movement of capital within the EU. In theory, this paved the way for the German sports car manufacturer, Porsche, to take control of Volkswagen. Porsche had already accumulated shares and share options which gave it a controlling interest in Volkswagen, but in 2009 large debts forced Porsche to abandon its takeover. The two companies then agreed a merger with VW as the dominant partner, an arrangement which effectively became a takeover when VW announced its intention to buy the remaining Porsche shares in July 2012.

In response to the European Court's decision, the German government introduced a revised VW law in 2008 allowing Lower Saxony to retain its veto, but in 2011 the European Commission reapplied to the Court to have its original decision confirmed – court action which the German government is likely to challenge.

In view of Volkswagen's prestigious position among Germany's corporate elite, the outcome of the battle between the EU and the German government could hardly be more important. On the other hand, the merger helps to reinforce the links that already exist within Germany's close-knit corporate community as Ferdinand Piëch is both chairman of Volkswagen's supervisory board and also a major shareholder in Porsche. Indeed, the first Volkswagen car was created by Porsche in the 1930s when Piëch's grandfather, Ferdinand Porsche, owned the company. Ownership of the Porsche company has remained within the family ever since. However, the future of the 'VW Law' is still uncertain.[28]

Question

● Is the EU justified in trying to open up the market for corporate control by removing VW's protected status or should it respect the consensus approach which underpins Germany's social market economy?[29]

on television or to provide assistance to its national airline, Air France, when it was in financial difficulties. Many Bolivians may also have been sympathetic to their government's decision to introduce a law allowing it to take control of the oil and gas operations of foreign investors in 2005. International opinion may be a little more sceptical. In all countries, however, there are times when selective intervention seems irresistible. As well as pouring money into struggling businesses where jobs are at risk, governments are sometimes tempted by a desire to 'pick winners' – to invest in companies that seem to offer a potential political or economic benefit or to become a future 'national champion' or 'national flag carrier'.

Airlines have often been viewed as national flag carriers, perhaps because of their visible presence flying in and out of international airports emblazoned with their national insignia. Governments have often been willing to support loss-making ventures in order to safeguard their national airlines or aircraft manufacturers. Thus, for example, the Belgian government subsidized its commercially unviable Sabena Airlines for most of its 78-year history (1923–2001). The development of the flagship Anglo-French Concorde aircraft was heavily supported by its parent governments but, although a technological triumph, it was less successful commercially. The European Airbus, built by aerospace companies in France, Germany, Spain, and the UK, has enjoyed considerably more success against its US rival, Boeing, but has experienced a number of organizational difficulties and both companies have been criticized for taking advantage of government financial support.[30] Clearly, governments have had mixed fortunes in promoting national champions.

Sometimes government support appears to be very effective for a period of time but the long-term effects are more questionable. This seems to be the case with some of the Japanese and South Korean companies supported by their respective governments during much of the post-war period. Like many Japanese companies, Nissan has been a member of a *keiretsu*, a network of companies with interlocking shareholdings providing mutual support. The Fuyo *keiretsu*, to which Nissan belongs, was headed by the Fuji Bank until it merged to form the Mizuho Bank in 2000. This relationship, which was encouraged by the Japanese government, allowed Nissan to expand both at home and abroad during the 1970s and 1980s. The provision of low-interest, preferential loans helped the company to invest in state-of-the-art equipment creating highly productive plants around the world. This was fine during the period of Japan's rapid economic development, but in the downturn of the 1990s the legacy of debt and overcapacity became a burden. This was one of the reasons why Nissan formed a joint venture with Renault in 1999, an alliance that has produced a major turnaround in Nissan's financial situation.

Daewoo Motors, formerly part of the giant South Korean Daewoo *chaebol* or conglomerate, provides a more dramatic example. Like Nissan, Daewoo was encouraged to expand abroad and incur mounting debt. At one stage during the 1990s Daewoo Motors was the largest single investor in the CEE countries but was producing its cars at a loss. By 1999, the company had become bankrupt and the car division was sold to General Motors.

Selective government intervention in East Asia has clearly produced some internationally successful companies and products. It has also resulted in excess capacity, misdirection of resources into selected industries, and an industrial culture which favours productivity and growth over profitability. Opinions are divided on the overall effectiveness of the East Asian industrial policy approach. During the industrialization phase it seems to have been highly effective. Whether it offers the best long-term prospects of economic success in an increasingly competitive international environment is a more open question.[31] Although different in many respects, selective intervention in Europe has produced equally mixed results.

4.6 Labour markets and labour market regulation

Labour markets are an important feature of the national environment. Two issues in particular need to be considered: first, the quality of the labour force; secondly, the way the labour market operates. The quality of the labour force depends on the quality of education and training available in a country but also on the extent to which organizations have developed their human resources. This combination of factors is encapsulated in the concept of human capital. Despite the dehumanizing sound of this term, the analogy between people and capital is in the importance of investment in both cases. Investment in people enables businesses and a nation to improve their stock of human capital in the same way as capital investment helps to improve the stock of physical capital (plant, machinery, and technology).

However, human capital has different characteristics from physical capital in that human beings are much more than their physical attributes. The key distinguishing feature is their ability to develop knowledge. Knowledge is an intangible asset which can be shared without loss to its original owner. This characteristic allows continually increasing returns to arise from the use of knowledge, something that does not normally apply to the use of other resources.[32] A machine may earn increasing returns as it is used more intensively but the returns from each additional hour of use will eventually decrease as the machine wears out or breaks down more frequently. Whilst this may in some respects also be true for an individual human being, the spread of knowledge and its increasing application to the development of technology mean that the benefits of knowledge continue to grow (see Section 10.4). The importance of human capital to a business and an economy should not therefore be underestimated.

The second key feature of labour markets is their ability to allocate labour to where it is needed. This issue is often discussed in terms of labour market flexibility, though it should be noted that flexibility may be derived from the knowledge and skills of the workforce as well as from flexible arrangements for the allocation of labour. Flexible arrangements may include the range of employment contracts available, the ease with which employees may be 'hired and fired', the flexibility of working hours, and the incomplete specification of contractual terms (allowing employers to use their employees in more flexible ways), among other things.

The UK generally has more flexible labour market arrangements than its continental European neighbours, though this varies considerably between countries. France, for example, has an official 35-hour working week, which was relaxed somewhat when President Sarkozy introduced a measure allowing tax-free overtime in 2008 – though the tax was reinstated by President Hollande in 2012. The UK has negotiated an opt-out from the 48-hour maximum working week under the EU organization of working time directive, allowing workers to work above this limit by agreement. In Germany and Spain, national collective agreements between employers and trade unions are common, whereas in the UK the few remaining collective agreements are largely confined to public sector workers. The UK has a higher proportion of part-time, fixed-term, and temporary employment contracts and more agency workers than most other EU countries. These arrangements allow employers greater freedom in their employment decisions and provide workers with more employment opportunities but less job security than in most other European countries (see Practical Insight 4.8). As with other aspects of the business environment, the attractiveness of different labour market characteristics will depend on the needs of particular investors.

4.7 Business, the national economic environment, and globalization

Macroeconomic stability is important for an economy, enabling it to achieve sustained growth without inflation and other problems associated with fluctuations in the economic cycle such as unemployment, a balance of payments deficit, or exchange rate volatility. It is also important for business. Stability provides a more predictable environment in which businesses can concentrate on the day-to-day operational issues and develop strategies on

Practical insight 4.8: The EU's temporary agency workers directive

Agreement on the EU temporary agency workers directive, first proposed by the European Commission in 2002, was finally reached in June 2008. The directive is intended to give agency workers the same employment rights as other workers. The proposal has caused particular difficulty for countries like Denmark, Germany, Ireland, and the UK which use a large number of agency workers. Governments and employers' organizations in these countries argue that the directive will reduce the labour market flexibility provided by agencies by discouraging employers from taking on agency workers. On the other hand, trade unions generally believe that agency workers should enjoy the same protection as other workers. The issue of protection for agency workers came to public attention following the decision of BMW, owner of the Mini, to lay off a number of agency workers as part of a package of measures to cut production at its Cowley plant near Oxford in February 2009. This is the type of situation where agency workers may receive the same employment protection as other workers, though the directive did not have to be implemented until December 2011.[33]

Question

● Why do you think it took so long for the EU countries to reach agreement on the temporary agency workers directive?

the basis of more reliable economic forecasts. Inflation, in particular, can have a detrimental effect as it not only increases costs and puts pressure on prices, profitability, and competitiveness, but also distorts price signals in input markets and labour and product markets, making it difficult for a firm to make accurate judgements when estimating the return on an investment or the profitability of a long-term contract, for example.

Macroeconomic stability also seems to be important during a time of major upheaval, as in the case of the CEE countries during their transition to market democracy in the 1990s. Countries like the Czech Republic, which managed to stabilize its economy relatively well, recovered from the initial economic downtown more quickly and with less price and exchange-rate volatility than countries like Russia or Ukraine, which were less successful in stabilizing their economies. Similarly, China has almost certainly benefited from a relatively stable economic environment during its rapid expansion since the 1980s. The need to restore economic stability as quickly as possible was also the rationale for the fiscal stimulus packages introduced by a number of governments during the 2008–9 world economic downturn, though the public debt incurred during this period will have to be managed carefully to avoid future instability.

Along with stability in the economic cycle, an economy's long-term growth rate is also important for business development. Economic growth creates incentives for business expansion and new business development. To achieve long-term growth it is necessary to invest in human capital, technology, and infrastructure, to stimulate competition, and to take a variety of other supply-side measures to improve the productivity of an economy. This chapter focuses mainly on the national picture, but we should not forget that most modern economies are open to international trade and foreign investment. In this context a stable, growing economy will provide a platform for exports and outward investment, and attract imports and inward investment. Inward investors will be attracted by the same healthy economic conditions that encourage indigenous business development. In this way, they will contribute to the host country's economic growth, both through the impact of their investment on income, output, and employment and also by stimulating competition and competitiveness.

Of course, the impact of globalization extends well beyond the effects of trade and investment. The increasing interdependence of the world's economies makes it even more important for a country to maintain economic stability and steady economic growth. Instability creates an unattractive environment for trade and investment and damages competitiveness. Poor growth performance creates a disincentive for foreign investors and indigenous businesses alike. The role of government in promoting a healthy national economic environment is therefore particularly important in the modern global economy. Of course, none of this is possible without political stability and well-functioning political, legal, and social institutions.

Summary

The national business environment depends on the type of political and economic system and the institutional environment in a particular country. Political and economic stability are essential prerequisites for a healthy business environment. Successful macroeconomic performance is important in raising living standards and encouraging business growth, though society's welfare is also affected by a wide range of qualitative factors. Economies normally experience short-term cyclical fluctuations and there is a general consensus that governments should conduct fiscal and monetary policy in a way that ensures the stability of the economic cycle whilst maintaining low inflation. In the longer term, sustained economic growth is achieved mainly through supply-side policies to improve the productivity of an economy, though active fiscal and monetary policy may also play a role when recovering from a financial crisis and recession. At any particular time, the industrial structure of an economy is affected by its stage of economic development. A country's industrial structure has implications for the patterns of output, employment, and international trade. Similarly, the structure of its labour market affects the quality of the labour force and the way in which the labour market operates. Government policy is sometimes used to influence industrial structure or the operation of labour markets. It is also important, in the modern world, to recognize that national economies operate in an increasingly interdependent global economy.

Discussion questions

1. In what ways does a country's political system affect its economic system?
2. What factors would you have to take into account when comparing the performance of the US and Chinese economies?
3. What policies should governments adopt in order to maintain stability over the economic cycle?
4. How can a country increase its trend growth rate over a period of time?
5. Under what circumstances should governments intervene to help industry?
6. What are the implications of globalization for national economic policy?

Suggested assignment topics

1. Using economic data for one of the developed countries, construct a graph to illustrate official short-term interest rates, inflation, and the GDP growth rate over a period of about ten years. What does the graph indicate about the relationship between monetary policy, inflation, and the economic cycle?

2. Choose a developing or emerging country and identify supply-side measures that would help to improve the productivity of its economy.

3. Gather data to indicate how a specific country's industrial structure has changed in recent years, then identify the reasons for the changes and their implications for the country's economy.

 Case study: The rise and fall of Europe's 'Celtic Tiger'?

The Republic of Ireland provides a fascinating example of how a combination of stabilizing and supply-side policies, together with favourable demographic and external conditions, can transform the performance of an economy. Not that the Irish experience has been problem free or that its development path has been without its critics, but its transformation from one of the EU's poorest countries in the 1980s to its second richest (after Luxembourg) in terms of GDP per capita from 2003–7 is remarkable by any standards. The real growth rate of the Irish economy between 1990 and 2007 averaged 5.9 per cent per annum and reached a little over 10 per cent per annum in 1999–2000. This was accompanied by falling unemployment and relatively low inflation (certainly by previous standards).

On the other hand, the Irish economy was badly affected by the financial crisis and recession. The economy was formally in recession from 2008–10, but the financial crisis had not been fully resolved by 2012. The rapid growth of the Irish economy enabled the banks to attract relatively high-risk capital, much of which was used to finance expansion of the property market. The international financial crisis then left the banking system on the verge of insolvency, whilst property prices collapsed and the economy stalled. The banking crisis subsequently made Ireland a casualty of the eurozone debt crisis, but unlike Greece whose debt was accumulated through years of overspending, Ireland's debt arose as a consequence of having to bail out six of its largest, heavily indebted banks. Banking debt thus became sovereign debt as the state assumed responsibility for the banking system – a policy which led to the Irish government seeking a €85 billion loan from the European Financial Stability Fund and IMF in November 2010.

A number of analysts have attempted to explain Ireland's rapid economic transformation during the 1990s. Certainly, the country benefited from its membership of the EU, its use of the English language, its historic ties with the United States, and the upturn in both the US economy and the world market for financial services, telecommunications, computers, and computer software. EU membership helped Ireland to reduce its reliance on the UK economy and the structural funds provided support for much needed infrastructure improvements. Irish government policies were also instrumental in a number of ways during the 1980s and 1990s: control of the public finances and inflation; more open economic policies in relation to trade, inward investment, and air travel (initially between Ireland and the UK – allowing one of Ireland's most successful indigenous companies, Ryanair, to enter the market); improvements in its outdated telecommunications sector; low corporate tax rates (initially 10 per cent for the manufacturing and selected service sectors, later set at 12.5 per cent across the board); and the expansion of technical and higher education. Some of these policies were encouraged by Ireland's influential inward investment agency, the Industrial Development Authority, in order

(continued...)

to attract foreign direct investment – a policy that has been particularly successful in attracting US investment in the financial services and technology industries.

Ireland's relatively high birth rate and the expansion of science and technology education, together with the return of well-qualified nationals who had previously emigrated, has helped to create a pool of young, highly skilled professionals to meet the needs of high-tech investors. Although Ireland has clearly benefited from favourable conditions not entirely within its control, the policies adopted during the 1980s and 1990s helped to improve the underlying conditions that allowed its economy to take advantage of the changing international environment.

Critics of Ireland's success have pointed to the country's over-reliance on foreign investment, both in terms of employment and exports, and the risk that high-tech investors may relocate to lower-cost countries as global competitive pressures increase. The economic boom fuelled house price inflation and other increases in the cost of living, especially around major cities like Dublin. The structure of Ireland's labour market is unusual for a developed country, with more employment in manufacturing and construction industries than comparable European countries – both of which were vulnerable following the banking crisis and the collapse of the property boom.

On a different front, Ireland's decision to join the euro may have made the control of inflation more difficult in the short term, as lower European interest rates helped to boost consumer spending in an already buoyant economy. It may also be argued that Irish governments have not pursued economic liberalization as avidly as they might have done in some sectors, notably in the country's rather centralized system of wage bargaining – though cooperation between government and trade unions has sometimes been credited with helping in the fight against inflation. Despite these criticisms, for most of the 1990s and 2000s the Irish economy enjoyed a new status as Europe's 'tiger economy'.

Since 2008, however, Ireland has struggled to recover from its banking crisis and recession, and the fiscal consolidation package required under the terms of the EU/IMF financial bailout has made life difficult for many ordinary Irish citizens. The Irish economy contracted by 8.3 per cent from 2008–10 and had recovered less than a quarter of this GDP loss by the end of 2012. The economic downturn resulted in a dramatic increase in unemployment from 4.6 per cent in 2007 to 14.8 per cent in 2012 and emigration was once again exceeding immigration, including many of the migrant workers from Poland and other CEE countries who had been attracted to Ireland during the boom years. Clearly, these problems will take time to resolve, but there has already been some improvement in the public finances and some of the factors that underpinned Ireland's economic progress during the 1980s and 1990s will no doubt provide a platform for the country's future development when economic recovery eventually gets under way.[34]

Case study questions

1. What role have demographic and external factors played in Ireland's economic success?

2. In what ways have Irish governments helped to stabilize the economic cycle since the 1980s?

3. What factors may have made economic stabilization more difficult?

4. In what ways have supply-side factors contributed to Ireland's economic success?

5. Inward investment has helped to transform Ireland's economy from agriculture and traditional manufacturing industries to financial services and high-tech manufacturing. Why do you think investors in these industries have been attracted to Ireland?

6. How do you account for Ireland's relatively unusual industrial structure and what are the potential risks for employment?

7. What internal factors are likely to constrain Ireland's future economic success?

8. What external factors are likely to constrain Ireland's future economic success?

Notes

1. Main sources: Peele, G., Bailey, C. J., Cain, B. E., and Peters, B. G. (2002), *Developments in American Politics* 4, Palgrave; Peele, G., Bailey, C. J., Cain, B. E., and Peters, B. G. (2010), *Developments in American Politics* 6, Palgrave Macmillan; OECD Economic Surveys: United States 2012; US Bureau of Economic Analysis; and US Bureau of Labor Statistics.

2. For a more in-depth treatment of political systems, see, for example: Held, D. (2006), *Models of Democracy*, Polity Press; Linz, J. J. (2000), *Totalitarian and Authoritarian Regimes*, Lynne Rienner; and Bruce, S. (2003), *Politics and Religion*, Polity Press.

3. An example of this approach can be found in Dalton, G. (1974), *Economic Systems and Society: Capitalism, Communism and the Third World*, Penguin Education.

4. For example, Hall, P. A., and Soskice, D. (2001), *Varieties of Capitalism: The Institutional Foundations of Comparative Advantage*, Oxford University Press.

5. A pioneering work in the field of institutions is North, D. C. (1990), *Institutions, Institutional Change and Economic Performance*, Cambridge University Press.

6. China's unit of currency is the renminbi yuan or RMB yuan, generally known as the renminbi internationally and the yuan within China.

7. For a discussion of the renminbi dollar exchange rate, see Goldstein, M. (2007), 'A (lack of) progress report on China's exchange rate policies', Petersen Institute for International Economics Working Paper, http://www.iie.com.

8. For example, the World Bank uses the 'Atlas Method', where average exchange rates in a given year and the two previous years are used, then adjusted for differences in inflation rates between the country concerned and a group of developed economies (the USA, UK, Japan, and the eurozone). Source: World Bank (http://econ.worldbank.org/).

9. http://www.oanda.com, accessed on 3 May 2009.

10. IMF, *World Economic Outlook: Focus on Transition Economies*, October 2000, table 7, p. 207.

11. Layard, R. (2011), *Happiness: Lessons from a New Science*, Penguin.

12. An introduction to economic cycles can be found in, for example, Gillespie, A. (2011), *Foundations of Economics*, Oxford University Press, ch. 21, pp. 341–56; a more detailed discussion can be found in Punzo, L. F. (2001), *Cycles, Growth and Structural Change: Theories and Empirical Evidence*, Routledge.

13. Venezuela's average inflation rate from 1990 to 2011 was 33.0% per annum, while Zimbabwe's inflation rate was estimated by the IMF at 10,452.6% in 2007 and some estimates have put it much higher (though inflation had come down considerably by 2009); sources: IMF, *World Economic Outlook*, 2008, table A7, pp. 269 and 272 and IMF, *World Economic Outlook*, October 2012, table A7, pp. 200 and 201.

14. Keynes, J. M. (2008), *The General Theory of Employment, Interest and Money*, http://www.bnpublishing.com, first published in 1936.

15. A trade-off relationship between money wages and unemployment was first observed by Phillips, A. W. (1958), 'The relationship between unemployment and the rate of change of money wages in the UK 1861–1957', *Economica*, vol. 25, no. 100, pp. 283–99.

16. See, for example, Friedman, M., and Schwartz, A. J. (1971), *A Monetary History of the United States, 1867–1960*, Princeton University Press; a number of Friedman's seminal papers can also be found in Friedman, M. (2008), *Milton Friedman on Economics: Selected Papers*, Chicago University Press.

17. The idea of a NAIRU was initially developed by Edmund S. Phelps in Phelps, E. S. (1972), *Inflation Policy and Unemployment Theory*, W. W. Norton.

18. For a useful discussion of the legacy of Keynesian and monetarist economics, see Wolf, M. (2006), 'Keynes versus Friedman: both men can claim victory', *Financial Times*, 22 November.

19. By September 2012, the US and UK authorities had injected $2.3 trillion and £375 billion respectively for the purpose of quantitative easing.

20. For example, while the OECD recognizes that 'policy action has rightly concentrated on dealing with immediate stability concerns', it continues to argue that 'productivity enhancing reforms [are needed] to support growth beyond the short term' (OECD, *Strategic Response to the Financial and Economic Crisis: Contributions to the Global Effort* (December 2008), p. 6).

21. The role of fiscal policy is discussed in more detail in Allsopp, C., and Vines, D. (2005), 'The macroeconomic role of fiscal policy', *Oxford Review of Economic Policy*, vol. 21, no. 4, pp. 485–508.

22. For a fuller discussion of the transmission mechanism, see, for example, Bank of England Monetary Policy Committee (1999), 'The Transmission Mechanism of Monetary Policy', http://www.bankofengland.co.uk.

23. For a discussion of the theory and evidence behind independent monetary policy, see, for example, Hall, S. G., and Henry, S. G. B. (2006), 'The New Monetary Policy Regime', *National Institute Economic Review*, 28 April, 196, pp. 63–5.

24. Rostow, W. W. (1960), *The Stages of Economic Growth: A Non-Communist Manifesto*, Cambridge University Press.

25. Sachs, J. D. (2004), 'Stages of Economic Development', transcript of a speech delivered at the Chinese Academy of Arts and Sciences, 19 June, http://www.earth.columbia.edu.

26. A discussion of South Korea's changing industrial policy can be found in Pirie, I. (2009), *The Korean Developmental State: From Dirigisme to Neo-liberalism*, Routledge.

27. A fuller discussion of industrial policy can be found in Andreosso, B., and Jacobson, D. (2005), *Industrial Economics and Organization: A European Perspective*, McGraw-Hill, chs. 15 and 16.

28. Main sources: *EU Business* (14 November 2008), 'Germany says new VW law in line with EU court ruling'; *Financial Times* (6 May 2009), 'Porsche and VW agree merger'; Bloomberg (21 March 2012), 'Germany will defend VW Law in European Court, Handelsblatt says', www.bloomberg.com; and *The Economist* (7 July 2012), 'VW conquers the world'.

29. For a detailed discussion of these alternative views, see Gerner-Beuerle, C. (2012), 'Shareholders between the market and the state: The VW Law and other interventions in the market economy', *Common Market Law Review*, vol. 49, pp. 97–143.

30. The WTO has ruled against illegal state subsidies amounting to $18 billion in the case of Airbus and $4.3 billion in the case of Boeing; source: *Financial Times* (12 March 2012), 'WTO affirms ruling on illegal Boeing subsidies'.

31. A useful discussion of Japanese selective intervention can be found in Flath, D. (2000), *The Japanese Economy*, Oxford University Press, ch. 9, pp. 184–213.

32. The concept of increasing returns from the use of knowledge and its application to technology has been extensively explored by Brian Arthur; see, for example, Arthur, W. B. (1994), *Increasing Returns and Path Dependence in the Economy*, University of Michigan Press.

33. Main sources: the *Guardian* (16 February 2009), 'Uproar in Cowley as BMW confirms 850 job cuts at Mini factory'; Directive 2008/104/Ec of the European Parliament and of the Council, 19 November 2008, accessed at http://eur-lex.europa.eu/en/index.htm.

34. Main sources: Fitzgerald, J. (1999), *The Irish Economic Boom*, Centre d'études et de recherches internationales, study no. 56; Burnham, J. P. (2003), 'Why Ireland boomed', *The Independent Review*, vol. VII, no. 4, pp. 537–56; The Economic and Social Research Institute, *Irish Economy Quarterly Economic Commentary*, Autumn 2012 (http://www.esri.ie); IMF, *World Economic Outlook Database*, October 2012; and Woods, M. and O'Connell, S. (2012), *Ireland's Financial Crisis: A Comparative Context*, Central Bank of Ireland.

Suggestions for further reading

Studies of the world's major political systems

Held, D. (2006), *Models of Democracy*, Polity Press

Linz, J. J. (2000), *Totalitarian and Authoritarian Regimes*, Lynne Rienner

Analyses of macroeconomic principles and policies

Blanchard, O. (2012), *Macroeconomics*, Pearson

Burda, M., and Wyplosz, C. (2012), *Macroeconomics: A European Text*, Oxford University Press

Miles, D., Scott, A., and Breedon, F. (2012), *Macroeconomics: Understanding the Global Economy*, Wiley

On industrial organization and industrial policy

Andreosso, B., and Jacobson, D. (2005), *Industrial Economics and Organization: A European Perspective*, McGraw-Hill

Lipczynski, J., Wilson, J. O. S., and Goddard, J. (2009), *Industrial Organization: Competition, Strategy, Policy*, Financial Times/Prentice Hall

An analysis of changing industrial structure and labour markets in a European context

Schmidt, V. A. (2002), *The Futures of European Capitalism*, Oxford University Press

Take your learning further: Online Resource Centre
http://www.oxfordtextbooks.co.uk/orc/harrison2e/
Visit the Online Resource Centre that accompanies this book to enrich your understanding of Chapter 4: The National Business Environment. Among other resources explore web links and keep up to date with the latest developments in the area.

Key terms introduced in this chapter

Absolute monarchy A political system where the state is governed by a hereditary ruler with absolute power.

Aggregate demand The total level of demand in an economy, consisting of consumer spending, capital investment, government expenditure, and exports minus imports.

Aggregate supply The total planned real output of goods and services in an economy.

Authoritarian A term used to describe a dictatorship or one-party political system where the government has absolute power.

Balance of payments A country's record of international receipts and payments arising from trade in goods and services (the current account) and investment and other capital flows (the capital account).

Central planning system An economic system where resources are allocated by central government rather than by market forces.

Communism A totalitarian political system where property and the means of production are owned by the state on behalf of the people.

Coordinated market economy An economic system where government intervention is used to regulate or otherwise influence the operation of markets.

Democracy A political system where the people influence the exercise of power either directly or through elected representatives.

Dictatorship A totalitarian political system where the people are governed by a leader with absolute power.

Direct democracy A political system where the people have a direct influence on policies and other issues.

Dirigisme A form of market intervention where government is involved in directing resources in conjunction with employers, trade unions, and other organizations (also known as indicative economic planning).

Economic cycle Short-term fluctuations of GDP around an economy's trend growth rate, including periods of faster and slower economic growth.

Economic growth rate The percentage change in a country's GDP from one year to the next, usually allowing for inflation (the real economic growth rate).

Fascism A totalitarian political system where the people are governed by a nationalistic leader with absolute power.

Fiscal policy The use of the government's budget (tax revenue and expenditure) to achieve economic stability or manage the level of aggregate demand.

Gross domestic product (GDP) The total value of goods and services produced within a economy in a year, including exports but excluding imports.

Gross national income (GNI) GDP plus net factor income from abroad, i.e. income earned abroad by domestic citizens minus income taken abroad by foreign citizens (also known as gross national product or GNP).

Human capital The knowledge, skills, and other attributes of labour that contribute to the development of a business or economy.

Inflation A persistent increase in the general level of prices, measured by a consumer price index, leading to a reduction in the purchasing power or 'value' of money.

Institutions The rules which determine how a market or economy operates, including formal rules such as the political and legal system and informal rules such as customs and practices.

Liberal market economy An economic system where resource allocation is determined by market forces with minimal government intervention.

Monetarism A free-market approach to economic policy placing emphasis on control of the money supply and a balanced government budget over the economic cycle.

Monetary policy The use of monetary instruments such as the interest rate or money supply to control inflation or increase bank liquidity (see quantitative easing).

Monetary policy transmission mechanism The process by which a change in the official interest rate raises or lowers the demand for goods and services in order to manage inflation.

Money supply The total quantity of cash and credit in an economy; credit includes bank and other financial deposits with varying degrees of liquidity, depending on the definition of the money supply being used.

Multiplier A method used to estimate the overall impact of an increase in aggregate demand on the level of national income over a period of time.

Oligarchy A totalitarian political system where the people are governed by a small group of leaders with absolute power.

Productivity The quantity of labour and other inputs required to produce a given level of output.

Purchasing power parity (PPP) A method of calculating an exchange rate between two currencies based on the amount of currency needed to buy the same 'basket' of goods and services in each of the two countries concerned.

Quantitative easing Expansionary monetary policy where the central bank creates new money (sometimes described as 'printing money') to buy bonds from banks and other financial institutions, with the intention of increasing bank liquidity, encouraging bank lending, and stimulating demand.

Real output The value of the production of goods and services in an economy after allowing for inflation.

Representative democracy A political system where the people influence the exercise of power through elected representatives such as members of parliament.

State socialism A political system where property and the means of production are owned or regulated by the state on behalf of the people – a term sometimes used in place of 'communism' (either with or without the prefix 'state').

Supply-side policies Government policies designed to increase productivity and the productive potential of an economy.

Theocracy A political system where the people are governed by a religious leader or group of leaders according to the principles and laws of a particular religion.

Totalitarian Authoritarian political leadership at either extreme of the political spectrum, including both communism and dictatorship.

Trend growth rate The long-run performance of an economy determined by its productive capacity.

Unemployment The number or proportion of the working population recorded as being out of work.

5 The Regional Business Environment

 Chapter learning outcomes

On completion of this chapter the reader should be able to:

- Discuss the factors that influence regional location
- Explore the causes and consequences of regional disparities within countries
- Discuss the role of regional impact analysis
- Evaluate alternative regional policies
- Assess the position of sub-national regions within the global economy

Opening scenario: Behind the scenes in China

Few people can be unaware of the story of China's recent economic success. China achieved a real GDP growth rate of around 10 per cent per annum from 1990 to 2011 and, despite the 2008–9 economic downturn, official statistics indicate only a moderate slowdown before growth resumed.[1] It is not as widely known that China's economic development has been very uneven across its varied geographical and cultural landscape. This is not unusual, as most countries have significant regional disparities, especially during their industrialization phase, but China's regional differences are particularly stark.

 Most of China's industrial development is occurring in its eastern and south-eastern provinces, notably along its eastern seaboard where Shanghai is located. These regions contain much of China's fertile land, most of its manufacturing industry, and about 90 per cent of its population. The people of these provinces are predominantly Han or traditional Chinese and are of Confucian cultural origin, whereas the people of western and northern China (north of Beijing) are mainly Mongols, Tibetans, and Uighurs who adhere to Islam or Buddhism. The western and northern provinces are generally mountainous and their rural communities are considerably poorer than those in the east and south-east. The population of the more prosperous regions has been swelled in recent years by eastward migration to provide labour for China's rapidly expanding factories. Taken as a whole, China's population growth is now slowing down, largely because of its one-child policy, but this policy has been less strictly enforced in the poorer rural areas, so population growth is still significant in western China. This tends to increase the income disparity between west and east.

 Within the eastern and south-eastern provinces, two regions have been particularly successful: the Pearl River Delta close to Hong Kong and Macao in the Guangdong province of south-eastern China, and the Yangtze River Delta, including southern Jiangsu, Shanghai, and northern Zhejiang provinces, along the eastern seaboard. The Pearl River Delta has attracted electronics, textiles, and other manufacturing industries, initially from Hong Kong but including many foreign investors, since the late 1980s. The Yangtze River Delta has been even more successful in attracting Taiwanese, Japanese, and many other foreign investors in service, high-tech manufacturing, and a variety of other industries since 1998. In this chapter we explore the reasons for uneven regional development, not only in China but in many different countries, and analyse the impact of regional imbalances for businesses and government policy.[2]

5.1 The regional location of industry

Regions within countries differ in a variety of ways. These differences may involve economic, political, legal, social, and other factors. Economic differences include their unique industrial structures, labour market characteristics, local taxes, and industrial infrastructures, among other things. Political differences include their systems of provincial and municipal government. Individual regions may also have their own policies, laws, social structures, and cultural identities. Regions are often highly distinctive and their inhabitants fiercely loyal. The differences between regions have generally developed over a long period of time, though they may be affected by particular events such as the discovery of oil or the decline of an industry. A region with a particular concentration of industry may attract inward investment by firms in that industry and the arrival of these firms helps to reinforce or complement its regional specialization. In this way, a firm affects its regional environment, but that environment also has an impact on the market and supply conditions facing the firm. Numerous explanations for the regional location of industry have been suggested. Some of the main explanations are outlined below.

5.1.1 Natural resource explanations

For many years proximity to natural resources was the favoured explanation for the regional location of industry. Clearly the location of many traditional industries like steel and textiles was influenced, though not entirely determined, by the location of natural resources. This is still true today for natural resource-based industries like fishing, mining, and petroleum extraction, though much less so for the processing industries that consume their products. Even the location of tourist destinations may be heavily influenced by the natural landscape and climate. However, not every attractive location has a well-developed tourism industry, suggesting that other factors such as the built environment, the quality of amenities, and the transport infrastructure are also important. Even established industries like motor manufacturing that still depend on natural resources are often located in regions with no natural resource advantages. This is certainly true of the Japanese motor industry, along with some of the country's other traditional manufacturing industries, as Japan has overcome its shortage of natural resources by building its economy on 'created assets' such as technology and skilled labour.

There also seems to be something of a **natural resource paradox** (sometimes known as the 'natural resource curse') that resource-rich countries are often underdeveloped, implying that natural resources may actually hold back economic development. Various causes of this phenomenon have been suggested, including the possibility that the income from natural resource exploitation lessens the incentive to develop other industries, the volatility of world commodity prices, or the effect of the discovery and exportation of a natural resource on a country's exchange rate. The last of these explanations is the so-called '**Dutch disease**', where the rising value of the guilder after the Dutch discovery of natural gas in the 1960s had a harmful effect on the country's manufacturing exports.[3]

5.1.2 Historical accidents of location

Industrial location may simply be an accident of history. Paul Krugman cites the example of the US manufacture of wind musical instruments, which is still predominantly based in the small town of Elkhart in Indiana where it became established in the latter part of the nineteenth century.[4] Boeing, the major US aircraft manufacturer, retains production facilities in Everett, near Seattle, where it was founded in 1916, despite moving its corporate headquarters to Chicago in 2001. Similarly, although established in New Mexico in 1975, Microsoft has had its company headquarters in Redmond, Washington state, since 1979. Once established, these companies attract supplier companies and a pool of skilled labour. This increases the incentive for them to remain in a particular location. Large companies like Microsoft and Boeing do of course invest in other locations both nationally and internationally, but the 'home base' still acts as a powerful magnet.

Sometimes global competitive pressures force the closure of a long-established factory; this happened to Clarks Shoes' last remaining UK production plant in 2005, but the company still retains its headquarters in the small Somerset town of Street, where it was founded in 1825. Another company with international operations, Cadbury, has maintained its main UK chocolate production at Bourneville just south of Birmingham since 1879, despite being owned by the US company, Mondelēz International, formed in October 2012 following a demerger from Kraft Foods which acquired Cadbury in February 2010. When deeply rooted in history, location can still exert a powerful influence even on a company with multinational operations (see Practical Insight 5.1).

5.1.3 Transport and communication costs

The cost of transport may affect a company's location decision, especially where its products are heavy, bulky, or perishable. Modern developed economies have vastly improved their transport infrastructures in recent years, but even within these countries it is not uncommon to find regions that are poorly connected to the national transport network. Differences in the accessibility of regions may be partly responsible for regional disparities. For example, Western Slovakia, with its capital, Bratislava, and close proximity to Austria, has attracted much more foreign direct investment than its less accessible eastern region (see case study at the end of this chapter). Accessibility, cost, and the time taken to complete a journey are taken into account by logistics companies when planning transport routes, along with political and economic risk factors.

Practical insight 5.1: Coca-Cola

Coca-Cola was first sold at a soda fountain in a pharmacy in Atlanta, Georgia in 1886 and the company still has its headquarters there today. Despite employing 49,000 people, selling its products in almost every country of the world, and having worldwide sales of $46.5 billion in 2012, the Coca-Cola company has remained loyal to its original location.[5]

Question

● Why do you think the pull of the original location is so powerful, even for a major multinational company?

The availability and cost of communication may also influence location, though communication technology has vastly reduced the importance of these factors in location decisions. Nevertheless, the type of communication media available in a particular region may still influence the effectiveness of a company's advertising or public relations.

5.1.4 Access to markets

Despite the declining importance of conventional location factors, market access has in some respects become even more important in recent years. The popularity of foreign direct investment over other modes of international market entry since the 1980s testifies to the fact that location still matters. Multinational companies have become increasingly aware of the importance of cultural sensitivity in their business practices and product and service design. Close proximity to a market enables them to employ workers with local knowledge and to gain greater cultural acceptance of their products. This is particularly important in countries with high-context cultures where it is difficult to do business without forming close relationships, as in China, or gaining access to networks, as in Japan's company networks or *keiretsu* (see Sections 6.4.1, 14.2, and 14.3 for further discussion of these issues). Regional differences between markets may also make proximity of location desirable.

The importance of establishing relationships has also been recognized in the emphasis marketers now place on relationship marketing: the building of long-term relationships that allow information and other benefits to flow between buyer and seller, helping to achieve loyalty from the buyer and commitment from the seller.[6] Close proximity to the market may be a factor in making this approach to marketing more effective. Of course, market proximity is even more important for conventional retailing, where customers generally live within a short radius of a retail store. The size and characteristics of the home market may also influence the growth of a new business, especially in the early stages of its development, as illustrated in Practical Insight 5.2.

Practical insight 5.2: Japan's dominance in the digital camera market

Of the top ten digital camera manufacturers in 2010, eight were Japanese and one was South Korean. These Japanese companies had a combined worldwide market share of 63.6 per cent.[7] Clearly, Japanese companies have chosen to specialize in this market, along with other electronic product markets. The origins of these companies could be described as accidents of history, but their combined success in the highly competitive digital camera market is significant. Japanese people are renowned for their love of photography, perhaps because of a natural curiosity and an eye for detail – traits which may also help them to excel at making intricate scientific and technological products (though around 40 per cent of worldwide digital camera production was outsourced to Taiwanese companies in 2010).[8]

Question

- Is it possible that the initial success of Japanese digital camera manufacturers was at least partly dependent on their home country's high demand for these products?

5.1.5 **Labour market characteristics**

In highly competitive international markets access to skilled or low-cost labour may be crucial to the survival of a business. An inward investor may also be looking for a flexible, lightly regulated labour market or workers who are reliable or compliant. Several examples of these influences can be found in the car industry: Nissan's decision in the 1980s to locate in north-east England, a relatively low-cost UK region with no history of motor manufacturing or the industrial relations problems of the established motor manufacturing regions; Audi's decision to relocate its assembly operations from high-cost Germany to low-cost Hungary in the 1990s; and Kia's decision to locate its European car plant in northern Slovakia rather than southern Poland in 2004, almost certainly influenced by Slovakia's lower wage costs, weak trade unions, and the pro-market orientation of its government at that time. In this respect relative labour costs and labour market conditions place sub-national regions in a competitive international environment, not simply within their national context, though competition between regions within a country may also be intense.

5.1.6 **Patterns of regional development**

A simple view of regional development might consider two basic types of economic activity: rural agriculture and urban manufacturing. A basic distinction between rural and urban development is that the former makes extensive use of large areas of land, whereas the latter makes intensive use of relatively small areas of land. Some regions are still predominantly agricultural, but the major influence on regional development during the nineteenth and twentieth centuries has been the growth of manufacturing and then service industries in the towns and cities. A common characteristic of urban development is the tendency for a central location to emerge, around which industrial activity and housing are located. An early attempt to explain this tendency is known as **central place theory**, published by a German geographer, Walter Christaller, in 1933.[9] Central place theory argues that the development of a 'central place' is dependent on principles relating to the market area, transport routes, and administrative efficiency, and that a number of smaller towns will surround the main town along the main transport routes. Whilst this theory represents a rather static, conventional view of urban development, its broad predictions can often be observed in practice.

The issues raised by Christaller are clearly important ones. Industry and people need space, but most people like to live within commuting distance of their place of work, so urban development is initially concentrated in a relatively small area. There also need to be linkages between different types of industrial and human activity, which helps to reinforce the concentration of activity around a central point or **growth pole**. This concentration or agglomeration of activity brings a number of benefits, sometimes referred to as **agglomeration economies** or economies of **spatial concentration** (see Section 5.1.7), and these benefits attract other firms and people. Over time, the more successful urban developments expand and join up with smaller neighbouring developments and sometimes with neighbouring central points to form a larger conurbation. A number of studies have investigated the potential synergies that may arise between neighbouring growth poles, forming what are known as **polycentric regions** (see Figure 5.1).[10] Of course, urban development is not uniform and the pattern of development depends on factors such as the suitability of land for particular uses, the

Figure 5.1 The Meuse-Rhine Triangle: a cross-border polycentric region

needs of particular industries, the demand for particular types of housing, the availability of transport, and people's willingness to commute, among other things.

Many of these factors will also change over a period of time. Improvements in transport and rising incomes have allowed commuters to travel longer distances and buy more desirable housing away from the city centres. Inner city areas have also been abandoned by traditional industries, including many of the larger retailers that favour out-of-town developments. More recently, young professionals have been returning to the city centres, where former docklands and industrial areas now offer exclusive modern housing. Regional development also reflects changing patterns of industry, and changing production systems and labour use. The central location of company headquarters and internationalization of company owner-ship have left some regions with **'branch-plant economies'**, without the security of the local industries they once enjoyed. Whatever the nature of change, regions are living organisms that develop and sometimes decline as the needs of people and industry change.

5.1.7 **Economies of spatial concentration (agglomeration economies)**

Concentrated pockets of economic activity in a particular location are common in many countries. Sometimes they are highly localized, sometimes spread over a larger area. This type of spatial concentration is now often described as a **cluster**, though it is by no means a new phenomenon. Many clusters occur naturally over a period of time, but some are created or encouraged by national or local government policy. Typically, clusters are made up of firms in a particular industry. Examples include high-tech clusters such as 'Silicon Valley' in California or Cyberjaya near Kuala Lumpur, the US movie capital, Hollywood, and 'Motorsport Valley' in England's East Midlands, home of the British racing car industry. On a smaller scale, the term 'cluster' might be applied to a group of motor car showrooms or restaurants which have located close to each other.

Whilst one might expect location to become less important as transport and communication improve, it seems that new types of cluster are continually appearing. This has led theorists and researchers to search for new explanations. It has also led some to argue that clusters may actually be a significant driver behind economic development and regional development in particular. Two of the leading figures in this field are the US academics, Michael Porter and Paul Krugman.[11]

Conventional explanations for the development of clusters have focused on three main areas:

- Knowledge spill over effects, where firms learn from each other or from a neighbouring university (for example, Stanford University supports Silicon Valley).
- The advantages of 'thick' markets for specialized skills, enabling new businesses to take advantage of a large pool of skilled labour.
- Backward and forward linkages, allowing businesses to find specialized supplies and a specialized market for their products.

These factors help to create a supportive environment so that, once established, clusters are more likely to persist. The larger the cluster, the larger will be the knowledge spill over effects, the pool of skilled labour, the potential market, and the source of specialized supplies. Large clusters will also tend to attract more firms and support services and are more likely to reach a critical mass that will enable them to become self-sustaining.

It has long been recognized that clusters benefit from external economies of scale or increasing returns from their external environment; that is, regardless of the size of an individual firm, a group of neighbouring firms benefits from its combined scale in that it attracts specialized labour, support services, and a more extensive local infrastructure. The economist, Alfred Marshall, was aware of this towards the end of the nineteenth century.[12] However, more attention is now being focused on internal economies of scale or increasing returns to scale at the level of the firm, that is, the benefits derived from the increasing size of a firm. Not only does a small firm benefit from external economies of scale when operating in a cluster with many other firms, but this environment also enables the firm to become larger by taking advantage of the market the cluster provides. In addition, firms, universities, and other agencies which operate closely with each other within a cluster are likely to experience network effects, where all members of the network benefit from the innovation of an individual member, for example.

The dynamic process by which spatial concentration reinforces itself may be described as the 'snowball effect'. It is likely that some clusters tend to be more stable and self-reinforcing than others; indeed, that they gather momentum over a period of time. A cluster may be reinforced where labour and other factors of production either are fairly immobile or earn higher returns at a particular location. The key questions for researchers are: (a) what factors determine the stability or rate of growth of a cluster; and (b) is there any recognizable pattern in the way clusters develop? For example, do they tend to move towards equilibrium? In dynamic models there may be several possible equilibria or, in fact, the search for equilibrium may be illusive. There may also be several clusters in close proximity, for instance two or more neighbouring towns each with a large industrial or commercial centre. Sometimes neighbouring clusters may feed off each other, as in the case of London's banking and insurance sectors. Sometimes they may be in competition, for example two rival shopping centres. The dynamic process at work within clusters is not yet fully understood, nor is it certain that clusters necessarily bring benefits that cannot be achieved outside cluster developments.[13] Practical Insight 5.3 considers the cluster around Cambridge University.

Practical insight **5.3:** Silicon Fen

The Cambridge Cluster, also known by its nickname Silicon Fen, is an example of a successful technology cluster located close to a leading university, similar to its more illustrious forerunner, Silicon Valley. Silicon Fen has helped to establish a large number of small businesses in fields such as computer software, electronics, and biotechnology. Only a few of these companies have achieved multinational status, but the strong pool of well-qualified and flexible labour allows new companies to draw on a ready supply of workers with highly specialized skills. The cluster's critical mass therefore seems to come from its large number of specialized businesses and workers.[14]

Question

- What does this tell us about the relative importance of internal and external economies of scale in this particular cluster?

5.2 Regional impact analysis

Studies of the economic impact of a major project have become increasingly common in recent years. An economic impact analysis might, for example, investigate the impact of a new leisure centre, conference centre, or airport on the demand for goods and services and the resulting income and employment in the region surrounding the new project. A similar analysis might be made of the impact of the closure of an industrial plant or other facility. These studies are often undertaken at the planning stage of a project to provide an evaluation of the estimated net benefits or costs of a project. They are generally focused on sub-national regions or even smaller localities, depending on the scale of a project. It is also recognized that the impact may be wider than an individual region and, in some cases, possibly even global. Increasingly, social and (natural) environmental factors are being included in impact assessments, as well as economic factors, as is the case with PricewaterhouseCoopers' impact analysis of the 2012 London Olympic Games.[15] This study assessed the likely impact of the London Olympics on the basis of six main 'accounts' (including estimated income and expenditure in each case):

- Global economic profile: the impact on the macro economy, infrastructure, inward investment, and tourism.
- Business support, innovation, and diversification: the creation of new businesses, supply chains, and clusters.
- People, skills, and employment: the impact on population trends, labour skills, and jobs.
- Sporting and cultural legacy: the creation of sporting and cultural facilities.
- Public health: the impact on physical and mental health and well-being.
- Environment: the impact on land use, ecology, transport, housing, waste, and other environmental factors.

Where possible, regional impact analysis focuses on quantifiable indicators such as employment or income levels, but social factors may require qualitative research methods such as interviews or focus groups to discover people's perceptions of the social impact on their

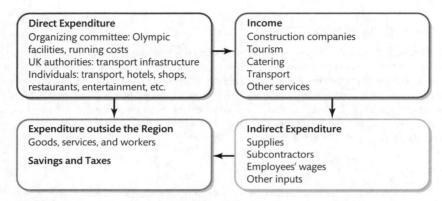

Figure 5.2 Illustrative expenditure on the 2012 Olympic Games

lives or communities. In order to quantify the economic impact, it is necessary to identify the industries and individuals directly and indirectly affected by a project. In the case of the London Olympics, for example, expenditure was made by the organizing committee on the Olympic facilities and the running of the Olympic and Paralympic Games, by the UK authorities on the transport infrastructure, and by individuals on transport, hotels, shops, restaurants, and entertainment during their stay in London.[16] This direct expenditure becomes income for the construction companies, tourism, hospitality, catering, transport, and other services, and is then spent indirectly on supplies, subcontractors, employees' wages, and numerous other inputs. Much of this spending will benefit the region concerned, but some of it will be spent on goods, services, and workers from outside the region. The impact on the region will be reduced by the 'leakages' of income, both to other regions and in terms of saving and taxes, for example. Figure 5.2 illustrates the main expenditure effects on the region around East London where the main Olympic stadium is located.

This process of output, income, and employment generation, including both initial direct effects and subsequent indirect effects, can be calculated using **regional multipliers**. Multipliers allow us to estimate the cumulative effects of expenditure over a period of time. Each time money is spent, it becomes income for other people, who in turn spend a proportion of their extra income. Even allowing for leakages in the form of saving, taxes, or expenditure outside the region concerned, the multiplier will normally have a value greater than one. When the original expenditure is multiplied by the value of the multiplier, it gives an indication of the total effect of the expenditure over a period of time. This process is similar to the Keynesian national income multiplier discussed in Section 4.4.3. An example of how the multiplier is calculated can also be found in Practical Insight 4.3. Regional impact analysis provides a useful picture of the impact of an investment on a region, especially in the case of an economically and socially disadvantaged region.

5.3 Causes and consequences of regional disparities

Regional disparities exist in most, if not all, countries. They also persist over long periods of time. Considerable efforts by governments and regional authorities are often insufficient to create balanced regional development. In part, this may be because the effort is

Table 5.1 UK regional disparities, 2010

Region	Gross Disposable Household Income per Head (Index, UK = 100)	Gross Value Added per Hour Worked, (Index, UK = 100)
London	128.8	133.3
South East	112.1	108.2
East of England	104.3	97.5
South West	99.6	92.0
Scotland	97.7	99.3
East Midlands	90.8	92.4
North West	90.2	87.7
West Midlands	89.3	86.0
Wales	87.7	83.9
Yorkshire & the Humber	86.5	88.5
Northern Ireland	86.3	81.0
North East	84.8	87.6
UK	100.0	100.0

Source: National Statistics website: www.statistics.gov.uk.

misplaced. Regional policy frequently tries to lure inward investors with the prospect of generous financial incentives without tackling the underlying reasons for a region's problems. It is also because some of the causes are intractable, perhaps because of a region's climate or remote location. However, there are also examples of regions, or depressed areas within regions, that have been regenerated and have taken on a new economic vitality. This is true of East London's docklands and similar inner city areas in Birmingham, Manchester, and Liverpool, for example. Table 5.1 illustrates two measures of regional disparity between UK regions. These measures indicate significant differences between prosperous regions like London and the South East and lagging regions such as the North East and Northern Ireland.

It is also possible that regional disparities are not as great as official statistics suggest. Whilst unemployment statistics or measures of social deprivation may suggest clear underlying economic and social disadvantages, indicators such as **gross value added** or household income and expenditure may overestimate the differences between regions. This is primarily because price levels vary between regions. Gross value added measures the difference between final output and intermediate inputs, that is, the additional contribution to output made by a particular firm, industry, or region. Output is valued at the prices charged in a particular region. If these prices are lower in some regions than in others, any given volume of output will have a lower value in a low-price region than in a high-price region. The low-price region therefore appears to be less productive than it actually is. A similar problem arises where household expenditure representing the same 'basket' of goods and services is lower in a low-price region and higher in a high-price region. Household incomes are also typically lower in low-price regions but less income is needed to buy the same goods and services, so the difference in the cost of living between regions may also be smaller than it appears to be. This problem can be resolved by valuing output, income, and expenditure on a 'purchasing power parity' (PPP) basis.

Purchasing power parity calculations are commonly used when comparing national income data, but rarely used with regional data. Statisticians would have to compare the cost of a basket of goods and services in Region X with the cost of the same basket of goods and services in Region Y. So, for example, if the goods and services cost €100 in Region X (the low-cost region) and €120 in region Y (the high-cost region), we can calculate a purchasing power parity regional 'exchange rate' of $€_x1 = €_y1.20$. We can then convert $€_x$ into a common $€_y$ currency by multiplying the value of output, income, and expenditure in Region X by a factor of 1.2, which will narrow the gap between the regions. These regional exchange rates are of course notional as regions do not normally have independent exchange rates. However, the important point is that differences in purchasing power may account for part of the disparity between regions.[17]

Gross value added per hour worked also depends on productivity. Productivity will inevitably vary with the balance of industries in different regions as it is sensitive to capital and labour intensiveness, levels of skill in the labour force, the use of technology, and other factors. Regions with low productivity will therefore have lower gross value added per hour worked than regions with high productivity. This does not mean that regional disparities caused by productivity differences are unimportant, simply that they may reflect structural differences between regions. Thus, for example, a predominantly rural region like West Wales, with its small-scale agriculture, tourism, and other service operations, will almost inevitably have lower productivity and therefore lower gross value added per hour worked than regions with high-tech manufacturing or service industries. In fact, the gross value added per capita index number for West Wales and the Valleys (a sub-region of Wales) for 2009 was only 62.8.[18] The entire industrial structure of West Wales would have to be changed in order to resolve this problem. Alternatively, the national or EU budget can be used to transfer income from richer regions to poorer regions.

Practical Insight 5.4 considers how differences between regions may also be exaggerated when comparing Western Europe with the emerging economies of Central and Eastern Europe. The reasons for the underlying differences between regions are now explored. Although a number of potential causes are identified in turn, regional disparities may

---

Practical insight 5.4:   Convergence between Europe's regions

If price differences between regions mean that some of the measures of regional differences exaggerate the disparity between regions, might this also be true of comparisons between Western Europe's high-income nations and Central and Eastern Europe's low-income nations? Although PPP data are available for these countries at the national level at a particular time, it is more difficult to estimate how prices and incomes will increase over a period of time. If prices and incomes in the CEE countries rise rapidly to the level of prices and incomes in Western Europe, estimates of the time it will take for their economies to catch up may be exaggerated if they are based solely on real economic growth rates that ignore the changes in PPP that will come from rapid price convergence.

Question

● Could it be that, for some of the CEE countries, economic convergence may come sooner than we expect?

reflect cumulative causation, where one factor is reinforced by another over a period of time.

5.3.1 Changing industrial structure

Perhaps the most important underlying reason for the regional disparities which exist in most countries is the changing industrial structure that is driven by new phases of economic development. In general terms this process can be described by what the Austrian economist, Joseph Schumpeter, called '**creative destruction**', where innovative companies prosper at the expense of lagging companies in a process of continual renewal and decline.[19] In this way, regions with a good record of innovation will progress as lagging regions decline. In the global economy industrial change can be even more fundamental as whole industries decline in Europe and North America and are reborn in Asia or Latin America. This has been the fate of the textile manufacturing and textile machinery industries and a long list of other manufacturing industries in recent years. Sometimes it happens on a continental rather than a global scale as, for example, with the European motor industry which has been gradually drifting from Western to Central and Eastern Europe since the 1990s. This process of de-industrialization in the former manufacturing heartlands and new industrial development in the re-emerging European countries or newly industrializing countries of Asia and Latin America represents industrial restructuring on an international scale. For the former core manufacturing regions of Europe and America, it represents industrial decline, unemployment, and social deprivation. Regions that are slow to adjust to the changing industrial structure experience persistent economic and social problems.

5.3.2 The core/periphery argument

It is sometimes argued that 'core' regions have a locational advantage over 'peripheral' regions. **Core regions** may be the centre of political power and the centre of a large market or industry, may have good transport and communication links, or may simply be established economic or cultural centres. Many countries have core regions located around their capital cities or major industrial and commercial centres. Historically, core regions were often located in the industrial heartlands as well as around the capital; this was the case in England's northern manufacturing regions in the nineteenth century, and is still largely the case in Italy's industrial north today. On the whole, however, commercial and financial centres have taken over from manufacturing as core regions in most of the developed economies. Generally, in industries where transport costs are high, economies of scale are limited, and most industries are well established, firms and industries are more likely to remain in their historic location than to move to the core. In industries where transport costs are low, economies of scale are important, and firms are 'footloose', the pull of core regions is more powerful. In many modern industries the economic pull of the core region is therefore significant and the authorities in **peripheral regions** have to be imaginative in their efforts to attract industry to or improve the performance of their regions.[20]

Core/periphery arguments have also been applied to countries, especially small countries with characteristics similar to sub-national regions. Thus, for example, Western

Europe's southern and western periphery has generally performed less well than its more central core states. However, the countries on the northern periphery seem to be an exception to the argument, and Ireland became Western Europe's star economic performer in the 1990s, so cores and peripheries appear to be less relevant at the country level. Core regions may also exist on the border between two or more countries, as in the case of the *maquiladora* **industries** along Mexico's border with the United States, where manufacturers take advantage of Mexico's low production costs and the lucrative US market within the free trade area of the North American Free Trade Agreement (NAFTA). In a different way, the geographical triangle linking Maastricht in the Netherlands with Liège in Belgium and Aachen in Germany (known as the Meuse-Rhine or Maas-Rhine Triangle – see Figure 5.1) provides a good example of a core cross-border region with strong business connections.

5.3.3   Economic, social, and political institutions

Thanks to the work of economists such as Douglass North, we now understand more clearly that, whatever its geographical location, the performance of a country's or region's economy is heavily influenced by its institutional structure.[21] The role of institutions is explained more fully in Sections 4.2 and 6.2. Economic institutions at the regional level include the transport and communication infrastructure, business and financial support networks, links with and dependence on other regions, and the quality and flexibility of a region's labour market. These institutions are both formal and informal. They are underpinned by social institutions such as the education system at the formal level and by attitudes to education, work, and business or career success at an informal level. Political institutions also play an important role at a regional level. The respective powers and accountability of national, regional, and local government affect the type of decisions that can be made at each level and the influence of a region's electorate on those decisions. Sometimes these powers are delegated to regional development agencies; this again alters the locus of decision making. Some writers have argued that the over-centralization of political power at the national level is damaging to regional prosperity and regional equality,[22] though too much decentralization may create institutional burdens on the local economy, especially where decision-making bodies have overlapping responsibilities.[23]

Clearly, a region with a poor transport infrastructure or poor links with other regions is likely to struggle either to develop its own indigenous businesses or to attract investors from outside the region. At the very least, the region will have to compensate for these disadvantages in some way. Typically, this is done with the help of financial incentives, but the benefit of these incentives may be short-lived. A more lasting solution is to improve the institutional environment. Informal institutions may also act as a constraint on regional development, especially where workers are reluctant to take entrepreneurial risks or develop their own education and skills. Even a poor regional image or perception, perhaps based on a region's industrial past, may inhibit business confidence and investor interest. The association of Germany's Ruhr region with heavy industry such as coal and steel, for example, has made it more difficult for the authorities to attract high-tech and service industries to the region. Examples from the Czech Republic and the UK are given in Practical Insight 5.5.

Practical insight **5.5**:   Image or reality?

In a recent conversation between the author and Jan Sucháček, a regional economist from the Technical University of Ostrava in the Czech Republic, close similarities were noted between the image problems of Ostrava and the author's university town of Middlesbrough. Both towns have a legacy of heavy industry, notably steel, and their reputation and physical environment bear the scars of their industrial past. These scars sometimes affect the confidence and aspirations of their inhabitants as well as the views of outsiders.

Question

● Is a region's image a real or imaginary problem? If it is real, how can it be changed?

5.3.4 **Inappropriate policies**

The most common solution to regional problems has been the provision of financial and other incentives to encourage business start-ups and attract inward investors. Often these incentives have been focused on investors in manufacturing industries in the belief that manufacturing is still the main basis of job creation in most countries. In the developed countries, however, many manufacturing industries are in long-term decline and are unlikely to continue to provide the large-scale employment they once did. A UK National Audit Office report in June 2003 found that 89 per cent of regional assistance had gone to manufacturing firms and that, despite a number of jobs being created in disadvantaged regions, regional assistance represented 'relatively poor value for money in generating productivity improvements'.[24] The policy emphasis on manufacturing possibly stems from the view that de-industrialization is a negative phenomenon to be resisted by governments, but evidence of the economic performance of advanced industrial economies suggests that it is more likely to be a natural consequence of industrial dynamism in a changing world.[25]

The problem is that, while incentives help to compensate for regional disparities in the short term, they fail to tackle the underlying regional problems. Improving the infrastructure may be a more expensive option and changing perceptions and attitudes a more intractable problem in the short term, but they may be necessary in order to correct regional disadvantages. If labour market and other institutional weaknesses are holding back regional development, ultimately the problem has to be addressed if a region is to prosper. The most appropriate policy approach is therefore to target the cause of the institutional problems rather than to compensate for them – unless the problems are genuinely insurmountable.

5.4 **Regional policy: alternative approaches**

The most common aim of regional policy is to promote balanced regional development within countries with significant regional disparities. Regional policy has also been used to promote industrial development more generally, especially in newly industrializing countries such as China and India. Various different approaches have been taken to regional policy. The approach taken depends on the aims of the policy and the prevailing wisdom at a particular time. Four of the more common approaches to regional policy are described below.

5.4.1 **The incentives approach**

Lagging regions are often characterized by higher than average levels of unemployment and by a lack of job creation by new or existing firms. Although unemployed workers have sometimes been exhorted to move to more prosperous regions to find work, in practice labour is much less mobile than capital. Greater emphasis is therefore placed on attracting inward investors into a lagging region. This is usually done by offering various kinds of financial incentive. Incentives may include the following: grants to cover part of the cost of an investment or to retrain unemployed workers; tax concessions such as capital allowances against corporate taxation or corporate tax holidays for a period of time; the provision of low-rent industrial units or support services.

This type of regional policy has been widely used in many countries and sometimes leads to incentive competition between neighbouring regions in an attempt to attract high-profile investors; this was the case in 2004 when the Slovakian government outbid the Polish government in its successful attempt to lure the South Korean car manufacturer, Kia Motors. Sometimes the financial assistance has been spread thinly across a number of regions with above-average unemployment, sometimes it is concentrated on the worst-affected areas. Sometimes it is allocated on the basis of strict criteria, sometimes it is discretionary. Since the 1980s it has been common for regional authorities and agencies to target foreign direct investors as FDI has been seen as a route to rapid economic development. This approach has increasingly been taken in China, with considerable success, as the Chinese authorities have gradually relaxed the ownership rules relating to foreign investment. The use of financial incentives to attract foreign investors in a region like the north-east of England has not always been quite as successful (see Practical Insight 5.6).

Practical insight 5.6:   FDI in north-east England

Regional development agencies in north-east England have been successful in attracting a number of high-profile foreign investors from the 1980s onwards. The investors have included Nissan (1986), Samsung (1995), Siemens (1995), and Wind Clipper (2010), but the story is one of mixed fortunes. Nissan's greenfield car plant near Sunderland was and remains one of the most successful foreign direct investments in the UK, making a significant contribution to employment, output, productivity, and exports at regional and national levels. Samsung made microwave ovens and computer monitors until world prices forced the company to transfer production to low-cost locations in CEE countries in 2004. Although Samsung stayed for nine years, far fewer jobs were created than was expected. Siemens' state-of-the-art semi-conductor plant in North Tyneside was the largest single greenfield investment by a foreign firm in UK history, but world market conditions forced it to close within three years. The US company, Wind Clipper, planned to manufacture giant offshore wind turbines in Newcastle upon Tyne, but shortage of funds during the economic downturn forced the company to abandon its ambitious plans. Each of these investors received large regional grants, some of which have now been repaid, but there is clearly a question mark over the benefits of financial incentives.[26]

Question

- Should financial incentives be used to tip the balance in favour of an investment if it is unclear whether the regional environment offers lasting benefits to the investor in a changing international environment?

Financial incentives have formed an important part of UK and EU regional policy, though both have moved towards greater emphasis on tackling a region's underlying problems. EU regional policy assistance is allocated through the structural funds. The structural funds include the following: the European Regional Development Fund (ERDF), the main fund for the disbursement of regional assistance; the European Social Fund (ESF), which supports employment and the operation of labour markets; the Cohesion Fund, which provides assistance for EU member countries where gross national income (GNI) per capita is less than 90 per cent of the EU average; the Instrument for Pre-Accession Assistance (IPA), which supports candidate and potential candidate countries preparing for EU member-ship; and the specialized funds for agriculture and fishing, the European Agricultural Fund for Rural Development (EAFRD) and the European Maritime and Fisheries Fund (EMFF). The Cohesion Fund is targeted at countries rather than sub-national regions and since its inception in 1993 the fund has supported Ireland (until 2003), Spain, Portugal, and Greece and, from 2004, it has been extended to the new member countries from Central and Eastern Europe and the Mediterranean.

5.4.2 Special zones and clusters

An alternative approach has been the policy of encouraging pockets of industrial development within concentrated areas. Examples of these areas include the UK and US enterprise zone policies initiated in the 1980s, China's, and more recently India's, policy of **special economic zones** established in 1980 and 2000 respectively, and the creation of science parks and other types of cluster in a number of countries. Enterprise zones offer an environment with minimal taxes and planning requirements and are designed to stimulate business activity without the normal fiscal and administrative burdens. They are mainly in the most disadvantaged regions, but, whilst often successful within the confines of the zones, their ability to spread the benefits to neighbouring areas has been limited. China's special economic zones, on the other hand, have been influential in promoting industrial development in the country's eastern and south-eastern regions, offering a variety of tax and customs incentives to local and foreign investors. India's special economic zones have been established more recently but they offer a similar range of incentives to encourage exporting and the location of offshore activities from the US and Europe. Clusters often occur naturally, but it has been common in recent years for governments to promote their development, especially in industries involving sci-entific and technological innovation.

5.4.3 Public sector growth and decentralization

The difficulty in encouraging private sector investment in lagging regions has led some governments to rely more on the public sector to promote regional development. Some-times this has involved the building of public amenities such as leisure centres, sports facili-ties, or art galleries, and a general increase in the level of employment in the public sector; this happened either by design or incrementally in Northern Ireland at the height of 'the troubles' in the 1970s and 1980s. Sometimes it involves decentralization of government functions and the relocation of government offices away from a country's capital city, as for instance when the Dutch government relocated some of its offices from The Hague and Amsterdam to Appeldoorn in the 1960s. These public sector activities create income and employment in their host regions, though they may 'crowd out' the private sector if they become too dominant in these regions. Apart from their economic impact, they are sometimes favoured by politicians as a way of bringing government closer to the people in regions that are remote from the centre of political power. Public-private partnerships, often involving predominantly private capital, have recently become a more politically acceptable method of using the public sector to promote new developments without the need for large amounts of public spending.

5.4.4 Creating the conditions for endogenous growth

More recently, the focus of regional policy has been turning towards the creation of conditions that are conducive to economic growth. Since the 1980s economists have been replacing their conventional ideas about economic growth with what has become known as the theory of **endogenous growth** or new growth theory (see Section 10.3.2).[27] Essentially, the theory argues that many of the conditions necessary for economic growth depend on 'endogenous' factors within a country or region. These factors are considered to be internal to a country's or region's economy rather than external ('exogenous'). In particular, endogenous growth appears to depend on the factors that increase productivity, especially the application of technology and improvements in labour skills. However, endogenous growth theorists focus on a variety of different factors, some emphasizing the competitiveness of free markets, others the importance of education or infrastructure. Any or all of these factors may contribute towards a region's competitive environment and the productivity of its industries.

This change of policy emphasis can be seen in both the UK and the EU. The 1997–2010 UK Labour government's refocusing of regional policy was set out in three government reports between 2001 and 2003.[28] In broad terms, the government promoted a change of emphasis away from reliance on inward investment towards the encouragement of indigenous development and the creation of 'enterprise areas' (designed to remove obstacles to new business development) and 'city regions' (combinations of small to medium-sized towns to form a critical mass). Regional development was seen as depending on five main drivers: skills, investment, innovation, enterprise, and competition. The policy was overseen by regional development agencies and particular emphasis was placed on addressing the problems of poor productivity and market failure in poorly performing regions.[29] Subsequent evidence suggests the policy was relatively ineffective in reducing disparities in regional gross value added per capita, but had a positive effect on urban regeneration and in reducing employment disparities – though largely by increasing employment in the public sector.[30]

In 2010, the Conservative/Liberal Democrat coalition government (2010–15) began the process of replacing the regional development agencies with a network of local enterprise partnerships (LEPs), bringing together businesses and local government, allowed the LEPs to create new enterprise zones, offering tax relief and simplified planning procedures, and introduced a regional growth fund, designed to support projects which generate economic growth and employment through private sector investment.[31] The new policy maintains the emphasis on economic growth and employment, but replaces what the government sees as a top-down region-wide approach with local initiatives and private sector investment. However, potentially positive effects on employment have, to some extent, been negated in the lagging regions by public sector job losses resulting from reductions in local government funding in the aftermath of the 2008–9 recession.

The EU also began to focus on endogenous growth in its revised cohesion policy for the period 2007–13.[32] The policy still coordinated significant financial resources, amounting to approximately one-third of the EU budget, but more emphasis was placed on improving the attractiveness of regions and encouraging innovation, entrepreneurship, and job creation. Particular attention was focused on the development of a knowledge-based economy and on the creation of a competitive environment. The revised cohesion policy was linked more closely to the EU's Lisbon Strategy, an ambitious attempt to create a competitive knowledge-based economy – later replaced by 'Europe 2020', an initiative aimed at improving employment, education, innovation, social inclusion, and sustainable development.[33]

The 2007–13 EU cohesion policy identified four types of region: Convergence Regions, which had a gross domestic product (GDP) less than 75 per cent of the EU-25 average (post 2004); Phasing-out Regions, which used to have a GDP less than 75 per cent of the EU-15 average and received Objective 1 assistance (the highest level of assistance); Phasing-in Regions, which now had a GDP less than the EU-15 average and also received Objective 1 assistance; and Regional Competitiveness and Employment Regions, a term that included all other regions of the EU.

The European Commission has now put forward revised proposals for the period 2014–20, which re-designate assisted regions as Less Developed Regions (with GDP per capita less than 75 per cent of the EU-27 average), Transition Regions, which replace the Phasing-in and Phasing-out Regions (GDP per capita between 75 and 90 per cent of the EU-27 average), and More Developed Regions (GDP per capita over 90 per cent of the EU-27 average). An illustrated map of these regions is shown in Figure 5.3. These proposals also attempt to simplify cohesion policy rules, to adopt a more coordinated EU-wide approach, and to bring cohesion policy more closely into line with the Europe 2020 strategy.[34] Despite the complexity of the EU cohesion policy framework, the intention is to promote improvements in the productive and innovative capacity of member economies and the balanced development of the EU as a whole.

5.5 Sub-national regions and globalization

Thus far we have mainly considered regions within their national context. However, in an increasingly open and interdependent global economy, even sub-national regions are increasingly being exposed to the forces of globalization. If there are few trade and FDI restrictions within a country, importers and inward investors can enter any of the country's sub-regions almost as though they were independent economies. Where regional authorities vie with each other to attract foreign investors, regions also enjoy a degree of political independence. This means that a region's firms are just as exposed to global markets, global capital

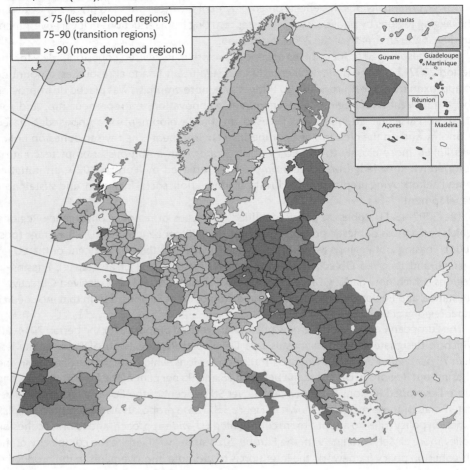

Eligibility simulation 2014–2020
GDP/head (PPS), index EU27=100

■ < 75 (less developed regions)
■ 75–90 (transition regions)
□ >= 90 (more developed regions)

Figure 5.3   EU cohesion policy eligibility regions, 2014–2020
Source: © European Union, 1995–2012.

movements, global labour migration, and global production decisions as national econo-mies. Multinational companies treat these regions almost as though they were countries. In effect, sub-national regions are part of a new international space, where many of the political, economic, and communication barriers have been removed. Like countries, they are partici-pants in the new international division of labour that results from the changing international structure of industries.

There are two main opposing views of the position of regions within the global econ-omy. First, the view that regions are being overwhelmed by globalization and, secondly, that a new 'regionalism' is giving them increasing autonomy. The first view sees regions, like small countries, as pawns in a global game of chess, unable to influence the activities of multinational companies. The second view is that regional governments may be in a better position to influence their own affairs now that they have effectively bypassed their national authorities. Both these views have been challenged by the influential work of Amin and Thrift,[35] who argue that regional economic prosperity depends on a region's ability to mobilize flexible institutional strategies. In effect, a region needs to create an environment that allows businesses to take advantage of globalization. In order to achieve this, a region may of course need some help from national government and supranational organizations like the EU.

Summary

The regional location of industry depends on a number of different factors. These factors include natural resource explanations, accidents of history, transport and communication costs, access to markets, labour market characteristics, and theories of the determinants of spatial concentration. Major investments, such as those associated with the Olympic Games, can have a significant impact on a region and regional impact analysis can be used to estimate the possible effects on income, employment, health, and the environment, among other things. The causes of regional disparities are often difficult to eradicate. Possible causes include the changing industrial structure of regions, the forces that attract industries towards core and away from peripheral regions, institutional problems within regions, and the use of inappropriate policies. The most common types of regional policy involve the use of financial incentives, the establishment of special zones or clusters, the use of public sector initiatives, and the creation of conditions that are conducive to endogenous growth. It should also be remembered that sub-national regions increasingly function as part of an international space within the global economy. This increases the need for regions to create a competitive environment for business.

Discussion questions

1. Why has access to markets become more important and access to resources less important as a location factor for modern industries?
2. What is the relative importance of internal and external economies of scale for firms within clusters?
3. The 2012 London Olympic Games was based in the Lower Lea Valley in East London. What lasting benefits from the Olympics are likely to come to this region and to what extent are the benefits likely to be dispersed to other UK regions?
4. What are the main reasons why some sub-national regions lag behind others?
5. Do you regard the recent emphasis on endogenous growth to be preferable to the more conventional incentives approach to regional policy?
6. What are the implications for regional policy of the increasing openness of sub-national regions in the global economy?

Suggested assignment topics

1. Choose an example of foreign direct investment in a particular sub-national region. Investigate the factors that are likely to have influenced the company's investment decision.

2. Choose an example of a major project involving the building of new facilities at a particular location. Estimate the economic, social, and environmental impact of the project on the region concerned.

3. Choose a lagging sub-national region and investigate the reasons for the relatively poor performance of this region.

 Case study: A regional perspective on Eastern Slovakia

Slovakia is one of Central Europe's re-emerging market economies that joined the EU in May 2004. Although slower to engage with market reforms than some of its neighbours after its separation from the Czech Republic in January 1993, Slovakia made substantial economic progress under the government of Mikuláš Dzurinda (1998–2006). Like other countries undergoing major change, Slovakia is experiencing significant regional disparities. These are illustrated in Table 5.2. There is a clear contrast in terms of GDP per capita between the capital, Bratislava, and the rest of the country. Bratislava is enjoying a political, economic, and cultural renaissance now that it has become a national capital after years in the shadow of Prague. It has become a magnet for FDI, especially in the financial services sector. There is also a marked difference between three of the most westerly regions (Bratislava, Trnava, and Trenčín) and the rest of the country in terms of unemployment.

   Eastern Slovakia is generally the least prosperous region, though the central region is not far ahead. The eastern region is the most remote not only from Bratislava but also from Western Europe. It contains Slovakia's second city, Košice, but is also close to Ukraine and Romania, where economic development has generally been slower. Eastern Slovakia includes a number of the country's poorer rural communities and has also been home to some of its older heavy industries, notably steel. The East Slovak Iron and Steel Works in Košice, acquired by US Steel in 2000, accounted for around 10 per cent of Slovak GDP in 1993 and is still the country's largest private sector employer.[36] This industrial and rural legacy has left its mark on the region.

Table 5.2: Regional unemployment and GDP per capita in the Slovak Republic

Area (NUTS 2)[a]	Region (NUTS 3)[a]	GDP p.c. (€, 2009)	Unemployment Rate (%, 2011)
Bratislava	Bratislava	28,443	5.5
West Slovakia	Trnava	12,928	8.6
	Trenčín	10,265	7.0
	Nitra	9,928	11.9
Central Slovakia	Žilina	10,038	13.2
	Banská Bystrica	8,425	15.8
East Slovakia	Prešov	6,654	18.5
	Košice	9,022	19.5

[a] EU regions are classified according to the Nomenclature of Territorial Units for Statistics (NUTS).
Source: Statistical Office of the Slovak Republic.

Eastern Slovakia is a peripheral region, both within Slovakia and in the EU as a whole. Whilst there are historic trade links with neighbouring regions in Poland, Hungary, Ukraine, and Romania (the Carpathian region), the locus of political and economic activity in the EU is much further west. The transport infrastructure in Slovakia also leaves the eastern region somewhat isolated, with an incomplete motorway network, few direct international flights, and slow (though extensive) rail connections. Despite these disadvantages, Eastern Slovakia has a well-educated, low-cost labour force and has been attracting an increasing number of foreign investors such as US Steel, Volkswagen, Siemens, Coca-Cola, and Tesco. The region also has a number of industrial parks designed to promote business activity. An interesting example is the Kechnec industrial park, located in the small town of Kechnec between Košice and the Hungarian border, which has been successful in attracting foreign investors such as Getrag-Ford, a German-US joint venture manufacturing gearboxes and Crown Bevcan, a subsidiary of the US company, Crown Holdings, which manufactures beverage cans for brewers and soft drinks companies.

Slovakia as a whole went to considerable lengths to create an attractive environment for foreign investors after the change of government in 1998. In particular, the political climate became more investor friendly and a unified flat tax rate of 19 per cent for income, corporate, and valued added taxes was introduced, providing businesses with one of the lowest corporate tax rates in Europe.[37] Membership of the EU has also opened markets for Slovakian exporters and created a low-cost export base for foreign investors. The influx of motor industry investors provides ample evidence of these benefits, though the major motor manufacturers have so far invested in the more accessible regions in the west and north.

A variety of businesses are also being developed by local entrepreneurs, but smaller firms are often beset with problems and uncertainties that their larger counterparts can more easily offset. Table 5.3 summarizes

Table 5.3: Perceived barriers to business development in Slovakia

Main Barriers[a]	Slovakia	Eastern Slovakia		
		Košice	Prešov	
Impact of district location on doing business	3.25[b]	2.49	2.00	(5)[c]
Perception of unemployment	3.02	2.36	2.06	(4)
Development potential of the district	3.05	2.51	2.20	(7)
Migration of skilled labour	2.76	2.28	1.88	(3)
Level of education	3.65	3.22	2.81	(11)
Level of competitiveness in industry	3.54	3.08	2.94	(10)
Level of competitiveness in services	3.64	3.24	3.20	(12)
Quality of road infrastructure	2.32	2.07	1.93	(1)
Interest of state institutions in the district	2.33	2.10	1.93	(2)
Bureaucracy and administrative delays	2.56	2.52	2.60	(8)
Law enforcement in the district court	2.23	2.31	2.34	(6)
Impact of corruption on authorities' decisions	2.84	2.84	3.05	(9)

[a] Barriers are ranked by the size of the divergence (from largest to smallest) between the average scores for Eastern Slovakia and the score for Slovakia as a whole.

[b] Numerical scores indicate the level of barrier on a scale of 1–6, where 1 is the worst score and 6 the best.

[c] Numbers in brackets rank each type of barrier from 1 to 12, based on the average score for Eastern Slovakia, where 1 is the lowest score and 12 the highest.

Source: Business Alliance of Slovakia (2011), *Competitive Regions 21: Yearbook 2010*, pp. 119, 378, 382, 384, 400, 401, 402, 403, 406, 415, 419, and 423.

(continued...)

the main barriers to business development reported by entrepreneurs in the two main administrative regions of Eastern Slovakia in a survey conducted on behalf of the Business Alliance of Slovakia.[38] The results indicate that the highest perceived barriers facing entrepreneurs (i.e. the lowest scores) are the quality of the road infrastructure, the lack of interest of state institutions at the district level, and the loss of skilled labour from these regions. The difficulties appear to be particularly acute in the Prešov region.

However, the scores for barriers listed towards the bottom of the table suggest that some of the problems exist at the national as well as the regional level. On the other hand, the greatest disparities between Eastern Slovakia and the country as a whole apply to barriers at the top end of table, including the impact of location, the perception (and reality) of high unemployment, and the negative view of the development potential of Eastern Slovakia. Whilst these barriers are not untypical of the problems faced by businesses in lagging regions, especially in a transitional economy, regional inequality of GDP per capita in Slovakia was among the highest in the OECD in 2011.[39]

Case study questions

1. What sort of political and economic conditions are likely to attract foreign direct investors to a country like Slovakia?

2. Why are countries undergoing major change likely to experience 'significant regional disparities'?

3. Why do you think the unemployment rate in Slovakia has been generally high since the end of the communist years?

4. How significant do you think Eastern Slovakia's industrial heritage is as a reason for its relatively poor economic performance?

5. How important do you think core/periphery arguments are in the case of Eastern Slovakia?

6. To what extent might local clusters of foreign direct investors contribute towards agglomeration economies in places like Kechnec?

7. Taking the first three barriers listed in Table 5.3, explain why each of them might be a problem for businesses in Eastern Slovakia?

8. Given that the barriers listed towards the bottom end of Table 5.3 are common to the country as a whole, to what extent, if any, are they relevant as factors affecting regional disparities in Slovakia?

Notes

1.   IMF, *World Economic Outlook Database*, October 2012.

2.   Main sources: Gamer, R. E. (2012), *Understanding Contemporary China*, Lynne Rienner; Naughton, B. (2007), *The Chinese Economy: Transitions and Growth*, The MIT Press; and CIA, *World Factbook*, 2012.

3.   A discussion of the natural resource paradox can be found in Sachs, J. D., and Warner, A. M. (2001), 'The curse of natural resources', *European Economic Review*, vol. 45 (4–6), pp. 827–38.

4.   Krugman, P. R. (1991), *Geography and Trade*, MIT Press, p. 9; most of these companies are now owned by Conn-Selmer, a subsidiary of Steinway Musical Instruments.

5.   Sources: Coca-Cola company website (http://www.coca-cola.com/index.jsp) and Fortune Global 500, 2012 (http://money.cnn.com/magazines/fortune/global500/2012).

6.   See, for example, Grönroos, C. (1994), 'From marketing mix to relationship marketing: Towards a paradigm shift in marketing', *Management Decision*, vol. 32, no. 2, pp. 4–20.

7.   The top ten digital camera manufacturers in 2010 were: Canon, Sony, Nikon, Samsung, Panasonic, Kodak, Olympus, Fuji, Casio, and Pentax (though Kodak decided to end its camera production after going into

'Chapter 11' bankruptcy proceedings in the USA in 2012); data source: IDC Japan via Bloomberg Japan (http://www.bloomberg.com/).

8. Source: Digitimes, 19 July 2010 (http://www.digitimes.com/).

9. Christaller, W. (1933), 'Die zentralen Orte in Süddeutschland', Gustav Fischer, translated by Baskin, C. W. (1966), *Central Places in Southern Germany*, Prentice Hall.

10. See, for example, Meijers, E. (2005), 'Polycentric urban regions and the quest for synergy: Is a network of cities more than the sum of the parts?', *Urban Studies*, vol. 42, no. 4, pp. 765–81.

11. See, for example, Porter, M. E. (2003), 'The economic performance of regions', *Regional Studies*, vol. 37, no. 6-7, pp. 549–78 and Fujita, M., Krugman, P. R., and Venables, A. J. (1999), *The Spatial Economy: City, Regions and International Trade*, MIT Press.

12. Marshall, A. (2009), *Principles of Economics*, Cosimo (first published in 1890).

13. See, for example, Hendry, C. and Brown, J. (2006), 'Dynamics of clustering and performance in the UK opto-electronics industry', *Regional Studies*, vol. 40, no. 7, pp. 707–25.

14. See The Silicon Fen Story, http://www.siliconfen.com.

15. PricewaterhouseCoopers (2005), *Olympic Games Impact Study: Final Report*, HM Government Department for Culture, Media and Sport, December.

16. See Blake, A. (2005), 'The economic impact of the London 2012 Olympics', http://www.academia.edu/375562/Economic_Impact_of_the_London_2012_Olympics. This analysis formed an important part of the PricewaterhouseCoopers study.

17. A discussion of purchasing power parity in relation to regions can be found in Gough, J. (2003), 'Measuring relative prosperity in the North East', *Northern Economic Review*, issue 33/34, pp. 32–44.

18. Office for National Statistics, Regional, Sub-Regional and Local Gross Value Added 2010 (http://www.ons.gov.uk/); gross value added per capita is not strictly a measure of productivity as it includes the economically inactive population, but it nevertheless provides a useful comparison between regions.

19. Schumpeter, J. A. (2010), *Capitalism, Socialism and Democracy*, Routledge (first published in 1942).

20. For a discussion of core/periphery issues, see Krugman, P. R. (1991), *Geography and Trade*, MIT Press, especially pp. 83–100.

21. North, D. C. (2010), *Understanding the Process of Economic Change*, Princeton University Press.

22. Massey, D., Amin, A., and Thrift, N. (1995), *Decentering the Nation: A Radical Approach to Regional Inequality*, Oxford University Press.

23. Rodriguez-Pose, A. and Gill, N. (2005), 'On the economic dividend of devolution', *Regional Studies*, vol. 39, no. 4, pp. 405–20.

24. UK National Audit Office (2003), 'Regional Grants in England', 17 June.

25. Rowthorn, R. and Ramaswamy, R. (1997), 'Deindustrialization: Causes and Implications', IMF Working Paper, WP/97/42.

26. For a fuller discussion of these issues, see Tomaney, J. (2006), 'North East England: a brief economic history', a paper delivered at the NERIP conference, Newcastle upon Tyne, 6 September.

27. For a fuller discussion of endogenous growth theory, see for example Romer, P. M. (1994), 'The Origins of Endogenous Growth', *The Journal of Economic Perspectives*, vol. 8, no. 1, pp. 3–22.

28. HM Treasury (2001), 'Productivity in the UK, No. 3: The Regional Dimension', November; HM Treasury (2003), 'A Modern Regional Policy for the UK', March; HM Treasury (2003), 'Productivity in the UK, No. 4: The Local Dimension', July.

29. For a fuller discussion of the change in UK regional policy, see Fothergill, S. (2004), 'A new regional policy for Britain', *Regional Studies*, vol. 39, no. 5, pp. 659–67.

30. See Crowley, L., Balaram, B., and Lee, N. (2012), 'People or Place: Urban Policy in the Age of Austerity', The Work Foundation.

31. UK Government White Paper, 'Local growth: realising every place's potential', 28 October 2010.

32. European Commission (2005), 'Cohesion Policy in Support of Growth and Jobs – Community Strategic Guidelines, 2007–2013', COM (2005) 299 final.

33. European Commission (2010), 'Europe 2020: A Strategy for Smart, Sustainable and Inclusive Growth', COM (2010) 2020 final.

34. European Commission (2011), 'Cohesion Policy 2014–2020: Investing in Growth and Jobs', http://ec.europa.eu/inforegio.

35. Amin, A., and Thrift, N. (1995), *Globalisation, Institutions and Regional Development in Europe*, Oxford University Press.

36. In early 2013 US Steel was considering options for the sale of its Košice plant, but agreed to remain for the time being in return for government concessions on energy and the environment.

37. Slovakia's 19% flat tax rate was abandoned in 2013 and taxes were increased as part of a package of budget deficit reduction measures introduced by Prime Minister Robert Fico (following his re-appointment for a second term in March 2012).

38. Business Alliance of Slovakia (2011), Competitive Regions 21: Yearbook 2010.

39. Main sources: OECD Economic Surveys: Slovak Republic 2012; Kirschbaum, S. J. (2005), *A History of Slovakia: The Struggle for Survival*, Palgrave Macmillan, ch. 13, pp. 273–310; Statistical Office of the Slovak Republic; and Business Alliance of Slovakia (2011), *Competitive Regions 21: Yearbook 2010*.

Suggestions for further reading

Specialist studies of regional and urban economics and policy

Armstrong, H. and Taylor, J. (2000), *Regional Economics and Policy*, Wiley Blackwell

McCann, P. (2013), *Modern Urban and Regional Economics*, Oxford University Press

Pike, A., Rodriguez-Pose, A., and Tomaney, J. (2006), *Local and Regional Development*, Routledge

Regional issues in the context of economic geography

Fujita, M., Krugman, P., and Venables, A. J. (2001), *The Spatial Economy: Cities, Regions and International Trade*, MIT Press

Knox, P., Agnew, J., and McCarthy, L. (2014), *The Geography of the World Economy*, Routledge

Regional policy in the EU

El Agraa, A. M. (2011), *The European Union: Economics and Policies*, Cambridge University Press, ch. 22, pp. 348–63

 Take your learning further: Online Resource Centre
http://www.oxfordtextbooks.co.uk/orc/harrison2e/
Visit the Online Resource Centre that accompanies this book to enrich your understanding of Chapter 5: The Regional Business Environment. Among other resources explore web links and keep up to date with the latest developments in the area.

Key terms introduced in this chapter

Agglomeration economies The economic advantages arising from internal and external economies of scale, knowledge spillovers, specialized skills, and forward and backward linkages within a cluster of firms.

Branch-plant economy A dependent region or country where most of the larger businesses are branches of companies whose head offices are elsewhere.

Central place theory The idea that business and residential development and smaller towns tend to be located around a main central town.

Cluster A group of related business activities located close together (also known as spatial concentration).

Core region A region which is at the centre of political and economic activity.

Creative destruction The process by which existing businesses are continually replaced by new businesses in a dynamic economy over a period of time.

Dutch disease A lack of export competitiveness because of an overvalued exchange rate caused by the discovery of a natural resource.

Endogenous growth Economic growth which arises from a combination of internal factors within a national or regional economy, including competition, the quality of technology and human capital, and the institutional environment.

Gross value added A measure of the difference between final output and intermediate inputs, that is, the additional contribution to output made by a particular firm, industry, or region.

Growth pole The central location around which economic development takes place.

Keiretsu Groups or networks of companies, often headed by a bank, to which many of Japan's larger companies belong.

Maquiladora industry A cluster of assembly plants which are located along the Mexican side of the border with the United States, taking advantage of low labour costs and the lucrative US market within the North American Free Trade Agreement (NAFTA).

Natural resource paradox The phenomenon whereby resource-rich countries remain underdeveloped, either because of the lack of incentive to diversify or because of the Dutch disease.

Peripheral region A region which is geographically distant from a core region.

Polycentric region A region with more than one main town or growth pole, often connecting smaller neighbouring regions.

Regional multiplier A method used to estimate the overall impact of regional expenditure over a period of time.

Spatial concentration A group or cluster of related business activities located close together.

Special economic zone A government-designated area in a country like China or India offering a variety of tax and customs incentives to local and foreign investors.

Part Two

Key Dimensions of the Business Environment

6

Contrasting Cultures and Business Models

○ **Chapter learning outcomes**

On completion of this chapter the reader should be able to:

- Understand the meaning and significance of culture
- Appreciate how culture influences a country's institutions
- Evaluate the essential elements of culture
- Apply methods of cultural assessment to the analysis of different cultures
- Engage in informed discussion of cultural controversies
- Undertake a comparative analysis of alternative socio-economic models

Opening scenario: France's management elite

In November 2011, Alexandre de Juniac became chief executive officer (CEO) of Air France. The new CEO was previously chief of staff for Christine Lagarde when she was the French finance minister and is a graduate of the *École Polytechnique*, one of France's élite *Grandes Écoles* which provide a rigorous education for many of the country's top public administrators and business managers. Whilst such a move might seem unusual among senior managers in many European and North American companies, France has long cherished its *Grandes Écoles* as the most appropriate training ground for its political, administrative, and business leaders.

In major French companies, it is not unusual for professional business managers to be brought in from outside the company rather than promoted internally, but their education at one of the highly selective *Grandes Écoles* is likely to have been extremely rigorous and intellectually demanding. A seminal 1991 article in the *Harvard Business Review* described how management in France is considered a 'state of mind' rather than a 'set of techniques' and how elite management education attempts to create 'a distinctive shared identity, a sense of belonging to the French managerial class'.[1] Even at many of France's less prestigious business schools, the curriculum is likely to have a stronger emphasis on the theory, history, and philosophy of management than is normally found at American and British business schools, where the focus is generally on more applied aspects of management.

There are, of course, exceptions to the traditional route into French senior management positions, as companies increasingly respond to global pressures to open up their recruitment practices and promote talented people with less regard to their background. Danone, for example, has taken steps to base its promotion policy on competence alone and the 2006 merger between French and US telecommunications equipment manufacturers, Alcatel and Lucent, resulted in a less hierarchical organizational structure than is common among French companies. Despite these exceptions, many French companies maintain hierarchical structures, where managers are remote from their employees, and even small family businesses often restrict promotion opportunities to family members.

(continued...)

Clearly, it is possible to identify both strengths and weaknesses of the French system of education for its élite political, administrative, and business leaders. However, at the heart of the French system are the unique cultural characteristics of the French way of life. The French top-down, hierarchical approach to its education system and business organization, and especially the education of its future business leaders, can at least partially be explained by cultural characteristics such as a respect for authority (power distance) and a desire to reduce uncertainty (uncertainty avoidance), though other cultural complexities may also need to be taken into account. In this chapter, we explore the nature of cultural differences in the national and international business environment in the hope of shedding light on the dichotomy between the converging forces of globalization and the persistence of cultural diversity.[2]

6.1 The meaning and significance of culture

A government department of 'culture' or a tourist brochure referring to 'cultural attractions' is likely to be concerned with art, music, theatre, or architecture. The classical arts, such as the music of Bach or the plays of Shakespeare, are sometimes known as 'high culture'; a Caribbean street carnival or the work of a graffiti artist may be described as 'popular culture'. This use of the term 'culture' is much narrower than the way it is used in this chapter, though the arts could be seen as a subset of culture and influenced by culture in its wider sense; aesthetics and creativity are in fact expressions of the culture of a particular group or society. **Culture** may be seen as an all-encompassing term, describing the complex set of values, beliefs, ideas, and social interactions which distinguish one society or group of people from another. In this sense, culture relates to an identifiable group of people rather than an individual, something that people share in common, though the behaviour of any individual is shaped by his or her own genetic make-up and personality as well as by culture.

An identifiable cultural group may be synonymous with a nation, but it may also exist at local, regional, or even transnational levels. Classifications of culture often focus on the nation state as the main cultural entity; thus, for example, it is common to speak of British, Italian, or Japanese culture. However, national culture is a convenient generalization of the more common cultural characteristics and does not necessarily reflect the variety of cultural groups in a particular country. Identifiable groups at the sub-national level might include Belgium's Flemish- and French-speaking regions (the Flemings and the Walloons) or Malaysia's Malay, Chinese, Indian, and other minority communities. Such groups may be labelled sub-cultures, though this term is more commonly used to describe groups whose beliefs are at variance with the predominant culture. Cultural groups may also transcend national boundaries, as for example Muslims, Jews, or Asians, though the latter term is rather imprecise as a designation of culture. At the transnational level, cultural groups are sometimes described as '**civilizations**', a term that is explored more fully in Section 6.3.3.

Geert Hofstede, a leading authority on the analysis of business culture, provides an alternative but complementary perspective on culture by describing it as 'the collective programming of the mind that distinguishes the members of one group or category of people from another'.[3] Collective mental programming describes the process by which people absorb their culture through family and wider social relationships, education, and various forms of social interaction. For this reason, it is generally believed that culture is 'learned' rather than 'inherited' – that we are born 'culture-free'. In more everyday terms, culture has also been described as 'a set of values as well as a set of practices: the food we eat, the clothes we wear, the kind of leisure we pursue, the rituals we abide by, the traditions we embrace or invent, and the ideas we follow'.[4]

At one extreme, culture involves apparently trivial customs and practices such as the way we greet people or the clothes we wear. At the other extreme, it represents deeply held beliefs and values. However, even a handshake or a deferential posture may reflect more fundamental values (see Practical Insight 6.1). For this reason it is sometimes useful to think of different layers of culture. A simple but effective way of visualizing the layers of culture is to use the so-called '**iceberg model**' of culture, with fundamental values and beliefs existing invisibly beneath the surface and behaviour, customs, and practices visible above the surface.[5] Like an iceberg, the cultural foundations below the surface are likely to be considerably greater and more immovable than the practical manifestations of culture that are more visible above the surface.

Practical insight 6.1: Deference to a Japanese emperor

During a visit to Japan in November 2009, US President Barack Obama bowed at an angle of almost 90 degrees to greet Emperor Akihito. In Japan, the angle of a bow represents the amount of respect shown to a person, so the US president clearly intended to show considerable respect to the Japanese emperor. In fact, earlier the same year, the president had shown similar respect to King Abdullah of Saudi Arabia during a G20 summit. On both occasions, President Obama was subjected to strong criticism in the US media by those who considered it inappropriate for the elected president of the world's main superpower to show deference to the hereditary leader of a lesser power. For some commentators the symbolism of the gesture was too much to bear, but the president remained unrepentant.

Question

● Do you consider President Obama's bow to be an appropriate cultural gesture or 'a shocking display of fealty to a foreign potentate'?[6]

An alternative, more sophisticated, way to visualize the layers of culture is to use Hofstede's idea of a '**culture onion**'.[7] As each layer of the onion is peeled away, deeper levels of culture are revealed. As in the iceberg model, the deeper layers are hidden. According to Hofstede, values represent the core of the onion and these values influence the layers above. Hofstede describes the outer layers as rituals, heroes, and symbols. Rituals include ceremonies and ways of greeting people and paying respect; heroes are real or imaginary people admired as role models; symbols are the most superficial and include words, artefacts, colours, and images. The three outer layers of culture are collectively described as practices, which are visible to the outside observer, but whose meaning is only fully understood by those within a particular culture.

Other researchers have also developed the idea of layers of culture. Trompenaars and Hampden-Turner split Hofstede's core layer into 'basic assumptions' and 'norms and values', basic assumptions being the underlying unchallenged basis of culture.[8] Spencer-Oatey combines basic assumptions and values as the core layer but adds 'beliefs, attitudes and conventions' and 'systems and institutions' as the next layers; the outer layer is then split between 'artefacts and products' and 'rituals and behaviours', representing tangible and behavioural expressions of culture respectively.[9] Spencer-Oatey's model is clearly built on the work of Hofstede and Trompenaars and Hampden-Turner but, by combining basic assumptions and values whilst separating them from beliefs and attitudes, it is possible to envisage a change in beliefs without requiring a change in underlying values. Spencer-Oatey also places the institutional framework of society more firmly within its cultural context and separates behavioural and non-behavioural expressions of culture.[10]

6.2 Culture and institutions

Political, economic, social, and legal institutions play an important role in any society. They are the rules by which a society or community operates. At the formal level they include political systems and laws, at the informal level customs, practices, and behavioural norms.[11] To a large extent, informal institutions are determined by culture and, as suggested above, are often grounded in more deep-rooted values and beliefs. Although customs and practices may seem fairly superficial, the core values on which they are based are often immutable. This means that informal institutions may persist despite considerable efforts to change them. Formal institutions are also likely to be culture related as governments and parliaments will create institutions that reflect their underlying values and beliefs, as for example in the French system of elite education for its political and business leaders described in the opening scenario to this chapter (see also Practical Insight 6.2). New laws are frequently created but they are influenced both by beliefs and attitudes which change gradually and by basic assumptions and values which are more resistant to change.

The relationship between culture and institutions is a complex one and powerful forces may have a significant impact on both. Perhaps the most persistent influences on a country's

Practical insight 6.2:   The EU takeover bids directive

The European Union Directive on Takeover Bids was finally adopted in April 2004 after 15 years of intermittent negotiations. This piece of legislation proved particularly controversial as many of the EU member states have different takeover rules and the final document is a watered-down version of the original European Commission proposal. Company takeovers may seem a curious issue to cause so much political consternation. However, takeover rules relate closely to corporate governance, which in turn reflects the way a country's economy operates. Industrial consensus among company stakeholders is an essential element of Germany's **social market economy**, whereas the UK's Anglo-Saxon economy requires the maximization of shareholder value (see Section 6.6 below).

The stakeholder and shareholder concepts (discussed further in Section 7.3.3) lead to very different conclusions on how a company should be allowed to defend itself against hostile takeovers and the extent to which an active takeover market is needed to promote effective corporate governance. In fact, a European Commission report on the operation of the Takeover Bids Directive found that, although the directive had been effective in clarifying the rights of stakeholders, it had been less successful in discouraging the use of defensive measures against takeover bids.[12]

Question

● To what extent do you think these different institutional arrangements are based on cultural differences?

culture and institutions are its history and geography. In this context, the countries of Central and Eastern Europe (CEE) provide a useful example. Political control in these countries has changed hands many times over the centuries. For example, the people of the present-day Czech Republic and Slovakia were citizens of Austria-Hungary during the years prior to the end of World War I. Czechoslovakia then became an independent state from 1918 until 1992, except during World War II when the Czech lands were overrun by Hitler's Germany and Slovakia was granted nominal independence. In 1993, the Czech and Slovak Republics became fully independent sovereign nations for the first time in their history. Each of these political changes brought about boundary changes, so the political geography of the region has been as volatile as its history. As a result, people of different cultural origins have found themselves in countries where they are a minority culture, often retaining their own language or religion as well as absorbing elements of the majority culture. Examples include the German-speaking regions of the Czech Republic (especially the former Sudetenland) or the Hungarian-speaking region of southern Slovakia. The physical environment may also form a natural cultural boundary and cultural characteristics such as stoicism may be influenced by extremes of climate.

The cultural impact of history and geography is generally carved out over a number of centuries, but powerful influences on culture are not confined to long periods of time. One of the most remarkable influences on recent CEE culture occurred over a period of little more than 40 years from the late 1940s to 1989: the period of communist rule under Soviet domination. Despite its relative brevity in a historical context, communist rule not only created an entirely new set of formal political, economic, and legal institutions, but also had a major impact on attitudes and behaviour. At a political level, communism affected beliefs as well as behaviour, as these countries were officially atheistic and religious practices were tolerated only in so far as they were not regarded as a threat to the state. The extent to which this approach suppressed individual religious belief or changed core underlying values is more debatable, but there is no doubt that communism had a significant influence on the outer layers and perhaps even some of the inner layers of culture. What is more certain is that the combined effect of history, geography, and politics on the culture and institutions of this region is likely to be substantial for the foreseeable future.

6.3 The essentials of culture

6.3.1 Culture as an expression of changes in society

Although the core elements of culture are deep-rooted, culture is not set in stone. Many of its elements, especially the outer, more visible layers of culture, evolve over a period of time. Forms of address in the UK, for example, became much more informal during the last quarter of the twentieth century. Whereas British university students now commonly address their tutors by their first names, this would have been rare, and students themselves would normally have been addressed formally by their tutors, only a generation ago. Values and beliefs change more slowly, if at all, but attitudes to important issues may change considerably over a period of time. For example, attitudes towards particular crimes, towards the role of women in society, or towards issues such as divorce, abortion, or gay rights have changed considerably among large sections of British society. Similar examples could be taken from many other countries, although in most Muslim countries attitudes towards many of these issues have remained firmer than in the west in recent years.

Culture is also adaptive in response to changes in society. This is particularly true in relation to changes in technology. Technology has enabled people to communicate more easily and over longer distances and has brought with it an endless stream of new production processes and products that have changed the work and home environment and the availability of leisure activities. Radio, television, cinema, DVDs, MP3 players, smartphones, and many other technological innovations have vastly increased our exposure to information, ideas, images, lifestyles, and music, among other things. Whether for good or bad is a more open question. These 'artefacts and products' have had a considerable impact on the way people live their lives, their expectations and attitudes, and perhaps even their sense of what is important. Assessing the effect of these changes on human behaviour and, more importantly, on beliefs, values, and attitudes is worthy of further study.

6.3.2 **The main elements of culture**

Language

The ability to communicate between members of a group helps the group to achieve cultural coherence. Since culture involves social interaction and shared experiences, a common language helps to facilitate the socialization process. It is therefore normal for cultural groups to be identifiable by their language, among other things, or by a particular dialect or accent. Languages are often associated with nation states, so for example most of the newer EU members have added their own languages to the EU's cultural mix. However, Europe has relatively few languages compared with Africa, where an estimated 2,058 languages were spoken in 2000.[13] Many of these languages are gradually dying out as isolated groups come into more frequent contact with larger groups and learn to speak more widespread African languages such as Swahili, Shona, Hausa, or Yoruba. In New Guinea, the large island shared by Indonesia and Papua New Guinea, there are more languages than in any other region of comparable size, with almost 1,000 languages but only around five million inhabitants.[14] The terrain in New Guinea is predominantly hilly and many small settlements live isolated from their neighbours, allowing them to remain culturally distinct. However, language is not always a distinguishing feature of culture, particularly at the transnational level. For example, Muslims from the Middle East, North Africa, and Asia speak a variety of languages, including Arabic, Urdu, Punjabi, Bengali, Indonesian, and Malay, though Arabic takes pride of place in Islamic culture.

Religion

Despite the decline in religious observance in much of the western world, religion is still the bedrock of many cultures, at sub-national, national, and transnational levels. Core values and beliefs predominantly stem from religious beliefs and precepts. Thus, for example, Christianity is still the dominant influence in North and South America and Europe, as Islam is in North Africa, the Middle East, and large parts of Asia. In some cases, the influence is mainly from a particular religious branch or denomination, such as Protestantism in the USA, Roman

Practical insight 6.3:   The role of religion in a secular state

The United States provides a fascinating example of the role of religion in a secular state. Former president George W. Bush (2001–9) is a self-professed evangelical Christian and the growth of the so-called 'religious right' or, more accurately, conservative evangelical Christians, had a significant impact on his election and policies. Sixty-eight per cent of white evangelicals voted for Bush in 2000 and 78 per cent in 2004 (though black evangelicals mainly voted Democrat) and evangelicals provided 40 per cent of his total vote in 2004. Evangelical theology also influenced some of his policies – for example, the strengthening of his support for Israel (as evangelicals consider the Jewish state to be the fulfilment of biblical teaching) or support for humanitarian causes in Africa, though not for the creation of supranational institutions to coordinate these causes (for similar reasons).[15]

President Barack Obama (2009–17), on the other hand, appears to hold liberal Christian beliefs emphasizing community, peacemaking, and human rights – beliefs which were couched in more pluralistic language in his inaugural speech at the beginning of his second term in January 2013.[16] According to exit-poll data in the 2012 presidential election, President Obama lost ground to his opponent, Mitt Romney, among most religious groups (achieving only 20 per cent of the white evangelical Protestant vote and 40 per cent of the white Catholic vote), but retained a high proportion of the black Protestant, Hispanic Catholic, Jewish, and religiously unaffiliated vote (95, 75, 69, and 70 per cent respectively).[17]

Question

- What do the above voting patterns tell us about the political influence of religion in the United States during the presidencies of George W. Bush and Barack Obama?

Catholicism in Latin America, Sunni Islam in North Africa, or Shi'a Islam in Iran. Religion may influence dress and other customs as well as fundamental beliefs and is often one of the main building blocks of a country's legal system. Some countries declare themselves to be officially secular, such as the United States, France, Turkey, or India, but this does not of course mean that religion is unimportant in these countries, simply that the state remains officially neutral in relation to religion (see Practical Insight 6.3).

Social structure and attitudes

Social structure describes the way a given society is organized: the extent to which it is stratified into classes or castes; the power relationships between those in authority and those under authority; the composition of family groups (whether extended or nuclear); the relative importance of individuals and social groups; practices relating to monogamy, polygamy, endogamy (marrying within the community), consanguine marriage (marrying within the family), or arranged marriages; and the degree of equality in society between men and women or between different social groups.[18] Many of the characteristics of social structure are reflected in the attitudes people have towards different issues. These may include attitudes towards equality, work, and leisure, the conduct of business, material possessions, or time and the future, for example.

The Nordic countries value social equality and consensus, while the US favours freedom and individual achievement. Anglo-Saxon countries in general like to separate work and leisure, whereas for an Arab work is a social activity. The rapid growth of Islamic banking, where the charging of interest in excess of the value of the amount borrowed (known as usury or *riba*), contrasts sharply with the emphasis on high rates of return in western business. Similarly, in Buddhist cultures, there is an emphasis on higher ideals rather than material possessions, unlike many western societies. Attitudes towards time and the future also vary considerably in different parts of the world, reflecting the degree to which cultures are mono- or polychronic (see Section 6.4.2) or ideas about whether the future course of events is predestined, as found in the teachings of Islam or Calvinism (a branch of Protestantism also known as reformed theology).

Education

In an informal sense education is a lifelong experience, in which the early years are particularly influential. Cultural mental programming occurs throughout this process and, in many ways, informal education provides the conduit through which culture is passed on from one generation to another or from one individual to another. Education is the means by which language, religious beliefs, and social structures and attitudes are passed on, as well as the source of understanding about the world we live in. Pre-school children make remarkable progress in learning their native language before starting their formal education. Of course, formal education at school, college, or university is also of vital importance. Without it, not only will individual and social progress be restricted, but our range of cultural experiences will remain limited. Literacy, in particular, allows culture and cultural creativity to develop as well as facilitating communication. Formal education is also used to promote national identity and values and may, in some circumstances, contain an element of censorship or propaganda. Even an apparently innocuous account of history may contain an element of national interpretation or manipulation.

Inspiration and creativity

Culture is also the source of inspiration and creativity in production and the arts. Anything from cooking to fashion, motor cars to buildings, or literature to music may be inspired by culture, and the creative skills and ideas behind them are expressions of culture. Thus, Celtic art or the paintings of Monet or Van Gogh may be seen as expressions of their respective cultures. The former has persisted, with variations, throughout the centuries, whereas the latter are products of particular artists at a particular time, but they are all nevertheless culturally inspired. Motor cars are of course more transitory, but their designs are still inspired by influences from their home or host cultures. Creativity is not restricted to the more enduring kind of artefacts or products. It may equally reflect changing trends in fashion, architecture, or music at a particular stage in a society's cultural development.

6.3.3 **Culture and civilizations**

The term 'civilization' is sometimes used to describe the broadest level of cultural identity, the largest grouping of people sharing common cultural characteristics.[19] The term is often used in connection with ancient civilizations, such as the Egyptian, Minoan, or Greek civilizations.

However, it is now increasingly being applied to transnational cultures or related cultural groups with one or more common cultural characteristics.[20] Some of these civilizations are confined to particular regions of the world, others are more dispersed. A number of them are characterized by current or historical religious beliefs, though members of a civilization may have many different languages and nationalities. The recent resurgence of religion as a powerful element of culture (discussed in Section 6.5.4) has led writers like Samuel Huntington to analyse the potential threats from a 'clash of civilizations'.[21] The existence of major civilizations may also affect the prevalence of particular languages, notably the influence of western civilization, or the United States in particular, on international business and the use of the English language.

Although there is some disagreement on what constitutes a civilization, Huntington categorizes eight major contemporary civilizations as follows:

- **Sinic (or Chinese) civilization** – this civilization includes present-day China, Chinese communities around the world, and the related cultures of Korea and Vietnam. A major influence on Sinic civilization has been Confucianism.

- **Japanese civilization** – this may be viewed as part of Chinese civilization, though it is now generally regarded as an offspring but independent of Chinese civilization.

- **Hindu civilization** – sometimes referred to as Indian or Indic civilization, Hinduism represents the predominant, though not the only, cultural influence in the Indian subcontinent. Like the Sinic civilization, it is not confined to a single nation, though at its core is the modern state of India.

- **Islamic civilization** – this is the most geographically dispersed civilization, being present in North Africa, the Middle East and several countries in Central, Southern, and South-East Asia.

- **Orthodox civilization** – although Christian (as is western civilization), Russia and some of its neighbours in Eastern and South-Eastern Europe are distinctive in that their cultures were less influenced by the Renaissance, Reformation, and Enlightenment.

- **Western civilization** – this is a geographical term, but western civilization has religious origins. Most of the countries of North America and Western and Central Europe have been influenced by Christianity, either Roman Catholic or Protestant.

- **Latin American civilization** – the countries of this region are sometimes included under western civilization because of their former colonial powers and the Roman Catholicism they left behind. However, the combination of European and indigenous Latin American Indian cultures, together with their more authoritarian political systems, suggests a distinct civilization.

- **African civilization** – more often regarded as a mixture of Islamic and western civilizations because of the spread of Islam in Northern Africa and the legacy of European colonialism in much of the continent. Sub-Saharan Africa may however be seen as an emerging civilization in its own right.

In the light of the Al-Qaeda attacks on the United States on 9/11 (11 September 2001), Huntington's 'clash of civilizations' has inevitably been interpreted as a clash between Islamic and western values. It should be remembered, however, that Huntington's first paper on this

> ## Practical insight 6.4:   A clash of world views
>
> Despite the fact that Al-Qaeda takes an extreme, atypical Islamic position, events since 9/11 have tended to reinforce the idea of a fundamental clash of beliefs and values between western and Islamic civilizations. At the very least, there is a fundamental difference in the world view of former President Bush and mainstream Muslim opinion. This was made clear by the reaction of many Muslims around the world to the US-led attack on Saddam Hussein's Iraq in March 2003, despite a general dislike of Saddam's regime. In many ways, this illustrates the difference between Huntington's thesis of the clash of civilizations and Francis Fukuyama's idea of the 'end of history', the view that western-style democratic capitalism has finally triumphed over alternative systems – a view that found favour with President Bush in his desire to rid the world of 'rogue states'.[22]
>
> ### Question
>
> - Which view of the world do you find more persuasive?

subject appeared in *Foreign Affairs* in 1993, so his arguments were made at a more general level. If Huntington's analysis is correct, however, civilizations in the modern sense may provide a new perspective on the international business environment. See Practical Insight 6.4 for further discussion of these issues.

6.4 Methods of cultural assessment

Several researchers have attempted to analyse the differences and similarities between cultures by focusing on particular 'dimensions of culture'. Some of the more important ideas arising from these studies are now discussed.

6.4.1 High-context and low-context cultures

Edward T. Hall, an American anthropologist, identified two important dimensions of culture. The first of these was the significance of the 'context' in which cultural exchanges take place; the second was 'time orientation' which is discussed in Section 6.4.2.[23] **High-context cultures** are those where the context in which communication takes place is more important than the words themselves and the meaning is conveyed more through the context than the message. **Low-context culture** is where the context is unimportant and the message is explicit in itself. Thus, for example, China has a high-context culture, so the environment in which business communication occurs – the form of greeting, social interaction, body language, even the seating arrangement – is of crucial importance. Doing business in such an environment is as much about showing respect, forming relationships, and developing trust as it is about completing a transaction. To an American, this process is more likely to be seen as time-wasting, as the important thing in a low-context culture like the USA is to make the deal; socializing can wait till later. A number of Asian and Middle Eastern countries have high-context cultures, whereas North American and European cultures tend to be lower-context. In reality, however, there are many gradations between high- and low-context cultures.

6.4.2 Monochronic and polychronic time orientation

Another key dimension of culture identified by Hall was the way in which people relate to time. He distinguished between '**monochronic**' and '**polychronic**' time orientations. 'Monochronic is characteristic of low-involvement peoples, who compartmentalize time; they schedule one thing at a time and become disoriented if they have to deal with too many things at once. Polychronic people, possibly because they are so much involved with each other, tend to keep several options going at once, like jugglers.'[24] Northern Europeans (or more specifically, the Germanic cultures) tend to be monochronic; they like to keep to a strict time schedule and deal with one thing at once. In the polychronic Southern European (Latin and Greek) cultures, order and deadlines are less important. Queuing is very much a Northern European trait. Trompenaars and Hampden-Turner use the terms '**sequential**' and '**synchronic**' in place of monochronic and polychronic, the former describing 'a line of sequential events', the latter a 'number of activities run in parallel'.[25] In sequential cultures, such as the USA, Sweden, or the UK, time is seen as a series of discrete events along a straight line and past events have little relevance to future events, whereas synchronic cultures like France, Spain, or Greece view past, present, and future events as occurring within the same time frame. This distinction may also help to explain why the British eat their meals quickly then move on to the next activity, while the Spanish regard their meals as a social activity where time is less important – or why French business schools teach the history of management as an adjunct to management theory and practice (see opening scenario to this chapter).

6.4.3 Hofstede's dimensions of culture

While working for IBM, Geert Hofstede conducted a major study of cultural differences involving over 100,000 IBM employees between 1967 and 1973.[26] Initially, Hofstede's analysis focused mainly on 40 countries, but it was subsequently extended to 76 countries. As a result of his original study, Hofstede identified four 'dimensions of culture' that enabled him to compare the essential characteristics of each culture: power distance, **individualism** versus **collectivism**, **masculinity** versus **femininity**, and uncertainty avoidance. A fifth dimension, **long-term** versus **short-term orientation**, and a sixth dimension, **indulgence** versus **restraint**, were also added, based on subsequent studies including World Values Survey data for 93 countries.[27] The following is a brief explanation of Hofstede's six dimensions of culture.

Power distance

This dimension relates to the willingness of individuals to accept authority, whether in the family, the organization, or the state. **High power-distance** cultures tend to be formal, hierarchical, and authoritarian; autocratic or paternalistic leadership is seen as caring. **Low power-distance** cultures tend to be informal and consultative, and there is likely to be a greater degree of equality. A number of Asian, Latin American, and Central and Eastern European countries are among the highest power-distance cultures, whereas the Anglo-Saxon and Western European countries are generally (though not uniformly) low power-distance cultures.

Individualism versus collectivism

This dimension concerns the degree to which individuals are considered to be more or less important than groups or society as a whole. Individualistic societies admire ambition and personal achievement and emphasize the importance of individual rights and responsibilities. Collectivist societies consider social cohesion and group loyalty to be more important than the needs of the individual. High power-distance cultures are generally more collectivist and low power-distance cultures more individualistic (with a few exceptions), and the United States is one of the most individualistic.

Masculinity versus femininity

Masculine values are considered to include assertiveness, competitiveness, ambition, and achievement, whereas feminine values include modesty, social responsibility, cooperation, and good working relationships. These are of course gender stereotypes, but cultures where 'masculine' values predominate are described as masculine cultures, whereas those where feminine values predominate are described as 'feminine' cultures. Among the more masculine cultures are Japan, China, Austria, Germany, and the Anglo-Saxon countries. Among the most feminine cultures are the Nordic countries, and the Netherlands.

Uncertainty avoidance

This dimension relates to the degree to which people prefer to avoid uncertainty and risk. In **high uncertainty-avoidance** cultures people are risk averse; they feel threatened by uncertain situations and create rules and procedures to minimize uncertainties. In **low uncertainty-avoidance** cultures people are risk takers; they are more likely to finance a business using risk capital (equities) and feel comfortable in a free-market environment. Japan, Russia, and a number of European, Asian, and Latin American countries have high uncertainty-avoidance cultures, whereas the Anglo-Saxon countries and, notably, China, India, Malaysia, and Singapore have low uncertainty-avoidance cultures.

Long-term versus short-term orientation

Although originally derived from Confucian teaching based on a study carried out in China, this dimension has now been generalized so that long-term orientation relates to societies where future rewards and persistence are valued, whereas short-term orientation represents an emphasis on past and present values such as respect for tradition, social obligations, and saving 'face'. Some of the East Asian cultures in particular have been found to have long-term orientations, including China and Japan, though Germany also appears to fit into this category.

Indulgence versus restraint

Indulgence relates to societies where citizens are allowed freedom to indulge their desires and enjoy life, whereas restraint describes societies where social control and social norms impose restrictions on these freedoms. The most 'indulgent' countries are generally found

Table 6.1 Hofstede's dimensions of culture for selected countries

Country	Power Distance	Individualism	Masculinity	Uncertainty Avoidance	Long-Term Orientation	Indulgence versus Restraint
Brazil	69	38	49	76	44	59
China	80	20	66	30	87	24
France	68	71	43	86	63	48
Germany	35	67	66	65	83	40
Great Britain	35	89	66	35	51	69
India	77	48	56	40	51	26
Japan	54	46	95	92	88	42
Netherlands	38	80	14	53	67	68
Sweden	31	71	5	29	53	78
USA	40	91	62	46	26	68

Source: Hofstede, G., Hofstede, G. J., and Minkov, M. (2010), *Cultures and Organizations: Software of the Mind*, McGraw-Hill.

in the Americas and Western Europe, while the most 'restrained' appear to be in the Muslim countries, Eastern Europe, and various parts of Asia.

The scores in Table 6.1 indicate relative rather than absolute values; the higher the score the greater the 'power distance' and so on. They should not be regarded as precise indicators, but as a broad indication of some of the main differences between cultures (see Practical Insight 6.5 for an example in the context of long-term orientation).

Practical insight 6.5:   International saving ratios

National saving ratios are generally much higher in Asia than they are in Europe or North America. In fact, estimates of gross national saving as a percentage of GDP ranged from 54.3 per cent in China to 33.6 per cent in India, 18.9 per cent in France, and 12.1 per cent in the USA in 2008.[28] Whilst there may be a number of possible explanations for international differences in savings ratios at a particular time, 'saving is fundamentally the outcome of inter-temporal optimisation'[29] – that is, the preference of individuals, businesses, and governments to engage in future as opposed to present consumption. The ratios also correspond reasonably closely to Hofstede's long-term orientation scores for the countries concerned.

Question

- In what other ways might long-term orientation scores be manifested in these countries?

6.4.4 **Trompenaars and Hampden-Turner's cultural orientations**

Fons Trompenaars and Charles Hampden-Turner follow a similar path in distinguishing between seven orientations or dimensions of culture.[30] Some of them are quite close to Hofstede's dimensions, others take a slightly different perspective. Trompenaars and Hampden-Turner describe these orientations as 'fundamental dimensions of culture', but some relate more to behavioural aspects of culture in the outer layers of the culture onion than to basic values. The first five deal with relationships with other people, the other two relate to time and the environment respectively. The seven cultural orientations are as follows:

- **Universalism versus particularism** – **universalism** involves a belief that some things are always right and must be observed at all times. **Particularism** is where the obligations of particular relationships or circumstances may be given priority over general rules.

- **Individualism versus communitarianism** – individualism gives priority to the role of individuals in society. In **communitarianism** (like Hofstede's collectivism), the community or society takes precedence.

- **Neutral versus emotional** – a **neutral culture** takes a clinical view of business objectives and efficiency is paramount. An **emotional culture** considers that human emotions are an acceptable and natural part of business negotiation.

- **Specific versus diffuse** – in **specific cultures** the main focus is on the details of the product or contract. In **diffuse cultures** the whole person is involved in forming a business relationship (in the same way as Hall's low- and high-context cultures).

- **Achievement versus ascription** – **achievement cultures** attach importance to what people have accomplished, their qualifications or employment record. **Ascriptive cultures** are more concerned with status, which may be conferred by birth, age, gender, or connections.

- **Attitudes to time** – in some cultures the past is unimportant (sequential cultures); what matters is the way a person is performing in the present or his or her future potential. In other cultures a person's past record is more important (synchronic cultures).

- **Attitudes to the environment** – some cultures emphasize the values and motivations that come from within a person, others attach great significance to the power and influence of nature or the external environment.

6.5 Cultural controversies

This section focuses on some of the contemporary debates surrounding cultural issues. Given the importance of culture in business and our everyday lives, it is not unusual for people to hold strong views or have particular concerns about cultural issues. In some cases, a view has become so widely accepted that it is rarely challenged; phrases such as 'we're all the same now' or 'everyone speaks English' are commonplace. In other cases, culture is thought to have a bearing on a country's political and economic development or to be responsible for divisions in society. Sometimes a new idea attracts our attention, such as Richard Florida's research on the role of the '**creative class**'. In many cases, the issue is more complex than it first appears. The purpose of this section is to explore the issues more fully and also to challenge accepted views.

6.5.1 Cultural convergence and diversity

It is a commonly held view that cultures are converging around the world. Globalization is often held responsible for this 'homogenization' of culture. The evidence for this view can be seen not only in our western dress and increasingly international diet, but also in the business practices of multinational enterprises, whatever their country of origin. Of course, there are plenty of exceptions, but cultures seem to be converging gradually and relentlessly. Convergence is also evident at the level of cultural groups and languages. Currently, there are an estimated five to seven thousand languages in the world, but the 60 most widely spoken languages are spoken by about 75 per cent of the world's population and many of the smaller languages are gradually disappearing.[31] Perhaps unsurprisingly, dominant cultural characteristics tend to survive at the expense of weaker ones.

In reality, however, the picture is somewhat more complicated. When cultures are isolated, they are more likely to retain their language, traditions, and distinctive artefacts. As they become more open, they adopt ideas, customs, and products from other cultures. However, even apparently isolated cultures may have been exposed to outside influences at some point in their history. The sculptural talents of the Inuit people, who inhabit remote areas of northern Canada, began to blossom after they were introduced to soapstone carving in 1948; this enabled the Inuit to use more permanent materials, allowing them to export their art and earn income to support their traditional way of life.[32]

The paradox of cultural openness is that, whilst foreign influences increase, so does the market for the home culture's products (including the creative arts as well as manufactured goods). Cultural products may need a large market in order to flourish; arguably, there is not much point in being a Puccini or a Picasso if the world is unable to discover your work. Technology has also played a role on the supply side as new methods of production and distribution have allowed unit costs of cultural products to fall, by spreading the fixed costs as the products become available in international markets. At the same time, changing demand and supply conditions may bring about product adaptations in response to different cultural influences. Persian carpet making provides a useful illustration of these demand and supply effects. This ancient craft experienced a revival in the late nineteenth century following renewed interest from wealthy western consumers and an injection of capital and design skills by western investors.[33]

International exposure clearly has a pervasive impact on cultures and cultural products. This may lead to cultural convergence as dominant cultures influence or even destroy weaker ones. It also leads to cultural diversity as new ideas and products complement existing ones or stimulate innumerable variations. The humble pizza, with its origins in Italy, is today served, with a variety of toppings undreamed of by its Italian inventors, in almost every corner of the world. Of course, not every effect of this complex pattern of cultural adaptation may be regarded as beneficial. It may be argued that dominant cultural 'products' such as cinema (Hollywood in particular) and television have led to a 'dumbing down' of culture. In theory, a mass international audience should ensure there are enough discerning consumers to discriminate between good and bad cinema and television, but the doubtful quality of many movies and reality TV shows suggests that even bad products may become dominant, at least in the short term. It is of course possible to choose alternative products; this is the beauty of diversity. It is also likely that the deeper layers of culture are more impervious to outside influences than those that are closer to the surface.

6.5.2 The 'rise of the creative class'

In his book *The Rise of the Creative Class*, Richard Florida claims that communities become more economically successful if they are able to attract the 'creative class'.[34] According to Florida, members of the creative class include people involved in a variety of activities ranging from technology to entertainment, journalism, finance, high added-value manufacturing, and the arts, among other things. What links them is the value they place on creativity, freedom of expression, individuality, and the desire to make a difference. Florida uses a 'creativity index' to measure the extent to which the creative class is present in a particular city, taking account of indicators of cultural openness as well as the proportion of workers engaged in the creative industries. He argues that these creative communities act as a major driving force behind regional economic growth and, by extension, may help to determine the economic fortunes of nations. In fact, in his subsequent book, *The Flight of the Creative Class*, Florida expresses concern about the loss of creative workers from a number of US cities as countries like India offer a more attractive environment for high-tech workers.[35]

Although the concept of a creative class relates to people of all cultural backgrounds and is not therefore culture-specific, creativity nevertheless has cultural roots and the characteristics of openness and tolerance that Florida believes are conducive to creativity may be more prevalent in some cultures than others. Of course, creativity is not restricted to open and tolerant societies, but a lack of openness may hinder it or steer it along a particular path. Whether this is necessarily a bad thing is a more open question. However, it may well be, as Florida argues, that creativity is more likely to flourish if a critical mass of creative workers are able to feed off each other's ideas and enthusiasm.

6.5.3 The ubiquity of the English language?

English is increasingly becoming the language of business, but what exactly do we mean by this? Indeed, does everyone now speak English? It is extremely difficult to estimate the total number of English speakers around the world. Clearly, there are those whose first language is English; in the main, these people live in the 'English-speaking' countries, the USA, Canada, UK, Australia, New Zealand, and a number of smaller former British colonies, or they are expatriates of these countries living elsewhere. Not all the residents of the English-speaking countries are native speakers of English; for example, they may be Spanish speakers in the USA, French speakers in Canada, or even Welsh speakers in the UK, though most of them will probably have a reasonable knowledge of English as a second language. The number of speakers of English as a first language has been estimated at 341 million, which in itself is a small proportion of the world's population, probably lower than the number of Spanish or Hindi speakers and certainly lower than the number of speakers of Mandarin Chinese.[36] The number of speakers of English as a second or subsequent language is much more difficult to estimate. Even if accurate statistics were available, the number would depend on how we define an English speaker, that is, the degree of fluency required.

The total number of those who speak English, as a first or subsequent language, is probably not more than 20 per cent of the world's population, but among people involved in international business and tourism, diplomats, scientists, airline pilots, and air traffic controllers, for example, it has become the 'lingua franca', the language of international and intercultural communication. It is also more likely to be understood by educated young people than by older people and is the main, though not the only, language used on the internet. However, the use of English is unevenly spread. It is widely spoken in the Scandinavian countries, the Netherlands, and former British colonies such as India, Hong Kong, Malaysia, and a number of countries in the Caribbean and sub-Saharan Africa. In China, francophone Africa, and the

Practical insight **6.6:** Language and the development of trade links

A study carried out by the UK National Centre for Languages found a noticeable difference in the value of UK exports and imports between countries where English is the main language of business and those where it is not. Exports exceeded imports in UK trade with the USA, Ireland, Australia, and India, for example, but imports exceeded exports in UK trade with Germany, France, the Netherlands, Belgium and Luxembourg, Spain, and Italy. Even more strikingly, per capita spending on UK exports in countries where English is widely understood (Denmark, Sweden, and the Netherlands) was significantly greater than in countries where English is less widely understood (France, Italy, and Spain). However, the most telling statistic was that UK exports to Denmark, a country with a population of five million, represented the same proportion of total UK exports (1.2 per cent) as UK exports to the whole of Central and South America, with its population of 390 million.[37]

Question

- To what extent do you think these differences can be explained by the degree of familiarity with the English language?

southern European countries, it is less widely understood. Even in countries where English is commonly used, such as India, there may still be a majority of non-English speakers.

As a tourist or business traveller, it is easy to think that 'everyone speaks English' and certainly it has achieved a dominant position as the main means of international communication since World War II and even more so since the end of the cold war. Whether it will continue in this position will depend on factors such as the future of US supremacy, the emergence of China, and developments in Latin America where Spanish and Portuguese predominate, among other things. However, no matter how dominant English may be in international business, it is always more difficult to communicate with people of another culture without some grasp of the host country's language (see Practical Insight 6.6). Cultural subtleties may elude even the most fluent speaker of a foreign language and a cultural chasm opens up when there is no common language. Even where a foreign host speaks English well, a faltering attempt to communicate in his or her native language is likely to create a favourable impression. A former colleague of the author was accorded great respect by colleagues in the Netherlands, where English is widely spoken, because he had taken the trouble to learn Dutch, a difficult language rarely attempted by foreigners.

6.5.4 **The resurgence of religion**

Religion has always been a core element of many cultures. At different times in history particular religions have influenced the development of political and legal systems and the behaviour of ordinary citizens to a greater or lesser extent. In the post-World War II western world the influence of Christianity appears to have been waning, with declining church attendance and the gradual acceptance of alternative perspectives on traditional Christian teaching. In terms of formal religious expression, the same trend was evident in the former Soviet bloc, albeit for different reasons, though Roman Catholicism was strong enough in communist Poland to enable Cardinal Karol Wojtyła to emerge as Pope John Paul II in 1978.

This picture of relative decline is not true of other parts of the world. In Latin America, Christianity still plays an important role in national life and Catholic bishops have enjoyed considerable political influence and popular support. In Africa, there has been perhaps the most dramatic increase in church attendance, though not commensurate political influence. Religion has also played a powerful role in conflicts in Northern Ireland, the Middle East, and the former Yugoslavia, where rival factions have been separated by their religious traditions, whether Protestant and Catholic, Muslim and Jew, or Christian and Muslim.

Perhaps the most remarkable developments in recent years, however, have been the revival of conservative evangelical Christianity in the United States (often known as the 'religious right') and the ascendancy of radical Islamic beliefs and practices in the Muslim world. Both these religious revivals are sometimes described as 'fundamentalist', implying that they adopt a more literal interpretation of the Bible or Qur'an, though in practice they encompass a wider set of religious traditions. Only a few years ago, most western politicians and scholars were adjusting their thinking to a world of declining religious influence, where 'trouble spots' like the Middle East were seen as political rather than religious conflicts in an otherwise secular world. This view now no longer seems tenable.

The 'new' influence of religion has important implications for the international business environment. Even in traditionally moderate or officially secular Muslim states, there is growing pressure to return to traditional Islamic principles, including Sharia Law, Islamic banking, and more modest forms of dress such as the *hijab*, *niqab*, and *burqa* increasingly worn by Muslim women. The election of a new Turkish president, Abdullah Gül, in August 2007 raised this issue in the context of Turkey's officially secular state. The country's military leaders have acted as the guardians of its secular constitution since the establishment of the modern Turkish state in 1923. The president's openly devout Muslim stance and the fact that his wife wore the *hijab*, which is officially banned in Turkish public life, raised concerns that government policy might become more overtly Islamic. However, while President Gul has been strongly critical of Israeli policy, he has remained loyal to the country's western allies and has supported the democratization process during the Arab uprising. Similar concerns have been expressed by defenders of the US secular constitution in response to the growing influence of the 'religious right', especially during George W. Bush's presidency. In both cases, those who support the religious resurgence see it as quite natural that religion should inform political and economic decision making. It is likely that the tensions between these opposing views will become more evident in the next few years.

6.5.5 Cultural explanations for economic development

The extent to which culture has contributed towards economic development has been hotly debated for many years. At one extreme, Adolf Hitler claimed the moral superiority of the 'Aryan' race (a term he defined rather narrowly). Others, with less sinister intentions, have pointed to the apparent success of a particular cultural group in science, business, and other fields, such as Jews in general, Protestants in Europe, or Asians (mainly from the Indian subcontinent) in Africa. One of the most influential writers on the role of culture, and religion in particular, in economic development was the German sociologist, Max Weber.[38] Weber argued that one of the main reasons for the success of capitalism in Europe and North America after the Reformation was the influence of Protestantism and, more particularly, the individual work ethic of its Calvinist and Puritan branches (generally described as the 'Protestant work ethic'). Countries with a predominantly Protestant population tended to be at the forefront of the industrial revolution, including Britain, Germany, and the United States. This has not, of course, precluded Catholic countries such as France, Italy, or more recently the Republic of Ireland, from catching up with their neighbours. If Weber's view has validity, it seems to apply predominantly to a particular period in history. The recent economic success of countries from a wider range of cultural backgrounds, especially those in Asia, suggests that it may not have more general validity. The influence of culture may, nevertheless, still be significant, either because of the values it instils or because of the way it helps to shape a country's institutions.

6.5.6 Asian cultures and economic success

During the 1970s and 1980s the business world's attention was turned towards the success of Japanese companies and the Japanese economy. Japan's success was soon followed by other East Asian economies, notably Hong Kong, Singapore, South Korea, Taiwan, Malaysia, Thailand, and Indonesia, some or all of which have been described as Asia's 'tiger economies'. These countries have achieved rapid economic development by emulating the success of the USA and Europe's major economies but using a different economic model. A number of factors distinguish their early routes to success: the western nations built their economies on heavy industries, relying largely on the innovative efforts of private sector pioneers, while the Asian 'tigers' developed selective industries such as electronics or financial services, either in cooperation with western partners or by marshalling the combined efforts of government, business, and workers. The Asian countries of course had the benefit of the western countries' experience, but the key difference between their approaches is a cultural one.

The Japanese economic model, so much admired until the end of the 1980s, lost some of its sheen during the years of economic stagnation that followed. The tiger economies continued to grow during the 1990s, but suffered a setback during the Asian financial crisis (1997–8). Most of them have recovered quite well since 1998, though sometimes after painful economic reforms. The leading Asian success story since 1990, however, has been China. China has followed a middle course between selective market liberalization, cooperative approaches, and state intervention. Nevertheless, a key element in this mix has been the legacy of Confucianism, with its emphasis on wise leadership, individual morality, and peaceful coexistence.

It has been suggested that East Asia's cooperative approach may be, at least in part, responsible for its rapid economic development. Hampden-Turner and Trompenaars liken the approaches of the west, or more particularly, the Anglo-Saxon countries, and the East Asian countries to 'finite games' and 'infinite games' respectively.[39] Finite games involve free-market competition, where short-term profit is paramount and the winner takes all, though the loser may discover a more suitable alternative; infinite games involve cooperation between the 'players', where the loser learns from the winner and society coordinates its efforts to achieve long-term goals.

East Asian economic success has not been without its critics. South Korea's Daewoo Motors (originally part of the giant Daewoo *chaebol* or conglomerate) illustrates how government-backed international expansion can leave a company with overcapacity and unsustainable debt. On the other hand, Daewoo's insolvency can be contrasted with Toyota's success in challenging the global dominance of General Motors and Ford. Whatever the successes and failures of the East Asian economies, cultural values seem to have played a significant role. Indeed, some of these values have been incorporated into western business practices as a result of the success of Japanese and Korean companies in particular. Whether East Asian values can be fully integrated into the western way of doing business is a very different question.

6.6 Alternative socio-economic models

Despite the cultural variation that exists within most countries, it is common to use typologies of national culture as a basis for analysing cultural differences in the business environment. Whilst imperfect, comparisons of national culture generally provide a useful indication of the different ways of doing business in different parts of the world. When the countries of the world could be divided into 'centrally planned economies' and 'market economies', the study of comparative economic systems provided an explanation of the economic theory underpinning state planning and market systems and the policy regimes in place to support these systems. With the demise of the main state planning systems in the former Soviet bloc and, to an increasing extent, in China, such studies have largely become redundant. This has left the way open for a variety of approaches to the classification of national differences. In the main, however, these approaches focus on the influence of culture and institutions on a country's business environment. The term '**socio-economic model**' is used in this section to categorize these cultural and institutional influences in a number of countries. The models have been selected not because they represent a complete typology, but because they include many of the main trading nations of the world and have been the focus of intensive study in recent years.

6.6.1 Varieties of capitalism

Peter Hall and David Soskice have been among the most influential researchers in this field.[40] They suggest a basic typology of 'coordinated market economies' and 'liberal market economies', with Germany and Japan as the former and the United States and UK as the latter. Although the essential distinction is between non-market coordination and market coordination respectively, Hall and Soskice's main contribution is their emphasis on the role of institutions in determining relationships within and between firms in the private sector, that is, relationships with employees, customers, suppliers, government, and a variety of other groups. They also recognize the importance of culture in shaping the institutional framework. Thus, for example, they focus on national differences in labour markets, social protection, or corporate governance and the way in which laws and other institutions are influenced by different cultural perspectives.

A more extensive typology is provided by Bruno Amable, who identifies five models of modern capitalism: market-based capitalism, Asian capitalism, continental European capitalism, social democratic capitalism, and Mediterranean capitalism.[41] Table 6.2 provides examples of each model, though the list of countries is not necessarily exhaustive. Market-based

Table 6.2: Amable's five models of modern capitalism

Market-Based Capitalism	Asian Capitalism	Continental European Capitalism	Social-Democratic Capitalism	Mediterranean Capitalism
Australia	Japan	Switzerland	Denmark	Greece
New Zealand	S. Korea	Netherlands	Finland	Italy
UK		Ireland	Sweden	Portugal
USA		Belgium		Spain
		Norway		
		Germany		
		France		
		Austria		

Source: Amable, B. (2003), *The Diversity of Modern Capitalism*, Oxford University Press, extracted from Table 5.1, p. 173. By permission of Oxford University Press.

capitalism corresponds closely to Hall and Soskice's liberal market economies and this group was found to be the most homogeneous in Amable's study. The other four models were found to have more diverse characteristics. The socio-economic models described in Sections 6.6.2 to 6.6.4, and represented in Figure 6.1, are broadly similar to Amable's typology, with some variation in the names and classification of the models.

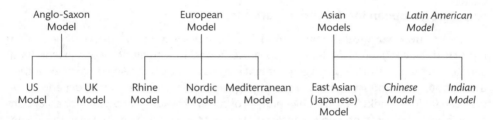

Figure 6.1 An alternative typology of the main socio-economic models: established and *emerging* models

6.6.2 The Anglo-Saxon model

The **Anglo-Saxon model** is almost synonymous with the English-speaking countries; in particular, it includes the USA, UK, Australia, and New Zealand, though Anglo-Saxon policies have also been used elsewhere, for example in Chile since the 1970s and some of the CEE countries since 1989. In some ways, the term 'Anglo-Saxon' is a curious one as it describes the early English settlers who originated from the area that is now northern Germany and Denmark, and many other cultures have also influenced the present-day English-speaking countries. Nevertheless, the term is widely understood in this context, though other terms such as 'Anglo-American' or 'neo-American' have also been used.

The Anglo-Saxon countries are broadly characterized by free product and labour markets, free trade in international markets, a market-based system of corporate finance and corporate governance, extensive property rights, relatively low levels of social protection, and a competitive mass higher education system. Of course, not all these characteristics apply equally to each country. The USA is generally seen as having the purest form of Anglo-Saxon capitalism and fits the model quite closely, though even here examples of market intervention can be found in the form of minimum wages or trade protection policies. The UK pioneered free trade (or 'laissez-faire') in the latter half of the nineteenth century, but adopted continental European welfare policies and nationalization after World War II, only to return to more liberal economic policies under Margaret Thatcher in the 1980s. Even today, the UK National Health Service is more 'European', in the sense of providing non-market social protection, than the health services of many continental European countries. Despite this, UK economic policy since 1979 has been distinctly less interventionist than that of most of its continental neighbours.

A particular feature of the Anglo-Saxon countries is their individualism. This provides the basic rationale for free markets, the priority of individual freedom over collective action, and the need for property rights to protect individual freedom and enforce individual responsibilities. In recent years, policies of privatization, market deregulation, trade liberalization, and flexible labour markets have come to be associated with the Anglo-Saxon approach. Indeed, some of these policies have been adopted by non-Anglo-Saxon countries, often at the behest of the IMF, the World Bank, or WTO. The EU has also embraced a number of liberal economic policies to complement its more conventional regulatory approach, notably policies associated with competition in the single European market. These policies have often received support not only from the UK, but from its Nordic members, some of its 'Rhine' members (especially the Netherlands and Germany), and from some of the newer CEE members.

6.6.3 The European model and its variants

The term ' **European model**' may be used as a loose designation for the common characteristics of the continental Western European countries. To a greater or lesser extent, these countries tend to use more active government intervention than the Anglo-Saxon countries, their labour and product markets are more regulated, companies are more dependent on loan capital from banks, there is a higher level of social protection, and policy decisions are more likely to be based on public consensus. However, the differences between the 'Rhine', Nordic, and Mediterranean countries may be considered significant enough for them to be described as distinct socio-economic models.

The Rhine model

Michel Albert, a French writer and businessman, coined the term '**Rhine model**', essentially to describe Europe's social market economies as typified by post-war Germany.[42] Albert then extended this concept to Japan and contrasted the Rhine model with the 'neo-American model' exemplified by the United States. In its original European context, the term 'Rhine model' is derived from Europe's longest and most prominent river which passes through or borders Switzerland, Liechtenstein, Austria, Germany, France, and the Netherlands before reaching the North Sea at Rotterdam. Here we use the Rhine model to describe the above list of countries, together with the neighbouring countries of Belgium and Luxembourg. Albert is less convinced that France is included in this model (though he wishes it were). A more dispassionate assessment would probably consider France to have more in common with the Rhine model than with the Anglo-Saxon model which Albert decries.

The core of the Rhine model is Germany's post-war social market economy. Germany's economy is essentially a market economy coupled with strong social protection for individuals and companies. The labour market provides the best example of social protection, with its long-term job security, extensive vocational training, generous sickness, unemployment, and retirement benefits, and internal company promotion structures. Consumer and environmental protection laws are among the strongest in the developed world and companies enjoy greater protection from hostile takeovers than in the Anglo-Saxon countries. Social consensus is strongly embedded in Germany's political system, with its proportional representation and coalition governments, and in its approach to industrial relations, especially the system of codetermination or *Mitbestimmung* where workers participate in company decision making. German companies are generally more dependent on bank finance than on equity capital and it is common for banks to play an active role in corporate governance, especially among the many middle-ranking firms (or *Mittelstand*), but also in some of Germany's larger companies.

When applied to the other 'Rhine' countries, the model varies to some extent in each case. Even in Germany itself, recent governments under both the left-of-centre Social Democrat, Gerhardt Schröder (1998–2005), and the right-of-centre Christian Democrat, Angela Merkel (from 2005), have been introducing market reforms to liberalize the country's rigid labour markets and reduce the heavy cost of taxation needed to pay for social protection. A similar reform process began in the Netherlands in the 1980s, though public support for social protection remains strong in most of the Rhine countries. France has its own distinctive version of the Rhine model, with a more centralized political and educational system, and close links between government and industry – a feature that has sometimes led to comparisons with Japan. There is often strong support for government intervention to protect French industry and the media from foreign dominance and a tradition of *dirigisme* (literally 'direction' or 'management', sometimes described as 'indicative planning'), initiated during France's post-war reconstruction when governments actively promoted industrial development.

The Nordic model

In many respects the **Nordic model** is similar to the Rhine model, with its regulated product and labour markets and its reliance on bank finance. However, the state welfare system is if anything more extensive and is based on a strong sense of shared responsibility for the well-being of society. This social partnership also translates into economic policy, where industrial and labour market decisions are determined by a process of collective negotiation between government and organizations representing the various interested parties. This process is sometimes described as the 'negotiated economy'.

As with the other models, there is significant variation between countries and Sweden is often regarded as the main representative of the Nordic model. However, economic problems and rising budget deficits led to austerity measures and the reining in of expensive welfare programmes in both Denmark (in the 1980s) and Sweden (in the 1990s), though Denmark has combined labour-market liberalization with social protection through its policy of 'flexicurity', which provides job flexibility along with security for workers moving between jobs. The Nordic countries have also followed different political and economic paths. Whilst they all belong to the Nordic Council, which allows free movement across its borders, Norway and Iceland have remained outside the EU (though within the European Economic Area)[43] and

Finland has broken with its fellow EU members, Denmark and Sweden, by joining the single currency. However, their common emphasis on generous state provision for higher education and scientific research has remained largely intact.

The Mediterranean model

The Mediterranean countries, Spain, Portugal, Italy, and Greece, share the regulated labour markets and bank-based corporate finance system of the other European models, but generally have more limited welfare systems and spend less on higher education. Public ownership of industry has also been more common in this region, especially in Greece, though these countries have been following their European neighbours in reducing the level of state ownership in recent years. Again, there are a number of differences between individual countries. Italy is perhaps the most distinct, with its more individualistic culture, extremes of left and right in politics, large family-owned corporations, and networks of small family businesses in industries such as clothing and footwear. The **Mediterranean model** is also characterized by bureaucratic administrative procedures and lax standards of corporate governance.

6.6.4 **The East Asian model**

The path to economic recovery followed by Japan after World War II has been variously described as the Japanese, Asian, or **East Asian model**. The approach pioneered by Japan, with US political and financial support, was then adopted by other East Asian countries, notably South Korea, Singapore, and Taiwan, from the 1960s onwards. Although there is not yet a clear alternative Asian model, the term East Asian model seems more appropriate as it is mainly associated with Asia's eastern and south-eastern regions. The East Asian countries are heavily dependent on bank finance, perhaps more so than their European counterparts, and workers are normally afforded a high degree of employment protection. Many Japanese skilled workers have enjoyed lifetime employment with the same company, though this practice is now gradually being eroded. Japan's relatively collectivist culture values mutual loyalty between a company and its employees, so the idea of making workers redundant, bringing in managers from outside, or promoting young employees to senior positions is alien to traditional Japanese culture (see Practical Insight 6.7).

The close links between companies and their employees also exist between different companies and between government and industry. Many Japanese companies belong to *keiretsu*, networks of companies with inter-locking shareholdings, often headed either by a bank (a *horizontal keiretsu*) or by a major company such as Toyota exercising a paternalistic oversight of its suppliers (a *vertical keiretsu*). A particular feature of the Japanese system, also common in other East and South-East Asian countries, is the way in which government works in partnership with companies. Japanese governments successively promoted the development of the steel, ship-building, motor vehicle, and electronics industries, among others, during the post-war years. When Japanese companies began to internationalize in the 1970s, it was no accident of the free market. Japanese companies were encouraged to venture abroad in tandem (the *convoy system*), supported by government and low-cost loans from their *keiretsu* bank (see Section 14.2). Governments have also been active in promoting industrial development in Taiwan, South Korea, and elsewhere, though not always in the same way as Japan. The Taiwanese government

Practical insight 6.7: Is Japan's corporate culture changing?

Even Japan's relatively collectivist, high uncertainty-avoidance culture is starting to change. In line with tradition, an employee of the Nichia corporation, Shuji Nakamura, was rewarded with only modest promotion, a small pay rise, and a tiny bonus of ¥20,000 ($190) after he invented blue light-emitting diodes (LED), one of the major inventions of the twentieth century. As an employee of the company, Mr Nakamura was simply part of the collective whole and was not therefore allowed to benefit much from his individual efforts. However, in February 2004, the Tokyo District Court made the landmark decision to require Nichia to pay him ¥20 billion ($190 million), equivalent to approximately half the profit the company could earn from his invention before its patents expired in 2010. The amount of compensation was subsequently reduced to ¥844 million ($8 million) by the Tokyo High Court in January 2005. Shuji Nakamura was offered a professorship at the University of California after he left Nichia, but the court decision made considerable waves in Japanese corporate circles.[44]

Question

- Is it necessary for Japanese companies to reward individual achievement in order to stimulate the country's collective innovation?

encouraged selective joint ventures with western companies to promote its embryonic electronics industry, whereas South Korea supported its giant conglomerates (*chaebol*), including Hyundai, Samsung, Daewoo, and LG, in the electronics, motor vehicle, and other industries.

This collective approach to industrial development has encouraged cooperation rather than competition in internal markets, and these markets are often highly regulated. Nevertheless, until the end of the 1980s in Japan and the Asian financial crisis (1997–8) elsewhere in the region, East Asian companies were often highly successful in international markets – and a number of them remain so. Their success was based on high productivity, advanced technology, efficient work practices, and continuous improvements in quality (*kaizen* in Japanese) rather than low costs and competitive prices. In the more difficult conditions of the 1990s, however, the 'soft' bank finance that had enabled them to expand rapidly became a liability as companies such as Nissan, Mitsubishi, and Daewoo Motors struggled to manage their vast debts, excess capacity, and poor profitability. Although the East Asian model has a number of apparent similarities with the European model, and especially France, the underlying cultural differences are significant and the East Asian countries rely much more on companies rather than the state to provide social protection, leaving 'public' services such as health and higher education largely to the private sector.

6.6.5 Socio-economic models in other regions of the world

A number of other candidates might be considered as alternative socio-economic models. Two major regions of the world have thus far been excluded from the above analysis: Africa and Latin America. Recent developments might also suggest the possibility that the experiences of China and India are sufficiently distinct to represent new variants of the Asian model. The case for Latin America, China, and India is considered in this section. The countries of Africa, whilst representing a variety of different traditions and experiences, have generally followed a dependent path, drawing on the legacy of their former colonial masters or Soviet communism, or the policy prescriptions of the IMF and World Bank. Many of them are also held back by climate, disease, conflict, corruption, and poor governance (see Section 15.4). There are of course a few exceptions, but even the relative success enjoyed by countries such as South Africa, or in former times Zimbabwe, probably owes as much to their European heritage as to their own distinctive characteristics. For these reasons it is difficult to demonstrate the existence of a distinct African model.

A Latin American model?

The Latin American countries, extending from Mexico in the north to Chile and Argentina in the south, represent a coherent cultural group or civilization. The Spanish language and culture predominate, while Portuguese is influential mainly because of South America's largest country, Brazil. Descendants of their former Spanish and Portuguese colonial rulers intermingle with native American Indians and descendants of black African slaves to form a unique cultural blend. Many of the Latin American countries achieved independence during the first quarter of the nineteenth century, but Spanish and Portuguese political power was soon replaced by economic dependence on Britain and later the United States. During this 'neo-colonial' period their economies became increasingly dependent on exports of basic agricultural commodities to Europe and North America. Export dependence was often accompanied by economic liberalism, enforced by British and American business and financial institutions and by local authoritarian leaders.

The Latin American economies turned inward after the Great Depression that followed the Wall Street Crash of 1929, pursuing domestic industrialization and import substitution. High protective tariffs remained until liberal economic policies re-emerged in the latter years of the twentieth century, notably in Chile from the 1970s onwards, but also more gradually in Argentina, Mexico, Brazil, and elsewhere. It is probably fair to say that each change of direction reflected the influence of external factors rather than an indigenous socio-economic model. The most recent liberalization is a response to global competition and US intervention, but the Latin American economies have struggled to maintain financial stability while opening up their economies. Although Latin American economic development has followed a dependent path and these countries have experienced difficulties in harnessing economic change, the recent emergence of Mexico and Brazil as international economic players suggests that it may be timely to consider the possibility of an embryonic Latin American model.

A Chinese model?

The gradual opening of the Chinese economy from 1978 after Deng Xiaoping came to power has enabled China to achieve an unprecedented rate of economic growth. The question is: has this success resulted from a unique Chinese model or from economic liberalization? Three main elements are present in China: its distinctive culture, its communist political system, and its embrace of economic liberalism. If each of these elements has helped to produce the country's economic success, there may indeed be a distinctive Chinese model. However, it is not at all certain that the three elements are equally responsible. Communist state control may in fact be more of a hindrance than a help in economic development, except to the extent that gradual relaxation of state control may have helped to avoid the chaotic inflationary conditions experienced by Russia and some of the other former communist states of Central and Eastern Europe.

In cultural terms, the Chinese share the common high power distance and collectivism of other Asian societies, but have a noticeably longer-term time orientation and are surprisingly less risk averse than their Asian neighbours. These characteristics almost certainly play a significant role in Chinese economic development. At the moment, however, the most significant factor accounting for their recent economic fortunes appears to be economic liberalism. As their economy develops and communist political control diminishes, it is possible that a specific Chinese model may emerge.

An Indian model?

India began to turn a corner in its recent economic development after the reforms introduced by prime minister Narasimha Rao and his finance minister, Dr Manmohan Singh, in 1991. Since then, India's economic growth has been significant, averaging 6.3 per cent per annum from 1992–2011, but always in the shadow of China's more spectacular economic performance. A major difference, however, has been the development of India's computer software and IT services industries as opposed to China's greater reliance on manufacturing. The early stages of India's modern industrialization occurred in the late nineteenth century under British rule when its textile industry began to challenge Britain's dominant position in world markets, though in other respects colonial rule and the traditional Hindu caste system have had more of a restraining effect on India's recent economic development. The caste system, which dates back many centuries, represented an orderly hierarchy in the labour market, where higher castes had positions of authority, middle castes conducted business, and lower castes performed more menial tasks in India's predominantly rural economy.

The British Raj (or 'rule') gave way to Indian independence in 1947, which was followed by a period of socialist-inspired economic planning or '*dirigisme*'. Active government intervention helped to improve India's poor infrastructure, but industrial development was based largely on inward-looking protectionist policies and import substitution. These policies left India with burgeoning public debt, rising inflation, and exchange rate instability. They also acted as a restraint on private enterprise. The 1991 and subsequent economic reforms have helped to create a more enterprising environment, though India still suffers from a bureaucratic administrative culture that is a remnant of both the British Raj and the hierarchical caste system. In this sense, India's past probably acts more as a constraint than as a contributory factor in its recent economic success and, as in China, rapid growth seems to stem mainly from liberal economic reforms. At the present time, therefore, the designation of a specific Indian socio-economic model may seem unwarranted.

6.7 Implications for business in the global economy

Culture clearly has important implications for the way business is conducted in different parts of the world. Culture affects the behaviour of consumers, the operation of labour markets, relationships between firms, the nature of corporate governance, and through its influence on institutions, the entire functioning of an economy. As political and economic barriers between countries are gradually taken down, globalization allows culture to flow across borders. This brings both convergence and diversity of cultures. However, whereas the outer layers of culture may adapt and evolve, it is by no means certain that the deeper layers are similarly affected. This is particularly evident in the main socio-economic models that have developed in the more established economies of North America, Western Europe, and East Asia. Even in the emerging economies of Asia, Latin America, and Central and Eastern Europe, where distinctive models are more difficult to discern, the complex mix of history, culture, and other factors may yet lead them to produce their own unique models or variants of existing models.

The problem with the above thesis is that recent successes in the emerging economies appear to stem from the introduction of liberal economic policies. To some extent this is also true in Germany, which has been struggling to reform its high-cost system of regulation and social protection, and in Japan and South Korea, where recession and corporate insolvency have forced them to introduce liberal market reforms. The lesson from each of these cases appears to be that free-market policies work better than other forms of capitalism – that the Anglo-Saxon model is pre-eminent. This conclusion seems to be reinforced by the success of 'Anglo-Saxon' business practices which have been increasingly adopted by multinational enterprises in the global economy, but has to be questioned in the light of the international financial crisis and economic slowdown of 2008–9 and the subsequent slow recovery in North America and Western Europe.

Despite the ascendancy of the free-market approach in recent years, it is important to remember that the way policies, laws, and markets work in different countries depends on the institutional environment in each country, which in turn is influenced by a country's distinctive culture. This means that free-market principles do not work in exactly the same way in China or India as they do in the United States. Similarly, organizational culture will inevitably affect the way Anglo-Saxon methods work in each individual company. It is therefore likely that there is no uniquely right way to run a country – or, for that matter, a company. Each country's or company's success will depend on a combination of factors, not all of which are within its own control.

Summary

Culture is an important element of the business environment. In its broadest sense, it is the complex set of values, beliefs, ideas, and social interactions which distinguish one society or group of people from another. When describing a large international group with common cultural characteristics, the term 'civilization' is sometimes used. Culture has been likened to the layers of an onion: as the outer, more superficial layers are peeled away, a deeper core of values and beliefs is revealed. Language, religion, social structure and attitudes, education, and inspiration and creativity are important elements of culture. Cultural differences may be analysed by focusing on the key dimensions of culture; these include the importance of context, time orientation, power distance, individualism and collectivism, masculinity and femininity, and uncertainty avoidance. Cultural issues are often controversial, invoking fears of cultural homogenization, linguistic dominance, and clashes between religions, or claims about the economic superiority of a particular cultural group. Culture also has an important influence on a country's institutions, its laws, political and economic systems, and business practices. These differences, and the effect they have on the way business operates in different countries, have led researchers to identify a number of distinct socio-economic models. The most generally recognized models include the Anglo-Saxon, European, and East Asian models.

Discussion questions

1. How useful are the iceberg and culture onion models as explanations of the main characteristics of culture?

2. In what ways does culture help to determine a country's formal and informal institutions?

3. To what extent is language a distinguishing feature of culture?

4. In what ways do monochronic and polychronic time orientations manifest themselves in countries with these cultural characteristics?

5. To what extent might culture provide an explanation for economic development?

6. Do you agree that multinational enterprises should adopt an Anglo-Saxon approach in order to be successful in the modern global economy?

Suggested assignment topics

1. With reference to a particular country, investigate the extent to which language represents a barrier to the development of the country's international business.

2. Undertake a cultural assessment of a specific country and investigate the extent to which business practice corresponds with this cultural assessment in the country concerned.

3. Choose a specific country that can be categorized under either the Anglo-Saxon, European, or East Asian model and investigate the extent to which this model provides an accurate description of the country concerned, bearing in mind any changes that have occurred in the country's socio-economic environment in recent years.

 Case study: The Renault-Nissan Alliance – a cultural enigma

The alliance between the French car manufacturer, Renault, and its Japanese counterpart, Nissan, was formed in 1999. Renault initially bought a 36.8 per cent equity stake in Nissan in return for Nissan's 15 per cent non-voting stake in Renault. Renault later increased its investment in Nissan to 44.4 per cent. The alliance is in effect a joint venture between the two companies, given the cross-shareholdings between them, but it is not a merger; each company remains legally separate with its own brands and market share, but the alliance is coordinated by a holding company, Renault-Nissan BV, a company registered under Dutch law. The alliance gave Renault management control of Nissan and, since 2005, the two companies have had a single chief executive, Carlos Ghosn.

The remarkable aspect of the alliance is the very different backgrounds of the two companies. Renault had been state owned and during the 1980s the company underwent major restructuring to improve its performance. In 1996, it was largely privatized, with the French government retaining a minority shareholding. Nissan, on the other hand, had reached the peak of its international success by the end of the 1980s, producing high-specification vehicles at its highly productive, state-of-the-art factories. The main things the two companies had in common were their status as symbols of national pride (especially in the case of Renault) and their roots in their respective national cultures.

(continued...)

By 1999, however, when the alliance was formed, Renault had become more adventurous, producing imaginative cars and enjoying its new-found commercial freedom in the private sector, while Nissan – still a highly productive company – had built up debts of ¥2,000 billion (then about $15 billion), a legacy of its reliance on loan capital to finance its domestic and international expansion. The alliance gave Renault an opportunity to venture into Nissan's markets, share technology and design skills, and achieve cost savings using common suppliers. Nissan was given a rescue line to allow it to return to profitability. Both companies became more significant players in the global car market, with their joint sales placing them close behind the market leaders, Toyota and Volkswagen, by sales revenue in 2012.

Carlos Ghosn was brought in as chief executive of Nissan in 1999 by Renault's long-standing chairman and chief executive, Louis Schweitzer. Schweitzer had transformed Renault into a successful company and Ghosn was expected to turn Nissan's fortunes round after the alliance was formed. Ghosn was remarkably successful in achieving this goal, helping to reduce Nissan's enormous debt and excess capacity, cut costs, and return the company to profitability by 2001. He then set about introducing new models. More recently, the alliance has been bringing its partners closer together, sharing technical expertise, production platforms, logistics, marketing, and information systems as well as the purchasing of components and other supplies. It has also been using its management and organizational synergies to form strategic alliances with Daimler of Germany and AvtoVAZ of Russia and when setting up new production facilities in countries such as Brazil, India, and Morocco.

The Renault-Nissan alliance represents a cultural conundrum. Carlos Ghosn's own cultural background is intriguing: he was born in Brazil to Lebanese parents, but educated in France. At Nissan, he gained a reputation as 'le cost killer', a curious amalgam of French and Anglo-Saxon cultures, both linguistically and socio-economically. Using an approach more commonly associated with the Anglo-Saxon model, Ghosn was able to build on the success of a French company to transform a quintessentially Japanese company. Surprisingly, he encountered as much praise as resistance from Japanese citizens when closing Nissan plants in Japan and making workers redundant, something normally alien to Japan's collective corporate culture. At the very least, the Japanese were starting to re-evaluate their conventional ideas. Japan had by this time already experienced a decade of economic stagnation and falling corporate profitability, and there was a growing realization that difficult times required drastic measures.[45]

Case study questions

1. Why did Nissan, along with other Japanese companies, get into difficulties during the 1990s?

2. In what ways have both Nissan and Renault benefited from alliance synergies since 1999?

3. Why do you think Renault and Nissan have decided to keep the two companies separate, despite their joint overall management?

4. Explain the differences and similarities between Japanese and French cultures in relation to the main dimensions of culture.

5. To what extent are Japanese companies in general likely to follow Nissan's example in leaving some of the country's conventional business practices behind?

6. Why do you think Carlos Ghosn decided to adopt elements of an Anglo-Saxon approach to the transformation of Nissan?

7. Does the experience of turning around Nissan's fortunes suggest that all companies should adopt an Anglo-Saxon approach if they want to be successful in the modern international business environment?

8. In the light of the Renault-Nissan alliance, to what extent is it still possible to speak of an East Asian or European socio-economic model?

Notes

1. Barsoux, J.-L., and Lawrence, P. (1991), 'The making of a French manager', *Harvard Business Review*, vol. 69, issue 4, pp. 58–60, 62–4, and 66–7.

2. Main sources: Barsoux, J.-L., and Lawrence, P. (1991), 'The making of a French manager', *Harvard Business Review*, vol. 69, issue 4, pp. 58–60, 62–4, and 66–7; *The Economist* (19 November 2011), 'The French way of work'; *Business Insider* (23 November 2011), 'Here's the real reason why France's economy is worse than Germany's'; and *Times Higher Education* (6 February 2013), 'Grandes écoles, grand designs: France told to think global'.

3. Hofstede, G. (2001), *Culture's Consequences: Comparing Values, Behaviours, Institutions and Organizations Across Nations*, Sage Publications, p. 9.

4. Sassoon, D. (2006), *The Culture of the Europeans from 1800 to the Present*, Harper Collins Publishers, p. xiii.

5. The iceberg model of culture is usually attributed to the Canadian sociologist, Guy Rocher: Rocher, G. (1969), *Introduction à la sociologie générale*, Hurtubise, vol. 1.

6. *The Washington Times*: editorial (7 April 2009), 'Obama takes a bow'.

7. Hofstede, G. (2001), *Culture's Consequences: Comparing Values, Behaviours, Institutions and Organizations Across Nations*, Sage Publications, p. 11.

8. Trompenaars, F., and Hampden-Turner, C. (1997), *Riding the Waves of Culture: Understanding Cultural Diversity in Business*, Nicholas Brealey, p. 22.

9. Spencer-Oatey, H. (2008), *Culturally Speaking: Managing Rapport through Talk across Cultures*, Continuum.

10. For a useful discussion of these alternative models, see Dahl, S. (2004), 'Intercultural Research: The Current State of Knowledge', Middlesex University Discussion Paper No. 26, 12 January.

11. See North, D. C. (1990), *Institutions, Institutional Change and Economic Performance*, Cambridge University Press.

12. European Commission (28 June 2012), Application of Directive 2004/25/EC on takeover bids, COM (2012) 347 final.

13. Janson, T. (2002), *Speak: A Short History of Languages*, Oxford University Press, p. 240.

14. Janson, T. (2002), *Speak: A Short History of Languages*, Oxford University Press, pp. 240–1.

15. Mead, W. R. (2006), 'God's Country?', *Foreign Affairs*, vol. 85, no. 5, September/October, pp. 24–43.

16. Butler Pass, D. (25 January 2013), 'In Obama's inauguration speech, a new American religion', *The Washington Post*.

17. The Pew Forum on Religious Life (7 November 2012), 'How the faithful voted: 2012, preliminary analysis', Pew Research Center.

18. For an extensive discussion of family and social structures, see Todd, E. (1988), *Explanation of Ideology: Family Structures and Social Systems*, Wiley-Blackwell.

19. See, for example, Braudel, F. (1995), *A History of Civilizations*, Penguin Books.

20. See Huntington, S. P. (2002), *The Clash of Civilizations and the Remaking of World Order*, The Free Press or Hoge, J. P., and Huntington, S. P. (2010), *The Clash of Civilizations? The Debate*, Foreign Affairs.

21. Huntington's ideas were first published in *Foreign Affairs*: Huntington, S. P. (1993), 'The Clash of Civilizations?' *Foreign Affairs*, vol. 72, no. 3, pp. 22–49, then expanded in Huntington, S. P. (2002), *The Clash of Civilizations and the Remaking of World Order*, The Free Press.

22. Huntington's *Foreign Affairs* article was in fact written in response to Fukuyama: Fukuyama, F. (2012), *The End of History and the Last Man*, Penguin (first published in 1993).

23. Hall, E. T. (1988), *The Silent Language*, Bantam Doubleday Dell.

24. Hall, E. T. (1988), *The Hidden Dimension*, Bantam Doubleday Dell, p. 162.

25. Trompenaars, F., and Hampden-Turner, C. (1997), *Riding the Waves of Culture: Understanding Cultural Diversity in Business*, Nicholas Brealey, pp. 123–4.

26. Hofstede, G. (2001), *Culture's Consequences: Comparing Values, Behaviours, Institutions and Organizations Across Nations*, Sage Publications.

27. The World Values Survey can be found at http://www.worldvaluessurvey.org/, but Hofstede's dimensions of culture are discussed in Hofstede, G., Hofstede, G. J., and Minkov, M. (2010), *Cultures and Organizations: Software of the Mind*, McGraw-Hill.

28. Guonan, M., and Wang, Y. (2010) Bank for International Settlements Working Paper No. 312: China's High Saving Rate: Myth and Reality, Table 1, p. 5.

29. Guonan, M., and Wang, Y. (2010), Bank for International Settlements Working Paper No. 312: China's High Saving Rate: Myth and Reality, p. 2.

30. Trompenaars, F., and Hampden-Turner, C. (2012), *Riding the Waves of Culture: Understanding Cultural Diversity in Business*, Nicholas Brealey.

31. Janson, T. (2002), *Speak: A Short History of Languages*, Oxford University Press, pp. 235–6.

32. Cowen, T. (2004), *Creative Destruction: How Globalization is Changing the World's Cultures*, Princeton University Press, p. 7.

33. Cowen, T. (2004), *Creative Destruction: How Globalization is Changing the World's Cultures*, Princeton University Press, pp. 34–7.

34. Florida, R. (2002), *The Rise of the Creative Class: And How It's Transforming Work, Leisure, Community and Everyday Life*, Basic Books.

35. Florida, R. (2005), *The Flight of the Creative Class: The New Global Competition for Talent*, Harper Collins.

36. Janson, T. (2002), *Speak: A Short History of Languages*, Oxford University Press, p. 260.

37. National Centre for Languages Report (2005), *Talking World Class: The Impact of Language Skills on the UK Economy*.

38. Weber, M. (2012), *The Protestant Ethic and the Spirit of Capitalism*, CreateSpace Independent Publishing Platform, originally published in 1905.

39. Hampden-Turner, C., and Trompenaars, F. (1997), *Mastering the Infinite Game*, Capstone Publishing.

40. Hall, P. A., and Soskice, D. (2001), *Varieties of Capitalism: The Institutional Foundations of Comparative Advantage*, Oxford University Press.

41. Amable, B. (2003), *The Diversity of Modern Capitalism*, Oxford University Press.

42. Albert, M. (1993), *Capitalism Against Capitalism*, Whurr, translated from the original French edition (Editions du Seuil, 1991).

43. Note that Iceland has now applied for full EU membership.

44. Sources: *Financial Times* (16 February 2004), 'Japan must reward bright sparks'; and Taplin, R. (2007), 'Transforming intellectual property in Japan', Thomson Scientific newsletter.

45. Main sources: 'The Renault Nissan Alliance', http://www.renault.com; 'Renault-Nissan Alliance', http://www.nissan-global.com; http://blog.alliance-renault-nissan.com; Magee, D. (2003), *Turnaround: How Carlos Ghosn Rescued Nissan*, Harper Collins; *Financial Times* (19 January 2004), 'Carlos Ghosn: A powerful motor for change'; *Financial Times* (28 March 2004), 'Renault's long shot romps home'; and BBC News (11 January 2012), 'Nissan-Renault alliance in sales record in tough year'.

Suggestions for further reading

Major works on culture in an international business context

Hofstede, G. (2001), *Culture's Consequences: Comparing Values, Behaviors, Institutions, and Organizations Across Nations*, Sage Publications

Hofstede, G., Hofstede, G. J., and Minkov, M. (2010), *Culture and Organizations: Software of the Mind*, McGraw-Hill

Trompenaars, F., and Hampden-Turner, C. (2012), *Riding the Waves of Culture: Understanding Diversity in Global Business*, Nicholas Brealey

A study of the impact of globalization on culture

Cowen, T. (2004), *Creative Destruction: How Globalization is Changing the World's Cultures*, Princeton University Press

An analysis of the role of civilizations in the modern world

Hoge, J. F., and Huntington, S. P. (2010), *The Clash of Civilizations? The Debate*, Foreign Affairs.

Huntington, S. P. (2002), *The Clash of Civilizations and the Remaking of World Order*, The Free Press

On institutions and their implications for economic performance

North, D. C. (2010), *Understanding the Process of Economic Change*, Princeton University Press

On the varieties of capitalism and socio-economic models

Amable, B. (2003), *The Diversity of Modern Capitalism*, Oxford University Press

Hall, P. A., and Soskice, D. (2001), *Varieties of Capitalism: The Institutional Foundations of Comparative Advantage*, Oxford University Press

Hancké, B. (2009), *Debating Varieties of Capitalism: A Reader*, Oxford University Press

Take your learning further: Online Resource Centre
http://www.oxfordtextbooks.co.uk/orc/harrison2e/
Visit the Online Resource Centre that accompanies this book to enrich your understanding of Chapter 6: Contrasting Cultures and Business Models. Among other resources explore web links and keep up to date with the latest developments in the area.

Key terms introduced in this chapter

Achievement culture A cultural orientation which attaches importance to what people have accomplished.

Anglo-Saxon model The socio-economic model found mainly in the English-speaking countries, emphasizing the importance of free markets.

Ascriptive culture A cultural orientation which is concerned with status conferred by birth, age, gender, or connections.

Civilization The largest grouping of people sharing common cultural characteristics.

Collectivism A cultural dimension where social cohesion and group loyalty are more important than the needs of the individual.

Communitarianism See collectivism.

Creative class A group of people whose work or other activities involve creativity, freedom of expression, individuality, and the desire to make a difference.

Culture In its broader context, culture is the complex set of values, beliefs, ideas, and social interactions which distinguish one society or group of people from another.

Culture onion A cultural concept which represents deeper and more superficial layers of culture as the inner and outer layers of an onion.

Diffuse culture A cultural orientation where the whole person is involved in forming a business relationship.

East Asian model The socio-economic model found in Japan, South Korea, Taiwan, and other East Asian countries, emphasizing the importance of coordination between firms, employers and employees, and government and industry.

Emotional culture A cultural orientation where people consider human emotions are an acceptable and natural part of business negotiation.

European model The socio-economic model found in continental Europe, associated with a social market economy.

Femininity A cultural dimension where values of modesty, social responsibility, cooperation, and good working relationships are predominant.

High-context culture A cultural dimension where the context in which communication takes place is more important than the words themselves and the meaning is conveyed more through the context than the message.

High power distance A cultural dimension where relationships are formal and hierarchical, and authoritarian or paternalistic leadership is seen as caring.

High uncertainty avoidance A cultural dimension characterized by people who are risk averse, feel threatened by uncertain situations, and create rules and procedures to minimize uncertainties.

Iceberg model of culture A cultural concept which distinguishes between values and beliefs which are hidden beneath the surface and behaviour, customs, and practices which are visible above the surface.

Individualism A cultural dimension which emphasizes the importance of ambition, personal achievement, and individual rights and responsibilities.

Indulgence A cultural dimension describing societies where citizens are allowed freedom to indulge their desires and enjoy life.

Long-term orientation A cultural dimension where future rewards and persistence are highly valued.

Low-context culture A culture in which the context is unimportant and the message is explicit in itself.

Low power distance A cultural dimension where relationships are informal and consultative, and there is a high degree of equality.

Low uncertainty avoidance A cultural dimension characterized by people who are willing to take risks and feel comfortable with uncertainty.

Masculinity A cultural dimension where values of assertiveness, competitiveness, ambition, and achievement are predominant.

Mediterranean model The socio-economic model found in the countries of southern Europe, associated with a regulated market economy and state invention in industry.

Monochronic time orientation A cultural dimension where people compartmentalize time and schedule one thing at a time.

Neutral culture A cultural orientation where people take a clinical view of business objectives and efficiency is paramount.

Nordic model The socio-economic model found in the Nordic countries, associated with a social market economy and collective negotiation at a national level.

Particularism A cultural orientation where the obligations of particular relationships or circumstances are given priority over general rules.

Polychronic time orientation A cultural dimension where people see the past, present, and future as part of a single time frame and keep several options going at once.

Restraint A cultural dimension describing societies where social control and social norms impose restrictions on individual freedoms and enjoyment.

Rhine model The socio-economic model found in Germany and its neighbouring countries, associated with a social market economy and political and industrial consensus.

Sequential time orientation See Monochromic time orientation.

Short-term orientation A cultural dimension where emphasis is placed on past and present values such as respect for tradition, social obligations, and saving 'face'.

Social market economy An economy where resources are allocated by a combination of market forces and social intervention.

Socio-economic model An economic system characterized by its social and political institutions representative of a particular group of countries.

Specific culture A cultural orientation where the main focus is on the details of the product or contract.

Synchronic time orientation See Polychronic time orientation.

Universalism A cultural orientation where there is a belief that some things are always right and must be observed at all times.

Business Ethics and Corporate Responsibility

Chapter learning outcomes

On completion of this chapter the reader should be able to:

- Apply ethical concepts to the analysis of business decisions and practices
- Evaluate alternative ethical positions as a basis for personal decision making in a business context
- Analyse the ethical basis for and the practical implications of corporate social responsibility
- Determine the appropriateness of alternative responses and policies towards the protection of the natural environment
- Evaluate the relative merits of voluntary and legal approaches to the promotion of ethical behaviour in business

Opening scenario: Cadbury

Cadbury is a British confectionery manufacturer whose origins date back to the early nineteenth century. In 1824 John Cadbury opened a shop in Bull Street, Birmingham, selling chocolate products, then a small factory making drinking chocolate and cocoa in 1831. In 1879 the factory moved to a new greenfield site which the company named Bournville, just south of Birmingham, where its main UK manufacturing operations remain to this day. However, after initial resistance, Cadbury's directors finally succumbed to a takeover bid by the US food giant, Kraft Foods, in February 2010 and Kraft split its international operations into two separate companies in October 2012, placing Cadbury with its demerged European arm, renamed Mondelēz International.

The takeover raised questions about the merits of the UK's liberal Anglo-Saxon takeover market, but the UK government resisted pressures to step in to prevent or influence the takeover, either to maintain British ownership of a quintessentially British company or to protect jobs in UK manufacturing. There was also tension between shareholder interests and the interests of the employees, suppliers, and other **stakeholders**. Kraft's takeover bid was essentially hostile, initially opposed both by Cadbury's directors and by its workforce and trade unions, though the directors later reluctantly recommended the takeover to the company's shareholders. It is worth noting that Cadbury's chairman, Roger Carr, said he felt obliged to recommend the takeover because of his duty to act in the interests of Cadbury's shareholders (the **shareholder view**). He also recognized that the takeover would inevitably lead to job losses, especially at the company's headquarters (tension with the **stakeholder view**).

Cadbury is no stranger to the ethical issues facing business decision makers. The company moved to its Bournville site in the late nineteenth century in order to create a pleasant environment for its workers, in sharp contrast to prevailing factory conditions in Victorian England. The Cadbury family were Quakers and held strong beliefs about social justice and the need for social reform. Initially, the company built houses for its key workers, but later bought more of the surrounding land and built an entire village, to be shared by its workers and the local community. The houses had large gardens, unlike most housing in industrial areas at the time, together with a variety of facilities such as shops, schools, sports fields, and almshouses for retired workers. The Bournville village and Cadbury factory can still be seen today, though its garden environment is now surrounded by Birmingham's sprawling conurbation.

The Cadbury family's benevolence towards its workers and the local community was motivated by powerful religious beliefs and was accompanied by a paternalistic concern, including compulsory prayers, Bible readings, and strict lifestyle requirements, that would seem intrusive to modern workers but was not untypical of social reformers at that time. Cadbury's social concern was rare among nineteenth-century British industrialists, but it was not unique. Other examples of company villages from the same period can be found at Port Sunlight on the Wirral, built by Lever Brothers, at Saltaire near Bradford, built by Titus Salt, and at James Reckitt's Garden Village in Hull. These industrial pioneers were inspired by a similar religious zeal and Salt introduced cleaner technology into his factory to reduce the terrible smoke and river pollution that was devastating the health of workers and communities in Britain's industrial towns and cities. Ethical concerns such as these, whilst different in some respects, are just as real today. This chapter explores the ethical principles underlying modern business practices and corporate governance and evaluates the arguments for **corporate social responsibility** and concern for the natural environment.[1]

7.1 Ethics and business

At the heart of business ethics is the question 'What is the purpose of business activity?' At first glance, it might seem reasonable to suggest that business is about making income or profit for the owner. On reflection, it is clear that the business owner's role is a means rather than an end. The purpose of business activity is to provide goods and services to satisfy people's wants and needs. There is therefore a social purpose behind business activity. In order to achieve this social purpose, people organize themselves into businesses of various kinds. Business owners take risks, and their businesses employ workers, borrow money, compete with rival firms to attract customers, and engage in a number of other activities. Each of these activities involves responsibilities towards other people or towards society as a whole. Some of the responsibilities may be legally enforceable, such as the rights of employees or consumers, but even if they are not, what is regarded as acceptable behaviour may be determined by the ethical standards of a particular group or society – or in some cases by universal ethical principles.

In this way, ethics are an important element both of the internal organization of a business and of its external environment. It is therefore surprising that the study of ethics does not always form an essential part of business education – the study of business and its environment. This is not to say that there is a single view of business ethics or of the nature of a business's responsibility towards its owners or other stakeholders. However, it does mean that there is an ethical dimension to business and the business environment. Ethical values are clearly crucial to our understanding of what this responsibility may entail. These values may include traditional moral virtues such as honesty, integrity, trust, and fairness, or may simply be what is acceptable in a particular context or community.

Of course, in a market economy economic agents are primarily motivated by self-interest: consumers want goods or services that provide value for money in meeting their requirements,

Practical insight 7.1:   Bankers' bonuses

One of the ethical issues to arise out of the international financial crisis of 2008 was the question as to whether large bonus payments had created the incentive for investment bankers to take excessive risks, possibly contributing towards the financial crisis. This concern has continued even after the crisis has abated as the bonus culture remains embedded in many of the institutions involved – in some cases regardless of the success of a particular investment strategy or a bank's overall performance. Bank senior executives often claim that large bonuses are necessary to attract the best people, but public concern is not assuaged by these arguments. The ethical tension is not only around the apparent disparity between the earnings of investment bankers and those of most other people, but also because of the disconnection between the rewards earned by the investment bankers (the risk takers) when things go well and the cost borne by taxpayers (the risk bearers) if governments are required to bail out an insolvent financial institution when things go wrong – an example of the problem of 'moral hazard (see Section 9.2.3).

Question

● How far should governments or the law go in regulating bank bonuses?

while producers seek to maximize the return on their investment. These activities are not mutually exclusive; they involve interaction between people and the actions of one person may very well have a beneficial or adverse effect on another person. There is therefore a mutual interdependence which relies on acceptable behaviour between the parties involved. Some would argue that the bounds of acceptable behaviour have been transgressed in the case of bankers' bonuses (see Practical Insight 7.1).

Marxists would take a more extreme position on the ethical problems of market economies. Karl Marx argued that the entire market (or capitalist) system was unethical as it allowed the owners of the means of production to exploit workers by retaining the surplus created by paying them a subsistence wage below the full value of their labour. Capitalism thus created extreme inequality between the 'bourgeoisie' (the capitalist class) and the 'proletariat' (the working class).[2] Even if we take a less extreme position, there is no guarantee that the pursuit of self-interest or business success is always compatible with ethical behaviour. It might be gratifying to believe that the 'good guy' always wins in the end, but this does not invariably appear to be true – except perhaps in the religious sense that virtue is rewarded in a future life. What is clear, however, is that many of the decisions we make, in business or everyday life, have ethical implications of one kind or another.

7.2 Difficult issues in business ethics

In some cases there is likely to be broad agreement on whether an action is right or wrong. For example, most people would regard theft of business property or fraud and other forms financial dishonesty as morally wrong. However, whilst some people may regard a little extravagance when incurring business expenses as morally acceptable, others may not. This issue received much public attention over concerns about the expenses claims of British members of parliament during 2009–10. Cultural differences sometimes present even starker contrasts between ethical values. Nepotism may be quite acceptable in a culture where loyalty to family and friends is highly valued, whereas strict adherence to equality of opportunity may be required in a more individualistic culture. The following are examples of cases where the ethical position may be unclear when considering alternative perspectives.

Universal standards of business practice

To what extent should a business adopt the same ethical standards wherever it operates in the world? To begin to answer this question we need to consider whether ethical standards are absolute or relative. **Ethical absolutism** describes a set of ethical values that are considered to be right regardless of the context. **Ethical relativism** refers to ethical values that vary according to the context. Is it wrong, for example, for a business executive to accept personal gifts (or 'bribes') under any circumstances? Does it depend on the type or size of gift or on the context in which it is given? Is it right for a multinational enterprise to employ workers under different working conditions in different countries or to take less care of the environment in a country with lax environmental regulations than in a country with strict regulations?

Clearly there is no universal agreement on the answer to these questions, though a common approach to resolving ethical difficulties is to look for the middle ground between absolutist and relativist positions. Thomas Donaldson and Thomas W. Dunfee, writers on international business ethics, argue that all organizations should respect core human values whilst at the same time allowing 'moral free space' for countries and communities to shape their own ideas of economic fairness.[3] A similar approach to defining universal minimum standards is taken by the United Nations Global Compact, in which companies are encouraged to sign up to its 'Ten Principles' concerning human rights, labour standards, the environment, and the fight against corruption.[4]

Corporate power

There has been a growing backlash against the power and influence of large business corporations in recent years. As the free-market revival and the associated 'Washington consensus' was reaching its peak towards the end of the 1990s, 'anti-globalization' protestors were becoming increasingly vociferous in their criticisms of the practices of giant corporations and their influence over the policies of governments and international institutions. Writers such as Naomi Klein caught the public imagination, arguing that business was taking over from government with its ability to influence people through the power of big international brands.[5] It has been argued that large corporations can use their vast resources to influence the policies of governments and international organizations such as the IMF or WTO – that, in effect, they set the international agenda in areas such as trade and economic development. Their multinational operations also allow them to outsource or offshore production, thereby transferring jobs to another part of the world, or to minimize their contribution to government revenues by transferring profit from high-tax to low-tax countries. Whilst these corporations are, in many ways, driving the global economy and the creation of wealth, understandable concerns arise if political and economic power is being transferred from legitimate governments to unrepresentative corporations.

The acceptance of risk

Risk is an integral part of most business activities. It can be mitigated by the limited liability of shareholders, health and safety provisions for employees, or consumer protection for customers. However, there are times when directors or employees may not be able to shelter behind the protection of corporate liability when acting on behalf of their employer or when an auditor or consultant may be held responsible for negligence despite the protection of a professional or contractual disclaimer. Such cases may hinge on the concept of what is a reasonable standard of behaviour, which is essentially an ethical concept (though it may also be a legal one). In some instances, an employee may be expected to take considerable risks when performing a task or may voluntarily take greater risks than would normally be expected. Such situations may raise the issue of what is an 'acceptable risk', given the type of work involved.

Risks may also take the form of threats to society, such as a nuclear accident, the effects of global warming, or an outbreak of BSE ('mad cow disease'), foot and mouth disease, 'bird flu', or 'swine flu', which governments and other agencies are expected to take responsibility for but often seem unable to manage effectively or to avoid (see Practical Insight 7.2).[6] The question here is the extent to which official agencies should be held responsible for events that are, in principle, avoidable but whose occurrence may be difficult to predict with any degree of accuracy.

Practical insight 7.2:   Rising sea levels

The global mean sea level has apparently risen by 10 to 20 centimetres over the last hundred years and by 3.2 millimetres per annum since the early 1990s. Rising sea levels are the result of increases in the earth's surface temperature, about 80 per cent of which is absorbed by the oceans. Higher sea temperatures lead to water expansion and the melting of glaciers and polar ice caps, resulting in rising sea levels.[7] This is a growing problem for regions that are close to sea level, such as much of the Netherlands and Bangladesh, Egypt's densely populated Nile Delta, the Maldives in the Indian Ocean, or the historic city of Venice.

Question

- On the assumption that global warming is mainly caused by greenhouse gas emissions which are the result of human activity, to what extent do governments, organizations, and individuals have a responsibility to change their behaviour or take alternative action to prevent the adverse consequences of rising sea levels?

7.3 Concepts in business ethics

7.3.1 Value systems

Values provide the basis for ethical behaviour. The two main approaches to the evaluation of ethical behaviour are the *teleological* and *deontological* approaches. Each of these approaches provides an alternative value system as a basis for judging whether an action is ethical or not. The two approaches and their ethical implications are now discussed.

Teleological or consequentialist theories

An ethical principle which holds that an action is morally right if the outcome or consequence of the action is desirable is known as a **consequentialist** or **teleological principle** (from the Greek word for 'goal' or 'end': *telos*). Thus, the consequence or outcome provides the justification for the action; the end justifies the means. Two examples of the teleological approach are '**egoism**' and '**utilitarianism**'.

Egoism

An action is treated as morally right if its consequences are desirable for the individual taking the action. Desirable consequences may include short-term desires as well as long-term interests. Acting in one's own self-interest is not necessarily the same as selfishness as, for example, a company may donate to a good cause because the directors believe it will generate good publicity, yet the action is not entirely selfish since it also benefits the good cause. Adam Smith (1723–90), one of the founders of free-market economics, argued that individual self-interest was generally good for society as market forces helped to bring the interests of producers and consumers into line with each other. Actions which lead to outcomes that are beneficial to society as well as to the individual concerned are sometimes described as 'enlightened self-interest' (or 'enlightened egoism').

Utilitarianism

An action is treated as morally right if it results in the greatest good for the greatest number of people – that is, greater good than any alternative action. Utilitarianism concerns the maximization of utility, where utility describes the satisfaction that people derive from consuming 'goods' – things that bring pleasure, happiness, or some other physical, psychological, or even spiritual benefit. This theory is associated with the British philosophers, Jeremy Bentham (1748–1832) and John Stuart Mill (1806–73), and has had a huge influence on classical and neoclassical economics over the last two centuries. In mainstream neoclassical economics the maximization of society's welfare (or total utility) is the goal of economic activity and this is achieved when perfectly competitive markets are in general equilibrium. On a utilitarian basis, it may also be possible to justify the use of animal testing in medical research or a progressive tax system that taxes the rich in order to provide greater benefits to the poor. The US-led invasion of Libya in 2011 may be justifiable on similar grounds if one accepts that it helped to prevent a greater wrong. Indeed, utilitarian principles can be observed in many of the policies associated with the Anglo-Saxon model.

Deontological or non-consequentialist theories

An ethical principle which holds that an action is morally right if it is based on moral obligations or duties is known as a **non-consequentialist** or **deontological principle** (from the Greek word for 'duty': *deon*). In this case, the consequence of the action is unimportant provided that the person taking the action has a moral obligation to do so. Moral duties may be derived from human reason or from religious beliefs. Deontological principles generally relate to rights or justice.

Rights principles

The idea of moral rights in relation to human beings was first developed as an ethical concept by the German philosopher, Immanuel Kant (1724–1804). Kant described the moral **rights principle** as a 'categorical imperative' (a moral law or law of nature), which could be expressed in the statement 'I ought never to act except in such a way that I can also will that my maxim should become a universal law'.[8] For Kant moral rights were about the right way to behave, but this also involved a duty of consideration for others. In a modern context, the emphasis has shifted towards the concept of human rights, with the focus on entitlements rather than duties, but even in this context the protection of human rights places a duty on all of us to respect the rights of others. The concept of human rights is enshrined in the United Nations Universal Declaration of Human Rights, adopted in 1948.[9] It has also been applied in a variety of other ways to describe the 'rights' of the mother or of the unborn child in the debate on abortion, or the 'right' to take one's own life in the context of euthanasia, though these usages are clearly more controversial.

An alternative view has been proposed by W. D. Ross, who argues that moral duties may be conditional or prima facie rather than absolute – that is, duties that must be respected unless overruled by a higher duty.[10] Thus, for example, a police officer may have a public duty to apprehend a criminal, but, if doing so involves a car chase that endangers the lives of other people, the duty to protect human life may override the duty to prevent crime.

Justice principles

Justice principles concern fairness, equality, and respect for the rights of others. The main types of justice considered in the ethical literature are 'distributive justice', 'retributive justice', and 'compensatory justice'. Distributive justice deals with the ways in which benefits or burdens are shared between members of society. This may be based on equal shares for all or criteria such as need, effort, or contribution to society, for example. Retributive justice concerns punishment for wrongdoing. A just punishment should be based on the certainty that wrongdoing has occurred, should be proportionate to the wrongdoing and consistent across wrongdoers, and the wrongdoer should have been capable of preventing the wrongdoing. Compensatory justice requires that the person injured by a wrongful act should be compensated and, where possible, compensation should be equal to the loss suffered.

The work of the South African Truth and Reconciliation Commission at the end of the apartheid era illustrates both compensatory justice, with its emphasis on reparation and rehabilitation for the victims of human rights abuses, and retributive justice, though in this case including the possibility of amnesty as well as punishment in order to encourage reconciliation. South Africa's approach has received widespread, though not uncritical, approval. On the other hand, Zimbabwe's land reforms since 2000, involving the expropriation of white farms and their 'restoration' to black Africans, represent an altogether more problematic attempt at distributive justice. Another example is provided by the WTO agreement on the compulsory licensing of drugs (see Practical Insight 7.3).

> ## Practical insight 7.3: The WTO and the compulsory licensing of drugs
>
> The World Health Organization estimated that approximately 34 million people were living with HIV in 2011, of whom about 23 million were in sub-Saharan Africa.[11] Although there is not yet a cure for HIV/AIDS, antiretroviral drugs can alleviate the symptoms of the disease and make life more tolerable for those affected by it. These drugs have been developed and produced by the large pharmaceutical companies that are mainly based in the United States, Germany, Switzerland, the UK, and other developed countries. Because of the extensive research and development required to bring these drugs to the market, they are also quite expensive and heavily protected by patents.
>
> Some of Africa's poorest countries have challenged the pharmaceutical companies over their high prices and this has sometimes brought concessions from the companies concerned. In other cases, these countries have preferred to produce their own copies of the drugs, but this raises complex ethical and legal issues. Under the WTO agreement on intellectual property rights (Trade-Related Aspects of Intellectual Property Rights or TRIPS), local production of copied drugs is permitted, provided the local producer has tried to reach agreement with the patent owner first and failed, and provided the drugs are only sold in the country concerned or exported to countries with no local production. This is known as 'compulsory licensing'. In the case of a 'national emergency', the first stage of negotiating a voluntary licence may be bypassed, but in any event the patent owner is entitled to 'adequate remuneration'.[12]
>
> ### Questions
>
> - Is the WTO agreement justifiable on utilitarian or human rights grounds?
> - Where does it stand in relation to distributive and compensatory justice?

7.3.2 **Social contract theory**

The idea of a **social contract** as an explicit or implicit agreement between members of a society has played an important role in political and ethical theory. Early writers on social contract theory include the British philosophers, Thomas Hobbes (1588–1679) and John Locke (1632–1704), and the French philosopher, Jean-Jacques Rousseau (1712–78). Whilst Hobbes and Locke emphasized the way in which individuals give up their rights to be ruled by an absolute sovereign (Hobbes) or by democratic consent (Locke), Rousseau's idea of the social contract as an expression of the general collective will is closer to what has become the more accepted meaning of the term in modern usage.

Modern social contract theory regards a social contract as an informal agreement between members of a society concerning accepted norms of behaviour based on shared values, beliefs, and attitudes. In this sense, individuals and businesses are expected to conform to accepted standards of behaviour in order to ensure social cohesion or the general welfare of society. The social contract thus helps to create 'social capital', the benefits to society that stem from relationships, networks, social action, and community initiatives that make a society more than simply the sum of its parts. Donaldson and Dunfee have been influential in developing 'integrative social contracts theory', which distinguishes between 'hypernorms' (universal norms of behaviour) and 'community norms' (norms of behaviour within small social or cultural groups).[13] They argue that community norms are acceptable provided they do not conflict with hypernorms. If this view is accepted as a basis for business behaviour, it implies that businesses may in some respects need to adapt to different standards of behaviour in different cultural (or ethical) environments – a degree of ethical relativism that some people may find unacceptable.

7.3.3 Shareholder and stakeholder concepts

The principles behind corporate governance provide two alternative ethical perspectives on the responsibilities of a corporation and, in turn, the nature of its corporate social responsibility. Whilst the underlying issues are much older, the debate on the relative merits of the shareholder and stakeholder approaches to corporate governance began to gather momentum in the 1970s and 1980s. These two approaches and their implications for business strategy are discussed below.

Shareholder value

In 1970, the US free-market economist, Milton Friedman, caused a stir by arguing in a *New York Times Magazine* article that the social responsibility of a business was to increase its profit rather than to demonstrate concern for the wider community.[14] Friedman had in fact expressed these views earlier, though with less impact.[15] His main argument was that the purpose of a business was to make a return on the owner's investment and that, in the case of a company, this meant making profit in order to increase or maximize the value of the company's shares. If managers used the company's resources to take on wider social responsibilities, they would be acting contrary to the interests of the shareholders. Indeed, Friedman argued that such action would ultimately subvert the capitalist system by deflecting attention away from profit making and the efficient allocation of resources.

Of course, if the shareholders agreed to accept wider social responsibilities, they would be free to do so, but if this policy was designed to promote the company's image in order to increase profit, it would be motivated by self-interest (egoism) and would therefore satisfy the requirement to maximize shareholder value. This view, whilst not usually taken to its extreme, is prevalent in the Anglo-Saxon economies; a carefully argued defence of the shareholder view can be found, for example, in the work of the *Financial Times* journalist, Martin Wolf.[16] It also provides a justification for the liberal US and UK takeover rules that encourage opportunistic (and often hostile) takeovers as a means of improving corporate performance and increasing shareholder value.

Stakeholder theory

The stakeholder approach was pioneered by Edward Freeman in the 1980s.[17] Unlike the shareholder approach, where the corporation's primary responsibility is to its owners, stakeholder theory considers that an organization has a responsibility to all its stakeholders. Freeman defined a stakeholder as 'any group or individual who can affect, or is affected by, the achievement of the organization's objectives'.[18] Stakeholders can be divided into two categories: direct stakeholders may include, for example, owners or shareholders, employees, customers, suppliers, banks, and competitors; indirect stakeholders may include the government, the community, and, if one extends Freeman's definition to the entire natural world, the environment (see Figure 7.1). These sets of stakeholders are not exhaustive and may vary

Figure 7.1 Direct and indirect stakeholders

depending on the organization concerned. In some instances, the community may include the national and international community as well the local community. The continental European countries have essentially adopted a stakeholder approach to corporate govern-ance. This is illustrated by Germany's policy of 'codetermination' (*Mitbestimmung*), involving employee representatives on the supervisory board of public companies, or Sweden's con-cept of the 'negotiated economy', where government, employers, trade unions, and other stakeholder groups participate in national policy making.

Whilst the stakeholder view may have intuitive appeal, any legitimacy it has is derived from legal, ethical, and economic arguments. A company's responsibility to its shareholders is not its only legal relationship. Its relationship with employees, customers, suppliers, and banks is also a contractual one and, if it behaves anti-competitively towards its competitors, it may well be subject to legal action in this area as well. The shareholder relationship is special in that shareholders carry ultimate responsibility for the company, but each of these relation-ships involves both legal and ethical considerations. There is also a powerful economic argu-ment concerning the company's wider responsibilities towards society. This relates to the problem of market failure, which is discussed more extensively in relation to corporate social responsibility in Section 7.5. If a company's activities cause harmful effects such as pollution and the company and its customers ignore these effects, the market will fail to deal with the problem. However, if the company takes into account the 'external costs' of its activities, tak-ing action to avoid or clean up the pollution, market failure will be avoided. Of course, this can also be viewed from an ethical perspective.

A number of more specific ethical issues relate to particular stakeholders. For example, an organization has responsibilities towards its customers concerning its product quality, pro-motional activities, and pricing policies, and towards its suppliers concerning its bargaining power and trading practices. Employers also have responsibilities towards their employees in relation to equal opportunities, sexual and racial harassment, data protection, redun-dancy and dismissal, the payment of wages, and freedom of conscience. The issue of labour

> ## Practical insight 7.4: Sweat-shop labour
>
> In June 2007, a report on working conditions in four Chinese factories was published by FairPlay 2008, an international alliance of trade unions.[19] The factories had been licensed to produce Olympic-branded goods for the 2008 Olympic Games in Beijing. The report was critical of a number of their work practices, including long working hours, forced and unpaid overtime, child labour, wages below the legal minimum, and dangerous working conditions. These four factories are, of course, not alone in operating 'sweat-shop' working conditions and the International Olympic Committee is not the only respected organization to have unwittingly (or carelessly) authorized goods to be produced in such conditions. In some instances, the factories were breaking their own national laws, but, more importantly, the treatment of their workers raises serious ethical issues.
>
> Working hours do of course vary between countries and families may even encourage their children to contribute to their meagre incomes. Long working hours and cheap labour allow developing countries to compete more effectively in world markets and to exploit their otherwise minimal comparative advantages. Indeed, China's economy as a whole has benefited hugely from the production and export of cheap manufactured goods.
>
> ### Question
> - Are sweat-shop conditions simply too high a price to pay for these benefits?

standards in different parts of the world is a more controversial issue and this is discussed in Practical Insight 7.4. The responsibility to engage in fair competition, which affects customers, suppliers, and competitors, is discussed in Section 9.4 and responsibilities towards society and the environment are discussed in Sections 7.5 and 7.6.

7.4 Personal ethics in business

It may be argued that, whatever ethical position is taken with regard to the responsibilities of a business organization, each individual member of the organization has a personal responsibility to act ethically within his or her own sphere of the organization's activities. Thus, in an ethical sense, individuals should not shelter behind the organization even where legal responsibility rests with the organization. Of course, in practice, this may be difficult as many 'whistleblowers' have found when exposing the unethical practices of their employer or fellow employees. Despite the practical difficulties, it seems reasonable to suggest that ethical principles should apply to individuals as well as to organizations. The following are some of the possible positions that might be taken in relation to personal ethics.

7.4.1 Moral virtue and alternative perspectives

The concept of moral virtue can be applied to the character and behaviour of a morally good person. Most people might agree, for example, that honesty, sincerity, and trustworthiness are moral virtues and are therefore desirable ethical qualities in any individual, whether in business or elsewhere. However, the basis for judging whether a particular character trait is a moral virtue depends on a person's ethical standpoint. For the Greek philosopher, Aristotle

(384–22 BC), often regarded as the founder of '**virtue ethics**', moral virtue represented a mean between the opposing vices of excess and deficiency that allowed a person to live the good life according to reason. Building on the work of his teacher, Plato (*c*.427–347 BC), Aristotle described the four 'cardinal virtues' as prudence, justice, courage, and temperance; courage, for example, represents a mean between cowardice and recklessness. Later, St Thomas Aquinas (*c*.AD 1225–74) added the Christian virtues of faith, hope, and charity (or 'altruistic love' in modern usage). Difficulties with the concept of moral virtue include the lack of a universally accepted definition and the fact that it relates to a person's character rather than indicating whether a particular action is right or wrong, though a characteristic such as honesty probably offers a reasonable guide to what is an appropriate action in many business situations.

Alternative perspectives on what constitutes a moral virtue can be found in feminist and postmodern approaches to personal ethics and also in 'discourse ethics'. Feminist ethics turns our attention to issues of more concern to women and might, for example, regard empathy, healthy social relationships, and care for others as moral virtues. **Postmodernism**, whilst difficult to define, represents a reaction to 'modernism', the late nineteenth and early twentieth century view that human beings are capable of recreating and reordering their environment with the aid of technology and other forms of knowledge. Postmodernism views the world as a complex and disorderly place where local events and provisional attitudes are more important than grand narratives or universal truths. In this context, ethics is rooted in moral impulses based on emotions and personal convictions rather than reason or religious beliefs. A further perspective comes from discourse ethics, which contends that moral norms should be established through mutual understanding as a result of a process of argument rather than based on the ideas of a single individual (making use of the concept of *dialectics* employed by philosophers from the ancient Greeks to Marx and Engels); from this perspective, ethical conflicts are settled through discourse and respect for the views of people from diverse cultural backgrounds.[20]

7.4.2 The 'Golden Rule'

The **Golden Rule** is the name given to the ethical principle of reciprocity – that we should treat other people as we would wish to be treated ourselves. This principle can be found in many religious and philosophical writings. Examples include the following:

- 'Do not that unto another which thou wouldst not have done to thyself' (Thomas Hobbes, *Leviathan*, 1651)
- 'I ought never to act except in such a way that I can also will that my maxim should become a universal law' (Immanuel Kant, *Groundwork of the Metaphysics of Morals*, 1785)
- 'You shall love your neighbour as yourself' (Matthew 22:39)

Although Kant's categorical imperative is an example of the Golden Rule (see Section 7.3.1), the Golden Rule should not necessarily be seen as a deontological principle or moral obligation. It may be considered simply as the demonstration of mutual respect for fellow human beings, a perspective from which human rights may also be viewed. However, the Golden Rule goes beyond 'basic' human rights to the idea of reciprocal treatment. In a business context, it

Practical insight 7.5: The wearing of a Christian cross

In January 2013, the European Court of Human Rights decided against an earlier ruling by a British employment tribunal in allowing Nadia Eweida, an airline check-in clerk, to wear a cross at work as a symbol of her Christian faith. Whilst the UK government argued that the wearing of a cross was not an essential requirement for a Christian, the court took the view that manifesting one's religious beliefs was a 'fundamental right' and that 'a healthy and democratic society needs to tolerate and sustain pluralism and diversity'. However, the court rejected a similar legal challenge by Shirley Chaplin, a nurse, on 'health and safety' grounds.[21]

Question

● What principles do you think should be applied to determine whether the wearing of a religious symbol should be allowed to breach a uniform code?

may provide an important guide to the treatment of employees, colleagues, customers, suppliers, and others who may not always receive such consideration in practice.

7.4.3 **Pluralism**

In an ethical context, **pluralism** is about the acknowledgement of diversity. Of course, from some ethical standpoints, particular views or issues may be seen as either right or wrong, but pluralism represents tolerance of the views, interests, and values of others without necessarily agreeing with them. A number of difficulties have arisen over the wearing of religious dress or symbols at work or school, for example. Sometimes the wearing of the Muslim *hijab* or the Christian cross has offended a uniform code and led to an impasse between those who argue that the uniform code should be strictly applied to all and those who maintain their right to wear religious symbols at all times. Pluralism implies that we should be tolerant of cultural and religious differences as far as possible. In some circumstances, the need to ensure personal safety when using dangerous machinery or community safety when a person's identity is obscured by a facial covering may override the need for tolerance of diversity. In general, however, tolerance helps to diffuse potential conflict. See Practical Insight 7.5 for further discussion of this issue).

7.4.4 **Autonomy**

In an ethical context, **autonomy** requires an individual to take moral responsibility for his or her own actions. Whilst apparently reasonable, the concept has been subject to a wide range of different interpretations. For Immanuel Kant (1724–1804), autonomy represented the ability to use reason to determine one's own actions without the influence of external pressures. For John Stuart Mill (1806–73), individuals could achieve autonomy by taking part in decision making through worker cooperatives and other forms of social participation, rather than relying on others to make decisions for them. In many cultures and religions, individuals are expected to show respect for accepted values or beliefs rather than to express individuality. However, if one sees autonomy not so much as the freedom to do what one likes but as being morally accountable for one's actions, the cultural and religious difficulties can more easily be overcome. In a business context, autonomy might be regarded as the need to accept personal responsibility for one's actions rather than hiding behind corporate responsibility. It may also be considered important that each individual be encouraged to take a personal position on ethical issues – to adopt a moral rather than amoral stance.

7.5 Corporate social responsibility

Corporate social responsibility (CSR) has been defined in many different ways. At its most basic level, CSR is about a business taking responsibility for the economic, social, ethical, and environmental impacts of its activities. A more demanding definition might require the total activities of a business to have a beneficial impact on society, though the measurement of 'beneficial impact' may prove difficult. A narrower, more conventional view was that social responsibility involved businesses acting philanthropically by giving back some of their profits to good causes. This view is no longer generally accepted. However, bearing in mind the contributions of nineteenth-century industrialists like Cadbury and Salt, it would be wrong to think of the more comprehensive view of CSR as a new concept.

A challenging view of CSR in the contemporary context was expressed by the former UK Prime Minister, Gordon Brown, when he was Chancellor of the Exchequer, where he argued that businesses had a responsibility not only towards their communities and the natural environment but also to help tackle global problems such as poverty reduction:

> Today, corporate social responsibility goes far beyond the old philanthropy of the past – donating money to good causes at the end of the financial year – and is instead an all year round responsibility that companies accept for the environment around them, for the best working practices, for their engagement in their local communities and for their recognition that brand names depend not only on quality, price and uniqueness but on how, cumulatively, they interact with companies' workforce, community and environment. Now we need to move towards a challenging measure of corporate responsibility, where we judge results not just by the input but by its outcomes, the difference we make to the world in which we live, and the contribution we make to poverty reduction.[22]

In its broader sense, the concept of CSR is an extension of stakeholder theory, especially in relation to the wider group of indirect stakeholders. In particular, the concept has been applied to a business's responsibility towards society and the natural environment. The arguments of Friedman and Wolf in relation to a company's primary responsibility to its shareholders (see Section 7.3.3) have also been used to make the case against CSR. In recent years, however, there has been growing intellectual, business, and popular support for the adoption of more extensive CSR policies. This is not to say that business decision makers always have altruistic motives, but that they have generally accepted the need to tackle problems such as pollution and that, by responding to the concerns of their customers and other stakeholders, their businesses are more likely to achieve financial success in the long term.

It is probably fair to say that all economic activity creates '**externalities**'. Externalities are the external consequences experienced by those who are not directly involved in a particular economic activity. Thus, for example, the use of fossil fuels to generate electric power may cause harmful carbon dioxide (CO_2) emissions. In this case, the power company and its customers are the parties directly involved, but the CO_2 pollution affects society as a whole – indeed, the effects may well be experienced beyond a country's borders. This is an example of a negative externality and, without some form of legal or political intervention, there is no economic incentive for the power company or its customers to do anything about the problem. In these circumstances, market failure has occurred. However, if the company and its customers can be persuaded to internalize the externalities – to pay for the cost of avoiding or cleaning up the pollution or searching for alternative sources of power – the economic problem of market failure will have been resolved and the ethical requirement to take responsibility for the adverse consequences of one's actions will have been met. CSR is about much more than environmental concerns, but this example illustrates the way in which a business can alleviate the harmful effects of its activities by taking responsibility for the external consequences.

The market failure argument provides a justification for corrective or avoiding action to minimize or neutralize the negative externalities of economic activity, but it does not provide a necessary or sufficient justification for all forms of CSR. More extensive support for communities or global initiatives may require conscious positive externalities to be achieved where there is no obvious market incentive. In this case, a business might be viewed as making a contribution to 'social capital'. The World Bank defines social capital as 'the institutions, relationships, and norms that shape the quality and quantity of a society's social interactions' and as 'the glue that holds [society's institutions] together'.[23] By engaging in CSR, businesses are helping to create social capital and promote the social relationships and collective values that support the development of a healthy society. This is clearly the rationale behind the UN Global Compact outlined in Section 7.2.

Seen in this wider context, it is easier to justify the more far-reaching aspects of CSR that businesses are increasingly expected to take on. It should be noted, however, that the development of social capital requires the commitment of individuals and a variety of public, private, third, and fourth sector organizations, not just business organizations, and that it may never be possible to measure the benefits, either to society or to individual businesses, with any degree of accuracy or objectivity (see Practical Insight 7.6).

Practical insight 7.6: CSR reporting

Increasingly, companies are starting to report their CSR performance publicly. A major international initiative providing a CSR reporting framework is the Global Reporting Initiative.[24] The current reporting guidelines at the time of writing are its fourth version, the G4 Guidelines, introduced in May 2013. These guidelines are now updated on an incremental basis. The G4 Guidelines cover a company's economic, environmental, and social performance and its impact. Social performance includes labour practices, gender issues, human rights, product responsibility, local community impacts, and compliance with standards relating to corruption, anti-competitive behaviour, and other regulations. This initiative has the support of a number of major companies, including Microsoft, GM, Ford, Shell, and Deutsche Bank.

Question

● To what extent do you think this type of initiative should be encouraged?

7.6 Responsibility for the natural environment

A particular area of corporate social responsibility that businesses are now being urged to address is their impact on the natural environment. The basic problem in a market economy is one of market failure. Harmful effects on the environment are negative externalities resulting from economic activity. These harmful effects include air and water pollution, resource depletion, waste products, and greenhouse gas emissions, among other things. Unless property rights are clearly assigned to all the parties involved in or affected by economic activity, and are legally enforceable (e.g. rights to pollute or to be protected from the consequences of pollution), there is no incentive for polluters to take account of the consequences of their actions. As a result, the level of output and of pollution is likely to be greater than the socially optimal level (the level at which the external costs of pollution are fully taken into account), and the price of the product is likely to be lower than the socially optimal price. This leads to a misallocation of resources and a higher level of pollution than is economically justifiable. It also means that society (including producers and consumers) is ignoring the external cost of economic activity and market failure has occurred. This is illustrated in Figure 7.2.

In a competitive market, efficient resource allocation occurs where price equals marginal cost, as this is where the marginal benefit to the consumer equals the marginal cost of producing the product and the net benefit to society is maximized. However, if organizations only take account of the **marginal private cost** (MPC) when setting their price and output and ignore the **marginal external cost** (MEC), the price (p) and output (q) will not represent an optimal allocation of resources for society. If they charge a higher price (p*) and produce a lower output (q*), taking account of the full **marginal social cost** (MSC), the resulting allocation of resources will be socially optimal. This does not of course mean that there will be no pollution, but it does mean that the market is able to price the product correctly. If consumers regard the price as too high, they will try to reduce their consumption, put pressure on the

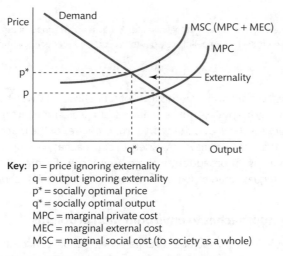

Key: p = price ignoring externality
q = output ignoring externality
p* = socially optimal price
q* = socially optimal output
MPC = marginal private cost
MEC = marginal external cost
MSC = marginal social cost (to society as a whole)

Figure 7.2 Graph illustrating a negative externality in a competitive market

supplier to use more environmentally friendly production methods, or look for an alternative product whose production causes less pollution.

Even where the market correctly prices a product by taking account of the externalities, society may consider that the environmental cost is unsustainable in the long term and that more drastic measures need to be taken. Thus, in the case of greenhouse gas emissions and their effect on climate change, the Stern Review concluded that 'the scientific evidence is now overwhelming: climate change is a serious global threat, and it demands an urgent global response'.[25] In fact several years earlier, the UN Framework Convention on Climate Change was initiated in Rio de Janeiro in 1992 (the Rio Earth Summit), which led to a number of countries signing up to the Kyoto Protocol on Climate Change in 1997. These commitments have been reaffirmed and extended at several subsequent conferences, including Bali (2007), Cancún (2010), and Doha (2012). Under the Kyoto Protocol, the developed countries committed themselves to a total reduction in greenhouse gas emissions (mainly CO_2 emissions) of 5 per cent by 2008–12 against a baseline of 1990; this commitment was increased to 18 per cent by the participating countries for the period 2012–20 at the Doha conference, though major polluters such as the United States, Japan, and Russia have not signed up to the second phase, along with developing countries like China, India, and Brazil, which are excluded.[26]

Practical insight 7.7:   The 'Skeptical Environmentalist'

The publication of Bjorn Lomborg's book *The Skeptical Environmentalist: Measuring the Real State of the World*, in 2001, caused consternation among environmentalists around the world.[27] Lomborg, a Danish statistician, claimed that the available data did not support the pessimistic predictions of mainstream scientists on climate change and a number of other environmental and social issues. Lomborg did not present alternative theories on global warming or world poverty, but provided statistical evidence to suggest that the accepted view on these issues was often exaggerated or misleading. In the main, Lomborg's 'evidence' has been dismissed as selective and therefore itself misleading,[28] though he at least raised the possibility that some of the evidence is not as clear-cut as is sometimes claimed.

Question

● Even if Lomborg turned out to be right that climate change is not as serious a threat as is generally believed, would there still be compelling reasons to take action to reduce pollution and protect the environment?

If scientific predictions are accurate, this level of reductions may well be insufficient to limit climate change and may in any case not be achieved, but nevertheless it represents a significant commitment that goes well beyond the short-term pressures of the market. A more sceptical view is discussed in Practical Insight 7.7. A variety of approaches have been proposed to tackle environmental problems. In broad terms, these approaches fit into one of four categories: regulation; market or quasi-market solutions; voluntary action; and technological solutions.

7.6.1 Regulatory approaches to environmental problems

Environmental regulation may include a range of legislation concerning air or water pollution, energy conservation, waste disposal, hazardous materials, packaging, and recycling, or even enforcement measures such as Australia's environmental service orders requiring offenders to engage in environmental projects.[29] Regulations have been hugely influential in reducing air and river pollution from many of Europe's heavy industries and in making its industrial towns and cities acceptable places to live. They are also helping to change behaviour in relation to the disposal of waste products and the design of new cars and buildings. Some of the most extensive environmental protection laws can be found in countries such as Sweden and Germany, where the wealth of legislation is sometimes seen as harmful to international competitiveness, but enhanced performance and a positive environmental impact can often compensate for additional cost in a world of increasingly sophisticated consumers. Even the cost of monitoring regulatory compliance may to some extent be mitigated if market forces or industry associations begin to take on this role.

7.6.2 Market or quasi-market solutions to environmental problems

Given the problem of market failure that arises when markets ignore negative externalities, some of the solutions to the problem have focused on the need for incentives to help markets internalize the externalities. One such approach involves the use of tradable pollution permits, commonly known as '**emissions trading**' or, in the case of carbon dioxide (CO_2) emissions, 'carbon trading'. Examples of emissions trading include the US Acid Rain Program, which limits sulphur dioxide (SO_2) emissions in the electricity generating industry, and the EU Emissions Trading Scheme, which covers a variety of industries responsible for about 45 per cent of total EU greenhouse gas emissions. The EU scheme is a 'cap and trade' system, placing an overall cap on the emission of CO_2 and other greenhouse gases each year, and issues allowances or credits to individual companies, giving them a pollution limit for the period concerned. Companies that have reduced their emissions below their limit may trade allowances with companies that are having more difficulty in reducing emissions. Thus, the authorities are able to control the total level of emissions, reducing it year by year, whilst at the same time providing an incentive for greater reductions in industries where these reductions can be achieved at lowest cost. The overall effect is that reductions in greenhouse gas emissions are achieved in an economically efficient way, using market forces to obtain this outcome. Despite the increasing popularity of emissions trading schemes,[30] there are also fears that the heavy-polluting part of an industry may be concentrated in a particular industrial area, with possible harmful effects on the community concerned.[31]

Governments also create incentives through the taxation system. Pollution taxes can be used to force producers and consumers to take account of the externalities in their decision making, in effect moving the marginal private cost curve (MPC) up to the marginal social cost curve (MSC) in Figure 7.2. This produces a socially efficient price and output if the pollution tax is equal to the external cost of the pollution. Pollution taxes are sometimes known as **Pigouvian (or Pigovian) taxes**, after the Cambridge economist, A. C. Pigou (1877–1959), who first identified this solution. Examples of pollution taxes include carbon taxes on CO_2-emitting industries, taxes on motor fuel and civil aviation, and charges at the point of use – such as road pricing or congestion charging. In some cases, road tolls are simply used to recover the road-building costs, especially where private finance is involved, but increasingly road pricing and congestion charging schemes are being used as a way of relieving congestion on busy roads or in city centres. Whether they simply divert traffic to other places or encourage people to use more environmentally friendly forms of transport is a more open question.

7.6.3 Voluntary action as a solution to environmental problems

In some circumstances, markets may achieve an efficient solution to the problem of externalities through a process of bargaining between the parties involved. For example, in the 1990s, Sweden reached an agreement with Poland, its former communist neighbour just across the Baltic Sea, whereby it would help pay for the cost of cleaning up Poland's industrial pollution. This 'bargain' is an illustration of the **Coase Theorem**, named after its originator, Ronald Coase (1910–).[32] The Coase Theorem states that the outcome of a bargain will be an efficient solution regardless of how the property rights of each party are specified, provided the agreement is to their mutual advantage and no transaction costs are incurred. Despite Sweden having to bear the cost of a problem of Poland's making, the outcome of the agreement was to their mutual advantage as pollution does not respect national boundaries and Poland was unable to bear the full cost itself. In reality, there are often transaction costs in such arrangements – including legal and other negotiation costs – but provided they are not excessive, the outcome may not be significantly affected.

Voluntary action may also arise where individuals or environmental groups choose to take action that is not necessarily or solely in their own interests, but which they consider important for society as a whole. This kind of social action is becoming more widespread and is increasingly regarded as socially desirable in the modern world. Examples of this type of activity include carbon offset schemes and campaigns to encourage supermarkets to buy locally sourced produce (see Practical Insight 7.8). Carbon offsetting involves the introduction of compensatory environmental benefits to offset the costs of environmental damage.

Practical insight 7.8: 'Food miles'

One of the consequences of living in an open international business environment is that the food we eat has often travelled halfway around the world before it reaches the dinner table. Exotic and seasonal produce adorns supermarket shelves throughout the year. This has led to calls for a return to local production and a reduction in 'food miles' to help reduce the CO_2 emissions from the international transportation of food. There are, of course, many benefits from locally sourced produce, especially traditional varieties that have been squeezed out of the market by lower-cost alternatives. Perhaps consumers in the developed world could also forgo the pleasure of having strawberries all year round or of buying cut flowers freshly flown in from South Africa. We should remember, however, that these activities are part of a much larger pattern of international business activity, where everything from cars to computer software is traded around the world – taking advantage of favourable production conditions as well as consumer preferences in a changing international environment.

Question

● How can we balance the benefits of international trade with the need to protect the natural environment?

Thus, for example, frequent air travellers may be encouraged to contribute towards energy efficiency projects or the planting of trees (which absorb CO_2) as a means of offsetting the 'carbon footprint' of air travel.

7.6.4 Technological solutions to environmental problems

Technological developments may help to improve the efficiency with which resources are used. For example, improvements in the design of motor vehicle engines or the aerodynamic properties of aircraft may lead to increased fuel efficiency. Perhaps a more significant, but controversial example of the impact of technological change can be seen in the recent growth of the biofuel industry. Biofuels are energy sources made from plants or animal waste products. The industry is increasingly using crops such as corn (or maize), sugar cane, and rapeseed to produce bioethanol, biodiesel, and other biofuels. Ethanol produced from plants is increasingly being mixed with petrol to help reduce the demand for petroleum and reduce the amount of CO_2 in the atmosphere.

However, the question as to the net contribution of biofuels to a reduction in greenhouse gas emissions is a controversial one. Whilst the growing of crops helps to absorb CO_2 from the atmosphere, the burning of biofuels and some of the processes by which they are produced add to CO_2 emissions. There is also concern about the effect of the biofuel industry on the demand for crops and agricultural land, some of which may be diverted from food production and much of which is likely to be in developing countries such as Brazil, where rainforests are already under threat from the expansion of agriculture and other industrial activities. Nevertheless, significant weight has been attached to the role of technology as a means of tackling environmental problems. In particular, the George W. Bush US administration (2001–9) decided to put its faith in technological solutions rather than incur the economic costs of the regulatory and other environmental policies required by the Kyoto Protocol.

7.7 Business ethics, voluntarism, and the law

Underlying much of the discussion of business ethics in this chapter is the question as to whether individuals or organizations can be expected to act ethically on a voluntary basis or whether some form of law or regulation is required. Clearly, government and other political institutions in most countries provide an extensive system of legal rules affecting business organizations. Sometimes these laws and regulations create a framework for the orderly conduct of business affairs, sometimes they interfere with efficient business practice, but in many cases they apply a particular set of ethical values or principles. Thus, for example, competition rules may outlaw practices such as price fixing or the abuse of a dominant position, or consumer law may impose an obligation on a supplier to deliver goods of merchantable quality. These are important safeguards and may provide a variety of legal remedies. However, there are many other practices involving ethical issues which may not be covered by the law. Two questions then arise: how far should the law go in regulating business practice and to what extent can **voluntarism** be relied on to achieve ethical conduct?

A particular difficulty relates to the issue of CSR. Most people would accept that a company's basic responsibilities to its employees or customers should be regulated by law, but what about its indirect stakeholders, including the community and society in general? Should the law be used to impose environmental responsibilities such as recycling, restrictions on the use of packaging materials, or the elimination of plastic bags at supermarket checkouts? Plastic bags are banned in Bangladesh, Bhutan, and several other countries, China has banned ultra-thin plastic bags, and the Republic of Ireland has introduced a government levy on plastic bags. In the UK, retailers such as Marks and Spencer and Tesco have voluntarily introduced charges for plastic bags – though admittedly under moral pressure from the government. Sometimes peer pressure or pressure from consumers and environmental groups is sufficient to bring about environmental action, or the desire to be seen as a market leader. At other times, legal action is required in order to bring about rapid change on a large scale, as in the growing number of countries which have introduced smoking bans in restaurants, bars, and other confined public places.

Summary

Whilst business activity is often about making income or profit for the owner, its ultimate purpose is to satisfy the wants and needs of society. It therefore has a social purpose and involves responsibilities towards employees, customers, and suppliers. These responsibilities require ethical behaviour by the parties involved. Many ethical decisions raise difficult issues, but a number of ethical concepts can be used to help make these decisions. Two alternative value systems that may be used for this purpose are the teleological and deontological approaches. The former holds that an action is morally right if the outcome or consequence of the action is desirable. The latter holds that an action is morally right if it is based on moral obligations or duties, regardless of the outcome. Social contract theory, the idea of an informal agreement between members of a society, provides another perspective on what might be regarded as accepted norms of behaviour. Considerable debate has occurred around the shareholder and stakeholder views of an organization and, in particular, the idea of CSR: the responsibility of an organization towards its wider stakeholders, including the natural environment and society as a whole. Environmental issues are then explored as a specific area of corporate responsibility. The chapter also includes some possible guidelines for individual ethical behaviour and some concluding comments on the relative merits of legal and voluntary action as a means of promoting ethical behaviour.

Discussion questions

1. To what extent, if any, should a business organization have a social purpose?
2. If we accept that business activity is essentially a means to an end, does it necessarily follow that the teleological approach is more appropriate than the deontological approach as a value system to guide business decisions?

3. Critically evaluate the idea of a social contract as a way of establishing accepted standards of behaviour within a particular group or society.

4. 'Even if one accepts that a company has a responsibility towards all its stakeholders, its primary responsibility must still be towards its shareholders.' Discuss.

5. To what extent does the ethical principle of pluralism provide a useful guide to employers seeking to regulate the conduct or dress of their employees?

6. Given the need to protect the natural environment, compare and contrast the relative merits of regulatory, market-based, and voluntary approaches to the solution of environmental problems.

Suggested assignment topics

1. Choose a specific multinational company. Identify differences in wages, hours of work, and other working conditions in the different countries in which it operates. Evaluate the extent to which these differences represent acceptable ethical variations between countries or whether universal ethical norms should be applied.

2. Identify an organization which publishes a CSR report on its activities. Examine a recent report, determine the extent to which its CSR activities are measurable, and evaluate the potential impact of these activities on the company and its stakeholders.

3. The globalization of business activity has inevitably led to an increase in international air and sea transport. This has led to calls for organizations and individuals to reduce their 'carbon footprint' by limiting air travel, buying goods produced in their domestic economy, and participating in carbon offset schemes. Investigate the costs and benefits of these ideas from business and environmental perspectives.

 Case study: Corus and the Tata Group

In 1999, British Steel and Koninklijke Hoogovens, a Dutch steel company, merged to form Corus. Within two years, the newly formed steel company had responded to difficult world trading conditions by making a number of cuts in its operations. The company's most controversial action was the announcement of 6,000 job losses in February 2001. Corus justified the job losses on the grounds that it had to reduce costs and improve efficiency in order to return to profitability when facing a high sterling exchange rate and a competitive world market.

The company's decision was accompanied by protests from the steelworkers trade union, the Iron and Steel Trades Confederation, and politicians, notably members of the Welsh National Assembly. There were also calls for the UK government to provide financial support for Corus, given the company's importance as the main national supplier of steel and the scale of the job losses in some of the country's already depressed regions. The British government might also have been considered to have some residual responsibility for the company, given its former ownership of the British Steel Corporation during a period of nationalization from 1967 to 1988 (and a brief earlier period from 1951 to 1953).

This scenario brings into stark contrast the commercial pressures on Corus to secure the company's profitability for its shareholders and its responsibilities towards its employees and other stakeholders.

(continued...)

In terms of maintaining shareholder value, the company appeared to have no option but to cut costs in order to ensure its long-term survival. On the other hand, from the perspective of its redundant workers and the communities where they live, survival of the company on a much smaller scale may seem a pyrrhic victory for its anonymous shareholders, especially if the country's steelmaking capacity can no longer meet the needs of its industry.

During the course of the next few years, the cost savings introduced by Corus, together with growing world demand for steel, helped the company to return to profitability. In 2007, after a bidding battle between India's Tata Group and Brazil's Companhia Siderúrgica Nacional (CSN), Corus was taken over by Tata. The Tata Group is based in Mumbai and is one of India's fastest-growing multinationals with interests in steel, energy, engineering, motor manufacturing, chemicals, information technology, financial services, the Taj Mahal hotels, and a variety of consumer products, including Tetley tea. The takeover of Corus has not only made Tata a major world steel producer, but also reflects a growing reversal in the direction of foreign direct investment, from developing to developed countries, as globalization changes the international structure of traditional, and sometimes non-traditional, industries. However, although still operating at a number of UK locations, Tata has been cutting back its UK workforce and sold its Teesside Cast Products plant to Sahaviriya Steel Industries (SSI) of Thailand in 2011 in response to difficult trading conditions in Europe and elsewhere.

A further interesting twist in this story is that Tata was founded with some of the same ethical principles as the businesses of the British philanthropists, Cadbury, Lever Brothers, Reckitt, and Salt, discussed in the opening scenario to this chapter. Jamshedji Tata, founder of the Tata company, built the company's first iron and steel works in eastern India during the early years of the twentieth century and created pleasant housing, recreation areas, and places of religious worship for employees in the city that became known as Jamshedpur, after its founder. The Tata Group now also supports a number of other charitable ventures. The various twists and turns in the story of Corus and Tata illustrate some of the complexities of business ethics in the modern world.[33]

Case study questions

1. What benefits might have been expected to come from the merger of British Steel and its Dutch counterpart, Koninklijke Hoogovens, in 1999?

2. How would you justify the plant closures and job losses that followed the merger between 1999 and 2001 from the perspective of the shareholder model?

3. How might these plant closures and job losses be viewed from a stakeholder perspective?

4. To what extent is it possible to reconcile the shareholder and stakeholder perspectives in this case?

5. What responsibility, if any, might the British government have been expected to take either for preventing the plant closures or for providing support for the redundant steel workers?

6. If Tata's takeover of Corus in 2007 is considered as an effect of globalization, is the fact that the predator is Indian rather than, say US or Japanese, likely to make globalization more ethically acceptable to some of its critics?

7. The city of Jamshedpur illustrates the concern of Tata's founder for the welfare of his employees. Given that present-day living conditions for most of Corus's European employees are likely to be considerably better than those facing Indian workers at the beginning of the twentieth century, what might be regarded as an equivalent form of corporate social responsibility today?

8. How far should a company like Tata be expected to go to fulfil its corporate social responsibility in the modern world?

Notes

1. Main sources: Cadbury plc website, http://www.cadbury.co.uk; Spartacus Educational, http://www.spartacus.schoolnet.co.uk; Bradley, I. (2007), *Enlightened Entrepreneurs: Business Ethics in Victorian Britain*, Lion Hudson; BBC News (6 December 2011), 'Kraft cuts 200 jobs at Bourneville, Chirk and Marlbrook'; and the *Observer* (4 November 2012), 'Nervous Cadbury sets in with a new owner as Kraft splits itself in two'.

2. Marx's ideas on the capitalist system were first published in Marx, K. and Engels, F. (1848), *Manifesto of the Communist Party*.

3. Donaldson, T., and Dunfee, T. W. (1999), *Ties that Bind: A Social Contract Approach to Business Ethics*, Harvard Business School Press.

4. See UN Global Compact, http://www.unglobalcompact.org.

5. Klein, N. (2010), *No Logo*, Fourth Estate.

6. This issue is discussed by Ulrich Beck in Beck, U. (1992), *Risk Society: Towards a New Modernity*, Sage.

7. Source: National Geographic, http://ocean.nationalgeographic.com/ocean/critical-issues-sea-level-rise, accessed 21 February 2013.

8. Immanuel Kant's 'categorical imperative' was developed in his 1785 work *Groundwork of the Metaphysics of Morals (Grundlegung zur Metaphysik der Sitten)*, first published in 1785.

9. UN Universal Declaration of Human Rights (1948), http://www.un.org/en/documents/udhr.

10. Ross, W. D. (2002), *The Right and the Good*, Clarendon Press, first published in 1930.

11. WHO Media Centre Factsheet No. 360, November 2012.

12. See WTO (September 2006), 'WTO compulsory licensing of pharmaceuticals and TRIPS', http://www.wto.org.

13. Donaldson, T., and Dunfee, T. W. (1999), *Ties that Bind: A Social Contract Approach to Business Ethics*, Harvard Business School Press.

14. Friedman, M. (1970), 'The social responsibility of business is to increase its profits', *New York Times Magazine*, 13 September.

15. Friedman, M. (2002), *Capitalism and Freedom*, University of Chicago Press, first published in 1962.

16. See, for example, Wolf, M. (2001), 'Sleep-walking with the enemy', *Financial Times*, 16 May.

17. Freeman, R. E. (1984), *Strategic Management: A Stakeholder Approach*, Pitman.

18. Freeman, R. E. (1984), *Strategic Management: A Stakeholder Approach*, Pitman, p. 46.

19. FairPlay 2008 (2007), 'No Medal for the Olympics on Labour Rights', 10 June.

20. For further discussion of these issues, see for example Crane, A., and Matten, D. (2010), *Business Ethics: Managing Corporate Citizenship and Sustainability in the Age of Globalization*, Oxford University Press, ch. 3, especially pp. 118–26.

21. Source: The *Telegraph* (15 January 2013), 'Christian wins right to wear cross at work'.

22. UK Department of Trade and Industry (2004), 'Corporate social responsibility, a government update', May, p. 2.

23. World Bank (2007), 'What is Social Capital?' PovertyNet.

24. Global Reporting Initiative, https://www.globalreporting.org.

25. Stern, N. (2006), *The Economics of Climate Change: The Stern Review*, Cambridge University Press, Summary of Conclusions, p. 1.

26. See UN Framework Convention on Climate Change, http://unfccc.int.

27. Lomborg, B. (2001), *The Skeptical Environmentalist: Measuring the Real State of the World*, Cambridge University Press.

28. See, for example, Cole, M. A. (2003), 'Environmental optimists, environmental pessimists and the real state of the world', *Economic Journal*, vol. 113, F362–80.

29. Abbott, C. (2005), 'The regulatory enforcement of pollution control laws: the Australian experience', *Journal of Environmental Law*, vol. 17, no. 2, pp. 161–80.

30. For example, China announced its intention to create a national carbon trading scheme by 2015 in its 12th Five Year Plan for 2011–15.

31. For a discussion of the wider health issues, see, for example. Corburn, J. (2001), 'Emissions trading and environmental justice: distributed fairness and the USA's Acid Rain Program', *Environmental Conservation*, vol. 28, pp. 323–32.

32. Coase, R. H. (1960), 'The problem of social cost', *Journal of Law and Economics*, vol. 3, part 1, pp. 1–44.

33. Main sources: Tata Steel website, http://www.tatasteel.com; Tata Steel Europe website, http://www.tatasteeleurope.com/en/; Tata Group website, http://www.tata.com; Tata in the UK Locations website, http://uk.tata.com; Will Hutton (4 February 2001), 'The lies behind Labour's Corus line', the *Observer*; the *Telegraph* (1 February 2007), 'India's Tata wins Corus in takeover battle'; *Financial Times* (2 February 2007), 'Indian pride fuelled Tata's push for Corus'; SSI UK website, http://www.ssi-steel.co.uk; and *Financial Times* (23 November 2012), 'Tata Steel cuts 900 jobs to reduce UK costs'.

Suggestions for further reading

Mainstream books on business ethics

Crane, A., and Matten, D. (2010), *Business Ethics: Managing Corporate Citizenship and Sustainability in the Age of Globalization*, Oxford University Press

Fritzsche, P. (2004), *Business Ethics: A Global and Managerial Perspective*, McGraw-Hill

Velasquez, M. G. (2011), *Business Ethics: Concepts and Cases*, Pearson

A variety of perspectives on the ethical issues raised by globalization

Dunning, J. H. (2003), *Making Globalization Good: The Moral Challenges of Global Capitalism*, Oxford University Press

On environmental issues and policies

Helm, D., and Hepburn, C. (2011), *The Economics and Politics of Climate Change*, Oxford University Press

Tietenberg, T., and Lewis, L. (2011), *Environmental and Natural Resources Economics*, Pearson

On corporate social responsibility

Crane, A., McWilliams, A., Matten, D., Moon, J., and Siegel, D. S. (2009), *The Oxford Handbook of Corporate Social Responsibility*, Oxford University Press

May, S. K., Cheney, G., and Roper, J. (2007), *The Debate Over Corporate Social Responsibility*, Oxford University Press

Take your learning further: Online Resource Centre
http://www.oxfordtextbooks.co.uk/orc/harrison2e/
Visit the Online Resource Centre that accompanies this book to enrich your understanding of Chapter 7: Business Ethics and Corporate Responsibility. Among other resources explore web links and keep up to date with the latest developments in the area.

Key terms introduced in this chapter

Autonomy In an ethical context, autonomy requires an individual to take moral responsibility for his or her own actions.

Coase theorem The economic principle that the outcome of a bargain will be an efficient solution regardless of how property rights are specified, provided the agreement is to the mutual advantage of the parties and no transaction costs are incurred.

Consequentialist principle See teleological principle.

Corporate social responsibility (CSR) The responsibility of an organization for the economic, social, ethical, and environmental impacts of its activities.

Deontological principle An ethical principle which holds that an action is morally right if it is based on moral obligations or duties.

Egoism An ethical principle which holds that an action is morally right if its consequences are desirable for the individual taking the action.

Emissions trading An environmental policy which grants pollution permits allowing firms to pollute up to a permitted level and to trade their permits if emissions are reduced below this level.

Ethical absolutism A set of ethical values that are considered to be right regardless of the context.

Ethical relativism A set of ethical values that vary according to the context.

Externality The external consequences experienced by those who are not directly involved in a particular economic activity.

Golden Rule The ethical principle that we should treat others as we would wish to be treated ourselves (the principle of reciprocity).

Justice principle An ethical principle relating to distributive, retributive, or compensatory justice which concerns fairness, equality, and respect for the rights of others.

Marginal external cost (MEC) The external cost of producing an additional unit of output borne by those who are not directly involved in a particular economic activity.

Marginal private cost (MPC) The internal cost of producing an additional unit of output borne by the organization and its consumers.

Marginal social cost (MSC) The total cost to society of producing an additional unit of output, including the marginal private cost and the marginal external cost.

Non-consequentialist principle See deontological principle.

Pigouvian (or Pigovian) tax A tax equal to the external cost of an economic activity, forcing the producer and consumers to take account of the full social cost of their activities.

Pluralism In an ethical context, pluralism represents tolerance of the views, interests, and values of others.

Postmodernism A view that represents the world as a complex and disorderly place where local events and provisional attitudes are more important than grand narratives or universal truths.

Rights principle In its modern context, an ethical principle which holds that human beings have certain rights which should be respected.

Shareholder view An ethical concept which holds that the primary purpose of a company is to maximize the return on its shareholders' investment.

Social contract An explicit or implicit agreement between members of a society concerning accepted norms of behaviour.

Stakeholder A group or individual who can affect, or is affected by, the activities of an organization, including direct stakeholders such as shareholders, employees, or customers, and indirect stakeholders such as society as a whole.

Stakeholder view An ethical concept which holds that an organization has a responsibility towards all its stakeholders.

Teleological principle An ethical principle which holds that an action is morally right if the outcome or consequence of the action is desirable.

Utilitarianism An ethical principle which holds that an action is morally right if it results in the greatest good for the greatest number of people.

Values The fundamental principles that form the basis of ethical behaviour.

Virtue ethics An ethical concept which holds that personal character traits such as honesty, sincerity, and trustworthiness provide a basis for ethical behaviour.

Voluntarism The view that individuals or organizations can be expected to act ethically on a voluntary basis without the need for regulation.

Internationalization of Business in a Changing Environment

Chapter learning outcomes

On completion of this chapter the reader should be able to:

- Appreciate the reasons why businesses venture abroad and the processes through which internationalization occurs
- Appreciate the role of country analysis in a changing international environment as a precursor to international market entry
- Analyse alternative modes of international entry and the influence of the business environment on the choice of entry mode
- Analyse and evaluate the contribution of theories of internationalization to an understanding of the internationalization decision
- Identify the ways in which the business environment affects the nature and scope of internationalization

Opening scenario: IKEA: The internationalization of a concept

IKEA has over 330 retail stores selling flat-pack furniture and other home products in over 40 countries in Europe, North America, the Caribbean, Asia, Australia, and the Middle East. It also has distribution centres and manufacturing facilities, as well as independent suppliers, in a number of different countries. With the exception of its Delft store in the Netherlands, all IKEA stores are operated under franchise agreements.

IKEA was founded by Ingvar Kamprad in Sweden in 1943 and opened its first retail store in Sweden in 1958. The company's international expansion strategy took it to Norway and Denmark in the 1960s and Switzerland, Germany, Australia, Hong Kong, Canada, Austria, the Netherlands, and Singapore in the 1970s. In the 1980s IKEA ventured into a number of other European countries as well as Saudi Arabia, Kuwait, and the United States. The early 1990s saw expansion into Central and Eastern Europe. Since then IKEA has ventured into China, Russia, Turkey, Japan, and other parts of Asia and Europe. Most of its production facilities are in countries with low labour costs such as Poland and China, but its products are still designed in Sweden.

The group headquarters are now based in the Netherlands, but IKEA retains its original concept of supplying low-priced, functionally designed, Scandinavian-style furniture and other home products from large retail warehouse stores. Manufacturing, transport, and storage costs are kept to a minimum, using the flat-pack format and a streamlined retail environment. The company also prides itself on its treatment of employees (or 'co-workers') and respect for the environment, though a report by Ernst

(continued...)

and Young disclosed that some of IKEA's furniture had been made with the use of forced prison labour, including political prisoners, in the former East Germany in the 1980s.[1]

IKEA's success in internationalizing its concept can be seen from the sometimes over-enthusiastic public attention that has accompanied the opening of a new store.[2] The company's international expansion raises a number of questions about how companies expand abroad, why they choose particular countries in which to design, manufacture, and sell their products, the sequence of countries into which they expand, the choice of international entry mode, and the degree of ownership and control they retain over their foreign assets, among other things. These questions are explored in detail in a variety of contexts in this chapter.[3]

8.1 Motives for going international

Businesses venture abroad for a variety of reasons and there is a large international business literature on this subject. In this section, we focus on the main factors that are likely to influence business decision makers in practice. These factors help to provide a broad overview of the topic. In Section 8.5, we consider the main theoretical explanations, which offer a more comprehensive rationale for the decision to go international. First, we distinguish between the main overarching factors and the firm-specific factors that affect the decision to venture abroad (see Figure 8.1). Fundamentally, this decision is motivated by an organization's mission and objectives: its overall aims and purpose and the detailed objectives it sets in order to achieve its aims. These are its primary motives for going international. The achievement of its aims and objectives, however, is significantly affected by the general international environment and by conditions within specific countries. For this reason, it is important to consider how the business environment affects a company's internationalization decision. A number of specific factors, including access to markets and resources and the need to reduce costs, will also influence this decision.

8.1.1 Overarching factors affecting the decision to go international

Primary motives

For most private sector businesses, profitability is of crucial importance. The opportunity to make profit by selling its products in a foreign market may therefore be attractive, especially if expansion in the home market is difficult because of slow market growth, market saturation, or regulatory obstacles. In some cases, significant business growth may only be possible through international expansion. International exposure also enables a company to achieve an international reputation, which may be important if it is to be regarded as an industry leader.

Profitability also depends on competitiveness, so international expansion may be a way of reducing costs in a competitive international market. Access to international markets allows increased scale of production, leading to lower unit costs. Economies of scale are particularly important for a company like Nestlé whose home market in Switzerland is relatively small.[4]

Overarching Factors

Primary Motives
- Profit-making opportunities
- Business growth
- International reputation
- Competitive advantage

The Changing International Environment
- International peace and stability
- World economic growth and emerging regions
- Reduction in trade barriers
- Technological developments and skills

Country-Specific Factors
- Political and economic stability
- Culture and institutions
- A country's stock of 'created assets'
- Supportive government policies
- Absence of 'nuisance costs'

Firm-Specific Factors

Access to Markets
- Large and emerging markets
- Access to a regional trading area
- First-mover advantages
- Need to follow the competition

Access to Resources
- Resources are core business
- Large quantities of resources are needed
- Specialized resources are immobile

Cost Reduction
- Access to low-cost materials, energy, or labour
- Financial incentives
- Avoidance of trade barriers

Figure 8.1 Factors affecting the decision to go international

Source: Adapted from Harrison, A. L., Dalkiran, E., and Elsey, E. (2000), *International Business*, Oxford University Press, Fig. 12.1, p. 256. By permission of Oxford University Press.

Scale economies apply not only at the level of the production plant, but more especially at the level of the organization as a whole. Access to international production allows international procurement of components and supplies, international relocation of production operations, or outsourcing of business functions that can be undertaken at lower cost abroad (known as 'offshoring'); these include not only call-centre operations, for example, but also many labour-intensive data-input tasks which are increasingly being outsourced to companies employing low-cost but highly skilled information technology workers in countries like India (see Section 8.4.5).

The changing international environment

In broad terms, the main nations involved in international business activity have experienced an unprecedented period of peace and stable international relations since 1945. From time to time conflict in particular countries has disrupted trade flows, notably in commodities like oil during periods of turbulence in the Middle East, but the United States, Western Europe, and Japan, which have until recently been the major trading nations, have enjoyed generally cordial relations with each other. This has helped enormously to increase the volume of world trade and investment, clearly having a positive influence on internationalization decisions.

The historic opening up of China and Eastern Europe since 1978 and 1989 respectively has also increased the opportunities for international trade and investment. The increase in international business activity has contributed to significant growth in the world economy over the post-war period. This growth has also been sustained by a general reduction in trade barriers between countries, thanks to the work of the General Agreement on Tariffs and Trade and the WTO, and the gradual liberalization of national trade and investment policies. The increased rate of growth in international business activity would not of course have been possible without significant developments in production and IT and commensurate improvements in the quality of human capital.

Country-specific factors

Whilst the general international environment influences overall internationalization decisions, the decision to do business in a particular country is primarily affected by conditions in the country concerned. A wide range of factors may be important, as indicated for example in the World Economic Forum global competitiveness report.[5] Among the most important factors are political and economic stability, culture and institutions, and a country's stock of '**created assets**'. The increase in economic activity, including foreign direct investment, that occurred in Northern Ireland (and to some extent in the Republic of Ireland) after the signing of the Good Friday Agreement in 1998 clearly indicates the importance of political stability. The implications of differences in a country's culture and institutions are considered at length in Chapter 6. Created assets, or what Michael Porter calls 'advanced factors', are assets which a country has developed through investment over a number of years.[6] They include tangible assets such as the transport or communication infrastructure and intangible assets such as education and skills, technology and the capacity for innovation, intellectual property, and business networks.

When comparing alternative locations, either between or within countries, government policies such as tax rates or financial incentives may influence the decision to invest; for example, the Republic of Ireland's 12½ per cent corporate tax rate (formerly 10 per cent) has undoubtedly influenced inward investment decisions in Ireland in recent years. In more difficult national environments, such as some of the former Soviet republics after the collapse of the Soviet Union in 1991, 'nuisance costs' have had the opposite effect by deterring foreign investors; these include bureaucratic obstacles, corruption, and mafia-style activities.

8.1.2 Firm-specific factors affecting the decision to go international

Access to markets

The lure of new markets either in large developed economies or in emerging economies with growth potential is often irresistible to businesses with international ambitions. Companies like Microsoft, Coca-Cola, or Toyota could not have achieved global leadership positions in their respective industries without selling their products in most of the world's markets. The opening up of China has attracted firms seeking low-cost production, but this advantage will in the longer term be dwarfed by the country's market potential as the wealth of China's massive population rises. The establishment of production facilities within a regional economic grouping also allows access to the region's entire market. Thus, for example, Nissan's UK investment allows the company to export a large proportion of its production to other European Union (EU) countries. Similar explanations can be found for foreign investment in Latin America in recent years (see Practical Insight 8.1).

In some cases, early entry into an emerging economy brings first-mover advantages and the possibility of market dominance before rivals have the chance to establish themselves. Tesco has achieved this position in some of the former communist CEE countries.

Practical insight 8.1: FDI in Brazil

By the end of the 1990s, many of the world's leading motor manufacturers had assembly plants in Brazil. Some, like Volkswagen, General Motors, Ford, and Fiat had come to Brazil much earlier, attracted by the size and opportunities of the Brazilian market and the difficulties in exporting to a country with punitive import tariffs. The 1990s saw a new wave of investment by companies such as Renault, Peugeot, Nissan, Hyundai, and Daimler, attracted by Brazil's growing economy and membership of Mercosur, South America's largest regional economic grouping formed in 1991.

Brazil's motor industry trade group, Anfavea, forecasts that car sales in Brazil will increase from 3.4 million in 2011 to 5.7 million in 2016, which would probably enable Brazil to overtake Japan as the world's fourth largest car market after China, the USA, and the EU. Volkswagen, Fiat, General Motors, and Ford have dominated the market for a number of years, with a combined market share of 84 per cent in 2007, but this dominance is now being challenged by newer arrivals like Kia, Hyundai, Honda, Nissan, and BMW. The new competition is also helping to improve efficiency and productivity. Despite or perhaps because of its protectionist tendencies, Brazil continues to attract the world's major car manufacturers and the country's economy has survived the world economic slowdown more or less intact.[7]

Question

● How important as a motive for foreign direct investment in Brazil are costs of production likely to be relative to market access?

Paradoxically, however, Pepsico's early advantage in the same region before the end of communism was swiftly displaced by Coca-Cola's aggressive expansion into the region after 1989. Sometimes, it is simply necessary to follow the competition so as not to be left behind.

Access to resources

Historically, a country's deposits of coal, iron ore, copper, precious metals, or other natural resources were the main attraction for foreign investors. Indeed, this is still true today in the oil and mining industries, or where large quantities of natural resources are consumed in the production process – though Australian or Colombian coal, for example, can now be economically transported halfway around the world. Perhaps a more generally important reason why a foreign investor may be attracted by resources is where a specialized resource such as highly skilled labour is relatively immobile. On the whole, resources have become less important as a motive for internationalization in the modern world, as highly transferable knowledge and technology have acquired greater importance than natural resources in many industries.

Cost reduction

It is not uncommon for a business to offshore some of its operations, obtain components and other supplies, or relocate a production facility to another country in order to reduce costs. For example, a number of British banks and insurance companies have outsourced their call centres to India and the British company, Dyson, has relocated its production plant to Malaysia, whilst keeping its research and design facility in the UK. Some companies have in fact been criticized for exploiting low-cost labour in developing countries where working conditions would be regarded as unacceptable in their home country. It should be remembered, however, that cheap labour is not necessarily attractive to capital-intensive businesses where relatively small amounts of highly specialized labour are needed – unless, of course, highly skilled labour is available at low wages, as has been the case in recent years with computer programmers in Russia or India, for example.

8.2 Multinational enterprises and the internationalization process

8.2.1 Multinational enterprises

Many of the firms involved in international business are multinational, that is, they have operations in more than one country. Firms which export but do not have a physical presence in another country would not generally be classed as multinational, but where they have facilities such as a factory, warehouse, or retail store abroad, whether owned directly or not, the term multinational is likely to be used. Multinational businesses are variously known as multinational corporations (MNCs), **multinational enterprises** (MNEs), or transnational corporations (TNCs). The term MNC is probably the most widely used, though the United Nations refers to them as TNCs, focusing on the transnational nature of their activities rather than their multinational locations.[8] Some leading international business scholars prefer the term MNE as it encompasses all kinds of multinational operation, including subsidiaries which are run as separate companies and **licensing** and **franchising** agreements where the foreign operation is not owned by the parent company and is not therefore strictly part of the corporation as a legal entity.[9]

The definition of a multinational enterprise also varies, in terms of both the minimum number of foreign operations and the degree of management control required. Richard Caves provides a basic definition of an MNE as 'an enterprise that controls and manages production establishments – plants – located in at least two countries'.[10] This is clearly a minimal definition, but it at least provides a basis for the study of multinationality. For example, UNCTAD ranks the world's largest TNCs by the ratio of their foreign assets, sales, and employment to total assets, sales, and employment in its 'transnationality index', indicating the extent to which a TNC's operations are outside its home country.[11]

8.2.2 The evolution of MNEs

Some writers have focused attention on the different types of multinational enterprise and what they tell us about the way in which MNEs develop over a period of time. One of the earliest attempts to do this was in the work of Howard Perlmutter, who distinguished between ethnocentric, polycentric, and geocentric approaches to internationalization.[12] An MNE with an **ethnocentric approach** would pursue strategies that view the world from the home country's perspective and would be likely to market products abroad that are produced in and developed for the home market without cultural adaptation. An MNE with a **polycentric approach** would be organized into separate divisions in different countries or regions, each using local resources and production, and marketing adapted to its own cultural environment. A **geocentric approach** would imply that the MNE has a global strategy for its worldwide operations, with international resourcing and production, and products designed for the global market, often with local adaptations. In effect, this typology represents the evolutionary progress of MNEs as they develop their international activities.

A more extensive typology is provided by Bartlett and Ghoshal, including multinational, global, international, and transnational companies.[13] A multinational company operates with a number of decentralized divisions, each operating in its own area and retaining knowledge largely within its own business unit. A global company is centralized, has global strategies, and retains knowledge at the centre. An international company centralizes its core functions and decentralizes others, adapts its strategies to take account of local differences, and diffuses knowledge to its foreign divisions. The transnational company has a unified global approach, together with local variations, but it organizes its operations so as to achieve overall global competitiveness and flexibility. While the multinational company is responsive to change at the local level, the global company is more efficient at the global level, the international company is able to influence and disseminate knowledge to its local divisions, and the transnational company achieves global flexibility and competitiveness. Bartlett and Ghoshal clearly see the transnational company as the most appropriate type of MNE in an increasingly globalizing world. Perlmutter's and Bartlett and Ghoshal's typologies are compared in Figure 8.2.

			Perlmutter's Typology
Ethnocentric Approach	**Polycentric Approach**		**Geocentric Approach**
Home country orientation	Host country orientation		Global orientation
No cultural adaptation	Local cultural adaptation		Global strategy, local adaptation
			Bartlett and Ghoshal's Typology
Multinational Company	**Global Company**	**International Company**	**Transnational Company**
Decentralized	Centralized	Centralized core	Global approach
Local operations	Global strategies	Local adaptation	Local variation
Local knowledge	Knowledge at centre	Diffused knowledge	Global competitiveness

Figure 8.2 Typologies of multinational enterprise

8.2.3 MNEs and globalization

MNEs play an important role in the process of globalization. Not only do they carry out much of the trade, investment, and other international business activity, but their operations also involve the international movement of people and the spread and adaptation of cultures. They are influenced by the international environment and also influence that environment (an issue that is developed in Section 8.6). During the early phase of modern globalization, international business activity was dominated by MNEs from the Triad nations of North America, Western Europe, and Japan, but MNEs from Russia, China, India, South Korea, Brazil, and other emerging countries are now becoming increasingly active around the world. This changing scenario is helping to make international business activity more global whilst, at the same time, altering the relative economic importance of MNEs and the countries they represent. HSBC provides an example of an MNE with roots in different parts of the world (see Practical Insight 8.2).

Practical insight 8.2:   HSBC

HSBC was ranked the sixth largest bank in the world with revenue of $110.1 billion in 2012.[14] The company started its life in Hong Kong in 1865 as the Hongkong and Shanghai Banking Corporation. Today, HSBC has operations in all the main regions of the world, a position it has reached largely through whole or partial equity investments in other banks. The group's corporate headquarters were moved to London in January 1993, after the takeover of the UK's Midland Bank the previous year. Key functions including strategic management, human resource management, legal affairs, and financial planning and control are now centralized in London, but other operations are decentralized. The HSBC Group has also adopted common technology throughout its banking operations and a uniform international brand and logo. However, the company likes to emphasize its responsiveness to local customs and practices in its international marketing and the global and local aspects of its mission are encapsulated in the strap line: 'The world's local bank'.[15]

Question

● What do these characteristics suggest about the type of multinational enterprise HSBC has become?

8.3 Assessing the international environment

8.3.1 Country analysis and international entry

Before doing business in a foreign country, it is a good idea to undertake an analysis of the environment in the country concerned. Country analysis may take many forms and a wide range of organizations provide general and sometimes specialized information on countries. These include government departments, international institutions such as the United Nations, the Organization for Economic Cooperation and Development, and the World Economic Forum, banks and leading newspapers which produce country profiles and surveys, and a variety of consultants and online services which offer analysis of what is often termed 'country risk'. Of course, detailed market research is required before launching a product in a foreign market, but the better the understanding of a country's political, economic, and cultural environment, the greater the probability of the product succeeding and the less risk to a company's profitability and reputation. The degree of risk may also affect the choice of entry mode in a particular country; for example, joint ventures, licensing, and franchising are more likely to be used than full ownership in high-risk environments. Here, we focus on the main types of country analysis, including both risk factors and the general environment.

8.3.2 Types of country analysis

Background information

In order to appreciate the context within which a country's political, economic, and social institutions have emerged, some understanding of its history, geography, culture, and demography is necessary. For example, when comparing Russia with the Czech Republic, there are clearly differences in the size and ethnic composition of their populations, their geographical size and climatic location, and their political, economic, and military importance. There are also significant historical differences, even in recent times. Both countries have experienced communism, but over a much longer period in Russia (1917–91) than in Czechoslovakia (1948–89), in the former as the dominant power and the latter as a reluctant satellite state. Before communism, Russia had a largely agricultural economy, whereas Czechoslovakia was a developed industrialized country. Perhaps most important of all, however, Russia had never experienced democracy until 1991 – changing from one form of totalitarian rule under the Tsars to another under Lenin, Stalin, and the one-party communist state – whereas Czechoslovakia had been a democracy since its inception as an independent state in 1918. These very different historical paths during the twentieth century help to explain why the Czech Republic more readily accepted democracy and the market economy after the end of communism, whereas, after a brief experimentation with a more open society under Boris Yeltsin, the Russians sought refuge in strong central leadership under President Putin when times became difficult.

The general political and economic situation

It is difficult to understand the business environment in a country without studying the current political system and institutions, major government economic policies, and a variety of data and other information on the country's economy. The latter may include statistics on gross domestic product (GDP), the GDP annual growth rate, GDP per capita, inflation, unemployment, consumer expenditure, and the volume of external trade, as well as information on particular industries, the competitive environment, and the financial system. This information is constantly changing, so it is important to keep it up to date and to study long-run trends to obtain an idea of how an economy is progressing over a period of time.

Cultural assessment

This would require an investigation into cultural elements such as language, religion, and social structure and attitudes. Language presents particular difficulties when venturing into a foreign country, despite the prevalence of the English language. Not only can partial knowledge of a language lead to misunderstandings and unwittingly cause offence, but in-depth understanding of a culture is difficult to achieve without a good level of linguistic ability. Failure to appreciate differences in religious beliefs and practices or differences in social status, relationships, and attitudes may also create cultural pitfalls when attempting to do business in an unfamiliar environment. Cultural differences between countries are sometimes described as '**cultural distance**', a factor which increases the risk of operating abroad and may either deter international entry or reduce the likelihood of success.

General product data and other development indicators

Various types of data can be used to give an indication of the standard of living in a country. These may include product data such as the number of passenger vehicles, television sets, telephones, or internet connections per 1,000 inhabitants or human development indicators such as life expectancy, the prevalence of particular diseases, or the literacy rate of the population. These indicators provide a picture of the level of economic and social development in a country.[16]

Risk factors

The potential risks involved in entering a foreign country vary greatly with the country concerned. Political risks may include wars, civil unrest, terrorism, and changes in government policy or the law. Economic risks range from exchange rate exposure to the risk of non-payment or financial instability. A particular problem in some of the emerging and developing countries, though not exclusively in these countries, is the problem of corruption. These are just a few of the potential risks that may face a business venturing abroad. Cultural mistakes, human error, and natural disasters are among a long line of other possible risks (see Practical Insight 8.3). Some of these risks may of course arise in any country but the nature of the business or physical environment may increase their probability of occurrence.

8.3.3 **Country analysis in a changing international context**

The changing international environment continually presents new opportunities and challenges for MNEs. On the one hand, there has been a huge increase in world economic activity, fuelled initially by MNEs and economic liberalization in the Triad countries, then by a new

Practical insight **8.3**: Guanxi

The Chinese concept of guanxi is used to describe the personal relationships and networks that are thought to be necessary when doing business in China. These relationships often require the exchange of favours, sometimes involving public officials, and they need to be actively maintained in the long term if they are to bring significant benefits. There is considerable debate, however, about the ethics of doing business in this way, the costs of maintaining active relationships, and the relative benefits of guanxi as opposed to having good products and a good marketing strategy.[17]

Question

- Relationships are important, in different ways, when doing business in most countries, but are they as important as is sometimes claimed?

economic dynamism in South-East Asia, China, the CEE countries, and Latin America. At the same time, there has been periodic financial turbulence, notably in Latin America (Mexico 1994–5, Argentina 2001–2), East Asia (1997–8), spreading to Russia and Brazil (1998) and international financial markets (2008–9), not to mention the internationalization of terrorism since 11 September 2001 ('9/11') and the subsequent increase in tension between the west and the Islamic world. These contrasting developments are compounded in a multiplicity of ways at the national level, creating enormous complexity for MNEs. Despite this, whilst some of the above events have brought a temporary slowdown in international business activity, the trend generally remains upwards. Rather than abandoning their international operations, MNEs tend to adapt their choice of country and entry mode to the changing conditions. What is clear, however, is that the need to understand the international environment has become more important than ever.

8.4 Modes of international entry

8.4.1 Direct and indirect exporting and importing

International trade, involving exporting and importing, is the oldest form of international business activity and is still of huge importance today. For many businesses, it represents the most straightforward way to benefit from international markets and resources, though it carries significant risks, especially if a firm is dependent on a small number of international customers or suppliers or on markets or supplies in high-risk countries. MNEs frequently trade either with businesses within their own group (intra-company trade) or with external customers and suppliers. **Direct exporting and importing** involve direct contact between the exporter or importer and the foreign customer or supplier. Large established MNEs often trade in this way. For smaller or less experienced businesses, **indirect exporting and importing** are often used; this involves the services of an agent or other intermediary, providing specialist knowledge and a safer and more convenient way for a business to engage in international trade, though there is inevitably some loss of control unless the agent is entirely trusted. In practice, exporting and importing are often combined with other modes of international entry, as MNEs may engage in FDI or a foreign joint venture to provide an export base for trade with neighbouring countries.

8.4.2 Foreign direct investment

The IMF Balance of Payments Manual defines FDI as 'the objective of a resident entity in one economy obtaining a lasting interest in an enterprise resident in another economy'.[18] FDI normally involves some degree of equity ownership on the part of the foreign investor and the IMF and UN regard a 10 per cent equity stake as the minimum requirement, though there is no universally agreed ownership requirement. More important is that FDI requires some degree of management control; this distinguishes direct investment from portfolio investment – the latter involving the purchase of shares or other financial assets but not control. Using the above definition, FDI may include the establishment of a wholly owned subsidiary (often called a 'greenfield investment'), a joint venture with a foreign partner (involving joint ownership), and a foreign acquisition or takeover. Examples include Kia Motors' greenfield investment in Slovakia from 2004 to 2006, Volkswagen's initial joint venture with Skoda in 1991, and Kraft Food's takeover of Cadbury in 2010. Each of these examples involves management control on the part of the foreign investor. FDI has become a favoured strategy in many parts of the world since the 1980s and some of the reasons for its popularity will become clear when we consider the theories of internationalization in Section 8.5 below.

8.4.3 Licensing and franchising

Licensing and franchising are contractual arrangements whereby a licenser or franchiser allows a licensee or franchisee to use its intellectual property in return for a fee or royalty and, in some cases, an initial payment. The two parties are independent businesses but have engaged in a contract for a specified period of time. In international business, the licenser or franchiser is using this type of arrangement as a quick and relatively low-risk international expansion strategy, using the country-specific knowledge of the licensee or franchisee to establish and run its business in an unfamiliar environment. This is probably the reason why Marks and Spencer used franchising when entering the unfamiliar markets of the CEE countries. The main risk, however, is to the reputation of the licenser or franchiser. Licensing is common in manufacturing and processing industries where the licensee is allowed to use a patent, trade mark, technical know-how, and other intellectual property under the terms of the licence. Many of Coca-Cola's bottling operations, for example, are licensed to independent companies in its foreign markets. Franchising is more common in service industries such as retailing, tourism, catering, and hospitality. It usually involves the use of a particular method of doing business, including not only a brand name but also corporate advertising, training, and other support services. Perhaps the best-known franchise is McDonald's, but other examples include IKEA, the Body Shop, Benetton, and Holiday Inns.

8.4.4 Joint ventures, strategic alliances, and other collaborative strategies

MNEs have increasingly become involved in collaborative strategies with foreign partners in recent years. As well as licensing and franchising arrangements which are discussed above, these may include joint ventures, strategic alliances, agency agreements, subcontracting, and project management contracts, among others. Joint ventures and strategic alliances have become particularly important international entry strategies and are now considered separately.

Joint venture

An agreement between two or more companies involving joint equity ownership and control is described as a joint venture or joint-venture agreement. Because a degree of control is involved, it may also be classed as a form of FDI if a company enters a joint venture with a foreign partner. This type of arrangement has been used as an international entry mode where full ownership is considered too risky or is not allowed in the host country, or where for some other reason the parties want to retain their separate legal identity. Joint ventures between western and local partners were very common in Russia during the transition years in the 1990s, especially in the oil, gas, and motor industries, were used as a way of attracting foreign expertise to develop Taiwan's technology industries in the 1980s and 1990s, and were a common form of entry into China in the 1990s before full foreign ownership began to be allowed. Volkswagen's initial investment in Skoda in 1991 involved a joint venture with the Czech government, with VW owning a 31 per cent stake in Skoda, though this later rose to 70 per cent in 1995 and became full ownership in 2000. The alliance between Renault and Nissan, formed in 1999, is also technically a joint venture, with mutual equity holdings, though Renault has management control of Nissan and, since 2005, the two companies have had a joint chief executive (see the case study in Chapter 6 for more details).

Strategic alliance

A non-equity cooperation agreement between two or more independent firms is generally known as a strategic alliance. The purpose of such an alliance is to gain a mutual competitive advantage through cooperation in production, research and development, marketing, or purchasing, for example. Sometimes, alliance partners may own equity stakes in each other, effectively making them joint ventures, though alliances are usually more fluid arrangements than joint ventures. Strategic alliances are often found in the motor industry, involving joint development of new models and common production platforms, and among commercial airlines, where code-sharing agreements, shared facilities at airports, and joint purchasing arrangements provide marketing benefits and cost savings. Alliances of this type are often crucial in creating competitive advantages, allowing the partners to develop new products, access new markets, and reduce costs. They also raise competition issues, as they encourage cooperation rather than competition. This can be a problem when alliance loyalties are involved (see Practical Insight 8.4). However, in some cases competition between firms is replaced by competition between alliances.

8.4.5 **Internationalization of production: outsourcing and offshoring**

Outsourcing, involving the contracting out of production operations or services to external suppliers, has been used for many years as a way of obtaining specialized expertise or reducing costs. In recent years, global competition has increased the pressure to reduce costs, leading to a vast increase in international outsourcing, and this activity has been made possible by

Practical insight 8.4:   Rolls-Royce

In 1998, Volkswagen bought Rolls-Royce Motors from Vickers after outbidding its German rival, BMW. Rolls-Royce had previously had an alliance with BMW to enable it to develop more efficient and environmentally friendly engines and allowing BMW to move further into the luxury car market. VW's purchase of Rolls-Royce ended this alliance, but BMW was able to use its close links with Rolls-Royce Aerospace, a separate company from Rolls-Royce Motors but the owner of the Rolls-Royce brand, to gain exclusive use of the brand. This left VW with the Rolls-Royce factory in Crewe, but only the Bentley brand and, since 2003, BMW has produced Rolls-Royce cars at its Goodwood production plant in south-east England. This case illustrates BMW's mixed fortunes with strategic alliances.[19]

Question

• What lessons can be learned from BMW's experience?

massive improvements in information and communication technology (ICT). When business operations are transferred to another country, either through outsourcing or by setting up a wholly or partially owned subsidiary, this is often referred to as 'offshoring'. The international relocation or offshoring of production operations is not new in the manufacturing sector, but the term offshoring has also been applied to the transfer of service functions to other countries in recent years. Technology has enabled a wide range of marketing and 'back-office' functions to be undertaken in low-cost countries; these include call centres dealing with customer enquiries or direct marketing activities, and IT services such as payroll processing, financial analysis, or software development.

Increasingly, higher added-value operations as well as more basic activities have been performed by well-educated workers in India, Russia, Poland, China, the Philippines, South Africa, and other low-cost countries with English language skills and/or strong technical capabilities. Ireland, with its low corporate tax rates and technology graduates, has also attracted offshore operations. Much of this offshore activity is being undertaken by companies in the United States and UK, taking advantage of the widespread use of the English language as well as their more cost-conscious Anglo-Saxon business model with its liberal employment laws and flexible labour markets. It was estimated that the US accounted for around 70 per cent of global IT and business process offshoring and that US companies could achieve cost savings of between 45 and 70 per cent in 2003.[20]

Offshoring raises a number of political, social, and ethical as well economic issues. When business operations are offshored, unemployment is created in the home country, but the lower costs enable the offshoring company to reduce its prices and improve its profitability. Consumers benefit from the reduced prices and spend their surplus income on other goods and services. For the host country the gains from offshoring are significant, though the benefits may be short term if the next wind of change takes the business elsewhere. Whether there is a net benefit for the home country depends on its ability to redeploy the redundant workers and on how one evaluates the social consequences for the workers concerned and their families. Politically, the negative impact of concentrated job losses tends to weigh more heavily on the minds of electors and politicians than the thinly spread benefits to consumers and producers. Even when an economy like that of the USA is successful in creating new jobs, pockets of unemployment often remain in the districts and states most affected by offshoring. The shedding of existing workers in order to save money may also be seen as 'social dumping', a morally questionable practice from a stakeholder perspective.

Despite the above issues, offshoring has become increasingly common in recent years, spreading from traditional manufacturing to banking, insurance, retailing, publishing, logistics, and a number of other sectors. This reflects the cost savings and productivity gains that can be made from offshoring, particularly in relation to relatively standardized, though not necessarily low-skilled, business processes.[21] Perhaps more than any other international business activity, offshoring is a response to globalization, reflecting the competitive pressures of operating in an interconnected global environment and also the reality that the developing countries are increasingly able to offer highly sophisticated but low-cost services in a world where the barriers between rich and poor countries are being flattened.[22] Essentially, offshoring represents a real-location of the world's resources, driven by technology and competition. Resource reallocation on this scale causes uncertainty and fear, but it means that resources are being used more efficiently. The present distribution of resources and business activity will of course inevitably change over time as costs rise in countries like China and there is growing evidence that some of the offshoring companies are beginning to repatriate their activities as cost differentials narrow and the advantages of proximity become more apparent (see Practical Insight 8.5).

Practical insight 8.5:   Is 'reshoring' replacing offshoring?

Despite the huge growth of offshoring in recent years, there are some signs that this process is starting to be reversed. America's General Electric, for example, has 'reshored' its production of fridges, washing machines, and heaters back from China to the USA. The company is also beginning to repatriate its IT operations, most of which were previously outsourced abroad. Similarly, Lenovo, the Chinese company which acquired IBM's personal computer division in 2005, has recently relaunched personal computer production in the United States.

The reasons for this growing trend are threefold: first, wage differentials between the developed countries and the major offshore manufacturing centres are narrowing and it is estimated that the difference in total costs (including shipping and other costs as well as labour costs) between the USA and China or India may be relatively small by the year 2015. It is also likely that the widespread practice of offshoring has driven up wage costs at the main offshore locations. Whilst low-cost advantages may simply shift to other countries like Vietnam, Bangladesh, or perhaps even some of the African countries, these countries cannot always offer the necessary supply chains or infrastructure. Secondly, even when labour costs are considerably lower at an offshore location, for many firms labour costs represent a decreasing share of their production costs as labour is replaced by technology. Thirdly, offshoring companies have sometimes been motivated by the 'herd instinct' and the expected benefits have not always materialized. Indeed, some firms are beginning to realize that their core asset (their customers) may not be best served by offshoring customer-facing activities such as call centres or that having production facilities close to design and R&D centres may create important synergies.[23]

Questions

- To what extent do you think the trend towards 'reshoring' is likely to continue?
- What are the implications for the changing industrial structure in the global economy?

8.5 Theories of internationalization

8.5.1 Conventional theories of trade and investment

The theory of comparative advantage, developed by David Ricardo in the early nineteenth century, still provides a fundamental explanation for international trade and investment (see Section 3.4.1).[24] The basic idea is that if each country specializes in producing goods in whose production it has a comparative advantage (that is, can use its resources more productively than in the production of other goods), then trades with other countries with different comparative advantages, the world as a whole will be better off. This is because the total output of goods produced from a given set of resources will have increased. Although this theory principally applies to countries rather than firms, it is firms that are actually engaged in production and trade, taking advantage of the comparative advantages of the countries in which they are based. It may also be argued that MNEs will be attracted by a country's comparative advantages when investing abroad, so the theory can be used as a basic explanation for FDI as well as international trade. The Heckscher–Ohlin theorem, also known as factor endowment theory, adds a refinement to the theory of comparative advantage by arguing that specialization will occur in industries where inputs are available at relatively low cost because of their abundant supply.[25] Conventional ideas about the sources of comparative advantage have tended to concentrate on the role of natural resources, proximity to which has become less important in modern industries. However, if the theory is adapted to take account of resources such as technology or human capital, it may still provide a plausible explanation for broad patterns of international location, if not necessarily for the motives of individual MNEs.

8.5.2 Internationalization in imperfect markets

The theory of comparative advantage was constructed with a world of perfect competition in mind. While this does not necessarily invalidate its general predictions, it leaves room for a number of possible alternative explanations of the behaviour of MNEs in practice. In a world of imperfect competition, with differentiated products, barriers to entry into international markets, and firms with varying degrees of market power, MNEs are likely to exploit their differentiated products, find ways of overcoming market entry barriers, and take advantage of their strategic position. For example, in the consumer goods and motor industries, MNEs in developed countries are able to achieve economies of scale by selling their differentiated products to consumers in other developed countries where similar but differentiated products are produced – a practice known as intra-industry trade. Intra-industry trade theory uses ideas from industrial organization theory, especially the analysis of oligopoly where markets are dominated by a few large firms, to help explain the behaviour of MNEs in international markets (see Section 3.4.2). Even smaller firms may be able to obtain external economies of scale by locating within an industry cluster, using the agglomeration economies of the cluster as a springboard to export their specialized goods or services (see Section 5.1.7).

International market entry barriers may include trade barriers such as tariffs, quotas, or local content requirements, exchange rate volatility or lack of currency convertibility, host country industrial policies that favour domestic firms, the existence of dominant competitors in the domestic market, or natural barriers such as geographical distance, transport accessibility, or language. MNEs can overcome some of these difficulties by locating their operations within the host country. This may also provide an export base for them to access a larger market in a regional trading area such as the EU or the North American Free Trade Agreement (NAFTA). In effect, MNEs use their international entry strategy as a way of exploiting their differentiated products, internal or external economies of scale, market position, and/or reputation to achieve their overall goals of international expansion and profitability.

A significant contribution to internationalization theory in imperfect markets was made by Buckley and Casson, who proposed a long-run theory of the development of MNEs.[26] Given that firms are operating in uncertain and sometimes poorly functioning markets, they will try to internalize the production of goods which incorporate substantial research and development or require specialized marketing techniques by retaining ownership through FDI as they venture abroad. According to Buckley and Casson, a firm's knowledge and innovation ability are its crucial firm-specific assets during the internationalization process and these assets can be protected and exploited through FDI. As well as making use of **resource-based** and **transaction cost** ideas which are discussed in Sections 8.5.5 and 8.5.6, this theory represents a significant departure from conventional theory by turning the focus of internationalization from countries to industries and firms.

8.5.3 **Vernon's product cycle hypothesis**

Raymond Vernon's product cycle hypothesis offers a possible explanation for the production cycle of a product.[27] His work was based on empirical studies of US industries in the 1960s and its relevance relates mainly to product innovation in developed countries. The product cycle consists of four main stages: (1) a new product is developed for high-income domestic consumers with inelastic demand (demand that is unresponsive to price changes) and production is based in the innovating country; (2) as the product becomes more successful and a dominant design is accepted, it is exported to other high-income countries to take advantage of economies of scale; (3) competitors in developed countries produce similar products as the technology becomes more widely available; (4) the product becomes more standardized and production is transferred to low-cost locations as price competition increases.

The international product cycle described above is often confused with the product life cycle used in marketing. Although apparently similar, the marketing concept is derived from the analogy with a biological life cycle and focuses on the development of markets, whether domestic or international, whereas the international product cycle focuses primarily on production in an international context. However, the two concepts may be considered in parallel in the special case of a product initially sold in the home market, then exported, subject to international competition, and finally sold at a more competitive price to prolong the product life cycle – relating Vernon's model to the introduction, growth, maturity, and decline stages in the marketing model. In effect, the transfer of production to a low-cost country in the standardization phase of Vernon's model may be seen as a way of extending the product life cycle and delaying the decline phase in the marketing model. The production and market perspectives of the two models are compared in Figure 8.3.

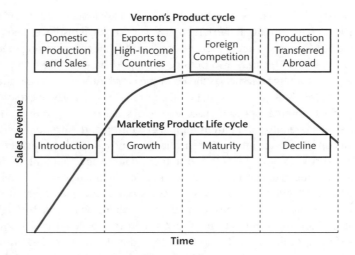

Figure 8.3   Vernon's product cycle and the marketing product life cycle

8.5.4 **Learning models of internationalization**

Some of the literature on internationalization focuses on the way in which MNEs learn by experience, proceeding cautiously at first to countries that are perceived to be similar or involving less risk, then becoming more adventurous as their international experience grows. These ideas are sometimes described as the Uppsala model, based on the work of researchers at the University of Uppsala in Sweden.[28] Whilst in some cases an MNE may begin by venturing into neighbouring countries that are geographically close, most researchers concentrate on the importance of '**psychic distance**' rather than physical distance. Psychic distance relates to a firm's perception of cultural and other business differences between its home country and other countries. Thus, for example, a British firm may be expected to venture initially into countries where English is widely spoken or understood, where the Anglo-Saxon culture predominates, or where historic ties have left a legacy of similar business practices; countries such as the USA, Ireland, India, Malaysia, or South Africa would satisfy one or more of these criteria.

The main focus of attention has been on the concept of 'cultural distance', a subset of psychic distance concerned with cultural differences between countries. One might expect MNEs to be more wary of entering culturally distant environments, especially during the early stages of internationalization, and to choose entry modes which involve less risk, such as joint ventures or franchising rather than fully owned subsidiaries. However, recent research suggests that the relationship between cultural distance and international entry is more complex.[29] In general terms, there appears to be no consistent pattern in this relationship, but when specific factors are isolated clearer links start to emerge. First, political and economic uncertainties in a country seem to have a greater negative effect on entry decisions than differences in culture. Secondly, there is some evidence to suggest that MNEs devote fewer resources and prefer low-equity modes of entry in countries with high cultural distance, though this appears to vary with the origin of the investor. Thirdly, MNEs in high-technology industries appear to be more reluctant to invest in culturally distant countries than MNEs in other industries, perhaps because of the scale of the capital investment required and the higher risk involved. Fourthly, MNEs are more likely to ignore cultural distance in developed countries than in developing countries, probably because market conditions and institutions are more similar and knowledge and resources are more readily available. Finally, MNEs are becoming more at ease with cultural distance as previously isolated emerging economies provide opportunities for expansion, more familiar markets become saturated, and cultural awareness increases.

There is also evidence to suggest that participation in an alliance or network may reduce the uncertainty otherwise associated with psychic distance, leaving 'outsiders' more vulnerable than 'insiders'. This is mainly because of the opportunities for trust-building and knowledge creation within a network or alliance.[30] These findings are consistent with the expected benefits of experience and learning, though they highlight some of the complexities of the internationalization process.

8.5.5 Resource-based theories of internationalization

In a world of imperfect competition, firms gain competitive advantage in the international environment by exploiting their firm-specific assets and capabilities. The idea that an MNE's decision to locate abroad and choice of entry mode is determined by its ability to take advantage of its firm-specific assets is derived from the resource-based view of the firm.[31] Firms acquire generic resources when they take on labour or purchase technology, but over time these resources become more specialized, giving a firm distinctive capabilities. Many of these firm-specific assets are intangible, including knowledge and skills, intellectual property, databases, customized computer programs, and relationships with other organizations. It may indeed be that competitive advantage depends not so much on individual resources, but on a particular combination of resources available to a firm, such as a team of researchers who have worked together on the development of a new drug in the pharmaceutical industry. In particular, the resource-based view suggests that a firm is more likely to locate abroad rather than to export at a distance in order to retain control of its marketing strategy, form local relationships, and ensure that its products reach the customer in pristine condition, especially where complex technical products requiring pre- and after-sales service are involved. Similarly, full-ownership FDI may be preferred to other modes of entry, allowing the firm to retain full control of its firm-specific assets.

The growing use of the internet for international business transactions enables a business to exploit its firm-specific assets in an international environment. By breaking down some of the barriers that restrict entry into foreign markets, the internet allows entry into markets that might otherwise only be accessible after incurring substantial investment costs. There may also be country-specific advantages that can be exploited when marketing culturally attractive products such as Celtic jewellery or African wood carvings to consumers hungry for new experiences. A study of internationalization by US-based internet firms suggests that country-specific websites may help to promote international expansion, though their success depends on factors such as a firm's reputation, the volume of website traffic, and the type of competitive or cooperative strategies employed.[32] Even with the internet, resources alone are not sufficient to guarantee success; the right strategies are also required.

8.5.6 **Transaction cost explanations of internationalization**

Whenever a firm undertakes a transaction with a customer or supplier, it incurs transaction costs in addition to the price paid for goods or services. These include the legal costs of drawing up a contract, the costs of going out to tender or searching for information on potential suppliers, or the cost of currency exchange or hedging, for example. In the 1930s Ronald Coase realized the significance of transaction costs for the very existence of firms, arguing that firms exist because they help to eliminate the costs of continually engaging in external contracting.[33] Firms are often described in the literature as 'hierarchies', consisting of structures with different levels of decision making, to distinguish them from the more transitory arrangements involved in market contracting.[34] In general, firms or hierarchies are regarded as preferable to market contracting where markets are characterized by imperfect information (*bounded rationality*), where incomplete or asymmetric information allows one party to exploit his or her advantage over the other (*opportunism*), or where dedicated assets and associated sunk costs are involved (*asset specificity*).[35] In these cases, firms are able to minimize the risks of doing business and the associated transaction costs.

In the context of international business, FDI allows an MNE to internalize its operations and avoid the transaction costs that would be involved in exporting, especially where the MNE has full ownership and control of its foreign subsidiary. Clearly, different entry modes carry different start-up costs, but ongoing transaction costs are minimized where an MNE's international operations are closely integrated within the organization as a whole. The internet also allows even small online businesses to export directly to international customers without the need for an intermediary, thereby reducing the transaction costs involved in agency contracts. Transaction cost theory is probably the most widely accepted explanation for the decision to retain ownership and control when venturing abroad. Recent studies generally support this view, though they emphasize that the success of an international entry strategy is affected not only by the ability to reduce transaction costs, but also by the suitability of the institutional context (particularly in relation to legal restrictions) and the cultural context (affecting the investment risk) in the host country.[36]

8.5.7 **Dunning's eclectic paradigm**

John Dunning, a leading international business scholar, has provided an eclectic view of the factors affecting the internationalization decision, with particular reference to FDI, by combining some of the above ideas into a single theory.[37] **Dunning's eclectic paradigm**, or the OLI paradigm as it is also known, focuses on the ownership (O), location (L), and internalization (I) advantages of FDI as opposed to exporting (see Figure 8.4). These advantages may be summarized as follows:

- Ownership advantages: firm-specific assets such as knowledge and skills, technology, intellectual property, management or marketing competences, and internal and external relationships (mainly intangible).
- Location advantages: a good geographical location with respect to production costs, market access, psychic (including cultural) distance, and the general political and economic environment.

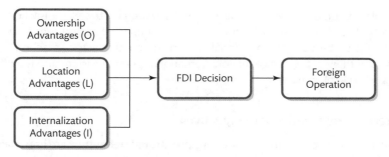

Figure 8.4 Dunning's eclectic (OLI) paradigm

- Internalization advantages: reduced transaction costs and the ability to protect management know-how and intellectual property.

Each of these advantages can be related to some of the internationalization theories outlined in this chapter. Ownership advantages can be derived from the resource-based view of internationalization and Buckley and Casson's long-run theory of MNE development. Location advantages can be found in several internationalization theories, including comparative advantage theory, learning models of internationalization, and ideas from **economic geography**. Internalization advantages incorporate the transaction cost view, but go further in relation to intangible benefits such as management know-how and intellectual property. Note that 'internalization' should not be confused with 'internationalization' – the former meaning that FDI enables a firm to internalize its operations and intangible assets, whereas the latter term refers to the process of going international, regardless of the entry mode involved.

Drawing on extensive empirical research, Dunning's OLI paradigm argues that FDI decisions can be explained by considering a combination of the above factors, rather than focusing on

Practical insight 8.6: A tale of two Hoffmanns

August Hoffmann began producing pianos in Sweden in 1838, but the company closed in 1988 and production was transferred to the Dongbei Piano Company in China, which was acquired by Baldwin Pianos, a subsidiary of Gibson Guitar Corporation of the USA, in 2007. Low-cost production allows this long-established brand to be marketed in North America, Europe, Asia, and Australia at modest prices. Having a German-sounding name is an asset in the piano business, alongside famous names like Bechstein, Blüthner, Bösendorfer, and Steinway (actually American, though its founder was of German descent). There was also a German piano manufacturer called W. Hoffmann, a more up-market brand than August Hoffmann, now owned by Bechstein but produced in the Czech Republic at the Bohemia piano factory (acquired by Bechstein in 2006–7). Some W. Hoffmann piano production is also outsourced to the Hailun Piano Company in China. These stories are not untypical of many other examples of international production and marketing.[38]

Question

- Which of the theories of internationalization could be applied to these examples?

one particular factor. By drawing on ideas from the resourced-based, transaction cost, and other approaches to internationalization, the theory implies that decisions to go international are affected by both organizational and environmental factors. Practical Insight 8.6 illustrates something of the complexity of internationalization decisions and the difficulty in applying a single explanation.

8.5.8 Internal organizational perspectives

Some research suggests that firm size and **organizational behaviour** are important factors in internationalization decisions. For example, there is evidence to suggest that large retailers are more likely to enter a foreign market through acquisition, whereas smaller retailers tend to use lower-risk strategies such as franchising.[39] A key aspect of organizational behaviour that is likely to influence a firm's approach to internationalization is organizational culture. The internal culture of an organization can be classified in a number of different ways. One approach is to distinguish between a *hierarchical culture*, based on rules, procedures, and control, a *clan culture*, based on loyalty, tradition, and collaboration, a *market culture*, orientated towards competition and achievement, and an *adhocracy culture*, which is entrepreneurial, innovative, and creative.[40] Whilst the latter two cultures are likely to produce high-risk modes of entry involving full ownership and control, the former two are more likely to lead to low-risk entry modes.

8.5.9 The economic geography of internationalization

Geographical location has always been recognized as an important factor in the decision to venture abroad. However, whilst in conventional theory location was the main focus, the dominant internationalization theories then turned their attention towards the role of the firm and its ability to exploit its resources or minimize transaction costs by internalizing the management of its foreign operations. Admittedly, location factors still played an integral role, as in Dunning's eclectic paradigm, but they no longer occupied a central position in the theory. The pendulum now seems to be swinging back towards location-specific explanations of internationalization behaviour – not exclusively so, but they are increasingly being integrated into established theory. The role of political and economic institutions and psychic distance is discussed in various sections above, but attention is also turning towards ideas from economic geography.

Two particular areas of interest are clusters and networks. Clusters are explored more extensively as an explanation for sub-national regional development in Section 5.1.7, but essentially they provide an opportunity for firms in a particular industry to feed off each other by supplying specialized services, cooperating in research and development, attracting a pool of skilled labour, and creating a market for each other's products within close geographical proximity. In an international context, the agglomeration economies created by clusters create opportunities for exporting and are likely to attract foreign investors to a particular location. In this way, spatial patterns of economic development act as one of the determinants of internationalization decisions (see Practical Insight 8.7). Networks, especially telecommunication networks, may also affect location decisions. MNEs dominate international telecommunications traffic and often lease telecommunication networks to support their international operations. The location of regional telecommunication hubs in countries like the UK or USA may then influence the strategic internationalization decisions of these MNEs.[41]

Practical insight 8.7: The Tees Valley process industries cluster

An example of the agglomeration economies created by clusters can be found in the Tees Valley process industries cluster in north-east England. Although formerly a major chemical complex dominated by ICI, the cluster now attracts firms of various sizes in a wider range of process industries. These companies complement and interact with each other in a number of related fields, including fine and speciality chemicals, pharmaceuticals, biotechnology, and a variety of supporting services. Among these firms there have been a number of inward investors, including BASF (Germany), ConocoPhillips, Dow Chemical, DuPont, and Huntsman (USA), Ineos Nitriles (Switzerland), Sembcorp (Singapore), and Vopak (Netherlands).[42]

Question

- What features of this type of cluster are likely to be attractive to inward investors?

8.6 Internationalization and the business environment

Several of the theories of internationalization acknowledge the importance of the external business environment. In some cases, the environment provides an explicit focus, as for example in conventional theory, where a country's resource endowments form the basis of comparative advantage, and learning models, with their emphasis on cultural and other psychic differences between countries. In other cases, environmental factors operate in combination with other factors. Thus, for example, production is located abroad as a response to international competition in Vernon's product cycle, hierarchies are compared with external market contracting in transaction cost theory, and location advantages provide an essential element of Dunning's eclectic mix. There is also a growing trend in recent research for environmental factors such as institutions, culture, and economic geography to be incorporated into explanations of internationalization and entry mode decisions. This is the case in recent work on transaction cost theory, for example, and in modern reinterpretations of Buckley and Casson's important work on the role of knowledge and innovation in the internationalization process.[43]

It is worth noting that the connection between firms and the environment may operate in both directions. In other words, the activities of firms may have an effect on their environment. It is often argued that large MNEs have the power to influence government policy to their advantage by lobbying politicians, funding political parties, or even engaging in corruption to further their objectives. Studies by the World Bank and European Bank for Reconstruction and Development (EBRD) have also focused attention on the problem of **state capture** in transition economies, where powerful corporate oligarchs 'capture' the authorities at the expense of the rest of the business sector by shaping the 'rules of the game' or bribing public officials to gain lucrative contracts.[44] At a more benign level, MNEs may influence the business environment by the way in which they compete or cooperate with other firms, the extent to which they exercise corporate social responsibility, or the way in which they develop strategies that influence the outcome of alternative future scenarios. One thing is certain: the international activities of MNEs both influence and are influenced by their external environment.

Summary

The motives for going international include both broad overarching factors and firm-specific factors. Whilst the search for profitability is often the primary motive for venturing abroad, international expansion is also influenced by the changing international environment and the business environment in a particular country. At a more detailed level, firms may be looking for new markets, specific resources, or opportunities to reduce costs. Different typologies of MNEs have been developed to explain the process of internationalization and how this process evolves over a period of time. MNEs need to undertake detailed country analysis before entering a particular country and this analysis will influence the mode of entry. International entry may take a variety of forms, including exporting, FDI, and various types of collaborative strategy. Outsourcing and offshoring are widely used strategies for improving competitiveness in an increasingly globalized world economy. A number of theories have been developed to help analyse patterns of internationalization and international entry decisions. Some of these theories focus on firm-specific factors, others highlight the importance of country-related factors. There is now a trend towards the integration of these two approaches. Whatever the precise combination of firm-specific and country factors, it is clear that the external business environment both influences and is influenced by the international activities of MNEs.

Discussion questions

1. In what ways are country-specific factors likely to affect a company's decision to venture abroad?

2. What are the advantages and disadvantages of the transnational company according to Bartlett and Ghoshal's typology of MNEs?

3. What kind of background information on a country might be useful to a company when undertaking a country analysis prior to investing abroad?

4. Under what circumstances might a company form a joint venture rather than engage in full FDI when venturing abroad?

5. To what extent does Dunning's eclectic paradigm provide a comprehensive view of the factors an MNE is likely to consider when investing abroad?

6. How important a role does the external business environment play in theories of internationalization?

Suggested assignment topics

1. Choose a specific MNE and investigate how its organizational structure has changed as it has internationalized. Apply appropriate typologies to describe how the MNE has evolved and evaluate the advantages and disadvantages of its current organizational structure.

2. Choose a specific country as a potential location for market entry by a foreign retailer. Undertake a detailed country analysis and recommend an appropriate mode of entry.

3. Choose a specific example of 'offshoring' by a company in the service sector. Identify: (a) the reasons for the company's decision to offshore some of its operations, (b) the impact of the offshoring on the home and host country's economies, and (c) a possible justification for 'reshoring' some of the company's activities to its home country.

 Case study: Wal-Mart's international expansion

Wal-Mart was the third largest company in the world ranked by sales revenue in 2012 and by far the largest retailer.[45] Its sales revenue of $447 billion was over three times the size of its closest rival in the retail sector, Carrefour of France. Wal-Mart opened its first store in Rogers, Arkansas in 1962 and by the end of the 1970s had 276 stores in the USA. By the mid-1980s the number of stores had increased to 882 and in 1990 Wal-Mart became the US retail market leader, but the company did not venture abroad until 1991. Its first international store was a joint venture in Mexico. This was followed by expansion into Puerto Rico, Canada, Hong Kong, Argentina, and Brazil, mainly through acquisition or greenfield investment. Wal-Mart then entered China through a joint venture in 1996, Germany through the acquisition of Wertkauf, and South Korea through a joint venture in 1998; this expansion was followed by the acquisition of Interspar in Germany and Asda in the UK in 1999. In 2007, Wal-Mart increased its equity stake in Seiyu of Japan to 95 per cent, having formed a joint venture with Seiyu in 2002 and acquired majority ownership in 2006, and opened its first store in India as a joint venture with Bharti Enterprises in 2010. The company also has stores in Chile (majority holding) and South Africa (acquisition), along with majority holdings in companies with extensive operations in Central America and Africa.

Wal-Mart has pioneered its own distinctive business methods. Many of its outlets are large discount stores offering a wide range of goods at low prices. It adopts a paternalistic management style towards its employees, describing them as 'associates', and prefers minimal involvement with trade unions. The company has extensive international sourcing arrangements in order to keep costs to a minimum. Its cost-control measures, large volume of sales, and streamlined business practices have helped to create a highly profitable business. However, like other MNEs, Wal-Mart has had to adapt its strategies to the cultural, institutional, and competitive environment it faces in different countries. Sometimes this has meant using a joint-venture agreement rather than full FDI, especially when first entering an unfamiliar environment. At other times, the company has built new stores on a greenfield site or has acquired an existing established retailer.

The European retail sector is dominated by a number of strong national competitors and Germany is no exception. Wal-Mart entered the German market through its acquisition of Wertkauf and Interspar, allowing immediate access to the country's mature retail sector. In addition to the established market leader, Metro, the German market includes successful discounters such as Aldi and Lidl. Germany also has a distinctive institutional environment with a highly regulated labour market and strong trade unions. In one instance, Wal-Mart met opposition when trying to introduce a new

(continued...)

ethics code for its staff, as the code was seen as overly restrictive by its German employees. Wal-Mart's paternalistic management style also sat uneasily with Germany's system of *Mitbestimmung* – involving the participation of trade unions in company decision making. Whilst Wal-Mart was able to use its vast resources and global scale to source low-cost supplies from China and other parts of the world, these strengths offered little advantage when it came to supplying German beer, Bratwurst, and the many specialized European brands that German consumers demand. This experience led Wal-Mart to sell its German operations to Metro in 2006.[46]

Wal-Mart's UK acquisition, Asda, sat more easily with the company's business model. Although the British retail market is also well established with a dominant player, Tesco, and other strong competitors, the institutional environment is closer to that of the United States and Asda had been modelling its business practices on those of Wal-Mart even before the takeover in 1999. Wal-Mart's position in the UK market, as number two to Tesco, is clearly different from its leadership role in the US market, but Wal-Mart has nevertheless consolidated its position as a leading discounter in the UK market. Like Tesco, however, Wal-Mart's expansion in China has been slower than expected, with both companies facing stiff competition, slower market growth as China's economy finally succumbs to the world economic slowdown, and cultural resistance from some of China's more traditional consumers.

These experiences illustrate the significant differences between the cultural and institutional environments in different countries and the way in which Wal-Mart has responded to these differences. In particular, the case study provides an insight into the pattern of internationalization of one of the world's most successful companies and the extent to which its choice of country and mode of entry has been influenced by the company's organizational structure and strategy.[47]

Case study questions

1. Why do you think Wal-Mart did not venture abroad until 1991, despite its success in the USA?

2. How would you explain Wal-Mart's choice of countries during the early stages of its international expansion in the 1990s?

3. On what grounds do you think Wal-Mart chooses between acquisitions, greenfield investments, and joint ventures when entering a foreign market?

4. Select two of the theories of internationalization and critically evaluate the extent to which they could be used to explain Wal-Mart's international expansion strategy.

5. To what extent is it possible or desirable for a company like Wal-Mart to use the same business model wherever it invests abroad?

6. Why do you think the German retail market proved to be a difficult environment for Wal-Mart?

7. Despite the cultural and institutional similarities between the USA and UK, what differences is Wal-Mart likely to have experienced in the UK environment?

8. Why do you think China is proving to be a more difficult market than expected for some of the world's major retailers?

Notes

1. *New York Times* (16 November 2012), 'Ikea admits forced labor was used in 1980s'.

2. For example, several people were injured during a fracas at IKEA's Edmonton store in North London in February 2005 when about 6,000 customers arrived for the opening of the new store; source: *Financial Times* (11 February 2005), 'MP to question Ikea over causes of stampede at store opening'.

3. Main sources: IKEA Group corporate websites: http://www.ikea.com, http://www.inter.ikea.com, and http://franchisor.ikea.com/franchising.html (accessed 22 February 2013); *Wall Street Journal* (18 September 2012), 'IKEA to accelerate expansion'.

4. 98 per cent of Nestlé's sales revenue was generated outside Switzerland in 2010; source: UNCTAD, *World Investment Report*, 2010, Annex Table 29: The world's top 100 non-financial TNCs, ranked by foreign assets.

5. World Economic Forum, *Global Competitiveness Report*, 2012–2013, http://www.weforum.org/reports/global-competitiveness-report-2012-2013.

6. Porter, M. E. (1998), *The Competitive Advantage of Nations*, The Free Press, ch. 3.

7. Forbes (22 October 2012), 'Why the world's automakers love Brazil'.

8. For example, UNCTAD, the United Nations Conference on Trade and Development, compiles data on TNCs in its annual *World Investment Report*.

9. See, for example, Caves, R. E. (2007), *Multinational Enterprise and Economic Analysis*, Cambridge University Press; Dunning, J. H., and Lundan, S. M. (2008), *Multinational Enterprises and the Global Economy*, Edward Elgar; or Rugman, A. M. (2012), *New Theories of the Multinational Enterprise*, Routledge.

10. Caves, R. E. (2007), *Multinational Enterprise and Economic Analysis*, Cambridge University Press, p. 1.

11. UNCTAD, *World Investment Report* (annual).

12. Perlmutter, H. V. (1969), 'The tortuous evolution of the multinational corporation', *Columbia Journal of World Business*, vol. 4, pp. 9–18.

13. Bartlett, C. A., and Ghoshal, S. (2002), *Managing Across Borders: The Transnational Solution*, Harvard Business School Press.

14. Fortune Global 500, 2012.

15. Source: HSBC Group website, http://www.hsbc.com.

16. See UNDP, *Human Development Reports*, http://hdr.undp.org/en/.

17. For a critical discussion of the concept of guanxi, see Fan, Y. (2002), 'Questioning guanxi: definition, classification and implications', *International Business Review*, vol. 11, no. 5, pp. 543–61.

18. IMF, *Balance of Payments Manual*, 5th edn (BPM5), 1993, p. 86.

19. Main source: *Motor Trader* (10 August 1998), 'VW buys Rolls-Royce but BMW wins the title'.

20. McKinsey Global Institute (2003), 'Offshoring: Is It a Win-Win Game?' http://www.mckinsey.com.

21. For a discussion of the productivity implications of business services offshoring, see Sako, M. (2006), 'Outsourcing and offshoring: Implications for productivity of business services', *Oxford Review of Economic Policy*, vol. 22, no. 4, pp. 499–512.

22. See Friedman, T. L. (2007), *The World is Flat: The Globalized World in the Twenty-First Century*, Penguin, pp. 141–50.

23. Main sources: *The Economist* (19 January 2013), 'Special Report: Outsourcing and Offshoring; and KPMG' (July 2012), 'The Death of Outsourcing', http://www.kpmginstitutes.com.

24. Ricardo, D. (2004), *The Principles of Political Economy*, Dover Publications, first published in 1817 under the title *On the Principles of Political Economy and Taxation*.

25. Ohlin, B. (1933), *Interregional and International Trade*, Harvard University Press.

26. Buckley, P. J., and Casson, M. C. (2002), *The Future of the Multinational Enterprise*, Palgrave, first published in 1979.

27. Vernon, R. (1966), 'International investment and international trade in the product cycle', *Quarterly Journal of Economics*, May, vol. 80, pp. 190–207.

28. Johanson, J., and Vahlne, J.-E. (1977), 'The internationalization process of the firm: A model of knowledge development and increasing foreign market commitments', *Journal of International Business Studies*, vol. 8, no. 1, pp. 23–32.

29. See, for example, Tihanyi, L., Griffith, D. A., and Russell, C. J. (2005), 'The effect of cultural distance on entry mode choice, international diversification, and MNE performance: a meta-analysis', *Journal of International Business Studies*, vol. 36, no. 3, pp. 270–83.

30. Johanson, J., and Vahlne, J.-E. (2009), 'The Uppsala internationalization process model revisited: From liability of foreignness to liability of outsidership', *Journal of International Business Studies*, vol. 40, pp. 1411–31.

31. See Barney, J. (1991), 'Firm resources and sustained competitive advantage', *Journal of Management*, vol. 17, no. 1, pp. 99–120.

32. Kottha, S., Rindova, V. P., and Rothaermel, F. T. (2001), 'Assets and actions: Firm-specific factors in the internationalization of US internet firms', *Journal of International Business Studies*, vol. 32, no. 4, pp. 769–91.

33. Coase, R. (1937), 'The nature of the firm', *Economica*, vol. 4, pp. 386–405.

34. See Williamson, O. E. (1996), *Industrial Organization*, Edward Elgar.

35. See Williamson, O. E. (1996), *Industrial Organization*, Edward Elgar.

36. See, for example, Brouthers, K. D. (2002), 'Institutional, cultural and transaction cost influences on entry mode choice and performance', *Journal of International Business Studies*, vol. 33, no. 2, pp. 203–21.

37. Dunning, J. H. (1979), 'Explaining changing patterns of international production', *Oxford Bulletin of Economics and Statistics*, vol. 41, pp. 269–95; a more extensive explanation of the OLI paradigm can also be found in Dunning, J. H., and Lundan, S. M. (2008), *Multinational Enterprises and the Global Economy*, Edward Elgar.

38. This case was investigated through a number of company and piano websites and resulted from the author being asked by a friend to check out a second-hand Hoffmann piano before purchase.

39. White, A. (1995), *Cross-Border Retailing; Leaders, Losers and Prospects*, Pearson Professional.

40. Cameron, K. S., and Quinn, R. E. (2011). *Diagnosing and Changing Organizational Culture: Based on the Competing Values Framework*, Jossey Bass.

41. The role of economic geography in internationalization decisions is discussed in Verbeke, A. (2005), *Internalization, International Diversification and the Multinational Enterprise: Essays in Honor of Alan M. Rugman*, JAI Press.

42. Source: North East Process Industry Cluster (NEPIC), http://www.nepic.co.uk.

43. See, for example, Henisz, W. J. (2003), 'The power of the Buckley and Casson thesis: The ability to manage institutional idiosyncrasies', *Journal of International Business Studies*, vol. 34, no. 1, pp. 173–84.

44. Hellman, J. S., Jones, G., and Kaufmann, D. (2000), 'Seize the State, Seize the Day: State Capture, Corruption, and Influence in Transition', World Bank Policy Research Paper, September; and Hellman, J. S., Jones, G., Kaufmann, D., and Schankerman, M. (2000), 'Measuring Governance and State Capture: The Role of Bureaucrats and Firms in Shaping the Business Environment', EBRD Working Paper No. 51.

45. Fortune Global 500, 2012.

46. Main sources: *Business Week* (11 April 2005), 'Wal-Mart: struggling in Germany'; *Business Week* (28 July 2006), 'Wal-Mart's German retreat'; *The Times* (29 July 2006), 'Wal-Mart pulls out of Germany at cost of $1bn'; and *Financial Times* (31 July 2006), 'Wal-Mart checks out from Germany'.

47. Main sources: Wal-Mart Stores corporate website, http://corporate.walmart.com; BBC News (14 June 1999), 'Wal-Mart bids for Asda'; *Financial Times* (22 October 2007), 'Wal-Mart to take full control of Seiyu'; the *Guardian* (14 May 2009), 'Asda lures customers from rivals'; and Bloomberg (19 October 2012): 'Tesco stumbles with Wal-Mart as China shoppers buy local'.

Suggestions for further reading

Comprehensive analyses of international business operations, international entry modes, and the international business environment

Daniels, J., Radebaugh, L., and Sullivan, D. (2012), *International Business: Environments and Operations*, Pearson

Hill, C. W. L. (2012), *International Business: Competing in the Global Marketplace*, McGraw-Hill

Rugman, A. M., and Collinson, S. (2012), *International Business*, Pearson

On country analysis for potential investors

Currie, D. M. (2011), *Country Analysis: Understanding Economic and Political Performance*, Gower

On multinational enterprises and theories of internationalization

Caves, R. E. (2007), *Multinational Enterprise and Economic Analysis*, Cambridge University Press

Dunning, J. H., and Lundan, S. M. (2008), *Multinational Enterprises and the Global Economy*, Edward Elgar

 Take your learning further: Online Resource Centre
http://www.oxfordtextbooks.co.uk/orc/harrison2e/
Visit the Online Resource Centre that accompanies this book to enrich your understanding of Chapter 8: Internationalization of Business in a Changing Environment. Among other resources explore web links and keep up to date with the latest developments in the area.

Key terms introduced in this chapter

Created assets Assets which a country has developed through investment over a number of years, including tangible assets such as transport infrastructure and intangible assets such as technological knowledge and human capital.

Cultural distance The cultural differences between an MNE's home and host countries.

Direct exporting and importing Exporting and importing involving direct contact between the exporter or importer and the foreign customer or supplier.

Dunning's eclectic paradigm The theory that FDI decisions are based on a combination of ownership (O), location (L), and internalization (I) factors (also known as the OLI paradigm).

Economic geography The study of the impact of geographical location on economic activity.

Ethnocentric approach An approach to internationalization where operations are based in the home country and organized from the home country's perspective.

Franchising A contractual arrangement whereby a franchiser allows a franchisee to use its intellectual property in a prescribed manner in return for a fee or royalty, commonly found in the retailing, tourism, and other service sectors.

Geocentric approach An approach to internationalization organized around a global strategy, international resourcing and production, and products designed for the global market.

Indirect exporting and importing Exporting and importing using the services of an agent or other intermediary between the exporter or importer and the foreign customer or supplier.

Licensing A contractual arrangement whereby a licenser allows a licensee to use its intellectual property in return for a fee or royalty, commonly found in manufacturing and processing industries.

Multinational enterprise (MNE) An enterprise that controls and manages production facilities in more than one country; the term 'enterprise' includes operations such as licensing and franchising as well as full ownership.

Organizational behaviour The study of the behaviour of individuals and groups within an organization, including organizational culture and relationships.

Polycentric approach　An approach to internationalization organized around separate divisions in different parts of the world, each using local resources and production, and marketing adapted to its own cultural environment.

Psychic distance　Perceived differences in culture, history, or business practices between an MNE's home and host countries.

Resource-based view　The idea that an MNE's decision to locate abroad and choice of entry mode is determined by its ability to take advantage of its firm-specific assets.

State capture　The phenomenon whereby powerful corporations 'capture' the authorities by influencing business rules or bribing public officials.

Strategic alliance　A non-equity cooperation agreement between two or more independent firms for the purpose of gaining a mutual competitive advantage.

Transaction cost　A cost incurred when undertaking a transaction in addition to the price paid for the goods or services; examples include legal costs, currency exchange costs, or information search costs.

Markets and Competition

⊙ Chapter learning outcomes

On completion of this chapter the reader should be able to:

- Appreciate the role of markets in the changing global economy
- Understand how markets operate under different conditions
- Analyse competition using a variety of theoretical approaches
- Evaluate the respective contributions of competition and regulation to the effective operation of markets

Opening scenario: Open skies across the Atlantic

The first phase of the EU–US Open Skies Agreement was completed in 2007 and came into effect on 30 March 2008. The agreement basically allows any US or European Union (EU) airline to fly across the Atlantic between any US and EU airport. Prior to the agreement, transatlantic flights between EU and US airports were restricted to relatively few airlines. For example, flights between London Heathrow and New York, the busiest transatlantic route, were confined to British Airways and Virgin Atlantic of the UK, and American Airlines and United Airlines of the US. As a result of the agreement a number of airlines, including Delta and Continental Airlines, moved some of their services to Heathrow and British Airways launched a new off-shoot airline called OpenSkies to fly between Paris and New York.

The second phase of the agreement came into effect on 24 June 2010. It allows EU airlines to participate in the 'Fly America' programme, which previously prevented US government-funded passengers from flying with non-US airlines. It also permits EU flights between the USA and non-EU countries and includes measures on environmental protection, safety, security, and labour standards, but important measures allowing increased access to internal US air routes and foreign ownership of US and EU airlines remain subject to further agreement and legislation. Foreign ownership is currently restricted to 25 per cent of US airline voting rights and 49.9 per cent ownership in the case of EU airlines. US airlines already have access to internal routes between EU countries.

Open skies across the Atlantic were preceded by the deregulation of civil aviation in the United States in 1978 and in the EU between 1987 and 1997. Previously, the right to operate on a particular route and the freedom to determine fares were tightly regulated by the civil aviation authorities. Deregulation opened up the market to greater competition, allowing airlines to fly on any route and set their own fares. As a result, a number of new airlines entered the market, some of the existing airlines were taken over or went out of business, and fares came down.

The intention of the Open Skies Agreement is that the consumer benefits of open competition will spread to transatlantic air travel. There are of course those who emphasize the costs as well as the benefits of the agreement. For example, some of the major airlines that have long enjoyed privileged access to key routes and airports fear a loss of business, and environmentalists are concerned about the increase in air traffic as competition increases and air travel becomes cheaper.

(continued...)

Even from a competition perspective, open skies will not automatically remove all the barriers to new entrants, as airport slots are often restricted and expensive. The agreement is bringing changes to an industry that has been characterized by a concentration of market power, but while new transatlantic routes have been opening up, US airlines have not taken advantage of internal EU routes and airlines have been using alliances and code-sharing agreements as an alternative to gaining direct access to internal markets. This may change if US legislators amend the rules on the foreign ownership of airlines – and the EU follows suit – though this is a sensitive political issue in the United States. In this chapter, we use a number of concepts and theories to help understand how competition works and why it sometimes does not.[1]

9.1 Markets in the global economy

Most of the world's economies are now, to a greater or lesser extent, market economies. This has not always been so and, even in recent history, was not so during the years following World War II when communist central planning dominated the Soviet Union, China, and a number of other states that came under their influence. Market economies are sometimes described by the more pejorative term 'capitalism', which focuses on the private accumulation of capital (wealth in the form of financial or physical assets), whereas the term 'market economy' describes the process by which resources are allocated and goods and services are exchanged between producers and consumers. Market economies had dominated international business long before World War II, but since the collapse of communism in the Soviet bloc in the years 1989–91 and China's gradual economic liberalization after 1978, market economies have become the predominant form of economic system in the modern world. Indeed, western newspaper headlines proclaimed the 'triumph of capitalism' after Europe's eastern bloc started to shed its communist central planning system in favour of market democracy. These events seemed to reinforce the revival of free-market economics that had accompanied the governments of Margaret Thatcher in the UK (1979–90) and Ronald Reagan in the USA (1981–9) and free-market ideas now permeate the policies of major international institutions such as the IMF and WTO.

As national barriers to trade and investment have fallen during the post-war years, a more integrated global economy has emerged. Multinational enterprises (MNEs) face open competition not only with their rivals in the developed world but increasingly with businesses in developing countries and the re-emerging countries of the former Soviet bloc. This is especially true in the natural resource and utility industries, where economies of scale and world demand foster the growth of large corporations; for example, two Chinese oil companies (Sinopec and China National Petroleum), a Chinese electricity company (State Grid), two Russian energy companies (Gazprom and Lukoil), a Brazilian oil company (Petrobas), a Mexican oil and mining company (Pemex), and a Venezuelan oil company (PDVSA) were among the world's 50 largest companies, ranked by sales revenue, in 2012.[2] In due course, these companies are likely to be followed by firms in other industries, including electronics and information technology, though in these industries the competitive gap between current world leaders and their newer rivals is still quite large (though narrowing). International competition has now become the norm in many industries, but the nature of competition varies considerably, depending on factors such as the number of firms operating in a particular market, the ease with which new firms can enter a market, the degree of differentiation between products, linkages between national markets or related product markets, and the extent to which consumers and producers have equal access to information. Competition therefore works in different ways in different contexts; these issues are extensively explored in the remainder of this chapter.

9.2 The role and operation of markets

Essentially, markets provide a mechanism for allocating resources in an economy. The basic market mechanism involves interaction between the forces of supply and demand (see Section 2.6). Some markets work more effectively than others in allocating resources and some of the possible reasons for this are discussed in Sections 9.2.2 to 9.2.5. Problems with the efficient allocation of resources were clearly evident during the 2008–9 international financial crisis and world recession, an issue which is considered in Section 9.2.5. However, even when there is price volatility in a market, it should not necessarily be assumed that markets are failing to work properly. It may simply be that the forces of demand or supply are changing rapidly in response to the changing environment. Whilst significant changes of this kind introduce uncertainty into markets, they may also send signals to producers and consumers that they should raise or lower their production or consumption or look for alternative products. Some of the reasons for rapid price movements are considered in relation to world oil prices in Practical Insight 9.1.

Practical insight **9.1**:   World oil prices

World crude oil prices approximately doubled between July 2007 and July 2008. This was the main reason for increases in the price of petrol, heating oil, and other petroleum-based products during this period, though their prices were also affected by national taxation. A number of alternative explanations have been given for the increase in world oil prices, but fundamentally the price is determined by demand and supply conditions. World demand for oil has been driven by the rapid economic growth of China, India, and other Asian economies, as well as the steady increase in international business activity generally. The world supply of oil has not always kept pace with demand because of the depletion of reserves in some of the major oilfields, a shortage of refinery capacity, and disruption caused by conflict in the Middle East and elsewhere. Central government control of oil production has also led to a lack of investment in the burgeoning oil industries of Russia, Mexico, and Venezuela. Other explanations for the rising oil prices include stockpiling as a precaution against future shortages, and speculation to take advantage of expected future price rises.

The world financial crisis and recession caused a rapid reversal in oil prices during the latter half of 2008, reducing the price of a barrel of Brent crude from around $145 in July 2008 to around $45 in January 2009. Oil prices then gradually recovered as economic growth began to return, spiking in early 2011 during the Libyan uprising, but slow economic recovery and reported increases in world oil reserves have generally moderated oil prices since 2011. Despite this relative stability, oil prices rose sharply in 2012 when the US and EU introduced an oil embargo on Iran and fell as oil production increased. Continuing turbulence in the Middle East and North Africa has also added to oil price volatility. This degree of volatility has a significant effect on transport and production costs, industrial output, inflation, exchange rates, the balance of payments, and world economic growth.[3]

Questions

- What factors have determined oil prices since 2012?
- What are the implications of oil price volatility for the search for alternative sources of energy?

9.2.1 **Markets and industries**

Before venturing any further, it is a good idea to define what we mean by a market and to distinguish it from the definition of an industry, two terms which are often used interchangeably but which are in fact quite distinct. A market involves the exchange of goods and services between producers and consumers and it includes goods and services which are considered to be close substitutes, goods which have similar uses, from the consumer's perspective. More technically, a market can be defined as a group of products with a *high positive cross-elasticity of demand*. **Elasticity** (ε) measures the responsiveness of one variable, such as the quantity demanded, to a change in another variable, such as price. **Cross-elasticity** of demand ($c\varepsilon_D$) measures the effect of a price change in one good on the demand for another, which can be calculated using the following formula:

$$c\varepsilon_D = \frac{\text{\% change in quantity demanded of good Y}}{\text{\% change in price of good X}} \tag{9.1}$$

If the goods are substitutes, such as Shell petrol and a supermarket's petrol, cross-elasticity of demand will have a positive value as an increase in the price of one good will cause an increase in the demand for the other. If the goods are complementary, such as cars and petrol, cross-elasticity of demand will be negative. The closer the substitutes, the higher will be the positive value as even a tiny increase in the price of X will cause a large increase in the demand for Y (though the precise definition of 'close substitution' is open to debate).

This type of calculation has been used in legal cases, the most famous of which was the du Pont case in 1956. In this case, a US court accepted du Pont's claim that it was not exploiting a monopoly position in the US market for cellophane, in which it had a market share of almost 75 per cent, because it was in fact operating in the larger market for 'flexible packaging materials', of which cellophane accounted for less than 20 per cent.[4] Of course, if the market is considered to be international, market shares are generally much smaller and the number of substitutes available to the consumer is correspondingly greater.

An industry, on the other hand, can be defined in terms of goods or services that have similar production processes from the producer's perspective. Thus, for example, the motor manufacturing industry produces a range of products, including motor cycles, cars, vans, trucks, buses, and caravans, using similar types of plant and machinery and similar skills, but these products are sold in a variety of different markets. More technically, an industry can be defined as a group of products with a *high negative cross-elasticity of supply* ($c\varepsilon_S$), using the following formula:

$$c\varepsilon_S = \frac{\text{\% change in quantity supplied of good Y}}{\text{\% change in price of good X}} \tag{9.2}$$

If the goods are made using similar production processes, cross-elasticity of supply will have a high negative value as an increase in the price of good X will create an incentive for the producer to switch production away from good Y and supply more of good X, which is now relatively more profitable.

Generally, an industry includes a larger group of products than a market, though industries may be defined at various levels of aggregation, ranging for example from the specialized manufacture of lighting equipment for motor vehicles (at a disaggregated level) to the general manufacture of motor vehicles (at a more aggregated level).[5] Occasionally, a market describes a broader group of products than an industry, such as the market for domestic heating, which includes the products of the coal, electricity, gas, and oil industries. From the perspective of competition, however, the market is the main focus of our attention and the distinction between markets and industries will become more important when we consider competition theories and policies in Sections 9.3 and 9.4.

9.2.2 Market efficiency and market institutions

In general, markets are remarkably effective in achieving efficient resource allocation. Ultimately, consumers determine what needs to be produced in a market economy. If they are unable or unwilling to buy a product, producers respond by reducing the price, improving the product, promoting it more effectively, or producing something else instead. In this sense, the consumer is 'sovereign'. Producers respond to consumer sovereignty by allocating resources to the production of goods for which there is consumer demand. Competition between producers then creates an incentive for them to use these resources as efficiently as possible, and the price mechanism determines how the goods will be distributed between consumers, depending on their willingness and ability to pay. In mainstream (neoclassical) economic theory (see Section 9.3.2), efficiency in the allocation of resources between the production of different goods is known as *allocative efficiency*, efficiency in the use of resources in a particular production process is known as *input efficiency* (or *technical efficiency*), and efficiency in the distribution of goods between consumers is known as *output efficiency*. If all goods and resource markets are perfectly competitive, these three types of efficiency enable a market economy to achieve a competitive general equilibrium.[6]

Of course markets are rarely, if ever, perfectly competitive (a term that is defined in Section 9.3.2). In practice, some producers have more market power than others and market efficiency is reduced by a number of other 'imperfections'. We should not, however, immediately jump to the conclusion that, if most markets are imperfect, the market mechanism is of no value. Even an imperfect market may allocate resources more efficiently than the next best alternative and, in general, the most developed market economies in North America, Western Europe, and East Asia performed much more efficiently than the planned economies of the Soviet bloc between the late 1940s and 1989. As explained in Section 9.3.5, some of the more **dynamic theories of competition** reject the conventional neoclassical analysis of competition, but they nevertheless argue that markets work efficiently over a period of time. Their disagreement with the conventional view relates more to the process by which efficiency is achieved.

In practice, the extent to which a market works efficiently will depend upon the institutional framework of the market. Institutions are the rules by which a market or economy operates. Formal institutions include consumer protection legislation, product liability laws, employment law, and contractual obligations; many of these institutions create **property rights** which are important in protecting the rights of consumers, employers and employees, and the parties to a contract. They exist to ensure that one party cannot abuse the rights of another without redress. Without formal institutions and the effective enforcement of

Practical insight 9.2:   The Bologna process

In June 1999 the EU member states signed the Bologna Declaration, committing themselves to the creation of a European Higher Education Area. This process involves the achievement of six main objectives in relation to Europe's universities: comparability between and mutual recognition of qualifications; a system based on bachelor's and master's degrees; transferability of credits between universities; staff and student mobility between universities; cooperation between national quality assurance systems; and the promotion of a European dimension to the higher education curriculum.[7]

The Bologna process has a number of potential benefits for graduates of European universities. It is also an important step towards the EU's aim of achieving the free movement of labour throughout its member states. Europe's higher education systems have travelled along different paths to reach their current position and comparisons based on length of study, breadth or specialization, and levels of qualification reveal significant differences between them. These differences form part of the institutional framework of the labour market in each country, helping to determine the quality of human capital, an individual's eligibility for employment, and the productivity of the workforce. By attempting to unify the European higher education system and break down some of the barriers, the EU is working towards the creation of a single institutional framework of higher education.

Question

● Is this likely to mean the end of diversity in the European higher education system or will culture and history still influence the operation of the graduate labour market in Europe's individual nation states?

property rights, even free markets will become chaotic and they will not work efficiently. Informal institutions include customs, practices, and ways of thinking, and they are influenced by national and local cultures, as are formal institutions to a certain extent. For this reason, institutions vary considerably from place to place and in different sectors of an economy.

Trust may also be an important informal institution, and a lack of trust between people or in the legal system, for example, may lead to market participants taking the law into their own hands if they perceive the market to be incapable of providing an efficient outcome. The way in which a market operates can be greatly affected by the framework of institutions, and differences in the law or local customs may account for significant differences between two apparently similar markets (see Practical Insight 4.1 on the institutional differences between the Scottish and English housing markets). The operation of an open-bid auction can also be used to illustrate the importance of institutions in a market. Whilst market forces are clearly very much in evidence, with successive bids quickly establishing an equilibrium price for a particular item at a particular time, the outcome of the auction is also influenced by the policies of the auction house, the skill of the auctioneer, the nature of the bidding process, and the trust of the participants in the legitimacy of the auction – all of which represent the framework of formal and informal institutions. A rather different example is provided by the Bologna agreement in relation to the operation of the European graduate labour market (see Practical Insight 9.2).

9.2.3 **Markets with asymmetric information**

In 1970, a US economist, George Akerlof, published a study on the problem of **asymmetric information** in the market for 'lemons' (poor-quality used cars that leave a bitter taste in the mouth of the unfortunate purchaser).[8] Akerlof found that, because consumers were unable to distinguish between the quality of good and bad used cars before purchase, they were only willing to pay low prices for the cars. In response, sellers of high-quality used cars looked for alternative ways to obtain a reasonable price for their vehicles. This left a higher proportion of 'lemons' in the main used-car market and drove prices down even further. This scenario describes the problem of **adverse selection** where unequal access to information between buyer and seller (asymmetric information) results in prices that do not reflect product quality, creating an incentive for sellers of low-quality products to enter the market and sellers of high-quality products to leave the market. For this reason, the used-car market was unable to operate efficiently under conditions of asymmetric information.

Asymmetric information is a common problem in many markets. Typically, the seller of a product knows more about the product than the buyer. This is especially true in markets for complex products, where product quality is variable, and where quality is difficult to determine without expert knowledge or close inspection. In some markets, the buyer has access to greater knowledge than the seller. This applies generally to insurance and credit markets, where the insured person or borrower knows more about the risks than the insurance company or bank (though lenders may have better knowledge of market conditions). In the case of life assurance, for example, adverse selection occurs because people with health problems are more likely to take out life assurance than those who are healthier; given the uncertainty facing the insurer, insurance premiums will be driven up because of the greater likelihood of claims. A further problem facing the insurer is that, once people are covered by insurance, they may be more likely to take risks and make claims; this is known as the problem of **moral hazard**, a problem that also faces international lenders such as the IMF or World Bank if debtor countries believe that their debts will be written off if they are unable to repay them. Similar concerns were expressed about the implications of government support for ailing financial institutions during the 2008–9 financial crisis.

In each of these cases, the market fails to deal adequately with the problem. There are, however, a number of ways of helping markets to deal with the problem of asymmetric information. The seller of used cars, for example, can offer a warranty as a sign of good faith to the buyer and the buyer may be willing to pay a premium in return for greater peace of mind. The insurance company will use a number of techniques to determine the risk more accurately and avoid adverse selection, such as basing premiums on the client's age, gender, health, or postcode, and can reduce the problem of moral hazard by discouraging claims (e.g. a policy excess) or by rewarding good behaviour (e.g. a 'no claims' discount). It is important to note, however, that the existence of asymmetric information is likely to cause some degree of distortion in the way a market operates.

9.2.4 The concept of market failure

Asymmetric information is an example of the problem of **market failure**. In mainstream economic analysis, markets are considered to fail, or at least to work imperfectly, in a limited number of situations. The most widely accepted cases of market failure are as follows:

The provision of public goods

Public 'goods' include services provided for the public at large such as defence, law and order, or street lighting. They have two essential characteristics: *non-rivalry in consumption* (consumption by one person does not preclude consumption by others) and *non-exclusion of consumers* (certain people cannot be excluded if others are not). If the provision of **public goods** is left to market forces, citizens benefit from them whether they contribute towards the cost or not (the **free-rider problem**), a problem which may result in under-provision of these essential services. For this reason, public goods are often provided by the state or at least under the supervision of the state, though this does not necessarily preclude private providers from being involved in the delivery of these services.

The provision of merit goods

Similar problems may occur with **merit goods**, such as education, health care, or refuse collection, though these 'goods' do not possess the characteristics of non-rivalry and non-exclusion; in this case, people who are unwilling or unable to pay may be left without education, health care, or other essential services. Although merit goods are sometimes provided by the private or voluntary sector, including private schools and charity-run hospitals, under-provision may again occur if these services are left entirely to market forces.

Externalities

Most economic activities have 'external' consequences for people who are not directly involved as producers or consumers. These consequences are known as externalities. Where those affected have no clearly specified property rights, the market participants have no incentive to take the externalities into account. As a result, the external costs are ignored and consumers pay too low a price for the goods, leading to overproduction and larger amounts of negative externalities such as pollution. This issue is discussed more fully in Sections 7.5 and 7.6.

Differences between individual and social time-preference rates

Producers and consumers may have a shorter-term perspective than society as a whole, leading them to make inadequate provision for the future. Examples include the need to plan future energy requirements or future pension provision. In each of these cases, the shorter **time-preference rate** of individuals will result in the market failing to make the socially optimal level of provision, so the state may need to intervene or at least to create appropriate market incentives.

Natural monopoly

A market may be described as a **natural monopoly** when the most efficient scale of production requires a single producer. The problem here is that, in the absence of competition, some form of regulation is needed to prevent the abuse of monopoly power. It used to be considered that railways and utilities such as water, electricity, and the telephone service were examples of natural monopolies, but now it is generally believed that only control of the infrastructure represents a genuine natural monopoly in these markets: the railway tracks, water pipelines, electricity grid, and fixed telephone lines. In other parts of these markets, it has been possible to introduce competition between service providers or power-generating companies, though competition is sometimes limited by factors such as the need for a single

Practical insight 9.3: The need for state support

Subsidies and other forms of state support have been used in a variety of industries to enable producers to remain profitable or to protect them from the threat of competition. One such industry is agriculture. In the EU common agricultural policy (CAP), for example, farmers have at various times received price support, export subsidies, import protection, and land set-aside payments to ensure continued food production or protect their income. Whilst large farms may be able to survive without such protection, the recent reduction in CAP support has brought into question the viability of smaller, more marginal farms.

Question

● Should agriculture be considered a merit good requiring state protection or should it be treated like most other private goods, with farmers being left to find their own ways of remaining profitable?

train operator on a particular route or the inherited dominance of a former state-owned telecommunications company.

Beyond the above cases, it is sometimes argued that the existence of monopoly power in general is an example of market failure, but here there are disagreements between the various schools of thought. In conventional neoclassical economics, monopoly is seen as potentially leading to market failure, especially where there are significant barriers to new entrants, whereas members of the Austrian school view monopoly as a normal part of the competitive process in dynamic markets. Indeed, the Austrian school argues that markets work efficiently provided they are free from interference by governments, trade unions, and other 'impediments' to market forces, and that what is generally described as 'market failure' is in fact the failure to allow markets to operate freely. This issue is at the heart of the EU–US Open Skies Agreement, outlined in the opening scenario to this chapter, where the debate focuses on the extent to which open transatlantic competition will moderate or exacerbate the dominance of the world's major airlines. Another contentious example of possible market failure is the case of state aid to industry. This is discussed in the context of the EU common agricultural policy in Practical Insight 9.3. Alternative perspectives on the competitive process are discussed more extensively in Section 9.3.

9.2.5 **Volatility in financial markets**

Financial markets seem to display characteristics that are not entirely explained by the normal operation of market forces. In a general sense, market forces are clearly at work in financial markets. For example, when a public company announces a fall in profit, some of its shareholders sell their shares (increasing the supply of shares) and the share price falls. This can easily be explained using conventional supply and demand analysis. The same is true for share prices in general when an economy is experiencing an economic slowdown. Foreign exchange markets behave in a similar way, with exchange rates rising or falling in response to changes in the demand for or supply of a currency.

However, other factors also seem to be at work in financial markets. One of these factors relates to the role of expectations. Whereas in most markets rising prices deter potential buyers, in financial markets investors are encouraged to buy in the expectation that prices will continue to rise. This effect is sometimes exaggerated by the activities of speculators; like or-dinary investors they are attracted by rising prices, but their skill is in anticipating when prices have reached a peak, at which point they sell their holdings in order to maximize their returns before the price starts to fall. In doing so they also make the fall in prices more likely and this leads to more widespread selling by investors.

Movements in share prices, commodity prices, and exchange rates over a period of time are less easily explained. Whilst it is well known that prices fluctuate more frequently in financial mar-kets than in markets for goods and services, the view that prices in financial markets reflect all the available information about future trends, known as the *efficient market hypothesis*, has increas-ingly been challenged in recent years.[9] Perhaps the most far-reaching challenge has come from the work of Benoît Mandelbrot.[10] Based on extensive studies of the price of cotton and move-ments in exchange rates, Mandelbrot found that the pattern of price changes was much more erratic than generally supposed. When illustrated on a frequency graph, the frequency of price movements contained far more outlying values than in the normal distribution or bell curve, indicating that extreme price changes were relatively common (see Figure 9.1). Whereas the 'nor-mal distribution' assumes a regular pattern where most values are clustered around the mean, Mandelbrot's research found evidence of long 'fat' tails where extreme values were the 'norm'.

However, if Mandelbrot's analysis is correct, price movements in financial markets are not as erratic as they appear to be. In fact, they exhibit the kind of irregular patterns found in the natural world, such as the irregular shape of a country's coastline or the earth's surface. These patterns are known as *fractals* and computer-generated patterns of this type are much loved by artists and designers. They are made up of irregular shapes, but also contain recognizable features which are replicated at different levels of magnitude. Mandelbrot argues that similar patterns can be found in price movements in financial markets (along with many other ap-plications). Particular patterns seem to recur repeatedly over different periods of time – ex-hibiting significant short-term fluctuations but greater long-term stability, suggesting it may be possible to model long-term trends using fractal techniques.

Whilst a complete economic explanation for the existence of fractals in financial markets is some way off, a relatively straightforward explanation of the phenomenon of financial bubbles can be offered. In 1999–2000, investors were frantically buying the shares of newly formed 'dot.com' companies as though it were a one-way bet, regardless of the underlying performance of the companies concerned. This collective optimism among investors drove share prices to record levels. However, when one or two of these companies began to fail, it soon became clear that many of them were not profitable, causing investors to sell their

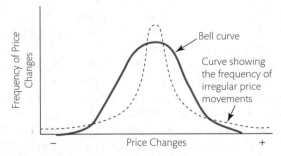

Figure 9.1 Irregular price movements superimposed on the bell curve

shares and the share price bubble to burst. This also illustrates the way in which a small event may ultimately lead to a much more significant event – the so-called 'butterfly effect', named after the idea that the flap of a butterfly's wings in one part of the world may create a tiny disturbance to the atmospheric system that results in the occurrence of a tornado in another part of the world.[11] This idea could equally be applied to the way in which mortgage defaults in the US sub-prime market acted as a trigger for much more serious turbulence in world financial markets in 2008–9.

9.3 The analysis of competition

9.3.1 Diverse approaches to competition

Competition is an important feature of most markets, enabling them to allocate resources with some degree of efficiency. However, there is no single view on how competition works and it may well work differently in different markets. A number of theoretical approaches to competition have been developed and the most important schools of thought are considered in this section. Several of the theories have influenced political and business decision makers over the years and their influence can still be seen in the industrial and competition policies of governments today. Despite a number of apparent contradictions, the theories also help us to gain an understanding of the nature of competition and its implications for producers, consumers, and society as a whole.

9.3.2 The neoclassical approach to competition

The mainstream tradition in economics that emerged from the ideas of Adam Smith and other classical economists during the nineteenth and twentieth centuries is known as neoclassical economics. Although not as dominant in competition theory today as it was up to the 1970s, the neoclassical approach is still commonly found in textbooks on microeconomics and has influenced thinking in related fields such as business strategy. In the field of competition theory neoclassical ideas underpin the conventional theory of the firm, which provides an explanation for the behaviour of firms under different types of competition. The main types of competition identified by neoclassical economists are **perfect competition**, **monopolistic competition**, **oligopoly**, and **monopoly** (see Figure 9.2).

Competition ⟵――――――――――――――――――――――――――⟶ Monopoly			
Perfect Competition	Forms of Imperfect Competition		Monopoly
	Monopolistic Competition	Oligopoly	
➢ Many sellers ➢ Many buyers ➢ Homogeneous product ➢ Freedom of entry and exit	➢ Many sellers ➢ Many buyers ➢ Differentiated product ➢ Freedom of entry and exit	➢ Few sellers ➢ Many buyers ➢ Differentiated product ➢ Entry barriers	➢ One seller ➢ Many buyers ➢ Product with no close substitutes ➢ Entry barriers

Figure 9.2 The neoclassical competition spectrum

Perfect competition and monopoly

The theories of perfect competition and monopoly offer the clearest predictions about the behaviour of firms and the way markets work, though they are the least likely to exist in practice, especially in the case of perfect competition. They do, however, provide a useful theoretical framework against which to measure the implications of different market structures. Perfect competition describes a situation where many buyers and sellers exchange identical (**homogeneous**) products with no restrictions on market entry or exit. When these structural characteristics of the market exist in a world of perfect knowledge, a single seller who makes even the smallest increase in price will soon have no customers and the smallest decrease in price will immediately be matched by competitors. The demand curve facing each individual firm in perfect competition is therefore perfectly elastic[12] and all sellers will charge the same competitive price, which is just sufficient to persuade them to stay in the market (with no incentive to raise or lower their price). This minimum acceptable level of profit is known as 'normal profit'; it is regarded by economists as the cost to the business of retaining the services and capital of the entrepreneur (an **opportunity cost**)[13] and is considered to be a cost of production. If demand or supply conditions cause the market price to rise, the established firms will make more than normal profit in the short run, but this will attract new entrants into the market, causing a return to normal profit in long-run equilibrium.

A monopolist, on the other hand, faces a downward-sloping market demand curve (as its product represents the entire market) and is able to raise its price by reducing output and moving up the demand curve. High **entry barriers** and the absence of competition allow the monopolist to make *supernormal* or *excess* profit (in excess of the opportunity cost of retaining the entrepreneur).

Figure 9.3 contrasts a perfectly competitive market with monopoly. The price in a perfectly competitive market is just sufficient to cover each firm's average cost of production (including normal profit) and the market demand curve determines how much consumers will buy in total. In a monopoly market, the price is likely to be much higher than average cost, allowing

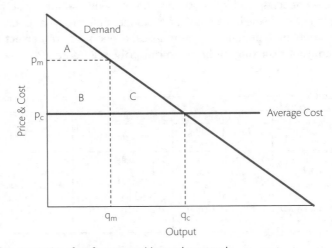

Figure 9.3 Welfare properties of perfect competition and monopoly

the monopolist to make excess profit under the protection of market entry barriers. In order to simplify the analysis, average cost is assumed to be constant at different levels of output and the same for firms under perfect competition and monopoly. In each case, the difference between the demand curve (the price consumers are willing and able to pay) and the market price (indicating what they actually pay) is called the **consumer surplus**. The consumer surplus is a benefit that consumers enjoy; it can be saved or spent on other goods and services. Under perfect competition, the lower price (p_c) creates a large consumer surplus (areas A + B + C), whereas, under monopoly, the higher price (p_m) leaves a smaller consumer surplus (area A); area B is a **producer surplus** (the excess profit in this case) and area C is known as the dead-weight loss from monopoly (a loss of surplus to society as a whole). Even if one accepts that monopoly profit is as beneficial to society as a consumer surplus, there is still a net **welfare loss** from monopoly when compared with perfect competition (equal to area C). This leads to the conclusion that perfect competition is better for society's welfare than monopoly.[14]

The welfare loss from monopoly

A number of studies attempted to measure the size of the welfare loss from monopoly between the 1950s and 1980s, based on the pioneering work of Arnold Harberger.[15] In this context, monopoly should be interpreted loosely to include markets where dominant firms have a significant market share (including oligopoly), rather than single-firm monopoly in the strict sense. Provided there is no compensating gain to the producer (a producer surplus), the welfare loss from monopoly equals the deadweight loss, area C, in Figure 9.3. This is sometimes known as the *welfare triangle* or *Harberger triangle*. Harberger estimated that the welfare loss from monopoly was only approximately 0.1 per cent of gross corporate product in the United States, suggesting that the negative impact of monopoly was minimal. Whilst other researchers have produced a wide range of estimates of welfare loss, depending on the criteria applied, this approach to the analysis of monopoly has now generally been abandoned. Nevertheless, the idea that monopoly or market power is undesirable is still influential in competition policy investigations and among consumer groups and anti-globalization campaigners.

Theories of imperfect competition

Considerable attention has also been paid to the issue of imperfect competition and, in particular, to the cases of monopolistic competition and oligopoly. Monopolistic competition has similar characteristics to perfect competition except that each firm has some degree of local market power (and therefore faces a downward-sloping demand curve) because of **product differentiation**. This form of market structure is commonly found in traditional retailing, personal and professional services, small-scale manufacturing, service trades, and more recently among the many dedicated online businesses which are often small in conventional terms.

However, the case of oligopoly (and in earlier studies the special two-firm case of duopoly) has received much more widespread attention. Oligopoly is common in natural resource industries, large-scale manufacturing, food retailing, telecommunications, financial services, and many other sectors. Much of the attention has focused on the interaction between the small number of dominant firms in oligopoly markets, ranging from the way they determine

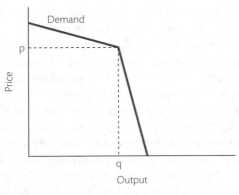

Figure 9.4 A kinked demand curve

prices or output to the extent of cooperation, collusion, or market leadership. At various times, particular oligopoly theories have been prevalent. One of the more enduring theories is *kinked demand curve theory*, which provides an explanation for price rigidity in oligopoly markets (see Figure 9.4). In this model, oligopolists take a pessimistic view that their rivals will immediately match a price reduction but not a price increase. As a result, the oligopolist's demand curve is relatively inelastic below the current price (leaving the firm with little or no increase in sales) and becomes more elastic above this point (with a significant fall in sales).[16] This creates a 'kink' in the demand curve and leads to the conclusion that oligopolists are likely to keep their prices constant, preferring to compete on non-price factors rather than to engage in price competition. This conclusion is reinforced by the fact that both an increase and a decrease in price will lead to a loss of revenue and profit for the oligopolist.[17]

The key feature of oligopoly is the interdependence between the few dominant firms in the market. This feature may lead not only to a lack of price competition, but also to the possibility of price leadership (where a dominant firm sets the price and others follow) or even collusive behaviour if the oligopolists believe it is to their mutual advantage to restrict competition. However, the conventional view of oligopoly has been increasingly challenged by alternative perspectives on competition, including developments in neoclassical economics as well as dynamic theories of competition and game theory, for example. These theories are discussed in Sections 9.3.4 to 9.3.6.

9.3.3 The structure-conduct-performance paradigm

The most significant development in competition theory in the neoclassical tradition has been the so-called **structure-conduct-performance (SCP) paradigm**, a theoretical approach sometimes attributed to the Harvard school.[18] The SCP paradigm postulates that there is a causal relationship between the structure of a market, the conduct or behaviour of firms, and the performance of firms in the market (see Figure 9.5). According to this view, market structure is the crucial determinant of conduct and performance. Structure is indicated by the number and size of firms, the degree of product homogeneity or differentiation, and the nature of entry barriers, among other things – in other words, the characteristics used to distinguish between various forms of competition and monopoly in the neoclassical theory of

Figure 9.5 The structure-conduct-performance paradigm

the firm (see Figure 9.2). Conduct relates to pricing policy and various methods of non-price competition. Performance can be measured by profitability, efficiency, productivity, and a number of other indicators. The SCP paradigm suggests that a monopolistic market structure will lead to high prices, excess profit, and inefficiency in the use of resources; a competitive market structure will lead to low prices, normal profit, and efficient use of resources, thus confirming the neoclassical view of competition.

Increasingly, researchers and competition authorities have focused not only on structure but also on conduct as a determinant of performance, either directly or by influencing structure, but the SCP paradigm became the dominant approach to the analysis of competition in industrial economics (or industrial organization) from the 1950s to the 1970s and beyond. Even today, its influence can be seen in competition policy cases, though decisions in these cases are now generally based on a more eclectic view of competition than in the past.

The SCP approach gave rise to numerous attempts to measure market structure in the belief that such measurements would indicate the potential for anti-competitive behaviour and the need for policy intervention. Until the 1970s, attention was focused mainly on the measurement of market concentration. For example, the simple concentration ratio measures the cumulative market shares (or shares of net value added) of the x largest firms in a market. For disaggregated data, the value of x is usually quite small (e.g. the three, four, or five largest firms), whereas for highly aggregated data relating to entire industries or sectors, x may have a value of 50 or 100. A five-firm concentration ratio of 80 or 90 per cent, for example, would indicate a high level of market concentration. Gradually, the focus of attention shifted towards the impact of entry barriers on market structure and this, in turn, led to the development of alternative views of competition. Practical Insight 9.4 provides an example of relatively high market concentration in the UK retail food market.

Practical insight 9.4: Supermarket dominance in the UK

A common feature of the retail environment in many countries is the growing dominance of the retail supermarkets, not only in groceries but increasingly in clothing, household goods, computers, financial services, and other product categories. The four leading UK supermarket groups, Tesco, Asda (owned by Wal-Mart), J. Sainsbury, and Morrison's, together had just over 75 per cent of the UK grocery market in 2012. The position of these four groups reached its present level of consolidation in 2003 when the fifth-largest store, Morrison's, acquired its fourth-largest rival, Safeway, after a Competition Commission investigation. The market has now become highly concentrated at the four-firm level, though competition amongst the nearest group of rivals, the Cooperative, Waitrose, Aldi, and Lidl, is also quite intense.

The market's oligopolistic structure is intensified by the barriers to new entrants. Although international rivals such as Wal-Mart, Aldi, Lidl, and Netto (bought by Asda in 2011) have been able to enter the UK market through acquisition or the opening of new stores, opportunities for entry are limited by the availability of suitable sites for retail development, especially in the more highly

(continued...)

populated areas of the UK. This problem has apparently been exacerbated by the practice of 'land banking' – the buying of prime sites by established supermarkets, ostensibly to prepare for future expansion but arguably to prevent rivals from locating close by.[19]

Question

- If one accepts the SCP paradigm in this case, the oligopolistic market structure is a cause for concern. To what extent do you think this concern is justified?

9.3.4 Developments of the neoclassical approach

Workable competition

The concept of workable competition was introduced by J. M. Clark in 1940 as a more realistic alternative to perfect competition.[20] Although workable competition may be seen as a second-best form of competition from a theoretical perspective, it sets out the kind of characteristics necessary for reasonably effective competition. Clark suggested a number of characteristics of structure, conduct, and performance, such as the maximum number of firms consistent with achieving economies of scale, and others have added to these characteristics over the years. The concept of workable competition has been quite popular from a practical and policy perspective, though the lack of agreement on the details and the limitations of the concept as a predictive theory have weakened its usefulness as an analytical tool. The main legacy of Clark's idea, however, is his view of competition as a dynamic process, in contrast to the more theoretical static analysis of the neoclassical approach.

The Freiburg school and 'ordoliberalism'

Although very much a product of its time in mid-twentieth-century Germany, the Freiburg school view of competition has renewed resonance today. This school of thought developed as a response to the increasing cartelization of German industry in the 1920s and 1930s. Members of the Freiburg school were essentially free-market economists but they were concerned about the growing power of cartels and industry associations in Germany at that time. Rather than government intervention, they advocated the need for constitutional liberalism (*ordoliberalism*): competitive markets with an institutional framework of rules. In the modern context, ordoliberalism has a parallel in concerns about the power of large MNEs, though it sees the solution not in pressure group lobbying or active public intervention but in institutions – a view that has gained increasing intellectual acceptance in recent years.[21]

Public choice theory

Rooted in the tradition of political economy, public choice theory uses economic principles to analyse political decision making. In the context of competition, public choice theorists are sceptical of the ability of governments to correct market failure. They argue that governments are influenced by political and social considerations when intervening in markets, making them less likely to reach optimal decisions in the economic sense. In democratic systems dominated by two political parties, such as the United States or the UK, governments try to attract the *median preference voters* (the group of voters in the middle of the political spectrum), adopting policies that are popular with the median voter rather than those which achieve market efficiency. As a result, according to public choice theory, government intervention often means that market failure is replaced by government failure.[22]

The Chicago school

The SCP paradigm and the concept of workable competition dominated the thinking of the competition authorities in the United States and elsewhere in the 1960s and 1970s. Their main policy prescription was that intervention was needed to promote competition and prevent the abuse of monopoly power. This approach was increasingly challenged by economists of the Chicago school from the late 1960s onwards. This clash of ideas between the Harvard and Chicago schools dominated industrial economics during the 1970s. The Chicago school challenged the neoclassical interpretation of entry barriers and the calculation of the deadweight loss from monopoly, arguing that the assumptions of perfect competition were unnecessarily restrictive.

Conventional neoclassical theory recognized four main entry barriers facing potential entrants: absolute cost disadvantages (start-up costs or less favourable access to supplies and capital), economies of scale (favouring large established firms), product differentiation (favouring established brands and reputations), and legal barriers (entry restrictions or established intellectual property rights). The Chicago school considered most of these barriers less restrictive than generally supposed. Start-up costs, economies of scale, and the lack of an established reputation may be barriers to a new business, but they are not barriers to a large firm already well established in another market; thus, for example, a supermarket carries its established reputation and resources with it when it ventures into petrol retailing or financial services. The main area of agreement between the two schools is on legal barriers, especially where regulations restrict the entry of new firms or the ability of firms to compete.

Similarly, the Chicago school challenged the idea that monopoly or market concentration was necessarily harmful, arguing that a dominant market position may be achieved by competitive pricing, superior products, and scale efficiencies; in other words, superior conduct and performance may determine market structure rather than the reverse. They also argued that the efficiency gain from economies of scale would compensate for any deadweight loss from monopoly. If the efficiency gain, area D, is greater than the deadweight loss, area C, in Figure 9.6, there will be a net **welfare gain**. For the Chicago school, the ideal market structure should therefore reflect the optimum number of firms required to achieve economies of scale rather than the many small competing firms required by the model of perfect competition.[23]

Contestable markets theory

In 1982, William J. Baumol proposed another view of competition which, like the Chicago school, challenged the conventional idea of entry barriers and the assumptions of perfect competition.[24] Contestability theory focuses on the importance of potential rather than actual competition. Baumol rejects the need for a large number of competing firms but, unlike the Chicago school, argues that the benefits of perfect competition can be achieved even with an oligopolistic market structure, provided there are no **sunk costs** facing potential entrants. Sunk costs are costs incurred when entering a market which cannot be recovered

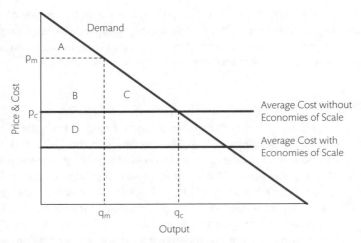

Figure 9.6 The Chicago school, efficiency gains, and deadweight loss

when leaving the market. According to contestable markets theory, the absence of sunk costs makes a market vulnerable to 'hit-and-run' entry, allowing firms to seize an opportunity to make profit, then look for opportunities elsewhere. Even if such entry does not actually occur, the constant threat of entry should keep the established firms on their toes, as though they were in perfect competition.

Along with most other competition theories, contestable markets theory recognizes that regulatory barriers may also restrict entry, but claims that, in the absence of entry restrictions and sunk costs, markets are more contestable than is generally supposed. Contestable markets theory emerged shortly after the US civil aviation market had been deregulated in 1978 and Baumol and others used this example to illustrate their new theory. Airline deregulation removed many of the restrictions that prevented domestic competition against the major US airlines. This left the problem of sunk costs. In the airline industry, the main sunk costs relate to the cost of airport facilities and runways, but provided new airlines do not incur the full cost of these facilities (only incurring usage costs such as take-off and landing charges), the market should still be contestable. In fact, a number of smaller airlines entered the US market, as occurred after EU airline deregulation in the 1980s and 1990s, followed by a period of consolidation in the form of mergers and alliances. The EU–US Open Skies Agreement is also encouraging the formation of airline alliances, though smaller airlines like Virgin Atlantic are concerned about the dominant position of the major airlines at the main hub airports. The key issue is the extent to which contestable markets exist in practice (see Practical Insight 9.5).

9.3.5 **Dynamic approaches to competition**

The Austrian school and Joseph Schumpeter

Although the foundations of the Austrian school were laid during the late nineteenth and early twentieth centuries by Carl Menger (1840–1921), Eugen von Böhm-Bawerk (1851–1914), and Ludwig von Mises (1881–1973), the most influential Austrian economist

Practical insight **9.5:** Contestable markets in banking

Contestable markets theory provided theoretical support for the policy of deregulation, or market liberalization, adopted by the US and UK governments during the 1980s, and later by a number of other European governments. UK examples include the deregulation of telecommunications, gas, electricity, buses, and railways, among others. Another example that attracted the attention of contestable markets theorists was the case of banking. Traditionally, UK retail banking has been separated into two distinct sectors: the joint-stock banks, which provide a wide range of financial services for business and domestic customers and profit for their shareholders; and the mutual building societies, which are owned by their members or account holders for their mutual benefit, take deposits from savers, and lend mainly for house purchase. This division between the two sectors was bridged when the 1986 Building Societies Act allowed building societies to 'demutualize' and become joint-stock companies. Demutualization allowed the former building societies to raise more capital and to spread their wings by moving into markets hitherto dominated by the banks.

The domain of conventional banks has also been 'invaded' by specialist internet banks, insurance companies offering savings policies linked to life assurance, supermarkets offering cash-back, credit, and other financial services, and by a variety of finance companies offering credit cards, loans, and other forms of credit.

From the perspective of the SCP paradigm, high-street banking was a classic oligopoly, dominated by a few large banks with a national network of branches. The conventional barriers to entry were significant, but the larger building societies already had a network of branches, so entry into the mainstream banking sector was not difficult. The arrival of the internet banks and other new entrants, however, suggests that the market is more contestable than might have been imagined. This is where the distinction between an 'industry' and a 'market' becomes crucial: the conventional banking industry has high entry barriers, but many of the markets in which banks operate do not. Thus, for example, the market for personal savings or consumer credit may be contestable even if the barriers to becoming a fully fledged commercial bank are considerable.[25]

Question

● To what extent do you consider the markets for financial services to be fully contestable in practice?

during the twentieth century was F. A. Hayek (1899–1992).[26] Austrian economists view competition as a dynamic process and reject the neoclassical idea of perfect competition in a state of stable equilibrium. According to the Austrian view, competition is a process of rivalry between market participants with imperfect knowledge. This process is one of discovery, where participants learn from their successes and failures and the actions of their rivals. Market structure is seen as largely irrelevant as it is continually changing. What is important is that the competitive process is unhindered by regulation, government intervention, and other forms of market interference. Austrians generally view competition policy with suspicion, preferring to allow the competitive process to operate freely. They also regard monopoly as a normal part of the competitive process, rejecting the idea of a deadweight loss from monopoly since comparisons with perfect competition are meaningless. In general, monopoly is considered to be the reward for success, which in the course of time will be weakened by competition if the monopolist fails to remain successful. This view of competition became the intellectual force behind Margaret Thatcher's privatization and deregulation policies in the UK in the 1980s.

Although not generally considered a member of the Austrian school, Joseph Schumpeter (1883–1950) arrived at similar conclusions but via a different process of reasoning.[27] Like the Austrians, Schumpeter regarded competition as a dynamic process, but he emphasized the way in which entrepreneurs develop new products and processes, creating disequilibrium as innovation makes the previous market conditions obsolete. In this way, entrepreneurs create new products and new businesses and destroy old ones – a process Schumpeter described as *creative destruction*. As one entrepreneur innovates, others must react either by imitation or counter-innovation, or by leaving the market. The policy implications of Schumpeterian analysis are similar to the Austrian view: that the authorities should generally leave competition to market forces. Dynamic theories of competition have the attraction of realism, especially in technology and other markets where innovation is continual, though their predictions are less clear-cut than more conventional theories.

Evolutionary approaches to competition

Increasingly, economists and other social scientists are adopting evolutionary ideas developed in the biological sciences to explain the competitive process.[28] In effect, these are an extension of the Austrian and Schumpeterian approaches. Evolutionary theories view competition as a process of adaptation and change where successful economic agents are those who are able to adapt as their environment changes; this view is similar to the Darwinian concept of *natural selection*. Unlike the neoclassical view of efficiency, which is achieved as a market approaches a perfectly competitive equilibrium, the appropriate concept of efficiency from an evolutionary perspective is **adaptive efficiency**. According to **complexity theory**, one of the main evolutionary approaches, the environment represents a complex adaptive system, consisting of independent elements which interact with each other and adapt to their changing environment. In a practical sense, competition involves organizations and consumers making decisions on the basis of their interpretations of fallible and situational knowledge, and responding to feedback from their environment and the reactions of rivals. This process enables their knowledge to develop as new ideas make old ones obsolete. As an explanation of the competitive process, evolutionary theory presents an apparently perceptive view of reality, though the policy implications are not yet well developed.

9.3.6 **Competition as strategic rivalry**

Porter's five forces model

Michael Porter's five forces model analyses competition from an organizational perspective, unlike most of the theories of industrial economics, which take the perspective of a detached observer.[29] Porter's model draws on ideas from the economics literature, deriving its basic structure from the SCP paradigm but taking a more eclectic and business-focused view than the more conventional Harvard school approach. The five forces that determine the nature of competition in Porter's model are as follows:

- The bargaining power of suppliers: those who supply labour, raw materials, components, and other inputs to the firm in question.
- The bargaining power of buyers: the consumers of the firm's products or services.

- The threat of entry by new firms: the extent to which there are entry barriers and potential rivals.
- The threat from substitute products: the nature of price and non-price competition and consumers' willingness to buy substitute products.
- Rivalry between firms: the nature of competitive advantages between rivals and the competitive strategies employed.

When represented diagrammatically, rivalry is normally placed at the centre, signifying that it is affected by each of the other forces. The five forces model provides a framework for the analysis of competition that can then be used as the basis for developing competitive strategies. However, whilst the five forces model is widely used as a practical tool for competitive analysis, its usefulness depends on the analyst's understanding of the underlying forces of competition.

Game theory

A wide range of political, economic, social, legal, military, sporting, and other situations lend themselves to analysis by game theory. The original idea was developed by von Neumann and Morgenstern, using mathematical analysis to solve economic problems, but it has since been applied in a number of other fields.[30] Game theory draws on the idea of competition between players to win a game. In some cases, as in the game of tennis for example, there is a winner and a loser; this is an example of a two-person zero-sum game – where the gain by one player equals the loss to the other (i.e. the net gain to both players is zero). This is the case in business where two (or more) firms bid for the same contract or franchise. In other cases, as for example where a group of supermarkets engage in price cutting, the total gains may increase, as total revenue will increase if market demand is elastic; this is an example of a multi-person (or *n*-person) non-zero-sum game. Game theory is essentially the analysis of the choices each player makes, bearing in mind that the outcome for each player is affected by the choices made by the other players. These choices are known as strategies, using the term 'strategy' in a more general sense than in the field of strategic management, though game theory clearly has implications for strategic decision making in business. Game theory views competition as a game of strategic interdependence between the players.

   In game theory, it is common to represent the strategies and outcomes (or *pay-offs*) for each player using a pay-off matrix. In Figure 9.7a we show the profits that can be achieved by two firms which have two alternative strategies: to charge a high price or a low price. We assume they are acting independently so do not know what strategy their rival will use, but they

Firm A → Firm B ↓	Low Price		High Price	
Low Price		8		0
	8		15	
High Price		15		10
	0		10	

Figure 9.7a Game theory pay-off matrix for two firms

Prisoner A → Prisoner B ↓	Confess	Deny
Confess	Light sentence Light sentence	Heavy sentence Light sentence
Deny	Light sentence Heavy sentence	Go free Go free

Figure 9.7b The prisoner's dilemma

are aware of the possible strategies available to their rival. The number in the top right-hand corner of each cell of the matrix is the profit (in € million) for Firm A; the number in the bottom left-hand corner is the profit for Firm B. This is clearly a simplified case, but it illustrates some of the issues involved. In the situation illustrated in Figure 9.7a, each firm is likely to choose a low price because the risk of choosing a high price when its rival chooses a low price is too great. Their best combined outcome would be to charge a high price, as this cell has the highest total value – best, that is, for the firms, not necessarily for the consumer or society. However, this would require cooperation or collusion between the firms.

Figure 9.7a is a business example of what is known as the prisoner's dilemma. In its original form, the game is played by two prisoners who have committed a serious crime, but whose conviction depends on the police gaining a confession through interrogation. The prisoners are interviewed in separate rooms and cannot collude. This is illustrated by Figure 9.7b. If both prisoners confess, they receive a light sentence (the top left-hand cell in the matrix). If prisoner A confesses and prisoner B does not, A receives a light sentence and B a heavy sentence (the bottom left-hand cell or top right-hand cell if the roles are reversed). If both remain silent, they go free (the bottom right-hand cell). As in the business game, they are likely to confess in order to avoid a heavy sentence. Ideally (from the prisoners' perspective), they would collude and remain silent. This is the dilemma they face.

These game scenarios can be adapted and developed in a number of ways, providing a range of possible strategies. Clearly, if the prisoner's dilemma is a cooperative rather than a non-cooperative game, the outcome is likely to be different. The outcome will also be different if the game is repeated; for example, if a firm knows it is likely to face retaliation from other firms during subsequent price rounds, it may well be tempted not to engage in price cutting. In some cases mixed strategies may be used in order to become less predictable to a rival, rather like a penalty taker in football who varies the direction of the shot in order to confuse the goalkeeper. At other times strategies may be used as a deterrent, such as a firm announcing a major expansion strategy in order to deter a market entrant. Of course, this strategy will only work if it is regarded as credible. These are just a few of the ways in which game theory strategies have been devised to provide an insight into the way competition works. Practical Insight 9.6 provides a different application of game theory in the context of trade policy.

Auction theory

Auctions provide another example of how competition works in particular circumstances. Auction theory is a development of game theory. Four main types of auction are generally

Practical insight 9.6: The prisoner's dilemma in trade policy

Let us characterize international trade policy as a two-person game where each player has two possible strategies. One player is Country A, the other is Country B, and each player may adopt a policy of either free trade or trade protection. In the short run, let us assume that Country A gains a large net benefit from trade protection if Country B adopts free trade, and a smaller net benefit if Country B opts for trade protection. These outcomes arise because trade protection safeguards domestic firms and employment in Country A, but export opportunities are restricted if Country B also adopts trade protection. Similar outcomes can be achieved by Country B. However, in the long run, both countries will gain from specialization and trade if they adopt a policy of free trade, and they would both be poorer if they pursued trade protection and not as well off as they could be if they are the sole country to adopt free trade. The best combined outcome in the long run is therefore where both countries agree to pursue a policy of free trade.

Questions

- What would the short-run and long-run pay-off matrices look like in this case?
- What are the policy implications of this scenario for multilateral trade negotiations at the WTO?
- Why might a country nevertheless decide to opt for trade protection?

identified: the ascending-bid auction or English auction, where the price is raised until a single bidder remains, as at a typical antiques auction; the descending-bid auction or Dutch auction, where an initial high price is gradually reduced until the first bid is made (so-called after the practice used in Dutch flower auctions); the first-price sealed-bid auction, where bidders make secret bids and the highest or lowest bid wins, a system which is often used when procurement contracts are put out to tender and is also used in the Scottish housing market; and the second-price sealed-bid auction, which operates in the same way as the first-price sealed-bid auction except that the highest bidder pays a price equal to the second-highest bidder's bid, a system used for example in stamp-collecting auctions because it is thought to encourage bidders to make a more realistic bid.

Apart from the many different examples of auctions, including wireless communication spectrum auctions[31] and internet auctions such as eBay, auction theory also has applications for competitive situations not normally considered to be auctions. For example, the internet is increasingly being used for the sale of motor vehicles, in addition to the more conventional motor dealership system. The internet offers a transparent marketplace where car sellers can easily compare each other's prices as though they were participating in an ascending-bid auction, where sellers make competing discounts until the last remaining seller wins the sale; although the price is 'descending' rather than 'ascending', the discount is increasing and the process is analogous to the ascending-bid auction in other respects. Conventional motor dealers, on the other hand, are less likely to know exactly what discounts their rivals are offering to a particular customer; this is more similar to a first-price sealed bid auction where the dealer may offer a more generous discount than strictly necessary. Counter-intuitively, auction theory demonstrates how the customer may receive a better deal from a conventional dealer than from a more open process such as the internet.[32]

9.4 **The need for regulation**

Markets need to be regulated by the authorities if and when they fail to achieve desired outcomes. These outcomes relate not only to efficient resource allocation, which tends to be the preoccupation of economic theory, but also to issues such as health and safety, intellectual property, product and service quality, financial security, or employment protection. Regulation provides the framework of formal institutions that helps to determine how a market operates. It is also used to promote innovation, as for example in the case of patents, where the encouragement of innovation has to be balanced against the benefits of competition (see Practical Insight 9.7), or to reduce risk, as in the case of genetically modified crops, though here the need for regulation depends on the balance of opinion on the scientific, economic, and ethical issues. Regulation is also used in former state-owned industries like telecommunications, water, electricity, and gas, where effective competition is difficult to achieve because of the natural monopoly element of these industries (see Section 9.2.4).

Competition policy, or antitrust policy as it is known in the United States, is used to regulate competition. The desirability of competition regulation depends on the theoretical perspective taken. From a conventional neoclassical perspective, regulation is necessary to prevent anti-competitive behaviour and avoid the welfare loss from monopoly. This view informed the early development of competition policy in the USA and UK, but it has been increasingly challenged by the Chicago, contestable markets, and Austrian views in more recent times. Chicago and Austrian school theorists have questioned the need for competition policy intervention, arguing that the authorities are more likely to interfere with market efficiency than to promote it. Contestable market theorists argue that regulation is needed to isolate the sunk-cost element of an industry, such as the railway network or electricity grid, but not to regulate the behaviour of firms. Of course, all but the most extreme adherents of these approaches recognize the need for intervention in some circumstances, but they generally prefer the competition authorities to be politically independent and favour non-discretionary rules over discretionary intervention. The rules-based approach to regulation provides clarity and transparency to market participants, though it may also encourage avoidance tactics.

The post-World War II years witnessed a significant increase in regulation in its various forms throughout the developed world, but the debate concerning the dangers of overregulation gathered momentum under the administrations of Ronald Reagan and Margaret Thatcher in the 1980s. Deregulation became the buzzword and one market after another was opened up to competition through the removal of price controls, entry barriers, and other restrictions on competition. In this context, a distinction was made between quantitative and qualitative regulation. Deregulation of the US, EU, and transatlantic civil aviation markets, for example, have allowed airlines to set their own fares and, in principle, to fly between any airports; they have not been about the removal of safety regulations. In recent years, the regulation agenda has moved towards the idea of better regulation rather than deregulation, using regulatory impact analysis to determine the cost effectiveness of a particular regulation and, in that sense, the justification for the regulation.[33]

Practical insight 9.7: The Apple/Samsung patent dispute

After a long rivalry with its more successful competitor, Microsoft, Apple has been fighting back with a series of innovative products, including the iPod, iPhone, and iPad, in recent years. It was not long, however, before Samsung and other rivals were producing their own versions of the smartphone and other hand-held devices. Perhaps inevitably, similar features appear on these electronic devices, but Apple's claim that Samsung has been breaching its patents has led to a lengthy battle in the US courts. In August 2012, a court ruled in favour of Apple, ordering Samsung to pay $1 billion in damages. However, this ruling was subsequently modified in relation to some of the patents and in March 2013 the damages award was reduced to just under $600 million. The outcome of the dispute is important for both companies, as well as for some of their rivals. Despite its earlier success, Apple's share price fell by 40 per cent between September 2012 and March 2013, so the dispute reflects the ongoing battle for supremacy in the market for the latest high-tech products.[34]

Question

● Do patents promote or hold back innovation in this rapidly developing market?

Summary

The market system now dominates the modern global economy. Markets are essentially a mechanism for allocating resources, where demand and supply are brought into equilibrium by price adjustments. The efficiency with which markets operate is affected by their institutional framework and the extent to which there is asymmetric information or other forms of 'market failure'. It should also be noted that financial markets tend to be more volatile than markets for goods and services. Competition is an important feature of an efficient market and a number of different theories have been developed to explain how competition works. The conventional approach, based on the neoclassical theory of the firm and the ideal of perfect competition, has given rise to the structure-conduct-performance (SCP) paradigm. This view has increasingly been challenged by the Chicago, contestable markets, Austrian, and other schools of thought. Other developments such as game theory have also contributed towards the analysis of competition as a process of strategic rivalry. The various theories of competition present different views on the rationale for and appropriateness of market regulation and competition policy.

Discussion questions

1. To what extent are markets an efficient mechanism for allocating resources?
2. In what way is market efficiency affected by formal and informal institutions?
3. To what extent is asymmetric information likely to lead to market failure and how might this problem be addressed?
4. To what extent do you think the structure-conduct-performance paradigm is valid in practice?

5. To what extent do you think the Austrian school view of competition is valid in practice?

6. What are the implications of contestable markets theory for market regulation and competition policy?

Suggested assignment topics

1. With reference to a specific market, investigate the reasons for price changes in the market concerned over the last five years.

2. With reference to a specific acquisition or merger, evaluate the extent to which the change in market structure is likely to increase or decrease the level of competition in the market concerned.

3. Select a specific competition policy investigation in a country of your choice and evaluate the outcome of the investigation using appropriate competition theories.

 Case study: Microsoft

In September 2007, Microsoft lost its appeal against the European Commission's finding that the company had abused its dominant position in the EU single market under Article 82 of the European Community Treaty. The Commission had originally ruled against Microsoft in 2004 after an investigation that began in December 1998. Microsoft had also survived an attempt by a US court to break up the company, following a series of investigative and legal proceedings dating back to 1991. In both the US and EU cases, the investigations were initiated after complaints from Microsoft's rivals. The European Commission originally fined Microsoft €497 million, its largest fine for anti-competitive behaviour at the time, then added a further €280.5 million because of delays in complying with the ruling. The original fine was then increased to €899 million in February 2008 as a penalty for overcharging for information after the Commission's 2004 ruling.

The EU case against Microsoft was twofold. First, Microsoft had made it difficult for rival software manufacturers to make compatible products because its software codes were not made available to its rivals; this lack of 'interoperability' restricted competition in the market for software, given that Microsoft had between 90 and 95 per cent of the world market for PC operating systems. Secondly, Microsoft had used its Windows operating system to extend its dominant position into related software markets by pre-installing its Media Player software onto its operating system; the 'tying' or 'bundling' of these two products discouraged consumers from installing alternative media software. Microsoft had protested that its software codes were a legitimate commercial secret, protected by patents, and that consumers were free to install rival media software if they wished. However, the Court upheld the Commission's ruling that Microsoft should make its codes available to competitors for a one-off fee of €10,000 and that the royalties that Microsoft had been charging for each copy sold after the 2004 ruling should be reduced from 5.95 per cent to 0.4 per cent.

The ruling was actually somewhat less far-reaching than it might have appeared, since interoperability information was only initially made available for work-group servers used by businesses and other large organizations, though its significance in terms of the European Commission's long-running competition investigation is considerable. The Commission's insistence that Microsoft should sell two separate versions of its Windows operating system, one with Media Player and one without, was more of a pyrrhic victory – especially as the two versions were sold with little difference in price. However, the European Commission then pursued a further investigation into the inclusion of Internet Explorer, Microsoft's web browser, in the Windows operating system. The case was finally resolved in December 2009 when the Commission accepted

Microsoft's proposal to make its interoperability information more readily available and to include a 'ballot screen' allowing users to choose from a list of popular web browsers.

The Microsoft case raises a number of issues. Clearly, Microsoft has a dominant position in relation to its PC and laptop operating system, though its share of related software markets varies depending on the product concerned. Its dominant position in many of these markets was achieved largely through its own success in making beneficial alliances and user-friendly products. The problem in technology markets is the role played by dominant technical standards. Whoever controls the dominant standard, in this case the Windows operating system, has a significant advantage over its rivals unless there is complete interoperability at a reasonable cost. However, Microsoft's dominant position is now being challenged by Google and other rivals as 'cloud computing' increasingly enables users to access software and store files on the worldwide web (see the case study at the end of Chapter 10). This makes interoperability with the Windows operating system less important.

A key question in this context is whether Microsoft's dominance has been in the interests of consumers. Has it given consumers the best deal in terms of price, product range, innovation, etc.? There is also the competition policy question as to whether the EU ruling is designed to protect Microsoft's competitors rather than its consumers (as some US observers have claimed), and the political question as to whether the European Commission is striking a blow against US corporate supremacy. Whatever the answer to these questions, some would argue that Microsoft's competitors have ultimately found a technological solution to the problem of Microsoft's dominance.[35]

Case study questions

1. To what extent has the level of market concentration been a cause for concern in the markets in which Microsoft operates?

2. To what extent have the lack of interoperability and the bundling of software products such as Media Player and Internet Explorer created a barrier to entry for Microsoft's rivals?

3. To what extent do you think the structure-conduct-performance paradigm provides a justification for the ruling of the EU competition authorities in the Microsoft case?

4. How might the case be viewed from the perspective of the Austrian school?

5. In what ways do dominant technical standards change the way competition works in technology markets?

6. To what extent do you think the European Commission rulings in this case have helped to promote innovation?

7. To what extent do you think consumers are likely to benefit from the rulings?

8. How would you evaluate the suggestion that the EU was trying to tame US corporate power in the Microsoft case?

Notes

1. Main sources: Dearden, S. J. H. (1994), 'Air transport deregulation in the European Union', *European Business Review*, vol. 94, issue 5, pp. 15–19; *The Sunday Times* (21 October 2007), 'Open skies ends a closed shop'; European Commission, Air Transport Agreement between the EU and USA, first and second stage agreements, http://ec.europa.eu; Association of European Airlines ,'Open Skies: The EU-US Air Transport Agreement', and http://www.routes-news.com/airlines/item/579-open-for-business, accessed 4 March 2013.

2. Fortune Global 500, 2012.

3. Main sources: Money Week, 'Oil price performance', http://www.moneyweek.com (accessed 7 March 2012); BBC News (2 January 2008), 'What is driving oil prices so high?'; *Financial Times* (27 June 2008), 'Oil shocks';

and *Financial Times* (10 May 2009), 'Oil prices'; US Energy Information Administration (21 August 2012), 'Crude oil prices peaked early in 2012', http://www.eia.gov; and WTRG Economics, http://www.wtrg.com/prices.htm.

4. *United States v. E. I. du Pont de Nemours & Co.* (1956).

5. See, for example, the UK Standard Industrial Classification (SIC), the EU Nomenclature générale des activités économiques dans les communautées européennes (NACE) or the UN International Standard Industrial Classification (ISIC).

6. For a more technical discussion of general equilibrium theory, see for example, Pindyck, R. S., and Rubinfeld, D. L. (2012), *Microeconomics*, Pearson.

7. The Bologna Declaration on the European Space for Higher Education, http://ec.europa.eu/education/policies/educ/bologna/bologna.pdf.

8. Akerlof, G. A., 'The market for "lemons": quality uncertainty and the market mechanism', *Quarterly Journal of Economics*, August 1970, pp. 488–500.

9. In its most developed form, the efficient market hypothesis is associated with Fischer Black and Myron Scholes in Black, F., and Scholes, M. (1973), 'The pricing of options and corporate liabilities', *Journal of Political Economy*, vol. 81, pp. 637–54.

10. See, for example, Mandelbrot, B. B. (2008), *The (Mis) Behaviour of Markets*, Profile Books.

11. The term 'butterfly effect' was coined by Edward Lorenz in his address to the Annual Meeting of the American Association for the Advancement of Science, Washington, 29 December 1979, though the butterfly analogy is much older; it relates to a central idea in what has become known as chaos theory.

12. Perfectly elastic demand means that the quantity demanded is highly responsive to a change in price (literally: infinitely responsive), so the slightest increase in price results in a complete loss of demand; the demand curve is therefore horizontal.

13. Normal profit represents the rate of return that is just sufficient to persuade the entrepreneur to invest in this particular business compared with the next best alternative; it therefore reflects the cost to the entrepreneur relative to the alternative investment opportunities forgone (the opportunity cost).

14. For a more extensive discussion of the theory of the firm, see for example Gillespie, A. (2011), *Foundations of Economics*, Oxford University Press, chs 11–14.

15. Harberger, A. C. (1954), 'Monopoly and resource allocation', *American Economic Review*, vol. XLIV, no. 2, pp. 77–87.

16. Demand is described as elastic if a price change leads to a greater proportionate change in quantity demanded; it is inelastic if a price change results in a smaller proportionate change in quantity demanded.

17. A price increase will lead to a fall in revenue (income) when demand is elastic as the fall in sales will outweigh the increase in price; a price decrease will also lead to a fall in revenue when demand is inelastic as the increase in sales will be insufficient to compensate for the price reduction. For a more technical discussion of theories of imperfect competition, see for example Pindyck, R. S., and Rubinfeld, D. L. (2012), *Microeconomics*, Pearson, chs 12 and 13.

18. The SCP paradigm is usually attributed to the work of Mason, Bain, and Scherer, all of whom either taught or studied at Harvard University, and the SCP tradition has been particularly associated with Harvard economists. Key works include: Mason, E. S. (1939), 'Price and production policies of large-scale enterprise', *American Economic Review*, Supplement 29; Bain, J. S. (1956), *Barriers to New Competition*, Harvard University Press; and Scherer, F. M. (1970), *Industrial Market Structure and Economic Performance*, Rand McNally.

19. See the Final Report of the Competition Commission Groceries Market Investigation, 30 April 2008 (http://www.competition-commission.org.uk).

20. Clark, J. M. (1940), 'Toward a concept of workable competition', *American Economic Review*, vol. 30, pp. 241–56.

21. A discussion of the Freiburg school can be found in Ahlborn, C., and Grave, C. (2006), 'Walter Eucken and Ordoliberalism: An introduction from a consumer perspective', *Competition Policy International*, vol. 2, no. 2, pp. 197–217.

22. Important works on public choice theory include: Downs, A. (1957), *An Economic Theory of Democracy*, Harper and Row; and Buchanan, J. M., and Tullock, G. (1962), *The Calculus of Consent: Logical Foundations of Constitutional Democracy*, University of Michigan Press.

23. See, for example, Stigler, G. J. (1968), *The Organization of Industry*, Irwin.

24. Baumol, W. J. (1982), 'Contestable markets – an uprising in the theory of industry structure', *American Economic Review*, vol. 72, no. 1, pp. 1–15; or for a more extensive treatment, Baumol, W. J., Panzar, J. C., and Willig, R. D. (1982), *Contestable Markets and the Theory of Industry Structure*, Harcourt Brace Jovanovich.

25. See, for example, Cruickshank, D. (2000), *Competition in UK Banking, A Review of Banking Services in the UK*, HMSO, March.

26. See, for example, Hayek, F. A. (2008), *The Road to Serfdom: Text and Documents: The Definitive Edition*, Chicago University Press, first published in 1944; or on the Austrian view of competition: Hayek, F. A. (1996), *Individualism and Economic Order*, Chicago University Press, first published in 1948.

27. Schumpeter, J. A. (1980), *The Theory of Economic Development*, Transaction Publishers, first published in 1934.

28. See, for example, Beinhocker, E. D. (2006), *The Origin of Wealth: Evolution, Complexity, and the Radical Remaking of Economics*, Harvard Business School Press.

29. See Porter, M. E. (2004), *Competitive Strategy: Techniques for Analyzing Industries and Competitors*, The Free Press.

30. Rubinstein, A., von Neumann, J., Morgenstern, O., and Kuhn, H. W. (2007), *Theory of Games and Economic Behaviour*, Princeton University Press, first published under its original authors, von Neumann and Morgenstern, in 1944.

31. For example, the UK's 4G mobile broadband spectrum auction in February 2013.

32. For a detailed discussion of auction theory, see Klemperer, P. (2004), *Auctions: Theory and Practice*, Princeton University Press; elements of this book can also be found on Paul Klemperer's website: http://www.paulklemperer.org/index.htm.

33. A more detailed study of regulation can be found in Malyshev, N. (2006), 'Regulatory policy: OECD experience and evidence', *Oxford Review of Economic Policy*, vol. 22, no. 2, pp. 274–99.

34. Main source: *Wall Street Journal* (1 March 2013), 'US judge reduces Apple's patent award in Samsung case'.

35. *Financial Times* (22 October 2007), 'Microsoft concedes defeat in EU battle'; *International Herald Tribune* (27 February 2008), 'EU fines Microsoft record 899 million euros'; the *Guardian* (16 December 2009), 'EU ends competition case as Microsoft offers choice of web browsers'; and Microsoft (16 December 2009), 'Timeline of European Commission Cases against Microsoft, 1998–2009'. http://www.microsoft.com.

Suggestions for further reading

An introduction to supply and demand analysis and competition theory

Gillespie, A. (2011), *Foundations of Economics*, Oxford University Press

More advanced treatment of markets and competition theory

Lipczynski, J., Wilson, J. J., and Goddard, J. (2013), *Industrial Organization: Competition, Strategy, Policy*, Pearson

Pindyck, R. S., and Rubinfeld, D. L. (2012), *Microeconomics*, Pearson

Varian, H. R. (2010), *Intermediate Microeconomics: A Modern Approach*, W. W. Norton and Co.

A useful survey of competition theory

Budzinski, O. (2008), 'Monoculture versus diversity in competition economics', *Cambridge Journal of Economics*, vol. 32, pp. 295–324

Take your learning further: Online Resource Centre
http://www.oxfordtextbooks.co.uk/orc/harrison2e/
Visit the Online Resource Centre that accompanies this book to enrich your understanding of Chapter 9: Markets and Competition. Among other resources explore web links and keep up to date with the latest developments in the area.

Key terms introduced in this chapter

Adaptive efficiency The ability of elements in a complex system to adapt in response to their changing environment.

Adverse selection Market failure resulting from the inability of consumers to determine the quality of a product in markets with asymmetric information.

Asymmetric information Unequal access to information between the buyer and seller of a product.

Complexity theory The study of complex adaptive systems.

Consumer surplus The difference between the market price and the price consumers are willing and able to pay, as shown by the demand curve.

Cross-elasticity A measure of the responsiveness of the demand for or supply of one good or service to a change in the price of another.

Dynamic theories of competition The study of competition as a continually changing process.

Elasticity A measure of the responsiveness of one variable to a change in another, e.g. the responsiveness of demand to a change in price.

Entry barrier A real or perceived obstacle to market entry, such as the cost of entry, sunk costs, product differentiation, or entry restrictions.

Free-rider problem The problem that arises when individuals are able to benefit from the private provision of public goods without contributing towards their cost.

Homogeneous product A product with identical substitutes.

Market failure The inability of a market to allocate resources efficiently in order to meet the wants and needs of consumers.

Merit good A service such as education or health care which is beneficial for society as a whole but which might be under-provided if left to market forces.

Monopolistic competition A form of market structure where there is freedom of entry and exit and a large number of small firms selling differentiated products.

Monopoly Pure monopoly is a form of market structure where there are high entry barriers and a single producer selling a product with no close substitutes; in practice, the term is also used to describe markets where dominant firms have some degree of market power.

Moral hazard Market failure resulting from a change in behaviour after receiving a benefit such as credit or insurance in a market with asymmetric information.

Natural monopoly A market where the most efficient scale of production requires a single producer.

Oligopoly A form of market structure where there are entry barriers and a few dominant firms selling differentiated products.

Opportunity cost The cost of a particular course of action valued in terms of the alternatives forgone.

Perfect competition A form of market structure where there is freedom of entry and exit and a large number of small firms selling homogeneous products.

Producer surplus The difference between the market price and marginal cost to the producer, which is equal to the average cost if the average cost is constant.

Product differentiation A characteristic of competition where products are perceived by consumers to be different with respect to their distinctive features or the context in which they are sold.

Property rights Legally enforceable protection of the rights of consumers, employees, shareholders, intellectual property owners, and others.

Public good A service such as defence or law and order where non-rivalry between consumers and the non-exclusion of consumers might lead to under-provision and the free-rider problem if left to market forces.

Structure-conduct-performance (SCP) paradigm The view that the structure of a market determines the conduct of firms which in turn determines their performance.

Sunk cost A cost incurred when entering a market which is irrecoverable when leaving the market.

Time-preference rate The willingness of an individual or society to consume resources in the present period as opposed to saving for a future period.

Welfare gain or loss The net effect of a price increase on the loss of consumer surplus (the deadweight loss) and the gain in producer surplus, if any.

Technological Change

 Chapter learning outcomes

On completion of this chapter the reader should be able to:

- Appreciate alternative perspectives on the process and implications of technological change
- Identify and analyse the main sources of technological change
- Evaluate the impact of technological change on productivity and economic growth
- Appreciate the relationship between knowledge creation, technology, and the knowledge economy

Opening scenario: The high-definition DVD format war

Toshiba launched its new format HD-DVD player in March 2006. This was followed six months later by Sony's alternative format Blu-ray high definition DVD player. For 18 months the two rivals fought for supremacy in the format war to find a high-definition replacement for the established DVD player. Toshiba finally conceded defeat in February 2008 after a number of important film producers gave their backing to Sony, allowing Sony's Blu-ray players to set the industry standard. This was in many respects a repetition of the battle between the Betamax and VHS formats for the video player which preceded the arrival of the DVD – except that in the 1980s Sony's Betamax lost out to JVC's VHS format.

In the end, the Blu-ray player won not necessarily because it had better technology or produced a better quality picture, but because of the backing it received from Walt Disney, Twentieth Century Fox, and Warner Brothers, key players in the Hollywood movie industry. Microsoft, whose operating system needs to be compatible with the new technology, especially to facilitate downloading from the internet, had in fact backed Toshiba, as had Warner Brothers until its pivotal decision to abandon Toshiba in January 2008. The support of the major film producers was ultimately crucial as, without a reasonable number of films being produced in the required format, the HD-DVD player would soon have become redundant. Other factors, such as Blu-ray's superior storage capacity and marketing success, including Sony's decision to incorporate Blu-ray into its market-leading PlayStation 3 games console, also helped to secure victory for the Blu-ray format.

This story illustrates the way developments often occur in markets for technological products. The high-definition DVD player is the latest generation in a series of devices for playing films. Although it contains features undreamt of when its earliest predecessors were developed, it is nevertheless an incremental innovation, building on previous technologies. Like any technological development, it is the product of a vast array of general and specialized knowledge, much of which is publicly available, some of which is protected. A particular feature of technological products is that one product acts as a platform for another, as the Blu-ray player does for films. This means that compatibility is important. Of course, it would be quite possible to have two alternative formats, each with its own set of films, but there are cost and marketing advantages in having a single format, especially if it attracts the majority of consumers. The dominant format then becomes the industry standard. This raises the issue of intellectual property rights, which should provide sufficient protection to encourage profitable innovation, whilst allowing the technology to be shared by a wide range of producers and consumers.

The next generation of 'ultra-HD' content may be accessed online, as film downloads are already replacing DVDs, but higher quality formats require increased internet bandwidth and high resolution monitors that are not always available, so discs and blu-ray players may still be required for a few more years. These issues, among others, help to create the distinctive characteristics of the technological environment.[1]

10.1 Perspectives on technological change

10.1.1 Technological 'revolutions'

Technological developments have occurred throughout history. Even in prehistoric times primitive tools made out of stone, wood, and other natural materials represented the technology of a particular period.[2] However, in modern times, the most productive period of technological development dates from the late eighteenth century to the present time. This period has been the most productive, not so much because of the number of inventions (which has been significant), but more especially because of the impact of technological developments on productivity, gross domestic product (GDP), and GDP per capita. The early part of this period, from the late eighteenth to the mid-nineteenth century is often described as the 'Industrial Revolution', which began in Britain, then spread to other parts of Europe and North America. The most significant aspect of this period, and indeed the period that followed the industrial revolution, is that technological and organizational change led to sustained economic growth and continual improvements in the standard of living in the countries concerned.

For centuries technological innovation had led to temporary or minor improvements in living standards, but these benefits had generally been cancelled out by conflict or population increases, leaving the majority of people little better off. This is starkly illustrated in Figure 10.1, which is based on Angus Maddison's estimates of GDP per capita from AD 1 to AD 2008.[3] According to Maddison, world GDP per capita was only about half as much again in 1820 as it had been in the year AD 1; this represents remarkably little economic progress during most of the first two millennia AD. The rate of increase was marginally higher in Western Europe, but Africa was slightly poorer in 1820 than it had been 1,800 years previously. By 2008, however, GDP per capita was about 20 times as high in the west (Western Europe and the USA), the cradle of the industrial revolution, as it had been in 1820. Latin America and Asia lagged behind, though their GDP per capita had grown significantly by the end of the twentieth century. African GDP per capita was just over four times as high in 2008 as it had been in 1820, though some individual African countries experienced little, if any, improvement over this period. These statistics illustrate the dramatic change that occurred after the onset of the industrial revolution, particularly in the west, and also the way in which some parts of the world have been left behind.

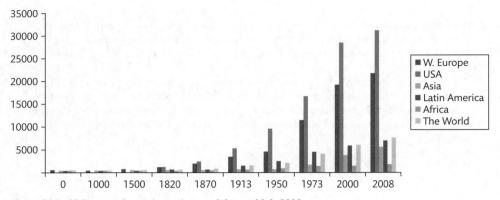

Figure 10.1 GDP per capita, major regions and the world, 1–2008 AD

Source: Maddison, A. (March 2010), http://www.ggdc.net/maddison/Maddison.htm. The vertical scale represents 'International Dollars' valued at 1990 prices.

For some economic historians, the industrial 'revolution' was more of a gradual process than the term 'revolution' implies.[4] Certainly, there is often a long time lag between an invention or discovery and the full extent of its applications. Joel Mokyr divides the industrial revolution into separate phases leading up to the present time, an approach which is useful in linking earlier developments with the recent growth of information and communication technology (ICT).[5] He describes the first industrial revolution as the period from about 1760 to the mid-nineteenth century, characterized by the development of coal mining, textile manufacture, the factory system, and the application of mechanical inventions such as the steam engine. The second industrial revolution, covering the period from the mid-nineteenth century to 1914, saw the development of industries such as chemicals and steel, the introduction of the telegraph and telephone, the discovery of electricity, and the development of the internal combustion engine, among others. The third industrial revolution covered the period from 1914 to the early 1970s, a period which included the introduction of assembly-line operations and product standardization as well as developments in medicine, air travel, nuclear energy, and many other fields. The period from the early 1970s to the present time is described as the 'Information Revolution' or 'Information and Communication Technology (ICT) Revolution'; this period is characterized not only by the widespread use of the computer, but also by the development of the '**knowledge economy**' (see Section 10.4), including the use of the internet and the way in which ICT has transformed work practices and everyday lives. Practical Insight 10.1 considers the application of ICT to the financial services sector.

10.1.2 **Technology as an application of knowledge**

A core feature of technology is that it represents the application of scientific or practical knowledge. As technological products and processes have become more sophisticated, the term 'knowledge economy' has been used to describe this phenomenon. Of course, technological knowledge is not unique to the economies of the late twentieth and early twenty-first centuries, but there is a perception that the level of human skill and technological sophistication required in the modern world is proportionately greater than in previous periods. The

Practical insight **10.1:** Electronic banking systems

Developments in financial services provide a useful illustration of the way ICT has been transforming our everyday lives. Electronic funds transfer allows salaries and payments of various kinds to be transferred directly from one bank account to another, and credit and debit cards are gradually replacing the need for payments by cash or cheque. Electronic systems enable us to do our banking online and allow call-centre staff to access our bank details from the other side of the world. They also link retail outlets to the banking system and are increasingly connecting the banking systems of developed and developing countries. Of course, these systems are not infallible and international connections sometimes involve delays and unexpectedly high costs, but electronic banking is undoubtedly changing the face of banking in many parts of the world.

Question

● What are the implications of electronic banking systems for competition in the high-street banking sector?

computer provides an illustration of the importance of knowledge relative to physical resources. Consider a personal desktop computer. The computer is made up of various physical materials and components and has an operating system and various software programs. The cost of the physical materials represents only a small proportion of the computer's total value. Most of its value is contained in the knowledge required to design and build the computer and its components, and to develop its system and application software. This is typical of many technological products.

Whereas a single piece of information contributes to our knowledge, the sense in which we are using the term 'knowledge' here is more than simply a collection of information. Instead, knowledge represents the way in which information and understanding combine to determine patterns and regularities in natural phenomena and their application to the solution of practical problems. Mokyr distinguishes between *propositional knowledge* (beliefs about natural phenomena) and *prescriptive knowledge* (techniques for applying propositional knowledge).[6] This broadly corresponds with the distinction between scientific knowledge and technological knowledge, though propositional knowledge may include practical knowledge gained through experience as well as scientific knowledge. The role of technological knowledge in economic growth and development is explored further in Sections 10.3 and 10.4.

10.1.3 **Spatial implications of technology**

One of the characteristics of the ICT revolution that seems to distinguish it from earlier industrial revolutions is the way in which it brings people, businesses, and other organizations around the world closer together. To some extent this also happened in earlier periods because of improvements in transport and communication, but the instantaneous flow of information provided by the internet and wireless communication seems to represent a revolution of an altogether different kind. Frances Cairncross has described this phenomenon as the 'death of distance', arguing that while the nineteenth and twentieth centuries witnessed the falling cost of transporting goods and people respectively, the twenty-first century will be characterized by the falling cost of transporting ideas and information.[7] Electronic commerce (e-commerce) bridges the physical distance between buyer and seller, including both retail and business-to-business transactions, enabling them to find each other more easily, make more informed choices, and reduce the cost of their transactions.

For Thomas Friedman, technology is a flattening process that removes the spatial and economic barriers that separate different parts of the world, especially between the western developed countries and technologically emerging countries like India.[8] In this sense, technology is starting to break down barriers between rich and poor countries, allowing a multitude of business services to be offshored across an increasingly 'flat world'. Not only is information transferred rapidly across vast distances, but so also are technological knowledge and economic wealth. This picture of a world where distance no longer matters is of course exaggerated; otherwise, there would have been no need for the huge increase in foreign direct investment (FDI) that has occurred in recent years. What is clear, however, is that businesses are now able to undertake operations and communicate between different parts of the world with relative ease. This facility is available to smaller organizations as well as larger ones and also to private citizens. Perhaps belatedly, citizens are now also being connected to local and central government much closer to home (see Practical Insight 10.2).

10.1.4 Technology and employment effects

In this section we consider the effect of technology on the labour market and the skills profile of industries and countries. It has long been feared that the substitution of technology for labour leads to unemployment. This concern dates back to the Luddites who tried to destroy the new power looms that were replacing handloom weavers in textile factories in early nineteenth-century England – a concern which has been expressed more peacefully in relation to the ICT revolution today. If one takes a narrow perspective on the immediate effects of the introduction of labour-saving technology at a particular workplace, it is clear that there are likely to be job losses for the displaced workers. However, when one considers the effect of technology on an economy as a whole, one sees that there seems to be little if any long-term effect on employment.

Practical insight 10.2: e-Government

The breaking down of distance barriers is not restricted to the private sector. A number of initiatives are being taken to link citizens with central and local government through e-government schemes. Citizens can increasingly apply for benefits, complete income tax returns, or exchange information with government departments online. e-Government is also being considered as a way of encouraging voters to engage with the electoral process, either through online voting, automated telephone voting, or electronic voting at polling stations. The potential benefits in terms of speed, efficiency, and cost saving are clear and late-night election counts could become a thing of the past.

Question

- To what extent do you think e-government will help to break down barriers between government and people and lead to greater public engagement by ordinary citizens?

This can be seen in Figures 10.2a and 10.2b in relation to employment and unemployment in the US economy over the period from 1946 to 2012. The US economy has maintained its ability to create employment, despite having probably experienced more technological change than any other economy over this period. The unemployment rate is more ambiguous, though its rise in the 1970s and early 1980s probably has more to do with the inflation and recession that accompanied rising oil prices at that time than with the impact of new technology. The ICT revolution gathered pace in the 1990s, when unemployment was generally lower, and the high unemployment in 2008–9 was clearly caused by the financial crisis and recession.

The lack of a negative impact of technology on overall employment, especially in the longer term, is probably due to the way in which markets and economies adjust to new technology. As well as reducing the need for direct labour in the production process, technology increases output and reduces the cost of production. Lower prices enable consumers to buy more, including new goods and services created by the new technology. The new products then generate employment opportunities to compensate for the loss of jobs in conventional production. In this way, the ICT revolution has helped to reduce employment in former labour-abundant industries such as car manufacturing or banking, and has created employment in the computer, electronics, telecommunications, and related sectors. In particular,

Figure 10.2a US employment level, 1946-2012

Source: US Bureau of Labor Statistics.

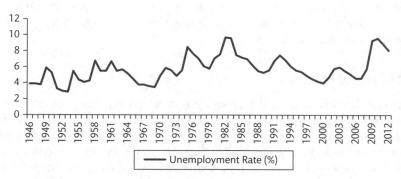

Figure 10.2b US unemployment rate, 1946-2012

Source: US Bureau of Labor Statistics.

modern economies are experiencing increased employment in the service sector as consumers demand more sophisticated leisure services and businesses add value to their products by offering support services to their customers. Technology also allows greater flexibility in the use of labour, enabling an increasing number of people to work from home or at other off-site locations. There is even some evidence to suggest that people who work mainly with technology work longer hours and are paid more than more conventional workers, though this may be because their roles generally require a higher level of professional commitment and attract people with higher skills.[9]

10.1.5 Technology and the working environment

One of the most significant effects of technology has been on the working environment. Most organizations have now vastly increased their ability to store, process, and share information. This facilitates communication with colleagues, customers, and suppliers at remote locations. For office workers, the computer has replaced typed documents and hand-written account books; for production workers it has replaced the draughtsman's drawing and the painstaking machining of precision products. Marketers use PowerPoint presentations instead of overhead projection and teachers have replaced their blackboards with electronic whiteboards. The use of computer-aided design (CAD) and computer-aided manufacturing (CAM) has transformed the manufacturing sector, allowing complex processes to be undertaken rapidly and accurately. Technology has also revolutionized many other areas of work, ranging from the use of DNA profiling in police investigations to Kuala Lumpur's driverless urban transit system.

Many tasks that were previously undertaken by teams of people or large organizations can now be carried out by an individual or small business in a fraction of the time. In this way, technology empowers small and medium-sized enterprises to take on work that was once the domain of large corporations. Even international markets are now within reach via the internet as long as customer requirements can be met either electronically or using the services of one of the many international logistics companies. In a similar way, technology is reducing the scale of conventional production operations, allowing steel producers to use more efficient mini-mills and motor manufacturers to produce differentiated finished products from shared production platforms. These developments enable efficiencies to be achieved with smaller scale at the same time as providing the customer with an individually customized product. In a variety of ways, therefore, technology is changing the relationship between inputs, output, and the consumer.

10.1.6 The global picture

It is clear from Section 10.1.1 that technological developments have not occurred evenly across different regions of the world. The US economist, Jeffrey Sachs, has suggested a classification of countries according to whether they are **technological innovators**, **technological adopters**, or **technologically excluded**.[10] Technological innovators are defined as countries with ten or more patents per million inhabitants and technological adopters are those where high-tech exports account for at least 2 per cent of GDP; the remainder are classed as technologically excluded. Whilst these definitions are somewhat arbitrary, they give a broad

Table 10.1 World internet usage, June 2012

Regions	Internet Penetration (% of population)	% of World Internet Usage
Africa	15.6	7.0
Asia	27.5	44.8
Europe	63.2	21.5
Middle East	40.2	3.7
North America	78.6	11.4
Latin America & Caribbean	42.9	10.6
Oceania/Australia	67.6	1.0
Total	34.3	100.0

Source: http://www.internetworldstats.com.

indication of a country's stage of technological development. The technological innovators account for about 15 per cent of the world's population and include the USA and Canada, most of Western Europe, Japan, Taiwan, South Korea, and Australia. The technological adopters include Mexico, Argentina, Chile, south and south-east Brazil, most of Central and Eastern Europe (CEE), South Africa, southern and western India, eastern and south-eastern China and much of South-East Asia. This leaves most of Africa, large parts of Asia, most of Central America, and much of the northern half of South America 'technologically excluded'.

The above picture is of course a changing one as countries progress from one category to another, as Taiwan and South Korea have done in recent years. A number of other indicators could also be used to determine the extent to which technology has permeated the everyday lives of a country's citizens. These might include the level of telephone, mobile phone, or internet usage, for example. Internet usage is now a prime indicator of technological connectivity, something which is becoming increasingly important in international business. Table 10.1 compares internet usage in each of the main regions of the world, though it is important to note that usage also varies considerably between individual countries. Despite the vast increase in internet usage since the mid-1990s, only just over a third of the world's population were using the internet in 2012. The reasons for the differences between countries and regions will depend on factors such as education, income, the availability of telephone connections and power supplies, and the level of peace and security, among other things. Remoteness of geographical location may also isolate some regions, even within a particular country, though joint ventures with multinational enterprises (MNEs) in innovator countries may accelerate the technological progress of an otherwise less developed country.

10.2 Sources of technological change

10.2.1 Uncertainties of technological change

Before we consider the factors that lead to technological change, it is important to note that technological change is affected by a large number of uncertainties at every stage of the process. First of all, it is unclear at the outset whether an idea or invention will realize its full potential or even produce more modest positive outcomes such as a quality improvement or cost reduction. Even if a product turns out to be technically successful, there is no guarantee it will be a commercial success. This was the case with the Anglo-French Concorde supersonic aircraft. The planning and design process for the Concorde began, with the support of the British and French governments, in the early 1960s. The aircraft went into service in 1976 and was finally withdrawn in 2004 after a period of uncertainty following a major accident near Paris and a number of technical problems.[11] Concorde was well ahead of its time technologically, but its commercial success was limited by the fact that most of its potential customer airlines withdrew their orders after a number of international airports refused it permission to land because of what they perceived to be excessive noise.

In some cases the eventual success of a discovery may be dependent on further discoveries in the future. Thus, for example, the drug aspirin was developed by scientists as an analgesic (pain killer) during the latter half of the nineteenth century, and was marketed successfully during the twentieth century until the launch of paracetamol and ibuprofen in the 1950s and 1960s. Its popularity was then revived in the 1980s after its effectiveness as an anti-clotting agent in preventing heart attacks and strokes had been established – something which was not foreseen by its original discoverers. Other possible uses in cancer treatment, for example, are now also being studied. Similarly, there may be unforeseen applications of a particular invention, such as the use of computer technology to create digital photography, or complementary inventions may create unforeseen synergies, as for example with the combined use of laser and computer technology to guide or track missiles and other weapons. Alternatively, a technology with significant potential may be held back by unforeseen problems or lack of public or consumer acceptance. This has been the case with the genetic modification of plants and animals, especially in Europe (see Practical Insight 10.3). Even when a new technology becomes commercially established, it is difficult to know how soon it will be replaced by a superior technology.[12]

Practical insight 10.3: GM crops

Genetic modification techniques have been applied to the development of synthetic insulin, human growth hormone, a number of vaccines and drugs, and the prevention of genetic disease, among many others. One of the more controversial applications of biotechnology has been the creation of plants which are resistant to pests and disease. This technology could reduce the need for pesticides and potentially bring increased yields, cost reduction, and security of supply to farmers and the food industry around the world. For the developed countries the potential benefits include increased productivity and profitability; for the least developed countries GM crops could help to create sustainable agriculture and ensure essential food supplies. Inevitably, the genetic modification of crops raises concerns about the potential dangers of GM crops 'contaminating' organic crops, encouraging the spread of increasingly virulent crop diseases, or causing harm to people, wildlife, and the natural environment. There are also suspicions about the motives of companies like Monsanto, which dominate the worldwide supply of GM crops. Whilst GM crops are now well established in the United States, the public is much more sceptical in Europe.[13]

Question

- In the light of these issues, how would you assess the future development potential of GM crops?

10.2.2 The process of technological change

A useful way to think about how technological change occurs is to use Joseph Schumpeter's terminology of **invention**, **innovation**, and **diffusion**.[14] Invention is the initial idea or discovery, perhaps including a prototype or trial to determine its feasibility. Innovation involves the commercial development of an invention, often by a large company rather than the original inventor; the term 'innovation' is also commonly (and confusingly) used to describe the entire process. Diffusion describes the spread of the innovation to other firms, products, or industries. Each of these stages is an essential part of the process of technological change and a number of factors may help or hinder the progress of an idea from one stage to the next. These factors include the nature of the invention, the level of potential competition, the availability of finance (risk or venture capital), the degree of legal protection available (**intellectual property rights**), the willingness of commercial enterprises to give their backing to the idea, and the role of government policy. These factors in turn will depend on the general economic climate and society's attitude towards risk taking. In reality, the process may be less linear than suggested by this three-stage approach, with different aspects of the process overlapping each other; indeed Schumpeter saw it as an evolutionary process – an essential part of the 'creative destruction' of a capitalist system, where change is driven by entrepreneurial foresight and the outcomes of good or bad commercial decisions.

It should not be assumed that all innovation is radically new. In fact, most innovation involves incremental changes to existing products, services, or processes. Whilst the first electronic cash dispensing machine might be described as a **radical**, **fundamental**, or **macro innovation**, the spread of cash machines to shopping centres, universities, and railway stations would be regarded as **incremental** or **micro innovation**. Of course, innovation is not restricted to technology; even a new type of financial product or a new marketing strategy might be described as an innovation. The development of technology is often an iterative learning process, where one innovation is followed by others over a period of time as new discoveries are made and new applications found. This is frequently the case with the discovery of new drugs or medical techniques. For example, in 1928 Alexander Fleming discovered the natural antibiotic properties of penicillin, though it was not until the 1940s, after a series of further studies and the need to treat wartime casualties, that penicillin was used to destroy disease-causing bacteria in humans, eventually leading to the development of other antibiotic drugs. A crucial element in this process is the way in which different technologies or discoveries interrelate with each other to develop the full potential of a product or process. This was the case with the discovery of DNA (see Practical Insight 10.4).

Practical insight 10.4: The discovery of DNA

Francis Crick and James Watson are generally credited with having discovered the structure of DNA in 1953. Along with Maurice Wilkins, who carried out further research in this area, they were awarded a Nobel prize for their work in 1962. Watson and Crick's discovery, however, was built on the earlier work of a number of scientists dating back to Gregor Mendel and Friedrich Miescher in the 1860s. Watson and Crick's discovery was in fact made possible by examination of X-ray images of DNA taken by Rosalind Franklin in 1951. Further discoveries were made in the ensuing years, notably the deciphering

(continued...)

of the genetic code by Marshall Nirenberg, Har Khorana, and Severo Ochoa in the 1960s and DNA cloning by Herbert Boyer and Stanley Cohen in 1973. These developments provided the foundations for the biotechnology industry and genetic engineering. The discovery of DNA has led to numerous applications in many fields.[15] One such application is DNA profiling (previously known as genetic fingerprinting), a technique which was discovered by Alec Jeffreys in 1984 but was not used in criminal investigations until the 1990s.

Question

● Why do you think there is often a time lag between a scientific discovery and its practical applications?

10.2.3 Path dependence and standardization

Processes of technological change are often 'path dependent', as are change processes in the social and natural sciences. **Path dependence** means that a sequence of events is shaped in a persistent way by a particular event in the past.[16] A classic technological example of path dependence is provided by the standard railway gauge, where the distance between the inside edges of many of the world's railway lines is 1,435 mm (4 ft 8½ in.). Although the origins of such an unusual measurement are unclear and a number of alternative gauges have been used, standard gauge began to emerge when George Stevenson was building his early public railways in England in the 1820s and has gradually become the dominant gauge since then. Having a standard gauge is clearly useful for manufacturers of rolling stock and to facilitate connections between railways in different regions and countries. Whilst there may be a number of advantages in having larger or smaller gauges, the cost and disruption caused by the changeover to a different gauge would be enormous.

Path dependence is not always as long term as the railway example. In some cases, new technology creates an opportunity for a new standard to be set. This is illustrated by the development of the standard video format in the 1980s (when VHS won the format war over the rival Betamax system) and the success of Sony's Blu-ray format over Toshiba's HD-DVD player in 2008 (see the opening scenario to this chapter). Even over a relatively short period, the advantages of having a single technical standard generally outweigh the benefits of having a choice between alternative systems. It should not be assumed, however, that path dependence necessarily precludes the option of an alternative system or prevents switching between systems. An example of the former is the persistence of Apple Macintosh computers in a market dominated by PCs and Microsoft Windows (mainly because of Apple computers' specialized uses); examples of the latter are converters that allow switching between 115 V and 220 V electricity supplies or between UK and continental European electric plugs.

The advantages of **standardization** are reinforced by the concept of '**lock-in**'. Once a particular standard becomes established, consumers and suppliers of complementary products, such as films in Blu-ray format, become locked into this format. Not only are the costs of changing to an alternative format high for producers, they are also high for consumers. How many of us have collections of old 33 rpm (or even 78 rpm) vinyl records, cassette tape recordings, or videos we can no longer play or afford to replace? Similar issues arise when an organization is choosing a new computer system, which is now typically a networked system used throughout the organization. Regardless of whether the system turns out to be the most effective, the initial decision creates lock-in effects which favour continued use of the system even when the technology is becoming outdated – unless relatively low-cost upgrades are available. Markets for technological products and services are often characterized by high fixed (sunk) costs in the form of set-up and switching costs, which help to reinforce the advantages of standardization, whereas the variable costs of producing multiple copies of films or software in a standard format are low.

The benefits of standardization also increase where networks are involved. Examples of technological networks include the internet and worldwide web, intranets within organizations, fixed telephone systems, and mobile phone networks. **Network effects** may also arise where compatibility or interoperability between hardware and software or between system and application software is required. This is the case with Microsoft's dominant Windows operating system, which is discussed in the context of competition theory in the case study in Chapter 9. Microsoft achieved dominance over its main rival, Apple, in the early 1980s after its deal to supply IBM, the dominant hardware producer at the time, with its DOS operating system. Although more difficult to use than Apple's system at that time, the Microsoft system gradually became established as the industry standard. This standard became a platform for Microsoft's and its competitors' software, a position which it has largely maintained to this day, though the development of smartphones and hand-held computer devices is now chipping away at this dominance. This example illustrates path dependence from the time Microsoft made its deal with IBM, the lock-in of consumers and competitors because of the need for compatibility, and the self-reinforcing network effects which are a particular benefit to users of Windows-compatible programs and files.[17] Further discussion of network effects can be found in Section 10.3.3. Another example of path dependence and lock-in which has stood the test of time is the well-known QWERTY keyboard (see Practical Insight 10.5).

Practical insight 10.5:   The QWERTY keyboard

The standard typewriter keyboard has an apparently peculiar arrangement of letters, often known by the first six letters of the top line of letters, 'QWERTY'. The first commercially successful typewriters to have this arrangement were produced by the Remington Company in the 1870s. Little did they know that the arrangement would become the standard for millions of computers around the English-speaking world, as well as the system taught on typing and computer courses, explained in typewriting manuals, and used in a variety of computer programs. Although thought to have been designed this way to achieve maximum typing speed, the arrangement has been criticized as inferior to alternative layouts such as the Dvorak keyboard, and alternative layouts have recently been designed for hand-held devices where thumb-typing is used. Whatever its relative merits, the QWERTY keyboard represents a prime example of path dependence and lock-in. Given that keyboards are now normally independent components which can easily be replaced, manufacturers could presumably devise alternative layouts at relatively low cost. From the user's perspective, however, lock-in may be a more difficult problem to overcome.[18]

Question

● How difficult do you think it would be to introduce an alternative, more efficient keyboard layout?

10.2.4 Open-source technologies

Technologies that are developed through a process of public cooperation are known as 'open-source technologies'. The open-source phenomenon is becoming an important alternative way of doing business. Perhaps the best-known examples are in the form of open-source software, such as the Linux operating system, Mozilla Firefox web browser (the re-birth of Netscape), Apache, which powers many web servers, and Sendmail, which handles a large proportion of e-mail traffic. The open-source approach can also be found in the area of product development, as for example CollabNet's coordination of collaborative software and cloud computing projects or, on a smaller scale, BMW's invitation to its customers to co-design the 'telematic' features of its cars (safety, phone, tracking devices, and other electronic equipment connected to computerized networks). In principle, open-source technologies are examples of collective action that can be found in a variety of fields, ranging from open-source online encyclopaedias (such as Wikipedia) to community social projects. In each case, members of the public contribute their time and expertise voluntarily to the development of the open-source project, improving and refining it over a period of time. The open-source nature of the project may then be protected by copyright restrictions to ensure it remains freely available. Some projects may be more coordinated, others may operate on a freer basis, but the outcome is always the result of collective effort.

Open-source products and projects are public goods; that is, there is non-rivalry and non-exclusion. The use of open-source software or a community facility by one individual does not decrease the benefit to other users (non-rivalry) and, once it is available, everyone can benefit (non-exclusion). Like other public goods, open-source projects may suffer from the free-rider problem, where some potential contributors shirk and still enjoy the benefits, but they may also achieve significant positive externalities – benefits to all users, not just to those who contribute towards the project's development. Whilst the public benefits are often con-siderable, it is not always clear why an individual contributor is motivated to do so. However, if the collective benefits to all contributors exceed the private costs of their individual contri-butions, this may provide sufficient incentive. Other incentives may include the desire to im-prove on existing (closed-source) products or the satisfaction of helping to create something that brings benefits to society.[19]

10.2.5 The evolution of technology markets

It is by no means certain whether new product development in technology markets is de-mand driven or supply driven. Is the consumer urging electronics manufacturers to produce high-definition DVD players because of the poor quality of existing DVD players, or are research and development (R&D) departments always trying to push forward the technologi-cal boundaries? Research by Paul Geroski suggests that new products are driven by supply-side technological developments.[20] In the early stages of the development of a new market, there is often competition to create an industry standard. Over a period of time a dominant standard emerges and competition gradually brings improvements to the industry standard. As a product approaches maturity, process improvements often become more important than product improvements and dominant firms concentrate on trying to reduce their costs. Product innovation then comes mainly from newer firms or firms outside the mainstream.

This pattern has been evident in the development of MP3 players, smartphones, and tablet computers, as companies like Apple, Blackberry, Samsung, and Asus challenge Microsoft's dominance.

On the other hand, Danny Quah argues that, unless there is sufficient demand for a new product or new technology, it is unlikely to take off.[21] China, he argues, has been at the fore-front of technological development throughout much of its history and was the world's most advanced industrial economy in the Middle Ages. However, according to Quah, for the next three or four hundred years, until recently, China fell behind Europe and America, largely because its feudal system did not provide the right demand conditions for the market to take off. Demand drivers may be at work at various stages of the development process. The internet, for example, was initially developed to meet the specialized needs of academics and the military, but as the technology improved it was gradually made available to businesses and the general public. However, it is unlikely that the internet would have continued to develop as it has if the public had not been keen to use the new technology.

10.2.6 Incentives and technological change

The system of incentives in a country is likely to have an impact on its technological development. In general terms, incentives are created by a country's institutional structure, including both formal and informal institutions. Perhaps the most important formal institutions in this context are the rules relating to intellectual property rights. Without the protection provided by patents, copyrights, licences, and trademarks, the incentive to innovate is considerably weakened, as the returns needed to justify the investment will quickly be lost to competitors. On the other hand, an overly protective patent could give the patent holder monopoly rights for an extended period of time and slow down potential diffusion. A balance therefore needs to be found between these two extremes. The commercialization of intellectual property (IP) developed by universities, research institutes, and new graduates is also becoming an important issue, leading to the development of science parks and business incubation units. In addition, informal institutions may be influential in encouraging innovation, particularly attitudes towards entrepreneurship and the taking of risks, and the possibility of significant rewards.

Governments and organizations such as the EU may also play a role in providing incentives. Governments can intervene by providing tax and other financial incentives when private financial institutions are reluctant to support new ventures. Short-term government intervention may help to provide seed capital or a protective environment for a new venture, but success in the longer term will depend on the market for the product. Competition provides an important element of the incentive structure, creating the rewards for success. Indeed, the level of technological sophistication, in relation to both products and organizational processes, has a key impact on an organization's competitiveness both at home and abroad. Research suggests a significant correlation between the level of technology (measured by R&D and patents) and international competitiveness as indicated by the trade performance of a variety of industrial sectors.[22] It should be noted, however, that countries with remarkably different government policies, competitive environments, and institutional structures, such as the USA and Japan, have been able to achieve significant technological development in recent years.

10.3 Technology and economic performance

10.3.1 Technology, productivity, and economic growth

There are basically two ways in which an economy can achieve economic growth: either by increasing the quantity of inputs such as labour, capital, and raw materials, or by increasing the productivity of its inputs. Thus, for example, China's manufacturing industries along its prosperous eastern seaboard have attracted labour from its northern and western regions to help maintain their rapidly expanding output. However, whilst an increase in the quantity of labour may be necessary in the early stages of new economic development, such a policy is unsustainable in the long term as even China's massive human resources are insufficient to sustain the country's recent rate of growth. In the longer term, continued economic growth requires higher productivity: output increasing at a faster rate than inputs. Indeed, increased labour and other inputs account for only part of China's recent economic growth. A growth rate of around 10 per cent per annum since the early 1990s would not have been possible without considerable productivity growth. Whether China will be able to sustain this growth rate in the future is a matter of debate; this issue is considered in Practical Insight 10.6.

Productivity is achieved through improvements in the capacity or quality of inputs, for example as a result of improvements in education and training or advances in technology. Whilst improvements in human capital are clearly of vital importance, technology has played a pivotal role in productivity improvements in many sectors since the industrial revolution. The term productivity is most commonly used to describe *labour productivity*, measured by output per worker or per hour worked; note the important difference between these two measures, as an increase in the number of hours worked will raise the former but may even reduce the latter. In studies at the national level, *total factor (or multifactor) productivity* is often used, though because of the difficulty in measuring the productivity of other inputs such as capital, it is sometimes measured as the residual – the amount by which an increase in output exceeds an increase in inputs. Using this method of measurement, however, total factor productivity may not be fully evident during the early stages of technological innovation, such as in the US economy when the ICT revolution was accelerating in the early 1990s, or when an economy is slowing down, as in the US in the early 2000s, despite the continuing pace of technological change.

Nevertheless, productivity improvements provide a significant element of the explanation for the long-run superior economic performance of the world's most successful economies, whether large or small.[23] However, it is important to distinguish between the many incremental innovations that help to increase productivity and economic growth on a regular basis and the more fundamental innovation which occurs at particular points in time. Innovations such as the steam engine, electricity, or the computer are sometimes described as **general-purpose technology** – technology which has a number of applications which are discovered over a period of time. Countries that have developed an innovative environment are able to generate continual improvements in productivity through a series of incremental innovations, whereas fundamental innovation in the form of a new general-purpose technology may initially cause a decline in productivity as resources are transferred from old technologies to new ones and old industries start to decline before the new industries have become established. This appears to have been the case with US labour productivity after the introduction of computer technology in the 1970s, but productivity then began to increase as the new general-purpose technology and its applications came into general use (see Figure 10.3).[24]

Practical insight 10.6: When will China overtake the United States?

Table 10.2 indicates that the US economy was roughly a third bigger than the Chinese economy in 2011, valued on a purchasing power parity (PPP) basis (see Section 4.4.1). It was in fact just over twice as big on an official exchange rate basis, though, given that the Chinese renminbi was almost certainly undervalued, PPP probably provides a more reliable indicator. However, the Chinese economy grew over four times as quickly as the US economy between 1990 and 2012, so at this rate China is clearly catching up with the United States. Using the following formula, it can be calculated that it will take China approximately four years from 2012 (i.e. until 2016) to become the world's largest economy on a PPP basis.

$$GDP_n = GDP_0(1+g)^n \qquad (10.1)$$

where GDP_n is GDP in n years, GDP_0 is GDP now, and g is the percentage growth rate expressed as a decimal.

Of course, this calculation assumes that both the Chinese and US economies will continue to grow at a constant average annual rate. In practice, this will depend on a number of factors. As the Chinese economy is coming from behind, it has been able to acquire technology from more developed countries, so most of its productivity improvements have resulted from technology transfer rather than home-grown innovation. This will become more difficult as China develops, so for this and other reasons its growth rate will almost certainly slow down.

Table 10.2: The Chinese and US economies

	GDP ($US billion) PPP basis 2012	GDP per Capita ($US), PPP basis 2012	Average Annual GDP Growth Rate 1990–2012 (%)
China	12,406	9,162	10.3
USA	15,685	49.922	2.4

Source: IMF, *World Economic Outlook Database*, April 2013.

Questions

- What factors are likely to determine how long it will take for the Chinese economy to become the world's largest economy?
- Why will it take much longer for China's GDP per capita to catch up with the United States?

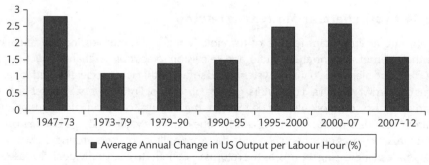

Figure 10.3 US productivity growth in the non-farm business sector, 1947–2012

Source: US Bureau of Labor Statistics.

10.3.2 The role of technology in theories of economic growth

A number of attempts have been made to explain why long-run economic growth occurs and why some economies grow faster than others. However, in recent years two explanations have dominated the debate. The first body of theory is known as **neoclassical growth theory** and is built on the work of Robert Solow.[25] Solow argued that about 80 per cent of US economic growth during the first half of the twentieth century could be explained by 'technical progress', with 20 per cent resulting from increases or improvements in labour and capital. Technical progress should be interpreted loosely to include changes in work practices and business organization, among other things, as well as technological innovation. However, neoclassical growth theory regards technological progress as an *exogenous* factor, something which is not specifically explained in the theory but which is a crucial determinant of economic growth. As the capital stock of a country depreciates, new investment is needed to ensure continued economic growth. The level of investment required to maintain constant economic growth depends on population growth and improvements in labour productivity as well as the rate of capital depreciation.

From the 1980s onwards, Paul Romer,[26] Robert Lucas,[27] and others developed what has become known as 'new growth theory' or '**endogenous growth theory**' as a way of explaining how economic growth occurs. In their model, technological progress is determined *endogenously* (within the model) as the outcome of a number of processes at work in an economy, in particular the level of technological knowledge and quality of human capital. Within this approach, the focus of attention turns to the way in which government policy, education, competition, intellectual property rights, and other factors create incentives to generate technological innovation. An important implication of endogenous growth theory is that, unlike neoclassical theory where capital depreciation leads to decreasing returns from capital investment, the conditions leading to endogenous growth may create **increasing returns** as various factors interact with each other to create a climate of continual innovation. The creation of knowledge is a prime example of increasing returns, as even R&D by private firms creates spin-off benefits for other firms and the economy as a whole. Clearly, technological progress plays an important role in both theories, but the concept of increasing returns presents a new way of thinking about how economies grow – an idea which is used extensively in complexity theory (see Sections 1.1 and 9.3.5).

10.3.3 Network effects and increasing returns

Networks are an important feature of technology markets; examples include telephones, faxes, the internet and intranets, radio and television, electronic exchanges such as eBay, credit cards and electronic banking systems, and software that is interoperable with operating systems on hardware such as computers, games consoles, or DVD players. Business and social networks are also common. Network effects are the benefits to individual users that arise as the number of users increases. Having a telephone is of little value if no one else has one, but its usefulness increases exponentially when there are millions of users around the world. This is an example of increasing returns, as the returns or benefits to each individual increase as the size of the network increases. Network effects are sometimes described as '**network externalities**' because prices charged for the use of a network do not necessarily fully internalize the benefits to all users, as the addition of a new user creates positive externalities for other users; the benefits to the owner of the network may, however, be fully internalized.

It should be noted that networks may grow rapidly as they approach a critical mass of users, but the more profitable connections are likely to be made first, leaving network growth to slow down as the remaining connections become less profitable. Whilst increasing returns may continue, their rate of increase is likely to slow down and returns may even start to decrease if the network's size leads to inefficiencies or other negative effects for users. In general, however, networks are likely to generate positive **feedback effects**, where the actions of individual users or interactions between users create benefits for the network as a whole, helping to produce increasing returns. Network effects, which are particularly important in technology markets, are therefore likely to reinforce the impact of technology in generating endogenous growth.

10.4 The knowledge economy

10.4.1 A new economy?

The ten-year upturn in the US economy which occurred throughout the 1990s was unprecedented both in its duration and in the fact that economic growth accelerated during the second half of the decade when one would normally have expected a downturn in the cycle. The most common explanation for this phenomenon was that the internet, the use of which grew more rapidly in the USA than elsewhere, had facilitated a huge expansion in the ICT sector, which in turn had led to accelerating improvements in productivity and economic growth. This view was reinforced by the fact that inflation had remained low despite low unemployment, presumably because of falling costs and competition, and by the boom in the number of dedicated 'dot.com' companies and their stock market valuations. The term 'new economy' has been used to describe these ICT companies, not only the dot.coms (a number of which went out of business when their share prices collapsed in 2001), but also companies in the computer, telecommunications, and other branches of the ICT sector. The new economy seemed to represent the new technology and its superior ability to increase productivity and add value, as opposed to the 'old' economy of traditional manufacturing, whose contribution to economic growth was declining.[28]

With hindsight, this characterization of the new economy seems out of place, not only because of the bursting of the dot.com bubble, but because ICT has increasingly spread to most parts of the developed economies and increasingly to the developing economies, including many of the 'traditional' industries. Perhaps a more useful term to describe the 'new' economy that has grown out of the ICT revolution is the term 'knowledge economy'. 'Knowledge' industries encompass not only computing and telecommunications but also the many manufacturing and services industries which use technological and other advanced forms of knowledge. Of course, knowledge industries have been in existence for centuries, but knowledge as a resource, embodied in educated and skilled workers and technology and other knowledge products, has become increasingly important in most modern developed and emerging economies. It has been estimated that knowledge industries, defined as high- and medium-tech manufacturing, high-tech services, financial services, business and communication services, health, education, and cultural industries, accounted for 41.4 per cent of total employment in the 15 established member states of the EU (EU-15) in 2005.[29]

10.4.2 **Knowledge as a quasi-public good**

If knowledge is fundamental to the process of technological change and the development of a modern economy, it is worth considering how it differs from more conventional resources. Most goods that are exchanged in a market economy are private goods. Private goods are normally both *rival* and *excludable*; that is, consumption of a good by one individual precludes consumption by others (rivalry) and particular consumers may be prevented from consuming the good if desired (excludability). This applies to resources such as labour, capital, raw materials, and manufactured components. Public goods, such as defence or law and order, are *non-rival* and *non-excludable*. Knowledge has many of the characteristics of a public good in that it is always non-rival and partially non-excludable. It may therefore be described as a '**quasi-public good**'. Although new knowledge is often generated by private individuals or businesses and competitors or customers can be denied access to it by intellectual property protection or password restrictions, once knowledge comes into the public domain it is non-rival; no matter how many people 'consume' it, each consumer has access to the same knowledge.[30]

Although the value of knowledge may depreciate if it is not kept up to date, new knowledge can immediately be shared with any number of users without necessarily diminishing its usefulness. The production and consumption of knowledge may therefore give rise to significant increasing returns to society as a whole. International spillover effects will also spread the benefits to other countries keen and able to take advantage of it. Where knowledge is developed through open-source technologies such as the Linux operating system or the Wikipedia online encyclopaedia, it is intentionally non-excludable and is therefore a pure public good. However, even when knowledge is partially excludable, its non-rivalry characteristic makes it significantly different from conventional resources. For this reason, the knowledge economy may have greater potential to create dynamic endogenous growth than an economy based on more conventional resources.

10.4.3 **Technological innovation and creativity**

The story of technological innovation involves the generation of new ideas, designs, inventions, and discoveries which combine human effort, accumulated knowledge, and other resources over a period of time. This is a creative process. Creativity is of course not restricted to technological developments. It can be found in the arts, sciences, and a wide range of business and social activity. A marketer who finds an imaginative way to promote a new product or a banker who develops an innovative financial product may be acting creatively. What is important is that, whilst the use of existing techniques or technologies in familiar ways may be routine, the continual adaptation or novel application of ideas and technologies is a creative activity.

Some researchers have argued that creativity, in its wider sense, is an important driver of local, regional, or even national economic development. Richard Florida has published extensively on this theme, arguing that the 'creative class', including creative professionals in a variety of fields, helps to stimulate the economic development of towns and cities and contributes to the economic success of nations.[31] Florida uses an index of creativity to indicate a region's creative and economic potential. The creativity index includes the 'creative class' share

Practical insight 10.7: A creative quarter for Middlesbrough

The author's university town of Middlesbrough in north-east England has introduced a number of regeneration initiatives to overturn its legacy of urban decay following the decline of traditional heavy industries like shipbuilding. One of the more ambitious initiatives is the DigitalCity project.[32] This project is jointly sponsored by Teesside University, Middlesbrough Borough Council, and a number of local business organizations. The DigitalCity project builds on the existing expertise of Teesside University in media technology and digital animation, and aims to combine this expertise with new and growing businesses by providing business units with close access to academic researchers. It will also serve as a vehicle for the commercialization of academic projects.

Although it was initially focused on the digital media, the intention is to promote creativity rather than purely technical expertise. Whilst initial developments involved the provision of specialist facilities on the university campus, the second phase of the project has involved the establishment of a creative district in a previously run-down area of the town. This district has been named the 'Boho Zone', aiming to combine Middlesbrough's (and its football team's) nickname, 'Boro', with the creative feel of London's famous Soho district. The Boho Zone incorporates buildings providing business units for specialists in digital media, digital technology, and other creative professions, and live-work studios for digital entrepreneurs alongside refurbished historic buildings, with the intention of establishing a supportive environment for creative activity of various kinds.

Question

● To what extent do you think a creative community of this kind is viable and on what factors is its success in regenerating economic activity likely to depend?

of the workforce, the proportion of high-tech industry, the number of patents per capita, and, more controversially, the proportion of gay people (the 'gay index') as a proxy for the degree of tolerance and openness. Whilst Florida's methodology and results have been criticized, the importance of creativity in technological innovation and economic development is nevertheless increasingly being recognized. Practical Insight 10.7 provides an example of an industrial town trying to recreate its creative history.

Summary

The development of technology through a series of 'revolutions', starting with the first industrial revolution in the late eighteenth and early nineteenth centuries, has had a significant effect on economic development, especially in the western world. Technology helps to break down spatial barriers and change work practices and its impact on employment is probably more beneficial than is generally believed. Technology also has a significant impact on the working environment as a whole. The process of technological change is surrounded by uncertainties and is often the product of a number of incremental innovations over a period of time. Industry standards are important in technology markets, allowing compatibility between related products. Standards often come about as a result of path dependence. Open-source technologies are becoming more widespread and technology often develops through a variety of demand- and supply-led processes. Technological developments are generally regarded as important in achieving improvements in productivity and economic growth. These benefits arise partly because of the increasing returns that stem from network effects. Technology is essentially the application of knowledge and knowledge is becoming an increasingly important resource as a quasi-public good in the modern world.

Discussion questions

1. What factors might need to be present to allow a technological adopter country to become a technological innovator?

2. What factors are likely to influence the progress of an invention from conception to full commercial development?

3. How important is path dependence in the technological development process?

4. To what extent is a high level of demand necessary to facilitate the development of technology markets?

5. What is the link between technology, productivity, and economic growth?

6. What is the significance of non-rivalry for the spread of knowledge?

Suggested assignment topics

1. Select a specific country which can be described as either a technological adopter or technologically excluded. Identify the changes that would need to occur for the country to become either a technological innovator or a technological adopter respectively.

2. Choose a specific example of a general-purpose technology (or fundamental innovation) and identify the main influences on its development.

3. With reference to a specific industry, investigate the extent to which knowledge has become relatively more important than conventional resources in recent years.

 Case study: The changing use of the internet

By the end of the 1990s, Microsoft had overtaken Netscape's early lead in the web browser market, using the dominant position of its Windows operating system as a platform to launch its Internet Explorer web browser software. By early September 2008, when Google launched its free Chrome web browser, Internet Explorer had an estimated market share of 58.8 per cent, but by early 2013 Chrome had become the market leader with 29.3 per cent of the web browser market. By this time, Internet Explorer's share had fallen to 26.6 per cent, followed by Mozilla Firefox (Netscape's open-source successor) holding steady at 19.7 per cent, Apple Safari (which can also be used on a Windows operating system) rising to 15.4 per cent in fourth place, and Opera in fifth place with 2.4 per cent.[33]

During this period, internet usage increased dramatically and the worldwide web was increasingly being used as an interactive medium rather than simply to make information available. Examples of

(continued...)

this trend include the use of blogs and podcasts, the development of social networking websites such as Facebook, LinkedIn, or Twitter, and video-sharing websites such as YouTube – developments which have collectively been described as Web 2.0. The popularity of this type of website has encouraged a number of businesses to consider ways of using them as a tool for marketing their products or for making links and sharing ideas with other businesses. Web 2.0 technologies are potentially useful for small businesses, enabling them to develop support networks with similar or complementary businesses.

Alongside these developments, the internet is increasingly being used to create web platforms, where applications such as word processing and databases can be accessed via a web browser rather than as desktop software. Web platforms provide greater integration between web-based and conventional desktop operations and allow documents to be stored on remote servers, enabling users to access files from anywhere via a web browser. This means there is no need to have particular software on each computer or wireless device with internet access. These developments are also known as 'cloud computing'. Of course, most of us already use 'cloud' services for emails, internet search, online multi-user games, blogging, or social networking, but cloud computing now offers the prospect of fully integrated web services for a wide range of business and personal uses.

A growing number of private and open-source web service providers now offer cloud computing services, including Microsoft, Google, and Amazon. Whether Microsoft will be able to establish a dominant position if web platforms gradually take over from desktop software is an open question. Computers will still need an operating system, but the choice of operating system may be less important if users transfer to web-based applications. A new struggle to achieve the dominant standard may emerge among web platform providers, though Microsoft may still hold on to its committed MS Office users for some time to come.

The full benefits of web-based applications may not emerge for some time. There will also be security issues if everything is carried out online and the need to speed up internet connections will become a pressing issue. These developments will also contribute towards widening the gap between technology users and the technologically excluded, both within and between societies. This probably increases the need for the least developed countries to be technologically connected. Whatever happens, however, business use of the web for networking and other computer-based activities is likely to increase substantially in the coming years. What is less certain is the impact these developments will have on the conduct of business, improvements in productivity, and economic growth.[34]

Case study questions

1. What potential benefits might social networking websites offer to small businesses?

2. Do you consider web platforms to be a fundamental or incremental innovation? Explain your answer.

3. Given that the full potential of web platforms is not likely to be achieved for some time, what does this tell us about the process of innovation?

4. There is considerable uncertainty about the way cloud computing will develop. What are the main reasons for this uncertainty?

5. How is cloud computing likely to affect work practices and productivity?

6. What benefits might arise for the web platform provider who achieves a dominant standard?

7. Are there any incumbent advantages for Microsoft when developing web-based applications, given the widespread familiarity with its Office software?

8. What are the implications of the increasing use of web-based applications for our access to knowledge?

Notes

1. Main sources: *Financial Times* (5 January 2008), 'Breakthrough for Blu-ray as Warner gives full support'; *Financial Times* (19 February 2008), 'Betamax memories erased as Blu-ray triumphs'; *Financial Times* (19 February 2008), 'Sony wins next-generation DVD battle'; and Coughlin, T. (18 July 2011), 'What is the future of optical disc technology and who will use it?' http://www.forbes.com.

2. The *Concise Oxford Dictionary* defines 'technology' as 'the application of scientific knowledge for practical purposes'.

3. For a more detailed discussion, see Maddison, A. (2007), *Contours of the World Economy, 1–2030 AD*, Oxford University Press.

4. See, for example, Lipsey, R. G., Carlaw, K. I., and Bekar, C. T. (2005), *Economic Transformations: General Purpose Technologies and Long Term Economic Growth*, Oxford University Press, p. 258: 'The Industrial Revolution was not a sudden event that came more or less from out of the blue. Instead, it was the contingent culmination of evolutionary paths that had been in place for centuries.'

5. Mokyr, J. (2004), *The Gifts of Athena: Historical Origins of the Knowledge Economy*, Princeton University Press, ch. 3, pp. 78–118.

6. Mokyr, J. (2002), *The Gifts of Athena: Historical Origins of the Knowledge Economy*, Princeton University Press, p. 4.

7. Cairncross, F. (2001), *The Death of Distance 2.0: How the Communications Revolution is Changing Our Lives*, Harvard Business School Press, ch. 2.

8. Friedman, T. L. (2007), *The World is Flat: A Brief History of the Globalized World in the 21st Century*, Penguin Allen Lane.

9. For a detailed discussion of the employment effects of ICT, see, for example, Freeman, R. B. (2002), 'The Labour Market in the New Information Economy', *Oxford Review of Economic Policy*, vol. 18, no. 3, pp. 288–305.

10. Sachs, J. (2000), 'A new map of the world', *The Economist*, 24 June.

11. For a comprehensive history of the Concorde project, see http://www.concordesst.com.

12. For a discussion of technological uncertainties, see Lipsey, R. G., Carlaw, K. I., and Bekar, C. T. (2005), *Economic Transformations: General Purpose Technologies and Long Term Economic Growth*, Oxford University Press, pp. 86–7.

13. For a discussion of the pros and cons of GM crops, see, for example, UK Cabinet Office (July 2003), 'Fieldwork: Weighing up the Costs and Benefits of GM Crops'.

14. Schumpeter, J. A. (2010), *Capitalism, Socialism and Democracy*, Routledge, first published in 1942.

15. A fuller discussion of the discovery of DNA and its applications can be found in BBC News, Special Report: DNA at 50 (7 January 2008), http://news.bbc.co.uk.

16. A fuller discussion of path dependence can be found in David, P. A. (2007), 'Path dependence – A foundational concept for historical social science', *Cliometrica, The Journal of Historical Economics and Econometric History*, vol. 1, no. 2, pp. 91–114.

17. Further implications of network effects in the context of technical standardization can be found in: Gandal, N. (2002), 'Compatibility, standardization, and network effects: some policy implications', *Oxford Review of Economic Policy*, vol. 18, no. 1, pp. 80–91.

18. A discussion of path dependence and the lock-in effect in relation to the QWERTY keyboard can be found in David, P. A. (1985), 'Clio and the economics of QWERTY', *American Economic Review*, vol. 75, no. 2.

19. See Myatt, D. P., and Wallace, C. (2002), 'Equilibrium selection and public-good provision: the development of open-source software', *Oxford Review of Economic Policy*, vol. 18, no. 4, pp. 446–61.

20. Geroski, P. (2003), *The Evolution of New Markets*, Oxford University Press.

21. Quah, D. (1999), 'The Weightless Economy in Economic Development', Centre for Economic Performance Discussion paper, no. 417.

22. Fagerberg, J. (1996), 'Technology and competitiveness', *Oxford Review of Economic Policy*, vol. 12, no. 3, pp. 39–51.

23. For a detailed practical discussion of the implications of increased productivity, see Lewis, W. W. (2004), *The Power of Productivity*, University of Chicago Press.

24. See Helpman, E. (2010), *General Purpose Technologies and Economic Growth*, MIT Press.

25. Solow, R. (1956), 'A contribution to the theory of economic growth', *Quarterly Journal of Economics*, vol. 70, pp. 65–94.

26. Romer, P. (1986), 'Increasing returns and long-run growth', Journal of Political Economy, vol. 94, pp. 1002–37 and Romer, P. (1990), 'Endogenous technological change', Journal of Political Economy, vol. 98, pp. S71–S102.

27. Lucas, R. E., Jr (1988), 'On the mechanics of economic development', Journal of Monetary Economics, vol. 22, pp. 3–42.

28. For a discussion of the 'new economy', see Temple, J. (2002), 'The assessment: the new economy', *Oxford Review of Economic Policy*, vol. 18, no. 3, pp. 241–64.

29. Brinkley, I., and Lee, N. (2007), 'The Knowledge Economy in Europe: A Report Prepared for the 2007 EU Spring Council', *The Work Foundation*, table 1, p. 7.

30. For a discussion of knowledge as a quasi-public good, see Romer, P. (1990), 'Endogenous technological change', *Journal of Political Economy*, vol. 98, pp. S71–S102.

31. Florida, R. (2012), *The Rise of the Creative Class Revisited*, Basic Books.

32. DigitalCity website (http://www.dcbusiness.eu/).

33. Source: Web Browser Market Share Trends, http://www.w3counter.com/trends.

34. Main sources: *Financial Times* (1 September 2008), 'Google launches internet browser'; *Financial Times* (27 January 2009), 'Business starts to take Web 2.0 seriously'; the *Guardian* (5 March 2013), 'Embrace the cloud computing revolution – with caution'; and BBC News (13 March 2013), 'Cloud computing's security pitfalls'.

Suggestions for further reading

Practical treatment of the impact of technology

Friedman, T. L. (2007), *The World is Flat: The Globalized World in the 21st Century*, Penguin

Schmidt, E., and Cohen, J. (2013), *The New Digital Age: Reshaping the Future of People, Nature and Business*, John Murray

More theoretical approaches to the process of technological development and the knowledge economy

Foray, D. (2006), *The Economics of Knowledge*, MIT Press

Lipsey, R. G., Carlaw, K. I., and Bekar, C. T. (2005), *Economic Transformations: General Purpose Technologies and Long Term Economic Growth*, Oxford University Press

Mokyr, J. (2004), *The Gifts of Athena: Historical Origins of the Knowledge Economy*, Princeton University Press

The role of productivity in a modern economy

Lewis, W. W. (2004), *The Power of Productivity*, University of Chicago Press

On Cloud Computing

Rhoton, J. (2010), *Cloud Computing Explained: Implementation Handbook for Enterprises*, Recursive Press

Take your learning further: Online Resource Centre
http://www.oxfordtextbooks.co.uk/orc/harrison2e/
Visit the Online Resource Centre that accompanies this book to enrich your understanding of Chapter 10: Technological Change. Among other resources explore web links and keep up to date with the latest developments in the area.

Key terms introduced in this chapter

Diffusion The spread of an innovation to other firms, products, or industries.

Endogenous growth theory An explanation of long-run economic growth where technological progress is determined by the outcome of internal processes at work in an economy, in particular the level of technological knowledge and quality of human capital.

Feedback effects In the context of networks, positive feedback effects are the benefits to the users of a network arising from the actions of individual users or interactions between users.

Fundamental innovation The development of a significant new discovery, product, or service.

General-purpose technology A technology which represents a fundamental innovation with a wide range of applications.

Increasing returns The outcome of an economic process whereby a set of inputs combine to produce a greater increase in output.

Incremental innovation The gradual development of an existing idea or product.

Innovation The commercial development of an invention or, more generally, the entire process of technological change.

Intellectual property right A legal right to the ownership of an invention, idea, name, or published work, protected by a patent, licence, trade mark, or copyright.

Invention An initial idea or discovery, sometimes including a prototype or trial to determine its feasibility.

Knowledge economy Economic activity involving industries or services in which technological and other advanced forms of knowledge are an important resource.

Lock-in The phenomenon whereby consumers and producers become dependent on an established industry standard.

Macro innovation See fundamental innovation.

Micro innovation See incremental innovation.

Neoclassical growth theory An explanation of long-run economic growth where technological progress depends on the rate of capital investment, which is determined exogenously (outside the model).

Network effect A benefit to an individual user of a network that arises as the number of users increases.

Network externality A network effect where the price charged for the use of a network does not fully internalize the benefits to all users.

Open-source technology A technology that is developed through a process of public cooperation.

Path dependence A sequence of events shaped in a persistent way by a particular event in the past.

Quasi-public good A 'good' such as knowledge which has the characteristic of non-rivalry but which is not necessarily non-excludable.

Radical innovation See fundamental innovation.

Standardization The setting of an industry standard which acts as a platform for the development of complementary products.

Technological adopter A country where high-tech exports account for at least 2 per cent of GDP.

Technological innovator A country with ten or more patents per million inhabitants.

Technologically excluded A country where high-tech exports account for less than 2 per cent of GDP.

11

Risk in the International Environment

 Chapter learning outcomes

On completion of this chapter the reader should be able to:

- Appreciate the meaning and significance of the concept of risk
- Appreciate the complexities of the concept of risk and its implications for the international business environment
- Identify and evaluate major risks emanating from the business environment at the global level
- Evaluate the nature of country risk in relation to political risk factors and the concept of international competitiveness at the national level
- Apply ideas on risk assessment and risk management to the analysis and evaluation of external risk facing business organizations

Opening scenario: The eurozone crisis

After a period of uncertainty following its launch in January 1999, the euro enjoyed a reasonable degree of stability throughout the rest of its first decade. This stability was shattered when the Greek prime minister, Georgios Papandreou, revealed a 'black hole' in his government's finances in October 2009. This was followed by a series of financial bailouts for Greece, Ireland, Portugal, Spain, Italy and Cyprus between early 2010 and early 2013.[1] In the case of Greece, Portugal, and Italy, the sovereign-debt crisis was largely the result of excessive government spending over a number of years, especially in Greece where successive governments had concealed the true state of the country's public finances.

This situation was brought to a head by the international financial crisis and recession of 2008–9, the reluctance of investors to buy government bonds, and the rising cost of financing sovereign debt. In the case of Ireland and Spain, government debt resulted from the need to bail out insolvent banks during the financial crisis rather than from excessive public spending. Cyprus is a special case – a small country whose large banking sector has attracted Russian and other foreign funds as an offshore tax haven; exposure to Greek debt and falling property prices have led to insolvency among the country's major banks.[2]

Although not primarily of the eurozone's making, the crisis has been felt throughout the eurozone, as well as beyond its borders. In addition to the burden on eurozone countries that provided funds to finance the bailouts (along with the IMF and European Central Bank), rising interest rates on government bonds reflected falling bond prices in the crisis-affected countries. These bonds were held by banks in other countries, notably by France in the case of Greek bonds; this helped to spread the effects of the crisis beyond the countries worst affected. The eurozone countries have also been criticized for failing to ensure that the EU stability and growth pact (requiring limits on budget deficits and gross public debt) was strictly enforced, both when a country adopts the euro and subsequently.

Each of the sovereign-debt bailouts has been accompanied by 'austerity measures' requiring governments to reduce their budget deficits and overall debt over a period of time. However, governments implementing these measures have faced considerable political resistance, both from opposition politicians and especially from ordinary citizens. This is hardly surprising, given the deflationary effects of the austerity measures, which have had some impact on reducing budget deficits (notably in Ireland), but in most cases overall debt has continued to rise as economic growth has slowed down. Slow or negative economic growth has taken its toll in terms of rising unemployment and poverty, business failures, and cuts in public services and welfare benefits. The eurozone's large, stagnant economy has also affected economic growth in neighbouring countries, as well as in the global economy as a whole. Clearly, the eurozone crisis poses risks for public, private, and voluntary sector organizations and its future course is still uncertain. This is an example of the type of risk facing organizations in the international business environment.[3]

11.1 Global and country risk in an uncertain world

All business activities carry a degree of risk, including the risk of production loss from a labour dispute, power failure, or major incident, financial loss from falling sales or financial mismanagement, and business failure as a result of an international financial crisis or civil disturbance in a politically unstable host country. In this chapter, we focus specifically on risks associated with the external environment, though we also consider the nature of risk and the extent to which risks can be managed or avoided. Political and economic instability is a major cause of risk in the external environment, whether it affects the international environment as a whole or the environment in a particular country. In unstable times, businesses are reluctant to commit significant resources to investment programmes or foreign ventures in high-risk countries. Even in more stable environments, risks are perhaps more common than we generally imagine. These risks are sometimes predictable but more often are not. Conditions within otherwise stable countries sometimes give rise to systemic risks, such as the liberal market environment and light regulation which may have contributed towards instability in the financial systems in 2008–9.

Risks may also be completely or seemingly unexpected, such as the terrorist atrocities in New York, Washington, and Pennsylvania on 11 September 2001 ('9/11'). The question for governments, businesses, and other organizations is the extent to which greater understanding of the issues surrounding these risks, and the consequent possibility of taking pre-emptive or precautionary action, might lead to a reduction in the consequences of risk, if not necessarily the likelihood of risk occurring.

The study of the business environment in particular countries has become a major preoccupation of politicians, business leaders, and economists in recent years. In particular, attention has been focused on the way in which political, economic, social, and legal factors combine to create an environment which is 'good' for business. Whilst there is inevitably disagreement about precisely what conditions make a good business environment, the search for the ideal environment has been pursued with some vigour. The term '**international competitiveness**' is now increasingly being used to describe the business environment at national and regional levels. Along with other techniques of risk analysis, studies of the international competitiveness of countries are increasingly being used to evaluate country risk. In addition to political and economic stability, factors such as the institutional environment and the health of a nation are regarded as important in determining the risks of doing business in a particular country.

11.2 Risk in the business environment

11.2.1 The concept of risk

Risk is a part of everyday life, whether in our personal lives or in business. The extent to which we face risk depends on our exposure to an event and the degree of uncertainty surrounding the event. The degree of uncertainty in turn depends on the likelihood of the event occurring and the consequences if it does occur (see Figure 11.1). Consider, for example, the possibility of bad weather. If we go out to sea in a small boat when stormy weather is forecast, we are taking a risk: first, because we will be affected if the boat capsizes (*exposure*) and, secondly, because there is *uncertainty* about the bad weather and its consequences. If we do not take part in an activity which is affected by bad weather, we can avoid being exposed to the risk. Similarly, a bank which lends money to someone who is unlikely to be able to repay the loan is taking a greater risk than one which lends more prudently. Of course, any business venture involves some degree of risk, as the business owner is exposed to financial loss in the uncertain event that the business fails. In this chapter, however, we are thinking mainly about risks facing an organization (or, to be more precise, the people involved in the organization) from the external environment, rather than risks which arise from business decisions.

A distinction is sometimes made between **risk** and **uncertainty**, risk being something which is measurable, uncertainty something which is not.[4] **Probabilities** are often used to calculate risk. For example, we may say there is a one in six (or 16.67 per cent) probability of scoring a 'six' when rolling a die. However, this distinction is not particularly useful in determining business or external environmental risks, as very few of these risks are quantifiable. An alternative distinction is sometimes made between **objective probabilities** and **subjective probabilities**, both of which can be considered as measures of risk. Objective probabilities measure knowable 'facts' about the occurrence of events, which result either from homogeneous data (such as the probability of winning the lottery) or inherent symmetries (such as the probability of scoring a 'six' when throwing a die), though even here the way the die is thrown or environmental factors such as an uneven surface may influence the outcome to some extent. Subjective probabilities are based on observations of past events or, sometimes

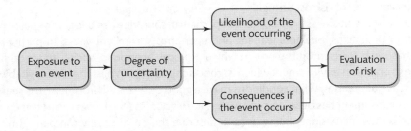

Figure 11.1 The nature of risk

more speculatively, on estimates or beliefs about future events which have little quantifiable basis. Observations about past events, such as the average daily rainfall in July in a particular place, have a quantifiable basis, but there is no guarantee that future rainfall will follow the same pattern. Indeed, external risks such as terrorism will depend on the changing dynamics of the underlying causes, so the past is not necessarily a good guide to the future.

11.2.2 Insuring against risk

The insurance industry, and actuarial science on which the industry depends, makes considerable use of the concept of probability when calculating insurable risks. Essentially, if the probability of a particular event occurring can be estimated with some degree of reliability, there is a potential basis for the risk to be insured. However, the willingness of an insurance company to provide insurance cover will also depend on the total amount of insurance premiums they can expect to receive in relation to the potential claims if the event occurs. The important concept here is the 'pooling of risk': if an insurance company receives sufficient premiums from all its policy holders to cover the claims of those who suffer loss as a result of the event occurring, it will have pooled or spread the risk. Of course, the greater the probability of the event occurring and/or the greater the potential loss if it occurs, the higher the insurance premium is likely to be. Insurance companies can also increase the 'pool' from which claims are paid out by investing the premiums in stocks and shares or other financial assets, including complex derivatives where insurance risks are transferred into bonds and other capital-market securities (a process known as 'securitization').

Where events occur with some regularity, such as flooding in low-lying areas or locations close to rivers, probabilities can be derived from observations of similar events in the past as well as similarities between areas which are considered to be 'at risk'. However, even when data on similar events is minimal, such as in the case of an earthquake or terrorist attack, it may still be possible to insure against such risks. In this case, insurers are likely to base their probability estimates on techniques such as *Bayesian inference*, where historical data from different parts of the world, logical interpretations of the consequence of scientific or other evidence, or even degrees of belief in the likelihood of particular events are used to determine probability. Whilst such estimates of probability clearly contain a larger element of uncertainty than in the case of more common risks, even the rarest of events can in principle be covered by an insurance policy if the insurance company is confident it can spread the risk and the policy holder considers the risk great enough to justify paying the required premium.[5]

11.2.3 Problems with the calculation of risk

Even when events occur with some degree of regularity and probabilities offer a reasonable prospect of accuracy, there are a number of pitfalls with the calculation of risk. The probability of an event occurring may change when more data or improved techniques become available; thus, for example, the probability of surviving a particular type of cancer may increase as medical knowledge develops. There is also a possibility that probabilities will be misinterpreted or misunderstood. If a weather forecaster says there is a 30 per cent probability of rain tomorrow, it is difficult to know precisely what this means in terms of intensity, place, or length of time. It is also common for people to draw wrong conclusions when comparing different types of risk. For example, some people choose to travel by road after news of a plane or train crash, despite the fact that the risk of being killed or injured in a road accident is considerably greater than when travelling by rail or air.

It is also important to understand the difference between **joint probabilities** (the probability of two independent events occurring) and **conditional probabilities** (the probability that one event will occur given the occurrence of another event). Joint probabilities are calculated by multiplying the two independent probabilities; for example, if the (subjective) probability of Andy Murray winning the Wimbledon men's singles tennis final in a particular year is one in four (1/4) and the (subjective) probability of the final having to be played under the all-weather roof is one in five (1/5), the joint probability of both events occurring is one in twenty ($1/4 \times 1/5 = 1/20$). Conditional probabilities are more difficult to calculate as they depend on the relationship between the two events. If the occurrence of one event makes the occurrence of the second more likely or if both events have a common cause, the probability of the second event occurring, given that the first has already occurred, will be greater. The probability of both events occurring in the first place will depend on the factors leading to their occurrence (see Practical Insight 11.1).

The probability of a unique event occurring, such as the terrorist attacks on 9/11, is impossible to calculate, though in some cases it may be possible to prevent an event occurring or to reduce its consequences through surveillance of the activities leading up to the event. For all these reasons, the calculation of probability is problematic. In the modern world, we have become accustomed to the use of statistical measures to quantify risk, partly because data are now more readily available and perhaps also because of a desire for certainty – a belief that

Practical insight 11.1: The misuse of probabilities when estimating risk

A UK lawyer, Sally Clark, was convicted of murdering her two baby sons in 1999, largely on the evidence of Professor Sir Roy Meadow, an eminent paediatrician who acted as an expert witness in the trial (as he had in many previous trials). Meadow had made his name through his work on a condition known as Munchausen Syndrome by Proxy, a condition where a parent might inflict gradual harm on a child in order to gain attention. Both of Sally Clark's sons had died of cot death (Sudden Infant Death Syndrome), the causes of which are not fully understood. There was also some disputed evidence of possible injury to the children. Meadow claimed that the probability of a single unexplained death of this kind in an affluent, non-smoking family was 1 in 8,543. He then estimated that the probability of two unexplained deaths was 1 in 8,543 squared, i.e. about 1 in 73,000,000. On this basis, Meadow concluded that it was extremely unlikely that the deaths were from natural causes.

Sally Clark was sent to prison for murder though she was released three years later after considerable public controversy and two appeals. She died of an alcohol-related illness in 2007, possibly having never come to terms with the events surrounding her sons' deaths. Meadow was struck off the medical register, though later reinstated after successful appeals. His probability estimate might have been valid if there had been no possibility of the two deaths having a common genetic, medical, or environmental cause. The fact that these causes could not be ruled out made the original court verdict unsound, especially in the absence of any clear evidence of abuse.[6]

Question

● In probability terms, what was the basic error that Professor Sir Roy Meadow made in this case?

we can control risk if we can measure it accurately and perhaps even eliminate it in some circumstances. In the case of external risks, the degree of uncertainty is generally greater, though as we shall see later in this chapter, there may be ways of managing risk that help to reduce either the likelihood or the consequences of risk.[7]

11.2.4 Attitudes towards risk

Attitudes towards risk vary between different people and different cultures. Some people are more risk averse than others, depending on factors such as gender, age, personality, religious beliefs, life experiences, and outlook on life. These differences can be seen in the type of jobs and leisure activities people do, the way they save their money, or their willingness to buy on credit. Some cultures are also more risk averse than others. Uncertainty avoidance was one of the cultural dimensions identified in Hofstede's research (see Section 6.4.3).[8] In high uncertainty-avoidance cultures people are more likely to use loan capital than risk capital (equities) to finance a business and their governments tend to have protective social welfare systems. In open, democratic societies a wealth of information is normally available from official sources and is often used to quantify risk, whereas such information is less likely to be available in more secretive and authoritarian societies. Public awareness of risk therefore tends to be greater in the former than in the latter. Even in similar types of society, there may be differences in the public desire to quantify uncertainty; weather forecasters in the United Kingdom, for example, are more likely to assign probabilities to their forecasts than they are in France.

11.2.5 Psychological and sociological perspectives on risk

Many of the early studies of risk, particularly in the context of financial markets, viewed risk calculations as an attempt by an individual to maximize the expected utility derived from a particular action such as an investment decision. Thus, a risk-averse investor would prefer a less risky investment to a more risky one with the same expected utility or would be willing to accept less expected utility in order to avoid risk. However, a number of researchers have challenged this rational economic view of risk. One of the more significant challenges came from a psychological perspective, notably the work of Daniel Kahneman and Amos Tversky, who argued that our perception of risk depends more on behavioural factors than on probabilities.[9] For example, investors will often systematically make poor decisions such as holding on to an investment for too long when its value is falling or, more generally, initial ways of dealing with a problem will tend to have a persistent influence on subsequent decisions – a form of behavioural path dependence (see Section 10.2.3). Kahneman and Tversky also found that people are generally more risk averse in decisions involving gains, preferring a certain gain to the uncertain probability of a higher gain, and are more likely to be risk takers in decisions involving losses. These ideas have become known as 'prospect theory', though the origin of the term is unclear.[10]

From a sociological perspective, the work of Ulrich Beck and Anthony Giddens has been particularly influential. Beck argues that we now increasingly inhabit a 'risk society' which is a product of modern industrial society and globalization.[11] He argues that '**manufactured risks**', which result from human activity or government policies, are becoming more of a concern than 'external risks' such as natural disasters. Manufactured risks include the risks from global warming, nuclear accidents, genetic engineering, foot and mouth disease, and terrorism – risks which governments often seem relatively powerless to prevent, but which may have long-term or even catastrophic consequences if they occur. For Giddens, the growing emphasis on risk in modern society stems from the belief that human beings can change society for the better.[12] He argues that the modern preoccupation with the future, as well as the desire for security, leads to a greater recognition of risk and of the need for risk management – based on a belief that the future can be controlled or influenced in some way. This view can be seen in the idea of sustainable development, involving economic development with minimal risk to the environment, or in the precautionary principle, as for example in the reluctance to accept genetically modified (GM) crops because of their uncertain consequences in the future.

11.2.6 The prevalence of uncertainty

In a business or political context, there is rarely any degree of certainty that particular outcomes will occur. For example, who would have predicted the future global success of Microsoft or Google when they were founded in the mid-1970s and the late 1990s respectively? Sometimes business success depends on a chain of actions which are influenced by particular events over a period of time. Such events are often difficult to predict in advance. Sometimes the factors leading up to a particular event, such as the crises caused by the outbreak of BSE or 'mad cow disease' in the UK in the late 1980s and early 1990s and of Mexican 'swine flu' in 2009, can be traced with some degree of accuracy after the event, but foresight is often lacking. In other cases, the potential consequences of a future event take on an apparent certainty that is difficult to justify on the basis of the available evidence. For example, whilst the majority of climate scientists subscribe to the view that greenhouse gas emissions are a major cause of global warming, estimates of their impact on future temperature rises are subject to wide variation. This does not however seem to constrain some of the more specific predictions about the impact of greenhouse gas emissions, which may satisfy an understandable desire for certainty but the basis of which is inevitably uncertain.

The principles underlying conventional ideas about the nature of risk are increasingly being challenged, in particular the idea that most events occur in a pattern that fits the so-called **normal distribution** or bell curve. The normal distribution implies that most data lie within a small range of the mean and that extreme values are relatively rare. This is the main basis for the reliability of probability estimates. The concept of the normal distribution has been challenged by scholars such as Benoît Mandelbrot, whose work on commodity prices suggests that extreme values are much more common than we generally imagine (see Section 9.2.5).[13]

Nassim Nicholas Taleb has gone further in arguing that randomness in the distribution of data is the norm rather than the exception.[14] He claims that too much reliance is placed on rational explanations of the pattern of events and that uncertainty stems from chance and unexplained phenomena more often than regular patterns. As a result, Taleb argues, we have a tendency to ignore **'black swan' events** – random events which occur infrequently (in the same way as black swans), but which sometimes have major consequences and may even influence the course of history.[15] Some 'black swans' are beneficial, such as a

Practical insight 11.2:   Could 9/11 have been prevented?

The Report of the 9/11 Commission, set up to investigate the terrorist attacks of 11 September 2001, concluded that 'the 9/11 attacks were a shock, but they should not have been a surprise' and that the 'most important failure [of leaders] was one of imagination'.[16] The report identifies a number of factors that could have acted as warning signals to the security services and political leaders before the event. However, despite the fact that the possibility of a major terrorist attack was recognized and there had even been a previous unsuccessful bomb attack on the World Trade Center in 1993, the idea of using civilian aircraft as weapons of mass destruction had not previously been imagined. If a string of security procedures had been in place or had worked more effectively, the attacks on 9/11 might not have happened. Whether it would have been possible to imagine any conceivable type of terrorist attack is a more open question. The 9/11 attacks are perhaps the most striking example of a destructive 'black swan' event in recent times.

Question

● With hindsight, actions could have been taken to prevent the 9/11 attacks, but is it possible to imagine such an event in advance?

major scientific discovery, while others are catastrophic, such as the 9/11 terrorist attacks (see Practical Insight 11.2). In particular, Taleb has argued that the interdependent global financial system, with its large concentrated banks, may be a source of stability in good times but increases the impact of a financial crash when some of the major institutions get into difficulties (as in the financial crisis of 2008–9).

11.3 Analysis of risk in the global environment

In this section we consider some of the more important risks in the global business environment and explore the nature of these risks. We then turn our attention to the issue of country risk. In Section 11.5, we consider the extent to which exposure to risk or to the consequences of risk can be avoided or reduced through some form of **risk assessment** and **risk management**. The likelihood of an event occurring and its frequency of occurrence are difficult to predict, as has been discussed at length, but the nature and consequences of an event are capable of in-depth analysis. Whilst the consequences may not always follow a unique path, it is possible to determine a number of plausible **scenarios** that can help an organization to make contingency plans or take avoiding action. Here, we focus on the analysis of some of the more important risks and their consequences.[17]

11.3.1 The changing world order

The factors which are driving globalization are also bringing about changes in the balance of economic (and potentially political) power in the world. The 'old order', dominated by the Triad nations of North America, Western Europe, and Japan, is gradually giving way to a world order influenced by a more diverse group of countries. Opinions vary on the extent to which this change is occurring, but it is difficult to ignore the increasing importance of emerging economies such as China and India, if only in purely economic terms.[18] This potential shift in the balance of world economic power is poignantly illustrated in a Goldman Sachs report on what they call the BRICs.[19] Based on estimates of the comparative economic growth rates of the G6 (USA, Japan, Germany, UK, France, and Italy) and the BRIC economies (Brazil, Russia, India, and China), the report concludes that the aggregate gross domestic product (GDP) of the BRICs will have overtaken that of the G6 by the year 2050, if not before; in fact, the Goldman Sachs report estimates GDP on an exchange rate basis, which probably underestimates the size of the BRIC economies. Some commentators view this change as a move towards a multipolar world, where economic power is distributed among a number of major economies rather than a world dominated by a single country or group of countries.[20]

The risks facing an organization arising from a changing world order are many and varied. Economic data can be used to plot and forecast the changing course of the world's economies, as well as trends in key variables such as demographic changes in the countries concerned. Some of the implications of these trends are more difficult to quantify but are nevertheless potentially far-reaching. The Goldman Sachs report argues that the growth in spending power and demand from the BRIC economies could offset slower growth among the ageing populations of the G6 countries, resulting in changing patterns of demand, increased investment flows into the emerging regions, and consequent currency realignments.[21] Other possible implications include a gradual shift in the balance of skills and innovative capacity from developed to emerging economies, and the increasing sophistication of consumers in the emerging economies.[22] These developments have potentially significant implications for multinational enterprises (MNEs). They may also have implications for the United States as the current leading world power and for US relations with the rest of the world. Practical Insight 11.3 considers the implications for US foreign policy.

Practical insight 11.3:   US foreign policy in a changing world

The period since the collapse of the Soviet Union in 1991 has witnessed significant changes in the global balance of power: first to a unipolar world dominated by the United States, then gradually towards a bipolar or multipolar world with the growing influence of China and other emerging nations. This does not necessarily mean that the world's main superpower, the United States, or the institutions of global governance have adjusted to the changing world. Ironically, while the generally conservative Roman Catholic hierarchy elected a non-European pope, Cardinal Bergoglio of Buenos Aires, in March 2013, the post of IMF managing director still alternates between Europe and North America. The United States also still retains much of its superpower role in trade and international relations.

US foreign policy became more aggressive in its fight against terrorism after the atrocities of 9/11. This was understandable after such a horrendous event, but American conservatives have continued to push Republican Party politics towards interventionist foreign and defence policy – despite their passion for minimal government intervention in domestic policy. Democrat President Obama, on the other hand, has generally been more 'dovish' in international affairs – what his opponents have described as 'weak'. However, despite a lack of success in dealing with legacy problems in Afghanistan,

Iran, and the Middle East, President Obama was apparently trusted more on foreign policy than his more 'hawkish' opponent, Mitt Romney, in the 2012 presidential election.[23] This tension between the interventionist tendency of the Republican Party and the more conciliatory approach to foreign policy taken by President Obama illustrates the difficulties the United States faces as it adjusts to the changing world order.[24]

Question

- How would you evaluate the risks to US foreign policy and the US economy as the country adjusts to the changing world order?

11.3.2 International financial crises

Financial crises occur with some degree of regularity, though relatively infrequently. Sometimes they are limited mainly to particular countries or regions, as in the eurozone crisis of 2009–?, sometimes they are more widespread, as in the 2008–9 international financial crisis. However, although each crisis is normally analysed as a unique event, a number of similarities have been found in the situation surrounding financial crises over a long period of time.[25] For example, factors such as credit expansion, inflation, and exchange rate depreciation have been found to precede commodity price collapses prior to a financial crisis. All these factors were present in the 2008–9 financial crisis. Depending on the severity of the financial crisis, it is also common for a crisis to spill over into the 'real economy', leading to a slowdown in economic growth (sometimes a recession), falling sales, and rising unemployment. Given the broad similarity both in the factors leading up to a crisis and in its consequences, financial market risks of this type can clearly be monitored to some extent.

11.3.3 Operational risks in the international environment

Many of the external operational risks in the modern world stem from globalization. As market liberalization increases, international competition becomes more widespread. Whilst the fiercest competition has until recently come from MNEs based in the developed countries, this situation is gradually changing. Consumers in the emerging nations are also increasingly demanding more sophisticated goods and services. In addition to the competitive risks in the changing international environment, supply-chain risks arise when a company's operations are located in different parts of the world. Careful logistics planning is necessary to ensure that supply disruptions in high-risk countries are minimized. Ongoing country risk assessments are therefore essential if a company is to manage a global operation successfully.

A number of other factors may need to be monitored in order to reduce operational risk. These may include risks arising from the following: technological developments that could mean the difference between gaining competitive advantage and being left behind; the cost and availability of energy supplies; exchange rate exposure; or the loss of intellectual property protection. Continual monitoring of developments is necessary in each of these cases, but energy and currency markets are sometimes especially volatile. Oil markets in particular went through an unusually turbulent period during 2007 and 2008, with Brent Crude oil prices rising from just over $50 per barrel in January 2007 to about $145 in July 2008, then falling to about $40 by the beginning of 2009. This degree of volatility has a huge impact on the fuel costs of the shipping, civil aviation, and road haulage industries and ultimately on consumers in general. Similar patterns were seen in the euro/US dollar **nominal exchange rate** over the same period, with the euro's dollar value rising from a monthly average of $1.30 in January 2007 to $1.58 in July 2008, and falling to $1.28 by early November 2008. This caused the dollar price of a €15,000 European car to rise from $19,500 in January 2007 to $23,700 in July 2008 and fall back to $19,200 by November 2008.[26]

11.3.4 Social and environmental concerns

There is growing pressure on all organizations to take account of their corporate social responsibility (see Section 7.5). Sometimes this pressure comes from consumers or interest groups of various kinds, sometimes from government policy. Provided one keeps abreast of public concern on social and environmental issues, in principle it is not difficult to monitor these concerns and to take appropriate action. A wide range of concerns may become the focus of attention, including issues such as community projects, emissions and waste management, resource depletion, or even support for projects in developing countries. However, there is a tendency for particular issues to rise rapidly up the public agenda after bad publicity has emerged. This has been the case when a manufacturer or retailer is accused of sourcing supplies from a company using child labour or other unethical work practices in a poorly regulated country. The ability to respond quickly to such concerns is therefore essential.

11.3.5 Security risks

Security issues generally fall into the category of risks that are difficult to predict but have serious or even catastrophic consequences. They include war and civil unrest, terrorism, technological risks such as computer hacking, computer viruses, or cyber attacks by another country, and fraud, money laundering, and other forms of 'economic crime'. Some of these risks might be described as 'black swan' events, especially where the time or place of their occurrence is unexpected. Whilst the possibility of a terrorist attack, computer virus, or fraudulent act may be well understood, these events often take us by surprise when they actually happen. Economic crime is more widespread than some of the other risks and is often committed by an organization's own employees. However, a number of external threats also exist. These include credit card fraud, counterfeiting, and various other forms of organized crime. A number of political risk organizations monitor these risks in specific countries and law enforcement agencies are now active in detecting and preventing crimes of this kind. Constant surveillance is clearly important as a means of minimizing security risks of all kinds. It may also be important to gain an understanding of the motives behind these activities and the mindset of those involved.

11.4 Country risk analysis

Whilst globalization poses a number of potential risks in the international business environment, many risks are specific to individual countries. Country risk is therefore an important consideration for any organization doing business internationally and, for this reason, it has been the subject of extensive analysis in recent years. The range of factors covered by country risk studies includes risks such as political and economic instability, government regulation and monitoring, infrastructure weaknesses, labour market difficulties, cultural pitfalls, currency instability or exchange restrictions, and nuisance factors like corruption or mafia-style activities. The range of organizations involved in these studies is equally broad, including political and business risk consultancies, debt-rating agencies, research institutions, and organizations such as the World Economic Forum (WEF). Indeed, the analysis of international competitiveness at the country level, for which the WEF and the International Institute for Management Development (IMD) are well known, provides a number of risk indicators that are useful when venturing into specific countries (see Section 11.4.3).

11.4.1 **Political risk factors**

A particular focus of attention has been the issue of political risk, a term which encompasses not only political instability but also the impact of government regulation and policy decisions as well as issues such as corruption. A useful framework which encapsulates the concept of political risk is Ian Bremmer's idea of the 'J curve'.[27] In this context, the J curve represents the relationship between stability and openness in a country. Countries which are higher on the graph are more politically stable and those to the right of the graph are more open. Political stability would include factors such as a political system based on the rule of law, a government which maintains order and a well-functioning economy, and a safe and secure domestic environment. These conditions may of course apply to a country with an authoritarian political system as well as to a liberal democratic country. Openness relates to individual freedoms and democracy within a country, the freedom to trade, invest, or travel abroad, and the extent to which a country participates in recognized international institutions.

Thus, a stable democracy such as the United States lies towards the top right-hand end of the J curve. A more authoritarian but stable country such as China lies at the left-hand end of the J curve. The greatest political risk arises when a country is at the bottom of the curve, where there is a significant level of instability. The situation in Zimbabwe, especially from 2000–9, provides an extreme example of political instability, where the rule of law effectively broke down and the economy was in crisis (though improving after 2009). This put Zimbabwe at the very bottom of the J curve. The case of Myanmar (Burma) is slightly different. Despite recent democratic reforms, there is little if any openness for Myanmar's citizens. The tight grip with which Myanmar's military leaders rule the country creates a degree of stability, but this veneer of stability obscures more deep-rooted unrest and economic failure which suggests that the country is only slightly to the left of the lowest point on the J curve.

The curve also illustrates the path that a country is likely to take as it moves from being a closed, stable country such as the former Soviet Union to being a more open but, in the short term, less stable society like Russia during the 1990s. Most of the former communist countries of Central and Eastern Europe (CEE) have progressed from left to right along the J curve since 1989, passing through the lowest point towards greater stability and openness. For some countries, the journey to stable democracy has been relatively smooth (i.e. the curve is higher on the graph), for others it has been more turbulent (i.e. the curve is lower).

Practical insight 11.4:   A brief profile of Mexico

Mexico is a country of contrasts. After turbulent economic and political fortunes in the 1980s and 1990s, Mexico's economy had been progressing quite well until the world financial crisis and recession of 2008–9. The country was also the world's sixteenth largest merchandise exporter, with 1.9 per cent of world trade in 2011.[28] After a period of excessive dependence on oil revenues, state-owned industry, and international loans, Mexico has created a more open free-market economy and modernized some of its manufacturing industry. It is also a member of NAFTA, the largest formal free trade area in the world, and has been able to attract inward investment from the United States and to a lesser extent elsewhere, particularly in the automotive, chemical, and food processing industries.

Despite these successes, Mexico has large inequalities between rich and poor, some sectors of industry are still relatively underdeveloped, and drug trafficking and its associated violence are deeply rooted in some parts of Mexican society. The country was also at the centre of the 'swine flu' outbreak in 2009, which caused considerable disruption to its economy as well as to the everyday lives of its citizens. Mexico offers a low-cost location with close access to the US market, but also stands at the dividing line between development and underdevelopment, both in an economic sense and in its location between the United States and Central America.[29]

Question

● How would you assess the risks of doing business in Mexico as compared with the United States?

The implications of this type of analysis for business organizations are complex. On the one hand, political stability creates an orderly business environment and openness allows greater freedom to do business, but stability without openness tends to increase the rigidity of the regulatory environment and increase the risk that a business will be unable to operate effectively. Even in a stable and open country, which in principle offers the most conducive business environment, there is no guarantee that particular restrictions will not limit what would otherwise be normal business activity. This may include restrictions on foreign ownership, most commonly found in closed countries but which also apply to the ownership of US airlines, for example (see the opening scenario to Chapter 9). Assessing the risks of doing business in an unfamiliar country is therefore complicated by a number of different factors. A further example of these difficulties can be found in Practical Insight 11.4.

11.4.2 The importance of international competitiveness

The concept of international competitiveness has been applied to firms, countries, regions, and even to cities or city regions in recent years. Fundamentally, international competitiveness is about the ability of a firm to compete in international markets. Why then should we apply the concept to a region or country? After all, it is firms that compete in business, not regions or countries. Regions or countries may 'compete' with each other to attract inward investment, using promotional strategies or financial incentives, but whilst these activities may support regional development, competition to offer the biggest incentives may be counterproductive if it influences short-term decisions without offering long-term advantages to investors.

Countries may also consider an increasing share of world exports to be an indicator of success, but herein lies the problem with this of the term 'competitiveness'. As Paul Krugman has forcefully pointed out, the idea of a country competing for export market share implies that its exports are to be encouraged at the expense of imports (i.e. another country's exports).[30] This contradicts the lessons from international trade theory that all trade (both exports and imports) is generally beneficial for individual countries and the world as a whole. If national competitiveness is measured by export shares, therefore, the concept is potentially harmful if it leads to import protection as a means of restricting imports from 'competitor' countries.

The concept of the international competitiveness of countries may be misleading in the context of international trade, but it has been increasingly applied to the quality of a country's business environment. In this context, it is about the ability of a country or region to provide an environment which enables firms to be internationally competitive – not only indigenous firms but also inward investors. Competition between countries to offer a high-quality environment for business seems entirely legitimate and healthy, and may even encourage countries with less attractive business environments to improve their performance. The concept of regional competitiveness has also attracted the attention of policy makers and development agencies, not only as a focus for improvements in the regional environment but also as a way of enhancing the reputation of a region (see Practical Insight 11.5).[31]

Practical insight 11.5: Should cities or regions compete?

It is common for cities and regions to offer financial incentives such as grants, tax concessions, or low-rent accommodation to incoming businesses. Whilst such incentives are perhaps understandable as a way of attracting investment, income, and employment to the region, competition to be the cheapest location is in some ways a 'race to the bottom'. This is especially true if one considers that cities and regions are located in an increasingly open and integrated global environment. Most cities in the developed world have little hope of being the cheapest location for companies operating in global industries. What they can offer, however, is a high-quality urban environment. The 'race to the top' to provide the most attractive environment is also more likely to improve the general economic welfare of the local community and of the country as a whole, as well as to reduce the risks for incoming investors. This type of territorial competition requires public authorities, development agencies, and community organizations to work together with private businesses to create the infrastructure, facilities, and networks that are needed to establish high-quality tangible and intangible assets in a city or region.[32]

Question

- Given that industrial specialization often occurs at the local or regional level, is city or regional competitiveness more important than national competitiveness?

11.4.3 The international competitiveness of countries

The economic approach

Comparisons of international competitiveness at the national level have often focused on quantifiable macroeconomic indicators. These relate most closely to the cost or price competitiveness of firms engaged in exporting or importing. One of the most important indicators at the national level is a country's exchange rate. An increase in the exchange rate between the euro and US dollar, for example, will make euro-area exports to the USA more expensive and euro-area imports from the USA cheaper. Given the volatility of freely float-ing exchange rates between the world's major currencies, export and import prices may vary considerably over relatively short periods of time. It is often thought that a depreciating ex-change rate is helpful to an economy, as it makes the country's exports more price competi-tive. However, this benefit may be short term if there are underlying productivity, product quality, or inflation problems in the country concerned, none of which will be resolved by exchange rate depreciation.

Market exchange rates, which determine the rate at which one currency can be exchanged for another at a particular time, are sometimes described as nominal or **bilateral exchange rates**. The rate of exchange between the British pound and the euro is an example of a nomi-nal exchange rate. Between July 2012 and February 2013 the rate fell from a monthly average of £1 = €1.27 to £1 = €1.16 (or from €1 = £0.79 to €1 = £0.86 if expressed in terms of the euro). The nominal exchange rate can be quite volatile from day to day or even during the course of a day if economic or political conditions are changing. Such changes have a major effect on the price of exports and the value of investments between countries. A high exchange rate in the home country makes exports less competitive but imports cheaper and it reduces the cost of investing abroad. A low exchange rate has the opposite effect and also brings imported inflation into the country. Nominal exchange rate movements therefore create a significant business risk, which is sometimes described as exchange exposure.

A broader view of how a country's exchange rate is changing with respect to its main trad-ing partners can be obtained by using an **effective** or **trade-weighted exchange rate**; this rate is calculated using an index to compare one currency's value in relation to a 'basket' of other currencies, weighted by the volume of trade between the countries concerned, over a period of time.[33] Relative inflation rates in exporting and importing countries also affect price competitiveness, so **real exchange rates** are sometimes used in place of nominal rates; the real exchange rate combines the nominal exchange rate with the relative inflation rate be-tween two countries and is therefore a more useful measure of international competitiveness than the simple nominal rate. The real exchange rate between the British pound and the US dollar can be calculated as follows:

$$RER_£ = (\text{£ price of UK goods}) / (\text{\$ price of US goods}) \times (\text{\$/£}) \qquad (11.1)$$

Thus, for example, if the UK inflation rate rises while the US inflation rate and the nominal exchange rate ($/£) remain unchanged, the pound's real exchange rate ($RER_£$) will rise and US citizens will pay more for UK goods. UK inflation will therefore have caused a loss of com-petitiveness for UK exporters. It is also possible to measure a country's international competi-tiveness in relation to a group of major trading partners rather than one country alone using a **real effective exchange rate**, which combines the real exchange rate with the effective exchange rate.

The official rate of inflation, measuring changes in retail or consumer prices, is not the only factor affecting price competitiveness within a country. Sometimes, indices of producer prices (especially prices of manufactured goods) are used in preference to consumer prices as not all goods and services included in consumer price indices are exported. Export prices are also affected by costs of production. Cost competitiveness can be measured by comparing unit production costs in different countries. Unit production costs are the cost of labour, materials, energy, and other inputs per unit of output. They therefore take account of productivity (labour hours and other inputs per unit of output) as well as costs of production. Thus, for example, Germany, with its high labour costs, can to some extent mitigate its lack of cost competitiveness by having superior productivity.

Determinants of national competitive advantage (Porter's diamond)

The search for a wider range of competitiveness indicators owes much to the work of Michael Porter. Porter and his team carried out extensive research covering ten countries, identifying four main determinants of national competitive advantage.[34] These determinants are sometimes illustrated diagrammatically as four points of a diamond and are commonly known as 'Porter's diamond'. Porter also recognizes the role of 'chance' and government policies, but he argues that governments should influence the main determinants rather than try to determine competitiveness directly. The four main determinants are as follows:

1. **Factor endowments** Porter distinguishes between 'basic factors', such as natural resources, climate, and the size of the labour force, and 'advanced factors', such as a high-quality infrastructure, advanced technology, and highly developed human capital; advanced factors were found to be particularly important for competitive advantage.

2. **Demand conditions** The quantity and quality of goods demanded by consumers and the expectations of consumers were found to be important in encouraging the development of innovative products and in creating growth in the home market which allowed firms to achieve economies of scale.

3. **Related and supporting industries** The close proximity of internationally competitive suppliers and firms producing complementary products or services in the home market was found to be important in establishing a strong basis for the competitiveness of firms.

4. **Firm strategy, structure, and rivalry** Organizational and industrial structure, including intense rivalry between firms and the need for effective competitive strategies, was also found to be influential in promoting innovation and other competitive advantages.

Whilst Porter's diamond provides a basic framework for the analysis of national competitiveness, a number of more specific factors can be identified and Porter's work in this area is now being developed through the WEF.

International competitiveness rankings

The growing interest in the international competitiveness of countries has led to a number of international initiatives aimed at analysing the differences between countries. These studies of international competitiveness now include both quantitative and qualitative factors, and attempt to provide a more encompassing view of the business environment, including the productivity and growth potential of an economy. The two most important organizations involved in this process are the IMD, an international business school based in Lausanne, and the WEF, an organization coordinating international gatherings of politicians, business leaders, and a wide range of professionals and community leaders, also based in Switzerland. IMD has been publishing its *World Competitiveness Yearbook* since 1989,[35] but the most extensive analysis of international competitiveness can now be found in the WEF's annual Global Competitiveness Report.[36] The Report includes the Global Competitiveness Index, which in 2012–13 ranked 144 countries according to 12 competitiveness criteria (known as 'pillars'), organized under three general headings:

1. **Basic requirements:** institutions; infrastructure; macroeconomic environment; health and primary education.

2. **Efficiency enhancers:** higher education and training; goods market efficiency; labour market efficiency; financial market development; technological readiness; market size.

3. **Innovation and sophistication factors:** business sophistication; innovation.

The above factors have been developed and refined in recent years. Some of them are measured using quantitative data, while the more qualitative indicators are derived from the WEF annual Executive Opinion Survey. The underlying objective of the Global Competitiveness Report is to identify the determinants of a country's productivity level in the belief that productivity is the main basis for sustainable economic growth and prosperity. Although this approach provides a broad view of the conditions under which businesses are likely to be successful, it is ultimately about national economic performance rather than simply the business environment. Perhaps inevitably, other factors could also be incorporated into indices of this type, especially bearing in mind the increasing emphasis now being placed on the role of social capital in national and regional economic development.[37] Practical Insight 11.6 considers the concept of international competitiveness in relation to the Chinese economy.

Practical insight 11.6: China's international competitiveness

In the 2012–13 WEF Global Competitiveness Index, China ranked twenty-ninth out of 144 countries.[38] Whilst this position is above most of the world's developing countries, it may nevertheless seem surprising to a western manufacturer accustomed to being undercut by low-priced Chinese exports. Clearly, in terms of price competitiveness, Chinese goods are among the more competitive in the world. Foreign investors can also take advantage of China's low-cost business environment. However, as China's economic development progresses, the demand for resources will inevitably raise the costs of production and China's long-term international competitiveness will depend on the quality of its institutions, infrastructure, and other advanced factors rather than on low prices. China received its lowest competitiveness scores for technological readiness, innovation, and institutions in the 2012–13 ranking, all factors that will become more important as the country's economy develops.

Question

● Do you think the WEF competitiveness rankings are less useful as a guide to the current business environment in a country than they are as an indicator of a country's future economic potential?

11.5 Managing risk in an uncertain world

11.5.1 Risk assessment and management

The concepts of risk assessment and risk management are well established in a number of fields. Risk assessment involves the analysis of potential risk, whereas risk management concerns the design and implementation of procedures for dealing with risk. Examples of the types of risk covered by these techniques include the following: health risks (e.g. risk factors in the onset of breast cancer or risks from hospital-acquired infections such as MRSA); technological risks (e.g. computer system failure); safety risks (e.g. hazards relating to a chemical or nuclear power plant or airport runway); electrical risks (e.g. from power failure or electric shocks); food hygiene (e.g. risks from harmful bacteria); environmental risks (e.g. pollution emissions); social risks (e.g. domestic violence or children at risk); and many others. Whilst the likelihood and consequences of risk can be reduced by risk management, they can rarely be eliminated. Risk reduction, however, may lead to significant benefits.

In some types of risk management, numerical calculations are used, for example, to monitor share prices in financial risk management or the incidence or spread of a disease in an epidemiological study. When there is considerable uncertainty about the likelihood of an event occurring, as in the case of the international business environment, probabilities based on numerical data may be of limited value. In this case, risk management is about insight rather than numbers. It is more important to gain an understanding of an issue or a possible course of events than to be able to predict the occurrence of an event. Of course, information gathering is an essential part of this process and it may sometimes be useful to categorize information in numerical form or to attach numerical values to the level of risk. However, the most important aspect of risk management in the context of the business environment is the development of insight, not only into the current dimensions of the issue but also into how the issue is likely to develop in the future. Despite the difficulties with the calculation of probability highlighted in this chapter, the concept (though not necessarily the calculation) of conditional probability may be of particular importance. This is because of the complex interaction between events in the business environment and the way in which the occurrence of one event makes another more likely.

11.5.2 Intelligence management

Intelligence management, the processing of information on risk, involves information monitoring and gathering, analysis of the information received, and application of the knowledge gained in the decision-making process of an organization. It is sometimes at this last stage of the process that risk management breaks down, partly because of the complexity of large organizations and partly because people are unsure of how to use their knowledge. The use of this knowledge is explored further in the context of developing scenarios in Section 11.5.3.

In general terms, it is important to look for **warning signs**, **triggers**, and **signposts** when considering changes in the external environment. Warning signs are events that provide an indication of a potential risk; in the context of the world oil market, evidence of falling oil stocks or the rapid expansion of China's economy might provide a warning of tight supply conditions and rising demand, leading to rising oil prices over a period of time. A trigger is an event that sets off an immediate reaction, such as a flare-up of military conflict in the Middle East; even if oil supplies are not actually disrupted, this news may cause panic buying and a sharp increase in oil prices. A signpost is something that provides an indication of a trend or future course of events, such as the decision of a major motor manufacturer to develop vehicles using alternative fuels – signalling a possible move away from oil-dependent technology. Whilst this is unlikely to have a short-term effect on oil prices, it may influence future research and investment priorities. Each of these factors creates either short-term or long-term risks for business.

In many cases an organization faces a number of different risks simultaneously or a particular risk is multifaceted. This situation requires complex risk analysis, breaking down the main risk components into their different stages or dimensions. The main elements of risk can then be evaluated and prioritized in terms of their likelihood and consequences. This helps an organization to focus its attention on issues representing greater risk. The most extensive work in this area has been done on country risk analysis. Typically, this involves the analysis of a number of key risk factors such as political and economic stability, government policy, ethnic and religious tensions, bureaucracy, and corruption. This type of country risk analysis was pioneered by William Coplin and Michael O'Leary at Syracuse University, but their approach is now used by a wide range of risk analysis consultancies.[39] The Coplin-O'Leary Model, or Prince Model as it is also known, attaches grade scores to each of the main risks within both an 18-month and five-year time frame. Further work in the area of political risk management at the country level can be found in studies carried out by the Eurasia Group.[40] These studies include analyses of issues such as regime vulnerability in countries like Ukraine, Pakistan, or Nigeria, rising populism and nationalism (including energy nationalism) in countries like Venezuela or Bolivia, and potential urban flashpoints in cities such as Istanbul, Cairo, or Manila.

11.5.3 Developing scenarios

Scenarios are a method increasingly being used to provide insights into a possible future course of events. This method involves the development of plausible alternative scenarios, drawing on information, analysis, and understanding of a particular issue, which can be used as a basis for risk management strategies. Through the process of scenario planning, an organization is able to identify alternative ways of planning its operations in order to minimize the consequences of risk or even to influence the likelihood of a particular event occurring. Each alternative scenario is intended to envision a possible course of events and its consequences. This process makes use of warning signs, triggers, signposts, and other indicators, but above all it requires insight and imagination. For this reason, it is often preferable to involve teams of people in developing scenarios in order to generate a wide range of ideas. The alternative scenarios represent a number of possible ways in which a particular issue may develop (see Practical Insight 11.7). Some scenarios may, of course, involve greater risks than others, but it is important for an organization to understand these risks and to put strategies in place to manage the risks effectively. It is also possible to include a few 'wild cards' when developing scenarios of the global environment: low-probability but high-impact events such as a terrorist attack or global epidemic that may disrupt the expected course of events.[41]

Practical insight 11.7: Scenarios for global risk

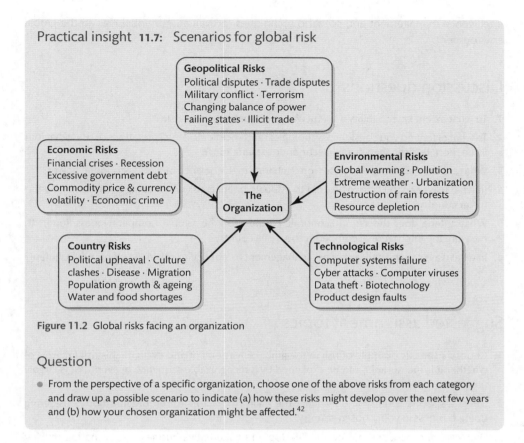

Figure 11.2 Global risks facing an organization

Question

- From the perspective of a specific organization, choose one of the above risks from each category and draw up a possible scenario to indicate (a) how these risks might develop over the next few years and (b) how your chosen organization might be affected.[42]

Summary

This chapter is concerned with methods of analysing the nature of risk in the international business environment. The national and global business environment gives rise to a wide range of risks and the concept and measurement of risk are explored at some length, including the uses and misuses of probability, differing attitudes and perspectives on risk, and the extent to which uncertainty is prevalent in the business environment. Several examples of risk in the global environment are analysed; these include the changing world order, international financial crises, operational risks, social and environmental concerns, and security risks. The analysis of country risk is then considered, focusing on the implications of political risk and the concept of international competitiveness. A distinction is made between the international competitiveness of firms, regions, and countries and alternative ways of analysing a country's international competitiveness are discussed; these include the risks posed by exchange rates, Porter's determinants of national competitive advantage, and the country rankings of organizations such as the World Economic Forum. Finally, we consider the extent to which the concept of risk management can be applied to the business environment, making use of intelligence management and scenario techniques to evaluate potential risks in the global environment.

Discussion questions

1. To what extent is probability a useful way to evaluate business risks?
2. To what extent do you consider psychological and sociological interpretations of risk behaviour to be more realistic than rational economic explanations?
3. What are the main risks that arise from a change in the balance of world economic power?
4. In what ways can the J curve be used to evaluate political risk when doing business in an unfamiliar country?
5. What criteria does the World Economic Forum use in its Global Competitiveness Report to measure the international competitiveness of a country?
6. In what ways can the concept of risk management be applied to risk in the global environment?

Suggested assignment topics

1. Choose a specific example of risk in the global environment and evaluate this risk in terms of whether it is measurable, can be explained by a recognizable sequence of events, or is largely uncertain.
2. Select a specific country and evaluate the main risk factors for an organization considering doing business in your chosen country.
3. With reference to a specific 'event', develop three alternative business risk scenarios, making use of available data as well as an understanding of the issues surrounding the event.

 Case study: A country analysis of Botswana

Botswana is a land-locked country in southern Africa. It shares a border with Namibia, Angola, Zambia, Zimbabwe, and South Africa. Like many sub-Saharan African countries, Botswana has an inhospitable climate and terrain (much of the land area is wilderness, including the Kalahari desert and Okavango swamps), a relatively poor transport and communication infrastructure, relatively low levels of educational participation and literacy, and a bureaucratic administrative system which makes starting a business a lengthy process. It also has one of the highest rates of HIV/AIDS infection in the world, which contributed towards a life expectancy at birth of around 53 years in 2012.

Despite this depressingly familiar picture in much of Africa, the reality is often more complex. Botswana has achieved a steady rate of economic growth, with an average annual growth rate of 6.0 per cent in the 1990s and 4.3 per cent from 2000 to 2010. This growth rate might well have been higher recently had it not been for the death toll from HIV/AIDS. Indeed, even though the educational participation rate is relatively poor, Botswana spends one of the highest proportions of GDP of any country in the world on education (8.9 per cent of GDP in 2009) and the country's estimated GDP per capita of $16,800 on a PPP basis in 2012 puts it into the World Bank's upper-middle income group. Among the countries of sub-Saharan Africa, Botswana ranks third in the 2012–13 WEF Global Competitiveness Index, behind South Africa and Rwanda (another country which has made remarkable progress, in this case since the genocide of 1994).

Botswana's economic success has been built on its good fortune in having abundant mineral resources, especially diamonds. Diamond production makes up more than one-third of the country's GDP, between 70 and 80 per cent of its export earnings, and half of government revenue. The country's wildlife reserves and wetlands have also become important tourist attractions. Although Botswana's dependence on diamond mining carries potential long-term risks, the country's governments have not allowed its natural resource revenues to distract them from pursuing policies of economic reform and careful management of the public finances. These policies have been pursued systematically since the country achieved independence from Britain in 1966.

Economic reform has included open-economy policies such as the encouragement of inward investment and foreign ownership, the removal of exchange restrictions, and trade liberalization, as well as pro-competition policies, low corporate taxes, and macroeconomic stabilization within the economy. Botswana is also an active member of the main regional economic groupings, including the Southern African Development Community (SADC), the Southern Africa Customs Union (SACU), and the Africa Free Trade Zone (AFTZ), formed between the 26 countries of SADC, the East African Community (EAC), and the Common Market for Eastern and Southern Africa (COMESA) in October 2008.

Corruption, both in business and among public officials, is a common problem in many parts of the world. In Africa, this is often one of the legacies of a history of autocratic and unrepresentative government, periodic conflict and crisis, as well as the unequal distribution of wealth that accompanies the abundance of natural resources. Whilst Botswana has natural resource wealth, it has also been one of the more stable democracies in sub-Saharan Africa in recent years and is the highest-ranking African country (i.e. has the lowest level of corruption) in Transparency International's 2012 Corruption Perceptions Index (ranked 30 out of 176 countries worldwide). This also puts Botswana ahead of the CEE countries and one or two of the countries of Western Europe.[43]

Case study questions

1. Using the latest WEF Global Competitiveness Report, identify Botswana's main strengths and weaknesses as a location for inward foreign direct investment (FDI).

2. Identify Botswana's main strengths and weaknesses from the perspective of the country's ability to maintain strong economic growth.

3. What factors are likely to hold back Botswana's general economic development?

4. What are the implications for Botswana's economic development of its membership of regional economic groupings such as SADC, SACU, and AFTZ?

5. What are the main business risks likely to be for a foreign direct investor in Botswana?

6. What other factors might a foreign direct investor consider before deciding to enter a relatively high-risk country like Botswana?

7. Corruption represents a lower-than-average risk in Botswana compared with other sub-Saharan African countries, whereas HIV/AIDS is a particularly high risk factor. How would you evaluate these two risks from a business perspective and to what extent are they measurable?

8. Describe two alternative business risk scenarios for Botswana over the next five to ten years.

Notes

1. Further bailouts for some of these countries may also be needed, especially for Spain and Italy.

2. The *Daily Telegraph*, National Post Wire Services (18 March 2013), 'Welcome to Cyprus: A sunny place for shady people'.

3. Main sources: the *Guardian* (2 November 2012), 'Eurozone crisis: a timeline of key events'; UN News Centre (17 January 2013), 'Euro zone's debt crisis and austerity policies continue to damp down growth'; *Money Morning* (25 January 2013), 'Eichengreen: eurozone debt crisis to "heat up again in 2013"'; *Time* (26 February 2013), 'Italy's political mess: why the euro debt crisis never ended'; and the *Telegraph* (15 March 2013), 'Debt crisis: EU leaders set to announce €750bn Spain and Italy bailout deal'.

4. This distinction was made in Frank Knight's seminal work, Knight, F. H. (2012), *Risk, Uncertainty and Profit*, Forgotten Books, first published in 1921.

5. For a discussion of risk and insurance, see Shirreff, D. (2004), *Dealing with Financial Risk*, Economist Books, pp. 92–5.

6. See http://understandinguncertainty.org/node/545.

7. A useful discussion of these issues can be found in Gigerenzer, G. (2003), *Reckoning with Risk: Learning to Live with Uncertainty*, Penguin Books.

8. Hofstede, G. (2003), *Culture's Consequences: Comparing Values, Behaviours, Institutions and Organizations Across Nations*, Sage Publications.

9. For example Kahneman, D., Slovic, P., and Tversky, A. (1982), *Judgement under Uncertainty: Heuristics and Biases*, Cambridge University Press.

10. See Bernstein, P. L. (1998), *The Remarkable Story of Risk*, John Wiley and Sons, p. 270.

11. Beck, U. (1992), *Risk Society: Towards a New Modernity*, Sage Publications, first published in German in 1986.

12. Giddens, A. (1999), 'Risk and responsibility', *Modern Law Review*, vol. 62, no.1, pp. 1–10.

13. Mandelbrot, B. B. (2008), *The (Mis) Behaviour of Markets: A Fractual View of Risk, Ruin and Reward*, Profile Books.

14. Taleb, N. N. (2007), *Fooled by Randomness: The Hidden Role of Chance in Life and in the Markets*, Penguin.

15. Taleb, N. N. (2008), *The Black Swan: The Impact of the Highly Improbable*, Penguin.

16. National Commission on Terrorist Attacks upon the United States (2004), Final Report: Executive Summary, pp. 2 and 9.

17. See also the latest World Economic Forum Global Risks Report, http://www.weforum.org.

18. Measured on a purchasing power parity (PPP) basis, China had the second largest and India the third largest economy in the world in 2012 (CIA, *World Factbook*, 2012).

19. Goldman Sachs Report (October 2003), 'Dreaming with BRICs: The Path to 2050'.

20. See, for example, a report by Accenture, a management consultancy, entitled 'The Rise of the Multi-Polar World', published in 2007 (http://www.accenture.com).

21. Goldman Sachs Report (October 2003), 'Dreaming with BRICs: The Path to 2050'.

22. See, for example, Accenture (2007), 'The Rise of the Multi-Polar World', http://www.accenture.com.

23. Pew Research Center's last pre-election poll found that 50% of voters trusted Obama on foreign policy and 42% trusted Romney (http://www.pewresearch.org).

24. Main sources: Drezner, D. W. (2013), 'Rebooting Republican Foreign Policy', *Foreign Affairs*, vol. 92, no. 1, pp. 143–52; Chayes, S. (12 March 2013), 'What Vali Nasr gets wrong', *Foreign Policy*; and Innocent, M. (14 March 2013), 'The GOP on foreign policy: rhetoric v. reality', the *Huffington Post*.

25. Reinhart, C. M., and Rogoff, K. S. (2011), *This Time is Different: Eight Centuries of Financial Folly*, Princeton University Press.

26. Data taken from http://www.thisismoney.co.uk/oil-price and http://www.x-rates.com.

27. Bremmer, I. (2007), *The J Curve: A New Way to Understand Why Nations Rise and Fall*, Simon and Schuster.

28. WTO, *International Trade Statistics*, 2012, table I.7, p. 26.

29. Main source: CIA, *World Factbook*, 2012: Mexico.

30. Krugman, P. R. (1996), 'Making sense of the competitiveness debate', *Oxford Review of Economic Policy*, vol. 12, no. 3, pp. 17–25.

31. See, for example, Camagni, R. (2002), 'On the concept of territorial competitiveness: sound or misleading?', *Urban Studies*, vol. 39, no. 13, pp. 2395–411.

32. For a discussion of city competitiveness, see Gordon, I. (2003), 'The Competitiveness of Cities: Why it Matters in the 21st Century and How we can Measure it', Cahiers de L'IAURIF, no. 135, March (http://www.iau-idf.fr/fileadmin/Etudes/etude_743/cahiers_135_EN.pdf).

33. Trade-weighted exchange rates can be found, for example, at *The Economist* website: http://www.economist.com/markets-data.

34. Porter, M. E. (1998), *The Competitive Advantage of Nations*, Palgrave Macmillan, first published in 1990.

35. International Institute for Management Development (IMD), http://www.imd.org.

36. World Economic Forum (WEF), http://www.weforum.org.

37. See, for example, the European Competitiveness Index of the Centre for International Competitiveness, based at the University of Wales Institute, Cardiff (http://www.cforic.org); this index includes indicators of knowledge and creativity, which are important elements of human and social capital.

38. WEF, Global Competitiveness Index, 2012–13.

39. Coplin, W. D., and O'Leary, M. K. (2005), 'Educational, research, and policy making activities of the Prince Project', *Policy Studies Journal*, pp. 311–16.

40. See Bremmer, I., and Keat, P. (2009), *The Fat Tail: The Power of Political Knowledge for Strategic Investing*, Oxford University Press.

41. See, for example, Laudicina, P. A. (2012), *Beating the Global Odds: Successful Decision Making in a Confused and Troubled World*, John Wiley and Sons, especially ch. 8, pp. 147–76.

42. See World Economic Forum, Global Risks Report, for further discussion of these issues, http://www.weforum.org/issues/global-risks.

43. Main sources: Human Development Report 2013, WEF Global Competitiveness Report, 2012–13; IMF Country Report No.12/234 (August 2012); IMF, *World Economic Outlook Database*, October 2012; CIA World Factbook, 2012; and Transparency International (http://www.transparency.org).

Suggestions for further reading

On the concept of risk

Bernstein, P. L. (1998), *Against the Gods: The Remarkable Story of Risk*, John Wiley and Sons

Gigerenzer, G. (2003), *Reckoning with Risk: Learning to Live with Uncertainty*, Penguin Books

On the analysis of global risk and risk management

Bracken, P., Bremmer, I., and Gordon, D. (2008), *Managing Strategic Surprise*, Cambridge University Press

Bremmer, I., and Keat, P. (2009), *The Fat Tail: The Power of Political Knowledge for Strategic Investing*, Oxford University Press

Laudicina, P. A. (2012), *Beating the Global Odds: Successful Decision Making in a Confused and Troubled World*, John Wiley and Sons

On the meaning and measurement of the international competitiveness of countries

Harrison, A. L., Dalkiran, E., and Elsey, E. (2000), *International Business*, Oxford University Press, ch. 13, pp. 272–91

International Institute for Management Development (annual), *IMD World Competitiveness Yearbook*

World Economic Forum (annual), *The Global Competitiveness Report*

Porter, M. E. (1998), *The Competitive Advantage of Nations*, Palgrave Macmillan

A guide to developing scenarios

Wilson, I., and Ralston, W. (2006), *Scenario Planning Handbook: Developing Strategies in Uncertain Times*, South-Western

An entertaining essay on expecting the unexpected

Taleb, N. N. (2011), *The Black Swan: The Impact of the Highly Improbable*, Allen Lane

 Take your learning further: Online Resource Centre
http://www.oxfordtextbooks.co.uk/orc/harrison2e/
Visit the Online Resource Centre that accompanies this book to enrich your understanding of Chapter 11: Risk in the International Environment. Among other resources explore web links and keep up to date with the latest developments in the area.

Key terms introduced in this chapter

Bilateral exchange rate A nominal exchange rate between two currencies.

'Black swan' event A random event which occurs infrequently, but which sometimes has major consequences.

Conditional probability The probability that one event will occur given the occurrence of another event.

Effective exchange rate An exchange rate calculated using an index to compare its value to a 'basket' of currencies, weighted by the volume of trade between the countries concerned, over a period of time.

External risk Risk that results from natural phenomena such as a natural disaster.

International competitiveness The ability of a firm to compete in international markets or the factors that determine a country's business environment and future economic growth and prosperity.

Joint probability The probability of two independent events occurring.

Manufactured risk Risk that results from human activity or government policies.

Nominal exchange rate A market exchange rate which determines the rate at which one currency can be exchanged for another at a particular time.

Normal distribution A pattern derived from the frequency of occurrence of a set of data where most data lie within a small range of the mean and extreme values are relatively rare (represented by a bell-shaped curve known as the bell curve).

Objective probability Probability that results from knowable 'facts' about the occurrence of an event resulting either from homogeneous data or inherent symmetries.

Probability The measurable likelihood of an event occurring.

Real effective exchange rate An exchange rate which combines the real exchange rate and the effective exchange rate.

Real exchange rate An exchange rate which takes account of both the nominal exchange rate between and the relative inflation rate in two countries.

Risk The possibility of an uncertain event occurring, sometimes though not necessarily considered to be measurable.

Risk assessment The analysis of potential risk.

Risk management The design and implementation of procedures for dealing with risk.

Scenario Analysis of a possible future course of events, drawing on information, insights, and understanding of a particular issue.

Signpost Something that provides an indication of a trend or future course of events.

Subjective probability Probability based on observations of past events or estimates or beliefs about future events which have little quantifiable basis.

Trade-weighted exchange rate See effective exchange rate.

Trigger An event that sets off an immediate reaction.

Uncertainty An unpredictable event, sometimes regarded as a risk that cannot be measured.

Warning sign An event that provides an indication of a potential risk.

Part Three

....

The Geopolitical Context

....

12 Europe: Unification, Crisis, and Beyond

 Chapter learning outcomes

On completion of this chapter the reader should be able to:

- Appreciate the major geopolitical and related developments which have taken place in Europe in recent years
- Evaluate the main implications of these developments for business organizations

12.1 Redrawing the map of Europe

The political geography of Europe has changed many times over the centuries. At no time has this been more true than since the end of the 1980s. Not only did the 'iron curtain' between Eastern and Western Europe come down, but it was followed by a process of political and ethnic fragmentation and changing allegiances between nations. The biggest fragmentation occurred with the break-up of the Soviet Union into 15 separate republics[1] and the conflict in Yugoslavia which led, over a period of time, to the creation of six independent republics, together with the disputed territory of Kosovo.[2] On a smaller scale, there was also the separation of the Czech and Slovak Republics (formerly Czechoslovakia). In one case, the ending of the east–west division brought about the unification of East and West Germany, enabling the first former communist country to join the European Union (EU) in October 1990.

Many of these newly formed states had enjoyed some degree of independence, or had been under different foreign occupation, in former times. Each change of political control had enforced a new national allegiance, but had left a legacy of ethnic tension in its wake. During the communist years, these tensions were generally kept under control by a combination of authoritarian leadership, censorship, repression, and an imposed sense of national purpose. When these strictures were removed, the ethnic tensions came to the surface. In most cases, differences were aired through political expression; in a few cases, notably in southern Russia (especially Chechnya), in the neighbouring states of Georgia and Armenia, and on a larger scale in the former Yugoslavia, they led to violent conflict. Even in some of the new states, successive border changes have left a patchwork of distinct ethnic groups in their territories.

Border changes have also occurred in Western Europe, though less so in recent years. By contrast with the east, Western Europe has been integrating rather than fragmenting. This process began after World War II as a deliberate attempt to prevent future conflict. Initially, cooperation occurred through the Organization for European Economic Co-operation (OEEC), formed in 1948 to coordinate the distribution of US Marshall Aid under the post-war

European reconstruction plan, which later expanded beyond Europe to become the Organisation for Economic Co-operation and Development (OECD). Then, in 1949, the Council of Europe was set up to promote the democratic principles set out in the European Convention on Human Rights. More importantly, post-war negotiations led to the formation of what we now call the EU in 1958. Although the EU is made up of sovereign member states, deeper and wider integration has inevitably produced a more coordinated approach to political and economic affairs in Europe and this has been achieved among an increasing number of European countries. More especially, European integration has brought together a group of countries from Eastern and Western Europe, which were separated by the 'iron curtain' during the cold war years and which had never before been unified by consent on anything like this scale.

Whilst several of the 'eastern' states have now been brought under the EU banner, there are of course a number of European countries which have been left outside. Some of these countries have expressed a desire to join the EU in due course, notably the countries of South-East Europe including Turkey, but some of the others have formed temporary, and sometimes fragile, alliances with Russia, their former political master. Twelve of the former Soviet Republics formed the Commonwealth of Independent States (CIS) (excluding the three Baltic states, Estonia, Latvia, and Lithuania) after the collapse of the Soviet Union in 1991, though whilst some of these states have inclinations towards the EU and the North Atlantic Treaty Organization (NATO), others have been keener to form their own economic and security alliances in the form of the Eurasian Economic Community and the Collective Security Treaty Organization.

12.2 The European Union

The EU began its life as the European Economic Community (EEC) in 1958 (established under the Treaty of Rome, 1957), though it grew out of the earlier European Coal and Steel Community (ECSC) which came into existence in 1952 (under the Treaty of Paris, 1951). Through successive enlargements, the EU has grown from its original six members to 28,[3] with membership applications from Iceland, FYR Macedonia, Montenegro, Serbia, and Turkey up to mid-2013.[4] The EU now has competence in a number of policy areas, including external trade relations, agriculture, fisheries, transport, and regional policy, and has been extending its influence in areas such as employment and environmental policy, justice, immigration, security and foreign affairs.

The EU is an important trading area within the global economy, accounting for 33.1 per cent of world merchandise exports and 38.5 per cent of world exports of commercial services in 2011 (including intra-EU trade in both cases).[5] The EU economy also accounted for 18.9 per cent of world gross domestic product (GDP) in 2012, making it roughly the same size as the US economy.[6] The level of economic integration between the EU member states brings a considerable degree of political integration, in terms of both policy coordination and representation at international institutions such as the World Trade Organization (WTO). Not only has this been a de facto development as the EU has extended its policy competence, it was also envisioned by the EU's founding fathers in the Treaties of Paris and Rome in the 1950s.[7] However, whilst some of the EU's founders supported the development of a federal policy-making structure, with a clear rationale for centralized and devolved power at the various political levels, the EU has tended to pursue a more pragmatic, functionalist approach in practice, with piecemeal decisions being taken at a pace acceptable to the member states.

12.2.1 The single European market

Undoubtedly, the most important achievement of the EU in the economic sphere has been the creation of the single internal market. This market extends not only to all the EU member states but also to three members of the European Free Trade Association (EFTA) – Iceland, Liechtenstein, and Norway. The extended single market is known as the European Economic Area (EEA). The fourth member of EFTA, Switzerland, whose electorate have rejected membership of both the EU and the EEA, has negotiated a series of bilateral treaties with the EU, giving Switzerland many of the benefits and responsibilities of EEA membership in practice. As at mid-2013, the extended single European market therefore included 31 member countries, plus Switzerland as an effective member. With a combined GDP of over $16 trillion, on a purchasing power parity (PPP) basis, and a population of almost 517 million, this makes the EEA the largest common market in the world.[8]

By removing tariff and non-tariff barriers, the single European market has brought about the free movement of goods, services, people, and capital between the member states' economies. Goods can move freely across internal borders because there are no tariffs (import duties), frontier controls have generally been removed, cross-border procedures and documentation have been simplified, product standards are being harmonized or are accorded mutual recognition, public procurement has been opened up to competitive tendering, and because of the free movement of transport. Along with the deregulation of transport and harmonization of transport regulations, other services such as telecommunications, electricity, gas, and other former publicly owned utilities are gradually being privatized and opened up to cross-border competition. The harmonization or mutual recognition of standards is also required to allow banks, insurance companies, airlines, haulage operators, and other service providers to operate freely across internal borders. The free movement of people allows business travellers, consumers, tourists, students, and workers to take advantage of the single market. Most EEA member states now belong to the Schengen area, which allows passport-free travel within much of the single market, and, to a large extent, the right to work or establish a business in another EEA country is being made possible by the mutual recognition of qualifications. The fourth freedom, the free movement of capital, allows individuals and businesses to transfer capital across internal borders without restriction.

For a variety of reasons, the single market is not as 'complete' as the above description would suggest. The free movement of goods and services is still, to some extent, hampered by the persistence of different regulatory and technical standards. These differences are evident in a variety of products ranging from electrical goods to cars, and in VAT, excise duties, and corporate and income taxes, though a degree of harmonization has been achieved in the case of VAT (where a majority of EU countries now have standard rates of between 18 and 21 per cent). One of the most protracted debates on opening up the single market has in fact been on the services directive, allowing the provision of cross-border services either at a distance or by setting up a business in another EEA country. The services directive was finally agreed in December 2006 and became legally enforceable in December 2009. The free movement of people will not be fully achieved until the transitional arrangements for the new EU members from Central and Eastern Europe (CEE) have expired in 2014 and further progress has been made on the mutual recognition of qualifications. Capital generally moves more freely than goods, services, or people, though occasionally local restrictions have the effect, if not always the intention, of discriminating against cross-border investors, and cross-border money transfers involve additional costs because Europe's banking systems are not fully integrated and the euro has not been universally adopted.

However, the excessively negative view that is sometimes portrayed by the EU's detractors should not obscure the significant progress that has been made since the single market project was given a new impetus by the Single European Act of 1986 and the series of measures that led to the symbolic opening of borders on 1 January 1993 (extended to the wider EEA on 1 January 1994). Despite the niggling obstacles that continue to make intra-EU trade more complicated than it need be, there is no doubt that cross-border trade and investment has blossomed in recent years and many of Europe's high-cost domestic monopoly markets have been transformed by more open competition. This is evident in road haulage, civil aviation, telecommunications, electricity, gas, banking, insurance, and postal services, where consumers are increasingly able to exercise choice and domestic industries are being restructured through cross-border mergers and alliances. The deregulation of European airways during the late 1980s and 1990s provides a vivid example of how competition has been transformed by mergers and the entry of low-cost airlines, resulting in lower fares, service innovation, and new flight destinations. Cultural and historic differences between EEA countries and the impact of these differences on the way EU policies are implemented will probably always represent a business challenge. On the other hand, these differences also help to create the EU's diversity and the distinctiveness of its regions. The EU has also established a deeper level of integration than any other group of independent countries in the modern world.

12.2.2 The euro

The creation of a single European currency has, in many ways, been a more ambitious and high-risk project than the single market. Trade and investment would have taken place between neighbouring European countries even without a single market, albeit on a significantly smaller scale, but confidence in a country's currency is crucial in maintaining internal price stability and external stability in the balance of payments.

The logic for a single currency is derived from the theory of optimum currency areas.[9] An optimum currency area exists where the monetary efficiency gains achieved by a group of countries adopting fixed exchange rates exceed the loss of economic stability from giving up flexible exchange rates. The monetary efficiencies arise because of the reduced risk from currency movements and the consequent reduction in currency transaction costs. These costs are further reduced in the case of a single currency (as opposed to fixed rates between separate currencies) as currency transaction costs are completely eliminated. Generally, the more closely integrated a group of economies, the greater the efficiency gains because of the larger volume of trade and investment between them. Closely integrated economies are also less likely to suffer *asymmetric shocks* requiring independent exchange rate flexibility; for example, their economic cycles are more likely to be synchronized, allowing collective exchange rate flexibility in response to a *symmetric shock*, such as an economic downturn, and avoiding the need for different policies to meet different economic circumstances in each country. However, if asymmetric shocks occur, each country is more likely to be able to cope with them if there is mobility of the factors of production, allowing labour and capital to move from regions where they are in plentiful supply to regions where they are in short supply.

The above conditions have not always been present in the euro area, leading to difficulties for the European Central Bank when setting the appropriate interest rate for a group of countries with diverse economic conditions. The strength of the euro has also created problems for businesses and economies such as Italy which might otherwise have benefited from a depreciating exchange rate. It should not, however, be concluded from this that the euro is necessarily bad for a country such as Italy. Allowing a depreciating exchange rate to compensate for weak industrial performance is only a temporary solution. In the longer term, underlying problems such as poor productivity must be tackled. It may therefore be argued that the euro has exposed these problems rather than caused them. Prior to the eurozone crisis, the euro was generally more successful than many observers expected. After an initial decline in its US dollar value during 1999 and 2000, the euro gradually strengthened and stabilized, making it a more sought-after reserve and trading currency during a period of instability for the US dollar. The relatively strong euro made extra-European exports more expensive, but a reasonable degree of internal price stability was achieved by the European Central Bank.

The future of the euro has become less certain as a result of the sovereign-debt and bank insolvency crisis since 2009 (see the opening scenario to Chapter 11). Although mounting government debt in Greece, Italy, and Portugal, and the banking crises in Ireland, Spain, and Cyprus began as domestic problems within these countries, the cost of borrowing to finance government spending and bank bailouts rapidly made national solutions to the problem unsustainable. Government insolvency and banking collapses would also have endangered the euro.[10] The eurozone crisis has put continual pressure on the more stable members, and especially Germany, to raise funds (along with the IMF) to support the countries in difficulties. Sluggish economic growth and uncomfortably high sovereign debt in some of the other eurozone countries are adding to these difficulties. It is therefore becoming clear that closer fiscal union and greater fiscal discipline will be needed to ensure that a tighter rein is kept on government deficits and public debt in the eurozone.

12.2.3 EU enlargement

From its origins in the 1950s, the EU has undergone a series of enlargements to include most of the countries of Western Europe, two small Mediterranean countries, Cyprus and Malta, and, more significantly, 11 former communist countries in Central and Eastern Europe.[11] Successive enlargements have inevitably changed the dynamics of the EU in political, economic, and social terms. These changes have brought about gradual shifts in emphasis in some of the EU's policies, notably the 'Anglo-Saxon' pressure for market liberalization, though the 'Franco-German axis' has, until recently at least, remained a dominant influence and older policies such as the common agricultural policy (CAP) have proved difficult to reform. With the exception of Iceland, the current applicants for EU membership (Iceland, FYR Macedonia, Montenegro, Serbia, and Turkey) come from south-eastern Europe and further applications from this region are likely in the near future. Future applications from former Soviet republics such as Ukraine or Georgia are also possible. Each of these countries will bring its own political difficulties.

Difficult issues arise over Turkey's EU membership application and over relations between Russia and some of its neighbouring states which have aspirations to join not only the EU but also NATO. Turkey is a member of NATO and is seen by the United States as a key western ally in the Middle East. The US is therefore keen for Turkey to join the EU in order to bring the country more firmly into the family of western nations. The European view on Turkish membership is more complicated for a variety of reasons. These include Turkey's human rights record, especially in relation to its Kurdish and other ethnic and religious minorities, its predominantly Muslim culture and institutions, its less developed economy, and its relations with Greece, especially over Turkish-dominated Northern Cyprus. However, none of these issues represents an insurmountable obstacle to EU membership and Turkey already has a customs union with the EU. In fact, EU membership may help to accelerate political and economic developments, as in other parts of south-eastern Europe. Russia's relations with the EU have generally been positive in recent years, though tensions occasionally erupt between Russia and its neighbouring states, notably disputes over gas supplies to Ukraine (which also affect supplies to other European countries) and over the disputed territories of South Ossetia and Abkhazia on the border between Russia and Georgia. In the light of these difficulties, further expansion of the EU to the east is likely to be problematic.

12.3 Transition in Russia and Eastern Europe

The post-World War II settlement, which ultimately led to the separation of Western and Eastern Europe, allowed the Soviet Union to extend its influence over the eastern sector from the late 1940s onwards. Communist central planning gradually spread throughout the region and Bulgaria, Czechoslovakia, East Germany, Hungary, Poland, and Romania remained under Soviet influence until towards the end of 1989.[12] Most of these countries had become industrialized before World War II, but increasingly their industrial output came under the central planning system and was traded mainly within the Soviet trading bloc, the Council for Mutual Economic Assistance (CMEA or Comecon as it was known in the West). The central planning system was effective in mobilizing resources to meet the priorities of the state, but the communist years left a legacy of inefficient work practices, over-manning (or hidden unemployment), poor productivity, the use of outdated technology, and, in some cases, recurring shortages of basic consumer goods (which encouraged the growth of black markets). State price controls kept energy, housing, and other living costs low, allowing the citizens of these countries to live comfortably even on relatively low wages, but encouraged inefficient energy use with harmful consequences for the natural environment. The lack of convertible currencies also made it difficult for them to obtain hard currency to buy imported goods. These problems, combined with slow economic growth and declining relative living standards, left these countries well behind most of their Western European counterparts in economic terms by the late 1980s.

The collapse of the communist governments and central planning systems in the Soviet bloc between late 1989 and 1991 initiated a long process of political, economic, and social reform. The transition process was quicker and more enthusiastically embraced in Czechoslovakia, Hungary, and Poland than it was in Bulgaria, Romania, and many of the former Soviet republics. In Russia itself, change occurred relatively quickly but somewhat chaotically under Boris Yeltsin's leadership. In general, there was greater public acceptance of change in Czechoslovakia, Hungary, and Poland, which had experienced less hard-line communist leadership and where Soviet domination had been periodically challenged.[13] These countries set about privatizing their state enterprises and liberalizing their domestic economies and external trade in the early 1990s, though they experienced a painful period of declining economic growth, high inflation, rising unemployment, and industrial restructuring before their economies began to return to growth from 1994 onwards. In Russia, Ukraine, Bulgaria, and Romania, the problems were more prolonged and public acceptance was more variable. In some former Soviet states, notably in Belarus, political resistance to change has been a major obstacle. Even where reforms have been pursued vigorously and with reasonable success, the transition has involved major economic and social upheaval, creating divisions between those who have exploited the new business opportunities and those who remain on low fixed incomes or have become unemployed.

Significant business development has occurred in sectors such as banking, retailing, and construction, alongside the decline of traditional manufacturing industries. The EU, the European Bank for Reconstruction and Development (EBRD), and foreign investors have brought significant amounts of North American, Western European, and Asian capital into the region. Foreign direct investment (FDI) has, unsurprisingly, been attracted more to west-leaning, pro-reform countries than to those where the political climate is more antagonistic towards western business and the economic nuisance costs are higher. For example, the cumulative FDI inward stock in Poland in 2011 was $198 billion, whereas the corresponding figure for Ukraine was $65 billion and for Belarus only $13 billion, though Poland's attractiveness was clearly helped by its EU membership. Russia, on the other hand, which had attracted slightly less inward FDI than Poland by 2000, had received inward FDI stock of $457 billion by 2011 – a figure achieved mainly as a result of large investments in Russia's oil and gas industries.[14] However, these investments have come under increasing pressure from President Putin, who is keen to repatriate the ownership of Russia's energy sector. Over the next few years, the political and economic differences between the former communist countries which have joined the EU and those which have not are likely to become more marked.

12.4 The future of European capitalism

The continental European economies have built their post-war success on their own particular version of capitalism. This has been variously described by labels such as the 'Rhine model', the social market model, or simply the European model. Numerous variants of the model can be identified in different parts of Europe (see Section 6.6.3), but the dominant characteristic of the European variety of capitalism is the way in which the political and legal institutions create a framework of social protection for consumers, employees, producers, and the economy as whole. The degree of social protection varies in different countries and at different times, but in most European countries there has been, and arguably remains, a broad consensus in support of the social market economy.

This social consensus has increasingly been challenged by business leaders keen to reduce production costs and taxes in the competitive global environment and by centre-right politicians keen to improve economic performance and the public finances. The social protection afforded to workers in countries such as France, Germany, the Netherlands, and in Scandinavia has provided job and income security for employees and low labour turnover for employers, but has increased non-wage labour costs and reduced flexibility for both employers and job seekers. In difficult economic times and competitive global markets, high labour costs and inflexible employment practices become a burden for businesses, especially when US, British, and other competitors operate under more flexible conditions. Protection for consumers, businesses, and an economy can also create problems. These forms of protection may restrict competition, for example by excessive regulation of price promotions or sheltering poorly performing companies from the rigours of the takeover market.

Flexibility, however, is not only about giving organizations more freedom to compete in goods and labour markets. It is also about workers having flexible skills and organizations having teams of workers that are able to respond flexibly to new developments and come up with innovative ideas. Indeed, one of the strengths of the mainstream European economies is their ability to produce reliable, high-quality goods and services using well-qualified, established, and productive teams and the latest advanced technology. Provided consumers are willing to pay high prices for high-quality products, there may still be a viable future for European firms in a competitive market. However, this still leaves the issue of regulation. Regulation can, of course, help to ensure the quality of a product or fair competition, but it can create a market entry barrier or otherwise restrict competition. Europe's highly regulated labour markets may provide long-term security for those in work, but they may also make it difficult for those trying to find work. Countries such as the Netherlands, Sweden, and Germany have all introduced reforms in recent years to make their labour markets less tightly regulated. The tensions between public expectations and business concerns, on the one hand, and between cost competitiveness and expensive but reliable products, on the other hand, suggest that this debate has not yet run its course.

12.5 European enigmas

12.5.1 Creativity and destructiveness

European development, whether in the political, economic, or social sphere, presents a number of enigmas. Europeans have pioneered democracy since its origin in ancient Greece, they have achieved sustained economic development following the British industrial revolution, and they have created masterpieces of art, literature, and music through the works of da Vinci, Shakespeare, Bach, and many others. European creativity in these fields is unsurpassed at an international level. Yet this creativity has to be juxtaposed with centuries of destructiveness in the form of war and barbarism. Of course, wars have not been a uniquely European preoccupation, but the two world wars of the twentieth century had their origins and centre of gravity in Europe. Indeed, the first half of the twentieth century was without doubt one of the most devastating periods in human history. These extremes of creativity and destructiveness are difficult to reconcile, but they serve as a reminder to us of the fragility of human endeavour. In this context, it is difficult to reach any other conclusion than that political cooperation is preferable to conflict. The period of peace most of Europe has enjoyed since 1945 and the improved relations between Eastern and Western Europe since 1989 clearly demonstrate this maxim. Political stability is also beneficial for economic relations between countries and is undoubtedly good for business.

12.5.2 Unity and diversity

Europe represents a highly diverse group of people culturally and linguistically. This is of course, to some extent, also true of the United States, but the cultural and linguistic differences are more distinct and there is generally less political cohesion in Europe than in the US. This makes cooperation in the EU more difficult and has been a contributing factor to many of the conflicts Europe has experienced in the recent and more distant past. Yet this diversity has given Europe a rich cultural heritage and many distinctive characteristics in its people and products. The combination of unity and diversity that the EU represents is another of the European enigmas. At times, EU decision makers have allowed their understandable desire for common product standards to mislead them into believing that the products themselves need to be standardized. This led to a plethora of regulations on the shape and size of fruit and vegetables, often the butt of jokes about the EU. Sometimes, of course, consumers themselves seem to want 'perfect' products, or supermarkets think they do, but the EU has recently decided to repeal some of these unnecessary regulations, recognizing that product standards do not necessarily mean that everything has to be the same.

12.5.3 **European secularization in a religious world**

Finally, one more of the many European enigmas is the way in which mainstream Europe has become increasingly secular while much of the world is still deeply religious. Of course, this is not universally true as evangelical Christianity and, more especially, Islam have become more influential in recent years. Nor was it true in the past as Europe played a significant role in the development of Christianity, notably the formation of the Roman Catholic Church in the first century AD and the Protestant Reformation in the sixteenth century. In recent times, however, the Christian influence on politics and society in Europe has generally been in decline. This is in sharp contrast to the resurgent influence of Islam on politics, law, and business in Asia, the Middle East, and Africa, the political influence of Roman Catholicism in South America, and the spread of evangelical Christianity in much of sub-Saharan Africa. Europeans have tended to downplay these religious movements, arguing that education and affluence free people from the need for religious beliefs. Yet Muslim, Hindu, Sikh, Jewish, and other religious intellectuals and business professionals generally place no such restrictions on the role of religion, and political leaders in the United States make a public demonstration of their Christian beliefs. European secularization is therefore untypical, even in the modern consumer age, and political and business leaders need to be aware of this contrasting picture in their international political and economic relations.

Emerging scenario: Europe coming of age

One of the biggest challenges facing Europe in the twenty-first century can be found on its eastern fringe, from Russia in the north-east to the Balkans and Turkey in the south-east. Many of the countries that make up these regions were communist republics in the former Soviet Union or Yugoslavia and they have generally followed a more difficult path to market democracy than their Baltic and Central European neighbours who have been joining the EU and NATO. Russia revived its fortunes in the early 2000s after economic and political upheaval in the 1990s by returning to a more authoritarian style of leadership under President (and for a time Prime Minister) Putin.

Some of Russia's European neighbours have also found it difficult to adjust to the post-communist era. Belarus's President Lukashenko has steered his country along an even more authoritarian course, scarcely embracing reform and maintaining the country's ties with Russia and the CIS rather than looking westwards. Tensions between Ukraine's ethnic Ukrainian and Russian populations came to a head during the 'Orange Revolution' towards the end of 2004 and the beginning of 2005, when the west-leaning Viktor Yushchenko narrowly defeated his pro-Russian rival, Viktor Yanukovych, surviving both election irregularities and an attempt to poison him. Political tensions between these rival groups have continued since then, with Yanukovych becoming president in 2010. Disputes between Russia and its neighbours led to military conflict with Georgia over the disputed territories of South Ossetia and Abkhazia in August 2008 and the periodic withdrawal of gas supplies to Ukraine between 2005 and 2009.

Further south the Balkan region has presented the greatest challenge to Europe and the international agencies. Even after the conflict in the former Yugoslavia in the 1990s, tensions remain between the tapestry of ethnic groups left by centuries of foreign occupation. This issue was highlighted by questions over the EU's insistence that alleged war criminals, including Radovan Karadžić and Ratko Mladić, should be brought to justice before Serbia could be considered for EU membership.[15]

Turkey is the other main EU neighbour where political tensions have held back EU membership – in Turkey's case a membership application dating back to 1987. Tensions between Turkey, Greece, and

Cyprus over the disputed territory of Northern Cyprus need to be resolved before Turkey accedes to the EU. Some EU member states also have reservations about Turkish membership in relation to other political and human rights issues. Despite these difficulties and Turkey's location across the boundary between Europe and Asia, Turkey has long been a western ally and has a customs union with the EU. It is also a member of the Council of Europe, the Organization for Security and Co-operation in Europe (OSCE), and NATO.

The issue for Europe, and for the EU in particular, is whether it has come of age in being able to bury these differences and build a more harmonious future. After all, virtually every European country has its own 'skeletons in the cupboard'. The question is whether Europeans can learn the harsh lessons from their past without allowing the disputes of the past to dominate the future.

Emerging scenario discussion questions

1. How far should the EU expand to incorporate its eastern and south-eastern neighbours?

2. Should the EU try to build political and economic bridges with Russia and other former Soviet republics along its eastern border?

3. Should the EU set aside its reservations and speed up the process of accepting Turkey as a full member?

4. What are the business implications of continuing tensions in Eastern and South-Eastern Europe?

5. Outline the most likely scenario for the development of relations between the EU and its eastern and south-eastern neighbours over the next ten to twenty years.

Notes

1. The 15 former Soviet republics are: Armenia, Azerbaijan, Belarus, Georgia, Estonia, Kazakhstan, Kyrgyzstan, Latvia, Lithuania, Moldova, Russia, Tajikistan, Turkmenistan, Ukraine, and Uzbekistan.

2. The former Yugoslav republics are: Bosnia and Herzegovina, Croatia, Macedonia (also known as FYR (i.e. Former Yugoslav Republic of) Macedonia), Montenegro, Serbia, and Slovenia; Kosovo declared independence from Serbia in February 2008, but to date has only received partial international recognition. Although a single unified state, Bosnia and Herzegovina is divided into two semi-autonomous regions: the Federation of Bosnia and Herzegovina and the Bosnian Serb Republic (Republika Srpska).

3. EU member states in mid-2013 were: Austria, Belgium, Bulgaria, Croatia, Cyprus, Czech Republic, Denmark, Estonia, Finland, France, Germany, Greece, Hungary, Ireland, Italy, Latvia, Lithuania, Luxembourg, Malta, Netherlands, Poland, Portugal, Romania, Slovakia, Slovenia, Spain, Sweden, and the United Kingdom.

4. Croatia became a member on 1 July 2013. Switzerland also applied for EU membership in 1992, but its application is 'on ice' because the Swiss people have voted against membership; Switzerland has, however, agreed a number of bilateral treaties with the EU on trade, security, and other issues.

5. WTO, *International Trade Statistics*, 2012, tables I.7, I.9, I.13, and I.15, pp. 26, 28, 32, and 34.

6. CIA, *World Factbook*, 2012, on a purchasing power parity (PPP) basis.

7. The ECSC was established by the Treaty of Paris, at least in part, to lock together Europe's key source of power (coal) and the main raw material of its manufacturing industries (steel) in order to prevent these industries being used to fight another war. The main Treaty of Rome, which established the EEC, states in its preamble its intention 'to lay the foundations of an ever closer union among the peoples of Europe'.

8. CIA, *World Factbook*, 2013; the North American Free Trade Agreement (NAFTA) is, however, the largest free trade area, by value, with a combined GDP of almost $19 trillion.

9. Mundell, R. A. (1961), 'The Theory of Optimum Currency Areas', *American Economic Review*, vol. 51, pp. 657–65.

10. The value of the euro fell from a monthly average of €1 = $1.49 in November 2009 to €1 = $1.22 in June 2010 during the initial phase of Greece's debt crisis.

11. The original six member states of the EU in 1958 were France, West Germany, Italy, Belgium, Netherlands, and Luxembourg; enlargements have been as follows: Denmark, Ireland, and the UK (1973); Greece (1981); Portugal and Spain (1986); Austria, Finland, and Sweden (1995); Cyprus, Czech Republic, Estonia, Hungary, Latvia, Lithuania, Malta, Poland, Slovakia, and Slovenia (2004); Bulgaria and Romania (2007); and Croatia (2013). Greenland also entered the EU under Danish sovereignty in 1973 but left after a referendum in 1985, and the former East Germany was integrated into the EU after German unification in 1990.

12. Yugoslavia and Albania had also originally come under Soviet influence, but later became non-aligned communist states outside the Soviet Warsaw Pact alliance.

13. Notable examples of resistance to Soviet domination were the Hungarian Uprising of 1956 and the 'Prague Spring' of 1968, both of which were ultimately quashed by Soviet forces.

14. UNCTAD, *World Investment Report*, 2012, Annex table I.2, pp. 173–6.

15. As at 22 March 2013, Karadžić and Mladić were still on trial at the International Criminal Tribunal in The Hague.

Suggestions for further reading

On the European Union, single market, and single currency

El Agraa, A. M. (2011), *The European Union: Economics and Policies*, Cambridge University Press

McCormick, J. (2011), *Understanding the European Union: A Concise Introduction*, Palgrave Macmillan

On transition in Central and Eastern Europe

Artis, M., Banerjee, A., and Marcellino, M. (2010), *Economic Transition in Central and Eastern Europe: Planting the Seeds*, Cambridge University Press

Bideleux, R., and Jeffries, I. (2007), *A History of Eastern Europe: Crisis and Change*, Routledge

For those who want to delve more deeply into European history

Merriman, J. (2009), *A History of Modern Europe: Volumes 1 and 2*, W. W. Norton and Co.

Take your learning further: Online Resource Centre
http://www.oxfordtextbooks.co.uk/orc/harrison2e/
Visit the Online Resource Centre that accompanies this book to enrich your understanding of Chapter 12: Europe: Unification, Crisis, and Beyond. Among other resources explore web links and keep up to date with the latest developments in the area.

13 Contrasting Developments in the Americas

◉ Chapter learning outcomes

On completion of this chapter the reader should be able to:

● Appreciate the major geopolitical and related developments which have taken place in North, South, and Central America in recent years

● Evaluate the main implications of these developments for business organizations

13.1 The US economy, the US dollar, and the world economy

By any measure, the United States economy is the largest national economy in the world.[1] It has held this position since overtaking China in the 1880s.[2] This dominant position and the commensurate influence of the United States in world affairs have given rise to the description of the twentieth century as the 'American Century'. It is possible that China will reassert its position as the world's largest economy in the next decade or two, but US influence is likely to continue well beyond this point. After a relatively lean period when the star performers were Germany in the 1960s and Japan in the 1970s and 1980s, the US economy re-emerged to achieve average annual growth in gross domestic product (GDP) per capita of 1.74 per cent from 1990 to 2003.[3] This was significant for two main reasons: first, because the economic boom was sustained throughout the 1990s and, secondly, because it was made possible by significant improvements in productivity. During this period the US also reasserted its technological lead over Japan. Although still outperforming Japan, the US economy has performed less well since 2000, especially during and after the 2008–9 international financial crisis and economic downturn that started in the US sub-prime mortgage market.

Throughout the post-World War II period the US dollar has been the dominant currency in international trade. It has also been used as an international currency for commodities like crude oil and is the major reserve currency held by central banks around the world. However, the US appetite for imports has far exceeded the country's ability to export in recent years, leaving the US economy with a huge balance of trade deficit. Many of the imports have been supplied by low-cost producers in China and other parts of Asia. This has left Asian central banks with large US dollar reserves, some of which have been used to invest in US bonds, allowing the US economy to attract sufficient capital to offset its trade deficit. This situation was acceptable while the US economy was growing rapidly, but has become more of a problem as economic growth has slowed down. As a result of the trade imbalance and weak US economy, the US dollar gradually weakened against the euro and other major currencies during the 2000s, falling from a monthly average of $1 = €1.13 in January 2002 to $1 = €0.63 by July 2008. The dollar's decline

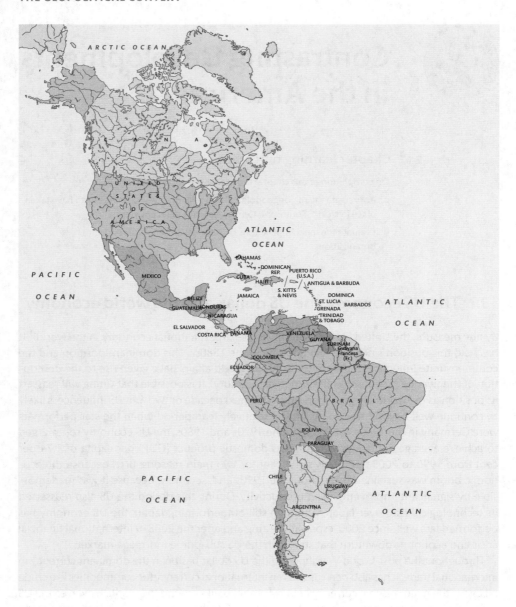

led to questions about its future as a reserve currency, though problems in the eurozone and the weaknesses of the European economies have allowed the dollar to recover a little since then.

Despite the US having the largest national economy, the value of US merchandise exports slipped into second position behind Germany in 2003, into third position behind Germany and China in 2007, with China taking over the lead in 2009.[4] Taking account of the relative size of these three economies, US merchandise exports as a proportion of GDP are relatively small compared to those of Germany and China. This may be partly explained by the size of the US domestic market, which allows even relatively large US multinational enterprises (MNEs) to conduct a significant proportion of their business in the home market.

Nevertheless, when comparing the similar-sized economies of the US and EU, the value of extra-EU merchandise exports was 44 per cent higher than for the US in 2011, representing 14.9 and 8.1 per cent of world merchandise exports respectively.[5] When it comes to foreign direct investment (FDI) the picture is somewhat different. The US is still the world's main outward investor and recipient of inward investment, with cumulative outward FDI stock 160 per cent higher and inward FDI stock 90 per cent higher than its closest rivals, the UK and China (including Hong Kong) respectively by 2011.[6] This position may well change in the coming years if China's economy continues to develop rapidly and becomes the favoured location for FDI.

13.2 US hegemony in international affairs

US economic influence also extends to the policies of a variety of international organizations ranging from the United Nations (UN) to the World Trade Organization (WTO). It is also the world's leading military power. During the cold war years, US military power was constrained by the balance of power with the Soviet Union, though the Soviet Union generally played a much smaller role in world economic affairs beyond its immediate sphere of influence in Eastern Europe. After the break-up of the Soviet Union in 1991, the end of the bipolar world left the US as the world's only 'superpower', though China is now becoming a more prominent world power. Whilst superpower status may seem desirable from a US perspective, it has created at least as many problems as benefits for the US in practice. As well as allowing the US administration to exert its influence in places like Afghanistan and Iraq, it has also imposed a heavy burden on the US in its assumed role as the world's 'policeman'. This role has added huge expense to the US national budget and the foreign policy agenda has inevitably distracted US presidents from domestic issues.

The US president is still expected to take a lead in trying to solve the world's problems, but it is likely that US influence in the world will gradually diminish as economic and political power is dispersed around an increasingly bipolar or multipolar world. This is not to say that US dominance is likely to disappear in the near future, but rather that the US will find it increasingly difficult to resolve world problems without the support of other nations such as China, Russia, and India, or regional groupings such as the EU or BRIC. For the time being, however, US influence in setting the world economic policy agenda is likely to continue, even if the Washington free-market consensus is diluted. Pressure for protectionist trade policies has been evident since the world economic downturn, but the vested interests of the major trading nations in maintaining a relatively open international trading environment may yet prevail as the world economy revives. This revival may, however, accelerate progress towards a multipolar world if China and other emerging nations manage to sustain a higher level of economic growth than the major developed economies.

13.3 NAFTA and prospects for inter-American free trade

The North American Free Trade Agreement (NAFTA) came into effect on 1 January 1994. It built on the earlier Canada United States Free Trade Agreement, effective from 1988, by extending the agreement to Mexico. NAFTA is essentially a tariff-free area, though it also removes investment restrictions and contains measures to protect labour and the environ-ment. It is now the largest fully operational free trade area in the world, with tariffs and a number of other trade barriers being removed by 2008, but it has not created the deeper kind of economic and political integration that exists in the EU. Opinions on the impact of NAFTA are varied. On the one hand, trade between the US, Canada, and Mexico has increased significantly since NAFTA was formed. Each of the three member states has also experienced a net increase in employment, though in the US case employment in the manu-facturing sector has been declining relative to the service sector. Opponents of NAFTA have attributed this decline in manufacturing employment to the southward drift of manufactur-ing industry to lower-cost Mexico. Indeed, a number of US firms have relocated to become *maquiladora* businesses close to Mexico's border with the US; these firms import duty-free materials from the US, assemble or manufacture their products in Mexico, then re-export them to the US market.

Like many of the world's developed economies, the United States would almost cer-tainly have suffered declining employment in manufacturing even if it had not been part of NAFTA, given the general shift of traditional manufacturing industry to Asia and other emerging economies. The early years of NAFTA in the 1990s also coincided with a period of significant economic growth in the US, though opponents have suggested that the wages of US workers have been depressed by downward pressure from wages in neighbouring Mexico. On a more positive note, Mexico's economic development appears to have ben-efited considerably from trade with the US and, to a lesser extent, Canada. The arguments about NAFTA became a contentious issue during the 2008 US presidential election cam-paign, with Democratic candidates taking the side of workers and trade unions aggrieved at the loss of manufacturing jobs; indeed, Hillary Clinton found herself in the invidious position of opposing the free trade agreement her husband, former President Bill Clinton, had cham-pioned. However, in early 2013, President Obama began his second term by promoting free trade when he endorsed the idea of a transatlantic trade and investment partnership between the USA and EU.[7]

Almost as soon as NAFTA came into operation, the US administration started to push for trade agreements with its neighbours in Central and South America and the Caribbean, and the concept of a Free Trade Area of the Americas (FTAA) was born. Whilst there was fairly widespread initial support for this plan, the idea gradually foundered because of concerns over NAFTA and fears that it was simply an attempt by the United States to extend its influ-ence in Latin America. This latter concern has been expressed by some of the Latin American countries most opposed to the United States, notably Venezuela and Bolivia, though Brazil, Latin America's largest country, has also expressed doubts. The United States has now turned its attention towards creating bilateral trade agreements with individual countries or groups of willing states, notably the Central American–Dominican Republic Free Trade Agreement (CAFTA–DR) between the US, Costa Rica, the Dominican Republic, El Salvador, Guatemala, Honduras, and Nicaragua, which is gradually removing trade and investment barriers be-tween these countries' predominantly agricultural industries and the United States. Bilateral free trade agreements also exist between the US and various individual Latin American coun-tries, including Chile, Colombia, and Peru. However, such agreements link together countries whose economies are very different in size and structure, so it is probably more accurate to see them as trading agreements rather than regional economic groupings.[8]

13.4 Regional integration in South America, Central America, and the Caribbean

The failure to create a free trade area of the Americas has not dampened the enthusiasm for integration between the countries of Latin America. Indeed, formal regional economic groupings have existed in Latin America since the 1960s. The most significant grouping is now Mercosur, Spanish for 'common market of the south' (Mercosul in Portuguese). Mercosur's members include Argentina, Brazil, Paraguay, Uruguay, and Venezuela,[9] which together make up over 70 per cent of the GDP of South America.[10] Mercosur has established a customs union and is in the process of creating a common market involving the free movement of goods, services, people, and capital, though a dispute between Paraguay and the other members is currently holding back developments. Mercosur has been moving towards deeper economic integration, though its coordinating institutions and policies are still relatively underdeveloped and the path to free trade has been hampered by periodic disagreements between its members.

The other main regional economic grouping in South America is the Andean Community (formerly Andean Pact), which has also created a customs union and includes Bolivia, Colombia, Ecuador, and Peru. Although older than Mercosur, the Andean Community is a much smaller economic area, but both the Andean Community and Mercosur belong to the Union of South American Nations, whose eventual aim is to establish an economic and political community similar to the EU.

The countries of Central America have also attempted to achieve economic integration, initially through the Central American Common Market (CACM). Like the Andean Community, the CACM is a customs union and dates from the 1960s, though it was effectively dissolved during the difficult years of war and political unrest in the region in the 1970s and 1980s. Attempts have been made to revive the CACM and Central American integration more generally since the early 1990s, with the most significant development being the creation of the overarching Central American Integration System (SICA) and CAFTA–DR (see Section 13.3).[11]

The other significant regional economic grouping in the Americas is the Caribbean Community (Caricom), which is in the process of establishing a common market or 'single market and economy' as it is known, among its 15 member states.[12] Despite a number of difficult issues and faltering progress, this patchwork of regional integration in the southern half of the American hemisphere has achieved some success in increasing trade, FDI, and economic growth, and demonstrates a commitment to cooperation in a region that has more often been associated with political and economic problems.

13.5 A new dawn for Latin America?

13.5.1 'Neo-liberalism' and the socialist backlash in Latin America

After centuries of political dependence on its colonial and neo-colonial masters (see Section 6.6.5) and economic dependence on agricultural commodities, Latin America began to develop its industrial capacity from the 1930s onwards. Industrialization was achieved largely through a policy of trade protection and import substitution, though after initial successes the region's economic growth was beginning to slow down by the 1960s. This was followed by large-scale public investment to promote the transition from import substitution to the export of manufactured goods during the late 1960s and 1970s. The new policy approach achieved significant success but was funded largely through international loans. This left the region heavily indebted and prone to hyperinflation, currency depreciation, and financial crises, notably the Mexican debt crisis of 1982 which rapidly spread to most of the other Latin American countries. Chile had responded to its growing debt problems by pioneering free-market reforms under its military president, General Pinochet, from 1973 onwards, though it was not immune to the debt crisis. The debt crisis throughout the region was managed by the IMF, which insisted on 'structural adjustment policies' in return for financial support. Financial instability was accompanied by a return to dictatorship and the spread of free-market policies throughout much of Latin America during the 1980s, policies which are often described – usually disparagingly – as 'neo-liberalism'.

Neo-liberalism in Latin America has now largely replaced the more interventionist policies of the period from the 1930s to the 1970s. The neo-liberal approach has been reinforced by the prevailing view in the USA and UK, especially since President Reagan and Prime Minister Thatcher in the 1980s, and by the Washington consensus that has prevailed at the IMF and WTO since then. It involves policies such as a balanced budget, often requiring large reductions in government expenditure, privatization, trade liberalization, and the encouragement of competition in domestic markets. These ideas are built on the classical 'liberalism' of economists in the tradition of Adam Smith, but they are also associated with conservative policies on the role of government and the need for individual responsibility. Whilst the region's dictators have now largely been replaced by democracies, neo-liberalism has in many cases survived the political transition, but its legacy has been the subject of much debate. On the one hand, it has helped to reinvigorate economic growth and has made some of the region's countries more attractive to inward investors. On the other hand, some of the less industrialized countries have returned to dependence on basic commodities and, in most cases, the gap between rich and poor has widened. Unemployment has also risen and Latin America continues to suffer from relatively high inflation and recurring financial crises.

President Hugo Chávez of Venezuela (1999–2013), a country heavily dependent on its oil reserves, led opposition to neo-liberalism in Latin America. Not only did President Chávez pursue a policy of socialism and nationalization at home, he also helped to deflect attention away from the US-inspired FTAA to form the Bolivarian Alternative for the Americas (now Bolivarian Alliance of the Americas) – a socialist orientated rather than neo-liberal regional grouping.[13] Whilst it is unclear what this grouping will achieve in practice, especially since the death of President Chavez in March 2013, it represents a backlash against both the policy of neo-liberalism and perceived US imperialism in Latin America. It is also noteworthy that China has increased its presence in countries such as Venezuela and Bolivia, which have valuable natural resources as well as like-minded political regimes. Many observers regard neo-liberalism as a failed policy because of the legacy of economic and social problems in Latin America. However, many of these problems have a long history and, as in Central and Eastern Europe, neo-liberalism could equally be regarded as a necessary but painful step along the difficult road to economic development.

13.5.2 Religion and politics in Latin America

Latin America has inherited its dominant religion as well as its languages from its former colonial powers. About 70 per cent of people in the region describe themselves as Catholic, though this includes 'cultural catholics', who observe religious festivals and traditions, as well as those with a more active faith.[14] Catholic bishops have long held influence with politicians and governments in the region because of the size and importance of the Roman Catholic Church and its influence in the fields of health care and education and in the lives of ordinary citizens. Even at a local level, priests and other church officials often exercise considerable influence in social and political affairs. As social divisions began to increase during Latin America's industrialization phase, 'liberation theology' began to take root among certain groups of Catholics – a radical form of Catholicism which emphasized social justice for the poor. Liberation theology became quite influential, especially in the 1960s and 1970s, and whilst actively discouraged by the Catholic Church hierarchy, has been instrumental in raising the profile and tackling some of the problems of the region's poor and persecuted. A number of evangelical Protestant churches have also sprung up since the 1960s and especially since 1980. These churches are often based in the poorer communities and are well established in countries like Guatemala, Honduras, El Salvador, Brazil, and Chile.[15] The Protestant churches tend to have more influence among local communities than at the national level, but together the various Christian denominations continue to have a significant influence on politics and the lives of ordinary people in Latin America.

13.5.3 Challenges facing Latin American society

Latin America's turbulent history has left a litany of problems in its wake. The military dictatorships and other authoritarian regimes that dominated the region's politics from the 1960s to the 1980s, or in some cases the 1990s, often exercised repressive control over their citizens, leaving physical and emotional scars that will take a long time to heal. Some of Latin America's economies have benefited from the economic reforms, but the gap between rich and poor has grown wider. Unemployment is particularly high in many countries in the region and there are high levels of crime, corruption, and social instability. Brazil's economic revival, which has attracted renewed FDI since the 1990s, provides a stark contrast with the poverty of those living in the *favelas* of downtown Sao Paulo or Rio de Janeiro. Industrialization has also left its mark on the natural environment with the destruction of some of the world's most extensive rainforests. In Colombia and its neighbouring countries in the Andean region, drug trafficking is a major problem. The drug trade has been accompanied by the destabilizing effect of the drug cartels and drug barons on the economies and governments of the region. Governments also continue to be confronted by the activities of paramilitary guerrilla groups, notably the Revolutionary Armed Forces in Colombia (known as FARC) and the Zapatista Army of National Liberation (known as the Zapatistas) in southern Mexico. It is likely that these problems will continue to act as a brake on Latin America's social and economic development for the foreseeable future.

13.5.4 Future prospects for Latin America

It is easy to be pessimistic about the future prospects for Latin America. Despite two hundred years of independence, the countries of Latin America remain economically dependent on their export earnings from commodities like oil and coffee, on the financial support of the IMF, and in varying degrees on the patronage of the United States. Social deprivation is a harsh reality for many people and the potential for authoritarian rule never seems very far from the surface. However, democracy is now established throughout the region and, notwithstanding periodic financial crises, signs of economic progress are becoming clearer. Perhaps the most promising developments have been in Latin America's two largest emerging economies, Brazil and Mexico, and the growth of regional integration, notably Latin America's most influential economic grouping, Mercosur. Although a free trade area of the Americas seems unlikely to materialize in the near future, there seems to be considerable appetite both for intra-Latin American economic groupings and for trade links with the United States. To a greater extent than most other regions, the nations of Latin America have inherited many common concerns as a result of their shared histories, cultures, and religions. Of course, this has not prevented them from fighting wars with each other or pursuing different political or economic courses, but the issues they face give them common cause to pursue social and economic development together. This may be an unrealistic view, but it is one that at least offers the possibility of a more optimistic future.

Emerging scenario: Challenges to US dominance

A report produced by the US National Intelligence Council in December 2012 concluded that, by 2030, 'There will not be any hegemonic power. Power will shift to networks and coalitions in a multipolar world.'[16] The report suggests that China and India are the most likely contenders to increase their political and economic influence in this multipolar world. The report also argues that 'the diffusion of power ... will have a dramatic impact by 2030, largely reversing the historical rise of the West since 1750 and restoring Asia's weight in the global economy and world politics'.[17] This is not the first time that claims have been made about the impending decline of US influence in recent years,[18] but the fact that this view now appears to be held by the US security establishment carries greater significance. The report is not arguing that the United States will rapidly cease to be an influential player in world affairs, but that its power will be tempered by the growing influence of other nations with large populations and economies.

The prospect of a multipolar world raises the possibility that the Anglo-Saxon free-market model may become less dominant in the policies of the major international institutions. The position of the free-market model has already been challenged by anti-globalization protestors and critics of the IMF's structural adjustment policies, among others, but it has increasingly come under threat, not from ideological opponents, but because of the practical economic necessity of government intervention to support failing banks during the 2008–9 international financial crisis and recession and the eurozone sovereign-debt crisis that followed. If more active state intervention is also seen as a source of economic success in China, India, and other emerging economies, as it was in Japan, South Korea, Taiwan, and other East Asian economies until the beginning of the 1990s, the Anglo-Saxon model is likely to lose favour in the coming years. Declining support for the Anglo-Saxon model would inevitably weaken the influence of the United States over the policies of the IMF and WTO. Arguably, this scenario has become more likely since the international financial crisis as the US economy has struggled to recover from the economic downturn.

Of course, US dominance has been threatened in the recent past both by the political, military, and to a lesser extent, economic power of the Soviet Union until the early 1990s and by the economic and technological power of Japan during the 1970s and 1980s. In reality, Soviet economic power was never really a threat to the United States owing to the vastly superior performance of the US economy, especially during the latter years of the Soviet Union's existence. The Japanese economy became, in many ways, much more of a challenge to the United States, with its significant technological capability and successful multinational companies. However, even without Japan's prolonged economic downturn since the 1990s, it is doubtful whether Japan is a large enough country for its economy to be able to overtake the US economy, let alone for Japan to become a serious challenger to US political dominance. China, on the other hand, is a different story. It clearly has the size and, if its economy continues to expand at a rate anywhere close to its recent performance, it is not only likely but almost inevitable that the Chinese economy will, in due course, recover its historical position as the largest economy in the world. Whether having the largest economy will necessarily mean that China carries the most political and economic influence is another matter.

Emerging scenario discussion questions

1. What factors are likely to contribute towards a relative decline in US world influence in the coming years?

2. To what extent do you think this decline is inevitable?

3. Do you agree that China and India are the countries most likely to challenge US dominance in the near future?

4. What are likely to be the business implications of a change to a multipolar world and the restoration of 'Asia's weight in the global economy and world politics'?

5. Outline the most likely scenario for the changing role of the United States over the next ten to twenty years.

Notes

1. US GDP on a purchasing power parity (PPP) basis was estimated to be $15.66 trillion in 2012; its nearest rival on this basis was China with $12.38 trillion. Source: CIA, *World Factbook*, 2013.

2. See Maddison, A. (2007), *Contours of the World Economy, 1–2030 AD*, Oxford University Press, figure 3.5, p. 158.

3. This compares with an annual GDP per capita growth rate of 1.42 per cent for Germany and 0.94 per cent for Japan over the same period (based on 1990 international dollars, i.e. PPP exchange rates adjusted for inflation). Source: Maddison, A. (2007), *Contours of the World Economy, 1–2030 AD*, Oxford University Press, table 7.5, p. 339.

4. WTO, *International Trade Statistics*, 2004–12.

5. WTO, *International Trade Statistics*, 2012.

6. UNCTAD, *World Investment Report*, 2012, Annex table I.2, pp. 173–6.

7. See Baucus, M. (3 March 2013), 'Transatlantic trade deal is a US priority', *Financial Times*.

8. The combined GDP of the Central American and Caribbean members of CAFTA-DR in 2012, for example, represented just over 2% of US GDP on a purchasing power parity basis; source: CIA, *World Factbook*, 2013.

9. Paraguay's membership was suspended over a political dispute in June 2012, leaving the way open for Venezuela to become a full member in July 2012; Bolivia was also in the process of becoming a member in early 2013.

10. Source: CIA, *World Factbook*, 2013.

11. The member states of CACM were originally Costa Rica, El Salvador, Guatemala, Honduras, and Nicaragua, but the Central American Integration System now also includes the other two countries of Central America, Belize and Panama, as well as the Dominican Republic as an associate member.

12. The member states of Caricom include Antigua and Barbuda, the Bahamas, Barbados, Belize, Dominica, Grenada, Guyana, Haiti, Jamaica, Montserrat, Saint Lucia, St Kitts and Nevis, St Vincent and the Grenadines, Suriname, and Trinidad and Tobago.

13. The Bolivarian Alliance of the Americas (ALBA in Spanish) is so called after Simón Bolívar, a hero of the struggle for independence from Spanish colonial rule in the early nineteenth century; it was created by Venezuela and Cuba, though its members now also include Antigua and Barbuda, Bolivia, Dominica, Ecuador, Nicaragua, and St Vincent and the Grenadines.

14. Hillman, R. S., and D'Agostino, T. J. (2011), *Understanding Contemporary Latin America*, Lynne Rienner.

15. Hillman, R. S., and D'Agostino, T. J. (2011), *Understanding Contemporary Latin America*, Lynne Rienner.

16. US National Intelligence Council (December 2012), 'Global Trends 2030: Alternative Worlds', p. ii.

17. US National Intelligence Council (December 2012), 'Global Trends 2030: Alternative Worlds', p. 15.

18. For example, much debate followed the publication of Paul Kennedy's influential book, The Rise and Fall of the Great Powers, in which he argues that 'the United States now runs the risk, so familiar to historians of the rise and fall of previous Great Powers, of what might roughly be called "imperial overstretch"' (Kennedy, P. (1989), *The Rise and Fall of the Great Powers*, Fontana Press, pp. 665–6).

Suggestions for further reading

On developments in the United States

Peele, G., Bailey, C. J., Cain, B., and Peters, B. G. (2010), *Developments in American Politics 6*, Palgrave Macmillan

A practical guide to Latin American history

Green, D., and Branford, S. (2013), *Faces of Latin America*, Latin American Bureau

A more in-depth analysis of the issues facing Latin America

Hillman, R. S., and D'Agostino, T. J. (2011), *Understanding Contemporary Latin America*, Lynne Rienner

For those who want a broad overview of the history of the Americas

Fernandez-Armesto, F. (2004), *The Americas: A History of Two Continents*, Phoenix

 Take your learning further: Online Resource Centre
http://www.oxfordtextbooks.co.uk/orc/harrison2e/
Visit the Online Resource Centre that accompanies this book to enrich your understanding of Chapter 13: Contrasting Developments in the Americas. Among other resources explore web links and keep up to date with the latest developments in the area.

14 Asia's Economic Potential

 Chapter learning outcomes

On completion of this chapter the reader should be able to:

- Appreciate the major geopolitical and related developments which have taken place in Asia in recent years
- Evaluate the main implications of these developments for business organizations

14.1 Asia's political, economic, and cultural complexities

Asia is the largest and most populous continent and is almost certainly the most varied region of the world in geographical, political, economic, and cultural terms. Geographically, it stretches from Turkey and the 'Middle East' in the west to Japan in the east, and from Russian Siberia in the north to Sri Lanka in the south and Indonesia and East Timor in the south-east. It also encompasses a landscape ranging from the Himalayas, the world's highest mountain range, to the West Siberian Plain, over 50 per cent of which is less than 100 metres above sea level. Asia's political systems are scarcely less varied, including the world's major remaining communist states, China, Laos, North Korea, and Vietnam, the world's largest democracy, India, Myanmar's military dictatorship, and Iran's Islamic fundamentalist state, as well as a number of hybrid forms of government which encompass different elements of these systems. Similarly in economic terms, Asia has one of the world's most developed economies, Japan, some of the largest and fastest-growing economies, including China, India, and the economies of South-East Asia, resource-rich countries such as Saudi Arabia or Brunei, and also some of the world's least developed countries, including Afghanistan, Bangladesh, Bhutan, Cambodia, Laos, Myanmar, Nepal, and Yemen.[1]

Asia also possesses a vast cultural diversity. This can be seen in its ancient Chinese, Hindu, and Islamic civilizations and the philosophies and religious beliefs that underpin them. These civilizations also bear testimony to the many centuries of human development that are represented by modern nations like China and India. China has been responsible for inventions such as paper, printing, gunpowder, and a number of other scientific and medical discoveries. India has a tradition of scholarship in fields as diverse as astronomy, cartography, and mathematics. It is not therefore surprising that these traits are re-emerging in modern-day China's manufacturing prowess and India's expertise in information technology.

Of course, diversity is also a product of Asia's religious traditions and its colonial past. In recent times, religious differences have been the source of tension in various parts of Asia, notably between Arabs and Israelis in the Middle East, between Shi'a and Sunni Muslims in Iraq, and between Hindus, Muslims, and Christians in India and the border areas between

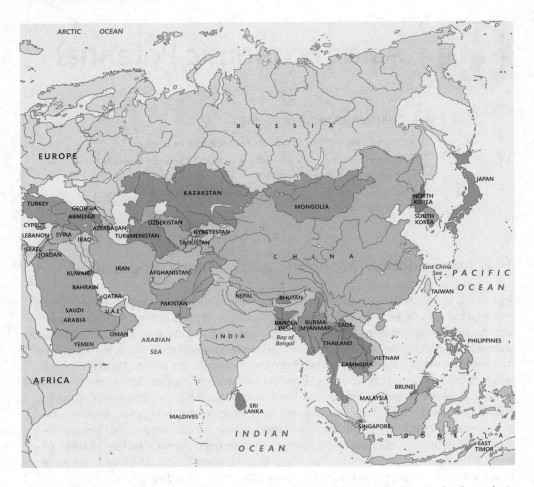

India and Pakistan. In places like Malaysia, where Malay, Chinese, Indian, and other ethnic groups live side by side, there is generally less overt cultural tension, though ethnic divisions are sometimes reflected in the type of work people do or their representation in public office. The influence of past colonial powers can be found in many parts of Asia, notably in the countries of former French Indochina (Cambodia, Laos, and Vietnam) and former British territories represented by present-day Hong Kong, India, Pakistan, Bangladesh, Myanmar, Malaysia, and Singapore. The legacy of US support for post-World War II development can also be found in countries like Japan, South Korea, and the Philippines.

Although more diverse culturally and economically than the world's other main emerging continent, Latin America, Asia has more obvious economic potential and is already a more significant player in world affairs. If economic growth continues as it has been doing in China, India, and South-East Asia, and the Japanese economy recovers something of its earlier success, the twenty-first century could well become the 'Asian century'. However, this prospect depends not only on the region's economic progress over the next few years, but also on the likelihood of political stability in the long term. In the Middle East and some of Asia's other troubled regions, political instability has been a major obstacle to progress. In China, stability has been maintained by tight political control. Whether and for how long state control can coexist with economic liberalism is a more open question. There are, of course, a number of more immediate difficulties that hold back economic and social development in Asia's poorest countries, which require sustained international effort to alleviate.

14.2 The rise and fall of Japan?

Japan was the first major Asian country to become a modern developed economy after 1945. It had in fact been a significant industrial and military power before World War II, but its rise to prominence as one of the so-called Triad nations (together with North America and Western Europe) came during the period from the 1950s to the 1980s. This was the period when companies like Toyota, Sony, and Mitsubishi became major international players and the Japanese or East Asian model (see Section 6.6.4) became the envy of western politicians and economists. Indeed, variants of the Japanese model have been adopted in several neighbouring countries, including South Korea, Taiwan, Malaysia, and Singapore. By the 1980s, Japan not only had recovered from military defeat in World War II and the devastation of the atomic bombs at Hiroshima and Nagasaki, but had graduated from being a technological adopter to a position of rivalry with the United States for technological leadership in sectors such as chemicals, electronics, and the automotive industry. Whilst Japan's more successful companies continued to achieve international success after the 1980s, the period since the early 1990s has been a time of sluggish economic growth, poor profitability, overcapacity, and periodic financial difficulties.[2] In fact, just as the Japanese economy was showing signs of returning to faster growth after almost two decades of lack-lustre performance, it was hit quite badly by the 2008–9 economic downturn.

Post-war Japanese industrial success was built on a combination of factors. Initially, Japan received considerable financial and other support from the United States to help rebuild its economy and public institutions during the period of US occupation from 1945 to 1952. The course taken by Japanese governments, however, has been much more interventionist than that followed by American governments during the post-war period as a whole. The Ministry of International Trade and Industry (MITI) was extremely influential in promoting the development of industries considered to be of strategic importance during Japan's rapid post-war economic development. At first, basic industries such as steel, petrochemicals, and shipbuilding were targeted, then attention turned towards the high-tech automotive and electronics industries. A variety of industrial policies have been used to encourage investment in these industries and later to encourage international expansion.[3] These policies have included import, foreign exchange, and inward investment restrictions, exemption from antitrust legislation, preferential tax treatment, public funds for research and development, extensive patent protection, and official encouragement of the provision of low-cost, preferential bank lending through the financial *keiretsu*.[4]

The financial *keiretsu* are groups or networks of companies headed by a major bank. Six main financial *keiretsu* have dominated Japanese business during the post-war years, four of which (Mitsui, Mitsubishi, Sumitomo, and Fuyo) are descended from pre-war *zaibatsu*, groups of companies most of whose shares were held by a common, family-owned holding company. The other two are Dai-Ichi Kangyo, which is an amalgamation of two smaller pre-war *zaibatsu*, and Sanwa, which was newly formed after the war. The financial *keiretsu*, or simply *keiretsu* as they are also known, often have cross-shareholdings in each other and provide a supportive network for their members, including the provision of finance on preferential terms. Despite the cooperative rather than competitive nature of these *keiretsu*, rival firms in the same industry sometimes belong to different *keiretsu*.[5] It should be noted that a number of other business groups are also referred to as *keiretsu*, including groups made up of a major company and its suppliers or distributors, sometimes known as vertical *keiretsu* to distinguish them from the more industrially diverse horizontal (financial) *keiretsu*. Some major companies, such as Toyota, are members of a financial *keiretsu*, as well as having their own vertical *keiretsu*. Although important during Japan's post-war economic development, the financial *keiretsu* have played a smaller role since their membership became more blurred after mergers between their leading banks during the 1990s economic slowdown. Some major companies like Nissan have also pursued a different course, leaving behind their *keiretsu* ties in favour of a joint venture with the French motor manufacturer, Renault.[6]

The *keiretsu* are examples of the close-knit relationships in Japanese society. These relationships can also be seen in the close links between government and business and between companies and their employees. The post-war Japanese tradition of lifetime employment for key workers with firm-specific skills, the provision by large companies of social, educational, and other benefits for their workers, and the low rate of labour turnover in Japanese companies all illustrate the importance of continuity of employment and loyalty between companies and their workforce. Together with Japan's protective industrial policies, this supportive environment helped to provide the capital, teamwork, and production chain necessary for the international expansion of Japanese companies in the 1970s and 1980s. Moreover, a key success of these firms was their ability to develop innovative business practices, including the emphasis on quality and continuous improvement (*kaizen*) and the *kanban* (signboard) stock control system, initiated by Toyota, which gives early warning of bottlenecks both in assembly-line production and in agreements with subcontractors. Stock control in relation to subcontractors, with whom Japanese companies traditionally have close ties, is also known as *just-in-time production* – a system which has now been adopted by many other manufacturing companies around the world.

Japan's financial system, along with those of Thailand, South Korea, Indonesia, and other countries in the region, was severely damaged by the Asian financial crisis of 1997–8, but Japan's prolonged economic stagnation during much of the 1990s and early 2000s suggests that the Japanese model has more fundamental weaknesses. Clearly, the supportive environment created by Japan's governments and close-knit business structure has been influential in the country's industrial success, particularly during the early years of post-war development, but they may also have distorted investment decisions, leading to excess capacity, high-cost long-term supply contracts, excessive corporate debt, and ultimately a misallocation of resources which caused favoured industries to over-expand and neglected industries such as agriculture and retailing to lag behind. Some of the above problems have been illustrated by companies like Nissan, which became heavily indebted before its joint venture with Renault in 1999 and has since been financially restructured under Renault's corporate control (see case study at the end of Chapter 6).

In addition to corporate restructuring, Japan has also been caught in a macroeconomic trap, with slow growth and low inflation, where even interest rates at close to zero per cent and a policy of quantitative easing have been unable to provide the necessary stimulus for economic expansion. The 2008–9 recession and the earthquake and tsunami of 2011 also made recovery more difficult, though Prime Minister Shinzo Abe's new government was elected on a platform of expansionary monetary and fiscal policy and structural reform in December 2012.[7] Provided Japan can return to a more sustainable economic model, the country's underlying strengths in technology and human capital suggest there is good reason to expect the country to retain its position as a major economy, albeit in a multipolar world economic system.

14.3 The Chinese phenomenon

China's recent economic development began after the country emerged from a period of increasingly repressive communist rule that extended from 1949 until the death of its first communist leader, Mao Zedong, in 1976. By the end of 1978, China's new communist leader, Deng Xiaoping, had introduced the first of a series of economic reforms that were to transform the Chinese economy over the ensuing quarter-century. The reforms were needed to improve the country's lagging economic performance, promote modernization, and raise living standards. There was widespread recognition that China's economic development had been held back during the early communist years and that change was needed. However, unlike the economic transition in Russia and Eastern Europe after 1989, China's transition has been largely restricted to economic rather than political reform. Although gradual economic reform was always the intention of China's leaders, the reforms were often a compromise between conservative and radical factions of the Chinese Communist Party, suggesting that the reforms might have been more rapid if the radical reformers had had their way. Nevertheless, the progress of economic reform, whilst initially slow, has produced remarkable results, transforming China from a backward, largely agricultural economy to the world's major manufacturing centre by the beginning of the twenty-first century.

China's economic reforms began with agriculture. A series of reforms allowed farmers greater freedom to make their own decisions and eventually to manage individual pieces of land rather than simply to work for the collective to which they belonged. Market incentives were then gradually introduced into other industrial sectors, allowing the creation of competition and decentralized decision making. Decentralization has been a particular feature of the special economic zones which were created at various stages of the reform process. These zones exist along China's eastern seaboard, providing a relatively open economic environment to encourage trade and inward investment, and similar free trade and development zones have also been established around major cities. The 1990s saw the beginning of the process of privatization of the country's state enterprises and the gradual encouragement of foreign direct investment (FDI) and international trade. This process has, however, been slow and China has been cautious in allowing foreign ownership of its businesses, generally favouring joint ventures rather than full foreign ownership in the varied group of industries it considers to be of strategic importance. China's 'coming of age' as a modern trading nation finally arrived after its tortuously negotiated entry into the WTO in 2001.[8]

Even China's radical reformers could hardly have foreseen the impact that the country's economic reforms would have. During the period 1973–2001, China's gross domestic product (GDP) grew at an average rate of 6.72 per cent per annum, its GDP per capita grew by 5.32 per cent per annum, and its share of world GDP increased from 4.6 per cent in 1973 to 12.3 per cent in 2001.[9] The corresponding figures for the United States are an annual increase of 2.94 per cent in GDP, 1.86 per cent in GDP per capita, and a fall in world GDP share from 22.1 to 21.4 per cent.[10] An almost twofold increase in a country's share of world GDP over a period of less than 30 years is probably unprecedented. This compares with a one and a half times increase in Japan's share of world GDP during its growth years from 1950 to 1973, which was itself also remarkable.[11] Of course, China's growth was made possible because of the country's huge human and physical resources, but the factor that made the difference between the 1970s and the beginning of the twenty-first century was economic liberalism rather than resources. In fact, China's economic growth accelerated from the 1990s onwards, growing by 10.3 per cent per annum over the period from 1990 to 2012.[12] Whilst the accuracy of China's official statistics has been questioned, there is no doubt that its economic performance over the last 30 years or more has, by any standards, been remarkable.[13]

China's rapid economic growth has brought rising living standards, which have been helped by the country's official single child policy and resulting slower population growth. However, as is often the case during a period of rapid economic development, the growth in living standards has been greater in the industrialized regions of eastern and south-eastern China than in its more rural regions. As might be expected, industrial development has also led to a number of social and environmental problems. Rapid industrialization has brought large numbers of migrant workers from the countryside to the towns and cities, sometimes working long hours and living in difficult conditions. Vast demand for energy and natural resources from China's emerging industries has led to significant air and water pollution and the Chinese government has sometimes resorted to controversial solutions to the problem of energy shortage; a high-profile example of this is the Three Gorges Dam and hydroelectric power station on the Yangtze River, which is a major technological feat but has caused the flooding of communities and historic sites.

The international significance of China's economic development is only just beginning to emerge. In economic terms, continued rapid growth will inevitably lead to China overtaking the United States as the world's largest economy in due course, though it will take much longer for China's GDP per capita to catch up. Whilst the 2008–9 world economic downturn appeared to have relatively little impact on China's economic growth, recent data suggest that the country's growth may be finally starting to slow down a little.[14] However, export surpluses, together with the propensity of Chinese people to save a high proportion of their income, have left China with vast currency and other financial reserves, and Chinese overseas lending and investment has helped to finance US demand for imports. Whilst this implies that the Chinese are effectively making sacrifices to allow Americans to live beyond their means, it also puts China in a strong economic position. In time, it is likely that China will play an increasing role in international organizations such as the IMF and WTO. Along with Russia, the Chinese government has already suggested it would like to see the IMF adopt a new international reserve currency in place of the current reliance on the volatile US dollar.[15] In this way, economic power may gradually lead to greater international political influence. The main 'fly in the ointment', however, is the question as to whether China's communist regime will be able to maintain strict political control in a country increasingly used to economic freedom.

14.4 India's contrasting fortunes

Like China, India is a large developing country which has experienced rapid economic growth in recent years, but has a relatively low GDP per capita. Whilst the growth was not quite as rapid as in China, India's GDP grew by 6.4 per cent per annum during the period 1990–2012 and 7.7 per cent per annum between 2002 and 2012.[16] However, in other respects India is quite different. Manufacturing industry started to develop in the late nineteenth century during the latter years of British colonial rule, but even today around half of India's workforce is employed in agriculture. Much of the agricultural activity takes place in small villages in India's rural communities, where the Hindu caste system is still in evidence. Manufacturing, including modern scientific industries as well as more traditional industries such as textiles and steel, continues to play an important role in India's economy, but the major contribution to the country's recent economic growth has come from the computer software and IT services industries, based in cities like Bangalore and Ahmedabad in southern and western India respectively. Western consumers are familiar with the Indian contact (or call) centres used by their banks and insurance companies, but American, British, and other companies now outsource many IT, financial, and legal services, including a wide range of back-office functions formerly undertaken at the companies' main offices in their home country.

India is also very different from China politically and culturally. As the world's largest democracy, India experiences the uncertainties of party politics and changes of government that sometimes make continuity of economic reform difficult. After a number of years of interventionist economic policy following independence in 1947, India embarked on a process of liberal economic reform in 1991. The reforms included tariff reductions, the removal of restrictions on private enterprise, the encouragement of inward investment, and a general move towards a more open economy. Although at times the progress of reform has been slow and the results have been mixed, India's path towards greater participation in the global economy has been inexorable. The liberal economic reforms have also helped to attract a growing amount of FDI into the country, taking advantage not only of the many low-cost IT service providers but also of India's highly skilled, English-speaking workforce. The widespread use of English and the political and legal institutions left by India's colonial past offer a significant advantage in attracting inward investment, but the cultural legacies have been more problematic – particularly the tensions between India's predominant Hindu population and its minority Muslim and Christian populations and the remnants of the Hindu caste system.

Like China, India has huge economic potential. India is also experiencing the social and environmental consequences of rapid economic development. However, the levels of poverty and illiteracy in India are considerably greater, as is the incidence of HIV/AIDS.[17] India also has a less well-developed transport infrastructure and less well-organized administrative system, which makes it more difficult to do business outside the major industrial centres. In this sense, India's economic development represents a picture of enormous contrasts. In political terms, India does not yet carry the same international clout as China. Perhaps this is because India has been progressing in China's shadow, because it has fewer financial resources and more intractable social problems, or because it has been less confident in shaking off its dependent past. Or perhaps we are simply left with a paradox: India is becoming a modern industrialized and service economy, but has been unable to translate its economic success into higher living standards for the majority of its citizens in the rural villages and urban slums. For these and other reasons, India has not yet been able to translate its growing economic power into international political influence.

14.5 Regional integration in Asia and the Asia-Pacific

Asia's political, economic, and cultural diversity makes regional integration among large groups of countries complicated, though as in other regions of the world, there are a number of trading arrangements between groups of neighbouring countries. Larger countries like China and Japan have tended to remain isolated from formal regional economic groupings. However, with US encouragement, the countries of South-East Asia formed the most firmly established regional grouping, the Association of Southeast Asian Nations (ASEAN) as long ago as 1967. ASEAN's original five members, Indonesia, Malaysia, Philippines, Singapore, and Thailand, were joined by Brunei in 1984 and by Vietnam, Laos, Myanmar (Burma), and Cambodia in the 1990s. ASEAN aims to promote trade and the mutual interests of its members, and it encompasses political systems ranging from democracy to communism, absolute monarchy, and military dictatorship. In practice, the member states do not generally interfere in each other's internal affairs, but their intention is to create an ASEAN Community, adding cooperation in security and socio-cultural areas to their current economic community by 2015. Despite its 45-year existence, the ASEAN Free Trade Area (known as AFTA) is not yet completely tariff free, though the intention is to develop it into a fully fledged single market.

Perhaps a more significant recent development is an agreement between China and the ten members of ASEAN to form a China ASEAN Free Trade Area, sometimes referred to as CAFTA (not to be confused with the Central American Free Trade Area, CAFTA-DR – see Section 13.3). The intention of the China ASEAN Free Trade Area is to extend the provisions of AFTA to China, though China will not be a member of the ASEAN Community itself. This agreement changes the nature of free trade in the region as China's economy dwarfs the size of the ASEAN member economies.[18] The balance of political power between these countries is also heavily biased in China's favour and the arrangement could be viewed as an attempt by China to extend its political influence in the region. The members of ASEAN may also consider it in their interests to have access to China's vast internal market and China may be conscious of the need to have good relations with its neighbours if their economies experience rapid growth in the coming years. Given the economic success of countries like Malaysia and Singapore in recent years and the economic potential of South-East Asia's largest country, Indonesia, the region could provide an important market for Chinese goods in the future. ASEAN also has similar agreements with India and Japan, and a number of other regional economic groupings exist, notably the South Asian Free Trade Agreement (SAFTA), including Bangladesh, Bhutan, India, Maldives, Nepal, Pakistan, and Sri Lanka.[19]

Asian regional integration took a different turn when Asia Pacific Economic Cooperation (APEC) was formed in 1989. APEC is a much looser organization than the other main groupings in the region, but it signifies Asia-Pacific cooperation on a much larger scale. Its members include countries around the Pacific rim that could hardly be more varied in terms of their size, political and economic systems, and level of development.[20] The stated aims of APEC are to promote trade, investment, economic and technical cooperation, and generally to encourage business development. Its members have formally agreed to create free trade and investment by the years 2010 and 2020 for developed and developing economy members respectively. However, given the difficulties in achieving this goal among such a diverse group of countries, it is unclear what it will mean in practice. More importantly, APEC symbolizes closer cooperation between North America and Asia, two of the world's three main trading areas. Some commentators have suggested that the third main trading area, the European Union, should be concerned about being left out of Asia, the world's major emerging region. Certainly, US political and economic involvement in Asia has tended to be stronger than Europe's in the post-colonial era, but this does not necessarily mean that future opportunities for European businesses will be curtailed. It may, however, mean that European governments need to be more active in cultivating relationships with Asian governments than they have sometimes been in the recent past.

14.6 Asian enigmas

14.6.1 Asia's 'tiger economies'

The term 'tiger economy' was first used to describe the rapid economic growth of Hong Kong, South Korea, Singapore, and Taiwan between the 1960s and the 1990s. These countries followed Japan's example in achieving rapid industrialization and are now officially classed as developed economies. The term has also been applied to Asia's larger economies, especially China and India, and to fast-growing economies in other parts of the world. In the Asian context, some of the less developed countries like Myanmar and Cambodia have also been achieving rapid growth in recent years, but the term 'tiger economy' is more commonly applied to newly industrializing countries (NICs) such as Malaysia, Indonesia, or Thailand. Even Vietnam, which is following China's example in liberalizing its economy while retaining its communist political system, has been going through a process of rapid industrialization (see Table 14.1).

This pattern of economic development has been a strong feature of Asia's gradual rise to prominence during the post-war years and has given rise to the view that cultural

Table 14.1 Growth rates of Asia's 'tiger economies', 1990–2012

Country	Real GDP Annual Growth Rate (%)
Hong Kong, China	4.0
Indonesia	4.8
Malaysia	5.8
Philippines	4.0
Singapore	6.2
South Korea	5.2
Taiwan	4.9
Thailand	4.4
Vietnam	7.2

Source: IMF, *World Economic Outlook Database*, April 2013.

characteristics may have been influential. Certainly, a number of common characteristics can be identified; these include high levels of general and scientific education, high saving and investment ratios, efficient work practices, the adoption of modern technology, and in most cases interventionist industrial policies. Whilst some of these approaches have been questioned more recently, most of these economies have managed to maintain strong economic growth despite the adverse impact of the Asian financial crisis of 1997–8 and the world economic slowdown of 2008–9. There is also a strong commitment to economic success at individual, corporate, and government levels.

14.6.2 Religious and political tensions

Asia is home to a variety of religions, including Islam, Hinduism, Sikhism, Christianity, Judaism, Buddhism, and Daoism (or Taoism). Its largest country, China, is also officially atheist. Except in one or two regions, adherents of these religions live peacefully alongside each other, though minority religious beliefs are sometimes suppressed. A significant development in recent years has been the growing influence of Islam. This has manifested itself in the adoption of Islamic (or Sharia) Law in a growing number of countries, the spread of Islamic banking and other business practices, and more overt support for fundamentalist Islamic beliefs. Whether fundamentalist or not, Muslims have generally become more active in their support for Islamic values and the contrast between Islam and western values and capitalism has become more pronounced.

An important factor in these contrasting world views is the ongoing conflict in the Middle East between Israel and the Palestinians, and the role of the United States in supporting Israel. The conflict encompasses a number of seemingly intractable problems: disputes over Israel's right to exist; the Palestinians' right to self-determination and international recognition; the Israeli-occupied territories and Israeli settlements; competing claims to represent the Palestinians by the Palestinian National Authority and rival Palestinian factions (Fatah in the West Bank and Hamas in the Gaza strip); missile attacks by Hamas and Israel's military response; varying degrees of hostility on the part of Israel's Arab neighbours; and the world's polarized supporters of one side or the other. This festering wound breeds resentment between Muslims and Jews and, at a wider level, between Muslims and the west.[21] The Middle Eastern conflict has also been used by extremists to provide a justification for terrorist violence, which has erupted in the United States, Europe, and countries such as Pakistan, India, and Indonesia.

Ongoing tensions persist in many other parts of the world, but of particular importance for international stability are problems stemming from the Arab uprising in North Africa and the Middle East, especially the civil war in Syria, and growing distrust between Iran, Israel, and the United States on the one hand, and between North Korea, South Korea, and the United States on the other hand. Both Iran and North Korea appear to have some (albeit uncertain) nuclear capability and both have chosen isolation from mainstream international politics, in Iran's case by its strict Islamic constitution, in North Korea's case by its own version of communist authoritarianism. Iran has declared its opposition to the existence of Israel and there has been an ongoing war of words, sometimes leading to military threats or incursions, between North Korea and its southern neighbour since the Korean War in the early 1950s. Both Iran and North Korea also see themselves as being under military threat from the United

States (arguably with some justification). For its part, the US finds itself embroiled in these issues because of its commitment to Israel and South Korea and its opposition to what it sees as 'failed' or 'rogue' states, as well as because of its assumed role as the world's policeman. In each case, the international business environment is made more difficult by uncertainty in the international political situation and the possibility of further conflict.

14.6.3 Asia's 'failing states'

Francis Fukuyama describes 'weak' or 'failing' states as those which 'commit human rights abuses, provoke humanitarian disasters, drive massive waves of immigration, and attack their neighbours'.[22] In varying degrees, Cambodia, Iran, Iraq (under Saddam Hussein), Myanmar, North Korea, and Syria may be regarded as having 'failed' in one or more of these ways. Of course they are not alone, and failing states are not confined to Asia. Indeed, many of the world's leaders have at some time in their history committed one or more of the above actions. However, countries which systematically behave like failing states and are impervious to international criticism tend to have poor relations with the world community and economic development is often faltering. Asia also has a number of states which, for a variety of reasons, are failing to create an environment that is conducive towards economic development. This is more likely to result from a legacy of social and economic problems than from political unwillingness. This group includes countries such as Bangladesh, Bhutan, Laos, and Nepal, which are among the poorest nations in the world. These countries are failing or struggling in the sense that they are sometimes unable to provide adequately for the welfare of their citizens. For different reasons, failing and struggling states generally offer a difficult business environment.

Emerging scenario: China's view of the world

Although China is seen as the most likely contender to match the power and influence of the United States if the current unipolar world becomes bipolar again, China itself has generally been reluctant to play this role. However, the 2008–9 world economic downturn left the United States economically wounded – both as the source of the initial problem in the US mortgage market and because of the damage done to its Anglo-Saxon free-market model. China, on the other hand, came through the downturn financially stronger and has been able to stand aloof from responsibility for the financial crisis. Not that the Chinese economy was unaffected by the economic downturn, but it was seen as part of the solution rather than the problem. Indeed, China's initial fiscal stimulus package, announced in November 2008, amounted to additional government spending of four trillion yuan. Even by Chinese standards, this represented a massive boost to the country's economy, setting an example to the more financially stretched developing countries as well as sending a signal that China had more than enough resources to weather the economic storm.

   Chinese leaders have been using this opportunity to express their views more forcefully and to criticize their western counterparts. Thus, the crisis allowed them to claim the moral high ground. Recent pronouncements from China's leadership have also gone further in describing the country as a 'great power'. However, this does not necessarily mean that China is ready to take on the mantle

(continued...)

of world leadership, even in a bipolar world. A number of events have suggested that China is still reluctant to assume a world role, other than to promote or defend its own interests. For example, when faced with a political crisis in countries such as Iran, Sudan, or Syria, China has used its veto as a permanent member of the UN Security Council rather than being willing to sanction intervention in another country's domestic affairs. China is also sensitive to criticisms of its policies and actions, preferring to shun foreign leaders of whose actions it disapproves rather than to challenge them openly or to rise above these concerns in the interests of international cooperation and conciliation. This was the case in May 2012 when Chinese government ministers refused to meet their British counterparts as a rebuff to Prime Minister David Cameron who had recently entertained the Dalai Lama, the spiritual leader of Tibet over which China asserts sovereignty.

China has certainly been extending its influence around the world – with investments in natural resource and other industries in countries as diverse as Argentina, Myanmar, Peru, Turkmenistan, the United Arab Emirates, and many parts of Africa. It should be remembered however that, although outwardly in control, China is struggling with a number of problems at home. Rapid economic development has brought a growing problem of inequality in Chinese society and many of the country's agricultural and factory workers have been left behind the rising middle classes. This is a recipe for social discontent and it has become worse as the Chinese economy begins to feel the effects of slower growth in the global economy. China's more affluent population has also been enjoying the benefits of western education and international travel. This is likely to raise aspirations for greater openness in Chinese society. There are also political tensions between liberals who favour continued economic reform and hardliners who want a return to a more egalitarian form of communism. Although China is likely to become the world's largest economy in the next few years, it is still a developing country and has many problems of its own to resolve before it can assume a more active role in world affairs. There are also other challengers in the race for international leadership, so a multipolar world may still be the most likely outcome.[23]

Emerging scenario discussion questions

1. To what extent did the world economic downturn of 2008–9 boost China's position as a world leader?
2. Why do you think China has generally been reluctant to play a world leadership role?
3. To what extent are China's domestic problems likely to hold back its bid for 'great power' status?
4. What are likely to be the business implications of China becoming a more significant world power?
5. Outline the most likely scenario for the changing international role of China over the next ten to twenty years.

Notes

1. United Nations List of Least Developed Countries as at 1 April 2013, http://www.unohrlls.org/en/ldc/25/.
2. Average real GDP growth in Japan from 1990–9 and 2000–11 was 1.5% and 0.8% p.a. respectively; the comparable growth rates for the United States were 3.1% and 1.7% p.a. and, for the advanced economies as a whole, 2.7% and 1.8% p.a. Source: IMF, *World Economic Outlook*, 2008, table A1, p. 259, and October 2012, table A.1, p.190.
3. For a detailed discussion of Japanese post-war industrial policy, see Flath, D. (2005), *The Japanese Economy*, Oxford University Press, ch. 9, pp. 185–214.

4. The word 'keiretsu' has no exact English translation, but means something like 'succession', i.e. a succession or chain of companies linked together.

5. See Flath, D. (2005), *The Japanese Economy*, Oxford University Press, pp. 238–47.

6. For a discussion of recent developments in the Japanese *keiretsu* system, see Lobo, R. (26 June 2012), 'Keiretsu for a new age', *World Finance* (http://www.worldfinance.com).

7. Source: the *Guardian* (2 April 2013), 'Japan to learn whether Abenomics will live up to pro-growth rhetoric'.

8. China was finally allowed to join the WTO after 15 years of negotiations.

9. Maddison, A. (2006), *The World Economy: Volumes 1 and 2*, Development Centre of the Organisation for Economic Cooperation and Development, OECD Publishing, table 8b, pp. 640, 641, and 643.

10. Maddison, A. (2006), *The World Economy: Volumes 1 and 2*, Development Centre of the Organisation for Economic Cooperation and Development, table 8b, pp. 640, 641, and 643.

11. Maddison, A. (2006), *The World Economy: Volumes 1 and 2*, Development Centre of the Organisation for Economic Cooperation and Development, table 8b, p. 641.

12. IMF, *World Economic Outlook Database*, April 2013.

13. For a discussion of the accuracy of China's official statistics, see Naughton, B. (2007), *The Chinese Economy: Transitions and Growth*, MIT Press, section 6.1, pp. 140–3.

14. IMF estimates of China's growth rate for 2013–18 range from 8.0% to 8.5% per annum; source: IMF, *World Economic Outlook Database*, April 2013.

15. In March 2009, the governor of China's central bank, Zhou Xiaochuan, proposed the creation of a new international reserve currency, under the supervision of the IMF, to help stabilize the international financial system, following a similar proposal from Russia; source: *New York Times* (23 March 2009), 'China urges new money reserve to replace dollar'.

16. IMF, *World Economic Outlook Database*, April 2013.

17. The proportion of 0–4-year-old children underweight for their age (suggesting malnutrition) in India was 42.5% in 2010; source: UNDP, *Human Development Report*, 2013. India's male literacy rate was 73.4% and its female literacy rate 47.8% in 2001, and an estimated 2.4 million people had HIV/AIDS in 2009; source: CIA, *World Factbook*, 2009. The corresponding figures for China are 3.8% underweight children in 2010, male and female literacy of 96% and 88.5% respectively in 2007, and 740,000 people with HIV/AIDS in 2009.

18. China's GDP, on a purchasing power parity (PPP) basis, was almost 3.5 times the size of the combined ASEAN GDP in 2012; source: CIA, *World Factbook*, 2013.

19. See WTO website (http://www.wto.org) for a complete list of notified regional trade agreements.

20. The members of APEC are Australia, Brunei, Canada, Chile, China, Hong Kong (China), Indonesia, Japan, Malaysia, Mexico, New Zealand, Papua New Guinea, Peru, Philippines, Russia, Singapore, South Korea, Taiwan (Chinese Taipei), Thailand, United States, and Vietnam.

21. Main sources: BBC News, 'A history of conflict: Israel and the Palestinians' (accessed 4 April 2013); and BBC News (28 February 2013), 'Palestinian territories profile'.

22. Fukuyama, F. (2005), *State Building: Governance and World Order in the Twenty-First Century*, Profile Books, p. 125.

23. For further discussion of these issues, see for example, *The Economist* (19 March 2009), 'How China sees the world' and 'A time for muscle-flexing'; and *The Economist* (23 March 2013), 'The power of China: Toasting the world (or not)'.

Suggestions for further reading

In-depth guides to the major Asian economies and their historical development

Flath, D. (2005), *The Japanese Economy*, Oxford University Press

Lal, D. (2005), *The Hindu Equilibrium: India c.1500 BC–2000 AD*, Oxford University Press

Naughton, B. (2007), *The Chinese Economy: Transitions and Growth*, MIT Press

A practical guide to Asian history

Crump, T. (2008), *Asia-Pacific: A History of Empire and Conflict*, Hambledon Continuum

An analysis of the shifting balance of power from the West to Asia

Mahbubani, K. (2009), *The New Asian Hemisphere: The Irresistible Shift of Global Power to the East*, Public Affairs

Take your learning further: Online Resource Centre
http://www.oxfordtextbooks.co.uk/orc/harrison2e/
Visit the Online Resource Centre that accompanies this book to enrich your understanding of Chapter 14: Asia's Economic Potential. Among other resources explore web links and keep up to date with the latest developments in the area.

15 Africa's Struggle for Reform

◉ Chapter learning outcomes

On completion of this chapter the reader should be able to:

- Appreciate the major geopolitical and related developments which have taken place in Africa in recent years
- Evaluate the main implications of these developments for business organizations

15.1 The African enigma

Africa is without doubt the world's poorest continent. Just over 60 per cent of the world's least developed countries (LDCs) are in sub-Saharan Africa[1] and, despite the Multilateral Debt Relief Initiative for the poorest countries initiated in 2005, many of these countries are still heavily dependent on foreign aid. The continent as a whole had received only 2.8 per cent of the world stock of foreign direct investment (FDI) up to 2011.[2] Most of this FDI has been in natural resource industries such as mining or oil extraction. Apart from mineral resources, African countries are often dependent on the production and export of agricultural commodities like coffee, cotton, tobacco, and tea. A few African countries earn significant income from manufactured goods, notably South Africa, Tunisia, Morocco, and Botswana, but in general African countries are much more dependent on the export of primary products than are exporters in the other main developing continents, Asia and Latin America. This heavy dependence on primary products has left many countries at the mercy of fluctuations in world commodity prices. Agricultural producers have also suffered from drought and flooding and have experienced growing competition from more productive exporters in Asia and Latin America. As a result, Africa's share of world merchandise exports fell from 7.3 per cent in 1948 to 3.3 per cent in 2011.[3] There are tentative signs that the continent's fortunes may be starting to change, particularly in the countries of North and Southern Africa, but the average level of economic development in much of sub-Saharan Africa has lagged well behind development in most other parts of the world.

From another perspective this picture may not be as gloomy as we have come to expect. Africa is often regarded as the cradle of civilization, where traces of the earliest human beings have been found. The part of Africa north of the equator was in fact one of the first regions of the world to develop land cultivation as hunter-gatherers gradually became farmers.[4] Africa has a rich history of human achievement, as evidenced by the pyramids of Egypt, the Benin bronzes of Nigeria, or the wealth of contemporary African art and literature. It is also a region well endowed with natural resources, including some of the world's most valued commodities

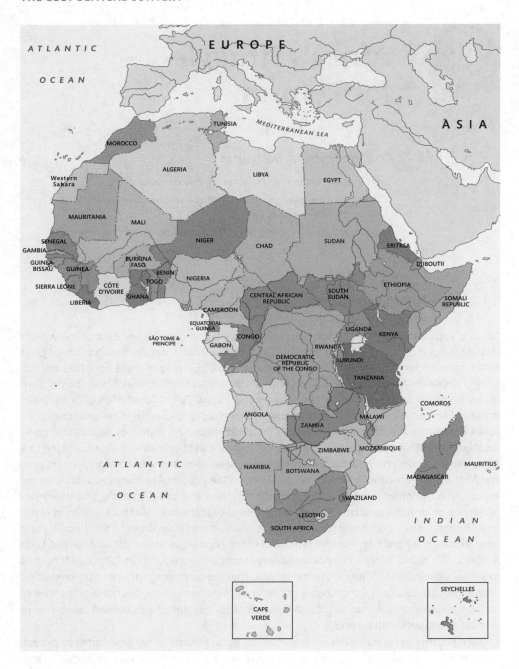

such as gold, diamonds, and oil, and some of the most spectacular tourist attractions, including the Victoria Falls on the border between Zambia and Zimbabwe and the wildlife reserves of Kenya and South Africa, among others. Clearly, history, geography, and politics have not been kind to Africa in recent times, leaving much of the continent excluded from the economic development of the last 200 years as well as the late twentieth century surge of industrialization witnessed in parts of Asia and Latin America. The reasons for Africa's lagging performance are complex and the subject of much debate. These issues and their implications for Africa's future development are explored in Section 15.4. However, it is important to appreciate that, like other continents, Africa is not a homogeneous region. We now consider the vast cultural, political, and economic differences between Africa's contrasting regions.

15.2 Africa's contrasting regions

15.2.1 North Africa and sub-Saharan Africa

The Sahara desert marks the border between North Africa and sub-Saharan Africa and these regions are separated by culture and history as well as by geography. The North African countries of Morocco, Algeria, Tunisia, and Libya (known as the Maghreb) are predominantly Muslim and Arabic speaking, like their Egyptian neighbours and the *Mashreq* countries of the Middle East. In addition to their cultural bond with the Arab world, the Maghreb are seafaring Mediterranean countries and have historical links with Southern Europe, especially Spain, France, and Italy. Algeria, in particular, has close connections with France, its former colonial power, and the French language is still widely spoken there. On the whole, the North African countries are more economically successful than their sub-Saharan counterparts. Egypt has in fact the second-largest African economy after South Africa on a purchasing power parity basis, but the Arab uprising has badly affected the country's manufacturing, construction, and tourism industries and its economic growth. In the case of Algeria and Libya, wealth has come largely from their oil and gas industries. Libya's large oil reserves have given the country one of the highest per capita incomes in Africa, though the uprising against Colonel Gaddafi and resulting civil war led to a temporary 60 per cent fall in GDP in 2011. In Algeria, progress has been adversely affected by political difficulties and civil unrest. Morocco and Tunisia have more diversified economies and are more industrialized, but significant economic and social problems remain in this region.

Sub-Saharan Africa's story is generally less positive, though there are some bright lights. The Central African Republic, Ethiopia, Rwanda, and Sierra Leone, for example, are among the world's poorest countries and 47.5 per cent of the population of sub-Saharan Africa were living on less than $1.25 per day in 2008.[5] All of the continent's LDCs are in sub-Saharan Africa. Nevertheless, 'bright lights' have been seen in Angola, Botswana, Ghana, Rwanda, Tanzania, and Uganda, among others[6] – in the latter case during the 1980s and 1990s after the despotic regime of President Idi Amin (1971–9), as well as more recently. One of Africa's many enigmas is the underperformance of its most populous country and one of its largest economies, Nigeria. Despite some progress in economic reforms, political instability has tended to hold back Nigeria's economic development. Like other oil-rich countries, Nigeria seems to suffer from the 'natural resource paradox', where dependence on oil has tended to deflect attention from industrial diversification and modernization of its economy (see Section 5.1.1). Sub-Saharan Africa has also generally suffered more from war, disease, and adverse climatic conditions than the countries of North Africa. These issues are explored further in Section 15.4.

15.2.2 South Africa and its Southern African neighbours

The end of apartheid and the election of the first representative government in 1994 brought South Africa into the family of African nations after years of colonial rule and racial segregation. South Africa had and still has Africa's largest, most diversified, and most inter-nationally integrated economy. The closest African economies in size are Egypt and Nigeria, though a handful of African countries have higher GDP per capita. The apartheid years left South Africa with a modern commercial sector, but also a legacy of inequality between its rich, predominantly white community and the large numbers of poor, mainly though not exclusively, black people living in shanty towns, squatter camps, and dispersed rural commu-nities. South Africa has been struggling to establish a new course and to reconcile old enmities since the end of apartheid, preoccupations which have held back the country's economic development. The South African government introduced liberal economic policies in 2000 in order to restart economic growth after a period of slow growth in the 1990s. This approach has been controversial and has failed to tackle some of the underlying problems, though it appears to have achieved a measure of improved macroeconomic performance.[7] For these reasons, South Africa is classed as a developing country, but it is undoubtedly Africa's most developed country both politically and economically.

South Africa has close economic and political ties with its neighbouring states, especially Namibia and its smaller neighbours, Lesotho and Swaziland. Mozambique and, in particular, Botswana have achieved some success with liberal economic reforms, though Mozambique remains on the World Bank's list of heavily indebted poor countries (HIPCs). The progress made by Botswana (see case study at the end of Chapter 11), together with the oil boom in Angola, and the underlying strengths of the South African economy, have given credibility to the view that there are signs of an 'African renaissance' in Southern Africa.[8] In the African con-text, one should of course always be mindful that progress is often halted by political turmoil or military conflict. Nowhere has this been more evident than in South Africa's other neigh-bour, Zimbabwe, where President Robert Mugabe's government oversaw the virtual collapse of the country's economy, especially from the late 1990s to 2008. The chaotic situation in Zimbabwe also caused a large displacement of people seeking better conditions across the border in neighbouring countries, though price controls and relative stability have brought some improvement in Zimbabwe's economy since 2008. Despite these difficulties, there have been encouraging signs of economic development in Southern Africa.

15.2.3 Francophone and Anglophone Africa

By the beginning of World War I in 1914, most of Africa was under European colonial rule and this continued until the 1950s and 1960s, or later in a few cases. France and Britain were by far the dominant colonial powers, though Belgium, Germany, Italy, Portugal, and Spain also had African colonies. French territories were mainly in North, West, and Western Central Africa, whereas the British controlled territories in North-East, East, and Southern Africa, together with one or two West African states, notably Nigeria. Many of France's former colonies form part of the Communauté Financière Africaine (CFA) and use the CFA franc, which is now fixed to the euro, though Algeria, Morocco, and Tunisia, all former French colonies, are notable exceptions.[9] The French language is widely used in most of the CFA countries, especially in government and commerce, along with native African languages. French political, economic, and cultural influence is still very prevalent in these countries. French is also spoken in Central Africa's most populous country, the Democratic Republic of the Congo (formerly the Belgian Congo and Zaire), a country divided by ethnic tensions and civil unrest for a number of years.

Anglophone Africa includes countries such as Botswana, Ghana, Kenya, Nigeria, South Africa, Uganda, Zambia, Zimbabwe, and to a lesser extent Egypt. British influence has also left its political and economic mark on these countries and their mines and crop plantations became a magnet for British and other European migrants from the late nineteenth century until the 1960s. Europeans were often responsible for developments in public administration, mining, agriculture, and commerce in many of these countries. However, white European migration also became the catalyst for apartheid in South Africa and the resentment caused by widespread land ownership by white farmers in Zimbabwe. In Zimbabwe's case, Robert Mugabe's ill-fated policy of land restitution to native Africans had the unintended consequence of destroying the economy of a country once known as the 'breadbasket of Africa'. Despite the mixed colonial legacy, political, economic, and linguistic ties with Europe serve as a basis for trade and economic development – though in practice aid has often been more in evidence than the wider economic benefits that might be expected to come from the international trading environment.

15.2.4 Christian and Muslim Africa

Religion plays an important part in African life. In addition to the many traditional African religions and one or two minority religions practised mainly by non-indigenous people, Christianity and Islam are by far the main religions in Africa. The influence of both these religions has been increasing in recent years. Islam is predominant in Northern Africa, including countries in the Sahel region to the south of the Sahara desert such as Mauritania, Mali, Niger, Chad, Sudan, and Somalia as well as the Maghreb and Egypt to the north. Christianity is predominant in Central and Southern Africa. Some countries, like Nigeria, are split fairly evenly between the two religions, along with the smaller indigenous African religions.

Among the oldest Christian groups in Africa are Egypt's Coptic Church and the Ethiopian Orthodox Church, but the main growth in Christianity in Africa came with European colonization in the late nineteenth century and has continued through the many American and European missionary organizations up to the present day. In the main, missionaries brought the mainstream Catholic and Protestant denominations, many of which are still prevalent throughout Africa, but the biggest increase in Christianity in recent years has come either from the more evangelical churches, notably Pentecostalism and the Assemblies of God, or from the growing number of independent African churches. Christianity has had a variety of influences on the political and economic development of Africa. At times, church leaders have appeared to cooperate with or even support authoritarian or repressive regimes; at other times, they have spoken out courageously against these regimes. Both of these extremes were evident during the apartheid years in South Africa.

Islam came to North Africa as a result of foreign conquest, but spread further south largely through the development of trade, through militant religious movements, or in the form of organized resistance to European colonization. In some countries, such as Sudan or Nigeria, Muslims have formed their own political parties, though on the whole political systems have remained secular in most predominantly Muslim African countries and Islam has often adapted to or accommodated African traditions. However, more fundamentalist Islamic groups have emerged in some regions, especially in Northern Africa and Sudan. In the case of Sudan, governments have been strongly influenced by Islamic fundamentalism and tensions between the dominant northern region of Sudan and the largely non-Muslim south have led to prolonged conflict, large-scale population displacement, and finally independence for South Sudan in 2011 (though not a complete end to violence). The spread of the conflict to the Darfur region of western Sudan in 2003, and the humanitarian crisis that accompanied it, brought the situation in Sudan to the world's attention. The Darfur war reflected a complex mix of ethnic tensions between the black African and black Arab population as well as religious differences and political grievances between rebel groups and the government in Khartoum.

Whilst there are apparent similarities between the growth of Christian and Islamic 'fundamentalism' in Africa, it should be noted that whereas strict Muslims are likely to support the idea of a theocratic state, evangelical Christians are more likely to see themselves as standing apart from the state. It is also interesting to observe that, while African Muslims are following the example of more radical Islam in other parts of the world, African Christians are in many ways at the forefront of Christian revival. In both cases, they have developed their own varieties of religious practice, inevitably influenced by African culture and traditions. The extent to which religious influences are likely to promote or hold back Africa's political and economic development is a more open question.[10]

15.3 Regional integration in Africa

The end of colonialism in the 1950s and 1960s left a desire among African states for cooperation to protect their fragile independence and promote economic prosperity. This led to the formation of the Organization of African Unity (OAU) in 1963. Although at times limited by its reluctance to intervene in the internal affairs of its member states, the OAU nevertheless survived the difficult years of political conflict and relative economic decline during the 1970s and 1980s. Its intention was always to promote political unity among its members as well as to create an economic community, at least in part following the example of the European Union. Although progress towards these ideals has been slow, the OAU took a step closer to its former aim by recreating itself as the African Union in 2002. The African Union includes virtually all the African states and has been in the process of establishing a number of coordinating institutions, including an Assembly (heads of state and government), an Executive Council (foreign affairs and other ministers), a Pan-African Parliament, an African Court on Human and People's Rights, and a Commission. Less progress has been made on the economic front, though a number of regional economic communities have been established with varying degrees of success over the years. The regional economic communities are part of an attempt by the African Union to establish an African Economic Community, ultimately with a common market and a common currency.

Africa's regional economic communities include the East African Community (EAC),[11] the Economic Community of West African States (ECOWAS),[12] the Southern African Development Community (SADC),[13] the Economic Community of Central African States (ECCAS),[14] the Intergovernmental Authority on Development (IGAD) in North-East Africa,[15] the Arab Maghreb Union (AMU),[16] the Common Market for Eastern and Southern Africa (COMESA),[17] and the Community of Sahel-Saharan States (CEN-SAD).[18] These communities have overlapping memberships, but are intended to link countries in all the main regions of Africa. Inevitably, the extent to which free trade, let alone further economic integration, has been achieved in each of the communities is variable and a number of difficulties will have to be overcome before anything approaching an African common market is possible. The first of these regional communities to be formed, the East African Community, illustrates some of the difficulties. At the time this community was formed in 1967, Kenya was a relatively industrialized country, Tanzania was a largely agrarian socialist state, and Uganda was an authoritarian state, initially under Milton Obote and later under the despotic regime of Idi Amin. The EAC collapsed in 1977 and Tanzania subsequently intervened militarily to overthrow President Amin's regime in Uganda. The community was later reformed in more stable times in the 1990s.

Despite its earlier setback, the EAC joined two of the other regional economic communities, SADC and COMESA, to form the Africa Free Trade Zone (AFTZ) in October 2008. The intention is now to extend AFTZ to include all Africa's regional economic groupings by 2018. This represents another step towards the goal of an African Economic Community, though of course there is still some way to go. A number of African countries also participate in preferential trading arrangements such as the African, Caribbean, and Pacific (ACP) Cotonou Agreement with the EU, the Generalized System of Preferences (GSP), and the US African Growth and Opportunity Act (AGOA) (see Section 3.3). Many of the African states are clearly convinced of the mutual benefits that can be derived from economic and political integration, but they are hampered by the huge differences between their economies as well as the litany of problems discussed in Section 15.4.

15.4 Constraints on Africa's economic development

There are many views on the causes of Africa's problems. One possible explanation relates to geography. Much of Africa is tropical, as are many of the world's poorest regions. Tropical regions experience high or relatively high temperatures all year round and are often subject to extremes of drought and heavy rainfall, though the climate varies depending on the region. Extreme conditions can make life particularly difficult for agricultural producers. Most of the world's richest nations, on the other hand, have more temperate climates. However, this does not necessarily explain why tropical regions of Latin America, Southern India, and South-East Asia are generally more prosperous than tropical Africa. Singapore, for example, which is located close to the equator, has achieved considerable economic success in recent years and is now classed as a developed country. Nevertheless, it may be significant that the two most prosperous regions of Africa, Southern Africa and the Arab countries of North Africa, are the only non-tropical regions of Africa. A tropical climate may make economic development more difficult, but it seems doubtful that this would provide the main explanation for Africa's problems.

Perhaps the most widely used explanation for Africa's lagging development, particularly by Africans themselves, is the continent's history. Long before the widespread colonization of Africa, Europeans were selling Africans into slavery. Slave-ships took several million Africans to the Caribbean and the Americas between the sixteenth and nineteenth centuries, though an East-African slave trade to the Middle East existed even before this time. Quite apart from the immorality of slavery, the slave trade deprived Africa of human resources vital to the maintenance of its already relatively well-developed economy. European colonization added to this problem by exploiting Africa's natural resources from the nineteenth century onwards. Of course, the colonial powers built a transport infrastructure and created commerce and political institutions, but they also left a legacy of economic dependence long after most of Africa achieved political independence in the 1950s and 1960s. In the long history of Africa, European colonial rule was relatively short, lasting less than a hundred years in most cases, but Africa's modern independent nations are even younger and many of today's political borders were artificially created by agreement between the European colonial powers. As has been found elsewhere in the world, politically convenient borders are not always conducive to harmonious relations between different ethnic groups. Indeed, colonial powers some-times exploited ethnic divisions as a means of exercising political control.[19]

The early post-independence period was a time when a number of African countries experimented with socialism.[20] This was to some extent a reaction against colonial capital-ism, but was also seen as a way of using the continent's resources for the benefit of the people as a whole after the unequal division of wealth left by colonization. Some of Africa's social-ist states were modelled on Soviet communism, notably Ethiopia under its military ruler, Mengistu Haile Mariam (1974–91). Soviet influence was in fact significant throughout the Horn of Africa during the 1970s and 1980s. For other African leaders, socialism was linked more to pan-African revival; notable among this group were Kwame Nkrumah (1960–6) of Ghana and Julius Nyerere of Tanzania (1961–85). Despite the ideals which brought socialism to post-colonial Africa, however, democracy was gradually replaced by single-party authori-tarian rule and economic development remained largely elusive. Socialism was in fact part of a wider nationalist movement in Africa as well as the pan-African ideals which led to the formation of the OAU (see Section 15.3). In some cases, nationalism has led to other kinds of authoritarian rule, sometimes with disastrous consequences. Whether these difficulties are primarily a consequence of Africa's colonial history or simply reflect the propensity of individual leaders or ruling elites to abuse their power is a matter of debate.

In more recent times, democracy has been gradually replacing authoritarianism throughout much of Africa, though there are still a number of 'failing states' which are unable to provide adequately for or abuse the rights of their citizens (see Section 14.6.3). The Fund for Peace lists Somalia, the Democratic Republic of Congo, Sudan, South Sudan, Chad, and Zimbabwe as the top six countries in its Failed States Index 2012.[21] These countries suffer from problems such as the mass movement of refugees, severe economic decline, and human rights violations. Even when Africa's more stable countries are included, much of sub-Saharan Africa suffers from poor access to education, poor housing and sanitation, lack of clean water, a low and often de-clining standard of living, poor public health provision, and a dysfunctional energy and trans-port infrastructure. The prevalence of HIV/AIDS,[22] malaria, cholera, and other life-threatening diseases also holds back Africa's economic development, not to mention the human and social consequences. When these problems are combined with the economic constraints imposed by dependence on basic commodities and international debt, it is not difficult to understand why many African countries have been unable to diversify and develop their economies.

A persistent concern for African development has been the problem of poor governance. This is not only a problem of poor economic policy. Indeed, often under pressure from the IMF or the World Bank, a number of African countries have followed their Latin American counterparts in pursuing 'neo-liberal' economic policies in recent years. However, with one or two exceptions, privatization, domestic economic reform, and especially trade liberalization have been relatively unsuccessful in the African context.[23] Among other things, this may be a consequence of the difficult institutional environment in many African countries. However, poor governance has more to do with the ability of politicians and public officials to maintain a stable and peaceful environment where the rule of law is enforced and people can go about their lawful business relatively unhindered. A particular set of economic policies may be less important than the ability of a government to root out corruption, respect human rights, and prevent or avoid creating conflict.

Authoritarian rule is generally inimical to good governance and Africa has had a long line of authoritarian rulers. Among the more repressive in the post-colonial era have been Joseph Mobutu in what is now the Democratic Republic of the Congo (1965–97), Jean-Bédel Bokassa in the Central African Republic (1966–79), Idi Amin in Uganda (1971–9), Mengistu Haile Mariam in Ethiopia (1974–91), Hissene Habre in Chad (1982–90), Charles Taylor in Liberia (1997–2003), Muammar Gaddafi in Libya (1969–2011), and Robert Mugabe in Zimbabwe (1980–). But these leaders are by no means alone. It is a sad fact of African post-colonial history that progress even in the more successful countries has been punctuated by periods of poor governance, often involving authoritarian rule of one kind or another.

15.5 An African renaissance?

In a world of economic globalization much of Africa has been left behind. Even where the continent appears to have a comparative advantage, such as in coffee and cotton production or diamond and copper mining, productivity has generally fallen behind that of competitors in other parts of the world. Heavy dependence on these commodities has left the African economies at the mercy either of world markets or of the natural resource paradox. In order to escape from financial disaster, African countries have borrowed large sums from the international financial institutions. This has left them heavily indebted, though some debt relief has been given to the poorest countries. Governments in the developed world, along with non-governmental organizations (NGOs), have also responded by giving aid to Africa, sometimes with strings attached. However, although aid is often essential to avert a humanitarian crisis and has sometimes been effective in tackling problems at a local level, the significant amount of development assistance that has gone into Africa in recent years has been relatively ineffective in promoting national economic development. The continent's natural resources continue to attract major multinational companies, but investment in other industries is only now starting to catch up. The Chinese have been at the forefront of this activity in recent years, seeing Africa as an opportunity to obtain resources for its rapidly industrializing economy, just as the European colonizers had done in the nineteenth century.

So, is there an 'African renaissance' anywhere on the horizon? In his thought-provoking book, *The Bottom Billion*, Paul Collier concludes that Africa suffers from four overriding problems: the 'conflict trap', where violence and wars plague fragile societies that are locked into a cycle of economic decline; the 'natural resource trap' facing countries that are resource-rich but policy-poor; being 'landlocked with bad neighbours', so that even well-run countries are held back by their wayward neighbours; and 'bad governance in a small country', where bad governance is compounded by problems such as commodity dependence, disease, skill shortages, corruption, or conflict in a country too small to tackle these problems on its own.[24] Collier's thesis builds on the work of others in focusing on the spiral of poor governance and economic decline, but he argues that good governance on its own is unlikely to be the answer.

Even when individual countries such as Ghana or Uganda have experienced periods of improved governance, they have had difficulty in overcoming the many competing problems they face. There is a broad consensus that Africa's future prosperity requires policies to tackle public health, education, productivity, governance, and a number of other issues. The extent to which the answer can be found through sustained political and economic cooperation between the African countries themselves is a more open question.

Emerging scenario: China's 'scramble for Africa'

The period between the 1880s and the beginning of World War I is sometimes described as the time of the 'scramble for Africa', when several European countries rushed to colonize most of Africa. A modern parallel may be drawn between Europe's earlier scramble for Africa and China's rapidly increasing presence in Africa since the early 2000s, though in China's case it has occurred through trade, investment, and lending rather than colonization. Further comparisons have been made between the EU–Africa summit held in Lisbon in December 2007, which was overshadowed by disagreements over trade and whether Zimbabwe's President Robert Mugabe should have been invited, and the more optimistic tone of the Forum on China–Africa Cooperation, including the July 2012 summit in Beijing attended by representatives of 50 African governments. The contrast between Europe and China illustrates the difference between Europe's post-colonial preoccupation with good governance and human rights and China's more pragmatic approach to cooperation without interfering in the internal politics of its trading partners. It is also significant that China's newly appointed President Xi Jinping made his first overseas trip to Africa in March 2013.

Africa's long-standing dependence on the west is now being challenged by China. Between 2000 and 2012, China's merchandise trade with Africa (including exports and imports) increased from about $11 billion to $198 billion. Over 60 per cent of China's imports in 2011 consisted of fuels, the remainder being mining products, and to a lesser extent manufactured goods and agricultural products. Chinese exports consisted mainly of machinery and transport equipment, clothing and textiles, and other manufactured goods.[25] In 2004, about half of China's FDI in Africa was in the oilfields of Sudan, but since then Chinese investors have diversified into a number of African countries in industries as varied as agriculture, mining, financial services, and manufacturing, as well as fuels. In fact, the largest number of Chinese investments in Africa is now in services and manufacturing.[26] China has also financed infrastructure developments such as dams, roads, railways, and other public works projects, and Chinese lending to sub-Saharan Africa exceeded that of the World Bank between 2001 and 2010.[27]

China's approach to lending has tended to be without the sort of conditions normally imposed by the international institutions and without regard to a country's political regime. This is in stark contrast to Europe's insistence on democracy and good governance. China's approach, of course, carries with it a number of risks for Africa's fledgling democracies as well as for western influence in the region. On the one hand, many African countries are attracted by China's financial profligacy and no-strings-attached approach, allowing them the freedom to make their own decisions rather than to depend on western post-colonial patronage. On the other hand, there is a danger that dependence on the west will simply be replaced by dependence on China and, whilst the direction of African trade may have changed, its composition has not. In time, rising production costs may persuade China to transfer some of its manufacturing plants to lower-cost Africa, leading to a new phase of globalization. Countries like Russia, India, Brazil, Malaysia, and South Korea are also showing an interest in Africa. For the time being, Africa is enjoying the attention of the outside world, but its new international relationships are not yet clearly defined.

Emerging scenario discussion questions

1. To what extent do you think China's activities in Africa are motivated by political as well as economic objectives?

2. To what extent do you think China offers a more attractive proposition for many African countries than their former European colonial rulers?

3. To what extent is Chinese investment likely to increase African economic development?

4. What are likely to be the business implications of China's African adventure from the perspective of multinational enterprises (MNEs) from other parts of the world?

5. Outline the most likely scenario for the next phase of globalization over the next ten to twenty years from an African perspective.

Notes

1. UNCTAD, *The Least Developed Countries Report*, 2012, p. xii.

2. UNCTAD, *World Investment Report*, 2012, Annex Table I.2, p. 173.

3. WTO, *International Trade Statistics*, 2012, Table I.5, p. 24.

4. See Oliver, R., and Fage, J. D. (1990), *A Short History of Africa*, Penguin Books, ch. 2, pp. 10–20.

5. World Bank data (http://data.worldbank.org).

6. *The Economist* (1 May 2013), 'Growth and other good things'.

7. South Africa's real GDP growth rate increased from an average of 1.4% per annum in the 1990s to 3.6% per annum between 2000 and 2010; source: IMF, *World Economic Outlook*, October 2012.

8. The phrase 'African renaissance' was used by South Africa's President Thabo Mbeki in a speech in Tokyo in 1998; it also appears in Mbeki, T. (1998), *Africa: The Time Has Come*, Tafelberg/Mafube, p. 248.

9. The countries of the CFA are divided into two groups, belonging either to the West African or Central African Economic and Monetary Union. Members of the West African group include Benin, Burkina Faso, Côte d'Ivoire, Guinea–Bissau, Mali, Niger, Senegal, and Togo. The Central African group includes Cameroon, Central African Republic, Chad, the Republic of the Congo (sometimes known as Congo-Brazzaville), Equatorial Guinea, and Gabon. Guinea–Bissau and Equatorial Guinea were in fact formerly Portuguese and Spanish colonies respectively.

10. For a discussion of the role of religion in Africa, see for example Moyo, A. (2012), 'Religion in Africa', in Gordon, A. A., and Gordon, D. L. (2012), *Understanding Contemporary Africa*, Lynne Rienner.

11. Members of EAC (formed in 1967, collapsed in 1977, reformed in the 1990s): Burundi, Kenya, Rwanda, Tanzania, and Uganda.

12. Members of ECOWAS (formed in 1975): Benin, Burkina Faso, Cabo Verde (or Cape Verde), Côte d'Ivoire, Gambia, Ghana, Guinea, Guinea–Bissau, Liberia, Mali, Niger, Nigeria, Senegal, Sierra Leone, and Togo.

13. Members of SADC (formed in 1980): Angola, Botswana, Democratic Republic of the Congo, Lesotho, Madagascar, Malawi, Mauritius, Mozambique, Namibia, Seychelles, South Africa, Swaziland, Tanzania, Zambia, and Zimbabwe.

14. Members of ECCAS (formed in 1983): Angola, Burundi, Cameroon, Central African Republic, Chad, Democratic Republic of the Congo, Republic of the Congo, Equatorial Guinea, Gabon, Rwanda, and São Tomé and Principe.

15. Members of IGAD (formed in 1986): Djibouti, Eritrea, Ethiopia, Kenya, Somalia, Sudan, and Uganda.

16. Members of AMU (formed in 1989): Algeria, Libya, Mauritania, Morocco, and Tunisia.

17. Members of COMESA (formed in 1994): Burundi, Comoros, Democratic Republic of the Congo, Djibouti, Egypt, Eritrea, Ethiopia, Kenya, Libya, Madagascar, Malawi, Mauritius, Rwanda, Seychelles, Sudan, Swaziland, Uganda, Zambia, and Zimbabwe.

18. Members of CEN-SAD (formed in 1998): Benin, Burkina Faso, Central African Republic, Chad, Côte d'Ivoire, Djibouti, Egypt, Eritrea, Gambia, Ghana, Guinea-Bissau, Liberia, Libya, Mali, Morocco, Niger, Nigeria, Senegal, Sierra Leone, Somalia, Sudan, Togo, and Tunisia.

19. For example, the tensions between Rwanda's majority Hutu and minority Tutsi people, which came to a head during the Rwandan genocide of 1994, may arguably have been exacerbated by the ethnic categorization of the population in the 1930s during the period of Belgian colonial rule.

20. The term 'socialism' rather than 'communism' is normally used in the African context, though it generally involved policies such as state ownership and collective farming similar to those used in the state socialist or communist systems of the Soviet Union or China.

21. The Fund for Peace Failed States Index 2012, http://ffp.statesindex.org/.

22. According to the World Health Organization Global Health Observatory, approximately 23 million people were living with HIV in Africa in 2011 (almost 68% of the world total); the prevalence of HIV among Africans aged 15–49 was about 4.6% (http://www.who.int/hiv/data/en/).

23. See UNCTAD, *Economic Development in Africa*, 2008: 'Export Performance Following Trade Liberalization: Some Patterns and Policy Perspectives'.

24. Collier, P. (2007), *The Bottom Billion: Why the Poorest Countries are Failing and What Can Be Done About It*, Oxford University Press.

25. WTO, *International Trade Statistics*, 2006, Chart 11, p. 11; WTO, *International Trade Statistics*, 2012, table A22, p. 249; and *Financial Times* (25 March 2013), 'China pledges more investments to Africa'.

26. UNCTAD, *Global Investment Trends Monitor* (25 March 2013), 'The Rise of BRICS FDI and Africa'.

27. Bloomberg (28 December 2011), 'China's EXIM lend more to Sub-Sahara Africa than World Bank, Fitch says'.

Suggestions for further reading

An in-depth guide to political, economic, and social developments in Africa
Gordon, A. A., and Gordon, D. L. (2012), *Understanding Contemporary Africa*, Lynne Rienner

A guide to post-colonial African history
Meredith, M. (2011), *The Fate of Africa: A History of the Continent since Independence*, Da Capo

Thought-provoking analyses of the problems facing Africa
Clarke, D. (2012), *Africa's Future: Darkness to Destiny: How the Past is Shaping Africa's Economic Evolution*, Profile Books
Collier, P. (2007), *The Bottom Billion: Why the Poorest Countries are Failing and What Can Be Done About It*, Oxford University Press

Take your learning further: Online Resource Centre
http://www.oxfordtextbooks.co.uk/orc/harrison2e/
Visit the Online Resource Centre that accompanies this book to enrich your understanding of Chapter 15: Africa's Struggle for Reform. Among other resources explore web links and keep up to date with the latest developments in the area.

Glossary

Absolute monarchy A political system where the state is governed by a hereditary ruler with absolute power.

Achievement culture A cultural orientation which attaches importance to what people have accomplished.

Acquisition The purchase of a majority ownership stake in another organization (also known as a takeover).

Adaptive efficiency The ability of elements in a complex system to adapt in response to their changing environment.

Adverse selection Market failure resulting from the inability of consumers to determine the quality of a product in markets with asymmetric information.

Agglomeration economies The economic advantages arising from internal and external economies of scale, knowledge spillovers, specialized skills, and forward and backward linkages within a cluster of firms.

Aggregate demand The total level of demand in an economy, consisting of consumer spending, capital investment, government expenditure, and exports minus imports.

Aggregate supply The total planned real output of goods and services in an economy.

Anglo-Saxon model The socio-economic model found mainly in the English-speaking countries, emphasizing the importance of free markets.

Ascriptive culture A cultural orientation which is concerned with status conferred by birth, age, gender, or connections.

Asymmetric information Unequal access to information between the buyer and seller of a product.

Authoritarian A term used to describe a dictatorship or one-party political system where the government has absolute power.

Autonomy In an ethical context, autonomy requires an individual to take moral responsibility for his or her own actions.

Balance of payments A country's record of international receipts and payments arising from trade in goods and services (the current account) and investment and other capital flows (the capital account).

Bilateral exchange rate A nominal exchange rate between two currencies.

Bipolar world order A world dominated by two powerful countries, as for example the United States and USSR during the cold war period.

'Black swan' event A random event which occurs infrequently, but which sometimes has major consequences.

Bond An interest-bearing investment in a company or public sector debt.

Branch-plant economy A dependent region or country where most of the larger businesses are branches of companies whose head offices are elsewhere.

BRICs/BRICS The four largest emerging economies, Brazil, Russia, India, and China, a term coined by a Goldman Sachs report in 2001, later joined by South Africa at their summit meetings.

Business environment The external political, economic, social, legal, technological, ethical, and other factors which affect an organization.

Central place theory The idea that business and residential development and smaller towns tend to be located around a main central town.

Central planning system An economic system where resources are allocated by central government rather than by market forces.

Civilization The largest grouping of people sharing common cultural characteristics.

Cluster A group of related business activities located close together (also known as spatial concentration).

Coase theorem The economic principle that the outcome of a bargain will be an efficient solution regardless of how property rights are specified, provided the agreement is to the mutual advantage of the parties and no transaction costs are incurred.

Collectivism A cultural dimension where social cohesion and group loyalty are more important than the needs of the individual.

Commercial services Traded services such as transport, financial services, or telecommunications.

Common market A tariff-free trading area with a common external tariff and the free movement of goods, services, people, and capital.

Communism A totalitarian political system where property and the means of production are owned by the state on behalf of the people.

Communitarianism See collectivism.

Comparative advantage theory The idea that countries should specialize in producing goods where they have a relative productivity advantage, then trade with each other.

Competitiveness When applied to an organization, the ability to compete effectively against rivals; when applied to a country, the ability to create an environment which is conducive to good economic and business performance.

Complex adaptive system A structure made up of many elements that operate independently and also interact with each other, absorbing information from their surrounding elements.

Complexity theory The study of complex adaptive systems.

Conditional probability The probability that one event will occur given the occurrence of another event.

Consequentialist principle See teleological principle.

Consumer surplus The difference between the market price and the price consumers are willing and able to pay, as shown by the demand curve.

Coordinated market economy An economic system where government intervention is used to regulate or otherwise influence the operation of markets.

Core region A region which is at the centre of political and economic activity.

Corporate social responsibility (CSR) The responsibility of an organization for the economic, social, ethical, and environmental impacts of its activities.

Created assets Assets which a country has developed through investment over a number of years, including tangible assets such as transport infrastructure and intangible assets such as technological knowledge and human capital.

Creative class A group of people whose work or other activities involve creativity, freedom of expression, individuality, and the desire to make a difference.

Creative destruction The process by which existing businesses are continually replaced by new businesses in a dynamic economy over a period of time.

Cross-elasticity A measure of the responsiveness of the demand for or supply of one good or service to a change in the price of another.

Cultural distance The cultural differences between an MNE's home and host countries.

Culture In its broader context, culture is the complex set of values, beliefs, ideas, and social interactions which distinguish one society or group of people from another.

Culture onion A cultural concept which represents deeper and more superficial layers of culture as the inner and outer layers of an onion.

Customs union A tariff-free trading area with a common external tariff.

Deadweight loss The loss of consumer surplus as a result of a price or tax increase.

De-industrialization A relative decline in the share of manufacturing output or employment in a country's GDP or workforce.

Demand curve A line or curve on a graph representing the quantities of a good or service that consumers are willing and able to buy at a range of prices.

Democracy A political system where the people influence the exercise of power either directly or through elected representatives.

Deontological principle An ethical principle which holds that an action is morally right if it is based on moral obligations or duties.

Deregulation The removal of regulatory barriers allowing open competition in a market.

Derivative A financial asset which is 'derived' from an underlying asset such as a share, bond, commodity, or currency, for example an option to buy or sell a share or currency at a fixed price on an agreed future date.

Dictatorship A totalitarian political system where the people are governed by a leader with absolute power.

Diffuse culture A cultural orientation where the whole person is involved in forming a business relationship.

Diffusion The spread of an innovation to other firms, products, or industries.

Direct democracy A political system where the people have a direct influence on policies and other issues.

Direct exporting and importing Exporting and importing involving direct contact between the exporter or importer and the foreign customer or supplier.

Dirigisme A form of market intervention where government is involved in directing resources in conjunction with employers, trade unions, and other organizations (also known as indicative economic planning).

Doha Round The latest round of trade negotiations at the WTO, which began in 2001.

Dunning's eclectic paradigm The theory that FDI decisions are based on a combination of ownership (O), location (L), and internalization (I) factors (also known as the OLI paradigm).

Dutch disease A lack of export competitiveness because of an overvalued exchange rate caused by the discovery of a natural resource.

Dynamic theories of competition The study of competition as a continually changing process.

East Asian model The socio-economic model found in Japan, South Korea, Taiwan, and other East Asian countries, emphasizing the importance of coordination between firms, employers and employees, and government and industry.

Economic cycle Short-term fluctuations of GDP around an economy's trend growth rate, including periods of faster and slower economic growth.

Economic geography The study of the impact of geographical location on economic activity.

Economic growth rate The percentage change in a country's GDP from one year to the next, usually allowing for inflation (the real economic growth rate).

Economic liberalization Policies designed to open up markets to competition, either through internal economic reform such as deregulation or privatization, or through the removal of external trade barriers.

Economic union A tariff-free trading area with a common external tariff, the free movement of goods, services, people, and capital, and common economic policies.

Economies of scale Lower unit costs which result from large-scale operations (internal economies of scale) or location close to other organizations engaged in complementary activities (external economies of scale); internal economies may be achieved either in the production process or in the sourcing, marketing, and strategic planning of the organization as a whole.

Economies of scope Lower unit costs which result from the use of a common production platform or standardized product to produce a number of differentiated variants.

Effective exchange rate An exchange rate calculated using an index to compare its value to a 'basket' of currencies, weighted by the volume of trade between the countries concerned, over a period of time.

Egoism An ethical principle which holds that an action is morally right if its consequences are desirable for the individual taking the action.

Elasticity A measure of the responsiveness of one variable to a change in another, e.g. the responsiveness of demand to a change in price.

Emissions trading An environmental policy which grants pollution permits allowing firms to pollute up to a permitted level and to trade their permits if emissions are reduced below this level.

Emotional culture A cultural orientation where people consider human emotions are an acceptable and natural part of business negotiation.

Endogenous growth Economic growth which arises from a combination of internal factors within a national or regional economy, including competition, the quality of technology and human capital, and the institutional environment.

Endogenous growth theory An explanation of long-run economic growth where technological progress is determined by the outcome of internal processes at work in an economy, in particular the level of technological knowledge and quality of human capital.

Entry barrier A real or perceived obstacle to market entry, such as the cost of entry, sunk costs, product differentiation, or entry restrictions.

Ethical absolutism A set of ethical values that are considered to be right regardless of the context.

Ethical relativism A set of ethical values that vary according to the context.

Ethnocentric approach An approach to internationalization where operations are based in the home country and organized from the home country's perspective.

European model The socio-economic model found in continental Europe, associated with a social market economy.

External risk Risk that results from natural phenomena such as a natural disaster.

Externality The external consequences experienced by those who are not directly involved in a particular economic activity.

Fascism A totalitarian political system where the people are governed by a nationalistic leader with absolute power.

FDI flow The amount of inward or outward FDI in a particular year.

FDI stock The cumulative amount of inward or outward FDI up to and including the current period.

Feedback effects In the context of networks, positive feedback effects are the benefits to the users of a network arising from the actions of individual users or interactions between users.

Femininity A cultural dimension where values of modesty, social responsibility, cooperation, and good working relationships are predominant.

Fiscal policy The use of the government's budget (tax revenue and expenditure) to achieve economic stability or manage the level of aggregate demand.

Fiscal stimulus An increase in government expenditure or reduction in taxation used to boost aggregate demand during a recession.

Fixed exchange rate system An exchange rate system where two or more currencies have an agreed exchange rate maintained by the authorities.

Foreign direct investment (FDI) The establishment or acquisition of production or other facilities in a foreign country over which the investing firm has some degree of control.

Fourth-sector organization An organization which combines business (including profit-making) objectives with social or environmental objectives.

Franchising A contractual arrangement whereby a franchiser allows a franchisee to use its intellectual property in a prescribed manner in return for a fee or royalty, commonly found in the retailing, tourism, and other service sectors.

Free-rider problem The problem that arises when individuals are able to benefit from the private provision of public goods without contributing towards their cost.

Free trade area A tariff-free trading area.

Fundamental innovation The development of a significant new discovery, product, or service.

Future scenario An evaluation of how alternative future events may materialize and their potential implications for an organization.

General equilibrium The situation where all markets in an economy are simultaneously operating under perfectly competitive conditions.

General-purpose technology A technology which represents a fundamental innovation with a wide range of applications.

Geocentric approach An approach to internationalization organized around a global strategy, international resourcing and production, and products designed for the global market.

Global governance Policies and rules set by supranational institutions such as the UN, IMF, and WTO.

Globalization A set of interrelated political, economic, and social processes involving international flows of goods, services, people, and capital which lead to the increasing interdependence of countries.

Golden Rule The ethical principle that we should treat others as we would wish to be treated ourselves (the principle of reciprocity).

Greenfield investment FDI involving the building of a new production plant or other facility.

Gross domestic product (GDP) The total value of goods and services produced within a economy in a year, including exports but excluding imports.

Gross national income (GNI) GDP plus net factor income from abroad, i.e. income earned abroad by domestic citizens minus income taken abroad by foreign citizens (also known as gross national product or GNP).

Gross value added A measure of the difference between final output and intermediate inputs, that is, the additional contribution to output made by a particular firm, industry, or region.

Growth pole The central location around which economic development takes place.

High-context culture A cultural dimension where the context in which communication takes place is more important than the words themselves and the meaning is conveyed more through the context than the message.

High power distance A cultural dimension where relationships are formal and hierarchical, and authoritarian or paternalistic leadership is seen as caring.

High uncertainty avoidance A cultural dimension characterized by people who are risk-averse, feel threatened by uncertain situations, and create rules and procedures to minimize uncertainties.

Homogeneous product A product with identical substitutes.

Human capital The knowledge, skills, and other attributes of labour that contribute to the development of a business or economy.

Iceberg model of culture A cultural concept which distinguishes between values and beliefs which are hidden beneath the surface and behaviour, customs, and practices which are visible above the surface.

Increasing returns The outcome of an economic process whereby a set of inputs combine to produce a greater increase in output.

Incremental innovation The gradual development of an existing idea or product.

Indirect exporting and importing Exporting and importing using the services of an agent or other intermediary between the exporter or importer and the foreign customer or supplier.

Individualism A cultural dimension which emphasizes the importance of ambition, personal achievement, and individual rights and responsibilities.

Indulgence A cultural dimension describing societies where citizens are allowed freedom to indulge their desires and enjoy life.

Inflation A persistent increase in the general level of prices, measured by a consumer price index, leading to a reduction in the purchasing power or 'value' of money.

Innovation The commercial development of an invention or, more generally, the entire process of technological change.

Institutions The rules which determine how a market or economy operates, including formal rules such as the political and legal system and informal rules such as customs and practices.

Intellectual property right A legal right to the ownership of an invention, idea, name, or published work, protected by a patent, licence, trade mark, or copyright.

International competitiveness The ability of a firm to compete in international markets or the factors that determine a country's business environment and future economic growth and prosperity.

Intra-industry trade International trade between firms in the same industry.

Invention An initial idea or discovery, sometimes including a prototype or trial to determine its feasibility.

Joint probability The probability of two independent events occurring.

Joint venture An agreement between two or more companies involving joint equity ownership and control.

Justice principle An ethical principle relating to distributive, retributive, or compensatory justice which concerns fairness, equality, and respect for the rights of others.

Keiretsu Groups or networks of companies, often headed by a bank, to which many of Japan's larger companies belong.

Keynesian policy Interventionist government policy used to manage the level of aggregate demand in an economy in order to stimulate economic growth and employment or control inflation and reduce a balance of payments deficit.

Knowledge economy Economic activity involving industries or services in which technological and other advanced forms of knowledge are an important resource.

Liberal market economy An economic system where resource allocation is determined by market forces with minimal government intervention.

Licensing A contractual arrangement whereby a licenser allows a licensee to use its intellectual property in return for a fee or royalty, commonly found in manufacturing and processing industries.

Lock-in The phenomenon whereby consumers and producers become dependent on an established industry standard.

Long-term orientation A cultural dimension where future rewards and persistence are highly valued.

Low-context culture A culture in which the context is unimportant and the message is explicit in itself.

Low power distance A cultural dimension where relationships are informal and consultative, and there is a high degree of equality.

Low uncertainty avoidance A cultural dimension characterized by people who are willing to take risks and feel comfortable with uncertainty.

Macro innovation See fundamental innovation.

Manufactured risk Risk that results from human activity or government policies.

Maquiladora industry A cluster of assembly plants which are located along the Mexican side of the border with the United States, taking advantage of low labour costs and the lucrative US market within the North American Free Trade Agreement (NAFTA).

Marginal external cost (MEC) The external cost of producing an additional unit of output borne by those who are not directly involved in a particular economic activity.

Marginal private cost (MPC) The internal cost of producing an additional unit of output borne by the organization and its consumers.

Marginal social cost (MSC) The total cost to society of producing an additional unit of output, including the marginal private cost and the marginal external cost.

Market equilibrium The point at which supply and demand are equal (where the supply and demand curves intersect).

Market failure The inability of a market to allocate resources efficiently in order to meet the wants and needs of consumers.

Market mechanism The process by which supply and demand interact with each other to allocate resources in a market.

Market signalling The process by which consumers and producers respond to price, quality, and other signals in a market.

Masculinity A cultural dimension where values of assertiveness, competitiveness, ambition, and achievement are predominant.

Mediterranean model The socio-economic model found in the countries of southern Europe, associated with a regulated market economy and state invention in industry.

Mercantilism The idea that exports should be encouraged and imports discouraged as a means of achieving economic prosperity, contrary to the ideas of comparative advantage theory.

Merchandise trade Trade in physical goods and resources such as food, cars, or oil.

Merger Either an agreement between two or more companies to form a combined company or the general term for a combination of two or more previously separate companies, including a takeover.

Merit good A service such as education or health care which is beneficial for society as a whole but which might be under-provided if left to market forces.

Micro innovation See incremental innovation.

Monetarism A free-market approach to economic policy placing emphasis on control of the money supply and a balanced government budget over the economic cycle.

Monetary policy The use of monetary instruments such as the interest rate or money supply to control inflation or increase bank liquidity (see quantitative easing).

Monetary policy transmission mechanism The process by which a change in the official interest rate raises or lowers the demand for goods and services in order to manage inflation.

Money supply The total quantity of cash and credit in an economy; credit includes bank and other financial deposits with varying degrees of liquidity, depending on the definition of the money supply being used.

Monochronic time orientation A cultural dimension where people compartmentalize time and schedule one thing at a time.

Monopolistic competition A form of market structure where there is freedom of entry and exit and a large number of small firms selling differentiated products.

Monopoly Pure monopoly is a form of market structure where there are high entry barriers and a single producer selling a product with no close substitutes; in practice, the term is also used to describe markets where dominant firms have some degree of market power.

Moral hazard Market failure resulting from a change in behaviour after receiving a benefit such as credit or insurance in a market with asymmetric information.

Multilateralism Trade and other international agreements made collectively by a group of countries, as for example at the WTO.

Multinational enterprise (MNE) An enterprise that controls and manages production facilities in more than one country; the term 'enterprise' includes operations such as licensing and franchising as well as full ownership.

Multiplier A method used to estimate the overall impact of an increase in aggregate demand on the level of national income over a period of time.

Multipolar world order A world where power is shared by a number of countries, possibly including the USA, China, and one or two other countries.

Natural monopoly A market where the most efficient scale of production requires a single producer.

Natural resource paradox The phenomenon whereby resource-rich countries remain underdeveloped, either because of the lack of incentive to diversify or because of the Dutch disease.

Neoclassical growth theory An explanation of long-run economic growth where technological progress depends on the rate of capital investment, which is determined exogenously (outside the model).

Neoclassical (micro) economics The mainstream economic theory of firms and markets in the tradition of Adam Smith and Alfred Marshall.

Network effect A benefit to an individual user of a network that arises as the number of users increases.

Network externality A network effect where the price charged for the use of a network does not fully internalize the benefits to all users.

Neutral culture A cultural orientation where people take a clinical view of business objectives and efficiency is paramount.

Nominal exchange rate A market exchange rate which determines the rate at which one currency can be exchanged for another at a particular time.

Non-consequentialist principle See deontological principle.

Nordic model The socio-economic model found in the Nordic countries, associated with a social market economy and collective negotiation at a national level.

Normal distribution A pattern derived from the frequency of occurrence of a set of data where most data lie within a small range of the mean and extreme values are relatively rare (represented by a bell-shaped curve known as the Bell Curve).

Objective probability Probability that results from knowable 'facts' about the occurrence of an event resulting either from homogeneous data or inherent symmetries.

Offshoring The relocation of production or other business operations to another country, either by outsourcing to an independent operator or by establishing a wholly or partially owned subsidiary.

Oligarchy A totalitarian political system where the people are governed by a small group of leaders with absolute power.

Oligopoly A form of market structure where there are entry barriers and a few dominant firms selling differentiated products.

Open-source technology A technology that is developed through a process of public cooperation.

Opportunity cost The cost of a particular course of action valued in terms of the alternatives forgone.

Organizational behaviour The study of the behaviour of individuals and groups within an organization, including organizational culture and relationships.

Outsourcing The contracting out of production operations or services to external suppliers either at home or abroad.

Over-the-counter market The sale of bonds or other securities via a bank, securities trader, or other intermediary without the use of a stock market.

Parastatal An agency, company, or other organization that is funded wholly or partly by government and performs functions of public importance, but has its own governance structure.

Particularism A cultural orientation where the obligations of particular relationships or circumstances are given priority over general rules.

Path dependence A sequence of events shaped in a persistent way by a particular event in the past.

Perfect competition A form of market structure where there is freedom of entry and exit and a large number of small firms selling homogeneous products.

Peripheral region A region which is geographically distant from a core region.

PESTLE analysis The identification of political, economic, social, technological, legal, and environmental factors as a basis for analysing an organization's external environment.

Pigouvian (or Pigovian) tax A tax equal to the external cost of an economic activity, forcing the producer and consumers to take account of the full social cost of their activities.

Pluralism In an ethical context, pluralism represents tolerance of the views, interests, and values of others.

Political union A group of countries with a unified policy-making structure.

Polycentric approach An approach to internationalization organized around separate divisions in different parts of the world, each using local resources and production, and marketing adapted to its own cultural environment.

Polycentric region A region with more than one main town or growth pole, often connecting smaller neighbouring regions.

Polychronic time orientation A cultural dimension where people see the past, present, and future as part of a single time frame and keep several options going at once.

Portfolio investment The acquisition of financial assets or commodities for the purpose of earning a return on surplus funds rather than to gain corporate control.

Postmodernism A view that represents the world as a complex and disorderly place where local events and provisional attitudes are more important than grand narratives or universal truths.

Preferential trading agreement An agreement allowing preferential market access for the exports of a particular country or group of countries.

Private sector organization A public or private limited company or unincorporated business owned by a private individual, group of individuals, or organization.

Privatization The transfer of state-owned industries, assets, or public services to the private sector.

Probability The measurable likelihood of an event occurring.

Producer surplus The difference between the market price and marginal cost to the producer, which is equal to the average cost if the average cost is constant.

Product differentiation A characteristic of competition where products are perceived by consumers to be different with respect to their distinctive features or the context in which they are sold.

Productivity The quantity of labour and other inputs required to produce a given level of output.

Property rights Legally enforceable protection of the rights of consumers, employees, shareholders, intellectual property owners, and others.

Protectionism A policy intended to restrict imports as a means of protecting output and employment in an economy.

Psychic distance Perceived differences in culture, history, or business practices between an MNE's home and host countries.

Public good A service such as defence or law and order where non-rivalry between consumers and the non-exclusion of consumers might lead to under-provision and the free-rider problem if left to market forces.

Public sector organization A central or local government department, public corporation, or other organization owned by the state.

Purchasing power parity (PPP) A method of calculating an exchange rate between two currencies based on the amount of currency needed to buy the same 'basket' of goods and services in each of the two countries concerned.

Quantitative easing Expansionary monetary policy where the central bank creates new money (sometimes described as 'printing money') to buy bonds from banks and other financial institutions, with the intention of increasing bank liquidity, encouraging bank lending, and stimulating demand.

Quasi-public good A 'good' such as knowledge which has the characteristic of non-rivalry but which is not necessarily non-excludable.

Radical innovation See fundamental innovation.

Real effective exchange rate An exchange rate which combines the real exchange rate and the effective exchange rate.

Real exchange rate An exchange rate which takes account of both the nominal exchange rate between and the relative inflation rate in two countries.

Real output The value of the production of goods and services in an economy after allowing for inflation.

Regional multiplier A method used to estimate the overall impact of regional expenditure over a period of time.

Regionalization Economic and other activities between groups of countries in specific regions of the world, as distinct from globalization if this term is used to imply activity between all the main regions of the world.

Remote development Undertaking all or part of a business operation at a distant location, often in another country.

Representative democracy A political system where the people influence the exercise of power through elected representatives such as members of parliament.

Resource-based view The idea that an MNE's decision to locate abroad and choice of entry mode is determined by its ability to take advantage of its firm-specific assets.

Restraint A cultural dimension describing societies where social control and social norms impose restrictions on individual freedoms and enjoyment.

Rhine model The socio-economic model found in Germany and its neighbouring countries, associated with a social market economy and political and industrial consensus.

Rights principle In its modern context, an ethical principle which holds that human beings have certain rights which should be respected.

Risk The possibility of an uncertain event occurring, sometimes though not necessarily considered to be measurable.

Risk assessment The analysis of potential risk.

Risk management The design and implementation of procedures for dealing with risk.

Scenario Analysis of a possible future course of events, drawing on information, insights, and understanding of a particular issue.

Sequential time orientation See monochromic time orientation.

Share An investment creating ownership (or equity) rights in a company.

Shareholder view An ethical concept which holds that the primary purpose of a company is to maximize the return on its shareholders' investment.

Short-term orientation A cultural dimension where emphasis is placed on past and present values such as respect for tradition, social obligations, and saving 'face'.

Signpost Something that provides an indication of a trend or future course of events.

Social contract An explicit or implicit agreement between members of a society concerning accepted norms of behaviour.

Social market economy An economy where resources are allocated by a combination of market forces and social intervention.

Socio-economic model An economic system characterized by its social and political institutions representative of a particular group of countries.

Spatial concentration A group or cluster of related business activities located close together.

Special economic zone A government-designated area in a country like China or India offering a variety of tax and customs incentives to local and foreign investors.

Specific culture A cultural orientation where the main focus is on the details of the product or contract.

Stakeholder A group or individual who can affect, or is affected by, the activities of an organization, including direct stakeholders such as shareholders, employees, or customers, and indirect stakeholders such as society as a whole.

Stakeholder view An ethical concept which holds that an organization has a responsibility towards all its stakeholders.

Standardization The setting of an industry standard which acts as a platform for the development of complementary products.

State capture The phenomenon whereby powerful corporations 'capture' the authorities by influencing business rules or bribing public officials.

State socialism A political system where property and the means of production are owned or regulated by the state on behalf of the people – a term sometimes used in place of 'communism' (either with or without the prefix 'state').

Stock A non-equity investment in a company or public sector debt, including bonds and other securities.

Strategic alliance A non-equity cooperation agreement between two or more independent firms for the purpose of gaining a mutual competitive advantage.

Strategic foresight The ability to develop future scenarios and/or influence the likely outcome of future events facing an organization.

Structure-conduct-performance (SCP) paradigm The view that the structure of a market determines the conduct of firms which in turn determines their performance.

Subjective probability Probability based on observations of past events or estimates or beliefs about future events which have little quantifiable basis.

Sunk cost A cost incurred when entering a market which is irrecoverable when leaving the market.

Supply curve A line or curve on a graph representing the quantities of a good or service that firms are willing and able to produce at a range of prices.

Supply-side policies Government policies designed to increase productivity and the productive potential of an economy.

SWOT analysis The identification of an organization's strengths and weaknesses and the opportunities and threats it faces in the external environment used as a basis for developing strategies or reviewing progress.

Synchronic time orientation See polychronic time orientation.

Takeover The purchase of a majority stake in another organization (also known as an acquisition).

Tariff A percentage tax or duty on goods imported into a country.

Technological adopter A country where high-tech exports account for at least 2 per cent of GDP.

Technological innovator A country with ten or more patents per million inhabitants.

Technologically excluded A country where high-tech exports account for less than 2 per cent of GDP.

Teleological principle An ethical principle which holds that an action is morally right if the outcome or consequence of the action is desirable.

Theocracy A political system where the people are governed by a religious leader or group of leaders according to the principles and laws of a particular religion.

Third-sector organization A not-for-profit organization such as a charity, cooperative, voluntary or community group, foundation, trust, or social enterprise.

Time-preference rate The willingness of an individual or society to consume resources in the present period as opposed to saving for a future period.

Totalitarian Authoritarian political leadership at either extreme of the political spectrum, including both communism and dictatorship.

Trade creation An increase in trade between the members of a regional economic grouping as a result of the removal of internal tariffs and other trade barriers.

Trade diversion Trade which is diverted from countries outside a regional economic grouping to countries inside as a result of the removal of internal tariffs and other trade barriers.

Trade-weighted exchange rate See effective exchange rate.

Transaction cost A cost incurred when undertaking a transaction in addition to the price paid for the goods or services; examples include legal costs, currency exchange costs, or information search costs.

Trend growth rate The long-run performance of an economy determined by its productive capacity.

Triad The name used to describe the major economies during the post-war period, including North America, Western Europe, and Japan.

Trigger An event that sets off an immediate reaction.

Uncertainty An unpredictable event, sometimes regarded as a risk that cannot be measured.

Unemployment The number or proportion of the working population recorded as being out of work.

Unipolar world order A world dominated by a single powerful country, as for example the post-cold war period dominated by the USA.

Universalism A cultural orientation where there is a belief that some things are always right and must be observed at all times.

Uruguay Round The last completed round of trade negotiations, signed in 1994 and leading to the creation of the WTO in 1995.

Utilitarianism An ethical principle which holds that an action is morally right if it results in the greatest good for the greatest number of people.

Values The fundamental principles that form the basis of ethical behaviour.

Virtue ethics An ethical concept which holds that personal character traits such as honesty, sincerity, and trustworthiness provide a basis for ethical behaviour.

Voluntarism The view that individuals or organizations can be expected to act ethically on a voluntary basis without the need for regulation.

Warning sign An event that provides an indication of a potential risk.

Washington consensus The free-market approach favoured by the US government and major institutions such as the IMF and World Bank.

Welfare gain or loss The net effect of a price increase on the loss of consumer surplus (the deadweight loss) and the gain in producer surplus, if any.

Index of Countries

General Index